Thro Alien Eyes

Wesley H. Bateman
Federation Telepath

Through
Alien
Eyes

Wesley H. Bateman
Federation Telepath

Cover Illustration by Alan Gutierrez

ISBN 1-891824-27-9

Published by

**Light
Technology
Publishing**

P.O. Box 3540
Flagstaff, AZ 86003
1-800-450-0985
e-mail: sedonajo@sedonajo.com
www.lighttechnology.com

Printed by

Sedona Color Graphics
■ ■   ■ PRINTING SPECIALISTS

2020 Contractors Road
Sedona, AZ 86336

To my daughter, Deanna.

Other Books

by

Wesley H. Bateman

Knowledge from the Stars

Dragons and Chariots

Through Alien Eyes

FIVE

SIX

SEVEN

EIGHT

NINE

THIRTEEN

FOURTEEN

Appendix A   461

Appendix B

Have You Dummies Heard the Latest?   477

Dictionary   485

P r e f a c e

This book reflects the personal views of a number of different types of extraterrestrials regarding the state of the local solar system and the state of the Earth. Each individual has described himself/ herself and how his/her particular culture relates to the universe in general, and how the culture desires to see the universal conditions for human life in the future.

At least one individual from each of the following cultures indigenous to the local solar system have agreed to give their views in Part I: Venus, Mars, Maldec, Jupiter (Relt radiar), Saturn (Sumer radiar) and Neptune (Trake radiar). Those of Uranus (Hamp radiar) have respectfully declined to participate. In addition, a person physically native to Earth who is presently living off the planet will participate.

Finally, a person who is not of this solar system will describe himself, the general Federation version of the way things are and what this institution's hopes are for the future. I have asked these extraterrestrials to relate some highlights of any of their past lives, particularly those they might have lived on the Earth. I have also requested that they describe their present life and their government, economy and religion.

I have never had the experience of communicating telepathically with a Gracian before. I have been advised by my Nodian associates that although the communication sessions with a Gracian should not be difficult, they could be somewhat confusing because the Gracians use numbers to explain things and to make a point. Therefore this communication will be monitored by several other extraterrestrials who will interject when necessary to clarify anything I do not understand. As I write this note I have no idea who will come to my assistance or when, so I will begin those interjected paragraphs with the ET's name.

In Part Two many (but not all) of the extraterrestrial accounts will originate from persons who have never spent any lifetimes on Earth that were influenced by the Frequency Barrier. They will mainly report on what occurred on Earth throughout the history of the Frequency Barrier and how these events affected their personal lives and those of other people of the open, unrestricted mental state of existence.

These extraterrestrial contributors will present both their personal opinions and the opinions of Federation officials about the affairs on Earth today and what will most likely happen in the near future. They will tell what they know about the Federation and dark-side agendas for the planet and will describe extraterrestrial bases on the Earth and elsewhere within the solar system.

As further information becomes available, it will be announced at www.geocities/Cape Canaveral/Hall/3324/ and Nefer's home page now [October 2000] under construction at www.realmofra.com.

P A R T   O N E

The Frequency Barrier of Planet Earth

As It Was and As It Is Now

The accounts given by extraterrestrials in this volume are about events that occurred in our solar system many millions of years ago. In that ancient time the solar system consisted of four planets and four "radiar systems" that orbited the central sun. The four planets of the solar system are known today as Venus, Earth, Mars and a now-totally shattered world that was called Maldec. The remains of Maldec presently exist in the form of the Amor asteroids that occasionally cross the solar orbit of Mars, the Apollo asteroids that on occasion cross the solar orbit of the Earth and the so-called Trojan asteroids that both precede and follow the radiar called Jupiter in its orbit about the Sun.

The term "radiar" applies to the astronomical bodies we presently call Jupiter, Saturn, Uranus and Neptune. The original satellites of these radiars are generally called moons by Earth astronomers, but the extraterrestrials prefer to call them planetoids.

Prior to the destruction of the planet Maldec, all four of the solar system's radiars were in entirely different solar orbits, where they generated sufficient heat and light to sustain both human, animal and plant life on their orbiting planetoids. After the destruction of Maldec the radiars and planets of the solar system gradually assumed totally different solar orbits in order to stabilize the system; that is, they adjusted for the absence of Maldec's mass in the gravitational pressure field produced by the sun. These adjustments prevented the inner planets from leaving their respective orbits and spiraling to their destruction into the sun. Even so, several planetoids separated from their particular radiar system and took up solar orbits like a planet. The planet we call Mercury was once a planetoid of the radiar system of Jupiter, and the planet Pluto and its moon, Charon, were both once planetoids of the radiar system of Neptune.

Presently the dysfunctioning radiars of Jupiter, Saturn and Neptune generate as much as three times the energy they receive from the sun. However, they do not produce enough energy to support life on their respective planetoids as they once did. Three of the radiars (excluding the fourth, which is Uranus) have unique surface features that are actually artifacts of their original energy-generating activities. These dynamic features are known as the great "red spot" of Jupiter, the "white spot" of Saturn and the "black spot" of Neptune.

Astronomical observations have revealed the existence of so-called binary star systems, where a smaller star appears to orbit a larger one. In truth, the orbiting star is not a star but a fully functioning radiar that most likely has orbiting planetoids. One well-known binary star system is Sirius, which has a central star called Sirius A and a smaller, less brilliant orbiting companion (radiar) referred to as Sirius B. When functioning correctly, the radiars of our solar system could also have been misidentified by an unknowing observer in some other solar system as being four smaller stars circling a larger one.

Spacecraft Observation of Earth through the Ages

Extraterrestrials in disk-shaped spacecraft have been visiting the Earth for thousands of years. During the reign of King Thutmose III (ruler of Egypt about 1500 B.C.) his scribes wrote: "In the year 22 during the third month of winter a circle of fire came out of the sky. Later it was joined by other circles of fire. When the king ordered his army to assemble around him, the circles flew skyward and disappeared." This ancient UFO sighting is described in what is called the Tulli papyrus. During the time of the Roman Empire and later during the Middle Ages, a great number of UFO sightings were also documented.

Today's technology has produced devices that could be used to map and totally analyze a distant planet in one five-day mission—that is, if we had a spacecraft that could carry all the required instruments to that planet. But we don't.

The question is, if these strange objects are really extraterrestrial spacecraft, why have their operators been coming to the Earth again and again for centuries? They have certainly long since finished mapping and analyzing this planet. The answer is that they are observing something that is constantly changing, something that we on Earth are totally unaware of.

In the mid-1940s UFOs were often spotted at locations where we were testing nuclear bombs and guided missiles. Theories arose suggesting that the extraterrestrials were concerned about our nuclear testing and/or our development of nuclear weapons. Extraterrestrials are interested in nuclear bomb tests only because those detonations produce effects similar to those produced by a natural phenomenon they have been observing long before nuclear bombs ever existed. This natural phenomenon is, of course, earthquakes.

The Significance of Earthquakes and Volcanic Eruptions

In the year 224 B.C. the Roman historian Pliny wrote that there were fiery chariots and shining shields seen in the sky when the Colossus of Rhodes was destroyed by a great earthquake. The Colossus, which is listed as one of the Seven Wonders of the Ancient World, was a large statue of the Greek sun god, Helios. The statue, which took the Greeks twelve years to build, is said to have stood in the harbor of the island of Rhodes in such away that ships of the time sailed between its legs.

Earthquakes occur when energy builds up in rock layers that compose an earthquake fault. Eventually the energy causes heavy stress in the rock layers and causes them to move (slip) or break, generating waves of energy that radiate from the quake's epicenter. Some waves move straight out from the epicenter. Others move outward, but in a side-to-side movement like a crawling serpent. These waves are called, respectively, push and shear waves (sometimes also primary and secondary waves, or simply P and S waves).

Most push and shear waves penetrate the Earth. Some bounce (deflect) off the planet's molten core. Others pass through the core as depicted below.

The push and shear waves that reflect off the Earth's core resurface at points about 7000 miles' surface distance from the earthquake's epicenter. Push and shear waves that pass through the planet's core are weakened in the process. This type of wave resurfaces about 9500 miles from the earthquake's epicenter. The area that lies between the two resurfacing points is called the quiet zone.

On March 20, 21 and 22, 1966, the *Los Angeles Herald Examiner* carried double headlines proclaiming the occurrence of massive earthquakes in China and UFO sightings that took place at Ann Arbor and Hillsdale, Michigan. In the fall of 1968 a Fort Lauderdale, Florida, newspaper carried articles side by

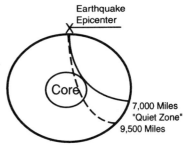

Push and Shear Waves

side on the same page, titled "Fiery Objects Seen in New York Skies" and "Philadelphia Shaken by Quake."

A series of phenomenal UFO pictures were taken by Agusto Arranda at Yungay, Peru, in the late 1960s. Within a year of this UFO activity at Yungay, the town was wiped off the face of the map by a tremendous earthquake and mudslide. The Yungay disaster is considered the greatest natural catastrophe ever to occur in the Western Hemisphere and is in the top-ten list of all natural disasters that ever occurred known history of the world.

UFO sightings correspond to points on the globe at which the strongest push and shear waves resurface and can be analyzed by the extraterrestrials.

In October 1989 a devastating earthquake occurred in San Francisco, California. Several days prior to this quake, newspapers and television reported a UFO landing at Voronezh, a city about 300 miles south of Moscow.

On October 5, 1973, the Orange County (California) *The Register* carried the headline, "Huge Dixie UFO: Law Officers Describe Sighting." Then on the following day the Long Beach, California, *Independent* carried the headline, "Huge Chile Quake." Over a period of several days prior to the Chilean quake of October 6, 1973, the southeastern part of the United States was blanketed with UFO activity. During this UFO activity, then-governor of the state of Georgia, Jimmy Carter, and ten others reported seeing a UFO in the skies over Leary, Georgia.

Most of the UFO sightings of October 1973 took place in the vicinity of the New Madrid fault. A moderate earthquake did occur there as the saucers moved about. This quake took place on a part of the fault that seismologists previously thought was inactive. This, of course, means that the extraterrestrials can predict when and where an earthquake is going to take place. This is confirmed somewhat by the destruction of Yungay in the 1960s.

Waves of energy pass more rapidly through material that is closely packed and more slowly through looser material or material with open spaces (gaps). Presently gaps or open spaces exist in the Earth's key strata. By measuring the strength and speed of push and shear waves as they pass through the key layers of the planet, the extraterrestrials can determine if the earthquake contributed any force that caused the fractures in the strata to close or become wider to any degree. The slightest closure of gaps in the planet's key strata will reduce the detrimental effects of the Frequency Barrier to some degree.

The extraterrestrials are also interested in volcanic eruptions, as they too generate push and shear waves. On different days just prior to the most recent eruption of Mount Saint Helens, triangular-shaped UFOs were reported only a few miles west of the mountain. The volcanoes of Mount Saint Helens, Mount Hood and Mount Rainier are all in the same mountain range. Remember, it was in the vicinity of Mount Rainier that Kenneth Arnold saw a fleet of nine "flying saucers" in June 1947.

On Wednesday, February 3, 1993, the *Arizona Republic* (Phoenix) published two articles, titled "UFO Sightings Are Raising Eyebrows in Wisconsin" and "Volcano Erupts, 25 Perish."

Basically, the UFO article described sightings near Waukesha, Wisconsin, on the evenings of January 31 and February 1, 1993. The second article described the volcanic eruption of Mount Mayon, located slightly north of Legaspi in the Philippines. It was reported that the eruption took place at 10:10 P.M. Monday, Arizona time. This means that the eruption of Mount Mayon and the UFO sightings in Wisconsin took place within an hour of each other.

The United States Science Foundation research ship, the El Tannin, was specially designed and built for the foundation's Antarctic research program. While conducting underwater photography 1000 miles west of Cape Horn along a major fault line that circles the Earth, a picture was taken of a strange device resting next to the fault at a depth of 13,000 feet. The device had an antenna with crossbars similar to a telemetry antenna. The scientists aboard the El Tannin were puzzled about what function the device had and who on Earth produced the technology to build such a device that could withstand the crushing pressures existing at those depths. It apparently did not occur to the El Tannin scientists that they had accidentally taken a picture of an extraterrestrial seismographic device.

An Added Factor: Nuclear Tests

The extraterrestrials have had to take nuclear detonations into account since the mid-1940s if they were to continue with their ages-old studies of push and shear waves as they pass through our planet.

In the 1960s the United States conducted high-yield underground nuclear tests at Jackass Flats, Nevada. These tests produced push and shear waves that resurfaced in the vicinity of Tashkent, a city located in the Uzbek region of what was then the Soviet Union. These waves gradually contributed energy to a fault line in the area that gave way under the strain, in turn producing a series of massive earthquakes.

Soviet underground nuclear tests at the same time in Siberia contributed energy to the fault lines in Turkey, Armenia and Afghanistan. The faults in these areas need very little encouragement, as they are naturally very active.

In 1968 a nuclear device was set off at Farmington, New Mexico. The project was called Gas Buggy and was officially described as an attempt to exploit a natural gas pocket in the area. Within a few minutes of the detonation at Farmington, the push and shear waves from the blast triggered an earthquake in India that killed 200 people. Such a quake would have eventually happened naturally, but the waves from the nuclear detonation hastened it.

It has long been realized that underground nuclear tests were really a failed attempt to develop a weapon system that would have employed push and shear waves as a means of destruction. Theoretically a high-yield nuclear device detonated underground at a strategic spot on the planet could produce push and shear waves strong enough to lift a city 7000 miles away a foot into the air, only to have it resettle in ruins. This type of weapon system would not require costly intercontinental missiles to deliver destruction. The devastated country of the enemy could be immediately occupied by troops, as there would be no hazardous radioactivity present at the target sites. The development of the system most likely failed because the means required to precisely aim and control the destructive waves was lacking—thank god.

Following are comments from several beings who were aware of the Maldecian catastrophe.

"The children of the elder race of Earth began to change. They were not able to be taught even to speak. They desired only to eat, fornicate, rave and kill those who possessed any form of reason. Such was their hunger that they ate carrion and even each other. All this happened as the Earth's skies were darkened by ash and smoke of hundreds of erupting volcanoes, and the planet was shaken by violent earthquakes.

"When we found the means to look into the ways of Earth once again, we found those of humankind who did survive the numerous geological calamities did so only because of the instincts of motherhood and other noble traits of love that were able to prevail amidst the insanity.

"I myself have looked into the vacant eyes of those survivors of Earth's elder race and other races of the solar system that sought false refuge on the planet. They feared me, though I would have done them no harm.

"As time passed, some of the good ways of man (those that please the elohim) began to resurface, but by this time all memories of the past were lost. At times we that are not of the Earth attempted to tell of these things to those of the troubled world. With these words we try once again.

"When my services are required, I enter the Frequency Barrier of the planet Earth and test its effects. I am pleased to see that the Earth is healing well. This provides me with the hope that at sometime in the future my home world will also be restored and support life once again. Believe me when I say, there are more of my kind who have envied your ignorance of these matters.

"I am Sycorant of Omuray (Titan), the largest of the planetoids of radiar you call Saturn."

"The princes and less exalted of the solar system came with those of their households, though unwelcome by the natives of the Earth and the immigrants who came before them. It was a time when the music and food of some left a bad taste in the ears and mouths of others. There was no order, and too many sought spiritual guidance from false gods and also sought protection from the strongest, who took their children as slaves in payment for their services.

"There were times when hundreds of vimana vessels of the Federation raised great dust clouds as they landed to unload their charitable cargoes. Though they came with concern and love, they did so to avoid the degradation that so greatly troubled their souls.

"I am Tortsigra, 128th female Lord of Devisement for the Trading House of Isotrex."

"I have memories of the most ancient of ancient times. My soul was young and danced on the firm foundation of my world. People were happy and the morning stars sang together. Then those who love the ways of the great deceiver shattered their planetary nest and brought terrible grief to us and to the angels. This deed also blinded the minds of those of the now-third world that is called Earth.

"These are the words of Omathra, daughter of Vey."

"We are products of millions of years of lifetimes. What we know from those times determines what emotions blend with our thoughts and energize the symbols of our dreams. Our personal experiences of past lives cause us to differ, as do the forms of snowflakes differ one from another. This, then, I must say: Because you have requested the views of many, expect to hear the same melody when they sing their song, but the lyrics of some might not always rhyme with those that are voiced by others of the chorus.

"I am Sangelbo of Temcain."

Following are a few explanations that will help the reader become oriented to the historical incident referred to in the chapters of this book.

1.   The names Radiant Ones, Watchers and Watcher Race relate to the people of the once-existing planet called Maldec.

2.   Maldec once held the fourth planetary orbit from the sun. It was shattered into pieces accidentally by its own people, who attempted to transmit a form of unique energy that they accumulated in, and transmitted from, the Great Pyramid of Giza in Egypt. The Maldecians built the Great Pyramid for this purpose and also to manipulate human and animal genetics.

3.   Mir is an ancient name for Egypt and Miradol for Teotihuacan.

4.   Vril energy is the highest form of energy in the universe. All types of energy are actually lesser forms of this supreme type of energy. It is the very creative energy of God, the creator of all that is.

5.   A vril stick is a wooden rod that has been chemically treated and tuned to both absorb and transmit vril energy.

6.   The Maldecians built the Great Pyramid on a strategic spot on the Earth where the most vril energy could be accumulated. When they transmitted the energy to their planet, it shattered. This is similar to an opera singer who, in sustaining a note, shatters a glass goblet. Because the energy originated from the Earth, the planet experienced feedback that caused key strata in the Earth's crust to fracture and separate. It also caused the molten core to begin vibrating erratically, sending out energy waves that were not harmonious with the bioelectrical activity of the human brain. These detrimental waves generated by the Earth's core are collectively referred to as the Frequency Barrier. The feedback phenomenon was similar to what is observed when a live microphone is held close to a connected audio speaker. Most people are familiar with the screeching sound that occurs when this is done.

7.   The term "Frequency Barrier" applies to a condition that exists solely on planet Earth. It is a byproduct of the destruction of the planet Maldec. Its presence on the Earth prevents humans living on the planet from using the higher mental frequencies necessary to permit the brain to function in ways that are presently considered to be extrasensory. The Frequency Barrier will be mentioned throughout this writing.

8.   Vimana is a name sometimes applied to an extraterrestrial spacecraft.

Wesley H. Bateman

O N E

Sharmarie, a Martian

We are products of millions of years of lifetimes.
What we know from those times determines
what emotions we blend with our thoughts
and energizes the symbols of our dreams. Our
personal experiences of past lives cause us to
differ like the forms of snowflakes differ from one
another. This then I must say: Because you have
requested the views of many, expect to hear the
same melody when they sing their song, though the
lyrics of some might not always rhyme with those that
are voiced by others of the chorus.
I am Sangelbo of Temcain.

In my first human lifetime I was born to shepherds of the nomadic Shem tribe. My mother, Scenra, was my father Ari-Lionent's only soul-mate, although one to seven female soulmates for one male is the way of the El of Mars. My father was killed during a hostile encounter with the mountain-dwelling tribe of my world, whom we then called the Burrs. This left my mother a very young widow of about twenty-three Earth years. Her physical beauty and marital status attracted the attention of one of several warlords (bar-rexes) that we had to contend with in those days. My mother eventually became part of that scoundrel's household, and I was given to my father's sister Tee-Robra to be raised among her eventual brood of fourteen children.

Aunt Tee-Robra was not physically attractive and had no permanent mate, but knew and taught the ways of fine weaving and tent-making and the arts of warfare to her children and many others who sought her out.

Our nomadic travels were dictated by the grass that grew beside the waterways fed by the seasonal melting of the polar icecaps and heavy winter snows in the mountains.

It took about three Earth months to drive our flocks of sheep (almost twice the size of any breed found on the Earth today), goats, donkeys and camels (one-hump dromedary type) to bridging points that allowed us to cross the waterways and reverse our direction of travel. Anyone caught crossing a waterway at any place other than the point authorized by the local bar-rex could expect to be either killed or enslaved for life.

Twice a year my tribe's southern travels would bring us to such an authorized bridge across a waterway; this one was the hi, or stronghold, of the bar-rex who was then my mother's protector. We had to contend with another bar-rex at the end of our northern journey. At these times the tribe would be taxed, and the young men would be looked at as possible candidates for military service. I do not remember how many times my mother's influence kept me from being selected when I crossed the southern hi. (It might come as no surprise to you that the path we took to reach a hi crossing point was called a highway.)

Because I was born when the tribe was traveling south, I wore a string of red beads about my neck until the age of about five Earth years; thereafter the beads were replaced by a tattoo on my right shoulder depicting a circle with a dot on its circumference, indicating the point on our traveling circuit at which I had been born. A child born while traveling north wore white beads until age five and then received the same type of tattoo on the left shoulder. By mutual agreement the bar-rex of the southern hi could claim only those with tattoos on their right shoulder for any form of physical service, and the bar-rex of the north could claim only those with the tattoo on the left shoulder.

The northern hi was a point where six waterways came together, whereas the southern hi was a point where only three waterways joined. This meant that the bar-rex of the northern hi had six tribes under his jurisdiction. He was a crusty old warrior who walked among the people and exchanged bawdy stories. I liked him and his eldest son, whom he called his "whip," and envied the white-beaders who would someday be in his service.

I left the tribe for two years and spent time in the hills, avoiding the military patrols from the south and visiting on occasion the young ladies of the Burr tribes. The Burrs paid tribute to numerous bar-rexes in the form of grain, fruit and manufactured metal goods. This exempted them from military service but did not stop their young men from rustling the Shem flocks when they had a mind to. It was during one such raid that my father was killed.

The military patrols learned from the disgruntled parents of several of my lady loves that there was a maverick Shem moving among them on occasion. (You never can trust a Burr to keep her mouth shut. "This day one might say Sharmarie has a Burr under his saddle." I can say, if it were true, you can be sure he is still alive and kicking.)

I rejoined the tribe and because of intercession by my mother, I escaped any punishment for my more-than-two-year absence.

My mother bore a daughter to Cap-Tonelarber, the bar-rex of the southern hi, a true princess who was named Wren-Shanna. In later times Wren-Shanna and I became the best of friends, and recently in our present lifetime visited together the site of her first-life birthplace. Wearing protective clothing, we stood among the hardly recognizable ancient ruins of her father's hi stronghold. As a fierce dust storm raged about us, we reminisced about what was good about that time.

My mother bought me several seasons of precious time, which I spent under the tutelage of So-Socrey, a tribal medicine man of great wisdom. He was a good friend of Aunt Tee-Robra and probably the only one in the universe who could outdrink her. It was he with whom I hid out in the hills until I finally rejoined the tribe during the southern trek. It was also he who taught me the medicinal values of plants and what he knew of the way of the elohim, how to pray for their magical assistance and when it was proper to do so. Once, So-Socrey tested my knowledge of what he had taught me by lowering me into a pit of poisonous snakes to harvest bulbs of a cactus-type plant. I succeeded in the retrieval of the bulbs and survived by becoming one with the reality of the serpents on their level of the universal life field. He brewed my collection of bulbs into a tea, which he drank. Then he became very intoxicated and proceeded to demonstrate how he could urinate any color at will. When he produced an endless stream of fire, I realized I still had a great deal to learn. The color changes I can presently duplicate (yellow is easy), but I have never found the necessary courage to attempt to duplicate my mentor's endless river of fire.

The day came when the tane (military overseer) of the bar-rex and two of his recent recruits sought me out during a hi crossing. He should have brought his army. I put Aunt Tee-Robra's and So-Socrey's teachings into action and physically disabled my unwanted would-be masters. After several days of being chased throughout the hi area, I was eventually subdued by their sheer numbers and a personal plea from my mother to surrender and refrain from hurting any more of my pursuers, who in some cases had once been my playmates in earlier times.

I was considered a loner and made very few friends. I was also considered to be a bit mad and dangerous. I was assigned to a camel patrol traveling north, to keep an eye on the flocks across the waterway that were moving south toward my master's hi. It was during this time that some of my comrades in arms and I learned how to swim from an old veteran. We yearned for the food, campfire stories and female companionship that the other side of the waterway so willingly provided.

The Earth at its closest approach to Mars appeared to be a bit larger than a harvest moon seen from the Earth. At its closest orbital approach to Mars, the planet Venus appeared to be about one-fifth the size of the same lunar observation. The then-fully functioning radiars you know as the planets Jupiter, Saturn, Uranus and Neptune blazed brilliantly in the night sky. Under the stars and the light provided by the planetary bodies of our solar system, those of the patrol would sit about our campfire and speculate as to whether life in any form existed elsewhere in the universe. (I can't help but fib a bit and say that we were sure that Earth was inhabited by little green men and gigantic purple women.) Some of my comrades recited ancient legends and stories and recalled bloody skirmishes with soldiers of other strongholds who had ventured too far into our territory, or when a patrol from our home hi had entered the jurisdiction of another bar-rex. There were also accounts of full-scale wars that had taken place between the bar-rexes, dictating the present status of the various rulers.

Among the stories was one that related the existence of mysterious silver-masked giants in purple robes who sailed sand sleds on the glasslike sands that began many miles from the grass-covered highways. Even the bravest of bar-rexes feared an encounter with these giants, who were said to live on the slopes of the sacred mountain called Daren. (This volcanic mountain is called Olympus Mons by those of present-day Earth.) The depiction of this mountain backed by two lightning bolts is the emblem that identifies our spacecraft and other things that require such identification.

Rancer-Carr, the Zone-Rex

Since very ancient times a special individual occasionally comes forth with great spiritual authority, which some bar-rexes willingly obey and others are forced to obey. Such a person is called a zone-rex.

In my first life, such a person in the form of a young man who was the son of a Shem copper miner (a profession practiced by special permit) was ordained by the silver-masked giants to rule and spiritually guide all who lived upon our world. This man lives today and is named Rancer-Carr. I never met or saw Rancer-Carr in my first lifetime. Little did I know in my first life of the relationship we would form in this present life, for on Mars I have lived only that first life. Each life thereafter (and there were many) were spent in the confines of the Frequency Barrier of the planet Earth.

Even though Mars is presently inhospitable to life without artificial life-supporting equipment, I am very pleased to be able to visit my home world whenever I can.

My life changed after receiving a gift from my mother of fine leather armor that was blood-red in color. This brought me a considerable number of jealous remarks and jibes from a few of my comrades, so I decided not to wear it in their presence. I would don the armor when returning to the stronghold so that my mother would be pleased. At one such time I found my armor missing and I became furious. I sought out the man I suspected of taking my property and we fought, to his eventual death. I did not learn until later that he had taken the armor as a practical joke. I was placed in chains, imprisoned and later sentenced to death.

One morning I was brought before the bar-rex and my mother. Also at the assemblage were three strange white-haired men wearing identical clothing made not of wool, but of a material with a type of weave I had never seen before. The words they spoke to each other sounded like gibberish. One approached me and touched a flashing rod to my forehead and everything went black.

I awoke with a great ache in my head among hundreds of other strange-looking characters who looked to me in most cases to be as small as children. I could not understand what they were saying and in some cases they could not understand each other. We seemed to be in a cave among metal boxes, and the walls gave off a soft eerie light. The white-haired ones gave us water and food I had never had before. After a time I learned to like the food and looked forward to its being passed out.

By and by, communication began to occur among the different types of "shorties," and I was able to pick up the fact that nobody knew where we were or what was happening to us. We lost track of time.

My Friend 63-92

From time to time I noticed moving among the mob a man who was taller than the shorties but not quite as tall as me. He wore a tattered and stained white wool robe and carried a black gourd with strange white symbols crudely painted on it. I learned later that these symbols stood for the numbers 63-92.

Sitting propped against a wall, I felt sad and longed to be once again with the people of my tribe. I placed my hands over my face to hide my emotions from those about me, and cried. As I was weeping, I felt someone touch the top of my head and speak my name. I looked up to see before me the man I would thereafter refer to simply as 63-92. He handed me the gourd, from which I drew nothing but air into my mouth. Though his lips did not move, I heard him say, "What do you want it to taste like?" I thought of a mild alcoholic drink that was popular on my home world and instantly my mouth began to magically fill with it, until I swallowed the liquid, and then the manifestation ceased.

I placed my fingertips to my eyes to salute this wizard as I would salute one such as my teacher So-Socrey. I asked how he knew my name and how he was able to speak to me without moving his lips. He replied, "The els know the names of everyone, and it is they who told me your name. I speak to you in your mind. Communicating in this way is an ability you will eventually acquire after you reach your destination. It is really not that difficult to communicate in this manner. Some of those presently about you which you call shorties can easily communicate in this way to each other."

I physically asked, "Who are the els? When will I be released from my confinement so that I can travel to the destination of which you speak?" Sixty-three ninety-two waved off my questions with a gesture and walked away, disappearing into the crowd.

The Planet Nodia

At one point during my imprisonment the walls of my confinement chamber began to hum and then produce a high-pitched sound that startled us and awakened those who were asleep at the time. One of the walls began to move and folded to both sides, producing an opening through which I could see a most wondrous sight. Towering buildings and silvery objects sparkled in the sunlight and seemed to float like feathers on the wind or move rapidly across the sky. You might say I witnessed what was to me at the time a sky filled with UFOs. Standing on a downward-slanting ramp were a number of white-hairs who motioned to us to come out. As I walked down the ramp, I turned to look at the place where I had spent my recent confinement. It looked like a large circular house (bigger than any house I had ever seen before) and it was covered with horizontal stripes, which were alternately colored red, white and black. Through numerous circular windows I could see white-hairs looking out at what was obviously their home world.

Suddenly before me stood 63-92. He mentally instructed me not to go to the left with the others, but to go to the right and ignore anyone who tried to tell me differently. My instructor then disappeared before my eyes.

Turning to the right, I came to a marketplace filled with stalls and vendors of every possible kind, mostly those who sold vegetables. I was drawn to a man selling flowers that emitted a marvelous fragrance that defies my ability to describe. Around me I saw others exchanging some form of currency for their purchases. Though I had no such currency, the vendor gave me a large yellow flower and shooed me away from his stand with a smile. At each stall or shop I was given whatever I had even the slightest mental interest in, then directed to leave. I soon became overburdened with my gifts and sat down, placing them around me. Within a short time, people came to me and pointed to one or more of my items, holding out to me various-colored currency disks (like plastic poker chips). A lot of good these disks did me: No one would take them from me, but preferred to give me whatever I wanted at no cost. What a world!

My travels eventually brought me to a large bakery that sold bread, cakes and pastries of kinds that no bar-rex of my home world could command to be placed before him. The bakery was staffed by pleasing, plump women and girls who directed me by hand movements to sit on the floor in a corner (all the chairs were too small for me to sit on). They brought me all I desired of their baked goods until I could eat no more. A finely dressed lady wearing sparkling rings on her fingers came down a flight of stairs and mentally asked me to leave. I gave her no argument.

Night seemed never to come on this world. There was a brief period of a kind of twilight lasting about twenty-nine Earth hours, followed by a gradual brightening of the sky. I experienced getting sunburned for the first time in my life. A street vendor, seeing this, gave me a large bottle of lotion. I thought I should drink the stuff, until my benefactor shook his head in the universal movement for no and acted out how I should topically apply it to my skin. I was also given a large-brimmed hat.

During the third twilight after my arrival on the planet Nodia, I settled down in a place where everyone seemed to be celebrating. Intoxicating drinks could be purchased, but my cup was continuously refilled at no cost.

I saw two men (non-Nodians) murdered. The bodies of the slain were stripped of their clothes and other belongings and moved elsewhere. Immediately thereafter I was approached by a group of **men** and women (off-worlders) who mentally offered me a large sum of **currency** to kill the murderer, who sat at a near table and continued to drink as if he had done nothing wrong. I mentally refused and also turned down their offer to guard them against any future physical harm that might come their way from the violent ones who also resided on the planet.

I awoke from my drunken stupor to find myself again incarcerated in a pit covered by metal bars. My numerous cellmates were a sad lot of various types of off-worlders. Their moans, cries, laments and loud conversations were deafening. The place stank, and I realized that I was probably one of the major contributors to the stench.

The bars that covered the pit were lifted and the place gradually became quiet. Standing at the edge of the pit looking down at its human contents were three white-hairs and several accompanying off-worlders. One of the white-hairs was young (my age, about nineteen Earth years old). The young white-hair (Nodian) wore a plain, loose-fitting beige shirt and matching pants bloused at the ankles. Standing beside him, to my surprise, was another Martian with a monkeylike creature on his shoulder. The Martian spoke to me in the language of my tribe: "He whom I stand beside offers you freedom if you serve him for the rest of your life and accept him as your only god." I mentally thought, *This fellow is really a self-important fool.* I also considered lying in order to gain my freedom. The young white-haired one called to me audibly in my native language: "You are not very far from wrong in how important I think myself to be. Come and join us, Martian. I am Rayatis Cre'ator."

A ladder was lowered, and I climbed it into the light of the sun-star Sost, and into the beginning of a new and most exciting life. Currency was exchanged with a group of jailers, and my previous cellmates climbed the ladder and spread in different directions.

Without saying another word, the Martian left our company. As we walked, the aroma of freshly baked bread filled the air. We soon arrived at one of my favorite places on the planet Nodia: the bakery where I had been generously stuffed at an earlier time. We did not enter the bakery, but instead went to the rear of the building and climbed a long flight of stairs to reach the fifth and uppermost story. Behind a plain door were large rooms decorated with furniture and art that was breathtaking to behold. These living quarters were occupied by quite a few Nodians and various types of off-worlders. There were elevators that went below ground level to endless corridors and rooms filled with Nodians doing one thing or another with one hand while eating a piece of freshly baked bread with the other.

Everyone seemed to take orders from a white-complexioned, red-haired man named Rick-Charkels and his mate, Orja. I was given a pallet and told by Rick-Charkels that I should sleep on one of the balconies. After I reluctantly bathed, I was given new clothing that perfectly duplicated that which I had been wearing since my arrival on the planet Nodia. One morning I found at the foot of my pallet the red armor that had been responsible for my exile to this place of marvels and subtle dangers.

I was rarely permitted to come into the living quarters and did so only to gain access to the stairs that led to the street. I would leave my living area to accompany Rick-Charkels, Orja and her kitchen crew as they did their marketing. My purpose and that of the crew was to carry the loot. I use the term "loot" because the vendors would not accept payment for their products and wares and would respond as if insulted if payment was offered.

I began to easily learn the Nodian spoken language, but found their form of telepathic communication to be frustrating due to my lack of education in so many subjects that required abstract thought.

Rhore, the Martian

One twilight time I was visited by Rhore the Martian, who had spoken to me on the day I was freed from the pit by my Nodian benefactor. Rhore gained access to my living quarters initially by crossing the rooftops of adjoining buildings and leaping onto the balcony from a considerable distance. During later visits he used a ladder for a bridge, storing it on the next roof until he needed it.

Rhore was a Shem, though not of my particular band. He estimated that he had been on the planet Nodia for nearly eleven Earth years. He was free to come and go as he pleased and chose to live about thirty-five miles away, in a forest filled with a countless number of different types of animals. He transported himself on a scooter that could fly about five feet off the ground but could not reach rooftop heights.

Once Rhore pointed out a bright star in the sky, which was in fact the sun that gave light and warmth to our native world. He told me that it would take nearly sixteen days by Nodian "star boat" to reach our home world. He said he would like to visit Mars someday to acquire a mate or two, but never to live there permanently. I was dismayed by his statement and asked him why he felt this way. He said, "Why live among the ignorant when you can live among the wise?"

During many a twilight time I rode on the back of Rhore's scooter as we traveled to his forest home and to other places of great natural beauty. We also visited places where star boats were being constructed and colonies of off-worlders existed. These excursions and endless conversations with Rhore helped me to better understand my new home and instilled within me the strong desire to learn as much as I could about everything I could.

I learned from Rhore that my provider, Rayatis Cre'ator, was really a different type of bar-rex. The mystery of the generous vendors was cleared up when Rhore explained that they were really Cre'ator's business partners. The whole system of Cre'ator's commercial enterprises was held together by what you might call the Godfather principle: He made his partners offers they could not refuse. Cre'ator, for many understandable reasons, kept a very low public profile. Even in his youth he had had five children: two sons and two daughters by a woman who lived on another planet in the same solar system, and a daughter by a Nodian beauty who was also absent from the household for the first year or so of my service. On the day she arrived with her red-headed daughter (red-haired Nodians are very rare), my life took another major turn.

I was assigned to accompany her with a considerable number of body-guards on shopping trips that on occasion ranged worldwide and also to nearby planets. She shunned security and ventured to places that caused the bravest of her Nodian guard to cringe. At first my job seemed to be to carry her offspring on my back or shoulders whenever the child kicked me in the leg. As time passed I discovered that I could assign this task to any of the other guards in the retinue. I soon thereafter realized that I was their commander. This was an astonishing revelation. I had been elected to the office by secret ballot of my fellow guardsmen.

Whereas Lady Cre'ator ignored security, she was highly interested in dressing her guards in outrageously colorful uniforms and dousing them with expensive perfumes. The latter practice was stopped when the "espers" (those who mentally probe the local surroundings for lurking dangers) complained that the smell was affecting their ability to perform their function.

A spacious room was given to me in the living quarters located above the bakery, and Rhore was allowed to visit me if he came bathed and dressed in clean attire. I had learned from Rhore early in our acquaintance that he had been brought to Nodia by women he had come across in the Martian desert who were harvesting those same intoxicating cactus bulbs favored so highly by my first teacher, So-Socrey. One of the women had asked Rhore if he would like to travel with her to far-distant worlds where she would sell the inventory of intoxicants. Without hesitation he had accepted her offer. The woman's name was Martcra, but she was generally referred to as Cherry Flag because she flew a banner with a red cherry embroidered upon it whenever she landed on a world and set up shop.

During one visit to Nodia, Cherry Flag, due to unforeseen legal circumstances, had found it necessary to depart the planet hastily, leaving Rhore behind. He had not seen her since. He was adopted and thereafter supported, as I had been, by the illustrious House of Cre'ator.

Rhore instructed me in the use of mental roms that helped me to rapidly fill my mental inventory with knowledge and experiences that would have taken an eternity to acquire in any other way. There was a never-ending supply of this mentally recorded material, and I absorbed it during every free moment that I was not attending to Lady Cre'ator.

One day I was awakened from sleep by a powerful mental command from Rayatis Cre'ator to come to the large council room. I had never been there before. On arrival I found an empty chair bearing my name tooled on its leather back support.

The Lords of Devisement

This council room was filled mostly by men and women whom Cre'ator called his Lords of Devisement. This body of devisers, or counselors, grew over the years until they filled an auditorium, and then to numbers that presently surpass my ability to comprehend. The Lords of Devisement originally numbered about thirty.

Meetings would last for days and were interrupted only when Cre'ator took a break. Many times important visitors would attend these daily gatherings; among them were Carlus Domphey, Trare Vonner (a Cre'ator brother-in-law) and Adolfro Blaclotter, as well as other dignitaries. Vonner and Domphey were in the same lucrative interstellar businesses as Cre'ator and were first considered to be friendly competitors. These relationships became very adversarial for a period, until the formation of the Federation restored (by threat of force and other means) a long-lasting peace between them, which exists to this very day.

Lady Cre'ator never attended the council meetings, but her daughter did, sometimes with her half brother Dray-Fost, whose raven-black hair and black eyes (physical traits of his off-world mother) caused him to stand out amidst the white-haired Nodians. I myself wished I had lived long enough to see those two children grow up and jointly take administrative control of the House of Cre'ator, as they did upon their father's death. Their first-lifetime stewardship of the assets of this now-great trading house played an important cooperative role in the rapid development of the Federation.

Just before the foundation of the Federation, the council meetings were attended by my old friend 63-92 and a lanky Nodian named Linc Core, who had a long white beard that reached to his knees. Linc Core had the same ability to disappear that I had seen demonstrated by 63-92 on that day I first arrived on Nodia. The pair would not verbally make a comment, but did speak to Cre'ator telepathically in a way that caused a variety of strong emotional expressions to form on his face. One could tell that they were forcing him to make some very difficult decisions.

One morning a man, introduced to the assembly as Cre'ator's half brother Opatel, arrived with another man whom Opatel identified as Sant, of the planet Maldec. Sant was physically beautiful, having golden hair and violet-colored eyes. He said nothing during the meeting but on occasion squinted his eyes and flicked the tip of his tongue rapidly against the center of his upper lip. This was not a nervous habit, but an indication that he was deeply concentrating on the subject under discussion. His presence seemed to make everyone but Opatel uncomfortable. At the close of the meeting Sant came to me smiling, and addressed me perfectly in my native language. He told me that we were planetary neighbors because his home world of Maldec orbited the same sun-star as my home world did. He said no more and walked away, leaving me speechless.

Nearly twenty years passed, during which the Federation was established and the form of economy was changed several times until Adolfro Blaclotter designed the system that is used today. The trading houses of Cre'ator, Vonner and Domphey expanded one solar system at a time until eventually they each had an outpost in every solar system in the Milky Way galaxy (as it is called on Earth) and several neighboring galaxies as well.

The opening subject of one of the daily council meetings pertained to the report that the planet Maldec had exploded into pieces. The report went on to say that all seemed to be well with the other planets of the system. I recall that only one Lord of Devisement asked, "What caused this catastrophe?" Getting no answer, he and the others put the subject aside and went on to the next order of business.

For several years following, I traveled with Rayatis Cre'ator and other officers of the trading house to countless different star systems, some located in other galaxies. I found the varying cultures we visited to be mentally stimulating and educational, but Cre'ator was tired to the depths of his soul. He was bored and spent most of his time in the presence of Linc Core, whom he could somehow summon at will.

Several days after returning to Nodia, Opatel arrived and related his first-hand account of the explosion of Maldec, which he had observed from the Earth. He added that the radiars and planets of the system were slowly taking new orbits and might even eventually spiral to their doom by crashing into the sun.

Cre'ator asked what the Federation was doing about this possibility, if anything. Opatel said that only the Earth appeared to be maintaining its natural orbit, so those who wished to leave the other worlds of the system were being moved to the Earth for safety.

Opatel personally told me that my home planet Mars was in jeopardy and that the Federation was considering putting two artificial moons in orbit around it to stabilize its solar orbit. He also said that a large number of my fellow Martians had relocated to the Earth and to a planet called Mollara in another star system.

Opatel told us that he was returning to Earth and that Lady Cre'ator wanted to travel with him and would return to Nodia after a brief visit. Opatel assured Cre'ator that there was no serious immediate danger. After some reluctance Cre'ator gave in to his wife's direct personal request to travel to the Earth with Opatel, on condition that I, Sharmarie, go with her. I looked forward to the trip and hoped that I would physically see and be able to talk to someone from the home world I had known in my youth.

On Earth with Lady Cre'ator

When we arrived on the Earth we were received as guests by the Maldecian governor of the Earth, Her-Rood. He had no apparent remorse about the fact that his home world was now circling the in bits and pieces. Since his planet's destruction he had occupied his time by hosting an ongoing orgy at his palatial estate, located in the area of the Earth now called southern Venezuela.

I spent the first six days on the Earth looking for Martians. I managed to find a few Shems and Burrs who told me that more than 100,000 of my people had left the Earth with the zone-rex, Rancer-Carr, about three weeks before for a planet called Mollara. They also told me there were thousands of Martians assembled at some location on the Earth, waiting for transportation that would permit them to make the same journey. They could not tell me where on Earth this assembling point was.

The Earth was filled with slave markets, and violence was rampant. To remove myself from the madness, I decided to return to the party and make inquiries of any half-sober person I could find who was still on his feet. I have never wanted to leave a place more than I wanted to leave the planet Earth. I strongly felt that something was going to go very wrong.

Then came the day when the sky filled with very dark clouds accompanied by thunder and lightning. The frequency of the thunder and lightning increased over a period of days until there was no silence. It was deafening. The rain was torrential and pelted the roofs of the buildings with such force that some of the structures cracked and slid off their foundations, to be swept away along with great waves of mud.

I sought out and found the Lady Cre'ator when the storm began, but could not locate Opatel. When we reached the place where our spacecraft had been left, it was gone.

Along with a number of other party guests, we acquired an aircar that was piloted by a man who kept the car airborne and flying by mentally focusing his life force through the detached but still-living brain of a dog. His energy lasted less than a day. About ten minutes after he landed the craft on a mountaintop, he fell asleep and then died. Because the car was being rocked violently by the wind and was rapidly turning around in circles in the mud, I decided that Lady Cre'ator and I should leave the car and look for some other kind of shelter. Shortly thereafter we watched as the car slid over a cliff and disappeared from our sight. I have since wished that we had stayed in the car and met our death when it plunged over the cliff.

We had walked a short distance when we saw in the sky the spacecraft that had brought us from Nodia. It was obviously trying to reach us, and its efforts brought us hope. But with every lightning flash, the craft rocked and gyrated radically. Several times it seemed to actually be struck by lightning bolts. Then suddenly it was gone, never to be seen again.

Lady Cre'ator walked to the edge of the cliff. I, of course, knew that she was planning to end her life in a fatal leap. Then the noise of the thunder and rain stopped, and a voice called my name. I turned to see 63-92 standing slightly above me, surrounded by an aura of white light.

He softly said, "Don't allow her to take her own life." I replied, "What should I do?" He answered my question by saying, "I cannot tell you what to do, but for the sake of her soul, do not let her take her own life."

I felt for my sidearm and took it from its container on my belt. As I raised the weapon, I thought, *She whom I swore to protect from harm I am now about to kill.* When I fired, her body arched and lifted from the ground. Her arms moved several times like the wings of a bird, then her body disappeared over the edge of the cliff. The noise of the thunder and rain resumed as I lifted the weapon to my temple. I activated the weapon again and again but nothing happened, so I threw it as far as I could and walked to the edge of the cliff, not to jump but to look for Lady Cre'ator's body. I could not see the base of the cliff, even in the light of the lightning flashes. As I walked I found myself chanting a Martian prayer for the dead I had learned so many years ago.

After several days of wandering I became very weak and fell face-down in the mud. Mud soon began to wash over me, holding me down in the process. I fell asleep and dreamed of enjoyable things that had occurred throughout my life. My body became disconnected from the universal life field and died, leaving my soul waiting upon the will of the elohim.

The lifetime I just described lasted for slightly more than 72 Earth years. It was not until my present embodiment that I learned of the first-life fates and later lives (reembodiments) of many of the people I interacted with in that first lifetime.

Understand that my 53-year association with the Trading House of Cre'ator and my numerous galactic travels that were sponsored by that organization brought me into contact with cultures and individuals that greatly impressed my spirit with the ways of humans who are bright and most holy, as well as the ways of humans who are dark and sinister. I found love with women of many worlds, but never fathered any children until this life I am presently experiencing.

Every life is important in the master plan of the Creator of All That Is. If this were not true, there would be no life at all.

Lives upon the Planet Earth

We of the "open unrestricted mental state" (not subjected to the

Frequency Barrier of the planet Earth) can recall each and every lifetime we have ever experienced. In fact, each life is to us really a part of one continuous life that has had no disembodied interruptions. Even though this is true for an individual living in the open mental state, it is not the case for those who live in the "closed mental state" that exists on the Earth today and has prevailed on the planet for hundreds of thousands of centuries.

I have made a comparison of the two types of mental states for you to understand that each and every life I have experienced on the Earth since the planet was subjected to the detrimental Frequency Barrier were lived under very much the same mentally restricting conditions (with very few exceptions) that a person of the Earth is subject to today.

Therefore, each life I have lived on Earth (and there were hundreds of such lives) began and ended in my ignorance of the fact that I had lived before and would surely live again and again in the physical human form.

Of the hundreds of lives I have lived on the Earth in the past, several (about five) stand out. I will describe these lifetimes briefly in the order in which they occurred. Some of these lifetimes were separated by thousands of years and they ranged from 14 to 534 years in duration.

The Prince

The time was so long ago in the past that stating exactly when it was would put your credibility and mine in doubt in the minds of those who are considered (or feel they are) authorities on the prehistory of the Earth. So I will give you nothing you must defend or waste time debating with those whose minds are closed and set to believe otherwise. I assure you that for several reasons no physical record of any type pertaining to that bygone civilization is recognizable, unless one considers such evidence as machine screws and machined objects found in deposits of anthracite coal.

The name of my father was Agrathrone. My mother Merthran was one of his hundreds of wives. I was the sixty-seventh of 182 sons. I had nearly twice as many half sisters and two full sisters. I had been named Urais. My father was more than an emperor; he was worshiped by his subjects as a god. Because I was his son I was also looked upon as a deity, as were all his wives and other children.

At that time my father's realm covered nearly one-third of the surface of the Earth, but he had plans to rule every square inch. The capital of the empire was located in the northern part of the country that is presently called Thailand.

My father had secret allies (gods) who came to visit on occasion in silver eggs that descended from the skies. From my earliest childhood I dreaded their arrival, as did everyone in the royal household. They brought immunization injections and tablets we had to take.

For several days after taking the injections the household was gripped by fear, because on occasion one or more of us would die from a violent reaction. If a child died, its mother usually died also. If a child died and the mother did not, she was immediately executed. To my father and the sky gods these deaths simply meant that those who died had an inferior biological makeup which did not fit into their plan of producing a biologically superior race that was totally resistant to any kind of infection or disease.

I was in my late teens when I learned that there was a plan to eventually infect and kill every other human on the planet with biological weapons that would not harm those of the empire who were biologically selected as superior (to begin with) and had received the immunizations over the course of many years. If a person survived an injection, they of course felt relieved, but with every injection they survived, they also began to feel that they were indeed more and more superior to other unimmunized humans. I was no exception.

The sky gods were always dressed in protective clothing and peered out from inside transparent helmets that totally enclosed their heads. Their semiannual visits never lasted for more than a few hours. One day they arrived in more than thirty silver eggs that were at least fifty times larger than any others I had seen before. They carried a cargo of vehicles and machines that when unloaded covered hundreds of acres. On that day the empire of Agrathrone instantly went from an ox-cart society to a technical level that would amaze the most imaginative physicist living on Earth today.

My brothers and sisters were assembled with others of noble houses, then a sky god walked among our ranks making selections for reasons that were not clear to us at the time. The sky god who stood before me and selected me by touching my chest was a beautiful man who flicked the tip of his tongue against the middle of his upper lip. He mentally spoke to me and said, "You will do very well, Martian. Yes, you will do very well." I did not know the meaning of the name he called me (the name "Martian" is used here only to correspond to the reader's references). He strolled away laughing, leaving me with a pounding headache.

Those of us who were selected (both male and female) were assigned to vehicles we were told could fly through the air. They were cylindrical in shape, about thirty-six feet long, had a diameter of about twelve feet and an olive-green exterior. We were given operation manuals written in our native language. The instruction in the closing chapter of the manual was "When you are sure you can operate the vehicle, do so."

I was not the first of my group to try to fly. It was somewhat humorous to watch one of my brothers or sisters rise from the ground a few feet and bump into the vehicles of one or more of the other fledglings. Upon landing they would argue and accuse each other of causing the collision.

When I made my first attempt to fly, it came easy; it was if I had always known how. My dreams from that time forward were filled with events of flying on the back of air scooters and in aircraft filled with white-haired people.

I enjoyed the thrill of flying and ventured hundreds of miles from the capital city at the highest and lowest altitudes that the automatic altitude governor would permit. Many times I wished I could climb higher and higher until I reached the land of the sky gods. Sometimes I would take with me a boy (in his early teens) on my practice flights. I thought at the time that he was my natural son. (Only in my present lifetime did I learn that the boy, whose mother was the first of my three wives, had really been fathered by one of my younger brothers. No matter, I loved him then as I do now.)

My flights never took us too far from my home base. This was because the villages and towns were filled with many low-caste nonimmune people who could not provide me or any of my passengers with the food and lodging befitting us who were of such an exalted station. It was interesting to watch the amazed expressions on their peasant faces when we slowly flew by and passed just a few feet over their heads. Some actually died of shock.

It was in the spring of my second year of flying when an older brother named Jasaul and I were summoned by my father. He and his advisors were seriously concerned about a rumor that had reached the court. They had heard that Mokaben, a governor of a distant province, was occasionally observed to tremble. We were ordered to fly to the province and find out if this was true. If so, we were to execute Mokaben and replace him with Jasaul as governor of that land. Jasaul was a stocky man with a moon face, which he chose to hide behind a coarse, wiry beard. He could not fly an air-car. This, of course, was why I was needed. Jasaul was very intelligent; he fascinated everyone with his knowledge.

We left our father's capital city in a fleet of eight aircars. Some of these cars carried special foods and others carried servants tightly packed into the vehicles.

The trip took about two and a half days (we got lost several times), and we arrived in the land of Toray at night. The landmark that identified our landing site was a large pyramid whose highly polished white limestone faces brilliantly reflected the light of a nearly full moon.

Electric lights were turned on below us, and we could see on the ground many men frantically motioning us away from the glowing structure. Not all the pilots of our flight got the message fast enough. Their craft first wobbled very erratically, then crashed in the high grass that bordered the nearby river. We lost four aircars in this way, and all of their occupants were killed.

As you might have realized, the land we then called Toray included the area you now call Egypt. The pyramid and river were, of course, what you would respectively refer to as the Great Pyramid of Giza and the river Nile, both of which still exist in that land today.

When we met with Mokaben, he made no effort to conceal the fact that his tremors lasted for up to about ten minutes. He had no doubt why we were there. He told us that during the 143 years he had governed the land of Toray he'd had to execute many people who had acquired the shaking sickness. Jasaul and I compared Mokaben's immunization record with our own and found them to be the same. It was his opinion that the sickness was caused by some effect generated by the Great Pyramid. Mokaben claimed his right as a noble to take his own life, and we granted his request. He added that he was probably a condemned man anyway, because he had angered the sky gods by not preventing the theft (five days before our arrival) of the Great Pyramid's crystal capstone.

That night I was introduced to another of the sky gods' marvels. Jasaul showed me a box that permitted him to talk to our father as if he were present in the same room (this was, in fact, a radio transmitter and receiver). My father instructed Jasaul to preserve Mokaben's body because the sky gods wanted to examine (autopsy) it. Jasaul requested and obtained permission to move the seat of government of Toray as far away from the Great Pyramid as possible.

Several days later I left Toray for home, accompanied by two of the remaining aircars. Jasaul kept one of the cars and a pilot with him. One of the aircars of my flight contained Mokaben's mummy-wrapped body and surgically removed organs.

The remaining two-thirds of the Earth's surface was governed by hundreds of different kings who were allied to twelve emperors, who in turn had a strong alliance between them. After many decades of primitive warfare (conducted with swords, spears, bows and arrows) between these emperors and my father, things were at a stalemate. This state of affairs was definitely something my father and his sky-god friends were planning to change and was the basis of their diabolical plan. Physically conquering the other people of the Earth was not part of the sky gods' agenda, for they had absolutely no need of those they considered to be racially (biologically) inferior.

About two years after Jasaul became governor of Toray, my father started to send aircars on missions that took them over the lands of his adversaries. These were training missions that were to acquaint the pilots with the geographical landmarks over which one day they would drop their biological weapons. The populations of these lands could do little but shake their fists at our aircars, which usually dropped human waste on them to simulate bombing. It was during the course of these training exercises that I received a message from Jasaul requesting that I come visit him along with six of my older brothers, whom he requested by name. We had no problem gaining our father's permission to visit Jasaul for a week or two.

After several days of wining and dining, Jasaul asked to talk to me privately. The story he related was at first overwhelming. He told me of other sky gods who had visited him and had convinced him that our father's plan to destroy the unimmunized of the Earth was wrong and would bring down upon us all not only their wrath, but the wrath of the divine power that created the world itself. I believed him and so did four of my six other full brothers. The two who thought we should remain loyal to our father did not join us for breakfast on the following morning.

Jasaul's sky gods had proposed that we return to our home with a device that, once activated amidst the stockpile of biological bombs, would secretly render them useless. Four days later this device was planted and did its job very well. When the day came about seven months later, the bombs were loaded on the aircars. But when they were dropped, they simply filled the skies with iridescent puffs of smoke that sparkled in the sunlight. My father and his sky gods were furious and made haste to produce more bombs (an obviously time-consuming task even for the gods).

The strange disappearance of the two brothers who did not return with us from Toray and the strange, guilt-ridden behavior displayed by several of my brother conspirators (who were then mentally tortured by the sky gods to confess) soon brought to light those of us who were responsible for the sabotage. We had anticipated that we would be discovered, so we collectively fled by aircar to the land you now call Japan (then attached to the continent you call Asia). We were later joined by Jasaul. Our three aircars, for some reason unknown to us, later failed to function, and over the many years that followed gradually disintegrated into unrecognizable piles of powdered metal.

Word finally reached us that our father and his empire no longer existed. The end of his reign occurred immediately after the two opposing types of sky gods battled with each other somewhere in the heavens far above the planet. Our father's war machines and aircars became inoperable and while unprepared, he was attacked by the allied forces of the other twelve emperors.

We were at a later time visited by a representative of the emperor whose jurisdiction we were living in. We were told not to be afraid, that no harm would come to us, for we were considered great heroes who were under the protection of the benevolent sky gods.

I lived to be 534 years old and died peacefully in my sleep.

Some centuries thereafter the Frequency Barrier took a drastic change for the worse and the people of the Earth were once again subject to a considerable degree of biological deterioration.

One More Golden Age

About 29,000 years ago the place I called home extended about 1200 miles southeast of the place you now call Florida. Another section of the kingdom extended about 650 miles southwest of the Iberian peninsula (Portugal and Spain). We called the two parts of the land separated by ocean Fe-Atlan and Ro-Atlan, respectively (meaning South Atlan and North Atlan). A part of southeast England was at that time still connected to the continent of Europe. Today, legends of this kingdom exist on Earth. The kingdom that is the subject of those legends you call Atlantis. We had colonies in the lands you call Egypt, Britain and Finland.

The rest of the world was our hunting reserve, and it was filled with animals and subhuman types left over from the last dark period brought about by the then-unpredictable Frequency Barrier. These subhumans were what you now call pre-Neanderthals, Neanderthals and primitive Cro-Magnon people. My people had a biological link to the latter. Cro-Magnons could be trained and were used as slave labor, mostly in Ro-Atlan mines located in the far north.

We of the Atlans did not need the assistance of extraterrestrials or sky gods (whom we knew to exist) to help us develop a very high technology that included aircraft, wireless radios, television, computers, nuclear power and a number of other forms of technology that utilized specially grown crystals and human psychic energy transmitted through higher levels of the universal life field. Mental telepathy was easily employed, but was wisely not practiced widely, in favor of not wasting the life force that would have to be spent in its performance. Even so, the priests carried on mental conversations regularly with the extraterrestrials. The extraterrestrials told us that they adhered to a law that they called the Prime Directive, which forbade interference in the natural development of a planetary culture. They did request to be permitted to visit the surface of the planet from time to time to obtain samples of various plants and animals. The priest granted them permission to do so.

I was born about 723 years after the beginning of this so-called golden age. Few were blessed with the biological ability to adjust to and benefit from this minor temporary lull in the course of the Frequency Barrier. I was called then Socrantor the Younger, born of Rosey (my mother) and Socrantor the Elder (my father). I had a younger brother named Macrantor.

The currency of Atlan consisted of precious synthetic gems and crystals that could be produced by secret processes known only to the king and the priests. The accumulation of wealth was the goal of every Atlanian.

My father was a captain of an oceangoing fishing vessel that also hunted fur-bearing animals such as otters and seals. His acquired wealth permitted him to buy my brother a place in the priesthood and myself a lowly commission in the king's army. My earliest duties included escorting and protecting groups of nobles on hunting trips in areas located on any continent you could name. The game was usually the hairy elephantlike creature you call the mastodon.

It was on one such hunting trip in central Asia that I was about to retire for the night when one of the nobles called the group's attention to an extraterrestrial spacecraft, which slowly passed over our heads and landed a short distance away. We commented on the huge size of the vehicle, and one of us said, "Let's go to bed. They won't bother us and we won't bother them." Another said that he wished that we of the Atlans had such a vehicle so that he could travel in space and visit other worlds. Another noble assured him that someday we would.

From within my tent I could see a soft white light rotating on the upper part of the alien craft. Its pulsing rhythm caught my attention. It soon began to pulse rapidly until I felt myself slipping into a state of consciousness I could not prevent, even with every bit of my summoned willpower. I then heard a voice speak to me telepathically: "Sharmarie, so there you are, old friend. You might not remember me now, but we knew each other in an earlier time. I am Rayatis Cre'ator. I wish I could take you with me when we leave, but I have no positive light of divine direction that would permit me to do so. I deeply regret this. Try to remember this mental contact, and try to remember me. Maybe we will be able to talk to each other mentally in the future. I have a great deal to tell you. Lady Cre'ator is back among us of the open state."

I remembered the mental contact of that evening but did not remember the one who called himself Rayatis Cre'ator. That night I dreamed of space-craft and white-haired people as well as aircars, painful injections and hel-meted sky gods who flicked the tips of their tongues against the centers of their upper lips.

For about twelve years after that night, all went well in my life. I rose in military rank and took a bride named Toriata. We had no children. Then some Atlan genius came up with the idea to punch two slanted holes into the Earth, using a number of successive nuclear detonations. One of these holes began in Iraq, and the other in Peru. He had determined that if he could reach the planet's magma, he could acquire one of the ingredients that the extraterrestrials used to propel their spacecraft, allowing the peo-ple of the two Atlans to travel throughout the stars. The energy extracted from the core was to be stored in large crystals housed underground in both Fe-Atlan and Ro-Atlan. The earthquakes, tidal waves and volcanic eruptions caused by his nuclear detonations were hard to ignore, as were the crazy ways the people of the two Atlans began to feel and act. The genius lost control of his project and his transmitter continued to send the core energy to the storage crystals. The two Atlans and its people literally vibrated into huge clouds of dust and volcanic ash, which covered the Earth and prevented the sun from warming the Earth, thus causing the beginning of the Earth's first ice age.

The ocean covered other parts of the land that were not disintegrated and the two Atlans were no more. I was 52 years old when this catastrophe occurred and took my life. Where is Atlantis? The answer: It is every-where.

A Soldier of Sparta

My name was Rembeylian. I was born in the year 462 B.C. to Menneva and Artaclean, who were, respectively, my mother and father. The place was the city-state of ancient Greece that was then, as now, called Sparta. I had three sisters. At the age of eight I was taken from my parents (with their willing consent) to live with other boys of my age in state-owned barracks where we trained to be soldiers.

We were first trained to use slings, which we used against any closely advancing foe that had survived the arrows of our long-range archers. We would actually stand just behind the short-range archers and hurl our stones over their heads, then run like hell to the rear of our own advancing javelin throwers and spear men. A wise general came up with the idea that the advancing javelin throwers should carry with them quivers of arrows to be handed to any grabbing archer running by. We could never get the javelin throwers to carry bags of stones for us slingers. I had experienced war many times before I reached the age of ten. By age fourteen I was an expert with the javelin and by nineteen was considered to be very good with a sword. To reach the age of nineteen in that profession you had to be very good at killing people and not getting killed yourself.

I liked horses and women. The women of the conquered were always part of a victorious soldier's pay. Captured horses belonged to the state and were ridden only by those of high rank. Horses had to be fed, watered, groomed and saddled. In those days Spartan saddles did not have stirrups, until one day one of our archers brought down a Scythian horseman and captured his mount, which wore a saddle that had these marvelous inventions attached. Why hadn't I thought of that? As I said, only high-ranking men rode horses.

Sparta did not have a cavalry because a common soldier had a hard time staying mounted on the beasts when they took off in a gallop. The use of stirrups permitted the formation of the first Spartan cavalry. I was selected as one of the members of this illustrious group that first numbered thirty and eventually grew to nine groups of 360 each. I learned to ride very well and eventually was assigned to teach others how to fight from the backs of the animals and when and how to get off a wounded horse and avoid being pinned under it when it fell.

In the year 432 B.C., what is historically known as the Peloponnesian War began between Sparta and the city-state of Athens. I was about thirty-one years old at the time. By this time the Athenians had a cavalry of considerable size and saddles with stirrups. I learned in the present lifetime that the war lasted twenty-seven years, ending with the Spartans defeating the Athenians, thus becoming the sole rulers of Greece. I was killed in the very first battle of this war while mounted on a horse, by arrows that came from my own archers (I think this is called friendly fire). The archery chief didn't calculate the angle of fire too well, and sent many a good Spartan horseman that day on a journey to the land beyond the river Styx.

A Soldier of Rome

I was Granius, born of a freeman named Robarius and his slave woman Sheila. The time was 236 B.C. The place was the farming village of Utherium, located about 70 miles north of Rome. From the age of about eight, my father hired me out for five years to a road contractor who was a friend. I was not treated as a slave, but more as a son badly in need of education. An education I got, especially when it came to designing and building bridges. These skills were not within the ability of my tutor Drancusus, so he always required special bridge engineers to come from Rome to tackle any bridging problem he might encounter in the course of the road he was constructing (usually roads running north and south, always to the north of Rome).

The bridge engineers were very learned men who spoke a dialect that was hard for me to understand at first. I was quick to learn their speech and they soon employed me to bark their orders to the slaves. Many of the stonemasons had dealt with them on other jobs and could comprehend what they were saying. While in close attendance of the bridge engineers, I learned to read their plans and was accepted as part of their luggage, so to speak. When my five years of service expired, I went home to find that my mother had died and my father was very sick. He died about two months later. I left before I could be sold by the state as just another slave of the household (I had no brand). I returned to the road construction crew and took up my old position as translator for the bridge engineers.

A time came when the chief engineer came to me and told me that the army needed bridge designers and builders. He told me that he would get me such a job, but the catch was that I had to join the army for twenty-five years.

I joined the army and was required to train as a combat soldier. I studied the construction of all types of bridges that could be built in haste and disassembled easily to be moved quickly to the front of the marching troops or as close to the battlefront as possible. (This was no small task.)

In the year 216 B.C. I was about twenty years old and commanded a squad of army engineers, about 75 slaves and 40 soldiers who guarded the slaves. We had about fifteen horse-drawn carts that carried our bridge-building tools. We were moving north under the command of Quintus Fabius Maximus Verrucosus to meet the army of the Carthaginian general known as Hannibal. Our army engaged his and stopped him in his advance. We fought and then strategically retreated south to food depots and weapons caches we had built and planted on our way north. We destroyed with fire or dismantled our bridges as we retreated. But Hannibal could also build bridges very rapidly.

It had rained for several days and it became necessary to abandon my carts and force the slaves to carry the tools. The army had already moved farther south. I took too long in making the decision to leave the carts, and we were overrun by the Carthaginians in great numbers. My slave guards either ran or surrendered on the spot. I was lassoed around the neck and dragged behind a horse. I gripped the rope with my hands until my body slammed into rocks and tree trunks, forcing me to release it. I heard the bones in my neck break, then everything went black. The moral I learned during this life is, don't take time to burn your bridges, especially if the Carthaginians are hot on your trail.

The Anasazi

The time was about A.D. 798. The place I was born was an Anasazi cliff dwelling whose remains are located in the northeastern part of what is now Arizona (Canyon de Chelly). My name was Moytensa. I had two younger brothers named Rocree and Rocreenal. (Yes, I know it is similar to saying, "I'm Larry. This is my brother Darryl, and this is my other brother Darryl.")

My parents were farmers, as were about 95 percent of the others of our tribe. The rest were far-ranging hunters who were absent during the warmest months, returning just before winter began.

This life was brief, but I recall it here to clear up a couple of questions pertaining to the Anasazi: What happened to them? Why did they disappear from their settlements? Did they turn cannibalistic?

In the spring of my twelfth year, the land was visited by grasshoppers that came up from Mexico and devoured our crops. The grasshoppers grew in number until from the highest hills they looked like a living ocean. Those of us who could went north, just ahead of this moving plague. The old and sick stayed behind, and yes, they ate those who had died of natural causes.

The game moved faster toward the north, northwest and northeast than we could. The northern tribes followed the game, not knowing of the horror headed in their direction.

At one point in our travels I sat down beside the trail and passed out, dying from hunger even though my stomach was filled with roasted grasshoppers. They contained something that poisoned us. Some of our tribe were killed or enslaved by the northern tribes, and some were benignly received and allowed to join them as brothers and sisters.

My Present Life

In this life my name is once again Sharmarie, which in my native Martian tongue means "a very small but important part of a very big thing" (or, as my three female soulmates, Quandray, Retkitta and Ogalabon, might say, "a large part of a very small, unimportant thing"; women do seem to have the same ways no matter which world they originate from). I have two twin sons by my mate Quandray; their names are Benner and Trocker. Trocker was born holding on to the foot of his brother at birth, and the seers see this as a great spiritual omen. The twins have had no previous human lives and are presently about nine Earth years old.

I was born into this life about 315 Earth years ago to the woman who was my mother in my first life and a fine man named Booke-Tasser. Booke-Tasser, who also fathered my sister Wren-Shanna in this lifetime, is one of those who on my world would be called a *ta father*. This type of parent would take many pages to explain. So let's let it go until some other time.

My place of birth this time was on the second planet of the sun-star Carrdovan, which is called Mollara. This star is the third in brightness of the seven stars you call the Pleiades. The name Carrdovan means in our language "Carr's star." It is not the name that was given to it by the natives of Mollara or the other planets of this system.

We call the star Carr's star because the Martian zone-rex, Rancer-Carr, brought, with the Federation's help, hundreds of thousands of Martians to this solar system after the destruction of Maldec so that they might survive. As you know, Mars moved to an orbit much farther from the sun than it originally had, which made it uninhabitable for any form of life.

Since my twenty-second year of this life I have been trained to fill the high position of monitor zero of my people. This is similar to being vice president or second in command to the zone-rex. I presently live most of the time in one of the Federation's underground Frequency Barrier-free bases on the Earth.

Many times in this lifetime I have visited the planet Nodia and met with Rayatis and Lady Cre'ator. She once asked me if I had ever learned to shoot straight. She humorously said that I had missed her completely on that rainy night on the Earth so many years ago.

As for Martian spiritual ways, we worship the Supreme Creator of All That Is and the El of our own world, who we know longingly awaits the time when we, her spiritual children, will once again walk the restored grass-covered highways.

We will never return to the life of nomadic shepherds. To put it simply, let me recall a lyric of an Earth tune: "How are you going to keep them down on the farm after they've seen Paree?" We, the Martians of the present, are too sophisticated in the ways of the wondrous universe and are sworn to join our energy to any and all who oppose the forces of darkness.

As for Earth, it has been a haven for millions of souls from its neighboring worlds who desperately needed a place to reside.

As for the future, it is my personal desire that Christ reality does in fact manifest into the molar-level plane of reality and remove any need for warfare between the Federation and those of the dark side at the end of the Frequency Barrier.

If this is not the case, look for the Federation defenders to fill the skies in those last days. And remember, the Martian craft will be marked with the symbol of a mountain backed by two lightning bolts. I wouldn't want you to throw rocks at the good guys.

Either way, let's get it over with once and for all—I truly want to go home.

I am Sharmarie.

T W O

Trome, a Saturnian

I am not of their kind, but I have lived among
them. When I first came they were not
strangers to the ways of war, but now they
totally shun the practice of war which they had
when their race was young. Their ways are not
rooted in cowardice, for they will risk every other
type of physical danger if in so doing the spiritual
purposes of the elohim are universally advanced.
Those of the Sumer radiar [the open-state name for
the planetary body we call Saturn] do not attempt to
change the ways of others and are kind and willing
hosts to those who are motivated as I to oppose with
force those who would impose their evil will upon us all.
I am Abdonel of Nodia, in service to Federation Black
Bow Harp Control of the Sumer radiar.

I am pleased to be asked to contribute to your project by relating some of my recollections of my past lifetimes. I am highly honored to be among those of the open state who are doing likewise, such as the great Martian lord, Sharmarie.

Call me a Saturnian if you will, but not saturnine, for I do not fit that definition, which in your language means to be melancholy or sullen, or having a tendency to be bitter or sardonic. Yes, I understand and can speak many of the languages of present-day Earth as well as several languages that have not been spoken for thousands of years.

Sumer (Saturn) and Omuray (Titan)

I was first born on the planetary body you know now as Titan, the largest of the twelve moons of the planet Saturn (Sumer radiar). We did not call the world Titan then or now, but prefer to refer to it as a planetoid.

For you to better understand how my kind lived during my first lifetime, I believe it would be appropriate to describe how the planetoids of the Sumer radiar system originally interacted with the core of the system, that is, with the radiar itself.

As you know, the Sumer radiar as well as the other three radiars of this solar system are not functioning normally, as they did prior to the destruction of the planet Maldec.[1] For a radiar to function properly, it must emit its life-supporting energy in pulses. Originally, the duration of the Sumer radiar's energy pulse was about thirty-six Earth hours long. This means that it took about eighteen hours to reach its maximum energy output (equal to the solar energy that reaches the North American continent on a day in late April). During the second half of the pulse cycle the radiar's energy emissions gradually decreased to about 30 percent of the maximum. Because Omuray's atmosphere and surface retained a considerable amount of the energy it received during maximum emission, its temperature did not vary much more than about 14°F. Other planetoids of the system had temperature variations that ranged from 6° to about 16°F.

The advance and decline of the pulse cycle could be physically observed from any of the system's planetoids. The surface of the radiar core was ringed with twelve pink bands (six on each side of the equator) that moved toward the radiar's equator until they reached about 19.5° north and south of the equator, where they merged at maximum emission and receded toward the body's axis poles during the waning phase of the pulse cycle. Because the bands of energy moved at a precise rate of speed in both directions, one could measure time by their movement. At the maximum point of its energy pulse, the radiar blazed a brilliant white, and at the minimum point it produced a soft white light that had a slight blue-green tint. A remnant of this original pulse cycle is evident by periodic radio-wave transmissions that presently emanate from the radiar's core about every 10.66 Earth hours (about one-third the time, or three times as rapid, as the original pulse cycle).[2]

When Omuray (or any other planetoid of the system) was located in its orbit between the central sun and the radiar core, it received light and energy from both sources. When the planetoid's orbit took it behind the radiar (when the radiar was positioned between the planetoid and the central sun), only then did Omuray experience what you would consider night. The length of such a night was dictated by the planetoid's rotational speed around its polar axis, which was about forty Earth hours (in other words, the length of Omurayan day). Any part facing away from the radiar during such an orbital position was in darkness, which allowed those of the world to see clearly the stars of the galaxy as well as the light reflected from other planets and emitted by the other radiars that compose our solar system. Omuray's orbit around the radiar was originally almost perfectly circular, and it took the planetoid nearly 108 Earth days (one Omurayan year) to make one full rotation about the radiar. It now takes Omuray only sixteen Earth days to orbit the dysfunctional radiar. The planetoid is presently situated about 759,000 miles from the center of the radiar's core, giving it a present orbital speed of about 149,000 miles per Earth day. Originally Omuray's orbit around the radiar was more distant and its orbital speed was very much slower.

Omuray (Titan) is second in size to the planetoid of the Relt radiar (Jupiter) that you know as Ganymede. Omuray still has a considerable atmosphere, about 1.6 times denser than the Earth's present atmosphere. The temperature at the surface is presently about 290°F. This, of course, makes the world totally uninhabitable by any type of life. Omuray has a diameter of 3195 miles, giving it a surface area of about 32,049,385 square miles, slightly more than one-sixth the size of the Earth.

My First Life

In my first lifetime the Sumer radiar had no rings, and Omuray had a human population of about 992,000. The world was governed by a democratically elected council of nine men and nine women. This council was affiliated telepathically with six similar councils located on the six other planetoids of our radiar. This grand council was called, then and now, the Council of the Seven Lights.

The council members, called *Babs*, were qualified to serve if they had the rare ability to look into the face of the radiar and psychically perceive images and visions in the form of scenarios that played out on the face of the fiery orb. These images and scenarios were produced by the Lord God El of the system, who used this method to transmit instructions to the seven councils and, through them, to the people of the system's planetoids.

The lifelong occupation of each Omurayan was assigned to him at birth by the Council of Babs. I was assigned to be a biologist, an occupation in which I presently still function on behalf of the Federation. Because the Sumer radiar is not functioning normally, the Council of Seven Lights is not at this time able to receive the Sumer El's holy instructions, so it relies instead on lights of divine direction provided by those of any world who can perceive the will of the creator of all that is.

In my first life we of Omuray did not rely on oxygen to live, but instead breathed nitrogen, which at the time had all the physical qualities that oxygen has on the Earth today. That is, due to the interactive relationship that the Omurayan atmosphere had with the unique form of light emitted from the radiar, nitrogen was altered chemically to perform as oxygen does on the Earth. Our water was composed of two hydrogen atoms and one nitrogen atom. Hydrogen is the only element that will not change chemically in the presence of various types of light or any other form of electromagnetic energy. These chemical variations were also due to the original orbital distance that the Sumer radiar system had to the central sun. To totally comprehend this, you would need more extensive knowledge about solar pressure fields, a subject beyond the scope of this communication.

The strength of the Omurayan gravitational field varied with its orbital position relative to the radiar core. At certain orbital positions the magnetic field of the radiar was stronger and the strength of Omuray's gravitational field increased proportionately. At other points in the planetoid's orbit, the radiar's magnetic field was less intense and the strength of Omuray's gravitation field became correspondingly weaker. We on Omuray who weighed 160 pounds during the time the gravitational field was at its strongest, weighed about 154 when it was at its weakest. (These variations in gravitational strength are similar to those that presently occur in the Earth's moon when it moves in and out of stronger and weaker parts of the Earth's magnetic field.)

During the weak-gravitational times, larger raindrops would fall slowly in the shape of a convex lens, and winds would increase slightly in speed. During the time of minimum gravitational strength, the Omurayan atmosphere's light-refracting conditions changed. It was during these times that the Babs would look at the radiar to receive their divine instructions from the El.

My Family, My Society and My Early Life

In that very first lifetime my name was Trome, son of my father Bulon and mother Sencreta. It is the way of the El of Sumer that once a female bears a child, she will become biologically unable to bear any others. Males can produce up to three children before they too become biologically incapable of reproduction. (This el-directed condition is the reason that the sperm count is going down in many types of people living on the Earth today—especially those who have Sumerian types of DNA.)

My father was a highly respected civil engineer who specialized in water management, but spent more time studying the subject than physically working at it. While waiting to be called by the Babs to work on a water project, he was one of several who administered several hundred fruit-producing orchards. My very first job was picking a crop of fruit that was very similar to what you call avocados. Individual tenders of several groups of trees would engage in contests to see who could produce the most fruit at harvest time.

Our society was what you might call communistic (we had no currency), wherein all food was distributed equally by the Babs. Other products were produced and owned by the state. We were a people obsessed by learning and competitive sports.

The ability to telepathically communicate was biologically (inherently) limited to those who were physically closely related to each other. Only the Babs had the ability to mentally communicate with anyone they pleased. Remember that although there were hundreds of Babs, only eighteen could hold governing offices at the same time.

Each home had a radio, television, computer and cellular telephone, but we transported ourselves mostly by riverboats and electric trains. We were capable of building aircraft and automobiles as you know them, but were forbidden to do so by the El. We used draft animals and lightweight metal weapons during harvest times.

We had a desire to visit the other planetoids of our radiar system as well as the other planets of the solar system, but developing the technology to do so was very slow during my first lifetime. Rocket travel that begins and ends on a moving planetoid is very different and poses a set of problems entirely different from what rocket scientists of larger worlds (planets that orbit a central sun) would have to contend with.

I was taught by my mother from the age of about three Earth years to read, write and operate a computer, and then passed on to other women teachers of our town to be taught basic religion, history, art and social graces (I learned to dance, sing, style hair and design clothes). From the age of about thirteen Earth years, my teachers were men.

Concentrating on the subjects of biology and botany, I learned to graft one type of tree to another and researched methods of artificial pollination. I specialized in the creation of plant hybrids and fertilizers.

Omuray had a considerable number of animal life forms such as insects and birds, as well as some forms of animals that would be familiar to a person of the Earth, such as cows (more like a pygmy buffalo), pigs (also of a small variety), elephants (pygmy in size compared to those of the Earth) and many other forms of grazing animals. We of Omuray were allowed by the El to slaughter and eat several types of animals six times a year (one revolution around the radiar). Even though this was permissible, killing and devouring animals was not widely practiced at any time of the year, but culling the herds six times a year was a necessity.

Celibacy was practiced until males and females were at least fourteen Earth years old. Thereafter sexual relations were permitted if the engaging parties mutually agreed. Pregnancy constituted marriage, and both parties were expected to be faithful to each other from that time forward. Widows and widowers were free to do what they wished. On very rare occasions a man might impregnate two or three women at the same time (before becoming married to any of them), thus becoming one of those who are fortunate (or unfortunate) enough to have more than one wife.

Along with my studies of biology and botany, I was trained in athletics and became a fairly good runner and rock climber. I was considered to be very good at these sports but failed to become the champion that my father dreamed of.

I liked wrestling, especially against female opponents. I must admit I lost more of these matches than I won. Omurayan women are very beautiful, but also pretty tough. These matches did help me prepare for married life, which I began at the age of seventeen Earth years with a woman called Graforet. From this union came a daughter we named Stenee, after my wife's maternal grandmother. Graforet was a beekeeper and expert in the production of rare types of honey. Her hives were located near our home, and their occupants hated me and would attack me unless Graforet called them off by mental command. I had been stung so many times that I became immune to their venom, thus becoming an unwilling subject of Graforet and her colleagues' numerous biological research projects.

The Nodian Visit, Prompted by My Fertilizer Development

When I was about thirty-eight Earth years old, Stenee became married and I received a high honor from the Babs for developing a photosensitive fertilizer that, once spread, lasted more than 53 Earth years and was time-released (activated from a state of dormancy) by certain radiar emissions. This honor is equivalent to winning a Nobel Prize upon the Earth. I did not know it at the time, but my fame became universal, and my fertilizer formula attracted the interest of people who were of an entirely different solar system. These people called themselves Nodians.

The Nodians arrived on Omuray on the day before Graforet's birthday and immediately contacted the Babs council. I was summoned to the council, and there I first laid eyes on human beings who came from another world.

We were offered many material things for the fertilizer formula, but accepted instead an unlimited number of trips through space in order to visit and meet the people of the other planetoids of our radiar system, planets of our solar system and those we now knew lived in other solar systems throughout the universe.

In order for this type of travel to be available to us when we were of a mind to take off, so to speak, the Babs allowed the Nodians to establish a base (about one square mile in size) on Omuray. It became quite a tourist attraction. (It was at that time that I met Abdonel, the Nodian ambassador who introduced this chapter, and his mother Taina-Soy, who was his constant companion and advisor.)

I accompanied the Council of Babs on our first space trip to the other six human-occupied planetoids of the Sumer radar system. We discovered that the then-remaining five planetoids were inhabited only by animal and plant life of types similar to those found on the seven planetoids inhabited by humans. The other planetoidlike bodies that now circle the Sumer radar (about eight of considerable size) and the ring system are actually pieces of the planet Maldec and chunks of its now-frozen atmosphere.

We nitrogen breathers of Omuray were easy adapters to the Nodian rad atmosphere that filled the interiors of their spacecraft. It was and still is necessary to breathe rad air, because once you move away from a radiar's various forms of physical influences, the nitrogen atom can change its chemical characteristics many times over, and in the case of those of Omuray, could no longer serve us as an oxidizer. Exhaled rad air is the same as the exhaled air that had initially contained any other type of oxidizer before being inhaled. That is, the exhaled air is mostly carbon dioxide, but in the case of rad air, several of the so-called noble gases such as neon, argon, krypton etc. (which are part of the rad formula) temporarily bond to the carbon dioxide molecule, then break away when entering the body of unbreathed air. Oxygen breathers have the most difficulty in converting directly to a rad atmosphere (the interaction could be explosive). Because of this, a person who has been relying on oxygen as an oxidizer must first breathe other oxidizer gases (such as nitrogen) with an oxygen chemical value before converting to rad air. These breathing conversions were not a problem for those of us from any of the Sumer planetoids because we were all nitrogen breathers.

The Nodians took the Bab council and some others of Omuray to visit the other planetoids of our radar system, and they eventually assigned a spacecraft capable of carrying up to forty people to each of the seven Bab councils. In the beginning these craft were always piloted by either Nodians, Vitronians, Regalians and the speechless Alperians, all natives of worlds located in the Nodian home solar system. As time went on, Sumerians were trained to operate these vehicles. Because the planets you call Venus, Earth and Maldec were oxygen-breathing worlds (Mars was not), we made no space trips to these worlds because the Nodians did not give us the technology to convert from breathing rad to breathing oxygen. (The reason for their withholding this process from us was due to what is now referred to as the Prime Directive.)

We of the Sumer planetoids who were now able to physically face one another found we had much in common, with the exception (in some cases) of language and history. Most languages of the Sumer planetoids were the same as the spoken language of Omuray (now called Sumer Basic). In the remaining languages of the system, only 10 to 43 percent of Sumer Basic words were used, and adjectives preceded nouns (contrary to Sumer Basic).

Four of the seven Sumer planetoids had experienced war, and certain groups on these worlds harbored ill feelings toward each other, totally ignoring their particular Bab council's divine authority. These hostiles later carried their disputes with them when they were forced to emigrate to Earth due to the destruction of Maldec.

After physical contact was possible between those of us of the various Sumer planetoids, the Grand Council of Babs received a communication from the system's El, permitting the people of the system to intermarry. From these intermarriages (mixing of DNA) came Sumerians of greatness. The Grand Council of Babs placed the other five planetoids of the system under their collective control and colonized them with people from every planetoid of the system. These colonists had to contend with something they had never had to contend with before: predators. Although man culled the animal herds on the other seven planetoids, several forms of carnivorous cats had this function on the remaining five worlds of the system.

Both my father and I, along with many other experts in our respective fields, were assigned by the Grand Council of Babs to develop these worlds and make them beneficially productive. Some of the colonists were hostiles who did not make things very easy for those of us who had lived our first life in peace. Murder and battles between various factions were frequent. Some did not care for the ways of others who were not native to their particular planetoid. The ways of the hostiles became contagious, and many who had known only the ways of peace took up violence, first in self-defense and later as a means to exert their will on others.

The Grand Council of Babs formed Sumerian military units to control the hostilities on the colonies. The Nodian Federation neither offered nor gave any form of assistance in these matters, again citing the Prime Directive.

One day a spacecraft bearing the insignia of the Nodian Trading House of Domphey landed at the Federation base on Omuray. Among the Nodians were a number of fair, delicate people from the planet you now call Venus (they called their world Wayda).

The Venusians brought with them equipment that would permit a rad breather to convert to oxygen. They installed this equipment in our seven spacecraft (reducing each craft's passenger limit from forty to thirty-one).

We were told that the gift of this equipment no longer violated the Prime Directive. The Venusians and most of us of the Sumer planetoids got along very well. We shared the common desire to understand and learn everything we could.

I was in the fifty-third year of my first life and one day was having a meal with several friends, two of whom were Venusian women. It was nearing the time for the Sumer radiar's energy bands to begin their waning cycle. Suddenly we all felt very ill and faint. The once-predictable movement of the radiar bands stopped for about twenty minutes, then they moved rapidly to their normal location during that time of day. At their normal point of recession, the bands of energy waxed and waned for another period of time, then corrected their position again and again. This stopping and catch-up action of the energy bands went on for about 90 Earth hours and then returned to normal.

The Babs announced that this phenomenon was caused by the explosion of Maldec. My friends and I wondered how such a thing could have happened.

Nearly 80 Federation craft left Omuray to inspect the physical condition of the other worlds in the solar system and to return to their home world. The majority of these craft never returned. The crews of those that did return related that the uncountable pieces of the ill-fated planet were moving at very high velocities in every conceivable direction, and currents of energy were producing very erratic forces; thus any attempt to pass through them was impossible. Dents, cracks and scorch marks on the hulls of the Federation spacecraft emphasized their terrifying accounts.

After a short time (about 2½ Earth months) Omuray suddenly had a constantly pacing companion in the form of a large Federation space vehicle (mothership) called the Commiva. This craft had a diameter of about six miles (tiny compared to present-day motherships). Four spacecraft from this mothership, of a type I had never seen before, landed at the nearly deserted Federation base. Among the hundreds of passengers they carried was a man named Tasper-Kane.

Tasper-Kane was a Nodian of great age who related to the Babs the concerns of the Federation as to the most likely detrimental future of the planets and radiars of the solar system. When he said that it might become necessary to move the entire populations of the Sumer planetoids to new homes elsewhere in the universe, the average Omurayan scoffed. After all, except for the fact that the planet Maldec was now represented by chunks of rock and a large gas and dust cloud, everything on the Sumer planetoids was perfectly normal.

The Babs stared for days at the face of the radiar, seeking the El's

This illustration depicts a reproduction of figures that are found on a clay cylinder originally produced in the ancient land of Sumeria. Trome's interpretation of these figures is as follows:

1. In the upper left corner are seven spheres, representing the planetoids of the Sumer radiar that were once populated by humans. Their triangular configuration also symbolizes unity under the authority of the Council of the Seven Lights.

2. Below the seven spheres is a sword with its tip pointing downward. This is a sign that those of the Seven Lights desire that warfare be abolished and that the people of Sumeria should live in peace.

3. The crescent moon to the right of the seven spheres indicates that the spheres, like the moon, are located in the heavens.

4. The depiction of the humanlike figure on the left represents a being who came from the seven spheres. One of the wings on the back of this being points to the group of spheres, indicating the place he had flown (come) from.

5. This angelic being holds one arm and hand in a protective gesture over a small fish headed in his direction. In his other hand is a container in which he will place the living fish for transport.

6. The feet of this individual are large, and his leg shows no calf muscle. These features are in sharp contrast to the large calf muscle and small feet of the figure at the far right. This indicates that the angelic (winged) being came from a place where the force of gravity is not as strong as on the Earth. The sphere that partially covers one of his feet represents the world from which he came or once walked that caused the leg to physically develop that way. One foot placed before the other is the scribe's way of describing the act of walking.

7. The table (altar) below the fish indicates that the creature is a gift to the gods and was transported to them by a winged vehicle [center right] shown with landing gear almost touching the table. The winged vehicle is, of course, the Sumerian scribe's way of depicting a spacecraft.

8. Below the spacecraft is shown a mature dolphin swimming toward the figure on the far right. The dolphin represents one of many types of animal life forms that were biologically conditioned by the gods to tolerate the Frequency Barrier and were reintroduced to the Earth after being deposited by a spacecraft in the planet's forests and oceans. The fact that the inhabitants of the Earth might not see the reintroductions physically take place is suggested by the dolphin swimming from under the table.

9. The figure on the far right points with one hand to the spacecraft located directly under the sun, and holds a written list in his other hand. The sun's six rays represent six solar years, which was the future time when the Sumerians could expect the spacecraft's return to pick up the animal life forms on the list.

instructions. When the divine message finally came, it essentially said: "Tell the people to start packing."

I was assigned to Tasper-Kane's planning staff, and what appeared to be an impossible task was begun. It was not just the movement of people from one planet to another, but every type of plant and nitrogen-breathing animal (including every form of microbe) had to be prepared for transport in order to be preserved. It was concluded that after the strongest of the various species were selected for transport, all others of their particular species would be left behind to perish.

Even though they knew of the dangers that lay ahead, a minority of people of the Sumer planetoids preferred not to prepare for emigration, but elected to die with their particular world when the time came. Other events prevented a large number of willing emigrants from leaving. Those who eventually left the slowly dying planetoids numbered about 3.8 million.

The Evacuation of the Planetoids

All of the preparation and transport planning took place aboard the Commiva. It was there that I came in physical contact for the first time with people who were natives of Earth, Mars, the Relt radiar (Jupiter) and the Trake radiar (Neptune). Aboard the Commiva were people from hundreds of worlds not of the local solar system. At first things were very chaotic, and it was frustrating for us to cope with the task and, for most of us, with the extreme differences that existed between our various cultures and individual personalities. Some would be quick to anger and some would simply sit down and cry for a while and then get right back to work.

About three Earth years after the destruction of Maldec, small pieces of the planet began to take up orbits around the Sumer radiar. Some of these pieces became meteors that streaked through the skies and vaporized. Some of them actually crashed on the surface of the worlds, leaving relatively small impact craters. The Federation advised us that these small fragments were a portent, as it was expected that very large pieces of the planet Maldec would eventually crash onto the planetoid surfaces and thus cause catastrophic effects, including considerable loss of life. The time to begin the mass emigration was shortened.

The primary destination of the human emigrants from the Sumer planetoids was the planet Earth. The plant and animal specimens, in both living and suspended embryo forms, were to be deposited on a nitrogen-breathing world located in a far-distant solar system. The name of that world is Simcarris.

Earth was selected for two primary reasons: (1) It appeared to be the only planet in the solar system that was maintaining its original orbit; (2)

the light of the central sun was composed of spectral energy better suited to the biology of its natives than would be the light of a different sun.

Nearly 600 Sumerians and 65 of my blood relatives (including Graforet) went through the process required to convert from breathing nitrogen to breathing the rich oxygen-laden air of the Earth. I converted from rad air, which I had been breathing on the Commiva, to oxygen. After this type of conversion it was necessary to be vaccinated to ward off diseases of Earth as well as those introduced by emigrants from other worlds. When this was accomplished, we left Omuray on a Federation spacecraft that had an interior atmosphere of Earth air. We arrived on the Earth just as the sun was coming up over the horizon.

Our job was to establish a reception depot for those from the Sumer planetoids that were to follow. Its location was in what you now call Iraq. A description of the preparations we had to make to receive and support 3.8 million people, even with the help of the Federation, is beyond the number of pages you have allotted to this writing. Basically, food production and preservation was a priority, because bacteria on the Earth caused it to spoil rapidly. Shelter and clothing were also very important, because for the first time in their lives, those of the Sumer planetoids were subjected to the changes of season. Winter temperatures on the Earth were hardly bearable, and many died because of them. Many of the living sought warmth from the funeral pyres of the dead. Most of those with medical training were kept on the planetoids. We learned that this was due to frequent Maldecian meteors that were raining down in great numbers on the worlds, causing a major number of deaths and injuries. First only the healthy came to the Earth, then the walking wounded along with some medical people, and finally those who, although severely injured, were able to tolerate the process of oxygen conversion. With the latter group came the medical personnel who had survived the meteor bombardments.

Our Life on Earth

One good thing was that more than enough electrical power was supplied by the seven spacecraft that were originally given to us by the Federation. The use of this energy played a very important part in helping most of us to survive, but it also caused envy in some of those of other worlds who had no electrical power sources. We shared this power with our neighbors until the seven spacecraft could provide no more. This good-neighbor policy protected our borders from invaders for several years.

Tasper-Kane moved his group of planners to the Earth and I rejoined them. As my people struggled to adjust and survive on the Earth, we of the group traveled the surface of the Earth and visited with the leaders of people who were once natives of the planets Venus and Mars as well as those of the planetoids of the Relt (Jupiter) and Trake (Neptune) radiars. Each of these transplanted cultures numbered in the millions and were suffering from the same adjustment and survival problems—and in some cases, more problems than we of the Sumer system were contending with. The purpose of these contacts was to establish a cooperative union for the mutual benefit of every culture. The resources of the Federation were taxed to their limits. It was becoming more and more difficult for them to provide transportation and differing provisions for millions of people as the various populations increased due to births and the arrival of more and more of their people from their particular home worlds.

Most of the natives of the Earth (but not all) resented our intrusions and chose to follow the counterproductive dictates of their Maldecian masters. Many Maldecians had survived the destruction of their planet by being either on the Earth or elsewhere when the disastrous event occurred. They showed no open regret for the fact that they had destroyed their own planet or the fact that they were responsible for the miseries and sorrows of so many people. They went so far as to demand material tribute from those of us who were forced to live among them. Eventually they extracted various forms of payment from us by the threat and use of military force. When they physically invaded our adopted land, it forced the Federation to remove the seven electric-power-producing spacecraft to keep them from falling into Maldecian hands. What was meant as a temporary measure became permanent. Many of our tools became useless, so we resorted to more primitive ways. One thing we really learned to do was fight. We readily accepted the tutelage of our Martian friends in the art of warfare. The Maldecians did not want to destroy us, but they did want to subjugate us. A dead slave was of no value to them.

Tasper-Kane and his first assistant, Abdonel, suggested that we take among us those who originally came from the planet Venus (Wayda). These poor souls were really at a loss about how to cope with the Earth environment and the belligerent Maldecians. By the time this meld was made, the original 1.1 million Venusians who had come to the Earth numbered about 390,000.

In the twenty-eighth Earth year after the demise of Maldec, the people of all races began to complain that things did not taste and smell as they once did. Graforet's bees did not reproduce and her hives became empty. Other types of animals developed very strange behaviors. Tempers flared, especially during full and new moon phases. These events prompted the Federation to take precautionary measures and begin to gather up Earth plants and animals for relocation and to search the universe for safe havens to which they could move the human populations of the present host world. The Martians were the first, along with a number of native Earthlings, to leave the Earth for a new planetary home orbiting one of the seven stars you call the Pleiades. This was called then, as now, Carrdovan, and the world was Mollara.

I assisted in the cataloging and gathering of the Earth's flora and fauna as I had done before with the similar types of life forms of the Sumer planetoids, only this time I did not accompany them to their final destination. I did not want to spend even one minute away from my people and family. I also wanted to remain on the Earth to do all I could to prepare them and the Venusians for another move to some undetermined place where we hoped and prayed that we might live in peace. The powers of the Babs were lost and they were unable to direct us as they once had. Bloodshed and slavery (both physical and psychic) prevailed on the Earth.

Nearly thirty years had passed since my family and I left our home world, and I was now 89 Earth years of age. A few years earlier, a large number of Martians and a comparatively small number of Venusians and those of Sumer had left the Earth to be relocated. Most of the worlds to which the latter had gone would accept only a small number of people. Therefore many from Mars, Venus and Sumer could not leave the Earth during that lifetime.

Maldecians now had aircraft with which to impose their dictates on those from other worlds. Everyone eventually accepted the fact that the Maldecians were in total control—even the Federation. The Federation continued to look for biologically suitable places they could transport us to and covertly provided us with goods behind the backs of our Maldecian rulers. They did this until the time of the Great Catastrophes. The beginning of these terrible events was described by the Martian Lord Sharmarie in his account of his first lifetime. I cannot improve on his description, but can only add that on the third day after the torrential rains began, I and my wife Graforet, huddled in our house of dried mud bricks, died as it crumbled down upon us.

The Beginning of the Frequency Barrier and Its Effects

The geological calamities that began on the Earth after my first lifetime continued off and on at various degrees of intensity for about 1750 years. And though these detrimental events did not totally cease, they did level off to the point that earthquakes occurred less frequently and hardly ever exceeded a magnitude of 6.2 on your Richter scale of measurement. The human, animal and plant life that had survived had experienced a drastic devolvement. Humans were reduced to heights that ranged between 3'10" and 4'5". Their bodies were covered with hair. Their ability to think and reason was very much impaired by the strong effects of the Frequency Barrier that prevailed then. The humans of that time survived more or less by instincts similar to those that are attributed today to wild animals. The average life span was about nineteen years. This time in history is referred to by those of the open state as the "first plateau of geological equilibrium."

Because the Frequency Barrier is mentally detrimental to all types of humans, the Federation and anyone else who could travel through space steered clear of the planet Earth and the local solar system as well.

Meanwhile, the Federation expanded into many other solar systems, some of which were located in other galaxies. Over time, the secular problems and considerations of the Federation, as they related to the various human cultures of the universe, became secondary to what were realized to be very important spiritual issues. For many reasons, these new priorities brought the planet Earth back into the spotlight. New technology was developed that permitted Federation spacecraft and their crews to operate for short periods of time within the influence field of the Frequency Barrier. Preliminary studies of the Earth's geological condition indicated that in some unknown course of time, the planet would heal itself of its Frequency Barrier affliction, and that the time would someday arrive when it and its detrimental mental effects would be totally gone.

From shortly after the beginning of the first plateau of geological equilibrium to the present day, the Federation has been monitoring the progress of the Frequency Barrier and the biological changes in the various forms of life on the planet.

It has been more than 8000 years since my last lifetime on Earth. I have since lived two lifetimes within the open, unrestricted mental state (unaffected by the Earth's Frequency Barrier). I was, and still am, in service to the Federation, involved in the study of the effects of the Barrier on plant and animal life, and with the eventual reintroduction of pre-Frequency Barrier types of fauna and flora that are presently in some form of preservation in the Federation's biological storage vaults or living in a number of game preserves located elsewhere in the universe. The locations of these preserves are highly classified.

I am at present 2108 Earth years of age, but physically would not be taken to be more than about thirty-five. If it were not for the Frequency Barrier, I could walk openly down a street in any city on the Earth (except maybe in the Orient) without attracting any curiosity or attention.

I understand that you wish me to relate the happenings and experiences of at least four lives I have lived on the Earth since my first life. There were many that were somewhat similar, especially the most recent. Even so, the most recent lives should help to clear up some questions that presently exist regarding the ancient civilizations of Sumeria and Babylonia.

The Dackeys

About 632,000 years after the beginning of the first plateau of geological equilibrium I was born in the mountainous region of the land that is now Turkey. My father's name was Tasido and my mother's was Masyna. We lived in a village of stone houses among about 450 people. We called ourselves the Dackeys.

I was told at a very early age that I was the great-grandson of a god. I was also informed that my great-grandmother had mated with a god she had encountered one late afternoon while tending her father's herd of goats. Her account ended with her description of her divine lover entering into the body of a silver bird and flying off into the sky. Great-Grandmother's experience was accepted as true because a number of other young women of her time and of our village also claimed to have had the same experience. In fact, many an argument occurred between women of all ages as to whose turn it was to tend the flocks.

Our religion and spiritual beliefs, for as long as anyone could remember, were influenced by legends of encounters with beings who came from the sky. We believed in reembodiment (physical life as humans after death) and that in some future lifetime we would earn, by doing good deeds and loving each other, the right to live among the gods in their heavenly abodes.

Up until about the age of ten, I never saw a god or any of the silver birds they rode to and from the Earth. At that time I observed, with many others, an egg-shaped silver object pass over our village. Many of my playmates also claimed divine descendancy, and we devised imaginary games in which we had godlike powers that permitted us to fly and perform miraculous feats. Older boys used their divine descendancy (signified by our soft, wavy black hair and beards) to inspire romantic interest in the young women.

The countryside surrounding our village teemed with many types of animal life, especially a species that resembled the present kangaroo. Also ranging about us were bands of humans we called the Zains. These people were very primitive and communicated with one another by grunts and hand gestures. They did not have the knowledge of fire, and in fact ran away from it, yelling and covering their eyes. I recall one time when a Zain who had been badly mauled by a predatory animal came to our village seeking help, which we were quick to render. While he was being treated for his wounds, a female, who was obviously his mate, moved about the outskirts of the village, wailing mournfully. Unable to save the Zain's life, we laid his body several hundred yards from the village. The Zain female sat by the body for several days and then left. That night the body disappeared.

It was suggested that the gods might come and live among us if we built them a suitable place to live. This thought inspired us to construct what might have been the very first temple or church to be built on the Earth after the beginning of the Frequency Barrier. Simple stone walls would not do, so stones were cut into blocks and meticulously dressed. The building took nearly eight years to complete.

The Crystal Sphere

On the very top of the pyramidal structure was a chamber where the gods could privately mate with any young woman of their choice from among a selected group of our most fair. Each one of this group of women (one at a time) would ascend the stairs to the upper chamber of the temple at sunset and stay until dawn. For many years none of them reported they had in any way encountered a god during their nightly vigil.

One morning a woman named Darrie descended the stairs of the temple, cradling in her arms a beautiful crystal sphere. Without saying a word, she presented the sphere to my father's brother Bellarbus, and then walked off into the hills, never to be seen again. It was assumed that she had gone off to physically join the gods.

My uncle Bellarbus would sit on the temple steps among other men and women of the village and stare into the crystal ball. He informed us that by doing so he could both hear and see the gods. No one doubted that he had this ability, because he could predict many hours in advance when the gods would fly over our village in their silver eggs. He told us that the gods were pleased that we had built the temple, and urged us to continue using it in the manner for which it was designed. The temple steps were cleared at sunset so that another priestess could climb to the upper chamber in the hope of meeting with a god.

I have learned since that my uncle Bellarbus was in a previous lifetime one of the Babs who sought divine directions from staring at the surface of the glowing sphere [Saturn] that was and still is the Sumer radiar.

In the years that followed, everyone in the village was given an opportunity on their birthday to peer into the crystal ball, and some reported a spiritual experience from doing so. Every one of my attempts to look into the crystal for a vision resulted in its clear transparency becoming blue and fogging up. Because everyone could see these physical changes in the ball, I became the object of considerable humor. Eventually the crystal sphere was stored at night in the upper chamber of the temple. It rested on an altar in the finely sculpted cupped hands that represented those of the woman Darrie who had originally brought this gift of the gods to the people.

At the age of seventeen I married a girl named Soogee, and we proceeded to add two girls and one boy to the Dackeys' growing population. The birth rate became quite high—even our flocks of various types of domesticated animals increased dramatically. But we noticed that the bands of Zains were reducing in size.

Our Move to the South

One morning Uncle Bellarbus called all the people to the temple and informed us that the gods had instructed us to abandon our very comfortable village and move to the south. We were told that this was to be done in order to avoid a large, murderous band of people who would soon come upon us from the east.

Three days later we burned our homes (but not the temple) and began our journey to a new land whose location was known only to the gods. Our rate of travel was slow because it was dictated by our flocks' need of food and water—items that became more and more difficult to find with every step we took south. The terrain was rugged and the land changed from sparse grass cover to barren desert. We relied entirely upon occasional rains to supply water for our needs. The much-needed rain seemed to occur during the times when the silver eggs of the gods hovered in the skies above our thirsty band.

About six months into our journey, grass and water once again became plentiful, and one of our advance parties returned to tell us that they had observed from a high hill a group of buildings in the distance. Uncle Bellarbus consulted the crystal sphere and reported that the buildings that lay ahead were our final destination. Though we were overjoyed, we approached the walled city with some caution. Before reaching its gates, we encountered many different types of tent-dwelling people, even some who looked like Zains. All types called to us in a multitude of languages that we did not understand. These people looked at us curiously but without fear. We were met by a group of tall, lightly armored men who carried spears. We had never seen anything like them before and wondered why they dressed in such an uncomfortable manner. I was among a small group of our band that was allowed to enter the city and escorted to a large house (palace) located in the city's center.

We were brought before the supreme ruler of the city and the grasslands surrounding it. King Rabbersinus was a kind and wise man. We were told that the city's name was Knoore. After a time, we learned to speak the language of the city and were invited to take up residence along with our large flocks in any area we wished outside the city walls.

We told the king about the dangerous invaders from the northeast who might invade his land. He was concerned about this possible threat, but told us that several hostile groups had tried unsuccessfully to conquer Knoore in the past. This was why he employed a moderate number of soldiers.

We learned from several sources that the ancestors of King Rabbersinus had come to the area about 200 years prior to our arrival and had found the ruins of an empty city. They subsequently rebuilt it and accepted the presence of other wandering peoples who showed up over the years seeking refuge and protection.

Rabbersinus listened to our claims that we were descended from the gods and to our stories of how we had built a temple and acquired our crystal sphere. He had seen silver eggs fly over his city in the past and wondered about them. He knew they were of divine origin, but had no idea what reasons they had for revealing themselves in this way to mortals. After Uncle Bellarbus predicted a number of future events that came true, he and the king became inseparable, and a new and grander temple than the one we had built in our homeland was begun.

Rabbersinus' oldest of seven sons, named Kalt-Rapanine, was the leader of a group of men who spent their lives studying the mysteries of life. From this group came such things as writing, paper, cotton clothing and the wheel. They established schools that taught medicine and art. Kalt-Rapanine greatly admired the sculpted stone hands of Darrie, which still held the crystal sphere that was our link to the gods. He gathered all who had seen Darrie before her departure and obtained from them her physical description. From their very vivid memories Rabbersinus produced a beautiful life-sized statue of the lady, which became the object of spiritual unity for all the people of the kingdom of Knoore. Kalt-Rapanine, like his father, was a good man. I am joyful in the knowledge that in one of his later lifetimes he achieved the infinite thought and that his eternal soul has reunited with the divine consciousness of the creator of all that is.

Over a period of many years the city of Knoore spread outside the confines of its walls. There was no thought about building protective walls, because the once-feared invaders from the east were never seen or heard of again. From time to time the gods in their silver eggs would fly over Knoore and the kingdoms' hundreds of types of people would shout praises at them, to which the gods responded with swaying motions and flashes of brilliant colored lights. In the new kingdom, as in our old home, an opportunity was given to each person on their birthday to look into the crystal sphere, and lines formed in front of the temple daily.

Before sunrise one morning King Rabbersinus and Uncle Bellarbus called their respective kinfolk together in the temple and bestowed their blessings upon us. The king gave the scepter of rule to Kalt-Rapanine, who was very reluctant to accept it. The elderly pair behaved like excited children. They kissed the crystal sphere several times and then went to sit in silent meditation in the corner of the temple. When the first rays of the sun danced off the surface of the crystal sphere, they rose as if in a trance and left us without saying another word. From the walls of the original city we watched them walk through the marketplace and then to the edge of the outer constructions. In a slow descent, a silver egg of the gods settled on the Earth before them. A doorway appeared in its side. This door framed the body of a beautiful woman with arms outstretched in a gesture of welcome. She was dressed in a fine sheer blue gown. All around me I heard a number of others of the assembly murmur, "Darrie—it's Darrie." Down our cheeks ran tears of joy as the craft carrying our beloved king and high priest rose into the sky and disappeared in the direction of the rising sun. From that day forward all the people of Knoore hoped and dreamed that someday the gods would come and take them to their heavenly home that existed somewhere above the clouds. Anyone who disappeared in the countryside without a trace in the years that followed was considered as possibly having been taken to paradise by the gods.

Kalt-Rapanine did not care for the time-consuming duties of a king but preferred to study with his group of scholars. He proclaimed that he would surrender the title to anyone who could truly contact the gods by means of the crystal sphere. This divine ability was soon demonstrated by Marqua, a teenage girl with a slightly withered leg. Marqua related to Kalt-Rapanine a surgical procedure she was told of by the gods that would restore her limb to a normal condition. This procedure was successfully performed without anesthesia while Marqua stared into the crystal sphere and directed the physicians in their work. Marqua reigned as queen and high priestess for a very long time and married a great grandson of my blood. I lived to about the age of 204 years and died peacefully in my sleep.

I have learned since that nearly 850 years after my death in that lifetime, the peaceful kingdom of Knoore was overrun by invaders who came from the east and was shaken into ruins later by many powerful earthquakes. The Frequency Barrier once again became drastically detrimental and the Earth and those who lived upon it were again biologically mutated and hurled into the dark places of ignorance.

Later Understandings

I learned later that those who came to Earth in the so-called silver eggs were not really gods, but those of the Sumer planetoids who were never born or died within the confines of the Frequency Barrier of the Earth. Their purpose of impregnating certain women of the Earth was not based on some lecherous desire, but instead to insert into the bloodline of the Sumer descendants living on the planet stronger forms of Sumer DNA they hoped would strengthen their Earthbound relatives against any future detrimental biological effects that could occur from the Frequency Barrier.

"And the sons of God found the daughters of the Earth to be fair, and from their unions came great men of renown." Those of the Sumer radiar system were not the only off-world culture to try to strengthen the DNA of their Earthbound kinsmen. Hundreds of other cultures employed similar methods to do likewise, including the Maldecians.

The Maldecians envisioned the creation of a master race that could conquer the planet from within and turn its rule over to them after the Frequency Barrier finally disappears. Some of these cultures are still very active in their various DNA-strengthening programs.

Those of the Sumer planetoids also include in their activities the preservation and DNA-strengthening of Earth's plant and animal life forms. From ancient knowledge of these animal-preserving activities came the story of Noah and his Ark. The story was changed many times to fit the references of those who could better understand an ark being used to save the animals than a spacecraft that took them to pastures on different worlds.

During several thousands of years I had quite a number of short lives. During many of these lives I was a member of hunter-gatherer tribes, often dying in infancy—and in some rare cases, due to miraculously surviving disease and other environmental hardships, I reached the ripe old age of twenty years or more.

I had lives during several so-called golden ages and dark ages before I was born, as was the Martian Lord Sharmarie during one of his lifetimes, in the kingdom of the two Atlans—that is, the place that is now referred to as Atlantis.

My Atlanian Lifetime

I was known as Mac-Densel, son of my father, Varman-Den, and mother,

Rita-Meesa. I was the third male child of four. To keep the time frame in focus, the kingdom, composed of the lands of Fe-Atlan and Ro-Atlan, had been founded about 135 years before my birth, and about 120 years would pass before the Martian Lord Sharmarie would be born into the life that he described in a previous writing.

I was taught from the age of four along with others in a state school to read and write. When we completed this course of learning, we were given a list of subjects that the state thought worthwhile. In order to learn more about these subjects it was necessary to visit the many libraries dotting the land. It was by this method that the youth of the Atlans taught themselves. Woe be to those who might say aloud, "I don't understand." The response of a parent or elder would definitely be, "Go to the library and don't come back until you do understand."

In order to visit a library it was required that one bathe and dress in clean clothes. Study groups composed of young men and women with the same interests gathered whenever and wherever they could. These meetings were also our means of socializing. When a student felt confident with what he knew and had the fee to pay for an official examination, he applied to the state to be tested. If applicants passed the examination (as I did, after several attempts), they were given the opportunity to attend classes conducted by a person considered to be a master of a particular subject. The catch here was that a considerable fee had to be paid to the master teacher on a yearly basis. Classes of this type were filled with people of all ages. Graduates were thereafter qualified to practice a particular profession. The soft, easy life of a priest was sought by most, followed by employment by the state in the capacity of bureaucratic official and then as officer in the army or navy. Medical doctors, scientists and engineers were elite classes that required years of expensive study.

I had a way with words and could take dictation, even if it was given at the speed of light. So I studied to be a scribe and historian. I amazed my master teacher and others with my ability to write down their thoughts before they could even utter a word. I know now that I was tapping into their thoughts telepathically.

To earn money for my education, I worked, as many did, digging canals and other forms of state-sponsored building projects. My father spent his entire lifetime as the assistant manager of a large sawmill that provided lumber for the construction of ships for the Atlan navy. When I completed my higher studies, I was sought after by the priests, who thought my ability to read minds was a spiritual gift from the gods. The government and the military also sought my services. I accepted a position in the army because, in truth, I enjoyed the power of ordering others about.

Sailing to Ser (Egypt)

In my twenty-fourth year of that life I boarded a large sailing ship that was also propelled by galley slaves chained to their oars. On the decks were several hundred more slaves, most of whom were considered minor criminals or simply Cro-Magnon types of humans who had been unfortunately caught in some Ro-Atlan slaver's net.

The destination of our voyage was the Land of Ser, where we were to found a colony and military outpost. The Land of Ser has had many names over the years, such as Mir and Tosh—and is presently called Egypt.

What is now the Mediterranean Sea was then about two-thirds its present size. We sailed across this sea and arrived at the mouth of the river now known as the Nile. We were met by a small group of our soldiers who looked as if they had been through hell. They had small wounds on their arms and legs. We thought at first that their condition was due to battles with the local natives. They were quick to tell us that the wounds were the result of thousands of monkeys who, for some yet-unknown reason, attacked people during certain phases of the moon. We went to the advance unit's encampment and put the slaves to work clearing away the thick foliage so that we could enlarge the site for the habitation of those of us who were newly arrived.

The Land of Ser was covered by a thick tropical rain forest that stretched for several hundred miles to the east and west of the great river. It seemed to be always raining. Rust and mildew were also problems we had to contend with.

The chief officer of the advance unit briefed us about the two types of people who were native to the area. One type was tall and blonde and the other was even taller and had black skin. They originally lived separate from each other and under a very shaky truce. Since the advance unit's arrival, warriors from both groups had been seen probing the borders of the Atlan camp together under one command.

One of the first assignments given to us prior to leaving Fe-Atlan was to seek out and find a number of pyramids that were built by the gods at some time in the ancient past. One morning we, along with a group of priests, soldiers and hundreds of slaves who were employed to hack a path for us through the jungle, began our search for these holy structures.

After several days and thousands of insect bites, we came out of the jungle and encountered a paved road about 75 feet wide. We were amazed to find this artifact from the distant past and used it to continue our mission. After some hours on the road we came upon a group of black warriors who first blocked our path and then marched in orderly ranks in front of us. Two of these black escorts stripped off their clothing and military gear and took off on a run.

Later we were alerted by the sound of drums and trumpets. Approaching us was a large group of people wearing clothes of every color. On a canopied litter was seated a very beautiful woman who, we later learned, was called Princess Rytoon. We were quick to learn why she did not fear for her safety: the jungles on both sides of the highway were filling with her warriors. I tried to read her thoughts but she immediately knew that she was being mentally probed. As if she had been trained to do so, she blocked my attempts.

By means of hand gestures, we were ordered to follow the parade down the road until we came to a town consisting of hundreds of thatched mud huts and one large building constructed of fine masonry. The outer walls of this building were covered with carved images of animals and people as well as images of creatures that had the combined features of animals and humans.

We entered this building to find sitting on a throne a woman of gigantic proportions. She weighed about 700 pounds. Princess Rytoon pointed me out to her mother, the Queen Soroona. I soon felt my thoughts being probed by the queen. I responded by thinking about the fact that we had come in peace in search of the Great Pyramids. I was a bit shaken by the fact that the queen could communicate with me telepathically. I had come to believe that I was the only one on Earth who had such an ability.

The queen addressed to me a number of mental questions as she pointed to the ceiling covered with painted stars. She asked, "Relt? Maldec? Nodia? Sumer?" I responded that I was from the kingdom of the two Atlans. She replied, "No, no; your spirit is of Sumer. I know of your kind." The name Sumer caused in me a very strong emotion that made my body experience a surge of energy both warm and pleasant. She then asked if we wanted to buy any dead human or animal bodies. When I told her that we had no such desire, she shrugged and mentally said, "No matter; your people who live above the clouds will buy all I have."

The queen could not rise from her throne, so she directed Princess Rytoon to take us to an enclosed courtyard filled with what appeared to be junk. When touching some of these strange items, they would light up and sometimes produce sounds. The junkyard attendant motioned that I could have one or more of these items if I traded him something in exchange. I was attracted to a small crystal sphere that turned blue and became foggy when I stared into it. I felt wonderful, but had no idea why. The attendant accepted from me in trade a gold medallion bearing the likeness of a one-time king of the two Atlans. We were told that the strange items came from the area where the Great Pyramids were located and from the sky people who traded them for dead bodies.

In another building were a number of dead bodies, both human and animal, that had undergone several stages of mummification. A body, when completely prepared and wrapped, was laid in a metal container that had a compartment at its foot in which were placed the internal organs of the deceased.

We stayed with the people of Queen Soroona for several weeks, during which we studied the strange items in her junkyard. I must confess, we never figured out what they were or what use they might have had. In my present lifetime I use similar devices to prepare food and look at the living activities of microbes.

My thoughts bored the queen, and she spent nearly all her time in mental communication making deals of more junk for bodies with those of the far-distant worlds in the sky that she called Sumer and Nodia.

We were warned that the place where the Great Pyramids were located was controlled by the blondes, who were not to be trusted. We were also informed that the blondes had recently entered into an agreement with the sky people to also provide them with cadavers. It was rumored that the blondes did not rely on natural death to occur and sometimes resorted to making war on people who lived farther to the south, even resorting to the murder of their own kind to fill out their shipments of bodies. The suicide rate went up among our slaves when they began to believe that if their bodies were preserved and sent to heaven, their souls would be free to follow and reside among the gods.

With a considerable escort of Queen Soroona's warriors as well as our own troop of soldiers, we once again proceeded south. After about a 1½-hour march, we came to a smaller road that took us just above the treetops. Below, we could see the blue waters of the River Nile and before us we could see three gleaming white pyramids. We passed by blonde sentries who made obscene gestures at the members of our escort, and even called in a friendly fashion to several of the group by name. Laughter was heard coming from the blonde sentries and from their black visitors as well.

The plateau upon which the pyramids stood was completely covered by multicolored tents. Between the paws of the Great Sphinx was a platform upon which sat a number of men. While these men sat dry under a canopy, we stood before them in the pouring rain.

The chief of those on the platform who was king of all the blondes was a man named Braymark. One of our escorts told us that Braymark, who looked to be about thirty-five, was really more than a thousand years old and the son of a god. With the will of his mind, Braymark caused us all to fall to our knees before him and place our faces in the mud. After about five minutes he had spent all his reserve energy demonstrating his godlike powers. When I mentally probed his mind he became alarmed over the fact that I could do so and momentarily became very frightened. He was quick to regain his composure and proclaimed to all about him that I was a brother god. I was invited to join him and his advisors on the platform. Braymark later confessed that he was not a thousand years old, but really closer to 800. He was obsessed with sex and claimed that it was from the sexual act that he obtained his godlike powers. He offered me the choice of any of the women of his harem, and being a young man, I was greatly tempted, and on quite a few occasions took him up on his offer. I found that Braymark was indeed correct about the sexual act being one of many ways to acquire the energy that permitted certain men or women to do things with their minds that could otherwise be done only by the gods.

Braymark was presently in a dilemma. His father's people, who called themselves Maldecians, competed for the bodies of the dead with another group of gods that flew about in black saucer-shaped vehicles marked with a silver triangle. The latter group offered Braymark treasures, whereas his father's people expected the bodies without pay. Braymark said that the Maldecians hated those who flew the black saucers for many reasons—one of the reasons being that they had at some time in the past stolen away the capstone of the Great Pyramid.

One night I joined Braymark and a group of his followers as they secretly moved several cartloads of bodies off the plateau and down to the river's edge, where they placed the containers on rafts. From beneath the water rose a black saucer-shaped craft that, by means of ropes, pulled the rafts out to the place where the vehicle seemed to float. By ropes attached to the other end of the rafts, Braymark pulled them back to shore along with box after box filled with precious gems and several boxes of candy. While returning to the top of the plateau, Braymark offered me a piece of the very delicious candy and remarked: "What my father's people don't know won't hurt them, will it?"

About two days later at about high noon, Braymark and his advisors sat on the platform between the paws of the Great Sphinx. Fortunately, I had not as yet joined them. I was on my way to do so when I saw in the sky a flash of sunlight reflect off the silver skin of a triangular spacecraft. The craft came down very low and hovered above the platform. Then as Braymark and his advisors waved a friendly hello, another flash in the form of a line of brilliant orange light came from the underside of the vehicle, and the platform and its occupants were instantly turned into a pile of smoking ashes. The craft then circled the plateau, dropping pieces of metal. On one piece was a silver triangle.

My group quickly left the area of the pyramids and returned to our encampment at the mouth of the river. I sent a report to the king of the two Atlans as to what I had learned about the Land of Ser and what I saw happen on that horrible day in the shadow of the Great Pyramids. With the arrival of the next ship I received orders to return to my homeland.

I was elevated to noble rank and began to serve the king as his mental ambassador to the extraterrestrials. Through my mental communications with the extraterrestrials I learned of the destruction of Maldec and all the problems that eventually befell the planets and radiars of the solar system. I was told that my psychic essence was native to the planetoid Omuray, which is part of the Sumer radiar system. During this time I telepathically arranged an agreement between the Federation and the king of the two Atlans. This agreement allowed the Federation, without conflict, to gather from time to time specimens of plant and animal life from within the confines of the kingdom.

One summer evening, at the age of 83, while sitting on the porch of my home with my wife of forty-nine years, Milly-Anet, and my only child, Mont-Bester, a son aged twenty-two, at their request I began to relate, as I had done many times before, the stories of my youth in the Land of Ser. (The story got better and better every time I told it.)

When I came to the part where I traded the medallion for the small crystal sphere, I had a desire to hold it once again in my hands. I sent Mont-Bester into the house to get the sphere, and I held it until I finished my story. I felt tired and asked to be left alone for a while. I spent some time staring into the blue fog that filled the sphere. Then suddenly the fog began to clear, and at the same time the image of a beautiful young woman began to form within it. While I looked at this radiant being in the sphere I heard a soft voice say, "It is time, Trome of Sumer, it is time." I fell to sleep and my soul went off again to swim in the river of time.

Monitoring the Effects of the Frequency Barrier

It was and still is difficult to take living things out of the Frequency Barrier. Humans who are suddenly introduced to the open, unrestricted mental state usually go completely insane. The farther one goes back in time, the more one could have expected this to happen. The Frequency Barrier is presently weak enough to permit some people from both the closed and open mental states to go into and out of the Barrier after a brief period of intense preparation (biological conditioning).

Because living humans went insane and usually died of uncontrollable bioelectrical brain activity (similar to epilepsy), it was impractical to bring live people out of the Barrier into the open state, where they would surely die a cruel and painful death.

At the time of the life I just described, those living in the open state had developed methods that made it practical to autopsy a dead body of one of the Earth and study the biological effects of the Frequency Barrier during a person's lifetime. These studies were carried out both to predict the rate of Frequency Barrier diminishment and to determine what patterns of DNA were best suited to tolerate its effects in the future. A genetically engineered human hybrid that could tolerate the effects of the Frequency Barrier was also on the agenda. The reasons for creating such a hybrid are too numerous to describe.

One might ask, "Why didn't the Maldecians and their open-state allies simply pick up living humans from the Earth? After all, they would not have been bothered by the fact that those they abducted would die." The reason they did not do this is because large numbers of specimens were required and they could not themselves function physically in the Frequency Barrier without suffering ill effects. This situation necessitated both of the opposing groups to enlist the aid of agents living on the Earth (tempered to the current degree of the Frequency Barrier) to act on their behalf and gather specimens for them.

Later, methods were developed to take living things out of the Frequency Barrier in a state of suspended animation, study them, biologically modify them and return them later to the Earth. This method was first employed about 12,000 B.C. in a place now referred to as Sumeria.

A Life in Bangur (Sumeria)

My name was Bello, and I was born about 10,000 B.C. into a family of wealthy merchants and moneylenders. Simply, my father Serakus and his brother Shavmenus were pawnbrokers. My mother's name was Qutata. We lived on an estate north of the capital city of the kingdom of Sumeria, which was called Bangur. It was in this city that my father and his brother maintained their business.

For more than 500 years prior to my birth, the priesthood of Sumeria interacted with the gods by providing them with sacrifices, both living and dead. Sumeria was the name the gods themselves gave to the kingdom.

I was educated along with an elder brother by private teachers. My mother died at childbirth, bearing my father a daughter. In his grief he gave the infant to the priests to be sacrificed to the gods so that they would treat my mother's soul well. My sister escaped death by being adopted and raised by a priestess of the goat-headed god known as Sitshay. Later my sister married a man who became king of Sumeria, and for more than 112 years she alone ruled the land while he lived for that period of time with the gods.

When I was about nineteen years old, my father received as a loan forfeiture a large vineyard. The vines barely produced fruit because the land had become saturated with salt that had percolated up into the topsoil. I asked my father to give me the vineyard, and he did. I had the overwhelming idea that I could actually bring the vineyard back to abundant production.

I started with a small band of slaves, whom I ordered to clean (at no charge) the horse stables of the wealthy and pick up manure from the streets of Bangur. From the manure I produced a composted fertilizer that I used later. I then had trenches three feet deep dug between the vines. I was very careful not to damage the roots. The contents of the trenches were removed from the site and replaced by a combination of topsoil and the fertilizer I had previously created. The rich soil was brought by horse-drawn carts from more than twenty miles away. Need I tell you that at the very next harvest the grapes were very large and sweet? The wines of Bello's vineyard became the most desired, and my money boxes overflowed.

I was solicited to donate money to the temple, which I did, and gained by this act a seat in the temple's inner chamber. After several visits with the priests I was accepted into a secret society. The society members were informed by the priests of the purposes of the sky gods in interacting with them. I became very excited about what I learned and attended every meeting of the society.

One night, while accompanied by the high priest of Rail, god of storms, members of the society gathered on the lawn of my father's estate. Above us circled four fiery spheres which, when they came close overhead, took on the shape of silver eggs that reflected the light of a full moon. After hovering for more than fifteen minutes, these "chariots of the gods" rapidly flew out of sight. We learned that the priests of Rail no more believed in the existence of such a god of storms than they believed they could jump high enough to touch the Moon. This ruse was perpetrated on ignorant believers by the so-called priests of Rail only to acquire their material support for the true activities behind the scenes.

There were temples dedicated to a god of just about anything imaginable. These buildings were mostly grouped together in what was called the temple compound; only the temple of Rail had an upper chamber which contained a large bed. On a nearby pedestal rested a pair of cupped hands cast from solid gold. The empty hands were continuously bathed by a fountain of water.

The priests told us that these items were simply symbolic and served to remind them that in the very distant past the gods had come to Earth to mate with the daughters of men. The bed had been provided just in case the gods wanted to resume this practice someday.

The Coming and Going of Sumerian Kings

One evening our society was visited by Cyrus-Orbey, then king of Sumeria. We, of course, fell to our knees and bowed our heads in his majestic presence. The king knew why he had been requested to come to the temple of Rail, but we of the society did not. We followed the king and a number of priests to a chamber located beneath the temple. It was a place I had never been before. In this chamber was a stone box large enough to hold a man. Without a word, the king sat down on a plush couch as the priests poured a blue liquid into a wine cup that the king held in his hand. By its aroma I knew the wine came from my winery, and I felt proud.

After drinking the contents of the cup, the king reclined on the couch. He soon fell into a deep sleep and appeared to be dead. His body was placed in the stone box, which was then covered by a stone lid. On the lid seven carved circles were grouped to form a triangle. The box was then tied by ropes made of the braided hair of priests and priestesses of the temple who had died in the temple's service.

Before leaving, a stone was removed from the floor, revealing a flight of steps, which ended in darkness. The door of the chamber was closed and sealed. We were each asked to impress our individual marks in the soft clay, which would harden and become the seal.

Eighteen days later the seal was broken and the ropes of hair were untied from around the stone box. When the lid was removed we found that the body of the king was gone. In the 284 years I lived during that time, I witnessed many openings of the stone box, only to find it empty of its recent royal contents.

I also witnessed the return of several of these kings. They would generally show up one day in the subterranean chamber or walk into the city from some remote point in the countryside. They seemed to know about everything that had occurred in the kingdom of Sumeria while they were away living with the gods, but could not recall what they did during their absence. I have learned since that some of these kings spent hundreds of years with the gods before returning to the Earth. They never returned to

Earth in the same order they left it. King Cyrus-Orbey returned during my lifetime: One day he walked into the city of Bangur, leading a large white bear that had blue eyes. Eventually the number of returning kings became quite large. Many had gone to live with the gods hundreds of years before I was born in that lifetime. This group of kings, for reasons of their own, called themselves Babs. After the decline of the Sumerian civilization, which was about two thousand years after my death, descendants of this group of kings founded the Babylonian Empire and once again resumed secret contact with the gods.

Not only kings were placed (while in a stupor) into the stone box; sometimes young animals that had never mated were sealed up in it. On several occasions the box was filled with water, and different types of living fish (or their eggs) were added to the water, and in this way they were dispatched to green pastures and blue oceans located somewhere in the heavens.

The farmlands of Sumeria became sterile, due mainly to the percolation of salt into the topsoil. Bad nutrition led to plagues. The kingdom was constantly at war to conquer surrounding lands that could provide food for its people. The gods recommended that the kingdom with all its people migrate to a land far to the south (a place presently called Kenya). The general population was confused as to which crazy god(s) of the many they worshiped were ordering them to give up their material possessions and travel to a strange land. It became harder and harder for the priests of Rail to mentally communicate with the gods. No one knew anymore what animals the gods wanted or when to place them in the stone box.

The priests resorted to sacrificing slaughtered animals and burning their bodies on altars in the hope that the smoke from the sacrifices would reach the gods and still contain in it the essence of the animal the gods required. It was a vain attempt to keep the gods happy.

The grapes of my vineyard became small and sour, and I lacked the ambition to restore them to a higher quality. Eventually Sumer was overrun by invaders. My father's estate became the headquarters for one of the invader's generals. Before he put the household to the sword, I attempted to save our lives by relating to him the story of the sky gods. He gave me about two hours of his time and then offered me a glass of wine he had brought from his homeland. I could not help telling him it tasted terrible. This angered him, so he had one of his soldiers cut my throat.

My Present Life

As I said earlier, I am presently 2108 Earth years of age. I live with Graforet, the wife of my first life on Omuray. Our home is called Simcarris, the eighth planet of the star you call Thurbal, located in the constellation of Draco (the Dragon). For all of this life and the one that preceded it, I have been involved with the Federation's project to monitor the continuing diminishing effects of the Frequency Barrier on the various life forms of the planet Earth. My last lifetime and the present one were not uneventful. I was able to observe the great and benign spiritual effects that the still-manifesting Christ reality has had on the people of the planet Earth.

I have also observed many of the evil activities that have taken place on the planet, initiated and encouraged by those who practice the ways of the dark side of reality. One recent evil activity that might still be fresh in the minds of many who read these words was created and carried forth in Germany of the late 1930s by a group who called themselves Nazis. Their goal of a master race and extermination of those they deemed to be inferior people was really a plan of the dark forces, which they have tried to recycle time and time again in many devious ways.

There are some of the Earth who would have you believe that the Holocaust did not really happen. Let me in sadness assure you that it did. The smoke that rose from those whose bodies were burned in Nazi ovens at the time might have smelled sweet to those of the dark side, but only strengthened the resolve of the Federation of Worlds to oppose every one of their evil projects, no matter where they are under way in the vast universe. If you find anyone who doubts that people of the Earth would in this day kill others because of their racial or religious differences, invite them to visit the mass graves that can be found in the land called Bosnia.

As I communicate to you I am looking out a window at falling snow. My home is in a remote mountainous region where the terrain is similar to that which is found in the country of Earth called Switzerland. Several hours ago a craft landed nearby that will take Graforet and me to the Federation mothership Regalus, which presently orbits the Sumer radiar (Saturn). This first leg of our journey will take about two Earth days. Six days thereafter we, among others, will land in a place located in the southwestern part of China. After landing we will meet with representatives of the Chinese government to relate to them the Federation's concerns about the warlike attitudes they are forming in relation to their neighbors. As I told you before, I do enjoy telling people what to do once in a while!

The date of this writing is March 25, 1996. So if you happen to be in southwestern China on April 2, 1996, keep your eyes open for a low-flying silver egg and give me a wave. One thing I have learned during my past two lifetimes is: It is better to be thought of as a sky god than a sky-god worshiper.

Please allow me to thank you for the kind attention you have given to my words. May the elohim bless you with good health and prosperity.

I am Trome of Omuray.

A u t h o r ' s N o t e s

1. In recent years Richard Hoagland, author of *The Monuments of Mars*, and a number of his associates extrapolated from the dimensions of the five-sided D&M pyramid located on the Cydonian plain of the planet Mars what they feel is a deliberate extraterrestrial message that pertains to the importance of tetrahedral geometry. They have inscribed a four-sided tetrahedron inside a sphere and discovered that a tetrahedron's four base corners would touch the surface of the sphere at points located at about 19.5° north and south of a sphere's or planet's equator. The Hoagland group realized that both Hawaiian volcanoes and the ancient pre-Columbian city of Teotihuacan are located at two of the 19.5° tetrahedral points on the globe. They also were first to recognize that the gigantic Martian volcano, Olympus Mons, is located at such a tetrahedral point on Mars, and the Great Red Spot of Jupiter is located at about 19.5° south of that radiar's equator. Hoagland refers to the 19.5° points on the globe as "energy upwellings."

2. In his description of the function of the Sumer radiar, Trome pointed out to me the following facts: (a) The energy upwellings of every planet range between 19.4920224569° and 19.570353825° north and south of its equator. (b) Ra mathematics states that the various spectral wavelengths of the elements are synonymous with degrees of a red pi circle. One red pi degree equals 0.008726646 units (red pi being 3.141592592). (c) The wavelengths of the first and second visible spectral lines of hydrogen are, respectively, 6561 red ra angstroms and 4860 red ra angstroms. The distance between these two lines is 1701 red ra angstroms.
   Returning to the first of Trome's energy upwelling points on a sphere (19.4920224569°), we find that when this value is multiplied by one red pi degree, the result is 0.1701 (1/10,000 of the distance that exists between the wavelengths of the first and second visible spectral lines of hydrogen). When Trome's second value of 19.5703353825° is considered in the following way: $\sqrt{19.5703353825}$ = 4.423839263; $\sqrt{4.423839263}$ = 2.103292482; $\sqrt{2.103292482}$ = 1.450273244; $\sqrt{1.450273244}$ = 1.204272911; and $\sqrt{1.204272911}$ = 1.097393690, we arrive at a very important result. The number 1.097393690 is known in quantum physics as the Rydberg constant for the element hydrogen. It is used in simple equations to determine mathematically the values of the spectral lines of hydrogen from the deep infrared to the ultraviolet. The reciprocal of this number is 0.91125. In the Ra system of measure, the weight of one electron is 9.1125 grams x 10-28. A unit of weight called the heavy qedet, which weighed 9.1125 grams, was used in ancient Sumeria and prehistoric Egypt to weigh gold and silver. The volume of the coffer in the so-called King's Chamber of the Great Pyramid of Giza contains an even number of these heavy-qedet units.
   Since Trome passed along this data to me, my Ra mathematical research (especially in the area of gravity) has been advanced by more than 100 percent.

THREE

Churmay, a Venusian

They are as if the most fragile of blossoms in
the human form. Their songs and words of
love express more reality about the great emotion than any I have heard or felt most sincerely
offered by those of any other world. I am sure the
Creator of All That Is from time to time calls for
silence and asks one of Wayda [Venus] to sing a song
of love. May the spiritual gentleness of those of Wayda
be an example for us all.
I am Tinsel of Nodia.

Know you that I speak only as a woman of Wayda whose past lives
were always influenced by the spiritual ways of my El. He instilled
those ways in my soul long before I viewed through physical eyes
the many realities that compose creation.

Only the Creator of All That Is truly knows the total number of worlds
that exist to provide the needs of life for men, women and their children.
Among the worlds of which I have some personal knowledge, the role of
women is seldom duplicated exactly. There are worlds beyond our solar
system where women totally govern. Within the structures of the
Federation and the trading houses there are women who sit as equals
among the Lords of Devisement and command the movements of space-
traveling motherships of great size. What might appear in some societies
to be a lack of equality for women in their relationships with men would
not in the least way be considered so by the females of that same society.

There are several reasons why this state of mind might exist. It might be the will of the Lord God El of that world that women function in life in such a way. These divine reasons can vary and be as numerous as sand on a beach. Also, on some worlds the psychic essence of the female half of a soulmate pair can subdivide into as many as seven parts. I myself am one of two such psychic subdivisions. Because of these subdivisions, there could be in such societies (such as in the Martian culture) as many as seven women for every man. If such a world is governed by a democracy wherein everyone has a vote, things seem to go very well.

I could never begin to describe the various types of relationships that women and men have with each other on the countless number of inhabited worlds that fill the universe. It is really the love that men and women have for each other and the tender care they give to their children that pleases the elohim. I recall hearing it once said, "It must be spring: Even the Amazons are fashioning their battle flags into wedding dresses." Male and female love for each other can really change the extreme ways of either or both parties for the better.

I have spoken of these things in order to emphasize that every life I have lived between the destruction of Maldec and my present life was spent on the Earth, within its horrible Frequency Barrier. During those lives it was mostly only women of considerable beauty, those with some remarkable talent, and those filled with the wisdom that comes with age who were able to change the course of Earth's history.

I was always one of those who observed the decisions and actions of kings bringing hardships on the people they ruled. Sadly, I can say that in most cases the sound advice of the wisest woman of the times would not have been heeded even by the males of her family, let alone by a king.

Remember, throughout the past the Earth has been occupied by both males and females whose psychic essence and DNA makeup originated on other worlds. All of the inherent ways of these various groups have in some way influenced the lives of the whole. At first the ways of others were confusing and to some quite laughable. Eventually men incorporated into their lifestyles and laws the ways of one group, which were not always fair to others. Then, in the false belief that they were serving divine higher powers, they did things that would not have been in their nature on their home planet.

While reading about those lives I have selected to relate, please do not believe that I regret living any one of them, because I now draw upon my memory and experiences of those times to better serve the elohim and the Creator of All That Is. I most humbly tell you that the great lords of the Federation and the trading houses know me by name and ask sincerely for my counsel.

Wayda

I spent the first thirteen Earth years of my first life with my father Rosolan, my mother Becrickta, and Alysybe, my father's second wife. I had a half brother named Juliopo and two full sisters, Sacriba and Loctensa, all of whom were younger than me.

We lived in a fishing village on the edge of a lake we referred to as Lake Samm. Our multistoried houses were built of both stone and wood and were arranged on the terraced hills that surrounded the lake. Beyond these hills were even higher hills that were covered by forests. Fish were so plentiful that two boats fishing once a week could catch the total needs of our village. Any additional fish were preserved and eventually traded for manufactured goods such as cloth and leather. My father, like most of the town, had two professions. He was both a fisherman and a shoemaker.

Some of the terraces behind our homes were used to grow vegetables. Elsewhere in the lower lands of Wayda, others of our world grew grain and raised flocks of animals. A major portion of Wayda's grassy and wooded landscape was left to wild animals such as gazelles, ostriches, lions, leopards and others such as you might find today on the African veldt of the Earth. The temperatures of the human living areas of Wayda (in those times) ranged from about 58°F to 82°F. Light snow did fall during winter in the highest mountains of the planet.

We of the planet Wayda worshiped the divine consciousness and order (El) that existed in every living and every inanimate object on our world. Our parents taught us to privately pray to this great spirit. Once a year the village gathered at sunrise and prayed together for about an hour, then danced, sang and feasted together for the remainder of that day and two more days as well.

Our village men had built a number of log cabins in the high mountains where those of the town could, with a previously made reservation, vacation in the winter. I had been to the high mountains twice before I was ten years of age and loved both the hiking trip and the ice cream we made from the snow. We girls sledded and watched and laughed as my father and Juliopo attempted to ski.

The young of the planet were taught by their parents to read and write. Our village traded fish for books on every conceivable subject. These books came from a city of nearly 800,000 people called Ansomore, located over a thousand miles from our town. My father and mother once visited this city and were gone for what seemed to me a very long time. When they returned, they repeated to us again and again the story of their trip and the sights they saw in the city.

Ansomore was really the seat of the world government of Wayda. Each village had an elected representative who spoke for the village in all types of governmental matters. These representatives had terms of office that were either two or four years in length, depending, respectively, on whether the elected man or woman was born in the winter/spring or in the fall/winter part of the Waydian year.

Horse-mounted couriers or merchants with carts would from time to time arrive in our village from Ansomore with public notices that would be read aloud by the head man or woman of the village. These notices contained mostly items the government wanted those of the village to think about and vote on. Political meetings took place about every two months. Later notices would carry the results and which villages had voted yea or nay on a particular matter. Nothing was resolved unless every village's vote was counted. I recall that a village named Ordover rarely sent its vote concerning anything to the government, and it was due to their lack of voting that many things were up in the air for even hundreds of years. My father, like his father before him, would say, "What's the matter with the people of Ordover? Somebody from our village ought to go have a talk with them." This statement usually was followed by looking up the place on a map. Ordover was located about 1900 miles from our village (it never got any closer), but its closest neighboring village, Iberlotin, was about 52 miles away from it. This would inspire my father to ask his next question: "Why doesn't someone from Iberlotin go to Ordover and have a talk with them?" So much for politics.

The notices sometimes contained news items and stories describing events that had taken place at some point on the globe. I really enjoyed hearing or personally reading these stories.

One day a notice arrived that stated very briefly that a spacecraft containing people from another world had landed near Ansomore and had contacted the central government of Wayda. I asked my father if he had known that there were people living on other worlds who could fly like birds. He replied that he and others suspected that intelligent beings lived on the large globe we called Teen (Earth), which Wayda periodically passed by during its faster orbit about the central sun. He said it was thought that the visible (then atmosphered) satellite of Teen, Luna, also contained some form of life. It was also believed that intelligent life inhabited our own moon, Oote, which orbited Wayda every 17.5 Waydian days and had an atmosphere. Flashing lights in the form of dots and dashes had been observed coming from the surface of Oote in the past, but no one could decipher their meaning, and eventually they stopped. My father said that he thought the visitors came from either Teen or Oote, but would wait for a future notice, which he was sure would inform us of the visitors' actual world of origin. He added that no matter where the space travelers came from, he was glad that they had chosen Wayda as a place to visit.

A Visit from Traders of the House of Domphey

A later notice stated that the star people came from a planet located in orbit about a distant sun and that they wanted to visit each and every village on Wayda, requesting a response from the people of each village as to whether or not they would be receptive to such a visit. Surprise, surprise: Even the people of Ordover immediately responded in the affirmative.

Several weeks later, at midmorning, a large black spacecraft settled down on the waters of Lake Samm. At several points on its hull were silver triangles that had an additional silver bar just below the base of each. This double-based silver triangle later became known to us as the insignia of the Nodian Trading House of Domphey.

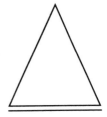

A small craft flew out of the larger vehicle and landed in the town square. There were gasps and nervous laughs when a door opened in the side of the vehicle and four smiling white-haired men, at least a head taller than my father, stepped out. I first thought their white hair was due to great age, but after looking at their faces I concluded that two of them were only a few years older than me. They were beautiful people, and I think I fell in love with all four of them. Everyone rushed to them. Then from out of the vehicle came Hocrolon, our village's elected representative to the central government of Wayda.

A number of chairs were brought to the square, and the visitors first sat on them as we of the village sat around them in a circle on the paving stones. Three of the visitors did not care for this and they joined us on the ground. One of the older white-haired visitors pointed to his back several times, as if asking our permission to sit on a chair. We all waved both our arms in the air which was the Waydian way of saying "yes, by all means."

One of the younger visitors spoke to us perfectly in our native language. From time to time he would look at his friends for some expression of approval.

The spokesman for the visitors told us that they were from a planet they called Nodia and that they personally represented a Nodian head man they called Carlus Domphey. He also told us that their Lord Domphey wanted our permission to bring to Wayda a number of people to plant, tend and harvest a certain type of grain that was not native to Wayda. It was said that the soil of our world was very well suited to producing such a crop in considerable abundance. For the right to plant and harvest this grain on our

world, they would give us in exchange a number of things we could hardly
fathom. The Nodian spoke and answered questions until sunset, concluding that they would display and explain their trade goods to us on the following day. Few of us slept that night.

At dawn the town square began to fill with items that were brought, trip
after trip, from the large spacecraft, which seemed to float on the surface of
Lake Samm. The square soon took on the appearance of a bazaar or, as you
now call them on Earth, a swap meet. Behind every group of items was a
trained Waydian from Ansomore and a male or female Nodian partner who
explained and demonstrated the various marvels. Essentially they were the
Nodian equivalents of electrical power plants, wireless radios, still-picture
cameras and document duplicators.

A New Kind of Learning and the Changes It Brought

The most exciting of all the items were the mental rom recorders and
players and the vast number of educational mental roms containing subjects pertaining to numerous off-world cultures. From the subjects of these
mental roms, we of Wayda learned of the existence and lifestyles of thousands of alien cultures with which the Trading House of Domphey had
some form of affiliation. Last but not least, the Nodians agreed to teach
anyone (after a preliminary rom study course) how to fly an aircar, one of
which they intended to give to each village. The Nodians said that these aircars would be delivered at a later time, and they were. Of course, we agreed
to permit these Nodians to farm certain lands, on the condition that they
did not endanger or bother in any way the wild animal life that lived in
those areas.

Our mental rom library provided us with instructions on how to use our
newly acquired power plants, radios and cameras. They also verified the
existence of other human cultures that existed in our local solar system,
including of the people of Teen (Earth) and those of our moon, Oote.

After the introduction of the rapid mental-rom method of learning,
Wayda was never the same again. Domphey provided airbuses that gave us
the means to visit any village on Wayda. Of course, my father set out to visit
Ordover to personally deliver his long-harbored complaints. Upon his
arrival he found three empty buildings and a message tacked to a door,
reading: "Gone to Ansomore."

The Domphey farming families were from numerous worlds and were
very friendly to us of Wayda. Those who came from the Sumer planetoids
seem to us to be very wise in the ways of growing things. The people of the
Waydian moon Oote looked like the people of Wayda but were a little
shorter in stature. Originally they did not speak the language of the mother

world, but they soon learned.

Those of Oote called themselves Whars and informed us that they had acquired the knowledge of electricity and wireless radio some hundred years in the past, and that the Nodians had responded to the radio messages they had been transmitting into space for more than seven decades. Because we of the mother world did not have this technology during that time, we of course had no idea that they had been doing this.

Within three years after the arrival of the Nodians on Wayda, there was hardly a man, woman or teenager who was not an expert in some highly technical field. As for myself, I left home at the age of thirteen to attend and live on the premises of a technical school in the rapidly growing city of Dankmis, about 325 miles from my home village. I enjoyed working with optics and worked at producing the gigantic magnetic lenses that were used in some way in the propulsion systems of the largest of Nodian spacecraft (motherships). We of Wayda loved to learn.

I was welcomed to visit the large Domphey mothership that from time to time assumed an orbit about Wayda, but due to the difficulty of converting from oxygen to rad atmosphere, I refrained from making such a visit. I did visit my family at least twice a month. My sisters were also away at school and my brother Juliopo had winged away into the stars on a Domphey spacecraft. He was expected to return in a little over a Waydian year.

The Day the Destruction Began

During one of my visits home, my sister Sacriba demonstrated a device that preserved flowers and fused them to fabric. Soon everyone present was wearing beautiful hats of her creation. The time was midafternoon when we of the family decided to take a walk through the village and down to the edge of the lake. We stopped on occasion to talk to others we encountered. Upon reaching the lakeside we joined other groups who sat about tables as their children splashed about in the water. Some of these groups had among them off-world people who had come up from the lowland farms to enjoy the day by the lake. Less than an hour after our arrival, the wind began to blow with such force that it overturned the tables and caused our fine hats to disappear from our heads. We had never experienced such a wind before. Everyone at the lake gathered up their children and headed for the village as best they could. The scene was one of bewilderment as we attempted to wade through flocks of water birds that fluttered about our feet, seeking refuge from the dry, hot winds that eventually reached hurricane speeds.

We and others took the nearest shelter available to us, which was a small house. We hastily closed the window shutters as airborne objects moving at high speed slammed into the building, producing considerable noise. As I was closing the shutters, I witnessed two aircars crash into the choppy waters of Lake Samm.

The wind continued with great force throughout the night. Little was said between us, and the sleepless night was spent by most in silent prayer. The wind gradually subsided the next morning and by midday ceased altogether. The world was gripped by an eerie silence, and the people were filled with apprehension and fear that the tremendous winds would start up again.

When we left our nearly roofless shelter, we were horrified by the devastation we beheld. Among the ruins of the village were the dead bodies of many of our friends and neighbors. In the days that followed, we moved about slowly as if in a trance. Whereas burial of the dead had always been our practice in the past, we put aside the custom and burned the bodies of those who had perished on that fateful night. From the decks of every fishing boat that would still float, we scattered their remains on the waters of Lake Samm and prayed that their souls would find peace.

Radio broadcasts soon informed us that other parts of Wayda were also being subjected to very high winds similar to those we had experienced. We were instructed to fend for ourselves as best we could until aid could reach us. During the days that followed, we experienced a series of mild quakes that in some cases crumbled most of the buildings that had been left structurally unsound by the great windstorm.

We eventually learned that our capital city of Ansomore was in total ruin. This same radio communique informed us that the terrible calamities we had experienced were a result of the planet Maldec exploding into bits. Our family was saddened to an even greater degree to hear of the fate of Ansomore, because my sister Loctensa had been attending school in that city. We never saw Loctensa again during that lifetime.

Abortions and premature births among the human and animal life forms became commonplace.

With the year that followed, the Trading House of Domphey established a number of bases on Wayda. After they were established, these bases were turned over to another off-world organization that came to be known as the Federation.

Evacuation to Earth

It first came to those of us of Wayda in the form of rumors, and later was officially verified, that our world was in great danger and that the Federation was making plans to evacuate the entire population of the planet to the world we called Teen (Earth). A census was taken of those who could respond, and it was determined that more than 600,000 people of Wayda and much animal life had died as a direct result of the destruction of Maldec. The day finally came when our family was flown from our village to one of the Federation bases. There we boarded a very crowded spacecraft that arrived on the Earth eleven hours later.

Our new home was the place you presently call the country of Argentina. This place was not occupied exclusively by us of Wayda. It was mostly populated by many types of off-worlders, who in some cases had belligerent and violent ways. The females of our world were continuously approached for sexual favors, and our menfolk were physically harassed in an attempt to intimidate them. When food became scarce, those who had the food supplies in their control increased their demands on us as well as on other types of off-world immigrants. Several types of immigrants fought back, but those of us who had never experienced the ways of those who follow the dark side of life were at a loss about what to do about the situation. Sadly, some of us eventually submitted.

Many of Wayda died of sexually transmitted diseases or died prior to bringing to full term a child fathered by one type of alien or another. Many of us died of starvation.

Several months after our arrival on the Earth, I saw a Maldecian for the first time. In fact, I saw five of them—three women and two men who came to our village of makeshift dwellings. With them were several people who were native to the Earth. They resided in fine white tents that had been erected for them on a nearby hill.

Word spread through the villages that the so-called Radiant Ones were seeking from among us those who had a particular ability or talent. My frail, starving father and mother begged me and my sister Sacriba to offer our services to these people in the hope that we could secure a way to survive. For weeks I sat with hundreds of others at the foot of the hill on which stood the Maldecian tents, waiting for my name to be called over a loudspeaker. One hot day my name was called and I assembled in a line of various types of people about a hundred yards from the nearest tent.

Becoming the Property of Jorhisa

After several hours, those of us still standing were looked over by a Maldecian woman who was carried about on a golden litter that was studded with jewels. An Earth man painted a white symbol on my forehead. Later, along with others bearing the same symbol, I boarded a large cart drawn by two elephants. That night we were given food and fell asleep from exhaustion. The next day those of us who could communicate with each other tried to become acquainted. Most of us wondered if we would ever see our families and friends again.

Eight days later we arrived at a huge estate surrounded by beautiful lawns and gardens. The trees were filled with brightly colored birds. We were led to a pool of water and told to bathe, both men and women together. This was embarrassing to some whose home-world morals frowned on such activities. The clothes we'd been wearing at the time of arrival disappeared. We later divided into two groups, one of men and one of women. We were taken to separate dormitories and fed twice a day by Earth women who covered their faces with veils whenever they were in the presence of men. I learned that I was now the property of a widowed Maldecian woman of great beauty named Jorhisa, whose brother Her-Rood was considered a god even by his fellow Maldecians. *[Jorhisa's husband was on Maldec when it exploded. —W.H.B.]*

I was eventually taken by two finely dressed Earth men to a large room to meet with Lady Jorhisa and a number of others of her planetary race. In addition, there were many present of very strange appearance who came from worlds located in distant solar systems. All listened in silence as I was questioned aloud by a Waydian man who translated my spoken words into the musical language of the Maldecians. His questions were basically aimed at learning everything I might know about the Federation, the Trading House of Domphey and the nature of those who called themselves Nodians. I was also questioned about the spacecraft propulsion-system lenses I had helped to construct on Wayda. When my answers became too technical, Lady Jorhisa became bored and called for a shelving of the subject.

Later I was quizzed on these same subjects by a Maldecian man named Vormass, who communicated with me by thought. He began by telling me in my spoken language that if I attempted to lie to him in any way, he would kill me instantly. At times he became angry when I truthfully could not answer one of his mental questions or when I realized that he already knew the answers and was asking me questions only to verify something he had learned from someone else.

Jorhisa thought it was beneath her to speak directly to a person of a lower rank and passed her wishes and instructions on to those such as me through a few highborn Earth men who acted as her overseers. The lady Jorhisa had a passion for music and for playing games of chance. My talent for singing was brought to her attention and I was called on several occasions to sing for her and her guests as they gambled. I never really kept track of how many times I had been lost and rewon by Lady Jorhisa due to the outcome of a bet. Simple games of chance such as those played with cards as you might be familiar with were not very interesting for those who had the mental ability to identify each card and its location in the deck before they were dealt. The game most favored by my Maldecian mistress was called Shadows. It was a game that involved an extremely high degree of mental concentration and telepathic ability. The progress of the game and its conclusion were displayed on a white wall in the form of kaleidoscopic holographic images of colors and the corresponding shadows of the images. I confess, I still don't know what really determined who won or lost in such a game.

One day I was informed by an overseer that the Lady Jorhisa wanted me to be trained to sing mentally, as was the way of her people. My teacher was a yellow-eyed half-Maldecian, half-Earthling man called Trowfor. I thought at the time that there was certainly no meaner person existing in the entire universe. His method of teaching included long periods of sleep deprivation, horrible-tasting foods and so-called mind-expanding drugs.

When I first performed using my new ability to mentally sing, I did so as if I were in a state of dreaming. The effects of such music on the nervous systems of those able to mentally listen to it is very stimulating sexually, even to the point of producing orgasms in both males and females. Because I could not perform without taking drugs and the possibility always existed that I might be called on to perform for Lady Jorhisa and her friends at any time of day or night, I was continuously in a drug-induced stupor. My health began to fail and I was literally wasting away. The more my life force declined, the more I was in demand. My death would have come as no surprise to anyone—and two more women of Wayda were being trained by Trowfor to take my place after I died.

During one late afternoon I sat in a dark corner of the room out of sight of Lady Jorhisa and her guests (my physical appearance now offended the lady). Among her guests were three I had never seen before: a Maldecian named Sant, a highborn Earth man named Tarm, and one man called Opatel Cre'ator, whom I recognized as being Nodian. Between the three of them they continuously beat Lady Jorhisa at her high-stakes games of Shadows.

Rescued by Opatel and Tarm, Marrying a Physician

I was informed that the Earth man Tarm had won me, sight unseen, as well as several forms of livestock. When the three men came to collect me, they ordered that I be placed on a litter and carried to an aircar. During a short flight I was injected with neutralizing chemicals that started me on the path of recovery from my addiction to drugs. Just before Sant and Opatel departed from Tarm's home, the handsome Nodian came to my bedside and placed a sealed envelope on my chest. He smiled and left without saying a word. When I opened the envelope I found a recent photograph of my brother Juliopo.

I was placed under the loving care of Tarm's uncle, Bey-Cannor, who was a physician and about twenty years my senior. After my recovery I helped Bey-Cannor in his work, and we were later married. Because of the damage done to my body by Lady Jorhisa's drugs, I was unable to produce any children.

Most of our remaining lives we spent gathering various types of plants and formulating medicines from their particular beneficial derivatives. We learned that certain medicines that were once helpful would not perform as well, or at all, a year or so later. Other formulas that were once thought useless sometimes suddenly acted in miraculous ways.

I went to the village where I had last seen my father, mother, sister Sacriba and stepmother Alysybe, but I did not find them. In fact, I found only a very few surviving Waydians. I learned that many from my world had gone to live among those of the Sumer planetoids in a far-distant land to the east. Bey-Cannor promised that whenever we could find a means of transportation to travel to the place my people now lived, we would go there. This was a sincere promise, but the means never materialized.

About a year before the Great Catastrophes began on the Earth, my brother Juliopo arrived at our home wearing a uniform of the Federation. After the joy of our reunion subsided, he told me that our father had died, but he had taken my mother and his mother Alysybe from the Earth and relocated them on a world called Drucall in another solar system. He told us that planet Wayda was now so hot that no life could exist on it. His efforts to locate our sister Sacriba had been entirely in vain. He offered to take both Bey-Cannor and me off the Earth, but my husband wanted to stay on his home world, and I loved him too much to leave him.

One day we were in the jungle searching for certain plants when the sky filled with dark clouds and a torrential rain began to fall, accompanied by continuous thunder and lightning. Our small band of twelve plant-gatherers never left the jungle. We died of fumes triggered by the extremely hot rain that fell on the long-dead vegetation beneath us. The fumes filled our lungs and we fell asleep and died quickly.

Life under the Eternal Stars

As do those who spoke before me and those who are yet to speak, I experienced many lives on the planet Earth, both in ignorance and in some cases with some degree of enlightenment as to the purpose that human life has in the master plan of the creator of all that is.

I have not chosen to speak of lifetimes that were influenced by primitive conditions and superstitious ignorance, nor have I chosen those brief times I lived when people of the Earth were able to send their thoughts to one another and to those living on other worlds.

My selection of the five lives I have still to relate was made with the purpose of connecting some of my past-life experiences to certain individuals of those same times whose fame has survived even to the present day.

Egypt during the Time of Imhotep

Those of authority on the Earth would place the time of which I will speak at somewhere between the years 2686 and 2613 B.C., though the period began about 650 years before that.

My name was Naya, the third child of an eventual twelve born to my mother Sybra and father Harcar. We lived in what was then and still is the fertile delta of the Nile River. In my infancy I swung from the ceiling of our mud-brick home in a basket made of papyrus reeds. After learning to walk, I was tethered by a papyrus rope to a post in front of our house as my mother went about her business of cooking, baking bread, weaving and making beer. She was assisted by the widows of my father's two older brothers, who had died in battles with invaders who had entered our land from the west. My father's sisters-in-law brought to our house two sons each. At the time of my birth, two of these boys were old enough to help my father in his work of producing fine metal daggers, swords and on occasion jewelry. My older brother, Yalput, also assisted my father when he was not fishing and hunting birds along the edge of the river.

My earliest memories of that life consist of my mother always calling out to the gods to change one of my siblings into a turtle for teasing me and pulling on my rope until I fell over. Tied to an adjacent post was a dog who was out of my reach. One day the dog chewed through his rope and took off on a run to the river, only to return later with my brother Yalput. The next day I too chewed through my rope and toddled to the river looking for Yalput. My excursion ended when I waded into the water and became bogged down in mud. I clung to the stalks of papyrus as crocodiles came close enough for me to touch them. (I did pass some time petting a very large one on his nose.) Many hours went by before my father found me. My scaly companion hissed at him a few times and slowly swam away. I was then called Naya, beloved of Sobek, the crocodile god. My father swore he would never eat crocodile meat again. He fashioned for me a copper bracelet in the shape of Sobek. As I grew I eventually could no longer get this piece of jewelry over my hand, so I wore it on a string about my neck.

Life as a preadolescent girl in that time was spent mostly at play, but as time went on I was called upon to assist the womenfolk of the household in their tasks and also to assist my father by sitting before a flat block of stone and beating odd-shaped pieces of gold into gold leaf. My father would trade this gold leaf to the royal carpenters of King Djoser, who used it to gild wooden furniture that they had fashioned. In exchange my father received small amounts of silver and copper, two metals he felt were much more valuable. Of course, the carpenters would provide my father with the gold in an unrefined form. He refused to refine it in their presence. His secret was to use a bellows to create the great temperatures that were required to melt the metal. After the carpenters had well departed the area, he would assemble his bellows of leather and copper tacks. His later version of a bellows had an outlet consisting of a copper image of a crocodile. Before he began to melt the gold, he would first face the river and shout "Sobek, it is time that we go to work!"

Girls were given dolls made by their mothers and boys were left to chase each other about with sticks. In this way they soon learned to fend off the blows of any attacker. By the age of fourteen, my brother Yalput had more scars on his body then any veteran who had survived the recent western wars. The only toy Yalput ever had (if it could be called a toy) was a papyrus reed boat about three feet in length. Though he had built it when he was less than ten years of age, he later pulled it through the papyrus reeds by a line attached to his waist. He used this floating vessel to carry his fishing catch of the day.

Sex at an early age was permissible as long as it was not an incestuous act. This is contrary to what are now believed to have been the sexual habits of the people of that time and place. Much later in time, such immoral practices were flagrant.

One early morning, just before dawn, we were awakened by loud voices. These voices belonged to a troop of soldiers who were looking for recruits for the surac's (king's) army. They came in the middle of the night to ensure that those of fighting age were still sleeping and not off hiding from them among the reeds of the river.

Only Yalput was recruited. He was happy about the whole thing. My mother cried and called out to the gods to protect her son from harm. My father went to his shop and returned with a very sharp, sickle-shaped copper sword he had made for Yalput in anticipation of this event.

Several months later a badly wounded Yalput arrived home between the arms of several of his comrades, who also were wounded to some extent. Yalput had several deep cuts and several flint arrowheads still embedded in his body. My father went in search of a physician. He returned home with a very tired old priest of Amon whom he found tending to other wounded soldiers who had managed to return to their homes throughout the delta. He looked at my brother and his moaning friends and asked for a cup of beer, which he drank and then fell to sleep. No one tried to awaken the old priest, for it was our hope that he would have a dream in which the god Amon would tell him what to do in order to save the lives of Yalput and his friends.

The Miraculous Healing of Yalput and His Wounded Companions

When the priest did awaken some hours later, he rose and chanted a few prayers, took a jug of beer as payment for his services and left us, saying, "The fate of these young men now rests solely in the hands of the gods." My mother threw a clay cup at him. He paid no attention as the cup missed him, struck the wooden door and shattered.

In the afternoon of the following day the dog began to bark. We looked out the door to see two men, one tall and dressed as a noble, and one much smaller, very thin man of very dark complexion, wearing only a leather skirt. Both men's heads were shaved in the fashion of the priests of Amon. The smaller man was gently stroking the dog. We asked the strangers what they wanted. They replied, "Don't you have wounded men here?" Did not Sabber, the priest of Amon, tell you that their lives were in the hands of the gods? As they spoke my mother began to arm herself with a number of throwable household items. My father restrained her with words of caution.

The little man asked us all to stand outside the house and pray to the gods as he and his tall muscular companion entered the building and closed the door. Twenty minutes later they came out. The little man handed my mother a clay cup that contained the arrowheads that were once in Yalput's body. She fell to her knees when she recognized that the undamaged cup was the very same one that had broken into several pieces when she had thrown it at the old priest. The two strangers asked to be left alone in the yard and told us to go to Yalput's bedside. We found Yalput and his comrades awake and talking to each other. Their once-gaping wounds were now closed. More noise caused us to look again into the yard. The area was filling up with soldiers and priests who were on their hands and knees before our magical visitors. The smaller man called to my mother and gave her a jar of rose-colored salve, instructing her to put the ointment on the wounds of those he had entrusted to her care. I heard a soldier on his knees call out to my standing mother: "Get yourself down, woman, before Djoser, King of Upper and Lower Egypt, and his holy companion Imhotep, beloved of the god Amon." After a moment of shock and bewilderment, she fell to her knees.

When the king, his soldiers and his priests departed on the backs of camels, we remained on our knees with our heads down, waiting for my father to tell us that it was safe to get up. When he did tell us to rise, we immediately hit the ground again, because there before us, sitting alone on the edge of our water well and holding out to our thirsty dog his cupped hands filled with water, was the man called Imhotep, the beloved of the god Amon.

Imhotep called softly to my father by name, then said, "Harcar, come to me and bring with you your daughter you have named Naya." As we began to slowly crawl toward him, he spoke louder: "Come to me walking."

He asked my father to sit next to him on the edge of the well and for me to sit at their feet. He patted me on the head and said, "So this is Naya, the beloved of Sobek, the crocodile god." He laughed and said, "I expected you to be covered by green scales." He laughed again when I felt my arms and looked under my tunic to see if any green scales were present.

Imhotep did not order my father, but in a soft voice asked him if he would come to him in the south and make metal stone-cutting tools for him. He told my father that he planned to build a mastaba (rectangular tomb) made of stone that would someday hold and protect the body of his friend King Djoser. My father without hesitation agreed to leave immediately.

Imhotep rose to his feet and said, "No, come in six days' time to the point in the river to the south where the boats of the tax collectors come ashore. Bring your bellows and Naya. Those of us who are beloved of the gods must share our great wisdom with each other."

Imhotep then said, "I believe you owe me a jug of beer." I rushed to the house and returned with a full jug of my mother's finest brew. We then watched as Imhotep walked off to the south to join with Sabber, the old priest of Amon. Imhotep gave the jug of beer to the old one. We continued to watch them until they were out of our sight.

Within a few days Yalput's wounds healed, leaving no scars. Even the scars that he had acquired when he played at war with boyhood friends disappeared without a trace. My mother placed the clay cup, still containing its contents of arrowheads, on a small wooden stool in the corner of the largest room in our house and prayed before it three times a day for the rest of her life.

Leaving the Nile Delta for Saqqara

On the morning of the sixth day following that day of miracles, my father and I embraced everyone in the household and began our journey to the south. My father carried a large pack on his back containing his bellows and fire-making stones, and I carried a reed basket filled with cheese, bread, onions and beer. Just before our departure, my mother said to us through her tears, "If you meet any more gods, tell them that we of this house have always done our best to serve them."

About an hour and a half later, my father and I came to the place where the tax collectors beached their boats. There we found, gently rocking to the rhythm of the waves of the river, a beautiful ship painted red and black. A gangplank extended from it, reaching just short of the bank, which required that we wade in the water a few feet before we could board the vessel.

We were met and greeted by a man dressed in fine white linen. He asked my father if he was Harcar and if I was Naya, beloved of Sobek, the crocodile god. My father told him that we were. Instantly the man called out to a man standing at the bow of the ship: "It is they. With the blessings of the gods we sail to the south." The man on the bow shouted out orders, and men with poles pushed the large boat away from the shore and into the northward current of the mother of all rivers. Once we were sufficiently away from the shore, oars were extended and a white sail bearing the brilliant green-and-black image of Sobek was unfurled, immediately filling with the wind that would carry us to new adventures.

We were the only passengers, and we spent that night listening to the rhythmic chants and songs of the oarsmen. That night a strange thing happened. A large globe of light rose from the water before our ship and at great speed disappeared into the sky, leaving all who saw it stunned with amazement.

I was awakened by the sound of the ship's crew walking down the gangplank in order to relieve themselves, bathe and breakfast. Their noble master was on the stern of the ship squatting over a small brazier, making what you call tortillas. He invited us to join him after we made a necessary visit to shore.

From the top of the gangplank I beheld a sight I will never forget. On the flat hill that was before us, illuminated by the first rays of dawn, were what first appeared to be three more hills that had pointed peaks. Two of these pointed hills were white, and the largest of the three was red. An oarsman who was at the bottom of the gangplank waiting for us to descend so that he could come aboard, saw the look of astonishment on my face and pointed to the objects, proclaiming with authority, "Those are the Great

Rens (pyramids) that were built long ago by the gods." My father said he had heard of these "mountains of the gods" and that he had told me and the others of our family about them several times. I recalled that when he'd told us of these things, I envisioned them to be very far from our home, in a place where only the gods were allowed to go. I thought at the time, *Am I allowed to see these holy things because I am the beloved of Sobek?*

As the sun rose higher in the sky, I could make out that the largest of the rens was not totally red in color but had thousands of painted red symbols that covered its sides. *[Note: These symbols were not on the Great Pyramid originally, but at the time prior to the demise of the two Atlans (Atlantis). I have been informed that they were painted on the structure during one of the so-called golden ages that occurred prior to the foundation of that ancient kingdom. — W.H.B.]*

At midafternoon of the following day, our boat once again came ashore. Several other ships (not so grand as ours) were beached, and the crews of these vessels were unloading cargoes that were being packed by others on the backs of more than a hundred camels. My father and I reluctantly mounted a camel; it was a first-time experience for both of us. We held on tightly to our gear and to each other as a man walked ahead and led the beast. After joining a single-file line of camels, we heard the sound of a beating drum, and our caravan started its journey to the west. I took one last look over my shoulder at the fine ship that had brought us to this place.

We traveled until nightfall and were invited to sit by one of the many campfires and partake of a supper of baked fish with boiled squash and onions. A few of the men at the fireside knew that my father was a sword-maker and treated him with great respect. I saw his eyes fill with pride as he announced, tapping his chest, that his knowledge of metals was not his only gift from the gods, that their greatest gift to him was here among the group in the form of his daughter Naya, who was beloved of Sobek, the crocodile god. His announcement was followed by murmurs and a considerable numbers of oohs and aahs.

Having the floor, so to speak, my father told the group about the globe of light we had seen rise from the Nile during the first night of our journey. Everyone responded, as they had to his earlier statements, but sat as if dumbfounded. One man ventured to say, "Only the gods and Imhotep know what it was."

Father then related the full account of Imhotep's visitation to our home and the invitation he had made us to come to work for him making metal tools. The group listened in silence as my father repeated the story again and again. One of the men asked my father for permission to tell a story about Imhotep that he had heard quite recently. His request made my father feel very important, and I was happy for him. My father gave his permission as a woman placed a bundle of sheepskins for the two of us to sit upon as honored guests and so we would be better seen by those seated farther away from the center of the group.

The man then started his amazing tale, "I have heard that when Imhotep was born he was like any other child, but when he was very young, the gods came to Earth and took him away. Many years passed and it was in the third year of the reign of King Djoser that Imhotep returned from the abode of the gods. His father and mother remembered him and rejoiced at seeing him again. He told them that the gods had bestowed on him much knowledge and had sent him home with a message for the king. While Imhotep was with the gods, his skin had become very dark, and if anyone dared to stare at the back of his head they would see the dark-blue symbols that some thought gave him his divine powers.

"When Imhotep came before Djoser, the king was in a very bad mood, for he was troubled by festering teeth and had lost many of them, making it nearly impossible to eat. If it were not for Imhotep's strange appearance, the king would certainly have had him beaten or even killed for daring to insist on a royal audience. Imhotep asked to be left alone with the king. When the court returned they found the ruler in very good spirits—his bad teeth were no longer bothering him, and within a week he grew another full set of teeth." The speaker then said that he had no more to tell us.

It was well known that from that time forward, King Djoser and Imhotep were hardly ever separated. Imhotep told Djoser that he could not and would not perform his magic at the king's command. This first disturbed the king, but later he accepted Imhotep's ego-deflating conditions and honored him with the titles of First of the King's Household and Grand Vizier.

At dawn we once again mounted our camel and ate pieces of date cake as we rode. Before noon we arrived at a level section of ground then called the "place of holy work," today called Saqqara. When we first arrived, the place was occupied by about 2500 people, and hundreds more arrived daily for at least a week. Our caravan was met by a young scribe of noble birth whose attending slave was calling out our names again and again. When we identified ourselves, the scribe crossed his arms on his chest and bowed as one would before a priest or noble. We returned his salute.

We were taken to the only standing stone building in the area, which stood behind a number of columns. The ruins of several other buildings surrounded it. The scribe told us that these structures had been built in the very distant past by the gods. We were also told that this was the home of Imhotep and were asked to wait inside. The interior was bare, except for Sabber, the old priest of Amon, who was fast asleep and snoring loudly.

Sometime later the scribe returned with two men whom he identified as Subto and Brugrey. These men were to attend to providing us with food and shelter and assist my father in his work. The scribe gave us each a papyrus scroll, which we were to show to any of the numerous overseers in order to obtain their cooperation or assistance. We could not read the glyphs on the scrolls, but whatever they said caused those who could read them to respond quite hastily to our requests.

Working in Saqqara

My father put our assistants to work building us a small house of mud brick. With a wave of one of our scrolls, the bricks, poles and palm-leaf roofing were assembled at our selected site in less than an hour. With these building materials came a number of additional laborers. By nightfall we were sitting by a fire in our fully erected new home. The next day mats, baskets and cooking utensils began to accumulate at the front of our door. Taking advantage of the situation, Subto and Brugrey also had a shelter built for themselves. Soon they were joined by their wives and a number of children. The women of their household cooked our food and washed our fine linen clothes, which we had found on our doorstep. When my father dressed in his fine clothes (which was seldom), it was a sign that he was not going to work that day.

My father found the detail and craftsmanship of much of the jewelry worn by the scribes and nobles to be inferior. He was positive that he could produce much better. He filled any spare time he had with designing and making clay figures that he hoped he would someday make molds from. When our house became filled with his creations, he was forced to place them in a mortar-lined pit covered with wooden planks located in the back of our home (an ancient Egyptian version of a closet). I mention this because it is one of my hopes to visit the Earth again when the Frequency Barrier is gone and retrieve these treasures, which I am aware still exist in the place in which he originally stored them.

Several months passed and the construction of the king's mastaba (tomb) was finally begun. My father worked at his forge from dawn to very late into the night, producing chisels and saws. One rainy afternoon as I sat talking with Tunertha, the wife of Subto, under the roof that extended out from the front of our house, old Sabber the priest of Amon came staggering down the path. Using gestures and slurred words, he got his message across—that Imhotep wanted my father and me to come to his house for an important meeting. Painted on the floor of Imhotep's house were plans for a metal coffin that could hold a human body. He wanted my father to produce twelve of them. He then asked that I and my servant women weave twelve lidded papyrus boats that the coffins could be placed within and which could be sealed with pitch to make them watertight. We later learned that our coffin-bearing boats would carry twelve mummified ancestors of the king down the Nile to awaiting gods, who would take them to an afterlife in a great globe of light.

The story of Imhotep's "boats of the dead" was passed on from generation to generation. People of later times placed their dead, their very ill, and their starving children (in times of famine) in reed boats in the hope that the gods would take them from the river to a place where they might live again. It is written that Moses, beloved of the El of the Earth, was set adrift on the Nile in such a manner to save him from being killed by the order of a king.

Each coffin and reed boat my father delivered to the house of Imhotep was gone by the time the next completed one was delivered. Though Imhotep required no more metal coffins, his need for reed boats of various sizes continued. The area about his house was covered with stacks of them, one on top of the other. On the bows my father placed metal figures of animals such as the ibis, cat, bat and bull. Inside the house a considerable number of priests of Amon were always very busy mummifying these same types of creatures, which were eventually set adrift on the Nile during the first night of a full moon.

During the three years we were engaged in Imhotep's special projects, the construction of King Djoser's mastaba and Heb-Sed courtyard were completed, and the king ran about the yard performing the rituals that were designed to renew his physical strength and confirm his divine right to rule Upper and Lower Egypt until the time the next Heb-Sed jubilee was scheduled to take place. During this same time my mother, four of my younger sisters and our very old dog came to live with us. My mother also brought her holy cup filled with arrowheads and later became the leader of a large group of cup worshippers. Our dog disappeared for several days, and when I saw it again it was in the company of Imhotep and the old priest Sabber. The old dog was hardly recognizable; it ran about and played like a puppy and never returned to our house again.

Time passed and my parents' household was increased by five more children. I was married to a glassmaker of my age, who was brought to me one morning and introduced by Imhotep. After saying that he thought we should be married, Imhotep left the fellow standing in front of our house on one foot and then the other. His name was Keerey, and my father immediately began to call him Son. They later collaborated in the production of glass and metal jewelry.

During the years that followed, Imhotep enlarged King Djoser's mastaba until it became a six-level stepped pyramid. Three days after the last white limestone casing stone was set into place in the pyramid, the king died. I asked why the king was buried in the pyramid and not sent down the river like his twelve ancestors. The old priest Sabber told me that the gods would come for the body of the king at some later time. After Djoser was buried, Imhotep and Sabber disappeared and were never seen again.

I had three children—two boys and one girl. Except for Yalput, our entire family came from the delta to live with us. We made a living selling glass and metal jewelry to the tourists who came to view the pyramid. Above our door was a wooden sign with the image of a crocodile, and glyphs that read, "This is the place of the father and husband of Naya, beloved of Sobek, the crocodile god." I lived to the age of 68 and my body was mummified. Because of my "holy" status, my corpse was placed in a lower chamber of King Djoser's pyramid, with the hope of my survivors that it would be taken by the gods along with the king's into the heavens. My father's and mother's bodies were also mummified and buried among his clay-mold models in the pit behind their dwelling.

A Life during the Reigns of Amenhotep III and IV

Those of authority are correct to place the reign of Amenhotep III between the years 1417 and 1379 B.C. It was during the rule of this great king that I was born once again in the land of Egypt. My name was Ymet, daughter of my mother Nansa and father Farneen, a soldier who had been killed several months prior to my birth. I had an older brother named Tobet.

I lived most of my youth with my mother's second husband, Kelneto. My stepfather was a taskmaster who spent his days beating on the backs of the slaves who carried baskets of rubble away from the sites of the elaborated tombs that were being hewn out of the rocky cliffs of the place now called the Valley of the Kings. At night Kelneto drank heavily and beat on my mother, my brother and me.

My brother and I shared a wish that the Nubians would someday invade our land and hack our stepfather into little pieces. My brother Tobet later garroted him to death one night after he had passed out from drinking. My brother was apprehended for this crime and sentenced to life in the copper mines in the south.

My mother reluctantly practiced what is now called the world's oldest profession and I got employment cooking for the masons and artists who built and decorated the tombs.

At noon I would take food to the tombs for those craftsmen who were working there. One day I was asked by an artist to mix some paint for him, which I did. He walked with me to the field kitchen and told the overseer that I would be working with him from this day forward. He thereafter called me Rainbow because of the many colors that spotted my clothes and body parts at the end of the day. I was allowed to enter parts of the tombs that remained secret from all others. Some of these hidden chambers are still to be located by those of the Earth called archaeologists.

Robbing a Tomb

Several years later my brother Tobet came to our house late in the night. With him were four other men who had escaped with him from their slavery in the southern mines. When they heard that I had knowledge of some of the hidden chambers in the royal tombs, they hastily devised a plan (which included me) to rob one of the tombs of as much gold and jewelry as they could carry. The tomb they selected was that of Amenhotep II. My brother and his companions dispatched to the gods the souls of two old soldiers who were sleeping at the mouth of the valley. In the darkness we could hear the snores and dream talk of the slaves in their barracks.

When we came to the tomb we were surprised to find several young noblemen already at work robbing the place. After knives and swords were drawn, one of the nobles began to laugh, and after a few words, our gang had four new members. I showed my accomplices the hidden room behind a plaster wall, and they broke through it by hitting and kicking it with their fists and feet. The room was not the burial chamber (really located several hundred feet below) but a minor storage room filled with thousands of small solid-gold statues of the king and the gods. We took our time looting the place but still left the valley under cover of darkness. When we passed the bodies of the guards, one of the nobles said, "You killed them? We had sent them a bottle of drugged wine by way of a slave and we were able to walk right by them." We followed the nobles over a hill to the place where they had parked three horse-drawn chariots. They put their share of the loot in their vehicles and said good-bye. My brothers and his friends filled a large sack with gold and gave it to me, then told me good-bye and vanished into the night. I went home and buried my ill-gotten gains in the earthen floor of our hut.

The next day when I reported for work, the place was filled with priests and soldiers. My master told me that the tomb had been robbed in the night but that the king's body had not been disturbed. Throughout that day and for many days that followed, I thought of the sack of golden gods that lived under my house. If I can insert some humor at this point, I am very glad they did not take fingerprints in those days. I know I must have touched or tried to lift every one of the items in that room.

I learned from my master, who was named Rort, the meanings of the glyphs that he painted on the walls of the tombs. He later allowed me to paint the art on the walls as he sat about and watched, or slept off a night of drinking. I eventually began to spend my evenings in the house of a fellow artist named Merelre. We never parted during that lifetime, and we had four children: three boys and one girl. Our house was located about a hundred yards from the tomb of Amenhotep II. I was afraid to bring my golden gods back into the valley where the ghost of the king might see them, so I did not bury them under my new home. Instead I reburied them in the hillside just below the valley's entrance.

When Amenhotep II died, his funeral cortege numbered in the thousands. They entered the valley accompanied by the sound of drums, cymbals and bells. The king's coffin of solid gold and his funerary furniture were placed in the tomb under the watchful eye of the now-widowed Queen Tiye. As she sat in her covered litter, she held an infant boy, later to be known as Tutankhamen. Though the queen was very advanced in age, she claimed the child to be naturally hers and that Amenhotep III was its father.

The Death of the King; Building a New Capital

Seated in another litter was her son, now King of Egypt; he was called Amenhotep IV. Our new king was very odd in his physical appearance. He carried the crowns of Upper and Lower Egypt on a lifelike clay bust of himself mounted on a gilded pole. He did this because if he placed the crowns on his head, he would have been unable to hold up his very large, elongated face. When I first saw him he was wearing a flowing white robe that covered his entire body.

When Amenhotep IV became pharaoh (meaning "he who lives in the big house"), he refused to have anything to do with his slightly younger brother Prince Smenkhkare. This brother later joined the pharaoh's enemies, who eventually overthrew him. During the first year of his rule, Amenhotep IV married the beautiful Nefertiti, the daughter of his mother's sister. They had six daughters and three sons.

It was well-known by all that Amenhotep IV was a hermaphrodite (of both sexes). Rumors said that he was able to breast-feed his own children. The people thought this to be true and were totally convinced that the pharaoh's so-called physical abnormalities were really gifts from the gods that made him more divine than any king who had come before him.

[*Note: As the reader may know, Amenhotep IV abolished the worship of the numerous gods of Egypt and declared that only one god, Aten (personified by the sun disk), would be worshiped in the land. The trouble this caused would require hundreds of pages to describe. Amenhotep IV changed his name to Akhenaten ("beneficial to Aten") and moved the capital of Egypt from Thebes to a place where he built an entirely new city of his design, which he called Akhetaten, meaning "horizon of Aten." The place where this city once stood is presently called Tel el-Amarna. —W.H.B.*]

Akhenaten put out a call for artisans of every type to come to the site of his new city and work for him. My husband Merelre was a member of a guild that swore allegiance to the pharaoh and ignored the possible wrath of the gods of old and their very vocal and disgruntled unemployed priests. For a short time the temple of Amon in Thebes remained in operation, until the death of Queen Tiye. Prince Smenkhkare at first defied Akhenaten's demand that the temple be converted to the worship of Aten, but under the threat of death Smenkhkare eventually departed Thebes and lived for a time in exile in the delta.

Before leaving the Valley of the Kings, I confessed my crime of tomb-robbing to my husband. We dug up the golden treasure and hid it among our belongings. Our trip to Akhetaten was in the company of hundreds of other people. Our route was hot, dusty and marked on occasion by the need to avoid the fast-moving chariots and horse-mounted couriers of the pharaoh coming and going from the new capital.

My husband and I became experts in the new style of art conceived by the pharaoh. Today this type of art is said to be of the Amarna style.

As the city of Akhetaten grew, the pharaoh paid little attention to the kingdom, and after several rebellions a great deal of Egyptian-occupied land in the east was lost. To prevent the kingdom's borders from dwindling any further, Akhenaten assigned full control of the army and many of the affairs of state to one named Horemheb. Little did he know that by doing this he was playing into the hands of the priests of Amon and his exiled brother Prince Smenkhkare.

Queen Nefertiti became very disillusioned with her husband and his never-ending radical ideas, departing for long periods to live with her children in Thebes. The pharaoh's physical appearance became more gross and he became nearly blind from staring at the sun for long periods of time, looking for some divine message from his god.

My husband and I shaved down some of our golden gods and bought horses, which we bred and sold to the purchasing agents of General

Horemheb's army. Our landholdings became considerable, as did our number of servants and slaves. Our home bore the sign of the god Aten above its door. (This act of placing this emblem of the king's favor on our house would later be regretted.)

The Murder of Akhenaten and the New King Smenkhkare

One day the king and several of his priests were taken by Horemheb to a tomb that was under construction for the king. Akhenaten and his priests never returned to the palace that night. Horemheb's soldiers went on a killing spree that lasted for days. When they came to our house, marked with the sign of Aten, we first tried to offer them bribes in the form of what was left of our golden idols. After seeing the idols, their captain added the charge of tomb-robbing to that of heresy and ordered everyone in the house put to the sword, including your humble narrator.

I have since learned that Prince Smenkhkare ascended to the throne for a very brief period and was then succeeded by his younger brother Tutankhamen. Tutankhamen's rule was followed by that of his very old uncle Aye, a high priest of Amon who later surrendered the throne to Horemheb, who in turn willed the kingdom to one of his generals, who became known as Rameses I.

After the time of Smenkhkare, the temples of Aten were converted to once again serve the old gods, and the name Akhenaten was stricken from every monument. He was thereafter referred to as the Great Enemy. Queen Nefertiti until her death was part of the household of Aye. Two of her daughters lived to become queens of Egypt by marrying Tutankhamen and Rameses I.

[Note: Because of Churmay's lengthy descriptions of the three lives just presented and the fact that space is limited, the remaining three lives she has selected to describe will be presented in the briefest form possible, touching only on the highlights that we have mutually agreed would be of interest to the reader. — W.H.B.]

The Great Wall of China

The year was approximately 222 B.C. My name was Ting Sue, the sixth of six children. I was married to a man named Key Shi at the age of eleven and bore the first of my three sons at the age of thirteen.

It was the time when the great warrior and emperor Shih Huang-ti ruled the land. This emperor decided to unite the existing walls of the provinces into one continuous wall that would run the full length of the empire. Though it was his intention to employ the wall to hold back invaders, its primary purpose was to control and tax any trade that would have to pass through any one of the strategically located gates.

For many years I worked with my husband and children as an independent stone quarrier. We used wedges of wood soaked with water to split blocks from the major body of rock.

My husband would first make a hole in the rock with a chisel and one of our sons or I would insert the wooden wedges and pour water on them. When the wood swelled, the stone blocks would break away in sizes that could be carried to our ox-driven cart. A full cart delivered to the construction site would provide us with a month's supply of rice and vegetables. Sometimes our rock supply was close to a building site and sometimes it was quite distant.

We considered ourselves lucky not to be one of the thousands of slaves who were forced to do the physical labor on the wall. We also thought ourselves to be wealthy because we owned our ox and cart.

The months of winter and spring were difficult for us because of the cold winter snows and spring rains that many times caused our cart to become bogged down in mud. One night during heavy spring rains our cart became mired in the mud. As we sought shelter under the rocky overhang, a light appeared in the sky. It gradually got larger and larger, then hovered over our cart for about five minutes, and then flew out of sight. My family clung to each other out of fright. Only I had the feeling that there was really nothing to fear. The next day we found our cart sitting on dry ground. The ground that lay in the direction in which we would travel was also dry for quite a distance. When we told our story to others, they thought that we were crazy, so we soon learned to refer to the incident only among ourselves.

I lived to the age of about thirty-eight and died of a heart attack while trying to get our very old ox out of some mud.

King Clovis of the Franks

The time was about A.D. 487. His name was Clovis, the first king of a number of tribes called the Franks. He was my mother's uncle on her mother's side, but that didn't matter—he really did not know she even existed.

My name was Dora and I had two older brothers. My father, Ambis, was an important soldier who fought with Clovis during his many victorious battles against the Romans and other Frankish tribal chiefs who had no love for him at all.

King Clovis married a royal princess of Burgundy and converted to her Christian faith, as did my mother and I. I never felt so sure of anything in my life as I did when I first accepted Jesus Christ as my lord and savior.

I raised my four children in the Christian faith and died of old age in the arms of my husband, Bormen.

When I returned to the open state and began to live my present life, I learned of the universal desire for the Christ reality to totally manifest in the molar level of perception. I am now filled with joy and hope that the spiritual energy I spent in the loving worship of the Christ during other lifetimes I lived on the Earth will collectively count with that of others to make this wonderful reality available for all of us of the universe.

Saladin the Magnificent

My name was Taydeena, daughter of Shabdar and his wife Nadja. I had no brothers or sisters. The year was A.D. 1188, and Islamic leader Saladin the Magnificent had been successful in repelling the Christian army of the Second Crusade from the city of Jerusalem. I, among others of my formerly wool-merchant family, was drafted to work on the construction and reconstruction of the city's defensive walls (my favorite job). A year later those persistent Christians once again came to our city gates under the command of Richard I of England (Richard the Lion-Hearted).

During my many trips carrying water to the workers on the wall, Saladin himself came to inspect our progress. With him was a young officer called Soldulah. After seeing me, this man spoke a few words to his chief, and the next thing I knew I was part of a very small harem consisting of two other girls and myself. Over the years our number increased to ten.

Saladin succeeded in repelling the crusaders again and went on to take firm control of the land of Egypt. Soldulah was appointed to the position of a very high official and sent to carry out administrative duties in the city of Alexandria.

One night as our ship approached the mouth of the Nile, prior to hugging the coast and sailing on to Alexandria, we witnessed a globe of light rise from the river and fly upward into the starry sky. We assured ourselves that the globe of light was a sign and blessing from Allah.

Eight years later Soldulah suddenly died. Before informing anyone, my sisters of the harem and I divided up his money and other belongings and fled in different directions into the night. Not knowing where I really was, I went south by boat.

During this trip I passed the Great Pyramids of Giza and had that feeling you call déjà vu. I settled in a small Christian Greek community near Luxor and eventually married a man named Callrus. My share of Soldulah's fortune set us up for life. I lived to the age of 83 and once again died naturally in the land of Egypt. (Do not believe the Martian Lord Sharmarie's story that I was eaten by a crocodile.)

I presently live, as I have for the past 187 years, on the eighth planet of the star called Thurbal. The planet is Simcarris, the same world on which live Trome of Sumer and his family.

I am once again living with my original Waydian mother and father, as well as both my sisters and my brothers from that first life. All of us on this world are engaged in the preservation of the animal and plant life of our home solar system and the monitoring of the biological changes that are continually occurring in the various life forms of the Earth.

Since I mentioned the metal coffins I once was involved in making for Imhotep, I'll add that a man of Sumer said he knows where one is presently stored and will see that it is delivered to me.

I am Churmay of Wayda.

F O U R

Thaler, a Neptunian

I witnessed the acts of their holy men of
magic, whom they call skates. My senses were
in every case overwhelmed by their powerful
illusions. Those of the great Trakel quicken the
spirit by their physical appearance, wisdom,
courage and fortitude. Anyone would surely waste
their time debating them on an issue on which they
had an opposing view. If you dare undertake such a
foolish task, I warn you, don't look into their eyes.
I am Howder of Delk.

My first human birth was on the planetoid you call Triton, the largest moon of Neptune. We called the place Mern. We were nitrogen breathers, as were those of the Sumer (Saturn) and Relt (Jupiter) radiar systems.

Trome of the Sumer radiar described the function of a radiar system very well. Therefore there is little to say except that the Trake radiar[1] that provided my people with light and energy performed in very much the same way as his native radiar.[2]

Some planetoids of the other radiars of this solar system are quite large in comparison to Mern. Mern has a diameter of 1,691 miles and a surface area just under 90 million circular miles. This makes it a little smaller than Earth's moon, Luna. Prior to the destruction of Maldec, the Trake radiar possessed two other planetoids of considerable size. They were ejected from the Trake system after the disastrous event and now orbit the central sun as Pluto and its moon, Charon. Two other planetoids of Trake took up orbits beyond Pluto and Charon and are called now, as they were originally, Banlon and Nylo. Another planetoid that broke away from its parent radiar to orbit the central sun is that world you know as Mercury, which, prior to the destruction of Maldec, orbited the Relt radiar (Jupiter).

At the time of my first birth the Trake radiar had no rings. The orbiting body you call Proteus, which has a diameter of about 240 miles, is a piece of Maldec that assumed an orbit around the Trake Radiar about 322,000 years ago.

The Trake planetoid we called Bove (Charon) had the largest human population, about 4,350,000 people. Mern, on the other hand, had about 238,000 inhabitants. The total number of Trakians living on all the system's planetoids at the time was near 10 million. There are more than 187 million Trakians embodied today, living on Earth and elsewhere in the universe. If the Trake radiar and all its eleven original planetoids were returned to the state they were in prior to the destruction of Maldec, the surface areas of planetoids of the system could never support the present number of Trakians or the millions more who will take human form in the future. Even subterranean living would not be an adequate solution.

Perhaps it is the true desire of the elohim that we of the Trake radiar and possibly humans of every other world are meant to eventually spread throughout the universe and peacefully interact with each other. If that is true, so be it, even though I personally find the ways and attitudes of some very benign other-worlders very hard to live with. Yet it is the differences that exist between people of every kind that will teach those like me to be tolerant and respectful of the spiritual rights of others to function as they will (or must) in complying with the master plan of the creator of all that is. I tell you this: I will never be tolerant of those who practice the ways of the dark side of reality.

We of Trake believe ourselves to have been programmed by our parent El prior to our human existence to be what you might call cosmic gypsies. This belief is physically supported by the fact that we are of a very rare type of human who has no problem whatsoever in converting from breathing nitrogen to even the most exotic types of atmospheres found on some other worlds. We can convert to breathing oxygen without so much as a cough during the multistaged process.

Skates, Teachers and Master Illusionists

During the time of my first human life I was called Thaler, the only child of my father Framer and mother Ibolue. Few families on Mern had more than one child.

All of the Trake planetoids were governed by a single body of people we called the skates. Whereas the Babs who composed the Council of the Seven Lights once governed the people of Sumer radiar by interplanetoid telepathic contact with each other and sought spiritual guidance from their el by staring at the face of their radiar, the skates of our system employed totally different methods to contact each other and receive divine instructions from the El of Trake. For the reader to comprehend the methods of the skates, it is necessary for me to explain what a skate actually is and how a person becomes a member of such a unique group.

Skates are masters of illusion who have a hierarchy based on how real they can make an illusion appear and how many observers they convince at the same time. A skate's position in the hierarchy is identified by a colored ring that appears naturally on a finger (or fingers) when he reaches progressively superior levels in this art. Twelve rings on the fingers of the left hand is considered the highest rank.

Skate initiates originating from the planetoids of the Trake radiar who have attained the basic knowledge required for pursuing higher levels of achievement have symbols physically tattooed on the back of their skull[3] that identify their teacher.

The natural manifestation of the rings of macro-level power (1 to 12) is a universal form of identification that indicates that the person bearing the rings has the ability to mentally reach and draw power (to some limited degree and at specific times) from the macro level of the universal life field (ULF). As the reader might know, the macro level of perception in the ULF is the dimensional plane in which the elohim interact. The Martian Lord Sharmarie is known to be marked with two rings of macro-level power and his teacher So-Socrey (when embodied) has four. Rick-Charkels of the Trading House of Cre'ator is known to bear seven macro-level rings. (Before continuing further, let me tell you that although I have a number of small tattoos on my arms and face, I have no finger rings of macro-level power.[4])

Skates of the Trake radiar eventually cover their entire bodies with tattoos[5] that assist them both to attain higher degrees of macro power and to produce their realistic illusions. On occasion tattoos manifest on a skate's body in the same manner as the rings of macro power described earlier.

The compulsion of many living on the Earth today to be tattooed (even quite artistically) has its basic source in the psychic instinct (possibly instilled in a previous life) to be spiritually favored by the elohim.

Even those who practice the ways of the dark side of reality use symbolic tattoos to solicit and acquire macro-level powers. It is the symbol, not the person, that is the medium. Those of the Nazi SS had the letters

"SS" tattooed on the underside of their left arms, stylized to also represent lightning.

During my first human lifetime the children of the planetoids of the Trake radiar were educated verbally in reading, writing, mathematics and history by minor-level skates, and their spiritual and religious education was left to the child's parents. After absorbing the basics of these subjects, the children were given a higher education in these same subjects by master skates.

The master skates employed illusion to create experiences and situations to force students to use every bit of knowledge and test the limit of their mental awareness.[6]

By the time I was about six Earth years old I had visited every planetoid in the Trake radiar system without ever being more than three miles from my birthplace on my home world of Mern. All my off-world explorations were made mostly by pedaling an imaginary bicycle or walking down illusionary roads that actually existed on real worlds. In fact, if a person were to physically walk one of those same roads when they existed, he would have seen that every smallest detail was identical to the generated illusion they experienced of that place. Because every one of the planetoids of Trake (through these illusionary experiences) knew everything about every physical feature of every planetoid, including the villages and towns located there, it was as if every individual in the entire system was actually one single population that lived on one world.

Eventually the time of illusionary education came to an end and the graduates were expected to use their knowledge and experience to get a job and make a living. Educational illusionary experiences were thereafter denied them and they were encouraged to develop their own skate powers whenever and however they could. The tattoo artists were always very busy putting magical symbols on the new generation of customers. Many sought out master skates to request apprenticeship.

Illusions cannot be recorded and played back like mental roms, which have been used for educational purposes for a very long time on some worlds. In the widely spread advanced cultures such as the Nodians', the technology to produce and play back mental roms existed hundreds of years prior to the foundation of the Federation.

Any scenario with any type of accompanying emotions can be recorded, edited and transmitted at a later time through certain micro-level planes of the ULF to any number of human receivers who are mentally tuned in to the transmission frequency on which the roms' components are being broadcast.[7]

The master skate of the highest rank of each planetoid of the system was automatically considered to be the supreme leader of the world. He or she would be the last word on any spiritual, legal or other type of secular matter.

Conditions on Our Worlds

During my first lifetime all of the Trake planetoids had plant and animal life. The people of two of the planetoids ate fish, but the people of the remaining nine worlds were vegetarians who also consumed milk products. Fruits were abundant, and we had a variety of tuber-type foods similar to potatoes, casavas and peanuts. Animals reproduced about every two Earth years, and most species never lived naturally longer than four years. Our milk supplies were obtained from four slightly different types of animals similar to what you call goats. Most of the worlds of Trake had a variety of different species of birds, but none were larger than a sparrow. We had no insect life. Our clothing was made from certain types of fiber obtained mostly from tree bark. Animal hides and bones were also used. All the planetoids of the Trake had vast deposits of iron, copper, silver and tin. We combined tin with copper and made bronze.

The two worlds whose people ate fish spoke different languages. These worlds were mostly covered by desert. The people lived in areas that were watered by geysers, which were triggered regularly by gravitational effects generated by the radiar. Beneath the surfaces of these worlds were large caverns and pools in which fish thrived among water plants and smaller forms of water life. The skates of these two worlds were very powerful. We called those of these worlds the "walkers," because it was the only way they could get around their sandy worlds. We of the other worlds, of course, built roads and used bicycles.

We had knowledge of electricity and electronics, but could not mentally tolerate the electromagnetic noise generated from devices such as a television set. Any type of electronic instrument we might have used to conduct a scientific experiment had to be first heavily shielded so that its emissions would not drive its users stark, raving mad.

At the age of about eighteen Earth years I was employed by a very high-ranking woman skate who was also an architect and a building contractor. She was paid for her services in paper currency backed by a beautiful but rare material found in limited amounts on every planetoid in the Trake system. After being separated from other materials, in its refined state it gleamed as if on fire when struck by light. This material, which we called *crare*, was physically formed at the same time that the planetoids themselves were created. Crare could be melted and formed into any shape. Essentially, crare was to my people what gold has been to those of the Earth for century after century.

My employer's name was Raind. She could design and construct a building on a chosen spot within minutes using her powers of illusion. Her clients could walk about the imaginary structure and relate their wishes, after which she would change her illusion to illustrate how their desires would look in reality. Once everyone was satisfied with the illusion, it disappeared. About two hours later the plan she designed by illusion was illustrated on paper. It was my job to physically build and install any windows the building plans required.

I spent a great deal of time reading and attending musical concerts. Very high musical tones beyond the hearing range of those living on the Earth today were favored by those of my age. Older Trakians thought this form of music to be senseless noise. Today I would agree with them.

It was the custom for women to ask men to mate, and my friends and I yearned to be asked. One afternoon while I was installing a window, the niece of my employer peered through the glass from the other side and smiled at me. Three months later we were married in a beautiful illusionary garden provided by the mind of her aunt Raind. My wife's name was Balis. She studied for many years thereafter under her aunt to become a skate. I was elevated to the highest job in the company: I became a roofer.

It was the custom of men to assemble every nine days in squares and teahouses and either talk privately to each other or request to speak to all who were assembled. It was during one of these assemblies that an event occurred that surely has a bearing on why I am communicating to you and not to some other person of my native system. The event was that of a first-time landing of a spacecraft from another world, and I was the first person of my world to hold a reasonably intelligent conversation with its occupants. Two others of my world came in contact with the visitors before I did, but what transpired between them could be used as a theme for what you would call a comic opera.

A Visit from Morris of Nodia

One day a longtime friend named Picer, in a very excited state, ran into the square shouting that down the road about two miles there were three very tall, strange men wearing even stranger clothing. He also said that he saw them "come out of a large metal circular thing." Everyone who heard his report began to laugh, thinking that he had been the victim of some skate's illusionary practical joke. He insisted that what he saw was real and not an illusion. He added that one of the strangers asked him mentally to direct them to whoever might be in political authority (in other words, "Take me to your leader"). Picer's emotional state soon began to convince many of us that he really had encountered something out of the ordinary.

A one-ring skate in the group spoke up, saying, "Take me to the spot where you had this experience and I'll tell you if what you saw was real or an illusion."

Our group of about fifty mounted bicycles and followed Picer and the skate down the road. When we arrived at our destination, things were really as Picer had reported. There was the large circular silver thing and three tall white-haired men standing by it with upraised arms, as if to say, "We surrender." The skate immediately proclaimed that these men were not an illusion, and everyone became very quiet. The skate shouted for everyone to stand back, because red lights were now flashing at several points on the rim of the metal thing.

The skate projected an illusion that at first startled the visitors. Those of the group who could see it were also startled. The illusion was that of the ugliest, most ferocious beast the skate could conjure. Where he got the idea for his illusionary beast was beyond us all, because there was nothing like it existing in reality on any of the Trake planetoids. After a minute or so one of the strangers walked up to the image of the beast and began to start hitting it with a hat. The other two strangers began to dance a jig around the image. As the skate realized that he was no longer fooling anybody, his imaginary creature progressively shrank in size and faded away. The strangers began to laugh and everyone present joined them.

I didn't know at the time what possessed me that caused me to walk to the strangers and stretch out both my empty hands. They did not shake my hands, but each touched their palms to mine. One of the group spoke to me in my native tongue and asked my name. I answered him, and he then told me that his name was Morris.

Morris spoke to one of his companions in his native language and the man entered their silver vehicle. The disturbing flashing red lights went out and a relatively large section of the hull of the craft split into two sections and separated, revealing its interior. We sat in the opening of the craft with our feet touching the ground.

Morris asked me to call my friends closer so that he could speak to us all. As the group came closer, I saw the skate and several others pedaling their bicycles as fast as they could toward our town.

Morris told us that he was from a world he called Nodia, which existed in a far-distant solar system. When I asked if he had come all that way in the craft we were sitting on, he said no. He then told us that he and his little ship had been carried to our world in a much larger spacecraft that was presently located beyond the orbits of any of the Trake planetoids.

When the subject got around to universal trade, I asked Morris what we had on Mern or on any other of the Trake planetoids that was of interest to him and his people. Before he answered my first question, I also asked him if it was our deposits of crare he was interested in. I was surprised to hear him say that crare could be found in great abundance on many far-distant worlds he had visited. He then told me that it was the people of the Trake radiar system that his employer, the Trading House of Cre'ator, was really interested in. It was thought by his employer that the ability of our skates to produce illusions could be very valuable when nontelepathic races were first contacted by the trading house and the illusions could be used to confuse the trading house's enemies during a hostile military encounter. I was bewildered to hear that people of other worlds sometimes killed each other. I had learned that dangers exist in reality that could cause accidental death, but the thought that one person would or could actually kill another was very troubling.

I pointed out to Morris that the number of existing skates, compared to the number of Trakians who did not have skate powers, was very small. He told me that he knew what I said was true, but he was sure that the basis of the skate's psychic abilities was in all native Trakians. He added that although it was not expected that all of us would develop the skate power to produce illusions, he was certain, as were his employers, that we could be trained to become excellent telepaths and espers, which were two types of people that a growing trading house greatly needed.

The Emigration to Vitron

Nearly an Earth year later, my wife Balis and I boarded a small Nodian shuttlecraft that took us to a cylindrical-shaped mothership about two miles long. We breathed out our last breath of nitrogen and drew in our next breath of rad air without even realizing we had made the switch. Aboard the mothership we came into contact with a few people of the Relt radiar (Jupiter) and some from the Sumer radiar (Saturn). The commander of the craft was not a Nodian, nor was she of the solar system from which the Nodians originated. Her name was Nella-Vo, and she came from a world called Orkintu, which was part of a solar system centered by a sun-star she called Tagmer. Nella-Vo had three preadolescent children who silently followed her about. (I think they were boys, but it was very hard for me or Balis to tell.)

The crew of the mothership was made up of people from hundreds of different worlds. Their various sizes and different eye and skin coloring made us feel that we were possibly among imaginary beings and actually experiencing some kind of fantastic illusion. The mothership was called by the Nodian name Shalope, which, when translated into your spoken language, means "lullaby." I have always thought that this name was very appropriate for a mothership.

The Shalope remained in our solar system for about eight Earth days. After departing our solar system, we stopped in two more solar systems before reaching our final destination, which was Vitron, a huge planetoid that was the only one orbiting the Ampt radiar. The Ampt radiar in turn orbited the sun-star Sost. The third planet of this solar system was called Nodia.

The planetoid Vitron has a surface area nearly thirty times that of the Earth. Because the encompassing magnetic field of the Ampt radiar is comparatively weak, Vitron's gravitational pull is only minutely stronger than that of Earth. For instance, the planet Nodia has a surface area about twenty-six times larger than that of Earth, but because it also has a weak magnetic field, little magnetic energy polarizes with the planet's weak nuclear force generated by its mass. Therefore Nodia's gravitational pull is weaker than that of Earth and comparable to the present gravitational attraction of Mars.

A major portion of the surface of Vitron was then and still is dedicated to agriculture. (It has been humorously said that one could actually live inside the shell of a Vitronian watermelon.) We were given an apartment in what was called the Cre'ator complex and found living among the Vitronians to be very pleasant. Vitronians look a lot like Nodians. They have slightly lighter skin and darker-colored eyes. When we asked about the planet Nodia, a Vitronian replied, "You don't want to go there. The Nodians are all right, but crazy, unpredictable things are always happening there. Too many off-worlders."

Balis and I were each given the Nodian version of a credit card, which allowed us to purchase only food and clothing. Housing and worldwide transportation was free. We spent more than an Earth year learning everything we could by using mental roms, the Nodian method of self-teaching. We found that the experiences provided by mental roms was similar to learning by illusion, except that here we could absorb years of experiences in minutes while we were in a deep hypnotic state. Illusions require real time to run their course and impress your senses when you are wide awake.

Eventually the Cre'ator complex began to fill up with Trakians. I was told that hardly anyone was still living on our home worlds. Using a term from nineteenth-century Earth, everyone wanted to "see the elephant."

For about two more years Balis and I trained to become telepaths, and we became quite good at it. It was at this time when a fresh lot of Trakians arrived at the complex on Vitron. They brought with them their eyewitness accounts of the destruction of the planet Maldec. They also told us of the mass migrations under way of the human populations of the planets and planetoids of the solar system. When I asked where everyone was going, one of the new arrivals said, "Really everywhere, but mostly to Earth." The Trakian planetoids were almost totally devoid of native Trakians, most of whom had been employed by either a Nodian trading house or by the recently formed Federation.

Ironically, the nearly vacant Trake planetoids were the last to feel the detrimental effects caused by the destruction of Maldec, so the House of Cre'ator and the Federation used the planetoids of the Trake as storehouses and staging areas for supplies they would eventually move to Earth to aid the hordes of refugees.

While this was happening, specimens of the plant and animal life of the Trake planetoids were being gathered by crews of Sumerians (Saturnians) and taken away for preservation in safe havens located outside their home solar system.

The Spies

One day those of us of Trake who were studying to be telepaths were requested to assemble in the large auditorium that was part of the Cre'ator complex. When Balis and I arrived, the place was filled with nearly a thousand Trakians.

We were addressed by a Nodian named Ostrocran. He told us of the sorrowful conditions that existed on the Earth and how Maldecians who survived the destruction of their world had taken total control of the planet and were making things even worse for the various types of immigrants.

Ostrocran then asked for volunteers who would go to Earth and telepathically keep the Trading House of Cre'ator and the Federation apprised of the ever-changing conditions there and anything about the Maldecians and their activities.

Everyone in the auditorium volunteered. We were divided into two groups. One group would go to the Earth and gather information and the other group would be scattered about on worlds in nearby solar systems. The latter group would telepathically receive information sent by those assigned to Earth and pass it on to Nodia. After some argument I convinced my wife Balis to remain with the receiving telepaths and allow me to go to Earth.

During the next two days both groups acquainted themselves by way of mental roms with everything that was known about the Maldecians, the Earth and the immigrants. When we thought we had learned all we could about these subjects, we were informed that we needed to absorb information about hundreds of different types of off-worlders (from other solar systems) living on the Earth who had come to serve the Maldecians before they exploded their home world.

After our conversion to breathing oxygen, under the cover of night forty Trakian telepaths stepped out of a Cre'ator shuttle onto Earth. Our landing spot was in the area now called Argentina. Prior to leaving the craft, I was handed what you would call a handgun. From mental roms I had learned how it worked and how to use it, but I had never actually held one in my hand before.

We were met by a body of men who were mostly Martians. Their leader was a Nodian who was convincingly disguised as a Martian, even down to the Mohawk-style haircut, which was considered a badge of honor among Martian warriors. He would have fooled anyone were it not for the white roots of his black-dyed plume. The Martians called him the Coate-Grol ("the sun cat").

Green Jacket and Prince Brone

We newcomers divided into five groups of eight. Each group left the landing site in half-hour intervals, led by a guide assigned to the group by Coate-Grol. The group I was in was led by Coate-Grol's second in command, who was a very handsome young Martian called Green Jacket because he wore a fine leather jacket of that color.

It was a cold night, and we whispered as we waited our turn to depart. Green Jacket sat apart from the group and seemed to be talking to himself, using two different voices. The mystery was solved when he stood up and turned to lead the way. Strapped to his back was a small chair in which sat a Martian dwarf. We learned later that the little man's name was Prince Brone and that he was a son of a one-time Martian bar-rex (warlord).

After about three hours of walking toward a glow on the horizon, we topped a hill. In the valley below for as far as we could see were thousands of campfires. From just about every mud hut we passed came the sound of coughing. Many of the Martians were finding it difficult to breathe the oxygen-rich air of their new home, and when they slept it was even worse.

We eventually came to a circular hut of wicker and mud that was large enough to hold about thirty-five people. Prince Brone was swung off his friend's back, still in his chair. Green Jacket then assisted him into a hammock and covered him with a blanket. I mention this because the loving friendship between these two men warmed my heart.

Coate-Grol entered the hut and asked that we surrender our handguns to him, which we did immediately. He smiled when he saw how clumsily we Trakians handled the weapons. He then told us that the weapons were being stored because they might not be needed for some time to come. He then pointed around the hut, saying, "For the time being we will rely on these."

On the walls hung bows and quivers of arrows, and stuck in the earthen floor were a number of finely crafted Martian broadswords. He added, "We will be going places that will bring us in contact with Maldecians, so it would not be good to be seen carrying sophisticated Nodian weapons. The Maldecians know of these types of weapons and probably have stockpiles of their own versions. Their leader has never needed these types of weapons to control the Earth natives because a mere look of displeasure from one of the so-called Radiant Ones is enough to cause an Earthman to jump out of his shoes. The Maldecian leaders do not even issue such weapons to their elite soldiers, called krates, because they anticipate the possibility that somewhere within their ranks might exist an ambitious rascal ready to wrest their power away and experience the thrill of running things his way." Coate-Grol then told a burly Martian standing next to him, "Go fetch our secret weapon."

Minutes later the Martian returned with another man dressed in the style of a native Earthman. He wore a turban, the tail of which covered the lower part of his face. He held his arms across his midsection, hands tucked into his sleeves. When he withdrew his left hand we saw that each finger was marked by a ring of macro power. He was a Trakian skate.

For several months that followed I was one of the group of Trakians who accompanied Coate-Grol and his band on nightly journeys into the surrounding hills to meet with Federation shuttlecraft. My job was to telepathically communicate with the crews of these vehicles and maintain the same form of communication with a Trakian telepath who was located in our distant camp. We unloaded cargoes consisting mostly of highly nutritious food capsules and medicines. On occasion a craft would carry passengers who would either join up with us or simply disappear silently into the night. Sometimes (but rarely) we could unload boxes packed with various types of weapons.

The day finally came when Coate-Grol told about fifteen members of the band, including Durdler, the skate, that we were going to take a trip to a town located about ninety miles from the Martian camp. I was very pleased to hear this, as life in the camp was emotionally unbearable for me and others of my kind. There was much sickness, and the stench of burning human bodies was hard for us to take. Coate-Grol told us of the trip while Prince Brone stood on a stool behind him, dyeing the roots of his hair black. We left at dawn on the following day.

As we walked north, the sky became cloudy and gray. Our path took us to a road on which we would periodically encounter other travelers.

Troops of Earthmen riding horses and carrying swords and bows would gallop past us in both directions. A few times one of these troops would stop and look us over, but after seeing the broadswords strapped to the backs of my fierce-looking Martian comrades, they usually departed without comment. As they rode off, Prince Brone, who was riding on Green Jacket's back, would make obscene gestures in their direction and make sounds like a pig.

Several times we came upon as many as four human bodies lying at the side of the road, some with embedded arrows. As we got closer to town, we passed the dead bodies of those who had been subjected to the Maldecians' favorite method of execution: crucifixion. We came upon a crucified woman who was still alive and in great pain. Green Jacket shot an arrow into her heart to put her out of her misery. I tell you of these horrors so that you will truly know how things were in those dark days on the Earth.

An Encounter with the Maldecians; Scouting Their Encampment

At sunset we entered a crowded town with cobblestone streets lit by torchlight. Almost immediately I got my first look at a real Maldecian, who sat on a balcony overlooking the street we were on. Prince Brone waved at him and he waved back. Our prince oinked like a pig under his breath.

The sounds of the town were a combination of laughter, violent arguments and mournful cries. People were doing everything imaginable. It was a madhouse. We entered a courtyard of a burned-down house and forcibly evicted a number of off-world squatters. We made ourselves at home around the fire they had built. From time to time throughout the night we were visited by people who wanted to either sell us something or wanted to make us some type of proposition. Just before first light a person selling bread came to us. We traded him three arrows for six loaves. Coate-Grol did not allow us to eat the bread, but instead put it in his backpack.

Our leader told us that it was now time to go, because we had gotten what we came for. His statement puzzled me. He then told us that there was a Maldecian military base located several miles farther north that he wanted to take a look at. One of the band told me that when they had first seen the base several months before, it was small and still under construction. We kept away from the roads and took a path into rolling hills. At midmorning we stopped at a stream and made a very bitter-tasting brew the Martians called tea. Coate-Grol took the bread from his pack and began to tear it into pieces, which he passed out to his hungry crew. From one of the loaves he took a small metal container. In it was a message that he read and then passed to me, saying, "For Nodia." I telepathically passed on the message to a Trakian telepath on Vitron, who mentally relayed it to Nodia.

The message was: "The Maldecians have begun a program to impregnate every healthy female living on the Earth, no matter what world she came from. They are offering food and shelter to any woman who will allow herself to become pregnant by a Maldecian male or by artificial insemination. When the child is born and turned over to be raised by the Maldecian governing powers, the woman will receive some type of material reward. Women who do not agree to take them up on their offer are eventually rounded up and forced to bear half-breed Maldecian children against their will."

Several hundred million Maldecians had been killed when their planet exploded, but about ten million of them survived because they were on Earth during that time. Knowing that the father determines where the psychic essence of the child comes from (native planet of the father), the Maldecians devised their plan to reembody those of their kind who had lost their lives when their world was destroyed. They wanted to do this as fast as possible.

That afternoon we lay on our bellies and looked across the plain at thousands of white tents. Beside one very large tent was an aircar. On a pole beside the tent flew a white flag bearing the images of two golden cobras facing each other. Coate-Grol whispered, "We and our people might be in for some real trouble. That flag is the emblem of Sharber and Rolander." Sharber and Rolander were twin Maldecian brothers who also happened to be very ruthless krate generals.

Our observations of the now-very-large Maldecian military base was interrupted when we were discovered by a krate perimeter patrol consisting of twelve men. They wore gold-plated armor and helmets.

Durdler, the skate, projected the illusion of twenty-four sword-waving krates, who stood facing our attackers. The real krates yelled at our illusionary krates, "What are you doing?" After hearing the phrase a few times, Durdler modified his illusion and had the imaginary krates yell back at the real ones, "What are you doing?" In the confusion we ran from the area as fast as we could. Durdler said that we had about a half-hour before his illusion would vanish. I have always wished I could have seen the faces of those real krates when it did.

We avoided the town on our trip back to our camp. On our return we did very little but send out telepathic scouts. We wanted to avoid a surprise attack on our camp by the massed forces of Sharber and Rolander. Nodia was informed telepathically of our expectations.

Landing of Federation Soldiers and
an Evacuation of Martians

Nine days later the sky over our camp was filled with Federation space-craft of every size and description. Hundreds of them landed on the plain and on the surrounding hillsides. Thousands of Federation soldiers called dartargas took up defensive positions north of the camp. As they did, I began to breathe easier.

A command post was established in the center of the camp and we of Coate-Grol's band were the first to visit it and talk to the supreme commander of the operation. The commander was a Nodian named Pen-Dronell, who also held the title of Second Lord of Devisement for the Trading House of Cre'ator.

Pen-Dronell told us that he was not there to fight the Maldecians, but he would if he had to. His real purpose for coming to the Earth was to evacuate as many Martians as possible. Some would be taken immediately to other worlds and some would be taken to lands in the east, to be left on the Earth until arrangements could be made to relocate them to planets whose native peoples would welcome them. He added that this could take some time to arrange.

Under orders, Coate-Grol left with Pen-Dronell on his return trip to Nodia and Green Jacket took over as the leader of our diminished band. The camp was like a ghost town. Green Jacket's first statement to us as leader was, "Let's get out of this place and let the Maldecians have these hovels." Prince Brone added, "Let's go and attack the Maldecians, oink, oink."[8]

Green Jacket scratched his head and pretended to be making a great decision. He then said, "I got it! The Maldecians are in the north—I think we'd better head south."

On our way to some undecided destination in the south, the weather became colder, so we changed direction toward the west for a while and then headed north. In our travels we came across scattered groups of off-worlders, some of whom told us that come spring, they were going to attempt to farm. Of all those we met, the most pathetic were the Gracians, who were brought to the Earth by the Maldecians to provide the knowledge and technology used to build the three great pyramids located thousands of miles to the east. As you know, the largest of those pyramids played the major role in the destruction of the planet Maldec.

It was during our stay with a band of Gracians that the skies began to blacken and endless rain began to fall. There was nothing we could do about it. I telepathically informed Nodia of the extreme weather conditions that prevailed on the Earth. It was my last contact. We perished from the effects of the rain and because we could find no food.

Shallo Bain and Trelba Sye

Thousands of years before the life that the Martian Lord Sharmarie experienced in the empire of Agrathrone, I too was born during a time of a so-called golden age. The population of the planet Earth was at an all-time low because the age was in decline and things were slowly reverting to what they had been during several previous times when the Frequency Barrier was at its worst.

In that life my name was Brace. I was born in the remote and secluded city we called Shallo Bain, which was located in the area now called Tibet. The city had been an artifact of pre-Frequency Barrier times that was reclaimed, restored and expanded in size over a period of several hundred years by my (then) biological ancestors. We had no idea who had originally built and lived in the city, but we knew it had been founded in a very ancient time.

Excavations in the city prior to my birth had uncovered several things that greatly influenced the development of our culture. Among the most important items were four inoperable dog-brain-powered aircars and maps of the planet's earlier terrain, which had changed drastically. Many other things were found that influenced the way we lived and thought, but a description of them would be too lengthy for this writing.

The aircars and the written language of the city's original founders were subjects of study for more than a hundred years. After we figured out the propulsion system of the aircars, we still could not make them work because we had no dogs, and even if we had, we didn't have the surgical skill or the biochemical know-how to keep an animal's brain alive.

After my birth in that lifetime an alternate propulsion method was developed for the aircars that used a specially grown crystal that substituted for the dog brain. This improvement over the original design allowed us to take to the air and explore the planet. Because I was one of those people called a "bright eyes," I was chosen to operate one of the restored vehicles. (The term "bright eyes" was given to those people who could still telepathically communicate to some degree or use limited telekinetic powers—

move objects physically through their will.) Many of us who had possessed these so-called extrasensory abilities for most of our lives were, for some unknown reason, losing them at an alarming rate. Due to mists and volcanic ash that blocked the sunlight, our food crops began to fail and the domesticated animals we used as food also stopped reproducing.

The area now called Tibet was then mountainous, but not with the present altitudes caused by geological upheavals that have taken place over the ages. In fact, the present land was not even situated at the same latitude. I will tell you more about this a little later.

Because our means for survival were disappearing, our leaders decided we should search the world by aircar for places (if any) that were not subjected to such harsh conditions, and also look for other people who might have solved the problems. Before beginning our search, we referred to the ancient maps for some likely places to look.

Prior to enlistment in the Shallo Bain air force I worked with my father and older brother making furniture and ceramic burial urns. I was married to a woman named Shrenala and had two children (a girl and a boy). My mother had died and my wife's mind was drifting; she would have extreme and sudden mood changes. This Frequency Barrier-caused condition at the time affected many of the younger women of our city.

I left my children and my mentally deranged wife in the care of my father and brother and left Shallo Bain on a hot summer morning. There were nine others aboard the aircar, and we flew eastward, sandwiched between upper layers of volcanic ash and a heavy mist that covered the land, making it impossible to see below.

We flew about ten hours a day and landed in the dense fog for a rest break. This was very hectic and dangerous, because it required us to enter the mist and visually search for a clearing, all the while watching out for trees and mountains. Crashing into such obstacles would of course have abruptly ended our journey. The terrain in those times was such that we had to pass over only small stretches of water.

After about five days of travel we started to feel depletion of psychic energy (life force) that was required to propel our aircar. Several of my comrades began to mentally drift. One fell asleep for more than twelve hours and then died. Babbor, our navigator, lost his ability to speak and gave his calculations to us in writing.

On the sixth day we came to a broad river, which we followed northward. We were sure that somewhere on the banks of this river existed an ancient underground city of Trelba Sye. Fortunately, the ground mist was light, but the sunlight was blocked by a thick ceiling of volcanic ash.

In the afternoon of that day we spotted a group of about seventy human beings grouped on the eastern riverbank. Farther east we could see images of men and women sculpted into the stone face of the cliff. These carvings seemed to go on for miles. We landed close to this group, which was obviously attracted to that spot by the bodies of dead fish washing ashore. When they saw us, they ran away in fear.

We also gathered some dead fish, which we ate before we started our search for an entrance into the city of Trelba Sye. We left Babbor with the aircar, and the remaining crew of eight climbed to the top of the cliff.

On the morning of the next day we found an opening in the top of the cliff that had been created by an earthquake. We searched for and found materials from which we could fashion torches, and then climbed down into the opening. At about forty feet we came to a broad ledge that provided us a place to stand and view the vast area beneath us. As far as we could see were buildings and streets cluttered with every sort of odd items. We realized that the ledge on which we were standing was actually a section of a crumbled roof. We dropped to the floor of the structure's uppermost story and reached street level by way of a stone staircase.

During our limited exploration of Trelba Sye we came upon many types of buildings and what were once living quarters of the city's original inhabitants. We also found several inoperable aircars and a circular vehicle, one of whose three spherical landing gears was lying several feet away. The vehicle emitted a low humming sound and was warm to the touch. We could not find a way into the craft and we were too exhausted to search long for its entrance port. Bodies of the original inhabitants had long turned to dust, as had most of their furniture and clothing. On occasion we would find a piece of finely crafted metal jewelry, and sculpted images of people and animals were abundant everywhere.

We found a small trickling spring of water and camped by it for several days while we tried to figure out what to do next. We were fully aware of the fact that none of us had enough psychic energy to propel our aircar back to Shallo Bain. We elected two of us to return to the riverbank for more dead fish, because we were totally out of food. But our food gatherers never returned.

The day after our group divided, the city suffered the effects of a great cataclysm. Many of the buildings crumbled about us and vast amounts of water rapidly flooded the city. From every direction came a deafening noise that sounded like a high-pitched human scream. I was tossed around in the churning floodwaters until I drowned.

I have since learned that the geological event that ended that particular physical life was a sudden northward rotation of the Earth's crust of over 1900 miles. The positions of the planet's geographic and magnetic poles did not change, but great stress caused the crust to slip over its underlying molten layer, which acted as a lubricant.

I am aware that you [Wes, the author] and others have visited the site of Trelba Sye on several occasions and have photographed some of the city's exterior features that are still recognizable. If you receive an affirmative light of divine direction to enter the place, be prepared to do a great deal of digging, as I am aware that eons of flooding has filled the place from floor to ceiling with very coarse sand. [Photographs of these cliffs are to be found in *Knowledge from the Stars* by Wes Bateman, Light Technology Publishing, 1993.]

Stoc and the Giant Monkey Men

About nine million years in the past people knew unseen realities that ranged far beyond their imagination and that could not be described in words. It was a time when talismans and magical chants of special people could cause certain types of animals (even those that were ferocious predators) to freeze in their tracks. The breath of the psychic hunter, when inhaled by the animal, or a magical word whispered in its ear would cause the beasts to fall asleep and die peacefully. Because these same powers (against which there was no defense) could be directed against humans, warfare between those with these unique powers was nonexistent. I was fortunate to have been born into a large tribe of people whose leaders possessed such powers. My name then was Stoc.

There were also many other species (groups) that did not have the magical powers of my of people. Humanoid species could not successfully interbreed. Some groups had populations numbering in the hundreds of thousands. Over 90 percent of the existing humanoid species lacked these powers and therefore would occasionally kill, and in some cases eat, those of another group even though edible animals were plentiful.

The various groups of humanoids varied in appearance. Most groups would be confused today with apes, gorillas and monkeys, but let me assure you that their ability to think and reason surpassed that of their present physical representatives. I have seen art produced by a humanoid creature similar in appearance to a present-day chimpanzee that would be envied by a master. The Earth in those times could easily have been called the Planet of the Apes.

In fact, there was one ape species of ancient Earth that never reevolved physically, but their mental ability surpasses that of their DNA ancestors, who originated on one of the planetoids of the Relt radiar (Jupiter). Their present exceptional mental ability permits them to perceive into the macro level of the universal life field (realm of the elohim). They are affectionately referred to as macro monks (English translation) and can mate with those of the Relt radiar, but seldom do.

Among the hundreds of humanoid species living on the Earth at the time were about six that looked similar to humans living on the planet today. My type (small in numbers) was one of these; we could walk the streets of any Earth city without drawing attention. We did not marry, and women and children were provided for by the community. In fact, we were a society where women and men shared equally in all things.

Because of the psychic powers of our leaders, the other humanoid species avoided us, leaving us in peace to roam the planet's woodlands and plains. It was as if the world belonged to us alone. The climate was very mild during each of the four seasons. My tribe's village was located in what would today be called northern Germany.

I have chosen to speak of this particular lifetime, not only to describe the various types of humanoids that coexisted at the time, but also to describe a rare event that few people of any other time on the Earth had ever experienced—and hopefully no one will in the future.

The event took place one day as a group of fourteen of my tribe set out to go fishing in a lake near our village. I was one of four men in the group; five were women and five were children. None of us had exceptional powers, but that didn't matter because those of the other species did not know that, and our very appearance would cause them to run and hide. We passed the time of our trip singing and yodeling.

The Crash of a Spacecraft and Death
by Radiation Poisoning

Suddenly we were overwhelmed by a terrible odor that burned our throats and lungs. The cause of our extreme discomfort was two plumes of yellow-colored smoke that billowed from the woods and was carried by the wind in our direction. We ran coughing and choking among numerous other types of humanoids and animals until we got upwind. The men of our group, after a period of recovery, decided to find out what caused the smoke, which had now disappeared.

We cautiously entered the woods from the opposite direction. We stopped when we heard voices speaking loudly in a language foreign to us.

Then we fearlessly headed in the direction of the voices, encountering on the way several trees that had been snapped off at their thick trunks. Closer to the source of the voices, we came upon trees with trunks that were scorched black and smoldering. Then we saw a totally unexpected sight.

Wedged between two large trees on its circular rim was a large metal disk spewing a red-hot substance from a tube that circled its underside. We used metal, but had never seen anything of this size made of it. The disk had a diameter of about twenty-five feet. The red-hot material dripping from the ruptured tube seemed to be melting the tube and other parts of the disk it touched. Even the Earth it fell on glowed red and turned to liquid fire. The heat was extreme.

We heard several excited voices calling to us, and then saw a man who was about eight feet tall waving us away from the disk, and three others of his size motioned to us to come in their direction, which we did as fast as we could run. By the time we reached them, our sandals were on fire and some of us had badly burned feet.

Those of us who were injured were physically carried by the giants back to our waiting women and children. On our way we passed many dead and dying humanoids and animals.

The giants themselves were injured to some extent and their strange clothing was ripped and scorched. Two more of their kind (one a woman) who were also badly injured came out of the woods to join us. These two giants were actually part of a crew of a second damaged disk that my group had not seen.

One of the giants pointed to the sky and shouted to the others. Hovering above the woods we had come from was another disk of considerable size. The giant who appeared to be their leader shouted and motioned to us all to hide among the rocks and brush. From our hideouts we watched as flashes of bright orange light came from the bottom of the flying disk, followed by two great explosions that lit up the ground beneath it. After disintegrating the damaged craft in the woods, the flying disk flew upward and out of sight at a fantastic speed.

Several of the giants had tears running down their faces. One of them came to me, took hold of my shoulders tightly and looked into my eyes. I heard him speak to me telepathically, accompanied by great sorrow. I somehow knew that he was speaking to me telepathically, and I experienced what you refer to as déjà vu (a feeling that I had done something similar before).

The giant told me that he was very sorry to inform me that everyone in my group would be dead in about ten days, because we had inhaled the fumes of the yellow smoke. He also told me that he and his friends would die sooner because they were suffering the drastic effects of biological mutation. He called me a Trakian and requested that I cremate their bodies after he and his comrades died—that, is if I was still physically able to perform the task. I agreed to do my best. He told me that his ability to communicate telepathically would soon fade away, and for that reason he was bidding me good-bye while he could.

On the following morning members of my group looked as if they had been sunburned, and they began to vomit. The giants were wobbling on their feet, their faces swollen. The growth of facial hair seemed to be accelerated; even the woman in their group had stubble on her face and forehead. She was in extreme pain because she had begun to menstruate unnaturally. The women of my group tried to help and comfort her.

By the second day the giants looked grotesque. They had removed their uncomfortable clothing, revealing that their body hair had grown to considerable length. To me they resembled several of the larger intelligent humanoid types that I had seen in the past on Earth. On the third day the giants began to die. On the fourth day we burned all of their bodies along with their clothes.

Even though the smell of decaying humanoids and animals was heavy about us, we made no effort to return to our village. We became delirious. As my life faded, the smell of burned human flesh brought forth a memory that had long slept in my soul: in my mind I saw a tall young man in a green jacket carrying a little man on his back who was shaking his fist in anger at the sky.

Devolution, Reevolution, then Devolution

Due to the waning and waxing of the strength of the Frequency Barrier, humans and every other form of life on the planet Earth have reevolved and devolved thousands of times since the explosion of the planet Maldec. Some species devolved into forms that would be totally unrecognizable when compared to the original forms first created by the elohim.

One example I might cite is that of the animal you call a horse. A pre-Frequency Barrier horse looked very much as horses look today on the Earth, except that the original creatures were about twice as intelligent. Harsh Frequency Barrier effects caused the original horse to devolve into a creature that was about the size of a large dog. Later, more favorable Frequency Barrier conditions permitted the animal's once-suppressed DNA code to express itself more. That is, progressive generations began to take on the appearance of the animal's earliest and most natural form.

Due to devolution, birds became lizardlike (some quite large) and then took to the sky as birds again due to reevolvement.

The human fetus goes through several stages of development. During one stage the fetus resembles a fish. At one low point in the history of the Frequency Barrier some human fetuses never developed beyond this stage and were carried to full term. From these humans in fish form came the intelligent dolphins. [See the dolphin on the Sumerian tablet in the illustration in chapter two.]

The Frequency Barrier has devolved and reevolved certain insects and strains of bacteria. Some insects such as scorpions have an immunity to Frequency Barrier effects. So-called new strains of bacteria and viruses are actually the biological products of frequency changes. Even benign changes can produce new forms of deadly bacteria.

The Frequency Barrier is responsible for the existence of radioactive elements on the Earth. The pulse of the Barrier makes certain atoms unstable. Elemental or molecular Frequency Barrier-generated decay, coupled with devouring bacteria that have come and gone, has left very little evidence of the numerous prehistoric human cultures in the so-called fossil record. If one could dig deep enough in the right spots, evidence in the form of human manufactured items could be found, and perhaps some uniquely preserved human body or body part contemporary with that time. Many other types of life forms do not exist in the fossil record for the same reasons.

It is interesting that several pre-Frequency Barrier artifacts still survive, unburied by time and available for all to see, in the form of the Great Pyramids of Giza and other ancient structures located elsewhere on the planet's surface.

Tamos and Cleopatra

The year was 72 B.C. and I was born in the city of Alexandria, Egypt, to Greek parents. My mother's name was Bemiss and my father's was Atrelos. I was their only child and my name was Tamos.

My teenage parents had emigrated to Alexandria from Athens, Greece, in 75 B.C. Both my parents could read and write Greek, and my father acted as an agent for his Athenian father in all matters of trade. My earliest years were spent accompanying my father around Alexandria making grain purchases and inspecting the cargo bays of ships for leakages. A cargo of wheat soaked in salt water would not have been well received by Grandfather, whom I had never met. For a time my parents grew rich, until Roman merchants with more gold began to compete for Egyptian grain. Business became worse when the illegitimate son of Ptolemy IX, Ptolemy Auletes, attempted to overthrow the then-ruler, Ptolemy XI. Bribing the Romans with grain, he bought their military support and thus took control of the kingdom in 59 B.C. Afterward the surplus Egyptian grain was sent entirely to Rome or to depots that would dispense it to their hungry legions who were busy conquering and enslaving the rest of the known world.

Because there wasn't enough wheat to ship to Greece even to make a loaf of bread, my grandfather kept his gold and wool and shipped my father several cargoes of Greek wine to sell. It took our family and friends about fifteen years to drink it all because the Romans prohibited the sale of Greek wine, nails, glass and pottery. Greek wool was another story, but Grandfather could sell it directly to the Romans in Athens without any shipping costs. My parents were faced with the decision to return to Greece or find some other way to make a living in Egypt.

My father eventually became employed as a minor minister of trade for Ptolemy XII. His ability to speak Greek, Latin, Egyptian, Persian and Hebrew soon propelled him to the rank of First Deputy Minister of Trade. This position was second to the Supreme Minister of Trade, Koffraf, who was a relative of the king. Because he didn't know the difference between a grain of wheat and a grain of sand, he gave my father full authority in all trading and shipping matters. (You can be sure that some shipments of grain intended for Rome arrived lighter in weight after the ships stopped a few days in Greece for emergency repairs.)

My parents sold their home and lived in the royal compound. I enjoyed this and spent a lot of time in the royal stables, where I learned about horses and chariots and also how to swear like a Roman legionnaire. (For that matter, I learned to swear in a number of languages.)

There were more gods to worship than I could keep track of. My parents favored Hermes (Mercury to the Romans) because he was thought to be both the god of healing and of commerce. On occasion we would get together and sacrifice some poor animal to him.

King Ptolemy had several children. One was a daughter who was three years younger than I. Her name was Cleopatra (born in 69 B.C.). She had been named for one of six Egyptian queens.

By the time her father became king, she was ten years old and I was thirteen. Cleopatra was taller than most girls and had a large frame. In her youth she spent a great deal of time with the other children of the royal compound (such as myself), playing games and getting into all manner of mischief. She was full of fun and enjoyed laughing. On occasion, though, she would play cruel jokes, some of which were deadly, on defenseless servants and slaves—such as ordering one who was in disfavor to retrieve an air-filled goatskin she had thrown into a pond filled with crocodiles. He never made it back to dry land.

It is true that when she matured, she was exceptionally beautiful. In her late teens she no longer fraternized with her childhood companions. She was always attended by a Greek scholar named Cyrol, who saw to her education and also planted in her the desire for ultimate power.

It is well-known that she married and murdered several of her brothers and became the mistress of both Julius Caesar and Marc Anthony of Rome. She bore sons fathered by both of these men.

During the time of Cleopatra's reign and amorous adventures, I visited with my father and mother the cities of Rome and Athens, where I met for the first time my fraternal grandfather and grandmother. While in Rome my father acted as an agent for his father to build a few ships for the Roman navy. Our trip to Greece was to fill Grandfather in on the deal. Both Rome and Athens were very enjoyable to visit, but of the two cities I liked Athens best. I liked my grandparents and spent many a happy hour listening to their stories of family history and their views of the world. Grandfather asked me to visit the great library of Alexandria (as I had done many times in the past) and copy for him all I could find concerning the religions of the Hebrews and the people of the land called India. I had not completed this lengthy work by the time he died.

While in Greece I married a girl named Marcela (half Greek and half Roman). She returned with us to Egypt, where she bore me two daughters. We later returned to Greece to carry on the new family business of shipbuilding.

In late August of the year 31 B.C., I was forty-one years old and sailed to the island of Cyprus in command of three galleys, two of which had been recently launched from my family's shipyard located at Actium in the southwest part of Greece. The purpose of my voyage was to deliver the two new galleys to the Roman governor of the island for payment.

When we arrived at Cyprus the harbor was nearly empty of ships. The governor told me that he could not pay me for the ships, nor did he have sailors to man them. He suggested that I sail the craft back toward Actium in the hope that I would find a large Roman fleet operating in nearby waters. He told me that the Roman admiral Agrippa would surely pay me for my ships. My crews were very unhappy, as most had expected the trip home would entail less work, because with only one boat to man, they could shorten the time each would spend on the oars.

On our return trip one of our lookouts spotted the sails of hundreds of ships. We, of course, thought that these were ships of Agrippa's fleet, so we sailed toward them. Night fell, and at dawn we discovered that we had made a dreadful mistake. We were actually about fifty yards from Cleopatra and Marc Anthony's Egyptian fleet en route to engage the Roman fleet in battle. We were captured and chained to the oars of our own vessels and forced to obey the orders of our new Egyptian masters. I pleaded with an Egyptian naval officer to get word to Queen Cleopatra. I hoped that I could trade on our friendship as children to gain our freedom. She responded, "Well, Tamos, it serves you right to be chained to an oar of a ship you built for the Romans—or were you bringing them to me as a gift? In either case, when we win this battle I will set you and your men free. You had better do a good job at rowing."

As history states, the battle of Actium occurred on September 2, 31 B.C. The outcome of this battle was the total annihilation of the Egyptian fleet by the Romans. The fact that we were in galleys of Roman design prolonged our lives to some extent, but when the Romans realized that ours were under Egyptian control, they attacked us mercilessly. I died chained to my oar as the ship sank to the bottom of the Mediterranean.

I lived another life within the times of your known history, but an account of that life would be of little interest. I presently reside on the planet Nodia, where I serve the Trading House of Cre'ator as a telepath.

It is my hope that I have contributed some additional knowledge of the way things were on the Earth in times long past.

I am Thaler of Mern, first born in the light of the Trake radiar.

A u t h o r ' s   N o t e s

1. The Trake radiar is the native name for the planetary body we call Neptune. It is called the Crobet radiar by the Federation.

2. See chapter 2.

3. In chapter 3, the Venusian Churmay mentioned that Imhotep, the Grand Vizier to the ancient Egyptian pharaoh Djoser, had dark blue symbols on the rear of his head.

4. For information pertaining to the Martian Sharmarie, So-Socrey and Rick-Charkels, see chapter 1.

5. Tattooed images generated the recall of some of the past lives of "the illustrated man" in Ray Bradbury's story of the same name. Bradbury used a similar theme of generated illusions in a section of *The Martian Chronicles*. In a television biography of his life, Bradbury explained how he educated himself by visiting libraries, where he spent countless hours reading. According to the Saturnian Trome (chapter 2), the youths of Atlantis, during one of his past lifetimes in that kingdom, educated themselves by visiting state libraries. It seems to me that Bradbury's writings were not based so much on his fertile imagination as they were on his experiences in previous lifetimes.

   During a telephone conversation in 1964 between television producer Gene Roddenberry and myself, I mentioned the ability of the Trakians skates to produce realistic illusions. Subsequently, several of the original Star Trek episodes adopted the idea of generated illusions. I recall that in the episode entitled "Shore Leave" Captain Kirk wrestles with an illusionary tiger that he thought was real.

6. According to Thaler, the advanced skate technique of teaching is similar to the fictitious holodeck images and scenarios produced by computer in the television series "Star Trek: The Next Generation." The difference is that the illusionary images and scenarios are produced by the mind of a master skate and not by a computer program. It would be difficult if not impossible for a computer to stimulate in someone the actual feelings of being kicked in the head by a horse or bitten by a poisonous snake, but it would take minimal effort for a skate to mentally affect the appropriate nerves in a person's body to add a greater degree of realism to an illusionary experience.

7. See the July 1995 issue of the *Sedona Journal* for the article, "The Rom Masters." There exists today a device that optically projects an illusion and also seems to explain how extraterrestrial spacecraft on occasion seem to instantly appear and disappear. The device consists of two aluminum bowls fitted together rim to rim. The upper bowl has a circular hole the size of a quarter at its center. The inner part of the bowl has fine computer-inscribed lines etched in it. When an object such as a penny is placed in the center of the lower bowl and the upper bowl is properly placed over the lower one, a projected image of the penny will appear to float in the air above the hole in the upper bowl. The image is so real that people

attempt to pick up the coin, thinking it real, only to be amazed when their fingers pass right through it. This, of course, is an optical illusion.

The optical properties of a planet's atmosphere can perform the same function as the two bowls. When these natural optical properties of the atmosphere are combined with the electromagnetic effects of an extraterrestrial spacecraft's propulsion force field, the image of the real spacecraft can be reflected off the ionosphere and appear thousands of miles away from where the craft is actually operating. If the penny is moved off the center of the lower bowl, its projected image disappears. So if a spacecraft moves even slightly away from the spot from where its image is projecting, that image, observed perhaps many miles away, instantly disappears from sight. The two-bowl device could be purchased eighteen years ago for about $45 at the gift shop of the Reuben Fleet Air and Space Museum in San Diego, California.

8. Thaler credits Prince Brone with being the originator of the joke recycled in modern times by W.C. Fields about children. Prince Brone's version was: "I like Maldecians, but it depends on how they've been cooked."

F I V E

Ruke, a Jupiterian

I will speak of the glowing orb of sleeping fire
called the Great Relt [Jupiter]. I will also think
for you a description of that first life, when
those bedecked with the bright feathers of birds
took me with them on their holy mission to the
planet you call Earth. I will tell you of several
times I have lived on the Earth because my spirit
was chained to the place by laws set by the elohim in
the beginning of eternity. I will think/speak to you
through Nedart, the Sumerian. It is my hope that you
find his translation of my images of remembrance to be
clear and in harmony with your wa*. I am Ruke of
Parn*.

[*Parn is a planetoid (moon) of the Relt radiar (Jupiter). Wa relates to
a person's most satisfactory state of psychic being.]

(Although I am Nedart, what follows are the memories of one Ruke of Parn.)

The place of my first life as a human being was called by my people Parn. This place, a moon of the planet Jupiter, is called Callisto by those of present-day Earth. As you were informed by those who have thought-spoken (telepathically communicated) to you before me, the body known as Jupiter is called by the Federation the Relt radiar. This name was given to the radiar by the people of Franet (the planetoid you call Ganymede). We of Parn called the radiar Robe.

At the time we of Parn had no knowledge of anyone living on any of the other planetoids in the Relt system. Later we learned that there were others, and that they were identical in appearance to us but spoke entirely different languages. I never encountered a person from any other of the Relt radiar system until I first came to the Earth. We of the Relt were all then, as now, about four feet in height with black skin. We actually resemble those of Earth who are known as Aborigines. In fact, those of that Earth those of Earth who are known as Aborigines. In fact, those of that Earth race are descendants of those of us from the Relt planetoids.

Parn and the Relt System

The Relt radiar is one-thousandth the size of the solar system's central sun and is still generating three times the energy it receives from that source. Presently the Relt radiar is about twice as close to the central sun as it was when it was functioning normally prior to the destruction of the planet Maldec. Parn (Callisto) is now located about 1,170,000 miles from the radiar's center and has a diameter of about 3,000 miles; it was originally located about 820,000 miles from the radiar's center and assumed its present, more distant orbit to compensate for the loss of the planetoid Sovia from the system. (Sovia presently orbits the sun and is called Mercury by those of the Earth.) Sovia was ripped away from the Relt radiar system due to a change in the sun's gravitational pressure field when Maldec was destroyed, upsetting the gravitational balance of the solar system. In its shattered form (asteroids) Maldec does not provide a concentrated mass for perfect solar gravitational balance.

Parn is now covered with ice, which covers what appear to be shallow craters. These craters are the result of the impact of the large meteors (pieces of Maldec) that struck the planetoid in its original orbit. I was not on Parn when this occurred.

About 59 percent of the surface area of Parn was once covered by rain forest and the remaining 41 percent was rivers and bodies of fresh water, now frozen. Parn originally orbited the Relt radiar about once every 37.2 Earth days and had an average temperature range of 85°F to 111°F. Parn rotated around its polar axis once every 5.4 Earth days. What would be considered night to you occurred on Parn only when the planetoid was blocked by its radiar from radiation from the sun and when part of its surface simultaneously faced away from the light of its radiar (Jupiter). Because Parn's angle of orbit relative to the radiar's equator varied 13.6 degrees north and south over a cycle of 112 Earth years, the weather difference and the differences in lighter and darker periods changed according to its angle. That is, the southern (or northern) hemisphere of the planetoid would gradually receive more energy from the radiar relative to its current position in the 27.2-degree orbital cycle of 112 Earth years. The effects of these changes in orbital angle are too numerous and complex to relate. Parn's (Callisto's) present orbit of the Relt radiar (Jupiter) does not include such remarkable changes in orbital angle.

The gravitational pull of Parn is vastly different today than it was when the radiar was functioning correctly. A person who weighed 100 pounds on my home world in those earliest of times would have actually weighed about 99 pounds 10 ounces on the Earth (6 ounces less).

In my first lifetime on Parn my father's name was Forn and my mother's name Shray. My name then, as it is now, was Ruke. Women of the Relt planetoids were biologically able to bear only one or two children at the most before becoming barren. I was my parent's only child. The average lifespan of one of Parn was then about 185 Earth years. Now it is about 370 years. I am now about 201 Earth years of age. Inhabitants of Parn and the other planetoids of the Relt radiar were nitrogen breathers, as were the people of the Sumer, Hamp and Trake radiar systems.

During my first human life on Parn we had no written language and could not telepathically communicate. I find it very difficult to use this form of communication today. (That is my reason for having Nedart relate my recollections telepathically to you.)

Parn provided us with a vast variety of wild fruits, vegetables and edible animal life (mostly an abundance of fish and hairless rodents that we called nubs). We wore brief clothing when Parn had a specific orbital angle relative to the radiar; at other times nudity was the norm. No matter where a person was on Parn, they could expect to be drenched with rain off and on for about two hours every thirty hours or so.

We lived in clans whose membership never exceeded more than 800 persons. The population of Parn never was greater than about 875,000 people, whereas Franet (Ganymede, presently the largest of the Relt planetoids) had a population then that was close to 1.1 million. Sovia (Mercury) had about the same number of people living on its surface, but they perished when the planetoid separated from the Relt radiar system and spiraled to its present orbit around the sun.

The clans lived in peace with each other. Each clan was led jointly by a chief and chieftess (not necessarily mates). Every ten years a clan would exchange (trade) an equal number of young men and women to avoid inbreeding. I was traded in that first lifetime to another clan when I was twelve Earth years old. At the age of seventeen, I fathered a daughter. My responsibility as a father was simply to catch fish and nubs and keep our family hut in good repair. My wife Croma spent most of her time with other women of the clan, who gathered fruits and vegetables for their families.

Our religion entailed the worship of the miracle of birth (fertility) and the creation of everything we could perceive with our five senses. No conversation about these things was considered worthwhile unless a woman who had borne a child was present and participated in the conversation. After such a conversation, anything that quickened the spirit of a participant could be related to others by the individual(s) experiencing it, but never by anyone not present during the original conversation. A second-party account of a spiritual experience was considered taboo. It was believed that anyone who listened to it would bring themselves lifelong misery.

Women whose presence during spiritual conversations caused the stimulation of emotions were considered to be ordained by a higher power and were greatly sought after. Spiritual gatherings of women were considered sacred. Any male who might dare to eavesdrop on such an assembly would thereafter be branded and shunned by every clan. (I believed in life after death without any doubt, solely because my mother told me so. Of course, I now know that she was right.)

Men, on the other hand, were free to study nature and discuss it in a secular, matter-of-fact manner. Laws and agreements made between the clans were devised and implemented entirely by the adult men of a clan but had to be approved by both its chief and chieftess before becoming official. Political activities were rare during my first lifetime. No new law or treaty had been proposed to the council of clan chiefs for hundreds of years. No one had found any reason to do so.

Parn's First Visitors, the Gracians

One day I was working behind our hut with several men repairing a fishing raft when we heard a commotion. We stopped working and went to see what was going on. Most of the people of their village were talking in an excited manner and walking toward the center of the 80-foot clearing around which our huts were built. I climbed a nearby tree to look over their heads and see what they were walking toward.

In the center of the clearing stood eight light-skinned men who were at least six feet tall, wearing fine clothing and hats trimmed with brightly colored feathers. They also wore shining objects on their necks, arms, legs and feet. With them were twelve strange-looking black-skinned men of my size wearing clothing and hats.

We of Parn never wore hats, but it was our custom to bury our dead wearing a hat woven of fronds, so my first thought was that these men might have come back from the dead and forgotten to take off their headgear. I learned later that the ornaments worn by the tall strangers were made of gold and multicolored gemstones, which I had never seen before. Nor had I ever seen such large, brightly colored feathers. I tried to image what the birds or animals they came from might have looked like. Several of the larger men wore capes of these feathers.

I watched as the chief of our clan approached the strangers and began to talk with them. About half an Earth hour passed before our chieftess joined the conversation. From the gestures made by the chiefs I was able to surmise that they were giving the strangers permission to speak to the crowd. One of the feathered men placed in the hand of the chieftess a small black rod with a red-and-gold ring attached to one end, after showing her how to hold the ring in front of her mouth. When she spoke, her voice sounded like thunder, which caused her to drop the rod and run toward the crowd, most of whom were also scattering, terrified.

Our chief picked up the rod and spoke softly. He told the crowd to reassemble and that they had nothing to fear. The chieftess returned laughing, and took over where she left off. She told us that the strangers came from a place located very high up in the sky. This brought an audible emotional reaction from the crowd, and each member of the crowd spent several minutes looking upward. The chieftess told us that one of the strangers, whose name was Moantalax, wished to address us.

We waited over an Earth hour for the stranger to speak. During that time a blue canopy was erected and several folding chairs were placed under it. These items appeared from backpacks that had been used as seats by the black strangers. We were amazed by these items and were even more astonished when several of the strangers put sticks in their mouths, set them on fire and from time to time exhaled smoke through their mouths and nostrils. I was certainly dumbfounded by all that I saw and wondered how the strangers could produce instant fire. (We of Parn produced fire by what would be called primitive and time-consuming friction methods.)

The reason for the canopy soon became obvious—it began to rain. I visualized how the fine, feathered garments of the visitors might have looked after being drenched by the downpour. We of Parn were used to rain and gave its frequent occurrence little thought.

Moantalax spoke to us in a soft, direct manner. He told us that he was from a world called Gracyea and had come to Parn to recruit laborers who would be employed in the construction of several mountains of stone on yet another world, much larger than Parn. He said the people who lived on that world called it Sarus (Earth). He told us that he wished to employ people of Parn because we were small in stature and very strong for our size. He said there would be much work to be done inside the mountains that required people of our size. He added that his people and those of Sarus were too large to do the work.

We were at first confused as to what "work" actually was. He told us that fishing, hunting nubs and gathering fruit were a form of work. He explained that if we agreed to work for him, he would give us things that would make us happier than we were. (This proposition appealed to me. I hoped he would let me work for him in return for showing me how to produce instant fire.) Moantalax related to our chief and chieftess what he would give us if we agreed to work for him. We never really learned what they bargained for.

The group of visitors then simply left and walked off into the forest, leaving their canopy chairs and several large chests behind. Everyone in the village took turns sitting on the chairs under the canopy. Many wished out loud that the strangers would return with canopies and chairs for everyone.

Several days later our chief and chieftess took exclusive possession of the canopy and its contents. Each family was told to come before them one by one. My wife, daughter and myself stood in line for a very long time. We were each given a string of blue beads (turquoise), which made us very happy. We were told that if I passed a test, my family and I would go with the Gracians to the world called Sarus and help them build their stone mountains. I was also told that the Gracians would return soon to conduct their tests.

The village was filled with joy. Everyone strutted about to show off their necklaces, and talked about building the stone mountains. Most thought the task that lay ahead would not take much time to complete because we assumed that the Gracians' mountains would not be larger than the largest hill near our village, which was about 65 feet high.

Only two Gracians and two of their smaller black companions returned to our village. They brought with them a black rod about six feet long and a number of silver-colored spherical objects. Each man of a family took turns bending the rod and taking a whiff of air through a face mask attached to one of the silver spheres.

With great effort I bent the rod. When I breathed the air through the mask, I first felt a little faint, but quickly recovered. One of the small black men measured my recovery time and asked my name. He spoke my name into a small silver box hanging from a strap that circled his neck. I learned later that the silver spheres contained oxygen-rich Earth (Sarus) air.

Amel, who was one of the strongest men I knew, failed to bend the bar and was excused from taking the breathing test. I knew he failed the test deliberately and so did the Gracians, but they never said a word about his deception. I asked Amel later why he deliberately failed the bar-bending test. He said that after seeing how some of the people reacted to the breathing test, he decided he didn't want anything to do with it.

The chief and chieftess told those of us who were selected to go to Sarus that we were to leave our personal possessions behind in the care of friends and bring back home everything the Gracians gave us in payment for our work. I entrusted my nub traps and fishing raft to my wife's father, Oker.

Preparing for Departure

At the time of departure for Earth, 425 people from our village assembled in the village center. We later followed two Gracians into the forest. We walked for about an Earth hour and a half before we came to a large clearing. Most of us were familiar with the place, but were totally unprepared to find the clearing totally occupied by a gigantic silver object (spacecraft) that had openings in its sides. Over 800 other persons of Parn (from other clans) had arrived at the site before us and were milling around and talking. There was much excitement in their voices.

Standing in groups and talking to each other around the spacecraft were hundreds of Gracians, along with a countless number of their small black companions. It was the first time I saw Gracian women. They were beautiful. Some had children, who clung to their fine skirts.

Standing at the top of the steps that led to one of the openings in the vehicle stood two giant-sized men (about eight feet tall). They were dressed in white shirts, trousers and thigh-length boots. Their skin was nearly the color of their clothes, but their hair was golden blonde. I learned later that these men were Maldecians, who operated the craft. I also learned later that although we of Parn worked for the Gracians, the Gracians worked for the Maldecians.

When we entered the craft we were taken to a large area located on the lowest deck in the circular vehicle. We entered a white room with metal benches, twelve at a time. When the door was closed, the place began to glow lime green and we felt weak for a few minutes. During our brief stay in the small room we converted from breathing the air of Parn to that of Earth. Another door opened and we were greeted by a black man who introduced himself as Barco. We learned later that he and the others of his kind came from the second planet of the sun/star system they called Lalm. They called their home world Morza.

Barco spoke our language well and told us that he and several others would be among us to answer our questions and help us deal with our new environment. We waited in a hallway until we were joined by several more groups that had gone through the nitrogen-to-oxygen conversion process.

We were then led to another very large rectangular room. The place was arranged with three-tiered bunk beds. We were shown by Barco that by pushing a button on the wall next to a set of bunks, the set would fold flat against the wall. Push the button again, and the upper bunk would fold down to become a bench, the center bunk would flip over to become a table and the bottom bunk, remaining stationary, would also serve as a bench. Push the button once more, and the table and benches would stack on top of each other and become bunks again. Barco and his friends laughed until they cried at the sight of more than 45 sets of these bunks going through their various stages of transformation again and again. Finally they put a stop to the button-pushing game. When their backs were turned, one of my people (who couldn't resist the urge) pushed a bunk button and ran and hid in the crowd. When this happened, we of Parn had a good laugh.

Next we were introduced to the separate (men's and women's) toilet and shower facilities. We of Parn were confused by these separate arrangements and by what we perceived to be baffling and totally unnecessary mechanisms. Those of us who forgot or didn't understand how to use the toilet mechanisms ignored them. (After all, when you've got to go, you've got to go.) No one took a shower; we preferred to wait until it rained. The lavatories were in an unbelievable state by the time we reached Earth. (We of Parn were very ignorant in those times.)

In the center of our barracks room were a number of tubes about five feet in diameter that ran from floor to ceiling. Mounted at 45-degree intervals on each tube's circumference were water fountains. Periodically doors would slide open in these tubes, which revealed slowly rotating trays of fruit and cooked nubs.

Barco introduced several of us to smoking the rolled Gracian leaves (you call it tobacco). Those of us who took up the habit were required to sit in a circle in a particular part of the barracks and have their cigars lit by Barco or one of his assistants. They didn't trust the new smokers with the instant firemakers. Though I didn't take up smoking, I spent quite some time with the group to watch them light up. I was fascinated by the making of instant fire, as were others, and hoped to learn how this miracle was accomplished.

I am sure that by this time you are aware that we of Parn in those days were very primitive and ignorant of the purposes and functions of man-made devices. Because we didn't understand them, we were awed by them. Although our first encounters with these things would be humorous to relate at this time, I prefer to speak of the marvelous transition my people went through during the earliest of times to the present. (Many of us from the Relt planetoids have since surpassed our educators in the knowledge of the most complex technology that exists.)

After boarding the Maldecian spacecraft, we waited many hours while others of my race went through the nitrogen-to-oxygen conversion process and environmental orientation. Speaking through an amplified sound device, Barco told us to face one of the barrack walls. The majority of the wall became transparent and we were able to look out at what we later learned was our very last view of our home world of Parn. The area around the craft was cleared of all my people, but not of Gracians. Groups of them were seen slowly walking away from the vehicle. They later went to Earth by way of another spacecraft.

Leaving Parn

Our transport first rose very slowly (about ten miles an hour) for about twenty minutes, giving us a visual experience of Parn that I will never forget. Some of us were crying, but none of us could explain why. After climbing above the cloud cover, there was a soft flash of red light, then a soft flash of blue light, each flash lasting about thirty seconds. Then there was a brilliant flash of green light that lasted only about a second. Suddenly we were in space and looking at the stars. At one point in our observations we saw the Relt radiar blazing brightly. It looked about twice the size of a full harvest moon as seen from Earth. Shortly after, the walls of our barracks began to glow and provide us with light.

After several hours we became used to the outward view, and when Barco's people gathered to sing, some of us accompanied the singers with stringed instruments and flutes. We found comfort in their music, and many of us fell asleep on the floor.

We of Parn normally slept about five hours in every twenty, but during our first sleep period aboard the spacecraft most of us slept nine hours or more. Some had to be awakened by Barco and his assistants. We did not eat food from the dispensing tubes immediately upon rising because they were opened only after each of us had swallowed a considerable number of tablets given us by our tenders. They looked into our mouths to make sure we had swallowed all of them. The capsules contained ingredients that would (and did) protect us from several diseases that we might contract on Earth.

A Maldec Layover

We had two more sleep periods before the spacecraft assumed an orbit around the planet Maldec. The vehicle remained in orbit for about six hours and then landed on the planet's surface. When the walls of our barracks once again became transparent, we saw one of the most beautiful worlds in all creation. To our left was a building constructed of caramel-colored blocks of stone that glittered like gold in the light of the sun. The building was multistoried and had a number of towers of different heights. Parts of the structure penetrated a hill covered with green grass and with trees that had red and purple leaves. Straight ahead and to our left as far as we could see was an endless lawn of grass. Not far in the distance were mountains, some of which had snow-covered peaks, and the sky was a brilliant blue.

I watched as several Maldecians from our craft walked toward the building and were met by several others of their race. Among those who greeted them were several beautiful Maldecian women. Among the welcoming party were also a number of tall, thin men and women who did not look in any way like the Maldecians. They were finely dressed, but were in fact servants, who were called Simms. The Simms were the only race of people the Maldecians would tolerate in their presence to physically serve them. Maldecians looked on all other races of people as inferior. This went for the Gracians as well, although the Maldecians showed false respect and affection for them when they were in their presence. This charade lasted only as long as it took the Maldecian to get what he wanted from the sincerely loving, highly spiritual and knowledgeable Gracians.

We were not allowed to leave the spacecraft even though Maldec had air similar to that of Earth. A Maldecian day and night cycle was about twenty-nine Earth hours long. In its night sky could be seen a small moon they called Malura.

After two days and nights parked on Maldec, the spacecraft once again lifted off into space and began its chase of Earth. The orbits of the planets and radiars were never very distant from each other (even for the earliest types of spacecraft). The distance between planetary orbits is one thing, but it is essential to know the exact location in their orbits of both the planet of departure and the planet of destination. Sometimes it is practical to travel to a spot in the orbit of the planet of destination and either wait for it to come to you or travel toward it as it approaches you. Had the Maldecians traveled the distance from their planet to the closest relative point in the Earth's orbital path, they would have had to wait more than nine months for the Earth to come from behind the sun and meet their craft. The Maldecians were not (and are not) people to be kept waiting, so they cut across the orbits of Mars and Venus to get into Earth's orbital path. They followed the planet for more than a month at a speed greater than Earth's speed.

Landing on Earth at Miradol

Eventually they caught up with Earth and landed at a Gracian colony called Miradol. (You know this place as the ancient Mexican city of Teotihuacan.) The Gracians were busy building the city and were nearly finished building several stone-block structures, one of which still stands and is presently referred to as the Temple of Quetzalcoatl (the feathered serpent).

I was told that such a creature did exist on the Gracians' home planet, and that it grew to be over thirty feet long and was covered with beautiful, iridescent scales and feathers. The Gracians didn't worship this animal, but employed its image as one of Earth would use a particular animal as a symbol or logo.

Barco was our supervisor and immediate superior. Everywhere he went, we went. When he stopped someplace, we also stopped, and we did not move until he told us to follow him. The group from my village on Parn set up camp about half a mile from the center of the Gracian construction site. We were told that we were not at Miradol to work, but to learn how to work. Barco selected twenty people (both male and female) to act as a cadre of overseers. Both my wife Croma and myself were chosen for such positions.

We learned that Barco's race had been associating with the Gracians for more than 500 years. They originally provided the labor for many Gracian building projects that had been carried out previously on worlds in other solar systems, most recently on the planet you call Mars. Barco's people had risen in rank due to their acquired understanding of the Gracian way of doing things. The Gracians were very highly paid building contractors who had a great deal of knowledge in the area of sacred geometry and how it related to the laws of nature. They were paid in gold and other elements they desired.

The Gracians had actually had the ability to travel in space hundreds of years prior to the Nodians. It was from the Gracians that the Maldecians obtained space-traveling technology. Even after the Nodians were able to travel in space, they never crossed paths with the Gracian race until they came in contact with each other on Earth.

I really don't want to give the impression that the Gracians were materialistic. In fact, I think of them today as one of the most spiritual races that ever existed in the universe. Their love for and study of sacred geometry has produced many wondrous things that have benefited the lives of the whole of universal humanity. They treated everyone as equals, even us once-ignorant louts from Parn.

Barco told us that there were several hundred Gracian construction crews, such as the one on Earth at the time, building things on worlds in other solar systems. The Gracian crew on the Earth referred to themselves as Itocot-Talan's people. Itocot-Talan was their very old chief and knew everything there was to know about sacred geometry and about building things according to its order. Some say he had the attention of the elohim, and possibly even that of the creator of all that is.

Native Earth People and Other Races

The native people of the Earth were for the most part gentle folk, though some tried to put on superior airs that mimicked the ways of their Maldecian rulers. There were a great number of Earth people living near

Miradol and also coming and going from the place where food and other items were delivered by carts drawn by horses, camels and elephants.

The native Earth people had customs and religions that were very strange to us of Parn. Their women covered their faces with veils and never ate in the presence of a man. They carried numerous charms and amulets that they believed had magical powers. Some of them carried so many of these things that they could hardly move about with their weight.

Various cults of Earth people actually worshiped the Maldecians as gods. If an Earth person got a Maldecian to bless one of his magical charms, he would become overjoyed. All types of Earth people referred to the Maldecians as the Radiant Ones. There was also a large body of Earth people who worshiped the Lord God El of their world. This group was headed by elder priests who practiced the oldest religion on the planet. But their demands for pious respect for the El was being rejected by the youth of the planet, who favored the worship of the Maldecians, which included the ritual use of drugs, alcohol and unbridled sex.

In truth, I tried alcohol in the form of wine, beer and that which is produced from various grains. I did this occasionally when I first arrived on the Earth. Eventually Barco kept our ration of the stuff very low, for good reason. When my life was coming to an end many years later, I drank myself into oblivion as often as I could.

Within a year's time thousands of others from the Relt planetoids began to arrive at Miradol. There were those of Franet (Ganymede) and Sovia (Mercury) as well as every other inhabited world that orbited the Relt. I could not tell the difference between a person from Parn and a person who came from any other planetoid of the Relt—that is, until we tried to talk to each other. It was frustrating, because we all spoke different languages. This chaotic condition continued until we all agreed to the meanings of certain hand signs that later were accompanied by simple words of the Gracian language.

Among the new arrivals was another black race from a radiar system located in a far-distant solar system. The central star of the system is called by you Sirius A. The circling radiar is presently called Sirius B. The descendants of these people live on the continent of Africa and are called the Dogon. Hundreds of years ago the Dogon were contacted by some off-world race (sorry, I don't know which one), which informed them of their most ancient DNA ancestry. Present-day Dogons included the configuration of this star/radiar system in their art and spiritual rituals.

Learning to Build Pyramids

My people were trained in quarrying stone, mixing mortar and measuring and moving stone by hand while it hovered suspended in the air by invisible waves of energy. Cutting and polishing stone blocks was carried out only by Gracians, who referred to architectural plans displayed on light-weight, breadbox-sized computers that hung from their necks.

During our period of construction training we interacted with Barco's people. From them we learned of the existence of the elohim and the supreme creator of all that is. From them we also learned not to come into contact with any Maldecian if we could avoid it. We were advised to leave the Maldecians to the Gracians to handle.

By the time we left the city of Miradol, its construction was well under way. The pyramid that expressed the key number of nature within its form was nearly finished and the base of a larger pyramid had been laid. This massive structure was intended to embody, and was described by, the language of sacred mathematics. A greater number of universal laws were in its form than were in the smaller pyramid. (The key number of nature of which I spoke earlier is, of course, the number you know as phi, or 1.618033989.) The smaller pyramid at Miradol (Teotihuacan) is now called the Pyramid of the Moon. The largest of the three pyramids, presently called the Pyramid of the Sun, was not completed by the Gracians. Its present state (after several reconstructions) can be attributed to a succession of civilizations that occupied the place throughout eons of time, including the Mexicans of 85 years ago. The Gracians are responsible only for its base dimensions and part of its first tier.

As you [the author] know, the base of the Pyramid of the Sun and the base of the Great Pyramid of Giza both have the same length of 763.407 red ra feet (243 x red pi, 3.333 x 1 red ram, 150 x 1 red ankh unit and 720 red hunab units). The number 763.407 is also equal to 229.0221 red rams (rams = ra meters). One red ram is equal to 1.0053745898 standard meters. The number 229.0221 is equal to 72.9 (27 x 2.7) red pi units. The number 729 (27 x 17) is the reciprocal of the fine-structure constant for the element hydrogen. The number 229.0221 also contains 45 red ankh units or 216 x 1.0602875 (1 red hunab unit).

The Land of Mir (Egypt)

The Gracians and Maldecians used low-flying aircars to move themselves about. A little more than six months after arriving on the Earth, we of Parn took a short flight to the land you call Egypt, which was then called the Land of Mir, in a fleet of aircars, each of which held about twenty passengers.

The Land of Mir was covered with rain forest and reminded me of Parn. The Giza Plateau on which you will find the Great Pyramids was higher by about four feet in some places than at present. The surface of the plateau was irregular. Our first task was to clear and level the plateau and remove the rubble. Before beginning this work, the Gracians spent several days taking magnetic compass readings, which they compared to the magnetic alignment of the molecules that composed the bedrock. From dusk to dawn they studied the positions of the stars, planets and radiars. Based on their astronomical observations, they determined what parts of the plateau they could cut, what parts they would have to include in the structures they were about to build and what part of the area they had to build up (though there was little need for that).

At dawn each day the Gracians would face the rising sun and pray with upraised hands. This would end when one of their stolfas (priests) sang a prayer to the sun. Instead of words, the hymn of the Gracian stolfa contained numbers and equations. After a time many of the different types of people from the Relt system, those from the Sirius system, and I joined the Gracians during their morning prayers.

Preparing the Site

Metal rods were driven into the bedrock to various, but precise, depths. Each rod was later capped with a faceted crystal shaped like a mushroom. When the rods were set, everyone left the plateau. We were given the day off, so I went fishing with my wife and daughter in the river now called the Nile. Thousands of my fellow workers also tried their luck, but with all that noise and commotion, there wasn't a fish to be had by anyone. From our position on the riverbank we watched as two Gracian aircars hovered over the plateau. For more than an hour we heard humming sounds and pops. After each pop a cloud of dust rose in the air. Giraffes ran about us in all directions and the angry bellows of elephants filled the air. Waterfowl and other river animals sought out places to hide.

On the following morning after prayers, we walked to the top of the plateau, only to find it covered with a fine limestone powder that was in some areas several feet thick. There were no signs of any of the thousands of crystal-capped rods that had previously been inserted in the bedrock. We wore face masks to keep from breathing the dust while we moved the dust into piles with large suction devices. (This limestone dust was later used along with other ingredients in the formulation of mortar that bonded the limestone blocks used for the core of the three pyramids.) The areas where the pyramids would be built were the first to be cleared of dust. After two days the leveled bedrock looked as if it had been polished. The Gracians were highly pleased.

Before leaving the plateau for a swim in the river to wash the dust from our bodies, we were informed that we had exactly 875 days (just under two years and five months) to complete the construction of the three pyramids.

Areas near the plateau were designated as quarries, not because their closeness to the pyramids was convenient for transporting the stone blocks, but because the Gracians wanted to use stone with the same magnetic orientation as the bedrock at the building site. Using all the highly technical and efficient building methods of the Gracians, the pyramids of Mir could have been built in about half the time allotted, but because only natural rock and specially formulated mortar was to be used, poured concrete was out of the question. By order of the Maldecians the buildings were to be constructed only with natural materials. At first the Gracians had no problem complying with this Maldecian order.

On the day after the dust was cleared, a Maldecian spacecraft arrived at the site. The head Gracian construction engineer, who was named Tarvmole, was summoned to the vehicle. He remained on the craft for more than two days. When he returned to the plateau he looked angry and very tired. He called his assistants together for a meeting, which took about twenty minutes. This meeting created even more angry Gracians. (I learned later that the Maldecians wanted some of their own engineers to participate in the redesign of some of the chambers in the pyramids and in the formulation of the mortar. In fact, the Maldecians insisted that no one but Simms mix the building mortar.)

Pyramid-Building

I was assigned to the construction of what is now referred to as the third pyramid of Giza. (The construction of this pyramid is erroneously attributed to the Fourth Dynasty pharaoh Menkaure—Mykerinos to the Greeks.) I worked on this structure until its completion. Because this pyramid was smaller than the other two, it was finished first. I then went to work on what is presently called the Great Pyramid. The second pyramid (in size) was finished next, freeing up additional workers to work on the Great Pyramid. In fact, there were now too many workers to keep busy full time, because they could hinder progress by getting in each other's way in the close confines of the various chambers. (Each of the three pyramids of Giza has numerous chambers. I understand that most of them have not yet been physically located and entered by anyone of the Earth of this time.)

High-frequency sound waves were used to first cut out and then cut and polish both the core and the casing stones. This was done in the following manner: A raw, unworked stone was obtained from a layer of limestone. A Gracian, using a sound transmitter, would send a sound wave of a certain frequency through the stone block. Feedback from the stone to the sound generator identified the exact frequency required to split the stone on the desired plane. Each stone had three specific fracture frequencies that had to be determined. Once they had been determined, these frequencies were used to cut the stone into the desired size and shape: one frequency established the block's length, another its width and the third its height.

The blocks were cut at the quarries so that the plateau would not become littered with mountains of rubble. Eventually the quarries close to the plateau were exhausted, so the quarried, cut and dressed limestone blocks had to be brought from more distant locations.

Levitating the Stone Blocks

The stone blocks were rendered weightless by canceling out the planet's gravitational pull on their mass. By using a key sound frequency, the gravitational equilibrium of the central molecule in the block's total mass was nullified. The central molecule in a mass is the only one that is surrounded by an equal amount of mass in every direction. Its role is passed to a number of other molecules close by when they move about due to the kinetic energy of the mass. When an established central molecule moves from its central position, the molecule that moves into its former space becomes the new central molecule. The key sound frequency does two things: (1) It suspends all movement of the molecules in the total mass, permitting one specific molecule to be established as the central molecule. (2) Its positive nodes cause the central molecule to stretch like a rubber band, whereas its negative nodes cause the molecule to contract.

This contraction and expansion of the central molecule denies the other molecules in the mass a central point of reference or orientation. Thus they begin to expand, contract and spin at a very precise rate. Molecules also spin at a specific angle on their axis relative to the pulsing central molecule. Due to the spin and consistent axis angle of the molecules that compose a block's total mass, the gravitational lines of force generated by its mass become out of phase with those generated by the mass of the planet, so the block becomes weightless. A small child could throw the block about like a beach ball. The key frequency that causes weightlessness is the reciprocal frequency of that frequency used to determine the fracture frequencies.

There were (and still are) two known ways to affect the central molecule of a mass, rendering an object weightless: (1) using a precise frequency of sound and (2) tapping the block three times with a vril rod charged with vril energy (the highest form of energy in the universe) while chanting certain words and numbers in the direction of the block. The Gracian stolfas accomplished this form of levitation with ease.

Levitation by sound was also used at the quarries to load large numbers of finished blocks on river barges. Each block was designated for a specific place in one of the three pyramids. Although aircars could lift only one or two cut stones (depending on their size and weight), they could pull hundreds of blocks at a time up or down the river on barges. At the receiving station located on the riverbank below the plateau, the specially designed barges were moved directly onto monorail transporters, which moved them to the base of the pyramids. These transporters were propelled electromagnetically (similar to Japan's present bullet trains). Those who built the pyramids rode these same transporters to and from the plateau. The transporters were remotely controlled (no onboard operator) and could reach speeds of several hundred miles an hour, but usually traveled about thirty miles an hour between the receiving station on the river and the base of the pyramids.

The Gracians were telepathic and used this method to notify the quarries what size and type of blocks they wanted cut; dressed and shipped to the building site of either of the three pyramids. If the block(s) that were ordered did not arrive at the building site within two hours, it was assumed that something in the system must have gone terribly wrong.

After reaching the base of the pyramid, the blocks were levitated by a stolfa onto an elevator platform suspended magnetically between two vertical rods that towered more than 800 feet into the sky. These elevators worked on the same magnetic principle as the ground transporters. The elevator suspension rods (guides) were only about an inch in diameter, but crashing an aircar into them at 2000 miles an hour wouldn't have moved them a millimeter.

These rods were able to tip to any angle and lock into the slots of a platform located on a currently incomplete level of the pyramid. The elevator platform, carrying a stone block, would automatically move over the receiving platform and come to rest on it. A stolfa would then levitate the block and workers such as myself would push the block to its designated spot in the pyramid. Block-pushers had to know exactly where the block was to go, because the stolfa had to keep his/her mind on the levitation process and could not be distracted. Any such distraction might result in the block falling and perhaps breaking, or falling on a worker and killing him. (I know of only three accidental deaths during the construction of the Great Pyramids of Mir.)

The main reason the stone blocks had to be levitated by a stolfa and not by generated sound was that after a block was mortared into its proper place, it became part of the total mass of all the blocks to which it was bound. The total mass increased daily in proportion to the number of blocks added to the pyramid. The total mass would in some cases absorb the sound energy or else reflect it, and no block could have remained weightless under such conditions.

After a block was set in place, a device similar to a tuning fork was struck against it. The vibrations of the fork were read by an electronic device and recorded. Any slight distortion in the desired vibration could be corrected by adjusting the mass of one or more blocks that would later be mortared to the block that was off. Finally, any accumulated vibrational distortions would be finally corrected when the crystal capstone was cut and set in place at the top of the Great Pyramid.

Only the Great Pyramid had a crystal capstone. The Gracians called the capstone the pyramid's "spiel." I learned that the second and third pyramids were built for two main purposes: (1) as aiming devices and (2) to absorb and disperse some type of expected feedback energy that would be transmitted by the Great Pyramid when performing some type of dynamic function understood at the time only by the Maldecians. It was speculated that the third pyramid (smallest of the three) might even vibrate into dust when the Great Pyramid was dynamically functioning.

Why Maldec Exploded Instead of the Third Pyramid

Therein lies the answer to why Maldec exploded. The third pyramid of Mir was to act like a fuse in an electrical circuit and disintegrate before anything disastrous happened to the Great Pyramid when it was employed to transmit Earth's vril energy reserve to Maldec. Consequently, Maldec exploded, not the third pyramid. This happened, of course, because the Gracians and we of the Relt don't build junk!

As recently realized on Earth, the three pyramids of Mir were designed, sized and positioned on the plateau to represent the three central stars in the constellation of Orion. The pyramids were built to be directly aligned with these stars at the summer solstice, when they were north of the Earth's equator. It had been calculated that at the time of the solstice Maldec would conjunct the largest of these three stars (the one represented by the Great Pyramid). However, when Maldec subsequently conjuncted that star, the planet disappeared because its reflected sunlight merged with the brighter radiated light from the star. (When Maldec exploded, it first appeared as if the star itself had exploded.)

After the second and third pyramids of Mir were completed, some minor work on the Great Pyramid still remained. Many of us of the Relt system were not needed and spent time fishing and talking—about what we would eventually be paid for our work and about going home.

Life in Mir

Construction on the pyramids went on around the clock, because the plateau was fully illuminated at night by floodlights and the interiors of the buildings were lit by portable electric lanterns.

During our stay in Mir we lived in two-room apartments made of mud bricks. Each apartment had a door that led to a walkway about sixteen feet wide. We were told that the apartments were built of this material because they were to be leveled when the pyramids were finished and we workers sent home. We were asked by the Gracians if any of us would like to stay on the Earth a while longer and help them finish the construction of Miradol (Teotihuacan). We were given time to think over their offer. Most of us of Parn wanted to go home because we were eager to use our newly acquired knowledge to build roads and beautiful buildings there. (While on the Earth we changed in many ways. One of the major changes was that we became very ambitious and wanted more out of life.)

We ate in a common mess hall. The cooks were of many off-world races but were under the direction of a chef native to Earth. We ate mostly fresh fruits, vegetables, rice, beans, garlic, spaghetti and fish. One thing we of Parn were introduced to for the first time was bread. We loved the stuff and couldn't get enough of it. We had wild grain on Parn, but had never done anything with it; we thought it had value only as bird and nub food. We couldn't wait to get home and show those who had remained behind how to make bread.

We sometimes went to the commissary, which was operated by Barco and his people. There we could trade in old, wornout clothes and shoes for new ones. At the commissary a worker could also purchase things such as popcorn, buns, cigars and sugar sticks (candy). Many types of food came vacuum-sealed with a picture on the wrapper of what was inside. Depending on the day of the week, a worker could obtain several quarts of beer. Purchases were made by exchanging blue strips, which were about the same size and shape of a piece of chewing gum [my reference—W.H.B.]. A worker would receive five of these "dids" at the end of a twelve-hour work shift.

Lavatories in the workers' village and on the plateau were large oblong units on wheels. Mechanisms in the units automatically processed the human waste, forming it into bricks. Then it stacked the bricks into a container that was taken several miles west by aircar and disposed of in a very large pit.

There were two types of shower facilities. One type employed sonic wands that attracted all foreign particles on the skin. When a person was finished using a wand, it was placed in a sheathlike holder where it was sonically cleaned. Teeth were cleaned by a smaller wand that operated in the same way. Near the river were showers that used river water mixed with a disinfectant and an insect repellent. (Earth bugs really loved those of us from the Relt radiar system.) Some of us off-worlders enjoyed bathing in the river. It was at first a bit dangerous for the bathers, until sonic force fields were generated by the Gracians to keep away the crocodiles (which were about two times larger than the present Nile croc), hippopotami and other creatures that have no current representatives in your animal kingdom.

The Gracians

Accidental injuries did occur, mainly due to falls. All forms of injuries and sickness were tended to by Gracian doctors, who employed marvelous medical methods. (Three out of five Gracian doctors were women.) They could heal bone fractures with sound within a day's time (a circadian cycle was required). Gaping wounds were sonically closed and healed without scarring in about three days.

From my descriptions I am sure you have come to realize that the Gracians had great knowledge of the electromagnetic spectrum and used their knowledge quite well. Gracians had exceptional visual and hearing abilities. They could see wavelengths in the deep infrared and ultraviolet that are invisible to most other races. They had the ability to control at will the opening and closing of the irises of their eyes (in most races this occurs automatically or involuntarily relative to the intensity of the light). By willpower the Gracians could also focus their eyes and use them like magnifying telescopes or microscopes.

They had eyelids like all types of humans do, but they had three additional sets of clear membranes under the outer lids. They could at will cover their eyes with any one or combination of the three membranes. Natural fluids flowed into the spaces between the membranes to produce what you might call instant contact lenses. These fluids produce the necessary optics for using their eyes telescopically or microscopically. When the membranes in their eyes contracted, the fluids ran down their faces like tears, but immediately evaporated, leaving no stains.

The Casing Stones

The casing stones of the Great Pyramid had to be precisely cut and dressed in such a way that their "tones" were individually and collectively perfect. The Gracian casing-stone cutters and toners were certainly a unique group. Even with all their care, after every casing stone was in position a finer tuning of the pyramid was still required.

Casing stones were not moved into their positions by the electromagnetic elevators described earlier. They already had a thin layer of mortar on their edges when the stolfas moved them upward level by level, using vril rods and chants. The massive, highly polished stones were set into place from the top down. Stolfas, toners and setters, wearing shoes made of soft, thick padding, set the blocks into place. To do the job we hung by soft, nonabrasive ropes. There were hundreds of teams working on the four faces of the pyramid to set these casing stones. Because most of the stone setters were blacked-skinned and the color of these stones was a brilliant white, from a distance an observer could have easily compared the scene to that of a giant sugar cube covered by hundreds of flies.

Periodically during the day and night the Gracians would electronically generate a frequency most people could not hear. The incomplete pyramid would respond to the generated electromagnetic wave by issuing an audible, loud (but very pleasant) sound. The frequency they wanted the pyramid to ultimately issue was 314.1592592... cycles per natural second of time (pi x 10 to the second power). *[The number 3.141592592... is known as red pi in the natural Ra system of mathematics and is considered the most sacred number of the creator of all that is. —W.H.B.]*

The Capstone Ceremony

When the day came to crown the pyramid with its beautiful crystal capstone, the plateau was flooded with dignitaries. There were noblemen and -women from Maldec, Earth and worlds of which I knew nothing either then or now. Among those present that day was Nodian Opatel Cre'ator and several others of his race. Opatel was attended by his giant servant, known as Corboslate. This group of Nodians kept very much to themselves.

There was much excitement when a golden spacecraft appeared over the pyramid. The capstone appeared from its underside, and after floating perfectly to its intended resting place, there was great applause and shouts of "Well done!" After the capstone was set, the Nodians left the plateau, taking flight in a spacecraft that appeared to be covered with shiny black enamel.

The capstone was beautiful beyond my ability to describe. It was actually made of a crystalline material called *astrastone*, which is the hardest material that exists in the universe (much harder than diamond). The original capstone of the Great Pyramid was removed by the Federation after Maldec's destruction. The Great Pyramid has had several other capstones over the years, each of which has been removed by the Federation. (I understand they have quite a collection.)

Normally, the Gracians themselves would have cut the pyramid's capstone in a way that canceled any discrepancy in the structure's overall molecular resonance frequency. But because the Maldecians had a time deadline and wanted to cut and shape the crystal capstone themselves on Maldec, a different way of tuning the pyramid had to be used. Thus when the pyramid with its capstone was toned, it issued a resonant frequency that was not quite perfect. This was corrected by carefully cutting out pieces of bedrock from the area in the pyramid now referred to as the subterranean chamber or Pit. (As a result of that cutting activity, the chamber gives an appearance of being incomplete, abandoned by the pyramid builders. I assure you that this chamber and the pit in its floor were built to be used as the last resort for tuning the total structure.) While the final tuning of the pyramid was being done, a nine-foot wall was built around it. This wall was covered with white plaster and painted with murals and strange Maldecian symbols.

The construction and fine-tuning of the three pyramids of Mir was accomplished in 842.6 days, 32.4 days ahead of the deadline. The extra days were used to dismantle and pack every type of construction equipment. About 90 percent of all the pyramid workers left Mir for Miradol, where some were returned to their home planets and planetoids by the Gracians.

My wife, daughter and myself were among those who remained behind to landscape the plateau with grass and trees. When we were finished the place was breathtaking. After the Gracians leveled the mud-brick apartments with sound waves, the area looked serene, as if no human had ever been involved in its creation. Thereafter more of the workers left Mir for Miradol. Only 22 of us workers, Barco's people (about 130) and 12 Gracians were left in Mir on the day the Maldecians took official possession of the pyramids. Four days remained until the summer solstice. Barco's people left the area at this time, along with ten of the remaining Gracians. Only the Gracian chief building engineer Tarvmole and his assistant Boinkalix remained. They were bent on finding out exactly what the Maldecians were going to do with their handiwork.

Prior to the completion of the pyramids of Mir there were two places on the plateau where a common worker was never allowed to go: the mortar-mixing area and the immediate vicinity of the Sphinx. At the mixing area the Simms, servants of the Maldecians, added ingredients to the mortar that were not part of the Gracians' original formula. (Some speculate even today as to what these additives were. Some believe human and animal blood and other biological materials were added to the mortar mix. I can personally tell you that sometimes it smelled like rotten eggs for about an hour.) The

Simms who worked with mixing the mortar looked pale and sickly, but refused to be treated by the Gracian doctors.

The Sphinx

Another group of Maldecian associates from a star system in the constellation of Lyra were employed to carve the Sphinx. This they did under a large tent that concealed their activities. They also were employed to build a number of secret chambers under the statue.

Anyone who dared to come too near the mortar-mixing area or the Sphinx encountered a considerable number of the elite Maldecian soldiers called krates. Usually they would threaten a person with electrical devices (like what you call cattle prods or stun guns). I seriously tell you this: a krate could be quite deadly. If one looked into their deep blue eyes, one would find no trace of emotion.

The Sphinx was unveiled two days before the solstice. Its original form was that of the body of a lion and the head of a woman. This head was recarved by a civilization that occupied Mir (Egypt) at some later time. I never did learn if its features were that of a woman who lived then or before. (Maybe she was in some way instrumental in the formulation of the Maldecian plan for the use of the pyramids?) In any case, the Sphinx was intended to symbolize and glorify the science of genetic engineering. Its headdress bore the image of the cobra, which is the insignia of the krates and also a sign of Maldecian royalty.

The Final Day

Prior to the day of the summer solstice, the Maldecians took up residence in a number of white tents that had been erected on the lawns bordering the Great Pyramid. They were eventually joined by a group of their elders, who arrived in a large silver spacecraft, bringing a new supply of healthier Simms. (The sickly Simms who had mixed the mortar mysteriously disappeared.)

Accompanying the elders of Maldec was the Maldecian youth known as Marduk. He was considered a god by his people, but why they did is totally beyond my comprehension even now. I do know that when Maldec exploded, Marduk's body and spirit were imprisoned in the pyramid for a long time, due to some universal law. After some time his psychic essence was able to be freed.

During the Maldecians' attempt to steal and transmit the reserve vril energy of Earth to their home world by way of the Great Pyramid, a pillar of brilliant red fire (energy) shot from the building's capstone into the heavens for miles. The Earth shook violently. About three minutes after these events began, there was a brilliant white flash of light that came from the direction of the constellation of Orion. The flash of white light was produced when the planet Maldec exploded, killing all things upon it. My family and myself watched these things happen from the bank of the river.

The Aftermath on Earth

After Maldec exploded, some of the Maldecians who had been at the site of the pyramids of Mir took their own lives. The elders of Maldec flew off to the west in their spacecraft. The next day the krates, by order of their commander Rolander, went on a killing spree. Their victims were anyone who had had anything to do with the construction of the pyramids. They blamed the disaster on the Gracians, not on their own arrogant stupidity.

We learned later that everyone who lived in the city of Miradol (Teotihuacan)—both Gracians and off-worlders—were murdered by the krates. Miradol's human population at the time numbered more than 100,000. This massacre left the city's construction incomplete. The chief Gracian construction engineer Tarvmole and his assistant Boinkalix were never seen after that day. A person close to both men who was at the base of the Pyramid of the Sun during the disastrous event related that Tarvmole threw his hands in the air and cried out to the Creator of the universe a series of numbers. As if the Creator had answered him, he then said in a normal voice, "What fools! What fools!"

We who survived did so only because we took refuge (as my family and I did) in a chamber under the Sphinx. (For some reason the krates wanted nothing to do with the Sphinx, fearing they might be psychically trapped in it in the same way that Marduk's psychic essence had become trapped in the Great Pyramid.) The chamber in which we hid was filled with thousands of small stone boxes and colored spheres that appeared to be glass.

We remained under the Sphinx for about three days before one of us ventured to look outside. The krates were gone, but the area was crowded with Earth people, who were stripping the dead of their valuables. One of the Earthmen (a merchant) told us that if we helped him quickly recover valuables from the dead before anyone else got them, he would transport us by aircar to Miradol. We took him up on his offer.

When it was time to leave Mir we discovered that his loot-filled aircar could carry only about 20 percent of the people who had helped him rob the dead. My family and myself were among those he took from the bloody Land of Mir. We sadly waved goodbye to those of Parn we left behind.

Arriving at Miradol, we found the same type of unholy activity going on. Not knowing at first what to do, we accepted permanent employment with the merchant, Beverjoanon, on the condition that he would return to Mir for our stranded people. He agreed to do this, though he never did.

Stripping the dead took months. The stench of more than 100,000 unburied bodies was awful. Beverjoanon never came into the city from his base of operations five miles away. He gave us food and alcohol for what we brought him, and we drank the alcohol to forget what we were doing. My wife and I left our daughter in the care of several of Beverjoanon's women so that she would not have follow us as we robbed the dead. Because there were other robber bands in the city, we often had to defend ourselves and our booty from the more violent ones.

One day while searching a building I found four bodies, which I recognized as krates. They had already been stripped of their golden helmets and armor, but I could not resist kicking their remains until my feet hurt. Gradually there was nothing left worth scavenging, and thus nothing left to trade with Beverjoanon. One night we found his base camp empty. He had gone, taking our daughter with him.

Our travels thereafter took us to many places on Earth, and most of the rest of our lives were spent avoiding slavers. We lived poorly off the land, dreaming that we would someday find our daughter and return to Parn to live happily. This, of course, could never happen. My wife and I traveled south from Miradol for over a year, during which time she became deathly ill from a disease contracted from the dead at Miradol. Normally we would have avoided contact with anyone, but because of her condition I dared to approach a group of very tall people, who at first appeared dangerous. I was proven wrong. They were Martians, who were also going south, where more of their kind lived. They couldn't help my wife, and she died. Although it was the Martian custom to cremate their dead, they helped me bury her, as was customary on Parn: Just before the burial a Martian woman gave me a hat of fronds to place on my wife's head. (I have never learned how the Martian woman knew of our custom.)

I traveled with the Martians for over a year. During our nightly conversations I learned much about them and how they came to be on Earth. I told them everything I could about my life, about the Gracians and about my experiences building the Great Pyramids of Mir. The Martians told me not to give up hope, because it was possible that the Nodians might take me back to my home world. (I know now that no one with the ability to travel in space at that time would have dared approach the Relt radiar or any of its planetoids. Ill effects generated by the dying radiar made it impossible for any type of field-driven spacecraft to operate anywhere in the radiar's vicinity. Besides, everyone was already dead on the Relt planetoids.)

One day during travels with my Martian friends, I stepped on a thorn that went through the sole of my worn-out sandal and penetrated deep into my left foot, which became infected. I could no longer walk, so the Martians took turns carrying me. One night in a weakened state I looked into the star-filled sky, hoping to see the light of the Great Relt, but the Martians could not help me pick it out among the thousands of stars. I fell asleep and died. I know the Martians buried me wearing a hat made of fronds.

At this time I live and work on the Federation mothership called the Pactra. As we speak, it orbits the Ampt radiar of the sun/star system of Sost, the home solar system of the Nodians. In this life I live with my wife Croma and daughter Rallee of my first life. The dream of happiness that we imagined those many years ago on the ancient Earth has been mostly fulfilled. I now exist only to be of service to the elohim and the creator of all that is.

I lived many lives on the planet Earth, many of which might interest you. Call on me anytime you wish me to relate my remembrances of those lives. I am Ruke of Parn.

I too would be honored if you call upon me again to assist you by relating the thoughts and memories of one such as Ruke of Parn. I have found pleasure in being of service. I am Nedart of Sumer. *Costrina blac sace mor mar rit trover*.

S I X

Jaffer Ben-Rob
of Earth (Sarus)

Before those of my world stabbed you with
forks of deception, the elohim strummed their
fire harps and sang of the beauty of your world
and of your devotion to the divine plan of the creator of all that is. May the veil that we caused to be
cast over your minds be soon lifted and carried away
from you forever by the wind that is now rising from
the depths of eternity.
I am Tob-Vennit of Maldec.

When I was born into human life for the very first time, the event occurred in the farming village of Tigrillet, which was located at the time on land now covered by the Atlantic Ocean. My village of birth (were it not submerged) would be closest today to Portugal. My name—Jaffer—was given to me by my mother, Marle, who was my father's second wife of four. My father's name was Rob Ben-Rob. I had two full brothers, three half brothers and six half sisters. In those days Earth females outnumbered Earth males five to one.

Maldecian spacecraft first landed on the Earth about 310 years before my first birth. During my teenage years, a family of four Maldecians moved into a villa on a hill north of our village. They referred to themselves as *ornas*, a name that applied to Maldecians born on Earth but educated on Maldec. An Earth-born Maldecian who had never visited Maldec (called a *toibe*) was considered by his kind to be somewhat incomplete as a person. An orna always bade a toibe farewell with the statement: "May you visit

Maldec soon."

The orna Maldecian family who lived by our village were a regal lot. They employed twelve people of our village as domestic servants and paid them very well. They had two aircars that the husband (Cro-Swain) and wife (Debettine) used individually and frequently to travel about the countryside and to attend "business meetings" in far-distant places. This Maldecian couple had a teenage son named Sou-Dalf and a teenage daughter named Valneri. *[Maldecian male names are hyphenated and the second name is capitalized at maturity. Female names are not hyphenated. —W.H.B.]* I never saw a Maldecian do any form of physical labor, but they continuously exercised. Sou-Dalf and Valneri would run for miles every day, rain or shine, passing through the village as they came and went from their luxurious home.

My father was not a farmer, as were most of his five brothers, but was one of two provincial magistrates. He also was deputy chief of our six-man police force. His jurisdiction covered over 300 square miles.

I was educated in what you call public schools until the age of fourteen, and then was taught a variety of vocational subjects at a local school. The educational courses selected for me by my father included the law and military science. I never completed any of these courses due to the fact that I was lured away from my studies to serve as a highly paid companion for Sou-Dalf, the Maldecian. It is because of my long-lasting relationship with Sou-Dalf that I was sought as one of those of the open state to relate to you some of the past lifetimes I have experienced on the Earth.

A Companion to Sou-Dalf, a Maldecian Teenager

My association with Sou-Dalf began the day I was called out of class by my father and taken to the Maldecian villa. My father told me that he had received a written invitation from Cro-Swain requesting that he come to villa, and that it would please him and his wife if they would bring me along.

That afternoon we dined with Cro-Swain and his wife Debettine, whose children were not present. Cro-Swain told us that he wished to employ me as a companion for his son, emphasizing that I would not be considered an actual servant, but that my role would be to simply talk to Sou-Dalf and pal around with him, so to speak. As a bonus for my service I would be taught the Maldecian language and would, in about six months, travel with the entire family to the planet Maldec. When he told us how much money I would receive (on a yearly basis), my father and I nearly went into shock. The amount was greater than what my richest uncle, Kanius, could earn in two years by farming. We immediately agreed to Cro-Swain's offer. I was told to return to the villa in two days and bring nothing but the clothes on my back. I did as instructed.

I was given a fine room with a balcony overlooking our village. From time to time I would stand on that balcony and look through the trees to catch a possible glimpse of a family member, but I rarely did. While at the villa I was forbidden to visit my family for any reason. All my attention was to be given to Sou-Dalf and no one else. At first this was not an easy thing to do. He said not a word to me for about two weeks, acting as if I weren't there. Except for when he slept, I was never more than ten paces from him.

Sou-Dalf never ate with his family and seemed to be avoiding his parents. He spoke only to his sister and to a tall, lanky Simm called Rubdus, who provided him and me with the clean clothes we would wear for the day. I learned later that our daily wardrobe and menu were selected by Sou-Dalf's unseen mother.

The villa had a fine stable of horses, but Sou-Dalf never rode them. His sister Valneri never got close to one of the animals because they would bolt as if in the presence of a rattlesnake, and if untied would take off on a run.

Valneri was a very beautiful girl, and I secretly fell in love with her. She was usually accompanied by a white Maldecian goose, which she sometimes kept on a leash. The goose, three times larger than any on Earth today, would attack anything at Valneri's command. From time to time the goose's beak and feet would be painted a different color, gilded with gold or some other decorative material such as powdered emeralds. I was always curious to see what the goose would look like next.

One afternoon I was walking on the villa grounds with Sou-Dalf and Rubdus, the Simm valet, when we came upon Valneri and her pet goose. The Simm told me to wait while Sou-Dalf went to have a private talk with his sister. Suddenly Sou-Dalf, Valneri and the goose came running at me and pushed me over the back of the Simm, who was on his hands and knees behind me. After I caught my breath, the great goose was sitting on my chest looking menacingly into my eyes, and Sou-Dalf, Valneri and Rubdus were laughing hysterically. I had been the victim of a long-planned Maldecian setup. Sou-Dalf's lack of communication with me had been part of an elaborate joke. I learned later that he decided to bring the joke to an end because he didn't want to explain his silent behavior toward me to his two sets of grandparents and an uncle, who were coming to the villa that evening.

After I was pointed out to Sou-Dalf's visiting relatives, I was dismissed. I spent the remaining evening talking to Rubdus and the other Simms. The servants from our village were sent home for the night and the Maldecians were served by special servants brought along by the visitors. Occasionally a young uniformed Maldecian would look in on us to make sure that we were minding our own business.

It was the first time that I ever talked to a Simm. There was a language barrier, because only a selected number of Simms were permitted to learn and speak the language of Earth. I was fortunate that Rubdus was one of those few. Simms were not telepathic. We of Earth in those days could telepathically communicate, but lacked the knowledge to do it correctly. It was an exhausting practice, so very few tried it except in an emergency.

Rubdus was about thirty-eight Earth years old. He told me that he had been in the service of Cro-Swain and Debettine for nearly three years. He had learned his trade during his stay on Maldec two years before. Earlier, he had lived on his home world, called Simm. He could tell me only that Simm was a planet in a distant solar system and orbited a sun/star called Druma. He told me that the fourth planet of that system was occupied by people who referred to themselves as Gracians. The Gracians had space-craft and had introduced the Maldecians to his people. The Maldecians liked the Simms' sense of loyalty and employed them as servants and minor functionaries. The Simms were not a primitive people, but lived in large towns and were already using electricity when first visited by the Gracians. Only certain areas on the Earth, including our village of Tigrillet, had hydroelectric power.

I asked Rubdus about conditions on Maldec. He whispered in my ear, "It's a very nice place to live if you are a Maldecian." He put his forefinger to his lips and shuddered a little. I know now that he regretted saying that to me, fearing the consequences. Rubdus said he had a ten-year contract to work for the Maldecians, with five more years before he would be trans-ported back to his family on Simm. He said he had not been selected by Cro-Swain, but had been assigned to serve the family by the supreme ruler of Maldec, Mic-Corru. Maldec was actually governed by Mic-Corru, three unrelated princes (Tra-Vain, Hol-Canter and Serc-Rhis) and Misshemoo, a princess of Mic-Corru's blood. Her husband was a very powerful person on his home world and on others. *[Note: I have heard the name of Misshemoo's husband many times in past communications, but for some reason have a men-tal block preventing me from telepathically receiving it at this time or recalling it from memory. —W.H.B.]*

During the months that followed that night's visit from Sou-Dalf's grandparents, a large building of Maldecian design was erected in the rear of the villa. It was a plush barracks that was later occupied by twenty-four Maldecian krates. Their commander, Sake-Kover, lived in the villa. The krates were new to the Earth and spent most of their time being instructed secretly about whatever in the strict privacy of their living quarters. They were also taught how to ride horses. When Sou-Dalf and I chanced to come in contact with a krate, he would salute Sou-Dalf, but give me a look that could freeze water.

Sou-Dalf and I spoke to each other about many things. His favorite subject was Earth women and any experiences I might have had with them. He would not discuss Maldecian women in any way. Lacking any sexual experience at the time, I made up some stories to please him. He knew I was lying but didn't care. Sou-Dalf refused to discuss anything of a spiritual or religious nature.

He told me of people from other worlds that his people had encountered while traveling aboard a Gracian spacecraft. When describing what he knew about the people of those other worlds, he would speak of them in derogatory terms. He was very insulting about the ways they lived. He was amused with his own dialogues and wanted me to laugh with him whenever he described an off-world cultural practice he thought was stupid. For all I knew at the time, I thought he might be right, and I laughed. When I asked why these people were not taught differently in the ways of Maldec, he became very serious. He told me that they were not created to be more than they were. They would someday fulfill their rightful place in the universe by serving the people of Maldec and possibly a number of other master races that would rule the universe with them. He inferred that he considered us of the Earth to be one of the so-called master races. I know now that he was lying.

Aircars carrying Maldecian dignitaries came and went from the villa on a daily basis. Two new aircars were delivered for the krates to use. I never saw the krates use these craft. They remained parked by the side of the barracks and were continuously washed and polished by the Simms.

Many times I saw Valneri being accompanied by a young krate officer named Mills-Bant. I was very jealous. Valneri knew this and so did Sou-Dalf. They got a perverse pleasure from my emotional pain and that of anyone else as well.

Through the grapevine (by way of Rubdus) I learned that the krates were present due to a situation that had arisen pertaining to some strange spacecraft that had been spotted in the vicinity of the Earth. There were more than ten of these vehicles that were painted with red, white and black horizontal stripes. They were bigger and faster than the twenty Gracian spacecraft that the Maldecians used. Furthermore, it was known that the UFOs (I couldn't resist that) were operated by people who were telepathic and also had the ability to esper (mentally view things at a great distance). The Maldecians were concerned because these newcomers had so far bypassed Maldec and appeared to be more interested in contacting the people of Wayda (Venus), Mars and the planetoids of the four radiar systems [Jupiter, Saturn, Neptune and Uranus].

I thought immediately that if these space travelers had the abilities that Rubdus described, they might be of one of the master races Sou-Dalf said were expected to join the Maldecians (and we of the Earth) in ruling the universe's vast population of morons and imbeciles. The fact that the Maldecians chose to be suspicious of the new arrivals and prepared for possible warfare made me wonder deeply. The Maldecians on both Maldec and Earth became even more paranoid when still larger spacecraft were spotted in the solar system. These craft were painted black and had no markings.

Our garrison of krates was rotated every two weeks, except for Sake-Kover, their commander, and Valneri's suitor, Mills-Bant. The krates were taken to some other location where they could relax and enjoy female companionship.

The proposed trip to Maldec (part of my bonus) was put off indefinitely. The village schools were closed and most of the young men were conscripted into a militia that was commanded for a very short time by my father. Later the militia was taken over by a krate of the lowest rank. (I learned later that a Maldecian officer's time was not to be wasted training such simpletons.)

One day an aircar landed on the front lawn of the villa. On its hull was the image of a serpent covered with brilliant-colored feathers. Rubdus and his people ran to the craft before they could be stopped by several krates who ran after them. When the occupants of the car stepped out, they were seen to be tall men dressed in feathers and jewels. These three men were Gracians. One of them took Rubdus into the aircar and the other two stood outside and stared down the krates. The krates saluted and backed off.

After about fifteen minutes a tearful Rubdus emerged from the car, accompanied by the Gracian. When he joined the group of his fellow Simms, he had to pass the krates. One of them struck Rubdus on the head with a baton and knocked him to the ground. A Gracian came to his aid and placed himself between the fallen Simm and the krates. The krates stood still for a moment and then walked away.

I learned later that Rubdus had tearfully pleaded with the Gracians to talk to the Maldecians on behalf of his people and himself for their release from their contract. Had I known then what I know now, such a request to a Gracian at the time would have surely been denied. Their philosophy was, a deal is a deal.

The Gracians stayed at the villa for about a week, during which time they were given permission to meet with Rubdus and his people. Whatever they told the Simms put smiles back on the latters' faces and the Simms would whistle while they worked when no Maldecians were present. The real purpose for the Gracians' visit was to discuss a building project they were going to direct for the Maldecians.

A Visit to Mir (Egypt)

When the time came for the Gracians to leave, Sou-Dalf told me that we were going with them. It was my first experience flying in an aircar. Our first stop was the Land of Mir (Egypt). The trip from Tigrillet to the Land of Mir took about two and a half hours. There we met with a number of other Gracians and Maldecians. They were living in tents on the banks of the river now called the Nile. By tents, I mean temporary buildings of waterproof material that contained every conceivable device for human comfort. There was a large tent that housed a group of beautiful women, many of whom were off-worlders and of races I had never seen before. These women were present solely to please the Maldecians. The Gracians were attended by their own kind, who were definitely their chosen mates for life.

We spent the night there and were awakened by a Simm who told us that something was happening that we should be aware of. Sou-Dalf and I, wrapped in blankets, left our tent and joined the gathering crowd that was looking toward the sky. Reflecting the light of a recently risen sun, a black circular spacecraft hovered overhead.

A Brief Nodian Landing

A Gracian stepped out of the crowd and walked in the direction of the vehicle, which had by then landed on the top of the plateau where the pyramids would later be built. He first put both his hands on his head and then crossed them over his heart in a salute. After a minute he continued to walk toward the landed craft. A door opened in its hull and two brown-complexioned men with snow-white hair stepped out onto the ground. One of the men began to walk forward to meet our Gracian emissary. They spoke (telepathically) for about five minutes, then shook hands and parted. The white-haired one reentered his vehicle, which instantly flew off to the west and was out of sight in seconds. The Gracian returned to those of us who were waiting to learn what was said during his encounter.

The Gracian smiled and told us that the stranger told him that they were traders from a world called Nodia, which was located in a distant sun/star system they called the Sost system. The stranger had told him that others of his kind had already made contact with the Maldecian governor-general of the Earth, Her-Rood, at his main headquarters (then located in what is now called southern Venezuela). The white-haired one said that he and his crew were attracted to our gathering by the sight of our fine buildings and thought they would stop by and say hello to everyone there. After the Gracian told the stranger that such a meeting would be inconvenient then because they were about to start work on a building project, the stranger said that he understood and would bother them no more.

That night Sou-Dalf did not sleep in our assigned tent. I did not see him until noon the next day. He told me that he had spent the night with several of the off-world women and therefore was looking forward to becoming an expert on all things of a sexual nature. It's the first time I ever saw him express true human feelings. He was happy and I was frustrated. He knew this, and it made him even happier. I wanted him to describe his experiences with the women, but he wouldn't. During our ten-day stay in Mir he never visited the women again. He wanted to, but was verbally restrained by an elderly Maldecian woman who seemed to be in charge of the women and their activities. To remove temptation so that the men could give their full attention to the project at hand, the women left the area by aircar on the eighth day of our stay in Mir.

The remaining two days were spent walking about the area, both below and on top of the plateau. The Gracians were making calculations and recording their observations electronically on devices similar to tape recorders. The Gracians would separate from the Maldecians in the morning and the evening to say their prayers. Late into the night they would sit outside their tents and talk numbers and smoke their cigars. They didn't mind who came by and listened. I did this once, then left because I couldn't understand what they were talking about. There were a few Simms and a group of small black fellows who seemed to follow their conversations and even participated in them. I tried smoking that night, but couldn't handle it. The Gracian who had given me the cigar took it and ground it out under his foot. Chuckling, he gave me another and said to try this one later. I placed it in my shirt pocket.

Later I walked alone to the south along the riverbank toward the distant glow of a number of campfires. The sound of my footsteps caused frightened hippos and crocs to take refuge in the river waters. I could not see these animals, but heard the splashes they made in their attempt to escape from me. As I walked I put the cigar into my mouth, but having no means to light it, I threw it into the river.

Visiting an Earth Tribe

After an hour of walking I came upon a tribe of Earth people baking fish over open fires. They spoke a dialect slightly different from mine, but I could understand them fairly well. They were curious about was going on downstream and about who we were. I told them that some of us were there to build something, but I didn't know what, nor did I know what function it would have when completed. They felt sorry for my ignorance and asked me why I was there. I told them of my job as companion to Sou-Dalf, and for some unknown reason told several young men about his recent sexual activities. Hearing this, one of the men asked me if I had ever been with a woman. I confessed that I had not.

I was just about to leave when an older man came and sat down beside me. He told me that he had recently taken a virgin orphan girl into his home. He said that he could tell by my clothes and manners that I was rich and of a high station. He said that he would give me this girl to be my servant if I would promise to care for her and treat her well.

After considering what Sou-Dalf and his parents might say about my having a female servant, I thanked the man for his offer, but refused. He told me to wait and give the matter a second thought after I saw the girl. He assured me that she was very pretty and fit to be the consort of a prince. He added that a fortuneteller (astrologer) had told him that the girl was to be kept virginal until a stranger from a distant place came and took her away with him. He confessed that trying to keep her a virgin was getting harder because her beauty was attracting much interest from the young men. Having never met a man from another land before, he was convinced that the man in the prophecy must refer to me. He added that if I took the girl, we would both surely find favor with the elohim.

Alfora and the Trip to Maldec

The girl's name was Alfora, and she was a fourteen-year-old beauty. She was frightened of me, but we managed to make conversation as we walked back to my camp. I sat on the riverbank until dawn while she slept, using her bundled belongings as a pillow. I spent the night trying to think about what I would tell Sou-Dalf. He was sitting in front of a tent when I walked up to him, Alfora behind me. He first looked stern and then began to smile, saying, "I see you have gotten yourself a pet. Take her to Mestvuker, the Gracian doctor, to be vaccinated. We are not returning to Tigrillet; we will depart for Maldec within a few hours."

During those few hours I avoided Sou-Dalf as long as I could, but he found me. He told me, "Don't worry, Jaffer. I'm not going cause you or your peasant pet any trouble. Just teach her how to behave in front of my parents and she will hardly be noticed." I agreed to teach Alfora to be obedient and courteous to all of her superiors.

Ten minutes after our conversation a silver, triangular-shaped Gracian spacecraft landed on the plateau. An hour later, with Sou-Dalf, myself and a very frightened and confused Alfora aboard, the Gracian spacecraft lifted into the heavens and headed for its next destination, the planet Maldec.

The interior of the Gracian craft had no metal or man-made materials, but was decorated by different types of natural wood. Many of the instruments used in the craft's operation were encased in cabinets carved with images of animals and people in exquisite detail. The carpeted floors had three-dimensional patterns that caused us at times to feel that by taking one more step, we would tumble into an endless void. After a time the mind would adjust to these illusions, giving us an excited sense of derring-do in defying this apparent virtual reality.

Alfora and I were assigned a small private bedroom and bath. We were allowed to go almost anywhere we wanted on the ship by ourselves. The Gracians preferred that we enter some areas of the craft only if we were accompanied by one of the crew. We learned that there were more than 70 people aboard the spacecraft, but only a small number of these passengers had Maldec as a final destination. The Maldecians aboard kept to themselves, and I rarely saw Sou-Dalf during the voyage.

We ate our meals with several Gracians and a number of small black-skinned people who smiled a lot but whose language I could not understand. Food was served buffet style. The Gracians were very friendly and made us feel welcome. I tried smoking their cigars, but never could get used to them. Even Gracian women puffed away on the things, using jeweled cigar holders of various lengths.

I was permitted to visit the control area of the vehicle, from which three young Gracians operated the craft. One appeared to be no more than ten Earth years old. The others appeared to be in their teens. My older Gracian escort told me that the craft would not land on Maldec but would, after our party departed, travel to its home base on Gracyea.

Within the first few hours of our flight a Gracian woman took Alfora under her wing and was gone quite some time. When I saw Alfora again she had been bathed and wore a fine feathered gown of Gracian design. Sou-Dalf looked at Alfora in a way that made me very angry. The Gracian lady told me that the way to protect Alfora from Sou-Dalf was for me to marry the girl by way of a Gracian ceremony, because at present the Maldecians honored Gracian ways. I followed her advice and married Alfora in less than an hour. We remained together throughout our entire lives. She was my only wife, as she is in this present day. As I relate my account of those earliest times, she is sitting near me, occasionally reminding me not to forget to tell you this or that about our first lifetime together.

Three Years on Maldec

As I was informed earlier, the Gracian spacecraft did not land on Maldec. Sou-Dalf's party, which included Alfora and myself, was transported by a Maldecian shuttlecraft into the planet's atmosphere, then to a complex of magnificent buildings and palaces. We landed on a large stone platform located in front of one of the most beautiful buildings I had ever seen. It had alabaster columns over 800 feet high. Parts of the building seemed suspended in midair. The smell of the place was marvelous, yet indescribable. Trees and flower gardens surrounded the place. (It would take many pages to describe the beautiful planet of Maldec and its magnificent architecture.) The planet and its buildings were breathtaking to any off-worlders, but the Maldecians dealt with these marvels in a matter-of-fact and emotionless manner. Every building there had been constructed in the distant past according to some master plan. I never saw anything being built; it was as if anything they ever wanted or would want in the future was already there—constructed by their industrious ancestors.

Upon landing we were ushered into the palace. The floors of the first grand room we entered resembled a deep, lime-green ocean with sky-colored ceilings more than 80 feet high. It was quiet and empty. We walked until we reached a conveyer, which we stepped onto. The conveyer was about eighteen feet wide and moved us silently past sculpted landscapes colored with paints that contained powdered gems fused to the sculptures by great heat. Our trip took about ten minutes, and we were met by an apparently unarmed krate in a white tunic and sandals of gold. Around each of his arms were coiled devices in the image of golden cobras. The heads of these cobras were attached to each forefinger. I learned later that these cobras were actually weapons of the palace guard. They could be activated by the contraction of a finger, injecting a quick-acting poison into an off-worlder's body and killing him instantly. The poison had no effect on a Maldecian.

We were escorted by the krate down yet another grand hallway to a room filled with hundreds of different types of off-worlders and a number of very worried-looking Maldecians. Although the room was filled to capacity, it was very quiet; everyone was talking in whispers. There was soft music coming from an unknown source. Alfora and I were told to wait in this room and Sou-Dalf went elsewhere with the krate. We learned that the people waiting in this room were there either because they had been summoned or because they had a personal reason to contact the Maldecian governing body. The worried-looking Maldecians were some of those who had been summoned. Simms walked about the room carrying trays of refreshing fruit drinks.

After waiting for about four hours, we were approached by an elegantly dressed female Simm who addressed me by name and asked me to come with her. Alfora and I followed her to an elevator that took us upward to one of those parts of the palace that looked like it was suspended in midair. On this open platform rested a small aircar with a male Simm at its controls.

The female Simm, who was named Orbeleen, got into the car with us. Shortly, we approached a building complex that went on for miles. The buildings were multistoried and had designs that could only have been copied from the memory of someone who had once visited a place built by the gods (elohim). I could not fathom how these places could have been designed or built by human beings. I then understood why an orna Maldecian would tell a toibe that he hoped the toibe would visit Maldec soon.

During several lifetimes since, I have visited other worlds, even the planet Nodia, whose people later became the Maldecians' bitter adversaries and who had already surpassed the Maldecians in all forms of technology at the time of my first life. The two worlds couldn't be more different. Nodian buildings were grand, but to this day they are continually modified because Nodians are always alert to improvements. Early Nodians were an arrogant lot, but their culture has mellowed with age. They have a sense of humor but can get instantly serious. In the present day, Nodians and some "reformed" Maldecians get along well with each other.

After settling down on a landing pad surrounded by beautiful trees and flowering plants, we were taken down a path to a house whose peaked roof was located at ground level and constantly bathed by twin waterfalls. We entered the house through a hatchlike door of red crystal located in the roof between the falls, then walked down a flight of steps. It was a split-level house and contained eight spacious bedrooms. The largest of the rooms looked out over a cliff that dropped 600 feet. The only way out of this mansion was the way we came in. I spent many an hour sitting before a window in the large living room, looking out over the beautiful Maldecian buildings and landscape below. As I sat there I contemplated Alfora's and my future. I wondered how my family would feel about my wife, whom they had never seen.

Orbeleen introduced us to our staff of three Simm servants, two young women and a much older man. It took awhile for Alfora to understand what a servant actually was. This was a revelation to a girl who, less than two weeks before, was living in a hut on a riverbank and cooking fish over a campfire.

The closets were filled with every manner of clothing sealed in transparent containers. Some were referred to as formal wear by Orbeleen, who said she would advise us when to dress in these garments. Before she left us that day she told us that any request we had should be forwarded to her through the old Simm, Tarnbero.

The other houses and apartments in this special area were occupied solely by people from other worlds. We gradually met many of the compound's inhabitants. We visited them in their homes and found that they also were attended to by Simms who directly answered to Orbeleen. Their place of residence, like ours, had only one way in and out.

We never left the compound in the three Earth years we spent on Maldec. Our social life revolved around meetings with groups of off-worlders in which we shared information about our home cultures. We learned of the existence of radios, television, photography, advanced medical procedures and religious practices. I wondered why the Maldecians did not have, or utilize, the knowledge of these wise off-worlders. In fact, no Maldecian ever attended any of these meetings. To us it was as if there were no Maldecians living on Maldec.

My interaction with the various types of off-worlders in the compound provided me with an education in languages that I could not have acquired elsewhere. The need to know what we of the differing worlds were talking about necessitated rapidly learning one another's speech. My acquired language skills eventually were utilized in the next phase of my life, which began when I returned to Earth.

During our stay on Maldec I saw only three Maldecians. They were escorting around the compound the newly appointed Nodian ambassador to Maldec and Earth—Opatel Cre'ator. On that day he was attended by six black-uniformed men of his race and his gigantic servant, Corboslate. Assigned to him as an interpreter was the Maldecian known only by the single name Sant.

I have learned that on that day Opatel was being shown housing for himself and his staff. I also learned that he turned down the most opulent palace in the off-worlder compound. He also refused a number of other grand palaces outside the compound. (I know now that he was not the kind of man who wanted to come and go from a single door.)

A clear spot on a hill near the compound was provided for him. On the hill he parked a large black circular spacecraft. On its hull was the insignia of the Trading House of Cre'ator, which was a silver triangle with a double left side. Opatel and his Nodians housed themselves and also conducted their diplomatic business inside the craft. Whenever Opatel's diplomatic duties took him to Earth, off he went bag and baggage, so to speak.

During the time I was on Maldec, twice I saw Opatel's craft leave and return to its perch on the nearby hill. I never laid eyes on Opatel again while on Maldec. About three and a half years later, I saw him twice again, once in his official capacity at the setting of the astrastone capstone of the Great Pyramid of Mir and once when we talked privately one night on the banks of the Nile.

While on Maldec we enjoyed meeting, talking and sharing knowledge with the various off-worlders in the compound. I even came to like and admire the Cryberants, a group of people who were at first very standoffish, trying to impress everyone that they knew the answers to the greatest secrets in the universe. For some reason I have yet to learn, the Maldecians had a little more respect for the Cryberants (who were very good telepaths) than for any other universal race of people.

The Cryberants were from a planet orbiting a sun/star system located in the constellation Lyra. As time passed, a considerable number of the Cryberants were taken to Earth and employed by the Maldecians to carve the statue now called the Sphinx, which had several secret chambers under it. I know now that when the chambers were finished, the Cryberants who built them were killed to prevent their revealing the locations of the chambers or their access routes. There were other chambers under the Sphinx that were not concealed, and it was in one of these that Ruke of Parn and his family hid when the krates slaughtered everyone involved in the construction of the pyramids. (As you know, the krates blamed the builders of the pyramids for the destruction of their home planet, Maldec.)

Alfora spent a great deal of her time gardening, and her flowers were abundant and very beautiful. During our stay on Maldec Alfora became pregnant. I learned later that her condition hastened our departure from the planet because the Maldecians wanted no off-world children born on their home world if they could prevent it. In truth, during my first lifetime I never saw a Maldecian child under the age of about twelve.

The planet Maldec had four seasons like Earth, but each season was longer due to the fact that Maldec had a larger orbit around the sun. Even so, Alfora's gardening activities went on year round because the weather in the compound was controlled. During the wintertime the entire compound area was covered by a force field of Gracian design. I enjoyed the Maldecian winters, for it was quite a beautiful visual experience. When the white falling snow came into contact with the force field, the snow would turn a brilliant blue, then green. The green rivulets of water would run down the outer surface of the dome-shaped field, warming in the process. After reaching a certain temperature near the bottom of the field, it would vaporize in a flash of yellow and red light.

We were given two days' notice by Orbeleen that we were going to leave Maldec for Earth. We arrived at our point of departure at night and found waiting a large triangular spacecraft that was not a Gracian vehicle, but one of Maldecian design. The craft's operators and passengers were Maldecians except for Alfora and me.

Onboard we met once again with Sou-Dalf, whom we had not seen for three years. He now wore the uniform of a krate officer. Sou-Dalf paid little attention to Alfora and me, and was seen mostly in the company of another krate officer of equal rank, whose name was Serp-Ponder. (I am compelled to say that if there was ever a Maldecian I came to admire, it was Serp-Ponder. Were it not for him, I would have been murdered in that first lifetime and my body added to the heap of bodies of the Cryberants killed to keep the secrets of the Sphinx.)

When we left Maldec the only thing we took was what we brought and about 100 packets of flower seeds. These seeds were lost during the flight and never found.

Back on Earth

Our flight from Maldec to Earth was quite uneventful. Alfora and I kept to ourselves and prepared our own food in our one-room living area. We were deposited about three miles from my home village of Tigrillet without even a good-bye. We stood in the open field along with our belongings as the Maldecian craft rose out of sight. Bewildered, I wondered if I should go to the home of my parents or to the villa of the Maldecians Cro-Swain and Debettine. I decided that I would go to the home of my family and introduce my wife. We started to walk toward the village as the sun set in the western sky. As we walked, we listened to the sounds of the night birds. The sounds from the woods around us made us feel good to be back on Earth once again.

When we entered the village we found it dark, though the villa on the hill was brightly lit and was now surrounded by a number of other multi-storied buildings. As we walked the empty streets, we heard someone singing and strumming a guitar. The melody was that of an old folk song of the Earth, but its lyrics had been changed and translated into the language of Maldec.

Coming to the door of my family home, I found a bag of acorns attached to its knocker. This was a sign that the owners of the house were not at home. Alfora and I spent the night there. By the number of burnt candles I was able to surmise that the electric power to the village had been off for quite some time.

On the following morning we walked toward the village square and encountered people going about their business as if everything were perfectly normal. The city hall was empty except for two krates, who occupied themselves playing a game similar to chess. We said nothing to them. After some inquiry we learned that my family now lived with my father's older brother, Kanius. Uncle Kanius' farm was located about twelve miles from the village. As we walked toward the farm we passed the small hydroelectric generating plant. The access road to the plant was guarded by two young uniformed Earthmen who looked as mean as krates. They gave us a cold stare, but managed a slight smile when I said hello in Maldecian.

About halfway through our journey we were overtaken by a carriage drawn by six horses. Its only passenger was Deybal Ben-Volar, who was once the chief of police of our village (my father had been his deputy chief). He recognized me and asked us to come with him, as he was on his way to meet with my father and Uncle Kanius. During the ride to the farm he asked me endless questions about my visit to Maldec. He was very disappointed that during our stay we had been sequestered in the off-worlder compound, because I could tell him little about Maldec or its native people. I sensed that my father's friend wanted to tell me something, but held back because he wasn't yet sure he could trust me.

Alfora and I were joyfully received by my family. They had been expecting us because that morning a chest of gold coins had been delivered for me there by a Simm. The money had been sent by Cro-Swain in payment for my services as a companion to Sou-Dalf. Uncle Kanius was boiling mad and advised me to put some of my earnings aside in order to pay the tax the Maldecians were levying on newborn infants. Only children whose parents paid such a tax would be taught to read and write and permitted to attend school. The tax could be paid at any time in the child's life (along with any accrued interest).

The Maldecian Takeover Plan

I learned that during my absence things had changed drastically on Earth. Claiming that the Nodians represented a great danger to Earth and its people, the Maldecians declared martial law. They suspended the governing activities of the Earth Council of Elders, and it was rumored that the temples would be closed to those who could not buy a pass. Hundreds of thousands of krates and off-world mercenaries had been brought to the Earth. The so-called taxes were to be used to provide for these "protectors." Only Maldecian installations had electrical power.

Any Earth person who contacted or dealt with any off-worlder not on the Maldecian list of friendlies would be immediately arrested and later publicly executed. One of the things that really angered my uncle was that the Maldecians wanted him to operate his farm with slave labor. The slaves were people who had violated some Maldecian rule or who were unable to pay some ridiculous fine or tax. My father told me that more than half the people he had known since he was a boy were now Maldecian slaves. It was also rumored that when the Nodian threat had passed, these people would be free to pursue their lives as before. The Maldecians proclaimed that these were emergency measures implemented only to deal with uncertain danger.

I know now that these cruel actions were really the final part of a 315-year-old Maldecian agenda for totally taking over the Earth and enslaving its native inhabitants. The presence of the Nodians in the solar system caused them to abandon their plan for a gradual takeover, accelerating it before the Nodians had a chance to find out and spill the beans to us or any other people of this solar system, which the Maldecians planned to conquer in the future.

A week after my arrival at the farm an aircar landed, carrying Rubdus the Simm. He brought a message for me from Cro-Swain, who was now the Maldecian military dictator of the local area. The message, written in Maldecian script (which he knew I could now read), offered me a job as a translator in the Land of Mir. I would be paid very well for my services and excused from paying any tax on my pending child. Cro-Swain's offer was one of the topics of the meeting later that evening.

Earth Freedom Fighters

At that meeting were Deybal Ben-Volar, Uncle Kanius, my father, two men who were previously village police officers, and myself. No one in this group was swallowing the trumped-up Maldecian story that the Nodians were going to invade the Earth. It was known that the power plant was operational, although the Maldecians claimed it had been sabotaged by Nodian agents. We also discussed the fact that shortages of certain types of food, medicines and other materials were also Maldecian fabrications. We were sure that these "problems" were invented to keep the population of the planet off balance, confused and worried while the Maldecians secretly tightened the noose about our throats. At the conclusion of the meeting all agreed that the Maldecians must be resisted even if it took force. We hoped that there was still time to spread the word worldwide and find some way to once again govern ourselves. My father suggested that we attempt to contact the Nodians and ask them for assistance in overthrowing our Maldecian rulers. We all knew that anyone caught making such a contact would be killed, but agreed that the chance should be taken.

I was the only one of the group who had ever seen a Nodian, and because I might come in contact with Nodians in the Land of Mir and confidentially relate our plight to them, it was decided that I would take up

Cro-Swain's job offer. The only good thing I could think of at the time was that Alfora might be able to visit the land of her birth and be with the people who were the friends of her youth. She was glad that our child would be born in Mir.

Uncle Kanius sent a runner to Cro-Swain with my acceptance of his job offer. The following afternoon Rubdus the Simm arrived by aircar to fetch Alfora and me. We were taken to the field where we had been deposited by the Maldecian spacecraft several days earlier. There we found a larger aircar waiting. This craft's operators were Maldecian and its passengers were a combination of Earth people and Cryberants.

During the time we spent with Rubdus he mentioned that he had about two years to go on his ten-year service contract with Cro-Swain, and was finding it very difficult to cope with the presence and cruel attitudes of the thousands of krates who now occupied the new buildings surrounding the villa. This was the last time I saw Rubdus. I learned later that while returning to the villa from an errand for Cro-Swain, he killed himself by diving his bomb-laden aircar into one of the krate barracks. His act killed several hundred krates, but in reprisal every Simm in a hundred-mile radius was publicly crucified. (I have also learned that the cargo of explosives Rubdus delivered to the krates that day were secretly made and loaded on his aircar by my father and Uncle Kanius.)

When we arrived in Mir we were housed northwest of the plateau (now called Giza) among a group of about 200 Cryberants and 100 Earth people. The Gracian and Simm housing area was to the north of us and the workers from the Relt planetoids and elsewhere lived east of the plateau near the river. The Maldecians, when they finally arrived in numbers, lived to the far north on the shores of the Mediterranean Sea (much smaller than it is today). A group of about thirty krates eventually took up residence in fabricated housing near the stone outcropping that would later be carved into the shape of the original Sphinx.

About fifteen miles east of the plateau was a large village of native Earth people. It was called Pankamerry, and its head man was Cark Ben-Zobey. All business that the Gracians had with food suppliers and other merchants was conducted in this village because the merchants were forbidden to come into the area of the pyramids. All Gracian spacecraft landed at and left Earth for wherever from the village of Pankamerry. Because I and two Simm assistants were assigned to see to the needs of the Cryberants, from time to time I went to the food depots in Pankamerry and visited among my own kind.

I knew that if I saw a Nodian I must never be seen talking to him or her, so I devised a plan to enlist the aid of either a Gracian or Cryberant to telepathically notify any Nodian that I wanted to meet with them secretly. The trick was to find a Gracian or Cryberant I could trust not to betray me to the krates. Of the two telepathic cultures, the odds were that a Gracian would be the more trustworthy. I spent many an evening listening to Gracians rattle off numbers to each other, pretending that I understood what they were saying and that I was enjoying their cigars. My real purpose was to pick out a Gracian among their number who might, on my behalf, telepathically contact any Nodian who might or might not show up in the area.

Over a period of about a month my search for a telepathic coconspirator came to an end when I was approached by an elderly Gracian named Ponalix. He asked directly what I wanted. He said it had become obvious to him and many of his kind that I was always in a state of high emotion whenever I visited their nightly gatherings. In friendship he thought he would tell me that I was unknowingly flashing an emotional danger signal that might be detected by the krates. I told Ponalix of my plan to contact any Nodians who might come to the area. Without hesitation he agreed to help me if I would calm down and not contact him until he sent me a message. I agreed and went home to bed.

One afternoon Alfora and I boarded an empty block barge that was to be towed by aircar upriver to a quarry, where it would be loaded with cut core stones for the pyramids. Alfora was certain that she would be delivering our child very soon and wanted to be with women of her own tribe. From the barge we could scan the riverbanks for her people, who were nomads that moved up and down the river fishing and hunting. The aircar moved slowly until we were out of sight of the plateau, whereupon its towline slackened as it moved over the barge and lowered to about three feet overhead. The door of the craft opened and Ponalix jumped onto the barge. The aircar then resumed its towing operation. Ponalix told us we would find Alfora's people about thirty miles farther south and that we should stay with them until we were contacted further. He told me that he had made arrangements with my immediate Gracian overseer to give me an indefinite leave of absence (longer than the four-day leave I had arranged).

Alfora's people welcomed us warmly. Mill, the man who had taken her into the care and protection of his family after she had been orphaned, was overjoyed to see us and spellbound when we told him of our trip to Maldec. He recalled that it had been more than three years since he had last seen us, and wondered, now that the building on the plateau had finally begun, how long it would take for completion. I told him that I had heard it would take about two and one-third years.

Three days after joining her people, Alfora gave birth to a daughter she named Barla. The following evening, as I was sitting and talking to Mill, a teenage boy came up to me and handed me a cigar. He told me he had gotten it from a man down by the river. He told me that the man spoke to him with a strange accent and told him to tell me to meet him on the riverbank.

An Appeal to Opatel for Nodian Military Help

The night was dark as I followed the boy to the spot he had been directed to bring me. I first saw a small boat anchored offshore. It held four people—I could only just make out their silhouettes. Then I was startled by the low voice of a man who addressed me by name. I turned to find a tall man dressed in black, his hooded headdress trimmed with a silver cord. He said, "I'm pleased to meet you, Jaffer. I am Opatel Cre'ator. I understand you have a serious Maldecian problem. How can I be of help?"

Opatel patiently listened to me describe how we of the Earth were being methodically conquered and enslaved by the Maldecians. After I requested Nodian military assistance to overthrow the Maldecians, he began to speak: "Jaffer, you are really a representative of one group among many of Earth people who have secretly come to us with the same request. Believe me, if I were in your position I would be doing the very same thing.

"First of all, it is our opinion that your people are not being conquered, but are in fact already conquered. In the second place, our technology has given you the false impression that we are capable of giving you superior military assistance. You must understand that because of our overwhelming numbers, our spacecraft could destroy the small Maldecian space fleet, but what would that accomplish? Millions of Maldecians would still be on the Earth. What would you have us do? Conduct planetwide ground warfare against them when more than 95 percent of your own people do not oppose their rule? In addition, convincing those who control the various military powers of Nodia to forcibly intervene individually or collectively in the political affairs of a planet in another solar system would be impossible. After all, the Maldecians have not given them any trouble."

As I listened to Opatel speak, tears ran down my cheeks. My hopes and expectations were totally shattered. He placed his hand on my shoulder and continued, "All is not lost, my friend. My younger half brother Rayatis is the prime director of a rapidly growing Nodian trading house, and I have discussed the ways and means of the Maldecians with him several times. It is Rayatis' belief that although the Maldecians are not a present threat to us of Nodia, they eventually will be. There-fore we have devised a long-range plan to deal with them. First, we have sent an envoy to the Gracian home world to establish diplomatic relations. We will use every means at our disposal to convince the Gracians not to give or sell any more of their advanced technology to the Maldecians. Hopefully we will succeed.

Rayatis will not oppose the efforts of the other two large Nodian trading houses to establish bases on Mars, Venus or any planetoids of the four radiars. This is a wise position to take, because if war eventually breaks out between the Nodians and the Maldecians, these otherwise-competitive trading houses will join with his trading house to collectively protect their own interests. The first phase of the plan is to keep the Maldecians bottled up in their home solar system and whittle away at their power."

Opatel had no false idea that the Maldecians were going to accept such Nodian actions lying down. The question was, how long would it take them to come up with countermeasures? Time would tell. Meanwhile he agreed to covertly supply any group of Earth people with anything he could that would help them undermine the Maldecian rule. He advised that it would be the task of these groups to convince other natives of the planet to reject the ways of the Maldecians and join the underground movement, which had the ultimate goal of restoring their rights and their liberty.

There were very many complex elements pertaining to the plan that Opatel and I discussed that night on the banks of the Nile, too many for this account. Even so, there were two pieces of information I received that night that I will relate, because I know that describing them will put the overall conditions of the time into a sharper focus for the reader.

Mars Construction and Word of Other Conquerors

Opatel told me that as we spoke, a Gracian construction team supported by workers from the Relt planetoids was building a large pyramid and other structures on the planet Mars. It was not known who was funding this construction, but he suspected that the Maldecians were behind the scenes. He told me that he had been informed that the pyramids of Mir and Mars were being constructed for the purposes of healing human physical ailments and prolonging life. Opatel was convinced that the structures were *not* being built for these purposes, but admitted that he had not yet discovered the Maldecians' real purpose. The Gracians, on the other hand, also seemed to be very much in the dark, but were caught up in a type of spiritual euphoria they would experience whenever they were building something whose form expressed the sacred numbers that describe every existing reality in the universe.

Opatel also informed me that Nodian space explorations had brought them into contact with many races of other worlds that had the same superior attitude of the Maldecians concerning people not native to their worlds. Some of these "superior races" had in one way or another taken control of entire solar systems and harshly ruled their human inhabitants. Opatel explained that it was presently beyond the physical means of the Nodians and their allies to directly take on these cultures. He added that he also knew the day would come when something must be done by someone to prevent those of the dark side from uniting into a single conquering force that at some time could spread like a disease and possibly take over the entire universe.

He also said that if it was true that we as humans would be reembodied after death and live again and again at future times, it would be very unpleasant to be born into a future life as a slave of those of the dark side. He caught his breath and said, "I could go on and on with all forms of speculation about the future and what can and cannot be done and what eventually must be done about those of the dark side. But such speculations won't help you and your people out of your present situation. Let us deal with what we know and find out as much as we can about the Maldecians' real agenda, then do whatever we must to keep them from making things even worse for your world."

Before leaving, Opatel told me to expect to be contacted by a man who would be recognized by his ability to prevent at will his physical form from projecting a shadow. I asked Opatel how the man could do such a thing. He replied, "I really don't know for sure, but I think he absorbs the energy of the sunlight into his interpsychic essence." Opatel then waded to the waiting boat. I heard the low purr of an electric motor and watched the boat move upstream and disappear from sight into the darkness.

When the carving of the Sphinx was completed, arrangements were made for the Cryberants and those who worked closely with them to leave the Land of Mir. Because I was one of those who worked with the Cryberants, my family and I were on the list of those who would depart. We assembled one morning to begin a walking trip north to the coast of the Mediterranean where, we were told, we would be transported by aircar to our respective homes elsewhere on the Earth or taken to ports where the off-worlders of the group would be transported to their home worlds by spacecraft. I was surprised to find that Sou-Dalf and Serp-Ponder, along with about fifty krates of lesser rank, were going to escort us.

Escaping Sure Death

As we started out, I kept my eyes peeled for a man who casts no shadow. Our path took us past Serp-Ponder, who stood in a regal manner on a small rocky hill and seemed to be counting or scrutinizing us as we went by. When he saw me, he called out my name and motioned me to come to him. He descended the hill and walked up to Alfora, who was carrying our infant daughter Barla. He looked at the baby and touched her gently on the forehead. As he did this he whispered, "Take your wife and child and go to

Pankamerry. For the sake of your lives, don't go with Sou-Dalf and the Cryberants. The Cryberants and all with them will be killed before they reach the shores of the sea."

He then asked us to follow him, which we did. He took us behind the hill and past the krate perimeter guards. He handed me a canteen of water and said, "Come back in a few days and join the group of Earth people who live north of the Gracian encampment. From there you will eventually be safely taken from Mir to your homeland." I hastily thanked him. Without saying another word, he turned and ran back to his previous hilltop position.

The road to Pankamerry went through a lush green forest that existed at that time. We had been walking this road for more than an hour when we came upon a little man wearing dirty yellow trousers and no blouse—and who appeared to be arguing with a tree in an unfamiliar language! At times he would strike the tree with a metal object, which later proved to be a flute. When he saw us, he stopped his ravings and violent actions and tenderly patted the tree as one would comfort a child. As the man stepped into the middle of the road I immediately noticed that neither he nor the tree cast a shadow, although we and every other object about us did. He smiled at us, motioned to the tree and said perfectly in my native language, "Sometimes it's necessary to show them who's the boss." I asked him his name and he told me he was simply called He Who Casts No Shadow.

As we walked along he told me that I could trust Cark Ben-Zobey, the head man of the town of Pankamerry, or anyone the latter said could be trusted. He Who Casts No Shadow knew of my home village and of the resistance movement directed by my father, Uncle Kanius and Deybal Ben-Volar. He told me that they were presently in hiding from the Maldecians, who had found them out after Rubdus crashed his aircar into the krate barracks. He advised us to stay in Pankamerry until Cark Ben-Zobey was sure it was safe for us to return to the pyramid building site. He said that Opatel Cre'ator and his brother Rayatis sent their regards and assurances that everything was under way according to plan to assist those of the Earth who were prepared to resist the Maldecian rule, and that every possible effort would be made to keep me informed of the progress of the plan. He Who Casts No Shadow then handed Alfora a small box and told her that it was a gift from Lord Opatel. The box contained a small silver triangle with two left sides (the insignia of the Trading House of Cre'ator). Alfora kept this treasure wisely concealed for the rest of that lifetime.

Our days in Pankamerry were spent as guests of Cark Ben-Zobey, his two wives and three fully grown unmarried sons. He Who Casts No Shadow visited us several times to inform us of what he had heard from

Nodia and what he had learned about the activities of the local Maldecians. It was during his first visit that he confirmed that the krates under Sou-Dalf's command killed the unsuspecting Cryberants and disposed of their bodies in the Mediterranean. We stayed with Cark Ben-Zobey and his family for about nine days and walked back to the plateau. We had our pick of any of the many empty houses that had been vacated by their previous occupants, who had either returned to their place of origin or had taken that fatal walk to the north with Sou-Dalf and his krates.

On the day the capstone of the Great Pyramid of Mir was set in place, Alfora and I were among a group of onlookers who stood several thousand feet west of the structure. Standing between us and the pyramid was first a line of krates and then the wall that had been built around the pyramid. On top of this wall at each of its corners stood a krate, all of whom were occupied for a while chasing workers from the Relt planetoids off the wall, where they had perched to get a better view of the proceedings.

I learned that the people of the Relt planetoids were not only selected by the Gracians for their size and strength, but also because the psychic energy they emitted naturally polarized with the toning frequencies that the Gracian stolfas used to levitate the massive blocks of stone. Had a person such as I tried to move or even touch a levitated block, it would have disrupted the process and brought the stone crashing to the ground.

An hour before the capstone was set into place a black spacecraft, marked with a silver triangle with a double left side, landed in a clear spot behind us. From the craft came Opatel Cre'ator and several others of his race. They walked directly through the crowd toward the pyramid. Opatel passed within feet of Alfora and me and looked me right in the eyes. He made a facial expression that I easily interpreted as meaning, "I know what the Maldecians are up to. "

Opatel and his group were met by a troop of twelve krates carrying a white banner that bore the images of two golden cobras facing each other. This escort stayed with Opatel during the ceremonies and for every second thereafter until he later entered his craft and flew away.

The Day of Destruction

The time of the summer solstice had been a worldwide holiday on the Earth for hundreds of years. Alfora's tribe also observed the day and the religious practices attached to it. We left the night before the solstice to spend the day upstream with Mill and his family. On the day of the solstice we feasted, bathed Barla in the river and proudly watched as an elderly holy woman of the tribe blessed our child with talismans and charms that were to assure a long and fertile life. Later the same priestess, during a mild trance, informed the gathered tribe that she was receiving powerful feelings that a disastrous thing was going to happen very soon. She told us that our lives would never again be the same. Mill told me that we should take the holy woman's spiritual feelings very seriously, because it was she who had told him years before to shelter Alfora until she was taken away by a stranger from a distant land.

Less than an hour later the Earth shook violently and waves of water from the Nile rolled over our campsite. We ran until we reached higher ground. From our new location we watched thousands of river animals and birds run and fly in every direction. Their cries were deafening. To the north we saw a pillar of red fire project into the blue sky, which was rapidly turning black. Then there was a brilliant flash of white light in the sky, and birds in great numbers fell onto the Earth and into the river. The river turned red with blood as the birds were devoured by crocodiles and other amphibious predators.

The pillar of fire was diminishing when we and the tribe set out to the northwest for the town of Pankamerry. En route we were joined by other tribes who had the same destination. There was a feeling in us all that the world was coming to an end. The sky was a dark and dismal gray color. Lightning was occurring continuously, but it did not rain.

We were very tired and frightened and sat down with others to rest. At this time I heard my name being called. I replied, shouting over the claps of thunder. Shortly after, we were joined by He Who Casts No Shadow, who told us that the Maldecians had shattered their home planet into bits. I admit that I felt glad to hear this at the time, but I also wondered if the Nodians might have had something to do with Maldec's destruction. While I was on the verge of hysterical glee, I was attracted to the sobs of my wife Alfora. I went to comfort her, saying, "Don't cry, the Maldecians deserved what happened to them." She answered, "It's not the Maldecians I feel badly about. I'm sad about my plants and beautiful flowers that I left behind on Maldec when we came home to Earth. Do you think the elohim might have saved them from being destroyed?" I was at a loss what to tell her. I comforted her by saying that I would help her plant a flower garden when we managed to return to our home village and my family.

When we reached Pankamerry the place was very crowded with Earth people and every type of off-worlder. There were about five or six Gracians in Pankamerry awaiting the arrival of spacecraft that would take them off the Earth and transport them to some other cosmic haven in space.

The next day was the one during which the krates went on their rampage, killing everyone on the plateau who had the slightest thing to do with building the pyramids. Word came to us in Pankamerry of these atrocities, and a warning that the krates were coming slowly in our direction.

Some of the men of the town armed themselves. Others of us decided to lose ourselves in the thick rain forest to the south. Just as we made the decision to move to the south, the expected but long-overdue Gracian spacecraft landed a few miles west of the town. After contacting the crew of the craft, we were accepted aboard along with Cark Ben-Zobey and his family. The Gracians took us northeast over the Mediterranean to a land that is now part of Iraq. They told us they would return for us after they completed picking up Gracian stragglers and moving them from harm's way. This craft never returned.

Aftermath

We spent several years in what was then a remote area of the Earth. We had no desire to move from this apparent sanctuary. With us were a number of people from the Relt planetoids and quite a few Earth people. From time to time someone would report the sighting of a Maldecian aircar, but such sightings were infrequent.

One night three large bright lights flew over our campsite. These lights descended to the top of a hill located about eight miles to the south. I, of course, recognized the lights as some type of spacecraft. We debated whether or not to investigate who was in control of these craft. A few of us men decided to go and look at the craft without being seen. We hoped the vehicles were Gracian or Nodian and not filled with angry krates.

The craft turned out to be Nodian transports that had come from the planetoids of the dying Sumer radiar. They were there to deposit several thousand Sumerians onto Earth. We met with the leader of the Sumerians, who was a man called Trome. *[See Trome's accounts of some early lifetimes he spent on Earth in chapter 2. —W.H.B.]*

My association with Trome and his people was very friendly and has existed even unto this very day. During the immediate months that followed, hundreds of thousands of Sumerians arrived on Earth by way of Nodian spacecraft. I was invited to join an advisory council headed by the Nodians Tasper-Kane and his assistant Abdonel.

Life with the Sumerians was easier than it had been for the past few years. One of the main reasons was that the Sumerians were able to generate electricity. For at least two years I traveled the Earth with the council by means of a Nodian aircar. I acted whenever I could as an interpreter. One of our trips took us to my home village of Tigrillet. I learned that my father and mother were still alive, but that Uncle Kanius had died of natural causes. The Maldecian villa and its outbuildings had been burnt to the ground. Some said that for some unknown reason they were burned down by the Maldecians themselves.

On one occasion we visited the ghost city of Miradol to find it totally empty of human life. On that same trip we flew south to the capital city of the Maldecian governor general, Her-Rood. The place was loaded with krates and many types of surviving off-worlders. One of the off-worlders in residence at Her-Rood's palace was the Nodian ambassador to the Earth, Opatel Cre'ator.

During the first afternoon at the palace the members of our council met with Opatel and briefed him on our accomplishments and future plans. He in turn told us that it had been determined that things were going to turn very bad on Earth. The surviving Maldecians intended to continue to rule the people of Earth, but this was not the worst of what was expected. Nodian scientists were forecasting that Earth was in for some geological calamities, but when in the future was still in question. The meeting ended with Opatel instructing the council to begin making plans to move as many off-worlders and as many Earth people as possible off the planet. He said that arrangements were being made in some other solar systems to receive any and all people who would eventually leave the ill-fated world.

It took years to make the arrangements Opatel spoke of. I myself gathered thousands of Earth people and accompanied them to a sun/star system in the constellation of the Pleiades, where they settled along with thousands of Martians. The planet Mollara (where I am now) is just a bit larger than the Earth and is inhabited by fair-skinned native people about five feet tall. They have always been kind and willing hosts. I visited Mollara eight times, each time transporting thousands of emigrants from the Earth.

Presently descendants of those emigrants and reembodied people from that first lifetime are participating in the study of the diminishing Frequency Barrier. Remember that to many of these people now living on Mollara as well as myself, Earth is really our home planet.

As the movements to take people off Earth were under way, the Nodians kept in close diplomatic contact with the Maldecians who lived on the planet. The Nodians never gave up hope that the Maldecians would in some way mellow out and live in peace with the other races on the planet. But the Maldecians kept up their program to subjugate the other races until that fateful day when the great rains began to fall and the world was constantly shaken by violent earthquakes.

Just before that terrible day, Alfora, Barla and I had gone by aircar in search of my father and mother. We and our aircar pilot (a Sumerian named Asentel) found them living in a small house on the edge of what was once Uncle Kanius' farm. We were happy to be together once again and spent hours telling each other of the experiences we had had during our absence from each other.

After the meal, Alfora brought us menfolk a bag of Gracian cigars she had saved from our time in Mir. Some of the cigars, which she had carried in a cloth pouch, were bent, broken or in powder form. She poured them out onto the table before us. Something caught the light of a nearby candle, and I picked it out of the mound of tobacco. It was a small silver triangle with a double left side, the very piece of jewelry that He Who Casts No Shadow gave Alfora the day the Maldecian krate Serp-Ponder saved us from death and sent us to safety in Pankamerry.

My father lit up one of the cigars and inhaled its smoke as if he had been smoking them all his life. He said, "If I live long enough, I could really learn to enjoy these things." He had just finished his sentence when the Earth beneath us shook with such force that the roof began to collapse. We managed to get outside the house and into the aircar, crowding into the vehicle and sitting on each other's laps.

Asentel took the aircar to about 4000 feet, where it was less turbulent than either above or below. Within a few minutes the car was struck by lightning. The first strike killed our pilot Asentel and the second and third strikes killed the rest of us. The aircar crashed, of course.

Well, there you have some of the highlights of my first lifetime on Earth. I have lived many lifetimes on the planet since then, and I will relate some of them to you in the future if it is your wish.

Jaffer Today

I was born into this present lifetime on the planet Mollara. I presently hold the position of chief counsel of trade for the House of Cre'ator on the planet Simm. I have yet to meet the reembodied Rubdus who, after being finally reborn on his home planet of Simm, grew to manhood and left his home world in the employ of a group of Gracians several years before I arrived here and began my present assignment.

Before ending this communication, I will answer your multiple question, which is, how long ago was the Great Pyramid built or, in other words, how long ago did Maldec explode? The simple answer is 252 million years ago (give or take a few thousand years). Think about this for a moment.

Many readers are ready to accept (or believe without doubt) that they have lived thousands of years before in such places as Atlantis and what is now thought of as ancient Egypt. Consider that those who live today and once lived as Atlanteans and Egyptians have also (in lives previous to those times) animated Frequency Barrier-mutated human life forms known as *Australopithecus afarensis* (dated at 4 to 5 million years ago) and *Australopithecus africanus* (dated at 3.5 to 2.5 million years ago). Then there are the prehistoric forms of Frequency Barrier-mutated humans known as *Homo habilus, Australopithecus robustus* and *Homo erectus.* These latter types of mutated humans are believed to have lived between two million and 300,000 years ago. Early Neanderthal types of humans are believed to have lived about 130,000 years ago.

As long ago as those times might seem, believe me, they are really quite recent when compared to the total time (about 11 billion years) that humans have lived on planets located throughout the universe. A person on the Earth today might say, "I don't want to die. I want to live forever." If not for the presence of the Frequency Barrier, the person with that desire would remember *every life ever lived in the past* and have no memory of those brief periods called death. You see, we *are* living forever, except that the beginning of my forever, and the beginning of the forever of many of those who are reading these words, started about 252 million years ago—or maybe even long before that.

During the great span of time that has passed since that first life of mine, universal humankind has advanced a million times a millionfold, both technically and in understanding the higher levels of the universal life field. I am pleased to say that these things inspire the desires of those who would follow the way of the master plan of the creator of all that is. I am sad to say that those of the dark side of life would (and presently do) use the knowledge and great achievements of humankind to continue their diabolical goal of universal conquest.

I leave you with this: There are no laughing gods who find humor in the sorrows of men. Ignore those who speak for them or pretend to manifest such things. I also find it necessary to say this: Those of the open state of awareness, including myself, are not will-of-the-wisp creatures residing in higher levels of the universal life field, nor do we come from some parallel universe and flit about in time. This is the last amount of precious life force that we will spend in response to such nonsense. Cut us, and we hurt and bleed as you do. Deny us the very same things that support your life, and we will die.

To those who think we have no right to correct their falsehoods and fantasies so that our eyewitness accounts are given a fair chance in the minds of those who seek truth, I warn you, do not make us your enemies, for we have humbled many who would play god. Indeed . . .

I am Jaffer Ben-Rob of Earth (Sarus).

Were you there when the fire of the first star in creation gave forth light, and its creator blessed it with kisses of power? Yes, for at the beginning of time you were one with the creator of all that is, and will be so again. I am Styler of Peckrant.

B efore continuing with my remembrances of past lives I experienced on the Earth, I will speak briefly of my present life. As I related previously, I am presently the chief counsel of trade of the Nodian Trading House of Cre'ator to the people of the planet Simm. My duties are mostly diplomatic, as items of trade move on and off this world about every forty-three Earth years. I head a staff of six: one Vitronian, two Alperians and three Simms. The Vitronian and Alperians are natives of the Sost system, which is the home solar system of the Nodians.

The farther one travels from the Sost system, the less one would find Nodians and other Sost natives established in Nodian trading house or Federation positions. The solar systems closer to the Sost system were, of course, the first to have been visited by the Nodians. Therefore the people of these systems were introduced early to Nodian technology and were also among the very first to be offered Federation membership.

Logically it can be said that there are only so many Nodians to go around, and they can't be physically everywhere at the same time. Presently, non-Nodian trading house Lords of Devisement outnumber Nodians in the same positions by several million to one. Many of the non-Nodian Lords of Devisement based in different parts of the universe have never laid eyes on a physical Nodian.

On their home planet about 80 percent of the Nodians (out of a population of about two billion) are totally engaged in either trading house or Federation activities. Even so, these Nodians represent only about 25 percent of the off-worlders living (based) on Nodia who are likewise occupied.

The trading houses and the Federation rely on a countless number of Lords of Devisement, with all their individual knowledge and resources, to telepathically keep things running as smoothly and diplomatically as is humanly possible. One might compare this system to a mental Internet, only in this case human brains replace computer terminals and information is stored on mental roms, not on what you call CD-ROMs. As you see, the present technology of the Earth is developing naturally in this direction.

My daughter Barla of my first life (and this life as well) lives on the planet Mollara, is married to a man of our race and has three children. Alfora never lost her passion for growing things. She will spend the next four Simm months (about thirty-six Earth days each) in her greenhouses, because a winter of snow and rain at our planetary location will begin very soon.

I will also add that the largest percentage of people in the Federation are ignorant of the fact that the planet Maldec exploded. Most of those who know of this event could not tell you when it shattered or where it once existed. Due to present Federation and dark-side interest in the Earth, more and more people of other worlds are seeking to know all they can about Maldec and Earth. They are especially interested in the new spiritual realities that are manifesting on Earth. I am proud that the highest form of spiritual consciousness has decreed that my home world of Sarus (Earth) will be the place where these new spiritual realities will come into the three-dimensional plane of existence.

I am presently 108 Earth years of age. All other of my lives that occurred prior to my present life took place on the Earth during times when humans and other life forms of the planet were either in a stage of deevolution or reevolution. The lifetime before my present one ended in America in the year 1862 when I was twenty-two years of age.

I can recall numerous primitive lifetimes when I witnessed strange lights traversing the sky and even times when we of limited reasoning thought these things were the flying huts of the gods who created the wind, rain, thunder and lightning. I have never lived during a time when the Frequency Barrier was weak enough to permit humans on the planet to telepathically communicate with each other or with extraterrestrials. In fact, there have been very few golden ages such as those experienced and described by the Martian Lord Sharmarie, Trome of the Sumer radiar and Thaler of the Trake radiar. Other than relating to you (as many others could) how frightening and miserable a primitive life with limited reasoning powers was, I will instead relate to you a few of my Earth lifetimes when I lived in cultures you might recognize, cultures that might be described (accurately to some degree) in the Earth's written historical record.

Being a psychic native of the Earth, there is always a strong possibility that after my next death I might again be born on Earth. If I am reborn on the Earth at some future time, hopefully the Frequency Barrier will be totally gone and those of the dark side of life will have lost interest in the planet's people and resources.

Mosh, of the Iron Age

My mother's name was Delme and mine was Mosh. I never knew or met my father. I was born in about 723 B.C. in the area that is now north-central Poland. My mother birthed me at the age of twelve. She had been orphaned two years before my birth when her parents died of the effects of a very hard winter. Until my mother of that life died at the age of sixteen, both she and I lived with an elderly woman named Merp.

When a single woman of the time died leaving very young children, the children were generally smothered and buried with their mother. Merp prevented me from suffering this fate. I was called Mosh because it was one of the first words I learned to speak, and I said it constantly. In our language, "mosh" meant "eat."

Merp and I survived by tending a small garden and by fishing in a nearby lake. Sometimes fishermen and hunters of our thirty-family village would provide us with fish and rabbits in exchange for our repairing their fishing nets or twisting by hand various materials into yarn and string. Animal skins (furs) were used to keep warm in the winter. We were fortunate to have a one-room log house that had been built by Merp's husband, who died before I was born. His fur coat covered me during the long winter nights and I wore it when I grew big enough.

At the age of eight I was sought after by some of the men of the village who had no sons to help them with their animal traps and fishing and hunting. Merp did not immediately accept their offers to employ me, knowing that when I grew older and larger I could either fend for myself and provide for her as well, or demand more from any would-be employer. Her wise strategy worked; our food supplies increased when some of the men of the village began to use food to influence Merp in their competition for my services. It is humorous to recall that even after I was sufficiently grown and started to hunt and fish on my own, Merp's food basket, which she kept just outside the entrance to our house, was filled from time to time by a passing hunter out of habit.

When I reached the age of fifteen, Merp got very sick and died. I stayed on in the house. I spent most of my free time in the company of the men of the village, talking about hunting and fishing.

One day after returning from a fruitless hunting trip, my three companions and I found the village filled with strangers. They were armed with weapons that I later learned were made of iron. We of the village knew of metal, but could see no practical use for it. Our fish hooks, arrowheads, spearheads and axe heads were made of stone, bone, horn and flint.

The leader of these strangers was called Torge. We all were astonished by the fact that some of the strangers rode on the backs of horses. I had brought down wild horses several times with arrows and later ate them, but I had never thought of capturing one and riding it about.

Moving to Torge's Village

Torge and his men did not speak our language, but after a few hours they were able to convey with hand gestures that they wanted everyone in our village to pack up and come along with them. It took them several days to convince us that we were in some kind of danger and that we should join with them for the sake of mutual defense. Only four families and I agreed to go with Torge. I thought at the time that I could always return if things were not to my liking. Torge and his men were very upset about the fact that they did not get the urgency of their message across to more of us. They muttered to themselves and shook their heads in disappointment.

After a week of traveling north we came to the home of Torge and his people. The place was a fortified town of more than a hundred log houses and buildings. The fortifications (walls) were built of logs. On the inside of the walls were ramps of dirt and stone. The streets of the town were built of logs, the spaces between filled by dirt and stones. Soon after my arrival in Bratel I learned why the streets had been constructed with logs. Torge's people had horse-drawn wagons—it was the first time I had ever seen a wheel, some parts of which were made of iron. Everywhere I looked I saw something made either partially or totally of iron, such as cooking utensils, door hinges and weapons. I estimate that I arrived in Bratel in the fall of the year 707 B.C. when I was about sixteen. I was left to find my own shelter. After walking about the town awhile, I came to an area where several men were working with a forge. It was with these men that I found a place to live and work for many years during that lifetime.

I was first employed digging out and loading iron ore onto wagons, then driving the load back to our forge, where it was smelted and fashioned into all manner of things. Those who worked in iron were paid in housing, food and clothing by Torge and his father Nort, who was considered the head man of the town. Iron and things made of it were considered signs of wealth. We also smelted copper and tin, creating a reasonably good bronze alloy.

I learned that the threat of well-armed invaders from the south was why Torge and his father sought out others to join them to help protect their stronghold. Over time, people from other areas came to Bratel, and it grew to more than 600 houses. Most of these new houses were built outside the town's defensive walls. Relocating the town walls to protect these new dwellings was always in mind, but due to the magnitude of the work and materials necessary, the task was never fully accomplished.

A year after I began working at the forge in Bratel, I took a thirteen-year old wife named Sata. The price I paid her father was one pig, one she-goat, two male dogs, an iron cooking pot (with a handle) and an iron shovel blade. It was one of the best deals I made in that entire lifetime. We had two sons, whom we named Ethbo and Rish.

Arbel, the Visitor Who Told Us about Gold

Torge and his father Nort did a good business in manufacturing and trading copper and bronze items in the form of jewelry and images of animals that were considered to have magical powers. One day a very strange-mannered man who had recently arrived brought to the forge an ore that was heavily speckled with a bright yellow metal. We were able to smelt the metal (which you call gold) out of the ore (elemental gold has a melting point of 1063°C). We called the shining metal *tur*. The man showed us the location where he had found the gold; it was very near our major copper deposit. This man said his name was Arbel and that he was from a land far to the southeast, a refugee from the warfare in his homeland caused by the scattering people and retreating armies that had been warring in the land you now refer as Assyria. That war lasted over a decade before it ended.

From Arbel I learned many things. First, he was part Assyrian on his father's side, but his mother's people came from a land farther south. He called the place "where the world began." I know now that the place is today called Egypt. Arbel said that he recalled his mother's stories of fine buildings and mountains of stone that existed in her parents' place of birth.

Arbel also told us that in his homeland, and in many lands he had heard of, tur (gold) was very valuable, and if a person had enough of it they could wear fine clothes and never have to hunt and fish for themselves again. He also told us that the rulers of some lands wore rings and bracelets of gold and also rings on their heads. He said that some of the head rings were set with colored stones that shine brilliantly in sunlight, stones that were also very valuable to his people. He asked me if I had ever seen any such stones near the town of Bratel. When I told him I had not, he said, "Mosh, some-day you and I should go looking for some. We can take them to my home-land, trade them and wear rings of gold on our heads." Everyone present laughed.

Arbel came by daily, and we sat spellbound at the forge as he related the stories and legends of his people. He told us of a time when the Earth was covered by floodwaters and a man saved his family and all types of animals by placing them in a large boat until the water subsided.

The stories that interested and fascinated me most were of sky gods that had visited his people in the distant past and still occasionally flew about in the sky over his homeland. When he told us that the sky gods flew in large metal houses bigger than than the whole town of Bratel, his listeners became skeptical whether he was telling the truth.

The chief of our group, Ock, after hearing about the flying metal houses of the sky gods, spoke up: "If there are such metal houses that fly through the sky like birds, then they must be made out of male iron." Ock rarely said anything, but when he did, those who worked for him paid close attention. I asked, "How can that be? If you put iron in water, it will sink to the bottom, not float in the air." Ock, looking very wise, said, "There are two kinds of iron. One kind that is female and and another that is male. The male type of iron will move on its own from a distance and attach itself to the female kind of iron. We who work here at the forge work only with female iron. Wait here, and I will go home and get some male iron. You will see that I know and can prove that what I said is true."

Less than twenty minutes later Ock returned with a small goatskin pouch. He emptied the contents of the pouch on the ground before us. There were two pieces of iron that appeared to be stuck together (one of the pieces was magnetized). Each of us took turns trying to pull the two pieces apart. We did, but enjoyed watching them reunite. (Remember, we were a group of men, so we laughed and made sexual comments that we thought were funny.) We got a number of small pieces of female iron and arranged them around the male iron to see if the male piece of iron liked one particular female piece of iron more than the others. At the conclusion of Ock's demonstration we all believed in the existence of Arbel's sky gods and were in total agreement that they flew through the sky in houses made of male iron. Ock told us that he had discovered his piece of male iron many years ago, before he came to live in Bratel. From that time forward, a day did not go by that that someone didn't show up and ask Ock to show them how two pieces of iron made love. Eventually he made Arbel greet the nosy visitors and tell them the story of the iron lovers, and also that the iron lovers were sleeping and would not wake up for many months.

Arbel came to me with a plan to gather up as much refined gold as we could (at least a large wagonload), go to his homeland and live wonderful, carefree lives thereafter. When he included the possibility that we might see or meet the sky gods, I agreed to his plan. We also agreed that we needed lots of gold, a wagon and some horses. We planned to live off the land as we traveled. We knew it could take us quite a long time to prepare for the trip. From that day forward we never stopped talking about the trip, what we would do and how we would live when we got to our destination.

One thing Arbel thought of was to teach both my wife Sata and me how to speak his native language. I surprised Arbel many times by using Assyrian words he had never taught me. I somehow knew these words and their meanings. It was as if I had been speaking Assyrian all of my life.

Every time I talked with anyone about the sky gods, I got very excited. I dreamt of their coming to me and taking me to the land of giant pyramids. In these dreams I climbed the smooth white faces of the pyramids and slid down them again and again into the arms of laughing little black people.

Arbel's fertile mind never stopped its scheming. He introduced the gods of his homeland to the people of Bratel in order to create a new market for idols and magical charms. Anyone wanting one of his winged lions or bulls with the heads of men or women could obtain one for a quantity of gold. My wife Sata made these things out of baked clay and my sons helped her paint them.

Ock thought us to be fools. He was quite familiar with gold and how to smelt it and fashion it into jewelry and such. He learned that in his youth when learning his metallurgy trade in his homeland (which I believe is now called Bulgaria). He admitted that the metal was nice to look at, but useless when compared to iron and bronze. Torge and his father Nort shared Ock's feelings, and in the beginning did not stand in the way of our sideline. Eventually their feelings changed.

Arbel taught a number of the people to pan the streams for gold, using iron pans and shallow clay bowls that he first provided free of charge, then later charged for. As the gold panners became proficient, more and more of the stuff became part of the lives of the people of Bratel, and they began to use it as currency. When it got to a point where a person could trade his neighbor a small amount of gold (in the form of a finger ring) for a heavier item made of iron or bronze, things began to hit the fan, so to speak. Nort and Torge began to get very angry when they realized that their wealth (in the form of iron and bronze) and their business of making items from those materials was becoming devalued and less profitable. To head off total ruin, they forbade Ock from smelting any ore that contained gold. But this did not take it out of circulation. Eventually it dawned on Nort and Torge that it was Arbel and me who had originally instilled the desire for gold over iron in the minds of the townspeople.

One winter afternoon Nort and a sword-carrying Torge came to the forge. Torge shouted at us and waved his sword in the air. I sat in a corner with my head bowed, waiting for a fatal blow. Arbel fell to his knees before them and prayed aloud to his gods. After a period of time Arbel raised his hands and spoke rapidly. His words caused Torge to stop shouting and waving his weapon. Arbel remained in a seated position on the ground and spoke softly to the pair of belligerents, who now appeared to be intently listening to him. Arbel called my name and motioned to me to join the circle.

Arbel Teaches about Levying Taxes

Once again the ways of Arbel's homeland became useful, and in this case saved Arbel and me from being hacked to pieces. He introduced Nort and Torge to the concept of taxes. He simply pointed out that everyone and just about everything grown or made could be taxed as it was in his homeland. He also pointed out that in order to make iron once again more valuable than gold, a person could pay their taxes in refined iron of a particular weight, or in gold twice the weight of the iron. This procedure would eventually dry up the limited supply of gold in circulation and any amount yet to be found in the surrounding streams.

In order to force the people to pay the taxes, they would be told that a failure to do so would result in being driven out of town and into the countryside to perish. Wintertime was the best time to tell the townspeople about taxes and the penalty for not paying them.

Arbel convinced Nort and Torge that once all of the gold was out of circulation and in the treasury, he and I would pack the worthless metal on a wagon and take it far away to a place where it would never again be a problem to them. Nort and Torge were wise men of that time, but not (as you would say) rocket scientists. They were certainly no mental match for Arbel. They were desperate, so they agreed to put Arbel and me in charge of collecting taxes from the people of Bratel. By the force of arms we eventually collected tribute for them from villages located over a hundred miles from their growing capital. I never went with Arbel into the countryside on his raids. Arbel, the dreamer of great grandeur, became ruthless and deadly in his quest for gold.

Within about six years nearly all of the gold that had been found in over 8000 square miles around the town of Bratel was in the treasury of Nort and Torge. During this period Nort died, and Torge acquired a taste for gold and items made of it. Arbel saw his plan to take the gold we collected to his homeland fade into dust.

Torge had a widowed sister named Olma, who had a son named Retvo. Both Olma and Retvo lived with Torge and his wife Carma. The latter pair had never had children who lived to puberty. Retvo grew up in the care of Arbel and accompanied him on many of his military campaigns and tax-collecting missions. One morning the word went about town that Torge had died in the night and that Retvo was now the headman of the town.

Departing with the Gold

Three days later Arbel, my family and I supervised the loading of three large wagons (about 12 feet long) with about 75 percent of the gold from the town's treasury. Each of these wagons was drawn by six horses. Three more wagons pulled by two horses each carried food and other necessities. Arbel planned our departure well, for it was summer and we did not have to contend with mud. We estimated that it would take us between two and three and a half years to reach Arbel's homeland. With us went fifteen men (guards) along with their wives and numerous children.

Traveling south, we came to the village of my birth. It had been burned to the ground by Arbel's tax collectors several years before. It was then that I realized how many people had suffered and died to fill our three wagons with gold. We had to avoid villages where Arbel's troops had visited in the past so that the surviving villagers would not take revenge on our small band.

For more than a year during our journey we were plagued by three invisible archers who would fire three arrows at a time at our group when we were moving or camped out. These attacks could occur daily or could be spaced as many as four days apart. Sometimes one of our group, horses or other livestock would be killed or wounded by the arrows from nowhere.

We soon learned to eat or burn our dead livestock so our enemies could not eat their carcasses. Many times we went into the forests to seek out and confront the phantoms, but we never found the slightest trace of them.

The horses were at times strung out in a single file on narrow trails. This sometimes caused the ropes that pulled the wagons to rub on their flanks, causing sores that eventually crippled them. Eventually we harnessed ourselves to the wagons. We kept our eyes open for wild horses to replace those we had lost due to hardship or arrows. Failing to capture any, Arbel eventually suggested that we raid villages for horses and supplies and take human captives as slaves. This we did, to my shame, and our wagons of gold moved onward to the southeast. After our ranks increased in number, the mysterious arrows concentrated their aim on the remaining horses, livestock and those of us they had been stalking for months.

Suddenly the attacks temporarily ceased for about six weeks. Our adversaries had moved far ahead of us to dig and conceal pits in the trail and prepare rock slides they could set loose on us whenever we were in a vulnerable position. The rock slides were indiscriminate and killed many of those we had enslaved. My youngest son Rish was killed by tumbling rocks. My wife was emotionally devastated and disappeared from the group along with my oldest son Ethbo. Arbel attempted to console me by saying that my share of the gold would buy me a thousand wives in his homeland. I did not take his attempt to console me well at all. The scouts that we sent out to look for pits and other dangers usually never returned. No one wanted to take on the job of scouting.

When we came to a river we learned to explore the area to determine if we were actually crossing the river, or ignorantly situating ourselves between two forks, which of course meant that we had to cross the river twice. At rivers we had to unload the wagons and carry the gold across on our backs. This led to the decision to pack the horses and slaves with the gold and abandon the wagons. To make this plan work, we needed more horses and/or slaves. When winter arrived we built several log shelters. We had no food for the horses, so we ate them first and then we ate the slaves. In the following spring there were five of us left alive (all men). We slept apart and well-armed, for very obvious reasons.

Arbel's Death and My Return Home

One bright spring morning we were sitting on our small mountain of gold when an arrow came out of nowhere and into Arbel's throat, killing him instantly. Two additional burning shafts set the roofs of our dwellings aflame. From the forest came the cry, "Tenny, for Tenny." This cry was followed by laughter. One of the voices was definitely a woman's.

The remaining four of us separated and went our own way. I started out for the town from which our trip of horror began, the town of Bratel. We left the hill of gold behind. I reached Bratel in the fall of the following year. I found my wife Sata and son Ethbo living with her sister's family. The ruler of Bratel was still Retvo, who was the only person who felt badly when hearing of Arbel's death. Retvo was also dying of some unknown ailment.

My wife was happy to see me and related the story of her trip back to Bratel. Two days after leaving our-ill fated group she and my son met the three phantom archers, who were an elderly husband, wife and son. The son's wife, Tenny, had been killed during one of Arbel's tax-collecting raids. They acted solely out of revenge. The next part of her story was amazing to me, but her very presence in Bratel supported her account very well.

After they separated from the archers, they traveled north, looking for the familiar landmarks we had passed during the trip south. One night as they slept, someone came to them silently and woke them by nudging her with a foot. She awoke to see a giant of a man standing over her. She said the man spoke Assyrian and told her not to fear him. He told her and my son to be patient and wait with him for a short while. She told me that the stranger wore something that covered his head and face, and on occasion in the region of his obscured face a small ring of light would pulse blue and then purple for a second or two. About twenty minutes later a bright, star-like object appeared in the sky. This object descended and landed in the nearby woods. It momentarily produced a light as bright as day, which diminished gradually until it was only a soft glow. The next thing she remembered was waking up about a quarter of a mile from Bratel. Both she and our son were wearing new shoes and colorful new clothes of a very fine weave. We were both convinced that she and my son had met Arbel's sky gods, who had brought them back to the home of her childhood.

Ock welcomed me back to work at the forge and over the years that passed got me to tell him about our trip south with the three wagons of gold. At one point I overcame my shame and told him of the cannibalism. He asked me if we ate Arbel. When I told him that we had not, he said, "Good; his flesh would have poisoned your bodies as his words poisoned your mind."

A fire broke out among the houses outside the original town fortifications. It was summer, and many of us went to aid those whose homes were burning. I entered a house that was not yet totally engulfed in flames to help a woman remove some of her belongings. A taller structure next to the house collapsed and fell onto the house I was in. The impact caused an idol of an Assyrian god to fall from a shelf and hit me on the head. I fell to the ground in a daze. Everyone thought I had gotten out of the house before it too went up in flames. As I laid there bleeding heavily and trying to breathe, I noticed that the idol that had struck me was made of gold and represented the Assyrian god of fire. I didn't even try to shout for help. I died of smoke inhalation. I was about thirty-five years old.

Nisor of Moor

Behind the veil of chaos there is yet another
and another of its kind. Be sincere and do not
falsely flatter or curse the divine, and I can then
assure you that once in every lifetime you will be
offered an opportunity to know all there is to know
to bring you spiritual peace. If you are restless in the
garb of a pilgrim (as are most of our kind), I say, be
patient and wait, for it is prophesied: The great mysteries will be revealed to all on that day when the high
priest of Ra will come forth at noon and shout, "Come all,
learn and know, for Isis is unveiled."
I am Benagabra of Delment.

I am Nisor of Moor, Lord of Devisement 862 of the Trading House of
Magail (a division of the Nodian Trading House of Domphey). My
home world of Moor is the ninth planet of the sun/star we call Ee,
which has no radiar systems. After several changes in course, a trip from
my home star system to the star system in which you live would take about
12.3 Earth days by the most up-to-date space-traveling vehicle.

I was selected to relate my first-life experiences and events of several
lifetimes that I have spent on Earth in the past because I was one of the first
emissaries from the Trading House of Domphey to visit the planet Venus
(Wayda). I was one of those who spoke to Churmay and her townsfolk on
the shores of Lake Samm so many years ago. I was also among those who
were employed after the destruction of Maldec to relocate those of Wayda
(Venus) to Earth.

During my first life I also spent a period of time with a number of
Gracian engineers who, with the help of laborers from the planetoid Parn

(of the Relt Radiar), built the five-sided pyramid and carved the immense stone face at the place you call Cydonia, located on the planet you call Mars. Later that same lifetime after the destruction of Maldec, I got stranded on Earth and worked for the Maldecian governor Her-Rood until I fell into his disfavor. As things transpired, I left the Earth several times in Nodian craft, and on my last return to the planet became stranded and remained there until my death.

The Fatal Pollution of Moor

I was the fifth son of eight born to my father Tramesent and mother Ticaree. We of our world practice clan marriage. That is, every male and female of the clan are considered married to each other, but sexual relationships are determined by age groups. Women do not mate for the first time until at least six of the oldest women of the clan give permission. The young woman would then be free to choose her first mate from any of the males of the clan who were in her age group. Thereafter, monogamous relationships for life can be established by a male or female if so desired. The mating arrangements are a little more complicated than I have described, but one might say that initially things are controlled by go-betweens or matchmakers. Mating outside the clan is forbidden.

We practiced several forms of religion that were generally based on prayers to our departed ancestors, when we requested that they speak on our behalf to the spiritual authorities we believed created our world and the universe as well.

About forty-five Earth years prior to the beginning of my first lifetime, Moor was devastated by continuous warfare. The multiple conflicts were caused by a long-lasting, worldwide drought brought about by industrial pollution of the world's atmosphere. The condition spurred multiple military actions to obtain water. Lack of enough water for crops and livestock resulted in famine and the death of hundreds of millions of people. Defoliation was occurring at an alarming rate. The world was littered with ruined buildings and war machines. The wars had stopped because no one had the energy to fight, and population control was strictly enforced. The population of Moor eventually diminished to about 200,000. The available water, from subterranean sources, was located in only four areas, and each could support only about 50,000 people. It was realized at the time that even the meager supply of water was running out and that total extinction of all forms of life on Moor would occur in less than fifteen Earth years.

What was left of my clan (the Shrives) lived at one of the water sources located in the southern hemisphere of the world. At the time of which I speak, my father was about eight Earth years old and my mother about five.

The Off-World Rescue Operation

My father related to me that one day just before dawn he and his family were startled by a number of very loud explosions. It was first thought that war had again broken out. In the distance could be seen billowing clouds of what first appeared to be white smoke. It was speculated that a forgotten underground ammunition depot had exploded. The columns of smoke continued rising into the sky throughout that day and the days that followed.

On the fourteenth day there was an unexpected light rainfall. It was brief, and there was no time to capture much of the rainwater before it evaporated. Within the next fifteen days it rained three more times. Each time, the rain became progressively heavier and lasted longer. The underground reservoir rose about one-fourth inch. The columns of smoke now appeared to be solid shafts that were spinning on their vertical axes at very high speeds.

A walking expedition was sent to the location of the phenomenon. The group reported back by two-way radio that the shafts looked like transparent smokestacks that radiated out of a black glass dome. The dome had a diameter of approximately 1500 feet and was about 150 feet high at its center. No one dared to approach it, so members of the expedition simply observed it for one more day and night, then happily returned home, washed clean by a two-hour rainfall.

Theories and rumors spread rapidly throughout the population about what the dome was and who was responsible for its presence. The most prevalent theory was that the dome was the product of divine intervention and was filled with the spirits of our ancestors. This theory was revised when the city was buzzed by a slow-flying airplane of a type you could describe as a World War I biplane. It was painted with black, red and white stripes. It flew in circles and even performed some aerobatics before departing. The people were totally bewildered.

Some days later a large disk-shaped aircraft, painted in the same manner as the biplane, flew silently about, showering the landscape with what later proved to be a variety of seeds. The rain that fell later tasted different and the people felt as if they had more physical vitality. The barren plains began to sprout grass, grain and flowers.

Once-dry streambeds again began to act as water channels, carrying water to depressions that grew into ponds and eventually lakes. The insects were the first forms of animal life to resurrect from their various states of naturally induced suspended animation.

On the day that the shafts of smoke disappeared, a group of our people who were camped about the dome praying to our ancestors witnessed the dome change from black to transparent, thus permitting them to see into its interior. The dome was occupied by many different types of strangely dressed men and women who ranged in height from four to eight feet. The average height of a male of Moor is about seven feet four inches. None of the strangers appeared to be a Moorian, either living or dead.

One of several of the strangers who seemed to walk right through the solid walls of the dome called to the crowd in their native language, using an electronic means of amplification (the dome was actually an energy field and not really solid). He assured them that they had nothing to fear and invited them to come into the dome. During the period when the hesitant crowd looked for someone brave enough to accept the stranger's invitation, they were entertained by Moorian folk music interrupted occasionally by a repetition of the invitation.

Two elderly women (Fogtra and Ermtay) walked heroically into the dome and into the Moorian history books as the first of our race to personally make contact with people from other worlds.

The group of strangers was made up of more than thirty different types of different extraterrestrial races. It was also learned that their recent activities on the planet Moor were sponsored by a syndicate of commercial trading houses from the planet Nodia. The Sost solar system in which the planet Nodia exists is identifiable as a star of medium brightness when compared to the other stars that can be seen in the night skies of my home world (even combined with the light of the Ampt radiar, which is also a part of the Sost system).

The leader of the off-worlders was a man named Rig-Nastbin, whose father and mother were, respectively, Nodian and Vitronian.

Remember that at this time the trading houses of Cre'ator, Vonner and Domphey were yet to be formed and the Federation was not yet in existence. The Prime Directive was not in force at the time.

The real purpose the off-worlders had for coming to Moor and restoring the planet to livable conditions did not become clear until many years later. No Moorian really cared; they were too grateful to be saved from certain death to have questioned their saviors. Fortunately, the motives of the off-worlders were benign.

The Time of Restoration

The period that immediately followed the arrival of the off-worlders was called the Time of Restoration. People from other worlds of the Ee system began to visit Moor, such as the highly spiritual Belps, who came from the smaller second planet of the system. They brought the knowledge of the universal life field and the worship of the elohim. For hundreds of Earth years thereafter, the people of Moor were a minority on their own world.

Each of the existing clans of Moor were given exclusive control of an industry that the off-worlders helped them start. Anytime another industry could be formed by two or more of the original industries, the clans who made the new commercial entity possible shared equally in its profits. Off-worlders could work for a Moorian clan, but had no ownership in any Moorian commercial enterprises. As the population of Moor grew, the number of off-worlders decreased, sent back to their respective home worlds by the dictates of the Federation (after the organization was founded). Today Moorians definitely outnumber the off-worlders who presently live on Moor. Any off-worlders living on Moor today are officials of either the Federation or the Domphey trading house.

Gradually the newly formed House of Domphey took over the various off-worlder activities and made contracts with the various clans for surplus products. In exchange Domphey provided the expertise and very advanced technology to rebuild the cities of the planet. Old cities were not restored, but left to crumble. New, well-planned towns and villages were built for thousands and grew over time to accommodate millions, as they do today.

I was born about twenty years after the beginning of the period of restoration. The Shrive clan (to which I belonged) controlled all forms of ground and water transportation. Atmospheric air transport remained under the control of Domphey for about twenty Earth years before the industry was equally divided among all the clans. The trading house wanted to be sure that no ill feelings existed between any of the clans because of the earlier wars. They did not want to see any clan bent on revenge dropping bombs on any other clan. When the trading house divided the aircraft production and air-transport industries among the clans, it did so in such a way that either one was able to shut the other's industry down by nonproduction or noncooperation.

When I was fourteen years old the House of Domphey informed the clans that they would accept qualified men and women of our race to be trained to travel in space and initially contact races of other worlds on behalf of the trading organization. The elected directors of my clan arranged for several males and females of my age group to be tested. I passed the written examination and waited for nearly a Moorian year (about 409 Earth days of about 28 Earth hours each) before I learned that I had been hired by the House of Domphey. My employment had one condition: that I be married to a female of my own race and that she accompany me so that we could be trained as a team.

It took the directors of the clan quite some time to find a young woman who would accept me as a mate. Finally, a girl who had also passed the

Domphey test and faced the same problem of finding a mate reluctantly agreed to become my wife. In the beginning we couldn't stand each other, but later fell deeply in love after we spent considerable time supporting each other emotionally as we journeyed into an unknown future. Three Earth weeks or so after Ivatcala agreed to be my mate, we dressed in light gray uniforms that were provided and walked up a ramp with six other couples into a Domphey spacecraft. Each recruit carried a personal suitcase. As I remember it, Ivatcala ran ahead of us all in order to claim the honor of being the first of us to go aboard, leaving me to carry both my suitcase and hers.

Leaving Moor for Vass and an Education

The starship lifted slowly at first, giving us a view of our world from a vantage point we had never had before. In an instant Moor was a bright spot about the size of the head of a pin and the sun of our system went from the size of a walnut to that of a small speck of light that disappeared among the millions of stars that filled our field of view. Suddenly the stars disappeared and we found ourselves peering into an endless black void. In the first few minutes we felt frightened, then very, very lonely. Ivatcala gripped my hand tightly and the fingernails of her other hand penetrated the sleeve of my tunic and dug deep into my forearm. Just as suddenly, the space around the craft was once again filled with stars. Twenty minutes or so later the craft assumed an orbit about a planet and remained in orbit for more than thirty revolutions, each taking about two hours. It had taken about forty Earth minutes from the point of departure to the time the craft arrived and began its orbit.

We were ushered from the small lounge by a fellow Moorian man we had never met before. He brought us before a tall, thin woman who had no hair on her head. She wore a plain dark green gown belted with gold birds that had brilliant green gemstones for eyes. The woman's name was Fan. As she spoke, she did so with her eyes closed, yet she pointed her head in the direction of each of us and welcomed us individually by name. She always prefaced a person's name by first stating their race, for example: "Moorian man Nisor, Moorian woman Ivatcala."

I noticed that Fan had but four fingers on each hand. On all of her fingers were rings studded with large, brilliant gems. We had never seen such stones before and their brilliance was breathtaking. After she welcomed us she asked if we were ready for a surprise. No one answered. She placed her jeweled hands in front of her eyes and slowly lowered them, revealing that the color of her eyes was a vivid yellow. We of Moor had blue, green, brown, gray or black eyes—in fact, on our world one's eye and hair color could be used to identify a person's clan. Fan told us that she would be our instructor. Later she told us that she came from a world called Ath. The star system in which Ath existed she called the Mel system. We learned later that Fan was considered a very important person by the directors of the House of Domphey, as was her daughter Frate, who at that time held the position of the Eighth Lord of Devisement for the trading house.

Fan was an exceptional telepath. We of Moor knew that the ability to telepathically communicate always existed in us, but we were never able to practice the art with any real success. During the Time of Restoration on Moor it was quite frustrating to witness many types of off-worlders tele-pathically communicating with each other and with people on different worlds located far away in the universe. When Fan finished with us, we of Moor were considered among the best telepaths in the Trading House of Domphey. That first-life's training as a telepath has served me well in many lifetimes and still does during this present life. (How am I doing?)

The planet we arrived at after our first space flight from Moor was called Vass by its native people. It was a very highly developed world compared to Moor either before the world wars or at the point of restoration reached by then.

The high development of Vass was totally due to its people's ingenuity and respect for each other and to the greater spiritual forces that existed in the universe. They were, then and now, fantastic at solving many a complex problem that might arise pertaining to any subject. Carlus Domphey rec-ognized a good ally when he came across one, such as those of the planet Vass.

Upon landing on Vass we were informed that we would be housed in a complex of buildings where we would also be taught our future profes-sions. We were surprised to learn that Lord Domphey and his wife Arita also lived there and not on their home world of Nodia. (It was not so sur-prising after we learned that Nodia was only about a three-hour space flight from Vass.)

We learned much about making first-time contact with people of another world. Worlds that showed some form of economic promise were isolated from lists of thousands of worlds not so promising. The worlds were on the contact lists because they were accessible from a Domphey planetary base of operation. There were only about eighteen such bases in existence in that first lifetime. Today the number of these bases is astro-nomical. There are more than ten million Domphey bases of operation in this galaxy alone, and just as many or more in about 250 million additional galaxies. *[Nisor was amused by my attempt to comprehend the vastness of the present Domphey economic system and added the following. —W.H.B.]* I did not want to overwhelm you as I did, but there are just as many of these bases of operation managed by the trading houses of Cre'ator, Vonner and millions of other trading houses whose names would not be recognizable.

It was the location of my home world of Moor and the fact that it would make a good base of economic operations that caused the off-world traders to make the effort to restore the planet to livable conditions. The early visitors (those who made first contact with my people) were referred to as second-phasers. Several years of first-phase covert studies of our race preceded their arrival. The second-phasers were not part of the House of Domphey, but independent contractors who specialized in such operations, which at times were very dangerous and in some cases fatal.

In order to eliminate the middle man and speed up second-phase operations, the trading-house directors decided to train their own teams of second-phasers. Ivatcala and I were among the first of many to be trained by the House of Domphey to deal with second-phase contact situations and problems.

Ivatcala and I were housed in one of several four-room apartments located above a number of classrooms, laboratories and an auditorium. Beneath these facilities were numerous chambers and rom study cubicles. All of us trainees ate in a common dining room similar to an Earth restaurant.

Three days after our arrival on Vass we boarded an aircar with Fan at its controls. After a short flight we landed on the lawn of a house composed of three white domes. Two of the domes were of equal size and the third dome, about a hundred feet in diameter, was about twice as large as the smaller two.

Meeting the Dompheys

When we stepped out of the aircar onto the lawn, the grass under our feet, though natural, felt like sponge rubber. One of the smaller domes split in two and separated, revealing a plush interior of fine furnishings. Fan had previously informed us of our invitation to the home of Carlus Domphey and had instructed us to be on our best behavior. Fan liked to surprise us, but in this case decided it was best to let us know what to expect.

Two Nodian men could be seen sitting on a large couch that had a view through the transparent dome. Beyond the dome were several plant-covered terraces, below which was a large swimming pool in which about thirty children splashed about. They were overseen by three beautiful Nodian women and a number of equally beautiful women of our host world of Vass. The Nodian men were laughing as they watched the children at play.

When we came within ten feet, they turned toward us, smiling. The only one who spoke our language, with a heavy accent, was Carlus Domphey, founder and First Lord of Devisement for the House of Domphey. He looked us over and said, "Nisor, let me look at your sleeve."

He took my arm and ran his forefinger over the three small holes that Ivatcala's fingernails had made when our spacecraft had passed between the solar lenses and we had the frightening experience of looking into the endless void. He asked me to remove my tunic and give it to the other Nodian, who was quietly standing beside him. The second man was later identified as Treno Domphey, a brother of the First Lord. Treno produced an object that looked like an icepick and stabbed the tunic several times. After examination, no holes could be found in it except those made by Ivatcala's fingernails.

Lord Domphey shook his head and addressed Ivatcala after rendering her a deep bow of respect. "Young woman, the only way those holes could have been made by your fingernails was if the act were accompanied by an emission of macro-level vril energy that you obtained from the realm of the elohim. You are a very exceptional person. If you wish, I will bring to you those who might be of service in assisting you in further developing your ability to perceive into those higher levels of the universal life field. I will not do this to employ you and your most holy ability, for you are worth more wealth than I have or will have if I live a thousand years." He bowed once again. He then smiled broadly and said, "Let's go swimming."

As we were about to leave the area, I turned to watch Treno Domphey once again try to produce punctures in my tunic. When he saw me watching, he laughed and threw the garment high in the air over his back. We left the room by stairs that led below the dome to an area where we donned what you would call bathing trunks. These items were provided for our Moorian modesty; Nodians normally swam in the nude.

During the remainder of the afternoon (about five Earth hours) we were given lessons, after it was realized that none of us had ever learned to swim. Lord Domphey swam circles around us and frolicked with the children. He reluctantly left us when two Nodian women appeared on the upper terrace and began to descend toward the pool. They were the ladies Domphey and Cre'ator, the latter being the wife of Lord Domphey's friendly competitor, Rayatis Cre'ator. The Nodian beauties stopped on one of the terraces and never came to poolside. With them was a tall, bronze-complexioned man with coal-black hair who carried a red-headed Nodian toddler. He came to the side of the pool and threw the naked child into the water. As she flew through the air she had time to scream, "I'm going to tell my mommeeeee."

Sharmarie [the narrator of chapter 1], the red-leather-skirted giant, once satisfied that the child had come to the surface and was swimming about like a fish, turned and walked away. The Nodian water sprite called to him, "Sharmarie, where are you going?" He replied, "To get you a big rock to hold onto." Later he entered the pool and conducted swimming races for the children. As the sun set, the Martian sat on the lowest of the terraces, cradling the sleeping little Nodian in his arms. A Nodian nurse took the child from him, after which a Nodian man who had been patiently waiting handed Sharmarie his sandals, blouse and a deadly pair of silver pistols, which he belted across his chest. He and the Nodian man followed the nurse and child to the uppermost terrace and then disappeared into the dome.

We ate a delicious meal of seafood and returned home in an aircar, singing as we flew, and bathed in the light of the twin moons of Vass.

Ivatcala was visited by what we first thought were the strangest people in the universe. Some came and went without saying a word. Others studied my wife with respectful awe. Ivatcala eventually became annoyed with her countless visitors and told Fan that she did not want to meet any more of them. Fan requested that she meet with only one more, so Ivatcala reluctantly agreed. One evening after a day of classes we entered our apartment to find a little man in a tattered and dirty black robe sitting on the floor. From a cord around his neck hung a gourd with the numbers 63-92 painted crudely on its side. The stranger asked us not to speak. He looked at my wife and said, "Wait, holy one, until you are much older and have gained greater wisdom before you seek to understand the mysteries of the elohim. You will know it is time when at a time in silence you first hear the sound of a crystal bell and then the strum of a harp replacing the sound of thunder after a flash of lightning."

He then requested three drinking goblets, which he filled from his gourd with a liquid that looked like melted gold. The drink tasted like peach brandy. He placed his gourd on a table and uttered a prayer in a language Ivatcala and I did not understand. He disappeared, and we noticed that he had left his gourd behind. Then the soft, disembodied voice of 63-92 came to our ears from every direction, "I forgot my gourd." The gourd seemed to melt like ice into a rising vapor that vanished before our eyes. We were astonished, as we had never witnessed anything so magical before (and rarely did in any lifetimes that followed).

After training to use telepathy and learning everything we could about second-phasing, we designed plans based on data provided by fictitious first-phasers concerning a number of imagined cultures. We played out numerous scenarios in which we did our best to respond to sudden emergencies.

After our training period, which took about two Earth years, we bade farewell to Fan, who was visibly proud of us as we boarded a small starship departing for the planet Nodia. Fan's final words were, "Don't try to second-phase the Nodians' children."

We had a brief stay on Nodia. Venturing outside our living area in the Domphey complex was hectic. Everyone seemed to be living on the edge and under the strain of some extreme urgency. The peacefulness of Vass was sorely missed. There were many areas on the planet that were controlled by other trading houses and that we were not allowed to enter. People from other worlds outnumbered the Nodians by about 150 to 1. The average Nodian disliked the fact that their personal lives were constantly disrupted by the presence of so many off-worlders with lifestyles and customs that were in some cases outrageous. The native Nodian had little good to say about the trading houses or anyone such as we who worked for them. But that was then. Today I would rather visit Nodia than any other world I know.

After a trip to the planetoid of Vitron, which orbited the Ampt radiar, which in turn circled the sun/star Sost, we boarded a spacecraft headed for the sun/star system that contained four giant radiars and four inner planets presently called Venus, Earth, Mars and Maldec.

A Visit to Wayda

Our precise destination was the single moon of the planet Wayda (Venus). We were responding to a radio-transmitted invitation received about eleven Earth years earlier. We expected no trouble from the inhabitants of the Waydian moon, but to avoid intimidating the culture, we landed in a small craft and were dressed in native clothing of designs provided by first-phasers. One of our ten-member team was able to speak and write the language of the culture. Two others were familiar with the language of those who lived on the planet Wayda itself.

The population of the Waydian moon was less than 100,000. They survived by vegetable farming. They transported themselves by electrically powered cars and they had telephones. The same technology did not exist on the planet this moon orbited. Wayda had been chosen as a world on which to establish a Domphey base of economic operations. Furthermore, it was known that the planet's rich soil would produce surplus grain in abundance.

We were received warmly by the people of the Waydian moon and we offered to take a few of them with us when we landed on Wayda itself. Those who were to go with us were selected by lottery.

We used the same approach when we landed on Wayda near the

world's capital city of Ansomore. We did not immediately disembark from our craft, but waited inside until we were discovered.

One afternoon a brave Waydian walked up to our vehicle and knocked on its hatch. We looked at each other with amusement, and our Nodian leader Morris said, "Well, I think it's time we meet the Waydians." The first to leave the ship were two men we had brought from the Waydian moon, who looked exactly like the natives of the larger world, but they did not speak the language of the Waydian herdsman who knocked on the hatch. Knowing this, we had taught our confederates how to say, "Hello, don't be afraid. Wait, we have someone who can speak your language." Our interpreter spoke to the herdsman from inside the craft and prepared the Waydian with the fact that we might look strange to him at first.

When we came out of the vehicle, the Waydian herdsman showed no sign of fear or concern. In fact, he treated us as if he had known us all his life. He offered to help us in any way he could. He told us that he could not leave his animals and suggested that we take a nearby path that led to his home. He told us to tell his three wives that he had sent us and that one of them should accompany us into the city of Ansomore. We said good-bye and he promised to look after our spacecraft. When we left him he was looking at his reflection in the polished silver hull of the vehicle.

The wives of the herdsman were no more emotionally moved by us than their husband had been. We waited as one of his wives, Gretrama, changed clothes and brushed her hair. During this time we were offered food and drink by the other ladies of the household. We were also offered toys and various forms of livestock by the family's children. Our chief of protocol advised us to accept at least one gift from the children. We chose a fowl similar to an Earth chicken. I think the children were pleased that we chose the chicken instead of one of their toys. I carried the restless bird several miles before I let it escape in the streets of Ansomore.

Many of the Waydians we passed on the street asked Gretrama who we were. She answered them with the statement, "They are visitors from another world." Those who had asked usually said, "Really?" or "I thought so."

The low humming sound of Waydians telling other Waydians who we were followed us as we walked toward the center of the city. If one of us turned to look back at the crowd, they stopped walking, fell silent and began to brush their hair or the hair of a person standing close by. Three times my chicken was returned to me. After the third time we kept the bird as a mascot. Morris named the rooster Bralph after one of his male relatives.

In much earlier times the city of Ansomore was a fortress surrounded by a wall, but it had long since grown beyond its original boundaries. We were met at the gate to the inner city by a man driving a four-wheeled cart drawn by four animals similar to Earth horses, only these creature had long lop-ears. We were invited to get into the cart, which we did. The silent driver delivered us to a large building. We were met formally by two elderly and dignified Waydians.

We were then escorted to a large auditorium that was gradually filling up with Waydians of both sexes. We were seated on one of two small stages that were the wings of a larger and higher stage. On the large stage sat two Waydian men and one very young woman.

The young woman called out the name of the person who mounted the opposite stage and asked us only one question. We spent hours answering questions—many times the question asked was the same as one that was asked before. Finally the Grand Council of Wayda welcomed us to their world and vowed to assist us in any way they could.

We were asked to not begin any unauthorized activities on their planet until all of the people of the world were notified of our arrival and what we wanted to do while in residence. The notification period took about three Earth months. We spent the time familiarizing ourselves with the ways of the Waydians and responding to their childlike interest in our various electronic devices. We spent some time ferrying Grand Council members back and forth to the planet's moon, which they called Oote. We also telepathically ordered a number of gifts for the Waydians from the House of Domphey. Thirteen Earth days after we made our request, the Domphey mothership Lamuma ("the great mother") took up orbit about the planet Wayda.

I had never seen a spacecraft of this size before. It had a diameter of about 1500 feet and a vertical height of about 400 feet. I learned later that this was a small craft compared to thousands of others that were then being operated by the Nodian trading houses. We of the second-phase team were permitted aboard the Lamuma and remained there until we received permission to travel about Wayda and visit the inhabitants of the world's many towns and villages. We were joined by some third-phasers—historians and psychologists who studied the culture's reaction to our presence and the impact of our technology on the individual lives of those of various occupations and religions.

During the time we were aboard the Lamuma, the mothership was approached on occasion by triangular spacecraft. We eventually learned that these were Gracian craft based on the planets Maldec and Mars. After their curiosity was satisfied, the Gracians went about their business.

I was called away from my duties of visiting Waydian towns and villages and was sent with the Nodian Cyper-Dale to the planet Mars to look into Gracian building activities known to be under way at the time. Rumors had also reached Nodia that the Gracians and Maldecians were going to build something of considerable size on the planet called Sarus (Earth). Sarus was of no real interest to Domphey because the House of Cre'ator had been first to send emissaries to Sarus and Maldec.

Mars was another story. None of the Nodian trading houses had any reason to subject their people to the hostile attitudes of the numerous Martian warlords. One of my prime reasons for traveling to Mars was to find out what the Maldecians and Gracians did to gain the cooperation of the warlords.

Before departing Wayda for Mars, I recalled Sharmarie, the bodyguard of Lady Cre'ator on that sunny day at Lord Domphey's swimming pool on Vass. I thought, *If the Martians are all like Sharmarie, what is there to worry about?*

I had no idea at the time that Sharmarie had been taken from his home world many years before the spacecraft of the Gracians, Maldecians and other off-world cultures began to visit the planet in an uncontrolled manner—which was totally against the wishes of its natives. Sharmarie was a rare person. He was more Nodian in his ways than Martian. I know now that during his first lifetime Sharmarie never returned to Mars and perished on the Earth.

On the Planet Mars

Cyper-Dale and six other people plus myself were deposited on a grassy plain on the planet Mars. We were about three miles from the Gracian/Maldecian building site. The building site was and presently is called Graniss by the Martians; you know it now as Cydonia. We stood for some time in silence as the craft that had brought us disappeared above a thick layer of clouds.

We covered our nearly one ton of supplies and set up several portable shelters. We also assembled two boats that we would use to travel on the nearby waterway to come and go from Graniss. We spent a cold, windy night. In the morning we carried our electric-powered boat to the banks of the waterway and launched them. We ate packaged prepared food as we proceeded southwest. A few minutes into our trip we heard a number of Martian women shouting at us and motioning to us to come ashore. We waved back at them and continued on our way.

I had just mentioned to Cyper-Dale that I was curious why the Martians didn't use these fine waterways to travel from place to place. Just then I heard a whistling sound and two thuds. The thuds were made when one

Martian arrow went through the muscle of my upper left arm and a second arrow went nearly through Cyper-Dale's left shoulder. On the left bank of the waterway stood five Martian archers, who were about to loose their arrows again in our direction. We yelled to them and those of us who could raised their arms as a sign of surrender. They lowered their bows and motioned us ashore. They grabbed each of us and threw us violently to the ground. One warrior went to a then-unconscious Cyper-Dale and quickly pulled the arrow from his body. The Martian then proceeded to wash the blood from the shaft in the waterway. Another of the warriors looked for a moment at the arrow in my arm and then into my eyes. He broke the arrowhead from the shaft and pulled the arrow out of my arm. I confess I almost fainted from the pain. The Martians kicked us a few times and yelled at us for a time. They were really mad.

The sound of a braying camel alerted me that there were nine animals being held by three more Martian warriors. After their hands were bound behind them with leather thongs, those of our party who could walk were herded along by two of our camel-riding captors.

The two of us who had been wounded were placed in our boats and pulled along behind. The boats first slid easily on the grass, but when we came to the end of the grass and started to cross a section of sand and rock, the material the boats were made of could not withstand the abrasion. Soon the boat bottoms were in shreds. We hung onto the surviving metal ribs of the boats whenever the Martians took a notion to gallop. They found it hilariously funny to see us bounce along behind.

About two hours after our capture we again came to grass and eventually to the banks of another waterway. Then we saw something unexpected. Stretched across the waterway was a metal bridge, a paved road from it on our side leading to large stone platform. On the platform rested a silver triangular-shaped spaceship. On its hull was the image of a feathered serpent, which we learned later was the emblem of the Gracians.

Beside the platform were several houses built of sandstone blocks. We could see three people at a distance sitting around a table in front of one of the houses. The Martians arrived at the place at full gallop.

The three people were Gracian, two men and one woman. They paid us little attention at first because they were occupied at repairing some device. One of the men looked up from his work and greeted our captors in the Martian language. After dismounting, the Martians assembled between us and the Gracians. We could hear them talking, but could not understand what they were saying.

The Gracian woman came to us and momentarily studied me. She then spoke to me telepathically, "They think you are part of of our building group. They are angry because it is forbidden to swim or cross a waterway by boat." She then asked me, "Who are you people and what are you doing here?"

I answered her questions. She looked at my wounded arm, then looked at Cyper-Dale, who was still unconscious and sweating heavily. She called to the Gracian men in her native tongue and they acknowledged her with a wave, followed by the universal signal for, "Wait a minute, will you?"

After the Martians were given several large boxes of Gracian cigars and had their pictures taken holding their giant broadswords over our heads (to show their warlord they had done their job), they galloped off, still dragging our boats behind them.

The two Gracian men brought portable cots to us and lifted Cyper-Dale onto one of them. The others of our group, realizing that they were now free, came to me to see what they could do and get instructions. One of the Gracian men telepathically told me, "While you are here and in our care, only I give instructions and orders. Accept this, or I'll give you back to the Martians." I agreed that he was the boss. For all I cared at the time, he could be supreme ruler of the world if he wanted.

The Gracian woman cleaned our wounds and treated them with sound waves. She and one of the men served us bowls of hot Martian lamb stew (I can still taste the chili pepper).

As night fell we were provided with a device that radiated heat. A lean-to type of shelter was erected over us. After dark the area was lit by lights mounted under and on the edges of the Gracian spacecraft. Just after dark two aircars landed and several people got out of them and went into the houses.

By dawn Cyper-Dale was awake and able to talk. I opened the flap door on the lean-to to see more than twenty Gracians facing the risen sun and chanting a prayer in unison. Afterward a Gracian man we had not met before came to our lean-to. He spoke to Cyper-Dale and me telepathically. He asked us if we were up to going with him to the building site. Cyper-Dale did not feel well enough, but I accepted the Gracian's offer. He told us not to tell any Martians about the telepathic ability we shared, because they would believe the ability was unnatural and probably cut off our heads so they could look inside for whatever made it possible. He advised us to learn the Gracian and Martian spoken language as soon as we could.

We left for the building site by aircar, leaving Cyper-Dale and the rest of my group behind. The flight took only about ten minutes. From the air I noticed that the paved road from the bridge did not go to the site, but ran on for miles across the flat grassland, then up into a distant mountain range where it vanished from sight. The Gracian, who was named Soakee-Loom, told me that the road was built by his people at the request of the local Martian warlord Trohawker. The road ended in the mountains at a small sandstone house where the warlord had been born.

Sight-Seeing at Graniss (Cydonia)

The Martian town of Graniss was as old as the Martian civilization. It was the only town that was not situated where waterways joined. No one could truthfully tell you who founded the town or when. Graniss was neutral territory, so the warlords would occasionally assemble there to discuss things, make bargains and exchange prisoners.

Graniss was the capital of the warlord of all warlords, who was called the zone-rex. A Martian zone-rex gained his position after being recognized as divinely selected. That is, he had the unique physical characteristics that were described in very ancient documents. To truly be the zone-rex, each of the numerous warlords had to swear him allegiance. The present zone-rex, a man in his twenties named Rancer-Carr, had not obtained the allegiance of every bar-rex (warlord). He therefore could do little about the deal the warlords had made with the Gracians and their partners, the Maldecians. I, of course, still wondered what the deal was.

Graniss was filled with Martian shepherds and soldiers who walked about, each followed by as many as seven wives and an army of children. These visitors were allowed to enter Graniss only by special permit, and then limited to a three-day stay. On the edge of town stood about 80 gigantic, hard sandstone obelisks on which were inscribed the history and deeds of the past 80 zone-rexes.

My first view of Graniss was comical. Among the crowds of Martians were numerous little black people from the Relt planetoids. At first I thought the Martians were doing a strange dance, but I soon realized that in order to pass a Reltian, the Martians would sometimes swing one of their legs over the little person or spread both of their legs and shuffle over the smaller person's head. Martian children who tried to copy their parents' actions would sometimes kick a Reltian in the head or back. I witnessed many a wrestling match between a Reltian and a Martian youngster. The child's parents would either continue about their business or stop to see how the match would turn out. Most of the time the Reltian would get enough and run off. The victor would then yell a war cry that would have curdled fresh milk and make the obelisks of the zone-rexes shake on their foundations. On the edge of the town was a walled complex in which lived the zone-rex. *[This walled area at Cydonia was photographed by NASA's Viking space vehicle and is referred to today as the Citadel of Cydonia. — W.H.B.]*

The building site was dusty because the Gracians and Reltians were leveling the area before beginning actual construction. They were using the same methods to level the Cydonian plain that were used at the Giza Plateau on Earth. (These methods were described by Ruke of Parn in chapter 5.) Soakee-Loom provided me with a mask for protection from the dust. I found it hard to breathe the nitrogen-rich air of Mars (nitrogen on Mars then had a different chemical value than that found on Earth today). I, like you, was originally born an oxygen breather. By the end of the day I was covered with dust. Along with the dried blood from my wound staining my clothes, I must have been a sight to behold!

I spent that night in a newly built one-room sandstone house at the base of one of the walls of the Citadel. Just before going to sleep I heard a noise on the roof. I thought it might be raining and that I might wash off some of the dust in the rain. I was disappointed to learn that the sound I thought was rain was actually caused by a number of Martians who were standing on the wall of the Citadel urinating onto the roof of my house.

By morning my quarters were covered with all manner of garbage and human waste. Soakee-Loom had the place demolished. I moved to a small cave that had Martian pictures and writing on its walls.

Several days later the dust settled and was vacuumed up. On that day the zone-rex, Rancer-Carr, came out of his sanctuary along with two giant bodyguards. They rode about the area on camels. Martians fell to the ground before him and warlords drew their swords and stuck them in the ground. Those who stood as he passed were those who did not recognize his divine authority, and those who knelt with their hands on the hilt of their weapons accepted him as their supreme commander.

When the zone-rex came to us, he reined up his mount, and after forcing the beast to kneel, got off and walked rapidly toward us. He had a serious look on his face, but spoke softly. Soakee-Loom interpreted his words for me, which in essence were: "What are you S.O.B.s up to today? Who is this man? I've never seen anyone like him before. Is he a Nodian?" Soakee-Loom saluted the chief warlord by crossing his arms across his chest. He answered Rancer-Carr's last question by telling him that I was not a Nodian, but was employed by a Nodian trading house. Hearing that, the zone-rex asked, "Vonner, Domphey, Cre'ator?" I replied, "Domphey." He then motioned me to follow him to his camel. I rode behind him back to the Citadel.

The interior of the place was plainly furnished. The furniture and floors were covered by sheepskins and brightly colored blankets. Colorful wool rugs covered the floors. The walls were covered with murals and broken, rusting swords. We were joined by an old Martian man named Mogent who had a sparse knowledge of the Nodian language. He tapped himself on the chest several times and said, "Vonner words. Vonner words." That night the zone-rex, Mogent and I dined on beans, lamb, cheese and a hard bread. My hosts drank more than a gallon each of a native beer they called drat. I could not stand the smell of it.

Through Mogent I figured out that the zone-rex wanted me to telepathically contact the Nodian Rayatis Cre'ator on his behalf, asking him to send a representative for talks. When I suggested that he might want to talk to a Domphey emissary, he replied, "No, I think only Cre'ator has the mind to deal with the Maldecians." When I asked him, "Who are these Maldecians?—I've never seen one," both the zone-rex and his interpreter hissed like a snake.

We were joined later by a number of young Martian women. The zone-rex left Mogent and me with the ladies and departed with his one and only wife, Saara. Saara was a quiet black-haired woman of great beauty. She carried in her arms their only child, a boy named Sharmack. Later they had a daughter they named Catransa.

Mogent told me that I could have my pick of any of the Martian women. I told him that I was mated to Ivatcala for life. He first looked bewildered, then said, "Take one of these women and pretend she is your wife. The elohim will not mind, and that is all that matters." I told Mogent of our meeting with 62-93, who had told Ivatcala she would someday be able to communicate with the els. Mogent thought again for a moment and said sadly, "You'd better leave, for the great spirits might tell your mate if you do otherwise. Wizards are too costly to have them remove your deeds from the memories of the elohim." I had no idea what he was talking about. Soakee-Loom advised me to keep clear of the Martian zone-rex, for it was rumored that some of the warlords were planning to assassinate him. He said, "I warn you to keep clear. You already know what a Martian arrow in your body feels like."

I attempted several times to send a telepathic message to the House of Domphey so they could pass on the zone-rex's request for a visit from a Cre'ator representative. I never was able to make contact. I know now it was due to the Martian air and food.

The warlords did attempt their coup, but it was the last thing they ever did in that life. The strongholds of the late defeated warlords were divided up among the bar-rexes who supported Rancer-Carr and he was proclaimed supreme ruler of the entire planet. He holds this position at this present time.

Cyper-Dale did visit the Gracian building site several times in the company of Tricklelemla, who had been a Gracian nurse. He and the Gracian lady had fallen in love and she was already with child.

The Gracians and Reltians had begun to carve the giant face at Cydonia using laser-type measuring and outlining instruments. The sculpting was actually accomplished by using specific sound waves to pulverize the rock and produce the individual features that later composed the entire form.

I learned that the Maldecians had secretly promised to each warlord who had opposed Rancer-Carr an armed aircraft whereby he could alone take total control of the planet. What was strange to me at the time was that each warlord secretly knew his own motive for agreeing to allow the Gracians and Maldecians to build their structures near Graniss—but why weren't any of them suspicious that the other warlords agreed so easily? I now know that each was given an exclusive Maldecian-scripted cover story. I regret that I never got to hear any of those stories.

Thirteen Earth months after I arrived on Mars a small black spacecraft marked with the symbol of the Trading House of Cre'ator landed by the Citadel home and headquarters of the Martian zone- rex. I knew immediately that he had found another telepath to send his request to Rayatis Cre'ator.

The Cre'ator craft remained there for several days. I kept an eye on it and eventually spotted two Nodians walking around it on a preflight inspection tour. They seemed to be worried about the craft's operational condition. I told them who I was and about the others in my group. I asked them to take us with them when they left the planet. They told us that they would, but that we all would be tightly crowded in such a small craft. I was so grateful that I would have volunteered to ride on the outside of the vehicle. As an afterthought, I asked one of the Nodians where we were going. He pointed to a large sphere that hung in the Martian sky, replying, "We're going there. To Sarus (Earth)."

Later they flew us to the place we had been taken many months before by our Martian captors. There we picked up the others of my group. Cyper-Dale decided to remain behind with his Gracian mate Tricklelemla. He was doubly fortunate in having found such a lovely mate and avoided the terrible events that occurred later on Earth.

Crashing on Earth

During the last half of the trip from Mars to Earth, the small craft's cabin filled with smoke and its rad atmosphere began to turn toxic. We managed to land on Earth just before the craft melted. The Nodian chief operator of the craft and I were the only survivors. Because I was a natural oxygen breather, the rich, oxygen-laden atmosphere of Earth saved my life. Sivmer-Binen, the craft's operator, coughed and vomited for days, but finally survived the ordeal. He never stopped saying, "I *told* them that thing was a worthless piece of junk!" *[a very mild English translation —W.H.B.]*. There were no dead bodies to take care of—they had been carbonized when the plasma-containment tube burst and spewed the superhot material into the vehicle's cabin.

Sivmer-Binen and I spent several days hunting for evidence of civilization. We stumbled onto a footpath that led into a thick jungle. We had no choice but to take the path. He estimated that we had crash-landed about 400 miles south of his intended landing site. As we walked I asked him if the meetings with the Martian zone-rex went well. He didn't know, because he had not been present at any of the meetings. He said that the only one who knew was his fellow Nodian, Neftener-Lype, who had perished when our spacecraft disintegrated.

We slept beside the path and were awakened in the morning by the voices of two men coming down the path in the same direction we had come. When they saw us they hastily put arrows in their bows. I thought, "Oh no, not again!" The older of the two lowered his weapon and pushed the other man's bow toward the ground. They were Earthmen, and I realized that I had yet one more language to learn. I was totally dumbfounded by their words. The younger of the two men had red hair and his face was covered with freckles. The bearded older man had white hair. They both wore knee-high boots, cloth pants with leather knees and rump patches and leather shirts.

We followed them for about half an hour, finally arriving at a house that had some upper parts (rooms) built upon the limbs of gigantic trees. We entered the house at its lowest level. The walls of the first room were covered with shelves of books. Lanterns were everywhere. The old man called out and we were soon joined by several elderly women and men. The oldest man was Brike Ben-Demus. The others of the household were his brothers and sisters. The red-headed youth was a grandson. We stayed several days with Brike Ben-Demus and his family. I tried to learn their language. Sivmer-Binen made no effort to do so, saying that he didn't think he'd be on Earth long enough to use the language and didn't want to fill his head with worthless information. (About five months later he was speaking the language like a native.)

Brike and his family had spent their long lives mining emeralds. Some of the upper levels of their home contained millions of the gems in both their natural state and cut and polished. These Earth people were considered very wealthy. One small emerald would feed and clothe them all for over a year.

Meeting Our First Maldecians

We were eating an evening meal when we heard a short trumpet blast. Brike opened the door to admit three tall blonde men wearing blue velvet cloaks. Quietly they scanned the room and its contents with emotionless eyes. One left, closing the door behind him. The other two stood at attention, one on each side of the entrance. When the door opened again, two women and a turbaned Earthman came in. The women, striking in appearance, refused Brike's invitation to sit down. One of Brike's sisters whispered in my ear, "Maldecians." I answered her, "So *this* is what they look like."

Brike left the room, returning with a small chest of his finest emeralds. He placed one at a time into the cupped hands of the turbaned Earthman, who then knelt before the women and held out his hands so the women could view the gem. Each stone they wanted was placed in another chest they had brought along. Those they rejected were placed on the floor at Brike's feet.

As if startled, one of the women looked up at me, her eyes first showing hate, then curiosity. She touched her companion's arm and nodded in my direction. Then they looked at each other and smiled.

Sivmer-Binen began to rise from his seat. In a flash the krates at the door were standing in front of the women with daggers drawn. I had never seen anyone move that fast. Sivmer-Binen slowly sat down. In very poor Nodian the Earthman who came with the Maldecians said to Sivmer-Binen, "Your presence, Nodian, offends my ladies. Sivmer-Binen said, "So what?" The krates began to rhythmically sway on the balls of their feet. You could have heard the sound of a feather falling. Without another word said, the room was filled with krates. Sivmer-Binen and I were bound by metal handcuffs and dragged to one of three very large aircars, each larger than the spacecraft that had brought us to Earth.

Our traveling companions were about thirty-five krates. During the flight one of them began to sing. His voice and the melody of his song was beautiful. Their leader, without saying a word, handed my fellow captive and me each a piece of fruit (I think they were peaches).

After landing, we were marching into a short tunnel that went through a hill and emerged on a platform. Below us was a building lit by hundreds of floodlights. A soft spotlight that fell on us signaled our krate guards to descend the stairs and approach the building. That same spotlight was afterward shone on Sivmer-Binen and me every day and night we spent there. If we became separated by a short distance, the light expanded to encompass both of us. If we were farther apart, it separated and became two spotlights. We never could determine where the source(s) of these lights were. Our handcuffs were removed and we were given a room to sleep in. We were allowed to roam free in some areas, where we saw others who were constantly bathed in their own spotlights. If we tried to converse with them, our lights would become an intense blue and we could no longer hear or see each other. Even gestures to each other was, as you say, a no-no. We learned eventually that we were being held in a Maldecian maximum-security prison. I can say this, though—the food was very good. We were incarcerated for about three weeks.

One late afternoon a krate led us to a large empty room. On the far side of the chamber was a familiar face. It was Brike Ben-Demus, the elderly gemstone dealer. With him was a Maldecian wearing the a uniform of a very high-ranking krate. Brike smiled and patted us on our backs. The Maldecian greeted us in perfect Nodian and announced that his name was Sant. He said, "Consider yourselves fortunate that you have made an important friend such as Brike Ben-Demus."

The only thing Maldecian about Prince Sant was his physical appearance and the fact that he flicked the tip of his tongue on his upper lip whenever he listened to something he thought was important. He told us that he was the only one of his race who had ever visited the planet Nodia, and he planned to go there again as the guest of his Nodian friend Opatel Cre'ator. He said we would be released from our prison into his care if we agreed to several conditions. These were that we live at the palace of Her-Rood, the Maldecian governor of Earth, and answer truthfully any questions we might be asked about any subject and that we would not try to leave Earth until at least fifty days after the last question they asked us. When we agreed to Sant's terms, he raised his hand and our spotlights disappeared.

Later Sivmer-Binen said, "I hope they want the design of that piece of junk we used to get here from Mars. I intend to praise that design and encourage them to build a fleet of thousands. The elohim work in mysterious ways. I know they gave me the idea."

Living at Her-Rood's palace was definitely pure luxury. Even so, we counted the days after the last Maldecian question. Many times in the more than two years we lived there we would count as many as forty-nine days before one of the bastards would ask us another question—such as, "What is your mother's name?" We were on a count of forty days since the last Maldecian question when the planet Maldec blew up. Then we were forgotten in the confusion.

We spent the remaining six days keeping a very low profile. We shouted for joy on the morning of the fifty-first day. The next problem we had was finding a way to get away from Earth and back to our life pursuits. We were to elated to be able to plan for our departure, but in truth had no idea how to begin such a plan.

We were the only people in the palace who had smiles on our faces or occasionally laughed, so our lack of remorse for the destruction of Maldec was easily detected. Her-Rood himself ordered our execution. He was advised that killing us might not set well with the Nodian ambassador, Opatel Cre'ator, who had recently arrived and was a guest of Prince Sant. Her-Rood rescinded his order and decided to turn us over to Opatel Cre'ator who, he was certain, would punish us harshly for not being emotionally devastated. Sivmer-Binen, with a twinkle in his eye, essentially said (as one might say on the Earth today), "Oh, please, most Radiant One, don't throw me into that briar patch."

Saved by Lord Cre'ator

We met with Lord Cre'ator, and Sivmer-Binen informed him that he had been a spacecraft operator for his brother's trading house. Opatel told him that he was glad to have him back and that his abilities would be sorely needed in the future. As for me, he promised that he would arrange to restore me to the care of the House of Domphey as soon as possible. But for the time being I should consider myself in the service of the House of Cre'ator. I agreed.

The day after our first meeting we flew over the Gracian construction site of Miradol (Teotihuacan). In the aircar with Sivmer-Binen and me were Opatel Cre'ator and the Maldecian, Sant. A Maldecian krate was at the craft's controls. As we flew low over the city we could see the thousands of dead bodies of those who had been slaughtered by the krates. We spotted a krate sitting on the lower step of the pyramid now called the Pyramid of the Moon. We landed near him. When we approached, the young man attempted to rise and extend his arm in a salute to Prince Sant. The wounded krate could not rise to his feet. Sant saluted the krate, who first nodded, then placed his hands over his eyes. Sant then went to him and cut his throat. He held the boy down with his foot until his body quit quivering. He threw the dagger away. Opatel said to Sant, "How could you do such a thing?" Sant replied, "He didn't want to live scarred and crippled." Opatel said, "I'm not talking about what you just did. I know of your ways. I'm asking you how your people could do this," sweeping his arm around him. Sant did not answer him verbally, but I saw tears running down both their faces.

The stench of the Miradol dead was overwhelming. Before leaving the base of the Pyramid of the Moon I took one last look at the body of the young krate. He had died smiling.

When we were again in the air, Opatel said, "I wish we had the means to totally burn and bury this place." Much later this was done [see "Additional Information" at the end of this chapter].

Sant dropped us beside Opatel Cre'ator's personal spacecraft. The two men stared at each other in silence for about five minutes before Sant entered his aircar and flew off to the south. About fourteen hours later aboard the Nodian craft, we arrived on the planet Wayda. The world was in ruins and its people were sad and confused.

Wayda In Ruins

During that first night on Wayda I spoke telepathically to my mate Ivatcala, who was on Nodia. It was the first time I had spoken to her for about six Earth years. Touching her loving psychic essence once again helped to restore my depleted spirit. She said she would make every effort to join me.

Then I contacted what was left of the Domphey third-phasers and was informed that help was on the way. I said good-bye to my long-time Nodian companion, Sivmer-Binen, who handed me a handwritten note in my native language that said, "Take care, Nisor of Moor, and may the elohim protect you." It was signed by Opatel Cre'ator.

When the small fleet of seven Domphey cargo ships arrived, they were commanded by my friend Morris, who had taken our second-phase team to Wayda on our initial visit. With him were a number of Sumerians (Saturnians) and Trakians (Neptunians). I had never met people of these races before, but I liked them immediately. When the last cargo ship landed, the last two passengers to debark were Fan and my wife Ivatcala. Fan put lvatcala's hand in mine and addressed us in her usual fashion before saying, "Take care of each other, children." She turned and reentered the spacecraft. We never saw her again during that lifetime.

During the weeks that passed, both Ivatcala and I worked at arranging transportation for hundreds of thousands of Waydians to, of all places, planet Earth. Each trip we made to Earth was worse than the one before. Watching those bewildered and frightened people carrying their children and personal belongings and leaving our care and security was terrible. After the portal of the craft was closed, we cried. They usually milled about the craft like lost children, until they had to be warned away for their own safety.

lvatcala and I escorted many loads of Waydians and Sumerians to Earth from their home worlds. The Sumerians were much better equipped emotionally to deal with the environmental and man-made conditions on the planet Earth. I know that they helped the Waydians survive in every way possible.

Ivatcala and I spent some time learning what the newly formed Federation was all about and how the House of Domphey related to it. The cities and towns of Earth in the days thereafter began to overflow with every type of off-worlder. I joined the group consisting of the Nodians Tasper-Kane and Abdonel, the Sumerian Trome [narrator of chapter 2] and Jaffer Ben-Rob of Earth [narrator of chapter 6]. Later we were joined by a Martian woman of high station known as Leeva. We attempted in every way we could to bring about an alliance between the various groups of off-worlders transplanted onto Earth. The one thing we tried to do was get everyone to accept one common language. Sumerian was chosen because there were more Sumerians on Earth than any other type of off-worlder. We hoped that their larger numbers meant more teachers. The Sumerians also had a greater ability than the others to understand Nodian technology. The Waydians had the same degree of ability but, sadly, their numbers decreased rapidly. As for the Martians, after we gave a piece of equipment to a Sumerian or Waydian, it was common for us to say, "Here, take care of this thing and don't let any Martians touch it or come near it."

The End

Both Ivatcala and I had an opportunity to leave Earth and go to a planetoid of the Trake [Neptune] radiar. Because we were very tired, we decided to remain behind on Earth and avoid the process of converting from oxygen to rad air and then to nitrogen. One day we were sitting on a bench in the front of our small house in what you call central Iraq when there was a flash of lightning. I never heard the clap of thunder that should naturally have followed the lightning flash. Ivatcala suddenly touched my arm softly and looked into my eyes. She spoke in low tones and said, "Dear one, I heard the bell and the strum of a harp. I now hear the words of the elohim. They tell me we are about to die, but that we should not fear the events to come, for all will be well in a future time."

I instantly believed her. We went into a dreamlike state and walked and danced in the wind and rain that came, laughing as we were knocked off our feet. At times we were airborne and imagined ourselves to be birds. We felt no pain when we we fell violently back to the ground. After one final collision with the surface, my life of that time ended.

I will tell you of several more lifetimes I lived on the Earth. Some of these times (but not all) should be somewhat familiar to you and to those who will read your words.

Gra Moy (Bear's Eye)

I estimate the time to have been about 5.8 million Earth years ago. I was born in the spring in the land that would be a part of the place now called Tennessee. My people lived in villages, and called themselves the Prenpossas (meaning "walking trees"). We were directed more than ruled by an elderly man named Harn Sloves (Dry Shoes). I was given the name Gra Moy because I was born in a cave that had been recently vacated by a hibernating she-bear, who returned to the cave's entrance to watch my mother give birth. Throughout my mother's labor she and the bear maintained eye contact. Therefore I was called Bear's Eye. My mother had sought refuge in the cave while my father, Meko Larm (Turtle's Shadow), ran some distance to our village to bring back his mother to assist mine.

The land of Tennessee in those days was mountainous and totally covered by forests. Our religion was the same as that of all primitive races of humans who ever lived on the Earth (or on any other world, for that matter). We worshiped anything that either frightened us or might help us avoid physical hardship.

Our village was located near a river, no longer in existence, on which we moved about in dugout canoes. The people I am describing were not, and did not look like, American Indians. We could have been described as very tall (males were about seven feet tall) black-skinned Japanese. We did weaving, pottery-making and metalworking in copper and iron. We also had crossbows, and during my infancy someone invented matches. There were times when there were small confrontations with other tribes, but actual all-out war was nonexistent.

We did not know it, but we were people of a period that would later be known as one of the golden ages. A "golden age" was a temporary condition during which the Frequency Barrier did not prevent some of the humans of Earth from using abilities that might today be called extrasensory.

With every golden age other-worlders came to Earth. The visitors were of two types. One type came in the hope that the Frequency Barrier was on a progressive path to extinction and wanted to help the planet and its people return to the open state of reality. The second type came with the same hope that the Frequency Barrier was ending, but wanted to gain control of the world before the planet's inhabitants became mentally capable of resistance.

Children such as I began to exhibit abilities that astonished our elders. Some of us were able to immediately locate game, reducing the time usually spent hunting. One girl of our village could call fish out of the water. Many children had visions and dreams that confused them at first, but later brought them wisdom and inventiveness. Some of the oldest people of our tribe were frightened of us and called us the ferts (monsters).

My generation established a tribe within a tribe. We shared our thoughts and what we first believed were fantastic dreams, later realizing they were memories of lifetimes we had lived on other planets and Earth. We found that the children of nearby tribes were also having the same experiences, so we united with them and formed our own community. Most of us brought with us our parents and less fortunate siblings because our parents were being blamed for producing us. In a very short time our village had electricity and plumbing.

We were certain that we would soon be visited by people from other worlds, and we were right. I recall one summer night in the light of a nearly full moon when the community was alerted to a sound similar to that of bees swarming. Looking up, we saw a large, triangular-shaped spacecraft hanging motionlessly in the light of the moon. After about fifteen minutes it flew away. The community had mixed emotions. The fact that the craft was triangular made some of us, including myself, very uneasy. We didn't know why at the time.

Several days later we awoke to find that we could not travel more than a hundred yards outside our town. We had been encapsulated in a restraining force field. Our electrical generating system stopped working. I was greatly troubled by something that nagged me deep within. Every effort we made to penetrate the force field failed, and we eventually resigned ourselves to waiting to see what would happen next.

We were later subjected to an odorless transparent gas that caused us to fall into a deep sleep. When we recovered, the force field was gone. Some of us eventually remembered being taken aboard the triangular craft and physically examined and injected with various colored fluids. Those who did this were light-skinned people shorter than we were. They had bright red hair and six-fingered hands, even though their leader was tall and blonde. I have learned since that the redheads were of a race known as Nivers, and their leader was undoubtedly a Maldecian.

Within a period of about 80 years after Maldec had exploded, the Maldecians got the message that Earth was going to hell. In spacecraft of Gracian and Nodian designs, of which they somehow obtained a large number, they left the Earth for different places in the galaxy. I'm sure it didn't take them long to wear out their welcome. But sadly, for the most part they succeeded in subjecting numerous solar systems to their rule and infected numerous cultures with their diabolical philosophy of life. We are still dealing with the results of their first contacts with other cultures.

It was more than twelve years before we ever saw another extraterrestrial spacecraft, and by then many of my generation were mated and had children. One evening another triangular craft appeared over our town, then two more. Suddenly they split up and took off in different directions. It was dusk and Wayda (Venus) was bright in the sky. We observed several brilliant flashes of light in several different locations in the sky. Several minutes after the last flash, a black disk came and hovered over our community. This craft landed and eight more hovered in the sky above. The craft were marked with a silver triangle, which I now know is the emblem of the Federation.

They remained in the same positions until dawn. The landed craft joined those that were hovering, and its landing spot was soon reoccupied by a black craft that had several vertical sky-blue stripes. Three men wearing transparent helmets emerged and walked toward us, motioning for someone to approach them. One of our people walked forward and they somehow conversed for about an hour. The extraterrestrials returned to their vehicle and took off straight up, along with their hovering companions.

The man of our town who had talked to them told us that the three people called themselves Sumerians and that others in the black disks were of several different off-world races. They told him they opposed those who had kidnapped us years before and that they had destroyed one of the three triangular craft hovering over our homes the previous evening. The visitors told us that we could expect to see both types of craft in times to come and that we should make every effort to avoid people from the triangular craft. They left after saying that they would return and talk to us again whenever it was possible.

In the many years that passed we saw numerous extraterrestrial craft of both types, but had no physical contact with their operators. Their flights over our village were frequent and became quite commonplace. When I was about 60 years old, I heard that some number of my generation and their children from another community were taken away and relocated by the extraterrestrials who flew in the black disks. This was just one of the many stories that circulated in those days.

Before my death by pneumonia at the age of 73, some of the younger people of our community had established telepathic communication with those of the Federation. Before I died I learned once again about the destruction of Maldec and what the Frequency Barrier was. As I lay on my deathbed delirious, I asked Branya, my wife of more than fifty years, if she heard a bell and the strum of a harp. She said, "No, I don't hear anything but thunder in the distance." These were the last words I heard in that lifetime.

Cronopius the Slave

I was born in the year that the cities of Pompeii and Herculaneum were partially destroyed by a great earthquake. The year was either A.D. 61 or 62. It was about two years after I was born that Nero burnt Rome to the ground. I was born to a slave girl named Melcenta. She was one of several slave girls that her master (later mine) Filbrius rented by the night to travelers who stayed at his inn and tavern.

Filbrius' tavern was located on a road about fifteen miles or so north of the thriving Italian city of Pompeii. Filbrius named me Cronopius in honor of a Roman gladiator he once saw fight in the arena at Pompeii many years before. He would often recount every slash and cut that he claimed he had seen. Others present remembered that the fight had taken less than ten minutes, but Filbrius' version of the battle took over an hour. Filbrius was quite a sports fan. He was really upset when a traveler from the north told him that my namesake had met his match and was killed in the Roman arena a few months before. I think Filbrius sacrificed a duck to the gods so that they would give Cronopius a fair shake in the afterlife.

My early years were spent brushing and feeding horses of those travelers rich enough to own them. I liked chariots and admired those who bravely sped about in them. Other than the fact that I was told what to do and got whacked quite a bit by Filbrius, I really didn't know that I was a slave.

One day a Greek named Criltrenos came to the inn and never left. He never ran out of money. He spent his time drinking, wenching, drawing and sculpting. Few men could equal him at any of those things. He eventually bought a piece of land across from the inn and built on it a very nice two-story house. After the building was finished, he went to Rome and returned with several fine horses and an old Greek woman who he said was his Aunt Dimathra.

Aunt Dimathra seemed to know more about my mother's profession than all the girls in the place combined. She would sit in the inn for hours drinking gallons of wine while advising and mothering Filbrius' girls. She took a liking to me and one day commented that I looked like a Greek. Filbrius said, "He could be part Greek." Dimathra offered to buy me on the spot, but my master refused to sell. Dimathra was like a dog after a bone. Every week or so her offering price increased a mite. I know now that Filbrius had other plans for me. Dimathra aggravated Filbrius, but he didn't want to lose her patronage or that of her wealthy nephew, so he usually smiled and waved off her offers.

He did give in enough to let the old Greek hire me to tend her menagerie of dogs, cats and assorted barnyard fowl. This arrangement was made after Criltrenos agreed to send me someday down the road to Pompeii and pay for my training as a wrestler. Filbrius liked the idea, because wrestlers were seldom killed during a match. He began to dream of owning a champion that could make him a lot of money.

I learned that Dimathra had two religions. She was secretly a Christian (not very much liked in those days), but openly worshiped the Egyptian god Osiris. She said that she came to believe that the gods of her people and those of Rome were nonexistent.

I was also fascinated by the fact that both Criltrenos and Dimathra could read. Once, in a drunken stupor, she tried to teach me to read Greek. It was a futile attempt on both our parts. I admit I didn't understand a thing—it was still all Greek to me! Just the same, during my association with Dimathra I learned to speak Greek quite well.

A year or so after I began to work for her, she bought two young slave girls from Rome. Criltrenos was disgruntled about her buying the girls. I think he thought two slave girls was one too many. I learned then that Dimathra was just as independently wealthy as her nephew. When I was twelve or thirteen she arranged my first sexual experience with one of her maids, Remisa. The buxom lass from northern Italy nearly killed me.

Criltrenos and Filbrius formed a partnership to manufacture and sell colorful mosaic titles to the artisans of Pompeii, Herculaneum and eventually Rome. Criltrenos supplied the technical know-how and built the required kilns. **Filbrius** supplied the labor. Soon the slave children of the household became **the** total labor force of the tile industry, because our mothers were constantly being called away to attend to their other duties.

I was selected with three others of my kind to load and drive the ox-drawn cart to Pompeii. Criltrenos and Filbrius always went with us. Filbrius wanted to be sure he was getting his share of the profits from the sale of the tiles. I know that Criltrenos was already rich enough and would never have cheated Filbrius.

Filbrius was always torn between watching Criltrenos making deals for the tiles and watching us to prevent me and my fellow slaves from running away. We had no intention of escaping. Where would we go? Besides, we believed, as every other slave child of the time believed, that the countryside was filled with wild animals that would kill and eat us. To ease his mind, Filbrius began to tie us together on a common rope around our necks, which he would then tie to some immovable object. Criltrenos thought this was ridiculous, and at times would give us several skins of wine just to watch Filbrius trying to herd with a string of drunken slave boys.

In the year A.D. 78 I was about seventeen years old. I was taken by Criltrenos and Filbrius to the southern part of the city of Pompeii to the Forum, which contained a temple, theater, concert hall, gladiator barracks and a wrestling school. The director of the school told Filbrius to take me home and feed me more, then bring me back in a year. Filbrius was not happy to hear this. He bought a very expensive scroll that contained illustrated wrestling holds and decided to train me himself.

During the year that followed I was either eating, lifting or throwing somebody around. My fellow slave boys were black and blue from head to toe.

Filbrius was continually having me demonstrate wrestling holds to his customers. He would challenge anyone of my size and weight to wrestle me. If my opponent looked puny, Filbrius would wager money. If my adversary appeared to have the slightest chance of winning, Filbrius would wager only a small amount of wine. I truly don't remember ever losing any of those matches. I did lose a few to Dimathra's maid (slave) Remisa. (But you can't really call our matches true Greco-Roman wrestling, because in that form of wrestling you're not allowed to use your feet and legs.)

The Eruption of Vesuvius

One evening in the year A.D. 79 the inn was shaken by three earthquakes spaced about forty-five minutes apart. The last quake caused the building to start to crumble. We of the household ran into the road, where we were joined by Criltrenos and Dimathra and her slaves. In the south the sky was glowing a bright red.

Criltrenos told us that we would all leave immediately and go north. He hastily told us that he had read that mountains such as Vesuvius (near Pompeii) sometimes belched fire, and that melted rock and hot ashes could kill everything around for miles. We left Filbrius sitting in the road looking south, still trying to make up his mind to leave or stay.

The road north went along the coast. The ocean had just come into view when Vesuvius erupted. The shock wave that followed knocked many of us off our feet. The air became hot and we could hardly breathe. The eruption of Vesuvius lasted nearly two days.

We continued north. I alternated between helping my mother and Dimathra. Both had a difficult time walking so quickly. Criltrenos told me that if we met any military patrols coming south to investigate the situation, I should tell them that I was his son and that my mother was one of his slaves. The next day we did meet several patrols. They were interested in rounding up slaves running loose as well as gathering up any valuables abandoned by those fleeing from the south.

It took us about sixteen days to reach Rome. A week later Dimathra died. Criltrenos sculpted and easily sold his work. I helped him in every way I could and learned some of the art myself. I earned some money teaching wrestling. Criltrenos sold the slave girls to a "good family." With full purses we bought passage on a ship bound for Greece. The ship was going to stop first in Egypt and then in the land of the Hebrews before sailing to Corinth.

During our journey we passed the spot where Pompeii once stood. Vesuvius was still smoking. Our ship also contained about fifteen Roman legionnaires en route to the land of the Hebrews. They were very unhappy about their assignment. We had a small cabin and the soldiers slept on deck in the open air.

Our ship docked at the port of Alexandria, Egypt, for about two days. The cargo hold was emptied of raisins and refilled with crocodile hides and some ivory. We stayed aboard the ship while it was in port. Criltrenos felt that we appeared too fat and could be mistaken for rich Greek merchants by the Egyptian thieves patrolling the docks.

When we left Alexandria our ship was powered by a new sail. The Roman, Greek and Hebrew sailors were very upset about this. There was a superstition that a voyage under a new sail usually resulted in disaster, but during subsequent voyages the age of the sail didn't matter. To appease his crew, the Roman captain took a small piece of the old sail and had it sewn onto the new one. I heard one of the sailors say, "What good does he think that trick will do? The gods will see through it, don't you think?"

Surviving a Shipwreck

Days later, with the land of the Hebrews in sight, our ship—along with its new sail—sank in a storm. My mother and Criltrenos were lost. Only a sailor who shared Roman and Hebrew parentage and I survived by swimming to shore. We stood on the beach in the rain waiting to see if anyone else would make it ashore. While we waited he said, "I told them that ship was a piece of junk" *[a mild English translation —W.H.B.]*. I had an overwhelming feeling of what you call déjà vu.

My fellow survivor's name was Ralno. He had been born in this land to a Hebrew mother and a Roman legionnaire who, in A.D. 73, was one of those who held siege against the Zealot stronghold of Masada. The outcome of that siege was the Roman takeover of that natural fortress after 960 or more Hebrew Zealots committed suicide.

The people of his homeland who knew the other half of his parentage made Ralno very unwelcome. For that reason he left home as a youngster of twelve and went to sea. I was grateful for his company, as he was with mine.

We lived off the land—that is, we stole chickens and raided orchards in the dark of night. We were only two out of hundreds who were making a living that way throughout the country then. The farmers protected their livestock with watchdogs, but made very little effort to guard their orchards. Their reasoning was that any passing troop of Roman soldiers would take what they wanted from the groves, anyway. As time went on, we recognized that the number of watchdogs was diminishing.

While with Ralno I learned much about the religion of his Hebrew mother. He personally favored the Roman gods because each of them were in charge of different aspects of life, whereas the god of his mother had full control over everything. He concluded that life was hard because a single god was overworked and probably not capable of keeping everything in order. He once said that if his mother's god wanted to reward or punish someone, he simply answered their prayers!

We eventually found employment cutting grain during harvest time. Our payment was our food alone. From our fellow workers we heard about those troublemaking Christians. I fondly remembered Dimathra, who was the only Christian I had ever known.

Ralno had traveled to many parts of the known world. He recounted with some pride that he was one of those who rowed the Roman general Agricola ashore to become the governor of Britain. Ralno had two vices, which were visiting brothels and drinking wine. He was frustrated because he had no money to do either. He got to the point where he began to devise plans to rob and kill if he had to to get his hands on a few shekels. Several times he convinced me to help him start a crime spree, but somehow no wealthy person came walking down the road in the dead of night wheeling a barrow filled with gold. We rejected the idea of going to sea, as the odds of being signed aboard a vessel were very low. There were many more sailors than there were ships needing their services. Ralno was sure that if he went back to sea it was only a matter of time until he went to a watery grave. In order to lift himself from poverty, Ralno joined the Roman army. He gave me a few coins out of several he had been given as enlistment pay.

A day or so after saying good-bye to Ralno I took to the fields to avoid running into any Romans who might press me into some labor gang. In the course of my journey I came upon an old camel that had very little life left in it. It followed me. When I stopped for the night, it lay down several feet from me. The camel had several strange brands on it. I concluded that the beast had been turned loose by an Arab who thought it was sick and ready to die. Only an Arab would have let the camel go. Within several days the old boy was nearly recovered. As I walked I began to talk to my four-footed companion. I was telling him the story of my life when he took off in a run. His destination was a string of twelve heavily packed camels moving across our path toward the seacoast. Their owners were a group of Hebrews. The men looked me over and decided that I was a Greek. I did not correct them. They spent some time deciding what to do with me. I thought that they were up to something they didn't want the Romans to know about. One of them produced a Roman shortsword and another tied my hands behind me. They insisted that I come along with them and that I not give them any trouble. When they searched me they found the coins that Ralno had given me. When they returned the coins to my pouch, I felt that I had little to worry about.

Several hours later we arrived at a small ocean inlet where several boats were beached. A ship bounced on the waves offshore. The Greek crew was nervous because my captors were overdue. When the camels were unloaded I saw that the loads consisted of Roman swords, spearheads and arrowheads recently acquired from a Roman armory. Those who had been guarding the armory were now receiving new orders in the afterlife from Mars, the Roman god of war. The Hebrews gave me over to the Greek captain of the ship, who knew I wasn't a native-born Greek. I helped them load the boats that would take their loot to the ship.

We sailed that night and unloaded our cargo on another beach. Those who accepted it were a multiracial band composed mostly of Hebrews, some blacks and even an Egyptian or two. Our ship, now empty, set sail for Greece. I asked the captain how old his sail was. He laughed and said, "You have been to sea before, haven't you?" I estimated my departure from Palestine to have been in the year A.D. 81 when I was about twenty. The Colosseum in Rome was completed the year before and descriptions of it had rapidly reached the empire's frontiers. The emperor Titus died later that year and Domitian replaced him.

In Greece I got a job first building ships, then cutting timber to build them.

One fall when my timber-cutting crew left an area, I stayed behind with a widow named Scora. I worked both at sheep herding and leathermaking. One day I accidentally cut myself while scraping a hide and the wound became infected. I came down with a fever and died several days later in my sleep. The year was A.D. 88 and I was probably twenty-seven years old.

Six Uncles, the Toltec

The year was about A.D. 784. I was born in the valley of Mexico to New Corn, my mother, and my father, Stone Snakes. I was called Six Uncles. We were of the people you call the Toltecs.

I must tell you Sharmarie's version of why I was called Six Uncles. He would have you believe that my parents were torn between naming me after one of six wealthy uncles they hoped would remember them in his will. So they called me Six Uncles to cover all their bases. In truth, however, I was given the name because my father had two brothers and my mother had four, and all were recognized as great warriors.

Prior to my birth the people of my tribe were sent south on a mission by the gods. Our numbers had increased beyond the capacity of our homeland (northern Mexico) to support. Before the migration south we consisted of a number of nonunited tribes that subsisted mostly by hunting. Farming was practiced, but few had the ambition to follow the laborious occupation. My ancestors of that time were simply lazy, preferring to rob others before putting their backs to any form of labor.

Our hunters out of necessity had at times traveled far to the north of our homeland and encountered the ancestors of the tribes you know as the Hopi, Zuni, Apache and Navajo. Many hunters never returned because they were killed either by the harsh land or by the people they had infringed on, or else they were absorbed into these other tribes.

In the days of my grandparents a group of about twelve long-gone hunters returned dressed in clothing made of cloth. They carried well-crafted weapons and shields painted with designs never seen before. They told their kinfolk of a meeting they'd had with several gods, who came to them from the sky inside a large egg. They described the gods as giants who hid their faces behind masks that glowed at times like a full moon (life-support helmets). The kindly gods lived in their egg, but came among them daily and gave them food and water. They said that the gods made them a large cave to live in, which was cool and comfortable.

During their stay with the gods and after their hosts began to talk with them, the hunters learned many things. The gods bought many magical things into the cave, some sparkling like stars in the sky. The hunters told the gods of the hardships of their people. The gods then gave them a picture (map) of the path they should travel that would eventually lead them to a new and prosperous homeland. They were told that they would know the place by the fact that they would find there "snakes made of stone." The gods also gave the hunters seeds to plant in the new land. After imparting to the hunters many other forms of knowledge, the gods flew away, leaving them to once again fend for themselves.

The hunters were made chiefs over our people. They visited other tribes and related their account of meeting with the gods. Those they contacted believed them and allowed themselves to be assembled into one tribe. This new tribe had twelve divisions, each led by one of those who had met the gods. Because the destination of our people was called "the land of the stone snakes," a number of males born at the time were named Stone Snakes, such as my father. (Honestly, however, one of the prime motivations the tribe had for moving south was based on the possibility of encountering an area that had an abundance of certain types of cactus plants, such as agave, that could provide them with an endless supply of alcoholic beverages.)

The plan of travel the gods had laid out for the twelve chiefs was arranged so that they could lead the people to certain areas to settle for a period of several years to farm, hunt and peaceably absorb any of the local people into the tribe before leaving the place and its natives better off than they had found them. The first settlement was located on the shores of what is now called the Gulf of Mexico. The place was called Atlan on the map of the gods (once a small part of the golden-age kingdom you call Atlantis).

During the tribe's stay at Atlan another group arose that said they had also met secretly with the gods. This was a total fabrication. The pretenders said the gods told them that they had changed their plan of gradual absorption of other peoples into the Toltec nation because it was too time-consuming. These people, who finally gained control of the Toltecs, established a religion that included human sacrifice. The new plan was to move south quickly, conquer any people they encountered en route to the land of the stone snakes and leave behind military garrisons to maintain control of the conquered peoples. The numbers in the military garrison left in Atlan later grew large, and several centuries later took on a new tribal identity. They called themselves the Aztecs and later went south in the footsteps of their Toltec ancestors into the valley of Mexico.

The twelve original chiefs of the Toltecs became very old, and their pleas to adhere to the original plan of the gods began to fall on deaf ears. None of the original twelve chiefs lived to see the land of the stone snakes.

Within four years after leaving Atlan, the conquering Toltecs entered the ancient city now known as Teotihuacan (Miradol). In the distance could be seen smoke rising from the volcano now called Popocatepetl. The city at the time was very rundown and had a population of about 18,000 people. They gave the Toltecs no organized resistance. Teotihuacan had housed many different cultures during its long existence, tribes drawn there by the city's buildings, which they believed were built in an ancient time by the gods. The various cultures that occupied the city at one time or another had died out from disease, famines or as victims of a countless number of conquerors, of which the Toltecs were simply the latest. On the day the feathered banners of the Toltecs were placed on the top of the edifice now called the Pyramid of Quetzalcoatl (decorated with feathered serpents carved in stone), they began to sacrifice the city's population. They did not stop until more than 1000 inhabitants had been killed. *[This bloodbath was probably caused by the stored psychic energy in Teotihuacan/Miradol. See the section "Additional Information" at the end of chapter. —W.H.B.]*

The Toltecs' chiefs did attempt to reconstruct some of the buildings of the city as well as complete the construction of the Pyramid of the Sun, as it is now called, which had been left unfinished by the Gracians after their slaughter by the Maldecian krates just after the dawn of time.

I was born during the three years the Toltecs occupied Teotihuacan. I was too young to realize what was occurring when I was gathered in my mother's arms as she fled the city with thousands of others. Those who looked back witnessed four giant space vehicles hovering over it. Three were black disks; the fourth was silver and triangular in shape and bore the emblem of a feathered serpent.

Those who were present related that they witnessed the city burst into flames. When those who dared to return to the place went months later, they found the city completely buried under several feet of soil. What now appeared to be hills covered the ancient buildings of Miradol. I now remember the statement made by Opatel Cre'ator on the day we visited Miradol during my first lifetime: "I wish we had the means to totally burn and bury this place." I have no idea how many times Teotihuacan has been buried by the Federation and reexcavated by later cultures during its long history.

During his conquest of Mexico Hernando Cortez, pursued by tens of thousands of Aztecs, took refuge among the buried ruins of Teotihuacan. He was unaware that the mounds of soil that surrounded him and his band actually contained ancient buildings. Leading a desperate charge, Cortez captured the Aztec war chief Snake Woman. The Aztec army disbanded and ran away in fear. They believed that Cortez had acquired magical powers from the gods during the time he camped within the buried city.

After the conquest the Aztecs told Cortez that the city of Teotihuacan was found buried when the Aztecs arrived at the valley of Mexico some two hundred years before. They said the city was a place "where men went to sleep and awoke in the presence of the gods."

After Teotihuacan was reburied during the time of the Toltec occupation, it was avoided and never again occupied by any large number of pre-Columbian people. Only after the turn of the last century has any real effort been made to uncover (excavate) the ancient site again. It is presently a great tourist attraction. (I can't help but wonder when the Federation will bury it again.)

After the Toltecs left Teotihuacan, they scattered and reassembled into a number of smaller bands. Many years later the groups were once again reunited by warfare. The reunification took place when I was about fourteen years old. The group of Toltecs to which I belonged lived in the area now known as Yucatan. We shared the area with those you refer to as the Maya. Some of our leaders married into the Maya aristocracy.

I was about nineteen and married a Mayan woman. We had no children. I had taken up the occupation of farming, growing mostly corn and cocoa. One day when I was drunk, I fell out of a tree and was badly injured. My three drinking companions, thinking me dead, buried me alive.

My Present Life

Presently I live on the planet Seron, which is located near the farthest boundaries of the Federation. I have lived here for about seven Earth months. I am about 331 Earth years of age. I am married and have two children, a girl and a boy (both more than 200 Earth years of age). My wife of this lifetime is from a planet called Distra. It would take nearly twenty-eight Earth days to travel from my present location to Earth.

As I mentioned in the beginning of my accounts, I am presently the 862d Lord of Devisement of the House of Magail, which is a subdivision of the Nodian House of Domphey. I deal very little with the commercial activities of the trading house. My duties are mostly related to acting as an intermediary between Seronians and any visiting off-worlders employed by the House of Magail. Soon the numerous types of off-worlders will be replaced by one particular type that the Seronians are the most compatible with. Thereafter even these off-worlders will leave as their positions are gradually taken over by Seronians themselves. When that occurs, I will leave this planet for yet another planet that is well into the fourth phase of Federation contact.

I was born into this life on my native world of Moor. My first life service to the House of Domphey qualified me for the position I presently hold. I had several choices of employment, but chose to come to the frontier to be part of the growth of the trading house and the expansion of the Federation.

I have kept abreast of the varying changes in the Frequency Barrier on Earth. It looks as if it will not be too long before it will be gone and we will be able to carry on a conversation face to face. Until then, I am Nisor of Moor.

Additional Information from the Federation

I am Macshallow-Brunto, Ninth Lord of Devisement of the Federation. You ask why the Federation would burn and bury the city of Teotihuacan?

This, then, is my answer. When any emotionally charged event such as a murder occurs, the psychic energy triggered by the emotion can impress the molecules of stone and wood in the vicinity of the event. The molecules act similar to the coating on a videotape in that certain life-field conditions that occur later (in cycles) can interact with the molecules that store the record of the event. The event can then replay at those times in the form of holographic images and can be seen by some or otherwise sensed by others. It is due to this phenomenon that people of the Earth see apparitions.

Constructions of stone and wood are fairly good recorders of such events because they usually have some mathematical order in their dimensions. But when a building is constructed on the order of sacred geometry, especially a building of stone, the structure is better attuned to psychic energy and is therefore a much more efficient storage vessel for the psychically impressed images.

The emotionally charged event of the slaughter of those at Miradol in very ancient times was recorded in the molecules of the so-called Pyramid of the Moon, the Pyramid of Quetzalcoatl and other buildings at the site which the Gracians had proportioned and constructed on the order of sacred geometry. Later, the emotions (psychic energy) generated during the countless human sacrifices performed in the vicinity were absorbed by the molecules of those same buildings. The playback of these terrible events into the universal life field could bring great feelings of misery to many sensitive people living on the planet. In some cases such adverse psychic playbacks could inspire unbridled violence.

By burning and burying a building of sacred construction, the effects of any form of akashic playback into the life field can be weakened or totally nullified, because the soil contains ingredients that interact with water and sunlight, causing seeds to become living plants that function (in life) in the universal life field. A seed contains within it many factors that pertain to sacred geometry (see Fibonacci numbers and ratios as they relate to plants and animals). Therefore, life-supporting soil that covers a building built on the order of sacred geometry can in most cases suppress the akashic replay of any past events stored into the building's molecules.

In the case of the so-called Great Pyramid of Giza, the removal of its capstone accomplished the same thing that would have been accomplished by burying it in soil. The absence of the pyramid's capstone distorted the building's energy matrix, destroying its ability to transmit any form of energy (akashic images).

Inaccurate reconstructions of buildings of Teotihuacan in recent times have helped to reduce the buildings' once-perfect ability to replay past events. Therefore it is very unlikely that the city will be buried again.

E I G H T

Tixer-Chock
of Gracyea

With numbers they pray and with joy in their
spirits calculate the wonders of the divisions
and multiples of one and zero. They say these
values are the basis of all that exists. I also
believe this to be true and forever so. With their
way of number many of their race have rejoined the
consciousness of the Creator of All That Is. In that
state of consciousness I pray they will subtract the
numbers of evil from creation and add
the numbers of eternal life that can only
be divided by the numbers of love.
I am Pris-Botu of Torco.

I am Tixer-Chock of Gracyea. My home world of Gracyea is the fourth
planet of the sun/star we call Lalm. The solar system of Lalm contains
one large radiar called the Bel Nec radiar by the Federation. Bel Nec,
which has eight planetoids, is in the sixth solar orbit from Lalm. It is from
one of these planetoids [Morza] that the man Barco originated [see chapter
5]. The planet Simm is the second planet of five that compose the solar system of Lalm. Including the radiar just mentioned, our sun has six major
orbiting bodies.

I am aware that the people of the planet Simm and their past relationship to the Maldecians has been mentioned by others in your previous
writings [see chapter 5]. The Simms were introduced to the Maldecians by
us of Gracyea.

I, Tixer-Chock, was the reward given to my parents for loving the elohim and each other. I have always sought to be worthy of the senses of perception they have given me to behold the wonders of the Creator of All

That is.

In that first lifetime I was the only child of Orydebbsa, my mother, and Crax-Milanto, my father. My grandfather Itocot-Talan, one of the great scholars of our race, directed the construction of the Earth city of Miradol (Teotihuacan). I was with him at Miradol when the Maldecian krates killed us. Those who died with us at that time might find it uplifting to know that for three days following our deaths, the elohim silently grieved for us. This is true and forever so.

You come to me with thoughts and questions that thrill me to consider. I have been excited during the time I have spent preparing for this meeting of our minds in the universal life field.

I will first dispel an assumption that most who are not of my world might make. We of Gracyea did not originally manifest the knowledge of sacred geometry into the molar (three-dimensional) level of perception. This wondrous knowledge was imparted to my people several hundred years before my first lifetime by a space-traveling race from yet another world.

The great teachers who taught us of numbers and their holy relationships to all that is seen and unseen found my ancestors to be industrious and peaceful. They asked for nothing from my people in exchange for the numerous gifts of enlightenment they gave them.

There were twelve of those ancient sages who invited us to come to their home world whenever we became able to use what they taught us—constructing spacecraft that could endure the journey. These teachers told our ancestors that they lived on several worlds that circled a radiar whose central sun can be seen even now as one of the most brilliant stars that appear in our night skies.

The ancient ones told us that when we came to their home world they would teach our people many more marvelous things. After making this promise, they left our world and never returned. My race was inspired and highly motivated by their promise, and we hastened to develop space travel so that we could meet once again and proudly show them we had accomplished what they had expected of us.

When the ancient teachers departed Gracyea, the people begin to build and build and build. They were obsessed with the desire to see sacred geometry expressed in buildings and enjoy the euphoric healing effects naturally generated by such buildings. The mathematical language of the creator of all that is became very much part of our lives and remains so today.

Our first adventures into space took us to the planet Simm. Those of that world were technically at the stage that those of the Earth were at the beginning of your present century. Simm had a one-world government and its people lived in peace.

Later expeditions took our space explorers to the other four planets of the Lalm system and also to the eight planetoids that orbit the Bel Nec radiar. We learned that those such as ourselves who had advanced knowledge had a great responsibility to contact those less fortunate. We found that we did not have the ability to immediately impart our knowledge of sacred geometry to others of the system, because they needed time to get over the shock of our arrival on their respective worlds and then achieve a basic understanding of many other things before they could learn the mathematical relationships one solid reality had to another and to the universe as a whole.

We devised a teaching plan whereby we could produce conditions that would encourage the planets' or planetoids' inhabitants to both consciously and subconsciously absorb and understand the divine power of numbers. We did this by constructing buildings based on sacred geometry on these planets and planetoids of the local system. It took some years before Barco's people no longer counted "1-2-3-4 and more than 4." In the beginning most people of the Lalm system simply enjoyed building with their hands and marveling at their beautiful handiwork, without understanding what powerful meanings their structures represented.

Those of these worlds who psychically phased into and became part of the living essence of the divine system of numbers became, like us of Gracyea, totally enamored with it. You [the author] and others of the Earth who are presently experiencing the same spiritual effects from your study of sacred geometry, know what it is like to be spiritually driven to learn more and more about the subject. I warn others who would pursue similar studies: Beware, for once you begin, you will never stop your research. The system provides a continuous flow of understandings that bring both mental satisfaction and a quickening of the spirit (thrill) that arises from the realization that the universe is not in a state of chaos, but was designed and functions on the order of sacred geometry established by the creator of all that is. I, Tixer Chock, say this is true and will be forever so.

From the time the ancient teachers departed from the presence of my ancestors, we employed the divine system of numbers that you call the Ra system in every facet of our lives. We benefited greatly from applying it to agriculture and medicine. So did others of the Lalm solar system.

Eventually we developed a field-drive spacecraft-propulsion system that would permit us to leave our native solar system and travel to worlds that circled other suns/stars. Our first destination, of course, was the home of our ancient teachers. Any other place in the universe would have to wait to be visited by us of Gracyea.

My youth was spent learning sacred architecture and developing ways to construct large stone buildings. People from the planet Simm who loved to grow things came to Gracyea and operated farms and ranches that provided the world with food. Our animal life is quite different from the animal life of present-day Earth. It would take considerable time and space to describe it entirely, so I will not do so during this communication. And Barco's people and others of the Lalm worlds enjoyed building things and assembling machinery. We all got along just fine.

Gracyea is also well-known as the place of the giant feathered serpents. It might surprise you to learn that these forty-foot-long animals are very timid vegetarians. They are the dragons spoken of in the ancient Nodian ode that says "I go to a world where the dragons fear the butterflies." This beautiful and benign creature has come to symbolically represent my race.

At the age of twenty-two Earth years I married a tobacco heiress on my world. At the time, few could equal her father in material wealth. Her name was (and is presently) Brevracarliss. (Yes, yes, yes, I will include here the falsehood and humor of the Martian Lord Sharmarie that her middle name is Nicotina. Thus I am permitted to retaliate with a little Gracian number humor: On the Earth there are those who have the aristocratic titles of count and countess. The Martians also have these same titles, but most of them are no-accounts!) But back to the seriousness of our communication.

Brevracarliss and I parented a daughter we named Denbrevra. I left my family behind on Gracyea when the time came for me to join with thirty-five others of my race and travel to the star system of the ancient teachers. The trip took about forty-nine Earth hours.

The Solar System of Our Ancient Teachers

After our arrival in the solar system of the ancient ones, we sought out one radiar of the four existing there, knowing from ancient records that the home planetoids of the teachers circled that particular blazing globe. We traveled from planetoid to planetoid of that radiar and found only beautiful forms of planet life, but no sign of animal life or any form of human construction. Thinking we might have made a mistake, we spent more than an Earth year covertly checking out the planetoids of the other three radiars. We found most of these planetoids occupied by humans, but none who fit the description of the ancient teachers. We then began to look for any sign of the ancient ones on each of the four planets that were part of that solar system. (This is the solar system of which Earth is a member, but before the destruction of Maldec. Mercury at this time was a planetoid orbiting

Jupiter, and Pluto and its moon Charon orbited Neptune.)

During our explorations we spotted some very old buildings, mostly in ruins, that had been designed and constructed on the order of sacred geometry. These minor constructions were located on the third planet of the solar system. On the fourth planet we found several large cities whose buildings and layout were designed and constructed on the order of the sacred numbers. We thought that this beautiful world must surely be the present home of the ancient ones.

We landed and made contact with the people of that world. You know today the name of that world as Maldec and its people as Maldecians. I am aware that some have spelled the name Maldec as Maldek (with a *k* and not a *c*). The "k" sound in the universal Sol-Tec language has a very harsh meaning—notice the way it is used in the English words *kick* and *kill* and that it is represented silently in the spelling of *knife*. Spelling Maldec with a *k* is very insulting to the Maldecians. The name "Maldec" is where the mathematical term *dec-i-mal* originated, meaning "they who have fractionalized (decimalized) the One."

The buildings of Maldec were very old, but due to the fact that they were built of hard stone and on the order of sacred geometry, they were in good repair. We found the Maldecian rulers to be strange, but they were friendly toward us. They told us that they too had been visited by the ancient teachers, who had helped them build their beautiful cities before leaving the planet with a promise to return. (It was later learned that when the teachers left Maldec, they did so vowing never to return. What happened between these teachers from Uranus [Hamp radiar planetoids] and the Maldecians never came to light in that first lifetime of mine. I will attempt to describe what happened somewhere during the course of this communication.)

One of the first things we noticed was the absence of Maldecian children below the age of sexual maturity. We eventually learned that at birth a Maldecian infant is visited by one who speaks for the El of that planet. If the child meets the standards set by the Maldecian El, it is allowed to live. If the child does not, it is put to death. Those who are allowed to live are psychically attached to the conscience of the El, where they remain in suspended animation until sexual maturity. They come out of their hibernation fully nourished, grown and educated in the ways of every Maldecian who ever came before them. The Maldecian children, who rarely awaken early from their induced sleep, are considered royalty and quite exceptional.

The Maldecians did not want any off-world child to be born on their planet [see chapter 6] because such a child's living presence in the planet's biosphere would disturb the growth of their own sleeping offspring.

The El of Maldec has been referred to on Earth as Lucifer ("the bringer of light"). The shattering of the planet Maldec has been interpreted by ancient cultures on Earth (such as the Babylonians) as "the casting of the Great Deceiver El, Lucifer, and his angels out of heaven."

Before our arrival the only things Maldecians did was grow food, produce fine clothing, exercise and produce other Maldecians. After we arrived they assigned the growing of food and the making of clothes to people who were not of their world.

We were happy to have found the Maldecians able to understand the meaning and importance of sacred geometry. They were lacking a few key factors that we understood quite well, and we wondered why the ancient teachers hadn't taught it to them. Their lack of this information kept them from developing any form of long-range space travel.

We were escorted around Maldec for several Earth months to take in the sights. After seeing and feeling the effects of their fine buildings, we concluded that we would pick up where the ancient teachers had left off and teach the Maldecians what they did not know about sacred geometry. We thought at first that we could work with them to mutually further our own understandings of the subject. We also thought that we could work collectively with them to find out what had become of the ancient teachers.

We took two Maldecians back to our home solar system and transported them to the planet Simm as well as all of the other human-inhabited bodies in the system. At first the Maldecians preferred to come to Gracyea to learn. Later they set up a place on their own world where they said our teachers would be very comfortable. Over a period of about thirty Earth years we shared with the Maldecians the propulsion system of our spacecraft, after which they built craft of their own and contacted their planetary neighbors, such as the people of Sarus (Earth). Unknown to us of Gracyea, they immediately began their program of taking over Earth. The Maldecians were very secretive about their long-range plans for planetary conquest. They pretended to have the same spiritual goals as we of Gracyea did. We respected their rules of controlled, limited contact to protect their particular ways of life from disruption. We dealt only with those their rulers selected for contact and had no contact with their general population.

We of Gracyea were happy to contact other planetary cultures to share what we knew of life and learn from them whatever we could. We never had the desire to rule others and could see no reason why anyone else would want to conquer and control someone else's world.

The Maldecians made trip after trip to Gracyea and to the planet Simm. They soon began to enlist the Simms in many subservient capacities. We learned later that the Simms who went to live and work on Maldec were secretly given chemically laced food that sterilized them and thus kept them from producing children during their stay on Maldec and even afterward.

Nothing new was really learned by us of Gracyea from our association with the Maldecians. For more than 300 Earth years after we made first contact with them, we explored other solar systems and contacted other cultures. We shared whatever these cultures could understand from our knowledge of sacred geometry. In order to satisfy our desire to build things designed on the order of the holy numbers, we found it necessary to ask those who would benefit from the structures to pay for the services of our engineers and our trained labor force. Payment was usually in the form of raw materials.

Building projects slowed our space explorations because our limited but growing numbers of spacecraft were employed mainly in transporting construction equipment and laborers to and from building sites on different worlds. During that 300-year period we of Gracyea were content. While we were going about our interstellar space exploration and building, we encountered hundreds of other cultures that had achieved some form of space travel, but we never encountered the Nodians during that period.

We of Gracyea have always been able to telepathically communicate with each other. The holy numbers that were passed mentally between us as thought forms are easily understood, but to those who do not have the molar-level (three-dimensional) references for such things, numerical thought forms are essentially meaningless. Thus, seeking long-distance mental contacts with another culture by way of the universal life field was for us a waste of psychic energy. It was simply that we could not mentally communicate in their way and they could not understand us.

The Physical Science of Sound

I was privileged to study under my grandfather Itocot-Talan, who taught me how to apply sound as a means to cleave, shape (tune) and levitate massive stone blocks of various elemental compositions. I also became expert in the formulation of mortars and cements, which had to be precisely mixed in order to be sound-compatible with the stone blocks used in a building's construction. Stone blocks and incompatible mortar just don't work. That is, they don't permit the building to live in sympathetic harmony with the universal life field.

The ancient teachers had told our ancestors of the existence of the elohim, who spiritually govern their respective worlds from the macro level of perception, and of the creator of all that is, who provides light to all things by way of the stars. We then found spiritual comfort in praying to the sun of whatever solar system we were in at the time, knowing that its blessed life-giving light was a divine gift to all things that absorbed and/or reflected it.

Those of our priesthood, called stolfas, spent many years meditating and practicing mental exercises that eventually allowed them to develop the ability to levitate an object of any mass and weight. They accomplish these mentally controlled and directed flights by acting as a mental filter. With their minds alone they are able to locate the proper frequencies and reject those that don't apply to their work.

All frequencies involved in the attraction of one mass to another exist between the local gravitational field of the sun and the gravitational field of the planet. Prayers to the rising and setting sun mentally attune those such as the stolfas to the sun's gravitational pressure field in the morning and separate them from it at nightfall. The stolfas can mentally identify the required frequency and provide the correct amount of psychic energy in the waveform of that particular frequency.

If the stolfa provides too little life force in that frequency, the object will not become weightless. If too much energy is applied, the stone will shatter to dust—as happened to the planet Maldec. A Gracian primary student could have told the Maldecians that would happen. The Maldecians had not told us of their intention to send vril energy from the Earth to Maldec by way of the Great Pyramid of Giza. They had told us that they wanted to build the pyramid for totally different purposes. Those "benign" purposes had interested us and we wanted to be part of their manifestation, so we eagerly cooperated.

I was about 325 Earth years old and the father of twelve additional children when the Maldecians proposed that we Gracians construct a network of life-field-compatible sacred buildings and pyramids, which would be built on Earth and Mars and eventually Venus. After hearing the Maldecians' reasons for wanting to do this, I admit we were thrilled to participate. This was a long-range project estimated to take as long as twenty-five Earth years.

The Nodians' Arrival

The Nodian arrival in the local solar system and their contact with the people of Venus (Wayda) put a hold on Maldecian plans to build a pyramid on Venus at that time. The Maldecians feared the Nodian presence and must have burnt out their mental circuits trying to figure out what to do about them. We of Gracyea admired the Nodians' technical successes, but originally found them very uptight about some things we cared little about.

Though we knew nothing about the Nodians prior to that time, they seemed to know quite a bit about us and our home planet of Gracyea. At the first physical meeting between the Nodians and ourselves, the Nodian representative greeted our representative eloquently in our language of numbers and swore by the light of the sun (as we also did) to be always nonaggressive in our dealings. This first meeting took place on Gracyea only weeks before the destruction of Maldec, and after that we became the closest of friends. Gracyea is now a member of the Federation and our holy constructions house Nodian representatives on many worlds as well as on their planet.

Basically, the Maldecians claimed that the constructions they proposed for Earth, Mars and Venus were originally part of a "plan" that the ancient teachers from Uranus imparted to them before leaving them alone to ponder the reason why. Because the ancient teachers had left us of Gracyea to develop spacecraft and other useful things on our own, we readily accepted as fact that they had done the same thing with the Maldecians.

The Maldecians told us that they had always known about the "ancient plan," but wanted to be sure that our cultures could get along. Furthermore, the teachers had told them that people from other worlds they had contacted would come and help them fulfill the divine plan. They also told us that when the buildings were completed, the teachers would return. We of Gracyea believed everything they said—after all, why would they lie about such holy things? We were very happy to be part of the plan of the ancient teachers and did everything we could to materialize it.

I was one of my race who visited the planets Earth and Mars to first determine and then prepare the appropriate locations for construction. On Mars, the area you know as Cydonia was perfect, evidenced by the fact that the ancient teachers had built there in ages past. The place called the Citadel, in which the the Martian zone-rex resided in that first lifetime, had been built by those of Uranus. It was they who had taught the early Martians how to select their supreme ruler and who had placed them on the path to greater spiritual development.

The Mars Construction Project

I remember that it was a rainy morning when our craft landed on Mars. We were greeted by four bar-rexes (Martian warlords), each accompanied by more than a hundred soldiers. These princes came aboard our craft bearing a signed and sealed written agreement they had made with the Maldecians that said we Gracians would be totally free to build whatever we wanted on a plain near the city of Graniss (Cydonia). The agreement was written in the languages of the Maldecians, Martians and ourselves, the Gracians, and we were aware that the Maldecians would not be present on the planet Mars during the period of construction.

[Aloiss-Mabray: In truth, the Maldecians considered the Martians dangerous louts with a primitive ability to reason, and they did not want the Martians to actively scrutinize them or seek out their underlying purposes. They were right to think that their physical presence among the Martians would eventually cause problems. The Maldecian belief that they were a superior race surfaced in the presence of Martians. If it served them, the Maldecians could be diplomatically tolerant of people such as the "civilized" Gracians or the bright inhabitants of the Earth, but the Martians were definitely another story.]

It rained for another two days, and the Martian army camped around our spacecraft. They occupied themselves telling stories, drinking and wrestling in the mud. They were very loud and argued among themselves, but there was no violence because they were on the neutral ground that surrounded the headquarters of the zone-rex.

We explored the proposed building site. Our explorations took us to the walls of the ancient citadel that had been built long ago by the teachers from the Hamp radiar (Uranus). It had been built of what we considered soft material. During its history it survived the abrasive Martian sandstorms, winds and rain only because of its holy design, which produced counteracting forces that shielded the structure. (The same type of counteracting forces presently protect the Great Pyramids of Giza, Egypt, even though they have been partially dismantled.)

We were met at the gates of the Citadel by guards of the zone-rex, who carried broadswords. The zone-rex had gifted us with several large skins of an alcoholic beverage called drat, along with a message that we should not come back unless he sent for us.

We spent several days "toning" the area and several days thereafter in our spacecraft making the tuning forks needed for cutting and levitating the local rock. After these tasks were completed, we visited the Martian city of Graniss to wait for others from our home world to arrive with other building equipment and a labor force from the planetoids of the Relt radiar (Jupiter).

By order of the zone-rex, no Martian was to physically assist us in our building project. Even though Rancer-Carr was not accepted as zone-rex by all the Martian warlords at the time, it was easy for the common Martian to accept his decree forbidding them to provide us with any form of physical labor. (The lumbering Martians would have just been in the way, anyway.)

While visiting the neutral city of Graniss we managed to engage some Martians in conversation. We asked them what they knew of the ancient teachers who had built the Citadel on the nearby plain. We were surprised to hear that the Martians believed that some of the teachers had never left Mars and lived in caverns in the sacred mountain they called Daren. (This mountain is now volcanic and is called Olympus Mons by those of present-day Earth.) They told us that they were sure that this was so because only a few years before, several of the teachers dressed in purple robes and wearing silver masks came to the copper mine. They spoke to hundreds of miners and called from their ranks a young man they proclaimed zone-rex. That young man was Rancer-Carr.

It was very frustrating that only several miles away was a man who had met and talked to the teachers but would not talk to us! We thought he might not understand that our entire race had been blessed by that ancient meeting with those who had also ordained him as the divine ruler of his people. We sent him a message in an attempt to inform him of our mutual respect for the teachers. His reply was, "Go away until I am declared zone-rex by all of the bar-rexes. Then we will talk together about the teachers."

The Swords in Stone

We took to the air and landed on the sacred mountain, whose base is about 370 miles across (about the size of the state of Arizona). There were many roads and paths that led to the mountain peak. Why and how these paths were built was a mystery to us. The summit (then covered with snow) is about 52,000 feet (9.85 miles) high. It was and is impossible for anyone to breathe at that altitude. Martians lived on the slopes at lower altitudes. There were seemingly bottomless narrow canyons in which the Martians dropped the bodies of their honored dead. They had been doing this for as long as any of them could remember.

Sticking in the rock walls that bordered the paths to these burial sites were numerous broadswords. Some of these weapons were forged and placed in their stone sheaths thousands of years before our visit to the mountain. These weapons were once wielded by Martian warriors and had been placed in the rock by shamans during the funeral of their original owners. Try as we did, we could not dislodge any of the swords from the rock. Young Martian males and females could be seen climbing the rocky walls in an attempt to draw a particular sword from the stone.

During our visit to the mountain we never saw anyone able to remove a sword from its ancient resting place. We met Martians later who had, and who proudly claimed a spiritual kinship to the warrior to whom the weapon originally belonged. This Martian practice is, of course, the basis for the story of Excalibur, the sword that made Arthur king of England after he pulled it from a stone, where it had been placed by Merlin the wizard.

We were not welcomed by the Martians we met on the sacred mountain. We chanted loudly a numerical greeting in the hope that if the teachers did live in the mountain, they would hear us and contact us physically. Our efforts only brought angry Martians to our campsite; they threatened us with violence unless we left.

After a few such encounters we returned to the city of Graniss. Several days later our supply ships arrived from Gracyea and several days after that the first contingent of our laborers arrived from the planetoids of the Relt radiar. We turned our work and knowledge over to the chief engineers who would be in charge of the construction at Cydonia, wishing them luck with their association with the Martians. We then left Mars for the planet Earth.

Working at Miradol (Teotihuacan)

On Earth I met with my grandfather Itocot-Talan, who was then more than 1200 Earth years of age. I joined him and others of my race at the place you now call Teotihuacan and we called, then as now, Miradol.

One thing different about the Earth compared to Mars was that there were Maldecians everywhere. At Miradol at the time of my first arrival were a number of large white tents that housed several hundred Maldecians and about half as many tents filled with Simms and Earth people. A number of Cryberants (who later carved the Great Sphinx of Giza [chapter 6] arrived at Miradol about two weeks later.

Several days after I came to Miradol the Maldecians requested an audience with my grandfather and me in order to be briefed on what was then occurring at our building site on Mars. During that meeting the Maldecians listened intensely to what I had to say about our joint building project, but when I alluded to my experiences with the Martians themselves, they excused themselves abruptly and left our presence.

I noticed that a tall thin man in strange attire was part of my grandfather's personal staff. He was always impeccably clean. He physically avoided the Maldecians, but occasionally would be seen talking privately to my grandfather. My grandfather saw that I was curious about the strange off-worlder and what he had to do with our building projects. My grandfather told me that this man, Brockmel, was a native of one of the planetoids of the Trake radiar. I was instructed to accommodate any of Brockmel's requests for information but to ask him no questions. I learned later that after night fell, the Trakian sent telepathic messages to the headquarters of the House of Cre'ator located on the planet Nodia.

Several days later Brockmel was found dead in his quarters, a "victim of something he had eaten." My grandfather turned down the Maldecian request to cremate Brockmel's body. Instead, he had the body physically examined by Gracian medics and sent to Brockmel's home planetoid by our next departing spacecraft. The forensic examination revealed that

Brockmel did not die of something he had eaten, but of cobra venom injected into his neck by a "one-fanged cobra." In those days as now, cobras were nonexistent in the vicinity of Miradol.

I spent several months at Miradol toning the local building materials and producing tuning forks compatible with the materials.

The Project in Egypt

Months later I performed the same type of work in the Land of Mir at the site where the three Great Pyramids were eventually built. I went to Mir in the company of the chief engineer of the Mir building project, Tarvmole-Bixor, and his assistant, Boinkalix-Ralsever. We were also accompanied by six Maldecians, one of whom was the krate general Rolander-Crobe. We were greeted upon our arrival by Somife-Rallee, the commander of about forty-five krates. On Rolander's orders the krates spread out in groups to warn the local people away from the Giza Plateau until further notice.

I visited the village of Pankamerry, located east of the plateau. There I met with the village leader named Cark Ben-Zobey to arrange the construction of temporary warehouses and to clear and level an area near the village where our cargo-carrying spacecraft could land. Afterward I spent weeks toning the natural rock formations of the plateau and those in the immediate vicinity. My estimates indicated that there would not be enough local material to construct the three proposed pyramids. This fact necessitated that I seek other sources of material in limestone deposits located upriver (to the south). The shortage was not in core stone, but in the limestone fine enough for cutting and polishing that would be used for the casing stones. The smallest of the three pyramids had to be constructed with other types of stone (granite and basalt) so we could have enough fine limestone to cover the faces of the two larger structures. *[It has been estimated that the four faces of the Great Pyramid were once covered by about 22 acres of fine limestone that came from an area up the Nile now called Tura. —W.H.B.]*

Until I could tell my Maldecian companions that there was enough of the right kinds of material in the vicinity for the pyramids, they were very uptight. The next problem they were unhappy about was that a certain type of labor force would be required and that we could not guarantee we could hire enough Reltians. The Reltians were ideal because they were small and strong, and size was important because the volume of passageways had to be kept to a minimum. Larger passages in some areas of the pyramids would have affected the overall tone of the structure. Nothing could alter the fact that the pyramids had to be solid in certain places to achieve the mass required to be in harmony with the vril energy that would eventually be drawn and concentrated within them. Reltians also had the proper emotional control, which assured us that they would not send forth counteracting psychic vibrations that would interfere with the thought processes of the stolfas when they were mentally levitating heavy blocks of stone.

The labor problem brought to light a malevolent characteristic of the Maldecians that we of Gracyea had never seen before in our more than 300-year association. They suggested that the Reltians be taken against their will, brought to the Earth and forced to work as slaves. It was lucky for the Reltians that the Maldecians breathed oxygen and not nitrogen. Otherwise they would have been rounded up by an army of merciless krates and brought to Earth in chains.

Another thing that saved the Reltians from this fate was the fact that the Maldecians would have needed Gracian spacecraft to transport the slaves to Earth. When we made it quite clear that we would have no part in such an action, the Maldecians backed off, claiming that they had suggested "benignly" enslaving the inferior Reltians because they were so overwhelmed with the holiness and importance of the building projects. They said that they would have released the Reltian slaves and rewarded them handsomely at the completion of the work. I myself pointed out to our Maldecian partners that no Reltian slave could provide the proper psychic state required to assist our stone-levitating stolfas.

The Maldecians finally agreed to leave the recruiting of the required Reltian labor force to us. We left the Land of Mir disgusted with them. We were not really sure that the pyramids could be built in Mir until the buildings were finished on Mars and the Reltians who worked there could be enticed to come to Earth. We know now that the Maldecians, who had a secret deadline for the completion of the pyramids of Mir, were holding their breath until the labor problem was solved. We of Gracyea considered breaking our agreement with the Maldecians, but our word was and is our sacred oath. Once we agree in the light of the sun to anything, we are eternally committed. So we decided to continue our association with the Maldecians and leave the future of our relationship in the hands of the elohim—as should be the way of all humans who get into situations they cannot honorably resolve.

As you now know, most Reltians who came to Earth to work on the building projects were mostly ordered to do so by their tribal chiefs and chieftesses who, in accord with our agreement with them, expected their people to be returned by us to their home planetoids within five Earth years. Because Maldec exploded, this part of our agreement with the Reltians was not completed. Therefore we of Gracyea even today consider ourselves in their debt and will settle our accounts with those good people as soon as possible. We have invested for them in certain commercial projects overseen by the Federation and the three major Nodian trading houses. Presently each individual Reltian is extremely wealthy by open-state physical standards, especially those who, due to no fault of their own, were psychically trapped in the Frequency Barrier of Earth and lived numerous harsh and miserable lives on the ill-fated planet.

We of Gracyea have also prepared a new planetary home where the Reltians can, at the end at the Frequency Barrier, reside together as one people until their home planetoids are somehow restored to habitability. We of Gracyea will do whatever we can to bring about such restorations.

Miradol and the Maya

When we were engaged in the construction of Miradol (Teotihuacan), we also built structures in several nearby locations. These structures were energy receptors of the universal life field that would sympathetically support the purposes of those buildings we were constructing at both Miradol and the Giza Plateau. Most of these outlying buildings were pyramidal. At our urging, they were later restored and copied by the people you know as the Maya. We hoped that they would build certain things on the order of sacred geometry that might lessen the effects of the Frequency Barrier.

By various means over a period of about two centuries we taught the Maya as much as they could understand about astronomy and mathematics. Their leaders misconstrued many of our teachings. Their addiction to drugs and alcohol caused their culture to fall apart. Their genetic qualities, which we once highly appreciated in the beginning of our contact with them, began to degrade quickly. The result of this self-created genetic devolution was what is now called the Maya gene. This unfortunate biological condition was partly due to the effects of the Frequency Barrier, but mostly due to the Mayan lifestyle. Within about two generations they changed from a race of high intelligence to one of hostility and stupidity. You can chalk up the Mayans as another Gracian blunder.

We are pleased that the descendants of the classic Maya have bred the bad Maya gene into near-extinction. The cruel European conquest of Central America and the forced acceptance of Christianity by the people of the area played a role in establishing certain disciplines that brought about positive biological changes in the Maya of today.

Follow well the Mayan calendar—it still represents something of value that we of Gracyea have given to the people of Earth. Our students, the Maya, used the calendar to determine the position of planetary bodies hundreds of millions of years into the past so they could accurately design and locate their buildings. Their projections of the planetary positions to the present are off by only about 33 standard seconds, or about 32.8 natural seconds of time. Most of this error is due to movements of the land under their observatories during the required 18-year observation period.

Because many of us of Gracyea began to feel ill after spending any amount of time with the Maldecians, we requested that medical specialists from our home world come to the Earth and get to the bottom of the matter. My wife Brevracarliss and several of our grown children arrived at Miradol with those medical specialists. Our mysterious illnesses miraculously disappeared before our medical people had a chance to make any examinations.

One afternoon as I was supervising the setting of stone blocks in the structure you presently call the Pyramid of the Moon, a Nodian spacecraft landed a few hundred yards away. Several Maldecians approached it (there were few if any krates stationed at Miradol at the time). The Nodians and Maldecians met for about thirty minutes, then the Nodians returned to their craft and left. I never saw a Nodian come to Miradol again.

I was happy to be with my wife and children again, and we built a small house north of the major building site. Other families from Gracyea also lived close by. We soon numbered about 100,000. As colder weather came to the area, the Maldecians and Cryberants departed for more favorable climes. Work proceeded slowly because those from the Relt planetoids were physically affected by weather they were not used to. Essentially, we of Gracyea and the Relt planetoids were, much to our content, left pretty much to ourselves every winter we spent on Earth.

I never left Miradol during that lifetime, not even to travel to Mir to see the progress in the building of the three great pyramids, although I did view videotapes showing the progress of these projects as well as those under way at the time on the planet Mars.

About two months before the Great Pyramid of Giza would be misused by the Maldecians to transmit Earth's creative vril energy to their home planet, the growing city of Miradol was ringed by thousands of white tents housing more than 10,000 Maldecian krates. From their encampments one could hear at first the sounds of their conversations and the loud humming sounds as they practiced drills. But for two days before the summer solstice, their camps were dead silent and dark at night. No one knew what they were doing in the dark, although we speculated they were all in meditation.

The Pyramid of the Sun and the Ra System

To meet the building schedule, we hastily completed the first level of the structure you presently call the Pyramid of the Sun. Its base length was 763.407 red ra feet, as is that of the Great Pyramid of Giza. The number 763.407 is very important. As a lineal unit of measure, it contains in it 229.0221 red ram units, which equals 916.884 red ra inches. In the body of 763.407 there are also 72.9 red pi units. (Red pi equals 3.141$\overline{592}$ [the line above the number indicates that it is infinite] and 0.729 is the 27th number in the Ra Table of Nines and the reciprocal of the fine-structure

Ra Table of Nines							
(1)	0.027	(10)	0.270	(19)	0.513	(28)	0.756
(2)	0.054	(11)	0.297	(20)	0.540	(29)	0.783
(3)	0.081	(12)	0.324	(21)	0.567	(30)	0.810
(4)	0.108	(13)	0.351	(22)	0.594	(31)	0.837
(5)	0.135	(14)	0.378	(23)	0.621	(32)	0.864
(6)	0.162	(15)	0.405	(24)	0.648	(33)	0.891
(7)	0.189	(16)	0.432	(25)	0.675	(34)	0.918
(8)	0.216	(17)	0.459	(26)	0.702	(35)	0.945
(9)	0.243	(18)	0.486	(27)	0.729	(36)	0.972
		(37)	0.999				

constant for the element hydrogen: 729 = 27 x 27.) The number 763.407 also contains in it 45 red ankh units (red pi x 1.62 = 5.08938, or red ankh). The number 763.407 also contains 216 red hunab units of 1.0602875 units each (216 is the 8th number in the Ra Table of Nines: 216 = 8 x 27). As a frequency, 10.602875 cycles per natural second [cpns] is that most commonly generated by a meditating human being. The sacred number of 763.407 also contains 141.4213562 red phi units (1.414213562 is the square root of the number 2).

The number also contains 360 rac 1 units (0.6317250 = rac 1), 400 rac 3 units (0.57255525 = rac 3), 500 rac 5 units (0.4580442 = rac 5). There are also 364.5 (27 x 13.5) red rac 2 units in the number 763.407. The value of red rac 2 is 0.6283185 and the number 364.5 is the Ra system's value for the Balmer constant for hydrogen. The number 364.5 is used in simple equations to mathematically determine the wavelengths of visible spectral lines of the element hydrogen. Rac means "ra cubit."

At Teotihuacan (Miradol) a line projected from the center of the Pyramid of the Moon down the so-called Way of the Dead is exactly 763.407 red rams in length, to a point where the same boulevard would be bisected by a line that could be projected from the center of the Pyramid of the Sun. The same boulevard is 48 hunabs in width, so 48 x 1.0602875 = 50.8938

(10 red ankh units).

The "platform" on which rests the Temple of the Inscriptions in the Mayan city of Palenque has the following dimensions: length 91.60884 red rams, or 12 x 7.63407 red rams; height 9.160884 red rams, or 1.2 x 7.63407 red rams. The height of the floor of the Temple of the Inscriptions above the plaza level is 76.403 red ra feet.

As a frequency of sound, the value 763.407 cycles per natural second of time is the third octave of the ra musical tone G. Therefore, anything precisely related to the dimensions of either 763.407 red rams, red ra feet, or red ra inches will also have a sympathetic universal-life-field relationship to the tone of ra G. One-half of the first octave of ra G is 95.425875 cycles per natural second of time. The number 95.425875 is the ra value for Hubble's constant, which is the astronomical constant (cosmic yardstick) used to determine the distances between the stars. There are exactly 9 red hunabs (1.0602875) in the number 95.425875. Remember that 10.602875 cpns is the average alpha brain-wave frequency produced during meditation, and 95.425875 (ra value of Hubble's constant) x 10.602875 = 485.65853971, which was the original height of the Great Pyramid in red ra feet. The green ra value for its height was 486 green ra feet. The number 486 is the 18th number in the Ra Table of Nines and also the wavelength of the second visible spectral line of hydrogen (Balmer M4), which is blue in color. If the green number of 486 is viewed as a red number (or as an omega major factor) and divided into the pyramid's base length of 768.407 red ra feet, the result is 1.5707962963 (half of red pi). I will leave it to one of Cre'ator to tell others about the Ra mathematical formats and their relationships to each other. I, Tixer-Chock, say that what I have told you of the sacred numbers is true and will be forever so.

The Night Maldec Shattered

It was night in Miradol when the Maldecians sent the holy creative energy of the Earth to their home planet of Maldec. When their world shattered, the completed buildings of Miradol sent a deafening screech that was hardly bearable by those of us not native to the Earth. To the Maldecians the tone was overwhelming. They walked about bumping into things and wailing, sounding collectively like a crying baby. Women and female animals in the area were tormented by the sound and felt a primal urge to help them. In most cases we had to physically restrain our women from going to their aid. Throughout the night the streets of Miradol were filled with wild female animals en route to the Maldecian encampments. The skies over the Maldecian tents were filled with female birds and bats.

By dawn all was once again quiet. My grandfather Itocot-Talan explained to us of Gracyea what had happened to the planet Maldec. We were attempting to form a plan to leave Earth and return home. We could not reach any of our people in Mir telepathically, but we did reach the Gracians on Mars. They related that their finished constructions also issued a loud screeching sound when Maldec exploded. We told the Gracians on Mars to keep our spacecraft stationed there and begin to systematically pick up those of us on Earth and take us home.

At about high noon of the day following the destruction of Maldec, the krates encircled the city of Miradol and closed in, killing anyone in their path. They performed their killing using swords, spears and axes and ejected liquid poisons from their finger injectors, which were in the form of cobras. They also used poison gas that killed everyone instantly except themselves. The slaughter took over two days and nights. We of Gracyea were unfamiliar with warfare and with the killing of other human beings. By the second day we had devised a means to use sound to disorient the krates and kill or wound them while they were in a state of confusion. We truly tried only to wound them. We learned later that it really did not make any difference, because the krates killed their own wounded, even those I would classify as slightly wounded, who could have recovered after being treated with toning sounds.

Our residential area in the north was not attacked until much later, and my wife and children had enough time to lose themselves in the dense forest. I learned later that my family and others from our colony joined Gracians living at several of our outlying construction sites, eventually traveling south into the area now called South America. There they lived as fugitives from the Maldecians until some were rescued by our people from Gracyea and Mars. Others, including my family, perished when the first catastrophe occurred on Earth, a delayed aftereffect of Maldec's destruction.

I was captured by the krates along with my grandfather. We were held for a ransom of thirty large spacecraft. My grandfather telepathically notified Gracyea of the Maldecian demands, but added that neither he nor I wanted our people even to think about paying for our release. We bought time by telling the Maldecians that our people were considering their demands (which they were, in order not to make our statements a detectable lie). The Maldecians eventually established a deadline and the time came and went. We were then taken to the palace of the then-Maldecian governor of the Earth, Her-Rood, where we were tied to stakes and burned alive in his presence. Neither my grandfather nor I had ever experienced physical death before. My grandfather said to me as we stood tied to our stakes, "They are going to burn us. Try your best, son, to smell bad."

Crazy Melth-Nakhefra, the Egyptian

I entered once again into physical life on the Earth in 2535 B.C. I was born to a noble family that served Khufu, who was then king of Egypt. My mother Solmara was the king's cousin, as she was the daughter of his mother's sister. I was named Melth-Nakhefra. My father's name was Semnaftut-Kanutra. He was the principal teacher of numbers and architecture to the king and his court. He had served Khufu's father, King Snofru [also Sneferu], before him. He learned of numbers and architecture from the scribes of Khufu's maternal grandfather (my maternal great grandfather), King Hu. I attended my father's classes side by side with Prince Khafre and his nephew Djenifre-Ptah (generally called Rededef).

It is generally believed that Khafre (Chephren) was Khufu's first son, but in fact Khafre was Khufu's younger half brother by his father Snofru's second wife. Rededef was a son of Khufu and Myva, the third of his four wives, who was a beautiful blond Libyan. Khufu's first three wives bore him only daughters, eight in number. Myva was the a mother of another of the king's daughters, named Tertmis.

Khufu's psychic essence was that of the Earth. He was not a good king; in fact, he was really not a king at all. Khufu spent most of his life in a drunken stupor, leaving domestic affairs and affairs of state to a man named Ameth-Thuth, who ruled in Khufu's "divine" name with an iron hand. Khufu was a small stocky man who was always squinting. By the end of his life he was totally blind.

The first real king of that Fourth Dynasty was Snofru, Khufu's father. Both Khafre and his son Menkaure, who succeeded Khufu to the throne after Djenifre-Ptah, did progressively better as kings because the vizier (regent) Ameth-Thuth died early in Khafre's reign. It took some time for the country to recover from the ill effects of Ameth-Thuth's years of control. His death left the governors of the provinces (nomes) without any watchful leadership, and they became very corrupt and rebellious.

Khafre spent most of his reign militarily reclaiming control of the nomes (provinces). He loved action, and after his total victory he became unhappy that there wasn't anyone close at hand left to fight. He became interested in shipbuilding; his plan was to build a fleet to carry his armies to distant places where they could provide him with his favorite sport—war. Egypt lacked the building materials for such a fleet, so he never fulfilled his dream. Even so, he built some fairly good oceangoing craft that carried crews to who-knows-where. Of five voyages of exploration, I know of none that ever returned to Egypt.

The Bent Pyramid and the Red Pyramid at Dashur

Immediately after Khufu's death his Libyan wife Myva took up with the regent Ameth-Thuth, causing him to ignore his other four wives. This union put Rededef (Myva's son) on the throne of Egypt. Rededef was the only king of the Fourth Dynasty other than Snofru who ever tried to build a pyramid. He made this effort at the place now known as Abdu Roash, located north of Giza in the Nile delta. His father Khufu had been buried in what is now called the Bent Pyramid located at Dashur. This bent pyramid was partially built by King Hu of the Third Dynasty. The upper section of the structure (which has a more acute angle than the lower section) was completed by King Snofru before I was born. Snofru was also buried in the Bent Pyramid. I know the structure well, and know that the remains of Snofru and Khufu still lie within it. Snofru was really the chief architect for King Hu. Snofru married Hu's oldest daughter Hetepheres and at the time of Hu's death became the first king of the Fourth Dynasty.

The Red Pyramid of northern Dashur was also built by Snofru at the direction of King Hu for use as a tomb. The rumor that Khufu's body was laid to rest in the Great Pyramid was started by Khufu's mother Queen Hetepheres (my grandmother's sister, who outlived her son Khufu by nearly eight years). Her reasoning made good sense at the time. The common folk held the three Great Rens (pyramids) of Giza as well as the Great Sphinx in awe and considerable superstitious respect. Few would come close to them, and none would have dared enter one for fear that they would anger the ancient gods who had built them. Rededef, Khafre and Menkaure played a part in dispelling the population's fear of the Great Pyramids when they brought workers to Giza to restore them and build a number of temples nearby.

Rededef

Rededef started his construction at Abdu Roash and assigned Khafre [his young uncle], my fellow student of numbers, to supervise the restorations at Giza. One of Khafre's assignments was to find the original entrances of the pyramids. I later became part of this search. Something in me that knew "told me" it knew where they were.

I married Princess Tertmis, which made Rededef my brother-in-law. After our marriage I became obsessed with numbers, astronomy and architecture when the priests of the sun god Ra put out the word that their deity wanted the land of Egypt to be covered by temples in which the people could worship him. It took nothing more than word that the sun god wanted something built to start me off in a new life that eventually caused others to refer to me as Crazy Melth-Nakhefra. I became so engrossed in my studies that I forgot I was married and at times could not remember my wife's name. Had it not been for the fact that Khafre demanded that Tertmis feed and care for me, I would have wasted away and died. Khafre liked my divine insanity and did not look on me as crazy. He was certain that I was under the spell of the god Ra and was acting as well as could be expected of a person under the influence of such a powerful god.

We of that time in ancient Egypt had known of the wheel since the time of Imhotep, but to us it was an impractical device. Early wheeled conveyances bogged down in sand and no one could construct a wooden axle that would not break when the cart was heavily loaded.

Prior to her death, my great aunt, Queen Hetepheres, had a tomb dug for herself at Giza and had placed in it many of her personal furnishings. At her death, however, Rededef buried her with her husband and son in the Bent Pyramid at Dashur. Her tomb at Giza was left empty and later sealed (concealed with rubble) until its discovery in modern times.

Khafre provided several of his boats and Rededef dismantled them and placed them in pits that dated from the building of the pyramids of Giza. They had originally been used as Reltian latrines until another type of facility was built at Giza. (Knowing the Reltians of the time, I am certain they never used those latrines.)

Rededef obtained a number of large stone blocks that once were part of a ruined Gracian building, a headquarters once located near the third pyramid, and used the blocks from that building to cover the pits. He buried the boats on the order of the high priest of Ra. I have never known why the high priest encouraged him to bury those boats; that was known only to them. Maybe they simply didn't want some perfectly good pits to go to waste. (What the hell, they were Khafre's boats, anyway.)

Khafre Takes the Throne

On the very day that Rededef died (at Giza) of fever, my wife Tertmis presented me with a son. I confess that I didn't remember fathering the child or even the son she bore me two years earlier. At the death of Rededef (who had no sons or daughters), Khufu's oldest living daughter Benranefifti should have become queen, but Myva schemed with Ameth-Thuth to put Khufu and her daughter Tertmis (my wife) on the throne. Before they could accomplish this, Khafre took control of the army, stopped them in their tracks and proclaimed himself king. The priests of Amon supported him in his takeover. Less than a year later Ameth-Thuth, once grand vizier to King Khufu, died. He was buried in a mastaba-type tomb in an area now called Saqqara South. Later King Shepseskaf, the son of Menkaure and his first wife, Queen Khamerernebty II, took over Ameth-Thuth's mastaba tomb, removed Ameth-Thuth's body and remodeled the tomb for himself, in which he was later laid to rest.

Because of our relationship, Khafre did not find my wife or her mother guilty of anything really serious, and with Ameth-Thuth gone, he did not consider them a threat. Myva settled down and accepted being the mother-in-law of "that crazy scribe," Melth-Nakhefra.

I stood before the Great Pyramid many times and pondered its outer dimensions. From time to time I would experience mental flashes that I know were strings of numbers and equations I had learned many, many lifetimes before on my home world of Gracyea from a very old man who faded each time from my memory with the parting words, "Remember, son, try to smell bad."

One night I was sitting by a fire at the base of the third pyramid of Giza. My companions at the fire were a young scribe and two male slaves who were sent by my wife to find me and give me some wine and a basket of food. My friends fell on their faces when they heard a feminine voice calling my name out of the darkness. Soon the light of the fire illuminated four armed soldiers bearing the litter of my Great Aunt Hetepheres, dowager queen of Egypt. For several hours we talked as I sat on the ground beside her litter. Her purpose for seeking me out was to ask me if my insanity was a misery I could not tolerate. She said that if it was, she would have the priests of Amon put me to sleep by giving me poison. I told her that I could not be happier. She kissed me good night and left.

Khafre put his faith in me to locate the entrances to the pyramids of Giza. I roamed about the area day and night, accompanied by several scribes and slaves assigned to record my thoughts and provide for my comfort. At my request both the scribes and slaves would take measurements. I was psychically urged to gather up pieces of different types of rubble that lay about. I tapped the egg-sized pieces together to create sound. Though I did not consciously know why I was doing this, subconsciously I was searching for a frequency that related to the material. I learned that this increased my hearing ability. Soon my assistants took up the habit of clicking stones together. When I asked them why they were doing so, they replied, "It makes us feel calm and sometimes takes away the desire to eat."

Mathematics at That Time

Egyptian mathematics of the time was quite primitive. We dealt mostly with the addition and subtraction of numbers that were rarely greater than 1000. Multiplication was accomplished by doubling and halving. The only fraction in the system that had its own unique hieroglyph was ⅔. I sub-consciously knew that the creator of the special symbol for the fraction ⅔ had done so with a purpose, because when written in decimal form it is expressed as $0.\overline{666}$. As you [the author] know, the number $0.\overline{666}$ is the 18th repitan (18/27) of what you call the Ra system of mathematics and the prime number of the molar level of reality. (The term 'repitan" means a sequence of numbers that repeats again and again. [For example, $0.037037\overline{037}$ (d27) or $1/0.81 = 1.234567m90\overline{1234567m90}$ or $8/0.81 = 9.8765432m09\overline{8765432m0}$.

Notice that the results of the divisions 1/0.81 and 8/0.81 (9 x 9 = 81) are, respectively, an upward sequence of numbers in which the 8 is missing from the string (m) and a downward-running sequence of num-bers in which the number 1 is missing. These number sequences are also referred to respectively as ra plus and ra minus sequences.

Earlier, Tixer-Chock pointed out that the number 0.729 (27 x 27) was the reciprocal of the fine-structure constant ($1/729 = 0.001371742112$) for the element hydrogen. Ra repitans and plus and minus sequences *in every case* are multiples of the fine-structure constant for hydrogen, as in the following examples: $0.\overline{037}/0.00137174 = 27$; $1.\overline{234567m90}/0.001371742112 = 900$; $9.\overline{8765432m0}/0.001371742112 = 7200$ and $0.\overline{666}/0.001371742112 = 486$. Remem-ber that the number 4860 ra angstroms is the wavelength of the second visible spectral line of hydrogen and that there were once 486 green ra feet in the height of the Great Pyramid of Giza. The first ra repitan $(0.\overline{037})$ squared also equals the value 0.001371742112 (fine-structure constant). —W.H.B.

The repitan $0.\overline{666}$ reverses the repitan numerical pattern of the 17 repi-tans that precede it. (Patterns are recognized when the first three numbers of the 27 ra repitans are placed in blocks of three such as repitan 0 or $0.\overline{000}$ over repitan 1 or $0.\overline{037}$, which in turn is placed over repitan 2, or $0.\overline{074}$. The number $0.\overline{666}$ must be put in a block by itself (with no other repitan) in order for the patterns to display the reversal just mentioned.

The creator of the special Egyptian hieroglyph for ⅔ ($0.\overline{666}$) must cer-tainly have been an ancient colleague from Gracyea who became psychi-cally stranded, as I did, in the Frequency Barrier of the planet Earth.

Saqqara

By foot, camel and boat I and my small band of assistants traveled far and wide throughout the land of the two kingdoms (Upper and Lower Egypt) visiting and measuring all buildings erected during earlier dynasties or in prehistoric times. I happened to be at Dashur near the Bent Pyramid when a royal funeral cortege arrived with the body of my Great Aunt Hetepheres. With the funeral party was Khafre, then king of Egypt, and his young son, Crown Prince Menkaure. Menkaure's mother (Queen Daamutyty) had died giving him birth. Unknown by me until then, my wife Tertmis and her mother Myva had become the young prince's nurses and reared him with my two sons.

I went to join the group of mourners and was met by my wife, who told me that I smelled bad because I had not bathed in some time. For some unknown reason I took this as a compliment. Seeing me, Khafre ask what progress I was making in locating the entrances to the pyramids of Giza. He was now certain that the pyramids contained many marvelous things left by the gods. Among those things, he was sure, existed a scroll that would describe how to live forever. I told him that I expected to return to Giza soon with the information he wanted. After our conversation he had a slave bring me a bundle, which I untied and unwrapped. It it were a number of papyruses and "papers" containing strange symbols that I later translated as being numbers. There were also a number of finely scored metal discs about the size of a coin. Among these treasures were a bottle of poison and a letter that said, 'I hope these things bring you happiness. They come from the time of Imhotep. My husband King Snofru many times tried to understand them. If they cause you to become more insane than you presently are, I leave you half of the potion I took during the last few painful minutes of my life. May we meet again in the presence of the gods. Hetepheres, daughter of Hu, the son of Ra."

At Saqqara I visited the ancient temple that once was the earthly residence of Imhotep, beloved of the god Amon. I sat within it and absorbed the geometric knowledge it radiated and exchanged with the universal life field, both consciously and subconsciously. I now know (again) that the structure was one of the outlying buildings built by my people, the Gracians, to bend by seven degrees certain magnetic lines of force of the Earth's magnetic grid, which would in turn reduce certain undesirable magnetic effects in the vicinity of the Giza Plateau. This was the same reason that some support buildings were constructed miles distant from Miradol (Teotihuacan). Another support building that crumbled when Maldec exploded was the so-called pyramid at Meidum [also Maydum and Maidûm]. Every Egyptian king after Djoser up to Snofru attempted to reconstruct the pyramid at Meidum. King Hu and Snofru made the greatest reconstruction efforts, but gave up when from time to time the structure crumbled again due to even the most minor of earthquakes.

My small group of five, including myself, depended on the local army commander to provide us with food and other provisions. On rare occasions we could also temporarily acquire a labor force from the army to help us move something. It was during a visit to to the headquarters of the small garrison stationed near the Step Pyramid at Saqqara that I noticed a group of men who, though captive, were being treated with respect. These men were travelers from the land you now call Babylon. They were arrested for entering the ruined temple and attempting to measure its interior. Even under guard they continued to look at the pyramid and temple from a distance and estimate their size. Those estimates they recorded on papyrus and on the ground in every direction around them. Their leader was a man named Hamarebuti. They were in luck that the local army commander was not a devout religious man, or he would have had them killed for their sacrilege.

I was first attracted to the group of Babylonians when I heard them chanting in the direction of the setting sun. I joined their group and felt good listening to their strange-sounding chants. At dawn I joined them again to repeat the ritual. My presence brought a smile to their faces. At night they would make observations of the positions of the stars and planets. I too had studied the positions of the heavenly lights and looked over their shoulders on several occasions at rolls of star charts they had brought from their homeland. I ordered the guards away and took these scholars into my custody.

When I did this, I motioned them to follow me to the temple in which they had such a great interest. When they realized that they were free and would be able to measure the temple, they became very excited and offered prayers of joy to the heavens. Among the group of twelve Babylonians was a small, thin, dark-complected man. At a glance one would have thought him to be a slave. I know now that he had come from the land you now call India. I had taken the measurements of the buildings at Saqqara many months before, but at first they were useless to my colleagues, who spoke a different language and used a different form of writing. This problem was solved to some degree when the high priest of Ra sent me Crubbo, an old priest-scribe who could speak but not write or translate the written language of the foreign scholars. We started our collaborations by agreeing to use the mathematical symbols for 1 to 10 that were provided by Bhafdat, the man from India. This was difficult for the Babylonians, who used a sexagesimal system which, I admit, was a better system than was then being used in Egypt.

[The Babylonian sexagesimal number system uses base 60, which is still used today to measure time (1 hour = 60 minutes, 1 minute = 60 seconds) and in measuring the degrees of a circle. —W.H.B.]

Crubbo, the scribe/priest of Amon, and Bhafdat, the "man of the East," huddled together, and after viewing my records and those of the Babylonians, proclaimed that the most ancient buildings of Egypt, including the Great Rens (pyramids), were built on the order of a decimal system (1 to 10) in which nine was the key number. I somehow knew they were right.

It was Bhafdat who told us of the existence of the greatest of numbers— pi (3.141592...) and other so-called irrational numbers such as the square root of two. I wondered why he had not told his Babylonian friends of these things before. It was then that I learned that Bhafdat did not come to Egypt with the Babylonians, but was arrested roaming around the Saqqara monuments several days after the Babylonians were arrested. After imparting his mathematical knowledge to us, Bhafdat mysteriously disappeared. We asked Crubbo if he knew what had become of him. He told us that Bhafdat went into a shaft (passage) that ran in the direction of the Step Pyramid built by Imhotep, the beloved of the god Amon. When Crubbo took us to the spot where he saw Bhafdat enter the passage, it could not be found.

Several days later my father came to me and told me that my mother had died and he had buried her near the pyramid at Meidum (south of Saqqara). With my father was a young man who constantly looked at me. I asked my father who the young man was and he replied, "You idiot, he is your son, Bredef-Karnut. I have brought him to you to be educated, as I educated you in the ways of numbers. I am old and tired and will soon join the gods." My father left us and went north a few days later. I never saw him again.

Our band of scholars increased and decreased in size many times due to the comings and goings of young men sent by the priests of Amon to either learn from us or spy on us. They didn't want us to learn how to gain entrance into the pyramids without their knowledge.

Back at Giza to Discover the Entrance

At Giza we built several small scale models of the buildings in the area. Over the time that passed, my group of Egyptians and the Babylonian group of scholars became able to communicate with each other quite well.

Many times King Khafre and his son Menkaure visited us at Giza. The king was impatient, but vowed his full and continuing support during our studies and investigations of the pyramids.

One morning, after a night of great anticipation, several Babylonians and I went to the north face of the Great Pyramid. Waiting for us there was Crubbo and the high priest of Amon. There were, of course, many more people present. A staff with a white pennant bearing an embroidered black scarab fluttered in the wind. The staff was located at the base of the pyramid in line with the structure's apothem line (a vertical line that runs down the middle of any face of a pyramid from peak to base).

I was given the honor of measuring off exactly 7.29 sacred units (green rams) from the location of the staff to the west. Remember that 0.729 (27 x 27 = 729) is the reciprocal of the fine-structure constant for hydrogen. At the point to which I measured we planted another flag embroidered with the head of a ram, which represented the god Amon Ra. A ladder covered with sheepskins and wide enough to hold three men abreast was placed against the sloping side of the pyramid by the staff of Amon. I climbed the ladder, slowly tapping the casing stones as I went. Several times I was pushed upward as extensions to the ladder were added below me.

Just under 17 meters from the base of the pyramid I found what I was looking for—one of the long-lost entrances to the interior of the Great Pyramid. The hatchlike door was really indistinguishable from the casing stones that surrounded it. When I was sure I had found the entrance and knew how to open it, I called to those below. King Khafre and Hamarebuti the Babylonian joined me on the ladder.

Even after so many years, the hatch lifted easily and slid inward on tracks or runners cut in the stone sides of the entrance. When the door reached the end of the tracks, it did so with a thud, bouncing back several times, with less and less force until it came to rest.

Inside the Great Pyramid

The interior was dark, but we could make out a small antechamber immediately inside. We waited some time for oil lamps to be brought up the ladder. Lamps in hand, we entered the room (now nonexistent), which was then $7.85398\overline{14}$ red rams (¼ red pi x 10) deep and 3 red rams wide. This chamber was vacant. At its southern end was a passage 1.06 meters wide and 1.34 meters high. These dimensions translate to 1.0602875 red rams wide (1.060660172 green rams or 1.0610329754 blue rams), height 1.332864854 red rams high ($1.\overline{333}$ green rams or 1.333801976 blue rams). The 1.0602875 red ram width of the passage is called a hunab unit and was used widely in the buildings and layout of the city of Miradol (Teotihuacan). (The value 10.602875 cpns is the most frequently generated alpha brain-wave frequency produced by a meditating human being.)

When the height and width of this passage in green rams are multiplied one by the other, the result is 1.414213562 square green rams. Those familiar with numbers should immediately recognize the number 1.414213562 as the square root of 2. Those who would argue that Egyptians during the time of the Fourth Dynasty did not know about irrational numbers such as pi and the square root of 2 would be correct. But we of Gracyea who built the Great Pyramids of Giza knew of these numbers thousands of millennia before the time of Khufu and his descendants, and the teachers from the Hamp radiar (Uranus) preceded us of Gracyea in knowing of these sacred numbers by many thousands of years.

The walls of the antechamber were of polished rectangular limestone blocks cut and shaped on the order of the phi proportion. They were 27 red ra inches long and 16.2 red ra inches high. Above the entrance of the downward-sloping passage was the triangular stone that bears what is now called "a mysterious tetragram."

[The tetragram consists of a "V" (shaped like an elevator indicator arrow), horizontally followed by an oval and a horizontal line sandwiched between two longer horizontal lines of the same length. This stack of three lines is followed by an oval with two vertical bars running through it. These are Gracian symbols that state, "Go down (downward pointing arrow) this open passage (first oval) until you come to three steps (three horizontal lines), where you will find a sealed passage (oval with vertical bars)." —W.H.B.]

The Descending Passage

Down the so-called descending passage of the Great Pyramid can be found three steps located directly under the entrance to the so-called ascending passage. This sealed passage was first discovered by the Arabs in the ninth century.

The triangular-shaped stone over the entrance of the descending passage (in which the tetragram is carved) has a base of 3.181980514 green rams and a height of 1.6495387 green rams. The stone's face thus has an area of 2.6244 square green rams There are 26244 green ra angstroms in the wavelength of Brackett's M6 spectral line in infrared of the element hydrogen. There are also 262,440 square green ra feet in the Great Pyramid's diagonal cross section. (The Martian Sharmarie's response to this information was, "Gee whiz, what a coincidence!")

Khafre, Hamarebuti and I stared downward into the darkness of the descending passage. The light from our lamps reflected off some metal object located near the right wall of the passage. Bending over, we made our way down to this spot, where we found a railing about 14.5 meters long mounted to the wall. *[Today one can still see the ten holes in which the railing described by Tixer-Chock was set. —W.H.B.]*

The railing was made up of six sections, each one made of a different metal alloy and detachable from each other. On each of the sections of railing were inscribed the measuring units dictated by the sacred numbers used to lay out the dimensions of the Great Pyramids. Later this railing was removed by Khafre and buried with him at Dashur.

The pharaohs built not the Great Pyramids, nor did their hands fashion the features of the Sphinx of Giza. How could primitive ignorance create such marvels? Think well of the words of Tixer-Chock and others who can correct these misunderstandings that are fostered by yet more ignorance. Do you want to know the truth of these things? If not, read no further. I am Pen-Dronell of Nodia.

King Khafre of Egypt, Hamarebuti the Babylonian and I (Tixer-Chock, who was then called Melth-Nakhefra), thought a bit about entering deeper into the descending passage of the Great Pyramid. I was willing, but my companions were hesitant. Total silence prevailed; we had to speak up in order to be heard because the low-frequency energy of softly spoken words was absorbed by the walls of the passage and the antechamber, to which we later returned.

Hamarebuti shouted down the passage, "Is anybody here?" His words and the laughter that followed produced no echo. It was King Khafre who insisted that we proceed to explore with caution and respect for the ancient gods who had built the pyramid. The king then called down to the crowd waiting outside at the base of the structure. He ordered several soldiers to climb the ladder and join us. I requested that my assistants also join us with more oil lamps, torches and measuring tools.

The temperature in the pyramid was pleasant to me, but the two lamp-carrying soldiers who preceded us down the descending passage, although stripped to the minimum of clothing, were sweating heavily.

I later measured the descending passage to find that its total length was 106.02875 red rams. As you might recall, the linear unit of 1.0602875 red rams is now called a *hunab* after the Aztec god of measure, Hunab-Ku. As mentioned before, most of the buildings at Teotihuacan (Miradol), Mexico, and some at Palenque, were proportioned on the order of the hunab unit of measure. I will also remind you that the alpha brain wave most frequently generated by a meditating human being is 10.602875 cycles per natural second of time (cpns).

The Horizontal Passage and the Subterranean Chamber

King Khafre, Hamarebuti and I followed the soldiers down the descending passage. We in turn were followed by my four assistants and Crubbo, the scribe/priest of Amon. At the end of the descending passage we came upon a horizontal passage that continued to the south. This passage is now called the subterranean horizontal passage. This passage has several features, including a niche located in its eastern wall, the depth of which is 38.88 green ra inches. The distance from the passage entrance to the point of the vertical axis from the apex is 7.63407 red rams. There are 763.407 red ra feet in the base length of the Great Pyramid as well as the Pyramid of the Sun at Teotihuacan. *[See page 253 for more information about the number 763.407 and its relationship to the measurements of many ancient Gracian buildings located on Earth. —W.H.B.]*

It is truly my wish that I could continue describing the sacred number relationships embodied in the features of the subterranean horizontal passage of the Great Pyramid. But the sacred numbers involved would have to be individually identified so that their relationships to each other could be fully appreciated. The time required to describe the unique meanings of these numbers would be quite lengthy. Therefore I will refer only to the sacred number relationships in certain features of the pyramid when I can be brief.

There are 3888 green ra angstroms (related to the depth of the niche previously mentioned) in the wavelength of the Balmer M8 spectral line of hydrogen (wavelength = $364.5 \times m^2/m^2 - 4$, wherein 364.5 (27×13.5) is the Ra version of the Balmer constant for hydrogen and m equals 8). (By the way, $m^3 = 656.1$ [$81 \times 81 = 6561$], $m^4 = 486$ [$18 \times 27 = 486$] and so on.)

Our band of explorers then entered what is now called the subterranean chamber. It looked then as it does now. Its irregularities make it appear unfinished. I believe it was Ruke of Parn who told you that its appearance was due to the fact that sections of its floor were cut as needed to fine-tune the total structure to the universal life field. These tuning cuts of different depths give the chamber an incomplete look. As you know, it is reported that there are several marks of the same size and shape in the ceiling of this chamber. These odd-shaped marks were made by an ultrasound pulverizer once held in the hands of Somarix-Tol, the Gracian in charge of the fine-tuning of the Great Pyramid.

Beyond the subterranean chamber is a passage that eventually comes to a dead end. The dimensions of this passage are 4.14213562 green rams long ($\sqrt{2} \times 10$), 0.074$\overline{074}$ green rams wide (2/27, or second repitan) and

0.763675324 green rams high, which is equivalent to the now-well-known value of 0.763407 red rams.

We searched for days for other hidden passages in the Great Pyramid, but we failed to find any during the first three months. We eventually gained access to other areas of all three of the Great Pyramids. I am aware that this has not been accomplished by anyone since.

The descending passage has a number of features that have long baffled those who have noticed them over the years: (1) a stone block set vertically (not slanted at the angle of the slope of the passage) and (2) immediately following this special block of masonry, a scored line in the passage wall. Why the builders went to the effort to create these features can now be answered. The distance from the original entrance to the scored line in the wall is 12.15 green rams. The length of the scored line is 1.215 green rams, and its width 0.01215 green rams. There are 1215 green ra angstroms in the most intense spectral line of the element hydrogen. The height of the passage is $1.\overline{333}$ green rams. When the length of the scored line is divided into the height of the vertically set block, the resulting ratio is 0.109739369, or the Ra value for the Rydberg constant for hydrogen. (Sharmarie the Martian says again, "Gee whiz, another coincidence!")

Discovering Imhotep's Work

In the course of sounding the walls of the descending passage to locate

Michael Tyree

possible hollow areas behind, I discovered an area of masonry that was not of the quality found elsewhere in the passage walls. This repair job was in the west wall of the passage and was located 6.561 green rams up from the bottom end of the passage. (The number 6581 is the product of 81 x 81, and there are 6561 green ra angstroms in the Balmer M3 spectral line of hydrogen.)

On one of the larger repair blocks was a carved inscription in a form of writing that we could not totally understand. The only symbol we recognized was the cartouche (signature), "imhotep, beloved of the god Amon." A scribe copied the inscription (by making a rubbing), which we later studied in our living quarters located near the second pyramid.

We were studying the copy of the inscription when Hamarebuti the Babylonian returned to our headquarters after a period of illness we then called Giza fever. It was this form of illness that had taken the life of the previous king, Rededef. After looking at the inscription, Hamarebuti declared the unknown writing to be that of his illustrious ancestors, the Sumerians. A member of his group named Armonamuri read the inscription and Crubbo, the scribe/priest of Amon, translated it into the language of Egypt. It took them many days because the symbols were very small and both translators were old and had failing eyesight. We solved the problem by having another scribe enlarge each symbol one at a time so they could be clearly seen. We waited impatiently for the translation to be completed and for Crubbo to inform the high priest of Amon first. It was a very impatient King Khafre, along with six sword-carrying soldiers, who interrupted the five-day meeting of the high priest and Crubbo. The high priest hastily departed from Giza and Khafre brought the translation to me. He placed the scrolls in my hands and said, smiling, "Tell me what they say, my crazy friend."

As I recall, the translated inscription basically read as follows. "Greetings to you, the gods that live beyond the clouds. He of Sumer brought your divine orders to me, your servant. As you have instructed, I have removed the remaining dangers of the Great Ren. My work lies beyond this stone. May it please you. I felt the soul depart of he who was imprisoned here. Beware; he may some day, by the will and mercy of the elohim, walk again in the flesh. Imhotep."

We leave Tixer-Chock at this point to insert information that supports his account of his life in ancient Egypt and provides mathematical data pertaining to the Great Pyramid that has never before been widely publicized except in my self-published four-book series, *The Rods of Amon Ra*.

A Cross Section of the Great Pyramid

The illustration here depicts the median cross section of the pyramid and its known passages and chambers. I have superimposed a Fibonacci logarithmic spiral over these features, which reveals a great deal.

A, the five relieving chambers, each constructed of numerous granite blocks weighing 70 tons each.

The relieving chambers are located over the so-called King's Chamber (**B**). The only object in this chamber is a box made of chocolate-colored granite of a type found only in the state of Minnesota. The southern wall is composed of 37 blocks of stone, the northern wall of 27 blocks (that's where the entrance is located). The east and west walls each contain 18 blocks. (The significance of the numbers 27, 37 and 18 will be explained shortly.)

C is the so-called Queen's Chamber. This chamber has a large niche in its western wall.

D is the horizontal passage to the Queen's Chamber.

E is the Grand Gallery (see closeup on page 275).

F is the outside entrance to the descending passage.

G is the beginning of the ascending passage, which was once plugged and impassable until the plugs were circumvented by tunneling around them.

H shows the three "girdle stones." Each of these once-solid stones have a carved, square opening, which Tixer-Chock will explain when his narrative resumes.

I is a natural cavity called the Grotto (at ground level). Running upward and downward from the Grotto is a shaft that starts at point **2** and ends at point **K** at the bottom. (It was at point **K** that Tixer-Chock found Imhotep's inscription.)

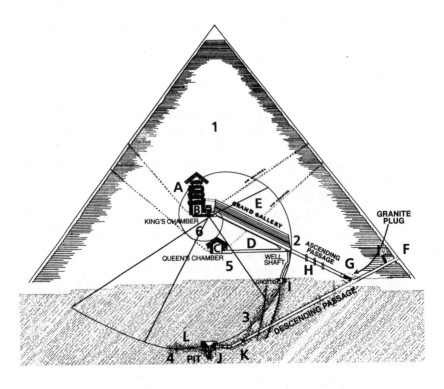

J is the subterranean chamber that Tixer-Chock says was dug out of the bedrock a little at a time as required to fine-tune the pyramid to the universal life field.

L is the dead-end passage mentioned earlier.

The shape of the force field produced by the Great Pyramid is that of a Fibonacci logarithmic spiral, seen in the shape of a ram's horn and the shell of the chambered nautilus. The vril energy transmitted to Maldec from the pyramid was first concentrated in this spiral shape. Notice that the top of the spiral (**1**) is at the same height as the pointed ceiling of the uppermost relieving chamber above the King's Chamber.

Following the spiral from the bottom to the right, we find that it intersects the ascending passage where it opens into the Grand Gallery. Notice that Imhotep dug the well shaft just inside the spiral and that it takes an abrupt turn downward at **3**, where it crosses the spiral. The spiral bottoms out on the floor of the dead-end passage (**4**) before it begins its upward swing.

A line projected from the center of the spiral to the bottom right corner of the Golden Rectangle just clears the roof edge of the Queen's Chamber and passes through what is referred to as the "mysterious step" (**5**) in the passage that leads to the Queen's Chamber.

At a glance one can see that the known passages and chambers of the Great Pyramid were constructed and positioned to correspond with the shape of a Fibonacci spiral.

The center of the spiral (**6**), located just below the "great step," is the only point on the spiral that cannot be physically viewed by anyone at present. I will return to Tixer-Chock so that he can describe how to reach that spot in the pyramid and what someone could expect to find there. —W.H.B.

The Well Shaft

We removed the masonry that Imhotep used to seal up the bottom of the well shaft. When the shaft was opened, there was a blast of hot air followed by a sweet odor of flowers. Eventually this pleasant smell vanished. We climbed the well shaft and emerged at the base of the Grand Gallery. I now know why Imhotep dug the well shaft and what he was referring to when he wrote, "I felt the soul depart of he who was imprisoned here."

He had dug the shaft just inside the still-active spiral to further dampen its detrimental effects—which can be seen by the fissures it produced in the bedrock beneath the pyramid. The digging at the well shaft might have prevented the still-active vril-energy vortex from causing the Earth to shatter as it once shattered Maldec.

Another Account of the Day Maldec Exploded

Following is a short account of the day Maldec exploded, given by Kevinar-Kale of Earth.

As was our custom, we gathered on the roof of the temple to pray and make music. We were of such an age that women gave us honor by walking among us unveiled. The plaza below was filled with visitors from many other worlds who came to hear the words of the Watchers. They would be disappointed this day, for the Radiant Ones [Maldecians] had all left to assemble in the Land of Mir to view the Great Pyramid they had raised for the sake of glory.

Michael Tyree

The day before, a legion of gaily robed elders of the Watcher race had arrived from their world, which is called Maldec. I myself watched servant Simms come and go from the Maldecians' spacecraft for the purpose of seeing to their comfort. At dusk I watched with my wife, Dovinta, as their silver craft rose, appearing first as a moving star, then passing out of sight over the eastern horizon. It was the day of the summer solstice, and there would be much feasting and merrymaking through-out the night. We of the temple would not join the revelry, but would talk and enjoy the starry sky till dawn.

Nearing the eleventh hour of the night there was a great light that appeared in the northern sky, and our spirits were stabbed with spears of foreboding and overwhelming concern. The light grew larger and brighter, and birds flew in circles, frightened from their nests by the deafening sounds of other animals and perhaps by the silent sounds made by the souls of men.

By dawn the only sounds heard were the inquiring voices of those who gathered below. In many languages I heard them ask, "What caused the great light? What did it mean? Was it an omen?" Then the high priest Savacanopy spoke to those who had gathered and advised them to come into the temple or seek a quiet place to pray, waiting for the Watchers to return, for they were wise in the ways of heaven. As he departed, I heard him murmur a prayer requesting of God permission

Michael Tyree

to cry.

Before sunset my sons Somencar and Adthro entered our home. They had been gone for several months serving the Watchers in the Land of Mir. They related to me a strange story. The elders of Maldec had joined others of their race at the place where the Great Pyramid stood. With them they had brought bundles of jeweled wooden rods they called vril sticks as well as vessels of water and soil from their home world. There were also vessels of soil and water from Earth, our home world, stored there in a white tent. A Watcher youth wearing a robe bearing strange symbols walked among his brethren and received their embraces and kisses.

Somencar also told me that he was one of those who took the vessels of soil and water into the pyramid and placed them as instructed in the twenty-seven pairs of slots in the curbs of the Grand Gallery. The vessels were alternated water of Maldec, soil of Earth, water of Earth, soil of Maldec. Two of the Watcher elders stood side by side, one by each slot, and held his vril stick inside his assigned vessel. The Watcher youth climbed the gallery and whispered to each in their ears. What he imparted is unknown.

At the exact time of the summer solstice, each pair of Watcher elders, without removing their sticks from their vessels, tipped them toward each other until they touched. When this was done the Earth shook violently and a red pillar of whirling fire rose from the pyramid's apex. Those on the surrounding plain were terrified and cried out to God. They also saw a great

Michael Tyree

light appear in the sky. The pyramid became very hot, driving away those gathered around it. The pillar of fire continued to reach skyward for many more hours and then gradually receded. A circle of dead Watchers were found later in the white tent. They had stripped naked and had taken their own lives.

My sons told me that Crennamer, the trader who dealt much with those who built the pyramids of Mir, came upon them and offered to bring them home and into my presence. Crennamer told my sons that a grieving and tearful Watcher had told him that they had destroyed their home world in error. Crennamer said that this must be true, as all know that the Watchers are wise to the ways of heaven.

Somencar and Adthro both suspected that it was Crennamer who provided the Radiant Ones with the poisonous potions that took their lives.

I lived for nearly fourteen more years after the world called Maldec exploded and shook the foundations of the stars. During that time tremendous cataclysmic events occurred on the Earth in the form of earthquakes, volcanic eruptions and great floods. I was spared the loss of my mind, whereas those who lived longer were not as fortunate.

At that time of life I did not know why the Watchers did what they did or in what way they had made their dreadful error. Even many lifetimes since, I think about that time and pray to God for permission to cry. I am Kevinar-Kale.

On page 226 of the book *The Wars of Gods and Men* by Zecharia Sitchin is found his scholarly translation of an ancient Sumerian manuscript that describes the digging of a shaft in the Great Pyramid that freed the demigod Marduk of his imprisonment in the structure. As you read the following, keep in mind the well shaft, the spiraling vril energy vortex and the Maldecian youth (Marduk) mentioned in Kevinar-Kale's account.

Sitchin: *Dalat biri iqa buni ilani.* ("A doorway shaft which the gods will bore.") [This tells of the well shaft dug in the Great Pyramid by imhotep much later at the instruction of the gods.]

Sitchin: *Shunu itasrushu ina biti etarba.* ("Its vortex they will lift off, his abode they shall reenter.") [This says that when the well shaft was dug into the center of the vril-energy vortex, its strength was weakened or its effects were totally canceled ("lifted off"). It also indicates that the psychic essence of the Maldecian youth called Marduk might also have been restrained by the spiral-shaped energy vortex previously generated by the pyramid.]

Sitchin: *Shunu hurrate ina libbi dalti uptalishu.* ("At the hollowing they will twistingly bore.") [The "hollowing" at which the well-shaft diggers would "twistingly bore" could mean either the center of the energy vortex or the natural hollow area at the surface of the bedrock called the Grotto. The hollowing of a vortex could be viewed as similar to the calm eye of a hurricane or tornado.]

Sitchin: *Quabu ina libbi uppushu.* ("Getting near in its midst, they will break through.") [At the point when the diggers broke through to the spiral-shaped vril-energy vortex generated by the Great Pyramid, the psychic shackles of vril energy were broken and Marduk's psychic essence became free once more.]

The following illustration depicts a closeup of several key features of the Great Pyramid. —W.H.B.

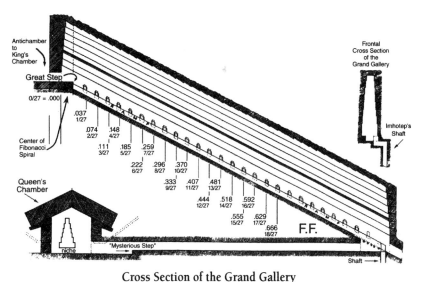

Cross Section of the Grand Gallery
The Grand Gallery with its 27 (28) pairs of slots and seven ceilings with 37 overlapping slabs.
The seven ceilings represent the seven periods of the Periodic Table of Elements (electron orbits K to Q).
The last pair of slots represents the repitan 0.999, or 0.037 x 27 (not 27/27).

More Pyramid Math

I am Tixer-Chock. Let us begin with the fact that the horizontal passage to the Queen's Chamber is 38.17035 red rams in length (38.17035 x 2 = 76.3407). This length is also equal to 127.2345 red ra feet or 12 units of 10.602875 red ra feet. When the 5.4 green ram distance from the "mysterious step" to the chamber is divided by the 38.1837662 green ram length of the total passage, the result is 0.141421362, or the square root of 2×10^{-1}. I am aware that it is presently believed on the Earth that the knowledge of irrational numbers such as the square root of two originated from the time of the Classical Greeks. We of Gracyea installed this knowledge of the square root of two in the design of the Great Pyramid. The knowledge of irrational numbers was later rediscovered by the Greeks. Those of the Fourth Dynasty in Egypt were completely ignorant of irrational numbers. I ought to know—I lived during those times and was considered a mathematical expert among my contemporaries.

The point **F.F.** in the drawing, located near the beginning of the passage to the Queen's Chamber, stands for "French find." Early in 1987 a French team of archaeologists, using ultrasound equipment, located what they call a hollow cavity below and to the west of the horizontal passage to the Queen's Chamber. Their discovery was made exactly where a line projected upward from the lower right corner of the Golden Rectangle (shown first in the illustration on page 270) crosses the passage. Because I had previously shared the information about the pyramid's inner features and their relationship to the Fibonacci spiral with Dr. Ahmed Kadry, then director of the Egyptian Antiquities Organization (E.A.O.), he invited me to speak at a symposium held in Cairo December 14–17, 1987. Later I was asked to write an article for the E.A.O's official publication on any methods I might think of to reach the French cavity without tearing apart the pyramid. Simple methods have been devised to enter the secret chambers of the Great Pyramid, but they have not yet been implemented as far as I know. I now return to Tixer-Chock, who will describe my favorite feature of the Great Pyramid—the Grand Gallery. —W.H.B.

The Grand Gallery is 157.0796$\overline{296}$ red ra feet in length. When its length is divided by the 127.2345 red ra foot-length of the horizontal passage to the Queen's Chamber, the result is 0.1234567m90 (ra plus sequence, m denoting the missing number 8). For that matter, when the ascending passage length of 125.6637037 red ra feet is divided by the 127.2345 red ra foot-length of the horizontal passage to the Queen's Chamber, the result is 0.98765432m09 (ra minus sequence, m denoting the missing number 1). Running the length of the curbs (banquettes) of the Grand Gallery, spaced evenly apart, are pairs of slots, 27 in all. These are the slots mentioned by Kevinar-Kale as those in which were put vessels of soil and water of Earth and Maldec. These 27 pairs of slots represent the 27 ra repitans—1/27, 2/27, 3/27 and so on. The Grand Gallery can also be viewed as 1884.9$\overline{555}$ red ra inches long. When the gallery's length in red ra inches is divided by 50893.8 (red ankh x 10^4), the result is 0.$\overline{037}$

(first ra repitan).

The distance between each pair of ramp slots is 69.813168724 red ra inches. When this distance is divided by red ankh, the result is 13.717421125, or the fine-structure constant for hydrogen multiplied several times by the power of 10.

The Grand Gallery has seven ceilings that once consisted of a total of 37 overlapping stone slabs. First of all, one ceiling would have been enough for a tomb, wouldn't it? The 27 slots represent the 27 Ra repitans that are multiples of the fine-structure constant for hydrogen. These repitans also represent mathematical factors related to such things as quarks and other particles/forces within the nuclei of atoms. On the other hand, the seven ceilings of the Grand Gallery represent the seven periods in the Periodic Table of Elements (electron shells K to Q).

The 37 slabs reveal the existence of a very important set of numbers in the sacred system of mathematics. These numbers that relate to electron dynamics comprise the list called the Ra Table of Nines. The numbers in the Ra Table of Nines are on page 253. The list of 37 numbers is called by that name because when each is added horizontally, they always total nine—for example, 27 (2 + 7 = 9), 54 (5 + 4 = 9), 81 (8 + 1 = 9) and so on. Remember, there are 37 blocks of stone in the north wall and 27 in the south wall of the King's Chamber, emphasizing the important relationship between the numbers 27 and 37. Eighteen is the number of blocks found in the east and west walls of the King's Chamber. The mathematical message here is that the number 18 and 2 x 18 (36) are also very important in the Ra system of mathematics.

There is a 28th pair of slots found in the Great Step located at the top of the Grand Gallery. This pair of slots represents the $0.\overline{000}$ ra repitan. The $0.\overline{000}$ repitan slots in the Great Step are situated directly over the center of the Fibonacci spiral shown on page 275. This identifies the Great Step as a very important feature of the Great Pyramid.

The Grand Gallery

After climbing up the well shaft, we came to the base of the Grand Gallery. Whoever dug the shaft to this precise location knew exactly where they were going. In other words, they worked from very accurate building plans. This upper opening of the well shaft is exactly 40 green rams from the beginning of the Grand Gallery, the point where the energy vortex spiraled upward (see **2** on illustration).

We climbed the Grand Gallery and the Great Step, but our way was blocked by a number of stone barriers (known in the literature as portcullises) that were in slots and resting on the floor of the antechamber.

With great physical effort we raised the stones and held them up with blocks. We then entered the King's Chamber. It was empty except for the granite box called the coffer. Its capacity was designed to equal a certain number of units of weight now called the *heavy qedet* (about 9.1125 grams in the m.g.s. [meters/grams/seconds] scale of measurement). This is exactly the weight of a heavy qedet in green ra grams.

The heavy qedet unit was established by the weight of the electron, which is 9.1125 green ra grams x 10^{-28}. The reciprocal of 0.91125 is 1.09739369, or the Ra version of the Rydberg constant for hydrogen.

The lid of the coffer was broken into small pieces and placed inside it. The ascending passage had been sealed during the pyramid's construction to permit the structure to resonate properly.

How people came and went from the structure before Maldec exploded is simple. Other entrances had become lost, then found by us of the Fourth Dynasty and lost again. Due to the secrecy enforced by the priests of Amon, a limited number of people knew the locations of the hidden entrances to the pyramids and the Sphinx. Acting as if they were on a holy mission, a gang of younger priests labored for years to seal the passages with rubble and the entrances with local limestone piled on a bed of mortar. When I inquired into why they did this, the high priest of Amon replied that he was acting on the direct orders of the sky gods. He added that in times to come, the gods would reveal these secrets once again to those of the Earth. At the time I did not know that I, Tixer-Chock, would play a part at this time in the fulfillment of that ancient prophecy.

The Ascending Passage

During our explorations of the ascending passage we noticed several markings on the passage walls just before both the first and second girdle stones (see **H**). Even without sophisticated equipment to assure us we were not on a fool's errand, we decided to give the walls between the girdle stones a push. Lo and behold, the wall moved inward! You see, the one-piece girdle stones support the weight of the passage's ceiling, so the walls bear no weight. I admit it took a number of very strong slaves to get the wall to budge. For several reasons, hydraulic jacks might be required to accomplish this task today. The priests of Amon used more than a dagger [see below] to block the numerous doorways and passages that still lay concealed within the largest pyramids at Giza.

King Khafre, Hamarebuti and I squeezed through the partially open doorway. Crubbo, the priest/scribe, was too fat to get through the narrow opening. He urged the slaves to push harder against the wall to increase the size of the portal. Unseen by Crubbo, King Khafre wedged his dagger under the stone door and, while smiling at us, told Crubbo to follow with the slaves as soon as he could. (Khafre must have had a bit of Martian DNA in his ancestry.) About ten hours later Crubbo came out of the pyramid to find us sitting under the king's canopy, having supper and talking about what we had discovered behind the secret door in the ascending passage. Crubbo was bewildered that we had gotten out of the pyramid without passing him.

We took pleasure in describing to Crubbo our journey and adventures of that afternoon. We did not have to elaborate in the slightest to maintain a look of awe on his face. Several times he asked where we came out of the pyramid so that he could backtrack and see for himself the wonders we described. As we talked, he summoned a courier to stand by with a camel. We knew that when we told him what he wanted to know, the high priest of Amon would be at Giza within a day. We deliberately prolonged telling him the location where we had exited.

That night we were joined by three young noblemen. One was Prince Menkaure, the son of King Khafre. I didn't recognize the other two until one of them said to me, "Father, Mother and Grandmother want to know if you are ever going to get over being crazy? I want to know when you will teach us about numbers." From that time until the day I died in that lifetime my sons rarely left my side.

Entering the Remote Access to the Underground Passages

The following morning my sons and Prince Menkaure were with our party of pyramid explorers as we trekked about a mile eastward to the remote entrance and a passage that eventually connected with several other passages located under the Giza Plateau. Wherever the passages joined was usually a small chamber. One slightly larger chamber has four passages stemming from it. These passages lead to the interiors of the Sphinx, the Great Pyramid and the other two large pyramids. We had not explored these passages and chambers the day before because our experiences in the Great Pyramid had taken a considerable toll on us, both physically and emotionally. The air had been stuffy in the pyramid's interior and had made us light-headed. Now that we had exposed the structure's interior to the outside air, we decided to let the place air out. This was during the fall of the year, probably early October. It was cool and it rained very hard that day.

Crubbo was with us, along with his small army of slaves, who bore him on one litter and food and lamp oil on a second litter. Seeing the large containers of lamp oil, we who had traveled this way before began to laugh. We knew that Crubbo would be in for a surprise, and we could hardly wait.

The lamps were necessary until we came to the first small chamber. When we entered the room it was automatically illuminated by light from a four-inch-long tube standing vertically in a corner. Crubbo wet his skirt and the slaves ran away in the direction from which we had come. Crubbo recovered from the shock and dared to touch the tube. As he approached it, it got brighter. When he touched it, it went out.

We made every effort to get the tube to glow again (even chanted some magic words), but it would no longer provide us with light. King Khafre forbade us to touch any more of these light makers that he knew (from the day before) we would encounter along our way. In some chambers the light tubes worked and in others they did not. We broke open one of the tubes and it bled beads of a silver-colored liquid that we chased about the floor until they disappeared between the cracks. The liquid was, of course, the element you call mercury. We of that time in Egypt had never seen it before.

Crubbo huffed and puffed. He had not considered that the mile-long trip through the passages would be so physically exhausting. Adding to his miseries, when the slaves ran off, they had taken with them his food and wine supplies. In the company of one of King Khafre's guards, he returned to the passage entrance.

Now I will tell you what King Khafre, Hamarebuti and I found within the Great Pyramid the day before, after leaving Crubbo stranded in the ascending passage.

Our Remarkable Discoveries

With the light of oil lamps we proceeded south down a passage that was tall enough for us to walk upright. After about 20 yards the passage came to an end. To our right (west) was a steep upward flight of steps flanked by stone pillars three feet high, which acted as hand grips as we climbed the stairs. At the top was another passage of the same size that continued some 24 feet to the west. As we approached its end, our presence activated one of the Atlantean light tubes. We were startled at first, but considered ourselves lucky because the passage ended at a platform beyond which was a sheer drop of 157.296296 red ra feet (50 red pi units). To the right and left of the platform were catwalks about three feet wide that ran north and south. We took the catwalk to the south, taking great care not to fall into the black void below. This vast empty area was the main resonance chamber of the Great Pyramid.

At the end of the catwalk three steps led to an oval room, which also had a light tube that automatically turned on. The floor of this room was covered with carved symbols arranged in a number of concentric circles. In the center of the innermost circle was a star chart, which had at its center the stars now referred to on Earth as the Belt of Orion. We followed a ramp leading upward and to the east. There we entered a beautifully constructed chamber with walls of highly polished white limestone. Its walls were devoid of inscriptions, but at its center was a stone "basin" resting securely on a four-foot-high pillar. On the circumference of the pillar's circular base were carved the images of four feathered serpents, each holding the tail of the preceding one in its mouth. When I saw these carvings I was moved to tears. I did not know at the time why I was so emotionally affected. I know now that the chamber was a chapel in which those of my home world of Gracyea came to pray to the creator of all that is. It is our way, then and now, to build such a holy chapel in each building we erect.

The chamber's dimensions are 31.41592 red ra feet (10 red pi units) x 16.9646 red ra feet (5.08938 red rams or 1 red ankh unit) x 16.2 red ra feet (omega major phi x 10).

A very small chamber measuring only 8.4823 x 8.4823 x 8.4823 red ra feet is centered on the pyramid's vertical and horizontal axis lines—that is, at the center of the Fibonacci vril-energy spiral when it was active. The place was very, very quiet during our visit. Its walls were encrusted with salt that had rust-colored stains (preserved dried blood) running throughout. It was as if an animal or human had exploded into microscopic parts that became embedded in the walls of the chamber.

A passage about fifteen feet long exits the chamber to the east, ending at a downward vertical shaft. At the very beginning of this passage is a steep flight of steps at its southern wall. At the top of these steps is a small platform located about six feet under the Great Step, which is located at the high end of the Grand Gallery. The depth of the shaft at the end of the passage is about eight feet, and it has handholds and foot slots in its western wall. At the bottom it connects with a gradually sloping passage that runs to the east and eventually levels off and connects with the subterranean hub chamber and the passage that leads to the exit/entrance I have previously described.

The Great Step is made of a solid piece of limestone that is actually a hatchlike door to the platform and stairs beneath. The so-called antechamber and its sliding "portcullis" (once resting in vertical runners in the chamber walls) is located immediately south of the Great Step. The sliding portcullises were not intended to seal off the King's Chamber, but were used as moving counterweights that raised and lowered the Great Step, which rests on stone protrusions (pivot bars) inserted into the masonry at each side of the slab (east and west). The two-piece granite leaf once acted as a scissors clamp that held tight the knotted lines of the counterweights (moving portcullises) to the hatch (Great Step). When the lines were clamped, the hatch remained open, allowing access to the inner parts of the Great Pyramid. The symbol presently found on the so-called "boss" of the granite leaf really tells the whole story. The symbol is T-shaped, which is the universal symbol for equilibrium, or balance.

Presently the Great Step cannot pivot to an open position because it is held in place horizontally by masonry blocks that now make up the lower parts of the north wall of the antechamber. Today the Great Step and the floor of the antechamber are slightly askew. This indicates that the Great Step has bounced on its pivots several times in the past due to earthquakes, and on at least the latest occasion did not settle back to a perfectly level position. The masonry blocks that hold it fast from tipping open were set in place by the Atlanteans, acting on the orders of the sky gods; and the portcullises were removed by the priests of Amon, who were directed to do so by the same heavenly powers.

The rest of the chambers that we found unsealed in all three Great Pyramids of Giza were vacant, but their walls and floors were covered with inscriptions. In one of the passages leading to the Third Pyramid (third in size) was found a fading painted inscription, which read, "In the 16th year of the reign of Djoser, King of Upper and Lower Egypt, Imhotep walked here with the king. Know you that the king had no fear of this place or its magic."

To describe the empty resonance chambers of the pyramids, whose walls contain endless rows of inscriptions, would not serve anyone at this time. I know there will be a time in the near future [this was said in late 1996] when someone will punch through the surface of the Giza Plateau and enter the subterranean passages that exist below. They will, of course, now encounter water of the Nile. The groundwater level has risen considerably since the time of the Fourth Dynasty. Those who succeed in entering the passages and gaining access to the interiors of the pyramids will also encounter passages that were sealed by the priests of Amon "at the direction of the sky gods." I know now that they were on a holy mission when they hid these things from those living at the time and from those who have lived since.

Dangers beneath the Sphinx

In the chambers beneath the Sphinx awaits death in the form of viruses and bacteria from the biological substances in the glass spheres I described earlier. These viruses and bacilli (life forms such as ourselves) are mutations generated by Frequency Barrier distortions in the universal life field at the time of the explosion of Maldec. Many of these microscopic life forms still exist there in a state of suspended animation. Beware—they will again become active in the presence of other forms of life that can act as a host. Let us thank the elohim that the present state of the Frequency Barrier is not friendly toward many strains of bacteria that once existed under the Sphinx. The only threat of this type to really be concerned with at present is the bacillus you call anthrax. Throughout the ages those with little immunity to certain bacteria (such as King Rededef) died of what was generally referred to as Giza fever. The Martian Lord Sharmarie told of the shaking sickness experienced by those living near the Giza Plateau when the land of Egypt was called Toray.

I say, enter the chambers under the Sphinx with biological caution. In them will be found thousands of broken glass spheres of many colors. But you will also find the only surviving writing from the kingdom of Atlantis.

I spent more than two additional years exploring the subterranean passages and the chambers of the Great Pyramids and the Sphinx. Many poorly fed slaves and priest-workers died of Giza fever. None among the royal family or my family were that unfortunate. At that time the pyramids inspired us to build temples nearby for our tombs.

I found great comfort in visiting the interiors of those ancient buildings, but as time went on, the Atlantean light tubes gradually began to fail. The priests of Amon removed them and placed them in a vault they built southeast of the plateau. It was their belief that the light tubes were created by their beloved imhotep, who would some day return to make them work once again.

I eventually gave up exploring the pyramids of Giza and settled down to study their dimensions and try to understand why the gods had built them. I rejoined my wife Tertmis, whose mother Myva insisted that her departed husband King Khufu still ruled the land (and she once thought I was crazy!). Tertmis and I got reacquainted, and we enjoyed (as she well deserved) the noble titles and pension I received from King Khafre for my services. My sons both became governors of lands in the south under King Menkaure.

I lived to about the age of seventy and died naturally one evening while I watched the sunset with Tertmis at the edge of the Nile.

More Ra Mathematical Data from the Author

At this point I will attempt to convey some basic Ra mathematical data to those who might wish to study the subject.

A red ram (Ra meter) unit of measure is 1.0053745898 meters in length. To find the red ram equivalent of a dimension reported in meters (1 meter = 3.280839895 British feet), simply multiply the number of meters by 0.994654142.

After converting any other type of unit of measure to red rams, simply divide the result by red pi (3.141$\overline{592}$, red ankh (5.08938), red hunab (1.0802875) or the red value for the square root of two (1.41371$\overline{666}$). In most cases these key numbers will divide evenly in the red ram result, verifying that the conversion was accurately made. Sometimes there might be a slight discrepancy of plus or minus a few thousandths of a decimal point because the reported measurement was either rounded off or not precisely measured in the first place.

There are five ra mathematical formats, which are presently called red, green, blue, omega major and omega minor.

The size of any dimension in any format is never greater than the size of a red ra unit (such as a red ram [ra meter], red ra foot or red ra inch). There are 3.$\overline{333}$ (3⅓) red ra feet or 40 red ra inches in a red ram. There are, of course, 12 red ra inches in a red ra foot. A green, blue, omega major and omega minor unit is just a different (smaller) division of a single red unit. There are five values for pi, five for ankh, five for the hunab and so on. I will list the five values for pi and leave you, the reader, to mathematically determine the ratios that exist between them: omega major pi = 3.125; red pi = 3.141$\overline{592}$; green pi = 3.142696806; blue pi = 3.143801408; and omega minor pi = 3.160493829. (The crop glyphs that have been found in English grain fields are mathematical expressions of the omega minor format.)

Once "Ra-mathized" (converted to Ra units of measure), the pyramids and buildings of Giza, the Mexican cities of Teotihuacan and Palenque and the ancient Bolivian city of Tiahuanaco—plus the buildings existing at Cydonia on the planet Mars—show that they were all built on the order of the sacred Ra system of mathematics and laid out by the same units of measure devised from that system. (Sharmarie: "Another coincidence?") There are thousands of calculations on record in my 22-year work (thousand-page self-published series titled *The Rods of Amon Ra*) that prove this to be true.

I will leave the subject of the Great Pyramid with the following marvelous mathematical facts. I will leave you, the reader, to determine how this mathematics was structured into these ancient buildings and how it can be revealed by studying their dimensional details.

When the 2550916.802 cubic green rams in the volume of the Great Pyramid is divided by the 52488 square green rams in the area of the pyramid's base, the result is 48.6. There are 486 green ra feet in the physical height of the structure. The number 486 is the 18th number in the Ra Table of Nines (18 x 27), and there are 4680 green ra angstroms in the wavelength of the Balmer M4 spectral line of hydrogen.

When the 2550916.802 cubic green rams in the volume of the Great Pyramid is divided by the 166707.449664 square green rams in the area of the pyramid's median cross section, the result is 152.6814, or two times the important number 763.407 divided by 10.

When the 2550916.802 cubic green rams in the volume of the Great Pyramid is divided by the 236619.6 square green rams in the area of the pyramid's diagonal cross section, the result is 108. The number 108 is the fourth number in the Ra Table of Nines (4 x 27).

When the 2550916.802 cubic green rams in the volume of the Great Pyramid is divided by the 85030.56007 square green rams found in the combined areas of the structure's four sides (faces based on the "ghost apothem"), the result is simply 30. (For an explanation of the term *ghost apothem*, see *The Rods of Amon Ra*.)

When the Great Pyramid's volume is viewed as 94478400.080 cubic green ra feet and divided by the total number of square green ra feet that are in the pyramid's four sides (faces) with 944784 green ra feet (based on the ghost apothem), the result is exactly 100.

The dimensions and layout of the buildings of the ancient Mexican city of Teotihuacan (the Gracian Miradol) are given by Hugh Harleston, Jr. in *The Secret of the Mexican Pyramids* by Peter Tompkins. Harleston believed the hunab unit of measure was close to 1.059 meters. We now know its size to be exactly 1.0602875 red rams or 1.0659861104 meters, which is a difference of only 6.9 millimeters greater than Harleston's original estimate. Remember, there are 100 red hunab feet in the length of the descending passage of the Great Pyramid and 216 red hunab rams in the base of the Great Pyramid. Notice on the map of Teotihuacan that there are also 216 hunabs in the base of the so-called Pyramid of the Sun. The number 216 is the eighth number in the Ra Table of Nines. *[Sharmarie: "Talk about coincidence!"]*

There are several other features whose dimensions consist of modules of hunab units. The so-called Way of the Dead is shown to have a width of 48 hunabs, or 50.8938 red rams (50 red ankhs). Remember, there are exactly 45 red ankhs in the 229.0221 red ram base length of the Great Pyramid of Giza and the Pyramid of the Sun at Teotihuacan. Also note that the square wall surrounding the so-called Pyramid of Quetzalcoatl is reported by Harleston to be exactly 378 hunabs long on each of its sides. The number 378 is the fourteenth number in the Ra Table of Nines. —W.H.B.

Before I continue with my account of two other past lives I have lived on Earth, I will respond to what has been falsely said by others on Earth who claim to know who built the Great Pyramids of Giza and who destroyed the planet Maldec and by what means. In the light of the sun I say these events came about *only* in the manner described by me and those others such as Sharmarie of Mars, Trome of Sumer, Churmay of Wayda, Ruke of Parn, Thaler of Trake, Jaffer-Ben-Rob of Earth and Nisor of Moor, who all spoke truthfully of these things before my account here. To those who declare that what we say is not the truth, let them dispute the sacred numbers that we alone have brought to your attention. Who but those who built the pyramids would know best about them? I, Tixer-Chock, say in the light of the sun that what I have said and what you [W.H.B.] have said is true about the sacred numbers and will be forever so. Let those who would say differently swear likewise, if they dare to displease the elohim.

Silmikos the Greek

By the will and sacred plan of the elohim I, Tixer-Chock, was born in the year 532 B.C. in the land you presently call Greece. My mother's name was Mermatha and my father, Kaltros. My father was a soldier who died in battle when I was about six years old. My name was Silmikos. In that life I had a sister named Osypala. For the first thirteen years of that life my mother, sister and I lived with my maternal grandparents. We made our living by farming.

My widowed mother eventually remarried another farmer, whose wife had died. His name was Aknostros. He was somewhat wealthy and owned several slaves. Aknostros had no children and we developed a good relationship.

One of Aknostros' male slaves was called Sepore. At the time he was about thirty-nine years old and was absent his right ear; he also had a withered arm. He spoke with a foreign accent, claiming to be of Egyptian descent. At the age of about twenty-five he had been captured along with other sailors, who were the crew of a raider of Greek ships. His handicaps kept him from the galleys and placed a price on him that my stepfather could afford.

Sepore was employed by my stepfather as an accountant. He could calculate numbers very quickly in his head; I marveled at his ability. When he wrote numbers down, he did so in symbols that were known only by him. His phenomenal ability with numbers was known far and wide throughout the country. Many people of wealth offered to buy or hire him from my stepfather, but Aknostros could not do without him.

One day in early spring a group of Greek soldiers and several well-dressed Romans arrived at our farm bearing an order from the local governor, who was directed by a higher authority in Athens to take the slave Sepore into custody after paying my stepfather a considerable sum of silver. The Romans and the officer in charge of the troops spent some time haggling with Aknostros and Sepore.

The bottom line was that Sepore would be returned to Aknostros in two years and that I would go along with him to see that he was not abused in any way. Aknostros, after hearing where Sepore was going, seized the opportunity to get me educated in accounting so that I could some day replace Sepore if necessary. I was about sixteen years old at the time.

Three days later Sepore and I climbed into an oxcart accompanied by a driver and two soldiers, who walked alongside the cart. We were treated with considerable respect by our escorts. I had never been away from home before, so I was very excited. I was told by my stepfather that Sepore and I were to be taken to the seacoast where we would sail to a town in southern Italy called Crotone. *[Croton is also the name of a plant, and a croton bug is a type of cockroach. —W.H.B.]* At Crotone we were to live for two years in the house of some unknown scholar to which the rulers of Athens and Rome were in some way indebted.

We were halfway to the coast when one of our escorts mentioned the name Pythagoras of Samos. Hearing this name, Sepore let out a barrage of words in his native language. In Greek he asked the guard to repeat the name. He slapped me on the back as he said over and over, "I knew that if he still lived, Pythagoras would remember me. Praise the gods of Olympus, Silmikos. We are on our way to paradise."

During our voyage to Italy Sepore told me that he had learned about numbers when he traveled with Pythagoras and several other Greeks to the land of Persia (Babylon). After having spent more than a year with the mathematical scholars of Persia, Sepore had enlisted at high pay to escort some of the Persian scholars to Egypt to study the dimensions of the Great Pyramids. When he left Persia, Sepore had left his friend Pythagoras behind, still engrossed in the study of numbers.

Sepore related that he and his Persian employers never made it to Egypt, because along the way they were attacked by bandits. The Persians were killed in the attack, and a wounded Sepore (minus an ear) was left for dead in the land presently called Lebanon or perhaps Syria. Several days later the bandits returned to find him still alive. They decided to patch him up and take him with them to the seacoast. There the bandits joined with a number of the seafaring version of their breed, who were Lebanese pirates. It was the plan of his captors to sell him as a slave if he became physically fit.

During the long and miserable recovery from his wounds, he said, he sailed about the Mediterranean Sea with the pirates as they attacked and plundered Greek fishing boats and small cargo vessels. It was during an attack on such a cargo vessel at anchor in a bay of a small island that the pirates were surprised by two Greek war galleys that swiftly came from the opposite side of the island and captured them without a fight. The pirate crew and Sepore were taken to the mainland of Greece and sold into slavery, at which time my stepfather Aknostros bought Sepore for less than he would have paid for two goats. After learning of Sepore's unique ability with numbers, he realized that he had made a very good deal that day in the slave market.

Life with Pythagoras of Samos

Sepore and our travelers reached Crotone three days after landing in Italy in midafternoon. The house of Pythagoras of Samos was a small four-room wooden structure, but to its rear a stone building of considerable size was being erected. The new building crawled with young men barking orders at each other. Workmen sat around with smiles on their faces. The noise stopped and the workmen jumped to their feet when several men came walking toward the building. One of the men, though obviously Greek, was dressed in the robe of a Persian, and from his right ear hung a large gold earring. This was Pythagoras of Samos.

He strode up to Sepore and shook his head in disbelief at Sepore's physical condition. He called to one of the young men nearby and ordered him kindly to bring us some wine and food. The rest of that afternoon Pythagoras listened to Sepore's account of what had happened after he had left Persia en route to Egypt. Pythagoras said to Sepore, "You will get to finish your journey. I promise you that we will sail for Egypt before the time I have agreed to return you to your master. But maybe the gods will provide a new plan for your future."

From 7:00 to about 10:30 in the morning a collection of young men would listen to Pythagoras speak about mathematics, music and astronomy and how all things were numbers. From that first morning I became Pythagoras' most devout student. (Thirty-seven years later I was at his side when he died on the first day of January in the year 480 B.C.)

From 10:30 to noon Pythagoras would occupy himself with his research and experiments. He lunched only on bread, vegetables and fruit when he could get it. He was a vegetarian, recommending the practice to his friends but demanding that his students eat as he did. It was considered an honor to sit with him during his lunch and listen to whatever he had to say informally about numbers and religion. He was a man of deep thought, and his dissertations were spellbinding. He would nap from from about 2:00 until 4:30 in the afternoon. When he awoke he would drink a large cup of wine and then go out to look at what progress had been made on the construction. He would then spend about a half an hour telling his students and building superintendents what they should accomplish on the building on the following day. He would always close his list of instructions with the statement: "If it rains tomorrow, stay home; if it's a holiday, don't get too drunk."

At about 5:00 in the afternoon Pythagoras would have dinner only with those he thought were the brightest of his students and the most interesting of his friends. About 7:00 he would pray for an hour in seclusion. He would then retire for the night. He believed that the soul is immortal and leaves the physical body at death. He erroneously believed that the soul incarnates into all forms of animal life until it has experienced life in the form of all creatures.

The construction of the stone building behind the small house of Pythagoras was being paid for by a syndicate of wealthy Roman merchants and aristocratic landowners who paid Pythagoras for its design and continued to pay him monthly for his supervision of its construction. It was their intention to use it as a money-making theater. Secretly, Pythagoras was in no hurry to finish the building. When one section of it was finally roofed, Pythagoras used it as a school.

His students came from far and wide. Locals paid their tuition in produce and livestock; foreigners paid their small tuition in gold and silver two years in advance. By the standards of the day Pythagoras was a very wealthy man, but he shared both his wealth and knowledge with those he considered serious seekers of truth. He had thousands of followers over the years to whom he taught basic things, but he imparted secret information to only about fifty of his special teaching staff. His school brought so much commerce to the area that those who originally financed the building of the theater gave it to him when they heard a rumor that he was planning to move his school elsewhere.

The logo of the Pythagorean school of mathematics was, as you know, the five-pointed star, or pentagram. The symbol was created by placing two Golden Triangles together in such a way that they formed the five-pointed star. A Golden Triangle is proportioned on the order of both the whole and decimal values for phi (1.618 and 0.618033989).

Basically, Pythagoras taught and demonstrated that vibrating strings produce harmonious tones when the ratios of the lengths of the strings are whole numbers, and that these ratios could be applied to other instruments. Pythagoras realized that any triangle whose sides were in the ratio 3:4:5 was a right-angled triangle (realized by the Egyptians as early as the Second Dynasty). The Pythagorean theorem states that the square of the hypotenuse of a right triangle is equal to the sum of the squares of the other two sides, but it did not originate with him. He acquired this knowledge in Persia, where he had studied for several years; the Persians had gotten the information from the Egyptians. (I would like to think that this mathematical knowledge was conveyed to the Persians by my once-friend and colleague Hamarebuti, who was with King Khafre and me many centuries before when we explored the Great Pyramids of Giza.)

Pythagoras had been greatly influenced by the Babylonian belief in astrology and taught his students about the periodic numerical relationships of the heavenly bodies. He referred to the stars and planets as the celestial spheres, which he said produced a harmony he called the music of the spheres. We of the open state of perfection call this macro-level activity the collective "song of the elohim." *[The word "universe" means "one song." —W.H.B.]* Pythagoras was convinced that the universe functioned on the order of three basic musical ratios, which are 4:3, 3:2 and 2:1. He also knew that the Earth itself was a sphere that orbits the sun. It was due to his astrological predictions that he gained favor with the ruling bodies of Athens and Rome. They relied on him from time to time to consult the stars on their behalf whenever they could not come to a decision about something on their own.

The Discovery of Irrational Numbers

One evening during dinner Pythagoras, after a period of deep, silent thought, decided to let us, his inner circle, in on a mathematical discovery he had made that morning. It was evident to all who were present that his discovery was bothering him. After some hesitation he began to tell us what he had come to know earlier that day. His discovery was that there existed numbers that were "irrational" (like the infinite numerical value of pi, which cannot be expressed accurately as a fraction). This discovery required the Greeks of the time to totally reconsider everything they previously believed about mathematics.

Pythagoras' own belief that whole numbers and their ratios could account for all geometrical factors was shattered. He had made his discovery when he found that the ratio of the diagonal of a square to its side was an irrational value.

Some present at the table actually began to weep. Others such as myself began to study the written calculations Pythagoras had made that morning. The words "no, no it can't be true" were repeated over and over. I was the first to state that I felt in the depth of my soul that there was a way to circumvent irrational numbers and revalidate our previous beliefs. My words caused Pythagoras to say, "I too believe this. Let us look for that way. We might find the answer in Egypt." He then said to Sepore, "Make arrangements for all at this table to travel to the land of the pyramids. Until we find the answer, let us keep what we have discovered about these endless numbers to ourselves." Pythagoras then left us and went to bed. Ha! Word of the discovery of irrational numbers spread rapidly among the scholars of Italy and eventually Greece, for most scholars in Italy at the time were Greek.

Pythagoras had to contend with visitors of every sort who came to Crotone to hear what he had to say about irrational numbers. The priesthoods of both countries proclaimed that the gods created irrational numbers to torment the minds of men like Pythagoras and his associates, who thought they were more clever than the gods themselves. There were thousands of sacrifices made to the gods to thank them for putting all of us heretics in our rightful place.

One morning Pythagoras spoke to his class and a number of visitors. During his presentation he declared that he could not as yet deal with irrational numbers mentally, but that he knew how and why they existed. He then went on to say, "The universe was created by one god, and prior to the creation of the universe the number 1 represented the maximum limit. The Creator drew within (inhaled) the nothingness (void represented by zero). This action produced all things that existed then and that will ever exist." By "things" he meant what people will be able to relate to with their five senses. All of these known and unknown things were individually describable by numbers (like the children of the numbers 1 and 0). He compared the symbols 1 and 0, respectively, to the male and female sex organs. It amused him at the time to do so when he saw his audience take greater interest in what he was saying.

The mating of the numbers 1 and 0 by necessity produced irrational numbers. Irrational numbers in turn describe the unlimited. Irrational numbers therefore really described the Creator and the Creator's purposes, whereas other numbers are related only to things that make up fractional parts of the Creator's infinite oneness.

Expecting the priests in the crowd to yell that he was a blasphemer for saying that there was only one god (which they did), Pythagoras had prepared the statement that Zeus (Jupiter) held the distinction of being describable by the number 1, or the irrational value of pi, and the lesser gods were describable by other whole and irrational numbers. This explanation satisfied the priests and planted the seeds of numerology as well as the ideas of even and odd numbers, male and female numbers, and lucky and unlucky numbers.

I, Tixer-Chock, tell you that there is some truth in all of this that Pythagoras spoke of that day.

Our trip to Egypt did not begin until things were favorable with the stars. As we waited for the right time to depart Crotone for Egypt, we also waited for a man named Philolaus to come from the north and take charge of the school. He was an old and trusted friend of Pythagoras. When he arrived he brought with him his family, which consisted of a wife and two daughters. His oldest daughter was named Valbra, who was about seventeen and already a widow whose husband of two years had died of sickness. After Valbra arrived at Crotone, we developed a loving relationship that led to marriage. When we Pythagoreans left for Egypt she was with me as my wife.

The Trip to Egypt

Before leaving Italy, Pythagoras had arranged for the services of twenty veteran soldiers from the garrison near Crotone. Pythagoras rejected several ships as being too unseaworthy before he chose one that had been recently built in Egypt and was manned by a crew of Egyptians. The ship did not sail directly to Egypt. It first crossed the Mediterranean Sea to the coast of Africa and then followed the coastline eastward. As we sailed along the coast, from time to time we passed large Italian galleys, low in the water because their holds were filled with Egyptian grain and other commodities from the east. Many of these ships flew pennants identifying the owner of the vessel and the vessel's cargo and destination.

Our Egyptian ship sailed directly into the mouth of the Nile River and docked about three miles upstream on the western shore. Sepore acted as our interpreter. It was enjoyable to see him interact with his own people. Pythagoras saw to it that he was dressed in the finest of clothes so that he could feel proud and make a good impression. His first two assignments were to obtain for us a number of donkeys and hire a number of porters. While we waited for Sepore to complete his tasks, we stayed in a small village near the spot where we had landed.

The land of Egypt was not in external turmoil, but it was in a state of confusion. The Cushites from the Sudan, who ruled during the Twenty-fifth and Twenty-sixth Dynasties, had recently been humiliated by their defeat by the Assyrians, who were still trying to figure out what to do with the land now that they had control of it. Conquerors came and went, but the priesthoods of the gods of Egypt always remained intact and guided the people through all difficult times.

About four days after our arrival we were visited by a group of Egyptian dignitaries headed by a eunuch priest of the Egyptian goddess Isis. He was a very old and wise man whose name was Dthermas. He introduced himself in Greek and handed Pythagoras a papyrus scroll on which was depicted in vivid colors a map of the area centered around the Great Pyramids of Giza.

When we left the banks of the Nile, Dthermas and his group accompanied us. Sepore learned from Dthermas that we would be met at the pyramids by other Egyptian scholar-priests. We Pythagoreans stayed in Egypt for about six months, seeking every type of mathematical information that we had never thought of previously ourselves. We learned of the additive series now called the Fibonacci series and its relationship to the physical forms of nature. We Pythagoreans all agreed that we would keep this information secret among ourselves. When we brought up the subject of irrational numbers to our most learned Egyptian colleagues, they responded that they had no idea what we were talking about. I cannot think back on that time without scolding myself for not realizing then that the answer to how to circumvent or utilize irrational numbers properly in the three-dimensional world existed before my eyes in the geometry of the Great Pyramid of Giza. I will explain what I mean further on in my historical account.

While at the pyramids we were taken into the largest of them, through the same hatchlike door I had personally rediscovered several thousand years before when I lived as "crazy Melth-Nakhefra" during the reigns of the Egyptian kings Khufu, Rededef, Khafre and Menkaure. The antechamber just inside the pyramid's entrance was still very much intact. By torchlight we made our way to the subterranean chamber. I now had a feeling that something was not quite right about the pyramid. I now know what I subconsciously sensed at the time—that the structure no longer absorbed sound, indicated by the fact that our spoken words echoed off its walls.

When we Greeks and Italians departed Egypt, we left behind twelve Pythagoreans to continue to seek out as much secret mathematical and medical information that we sensed existed but had not come to our attention during our visit. Pythagoras left Sepore in charge of the twelve who had remained behind. He also gave Sepore most of the gold and silver left in our coffer. When I asked Pythagoras how he would explain why Sepore was not to be returned to my stepfather as per the two-year agreement, he replied, "Sepore? Sepore? Oh yes, that fellow. I have often wondered what became of him. I guess I will have to make some sort of monetary restitution to your stepfather, because he (Sepore) is no longer in my custody."

Visiting Greece and My Family

After leaving Egypt, we first went to Greece, where Pythagoras wanted to meet with a Greek scholar named Altranmis and pose him some questions concerning things we learned in Egypt. While in Greece Pythagoras and all who had traveled with him stopped by to visit with my family. Pythagoras arranged and paid for a three-day feast that was attended by everyone for miles around. My mother and sister as well as my stepfather Aknostros were very happy to see me again and meet my wife Valbra, who was now several months with child.

Pythagoras met with my stepfather Aknostros and financially arranged to extend the Sepore agreement for another five years. After receiving a chest filled with gold from Athens, we said our farewells to my family and returned by ship to Italy. From time to time we received coded messages from Sepore. After about three years we never heard from him again or any of his twelve Pythagorean colleagues.

I lived out my life studying and teaching at Crotone. Pythagoras married a Greek woman named Estrelmis. They had no children, but Valbra and I parented two sons and one daughter. My life in Crotone was easy and intellectually stimulating.

One morning Pythagoras did not come to the school, but his wife did, seeking out Philolaus and me. She told us that Pythagoras was unable to rise from his bed. Our master was awake and he smiled when we entered the room. Saying nothing, he held out both arms toward us and grasped our hands. As he closed his eyes, his grip relaxed. In this way did Pythagoras of Samos cease to live among us. Pythagoras was actually eighty-one (9 x 9) at the time he died. I was about fifty-two years old at the time.

We of the teaching and administrative staff of the school were at a loss without Pythagoras to lead us. Because my father-in-law Philolaus had gained the experience of directing the affairs of the institution when we went to Egypt many years earlier, he was elected as the chief administrator. Eventually, running the school became too much for him or any of us of the original inner group. We closed the school but stayed together studying and writing down all we could remember about what Pythagoras had said and taught us. Even those things once considered secret were set down in writing.

One morning just after I returned from feeding our chickens I remember sitting by the fire holding a bag of chicken feed. I took a handful of the grain and threw it into the fire. The fire flared up each time I fed it grain and chaff. I began to throw the grain into the fire in a constant rhythm and saw in the flames numbers that seemed to have a meaning. When I stopped giving the fire more grain to feast on, the flames contained only zeros. Valbra came into the smoke-filled house and said, "What are you doing, you crazy old man?" I responded, "The pyramids of Egypt explain how mortals can deal with irrational numbers. I had better go and tell Pythagoras; he will be overjoyed to know this." These were my last words. I passed from that lifetime as Silmikos the Greek during the month of December in the year 469 B.C. I was sixty-three years old.

It was said earlier in this writing that the Ra system of mathematics consists of five known formats. A person using any of the formats of the system will in certain calculations be confronted by factors that have irrational values. When this occurs, the mathematician need only convert the irrational number to one of its rational representatives that exists in at least one of the other formats. They can then continue with their calculations rationally and accurately. Switching from one Ra format to another can be done whenever necessary. For instance, green pi (3.14269680) is an irrational number, but its representative in the omega major format has the simple rational value of 3.125, or 3⅛. — W.H.B.

Smoke Bird of the Maya

I will tell you of my short lifetime as Smoke Bird of the Maya, because it was during this lifetime that I witnessed the landing of a spacecraft from another world and left the Earth inside it.

The year was about A.D. 404 and the place was called "the well where the gods come to drink." The place later developed into the Mayan city of Chichen Itza. I got my name because my mother went into labor while she was roasting a game bird on a spit. My father found his dinner burnt to a crisp and smoking. He thought that this was a sign that the gods wanted me, his newborn son, to be called Smoke Bird.

I was a skinny youth who learned the ways of stonemasonry from my father. Both he and I were in the service of the priest king, Jaguar's Tongue. During the last year of that lifetime (my ninth year) I worked on the construction of the first primitive astronomical observatory that was built in the city. This observatory was eventually rebuilt, and the ruins of this later observatory can be seen today.

At the end of one workday I was not feeling very well, so my father carried me on his back out of the city toward the house of a woman who was known to cure the sick.

As we took the path into the forest, a bright light appeared over our heads. My father ran farther and attempted to hide us. The light moved out of view, but it later radiated through the trees. I passed out. When I awoke my father was not with me. Standing over me was a man wearing a feathered cape. He knew I would not be able to understand his words, so he did not speak. In my mind I heard, "Go to sleep, Tixer-Chock; your time on the Earth is over. We will take you home now." I went to sleep and died.

When I was once again born into human form it was on my home world of Gracyea, where I live at this time. I estimate my present age to be about 1582 Earth years. I, Tixer-Chock, say that what has been said here about the sacred numbers is true, and will be forever so.

N I N E

Doy, a Woman of Maldec

The story of the planet Maldec: Broken promises, shattered dreams, broken hearts, shattered world, broken spirits. It is now we who must repair these things.
I am Molacar of Vitron.

[To expedite the acquisition of the accounts of the past lifetimes on Earth of Doy of Maldec, some of her recollections will be mentally relayed by Sanza-Bix of Gracyea. Sanza-Bix will also include his own first-lifetime experiences on the planet of Maldec and the planet Mars up to and including the time that Maldec was destroyed. —W.H.B.]

I awoke in semidarkness and rose from my bed. I touched a control and the draperies pulled back, allowing the room to be filled with sunlight. On the veranda below were several people who were having breakfast. I knew who they were, though I had never seen them in physical form before.

I put on a yellow tunic that hung on a hook in the form of a swan's neck and opened the door. This was the room in which I had slept continuously for more than thirteen Earth years, and I had never left it before.

I joined my father Nass-Kolb, mother Orma and older sister Sibrette on the veranda. As was the custom of our people, the father of the newly awakened (if available) was the first to speak to the new addition to the family. My father smiled at me and said, "Are you well, Doy?" I responded, "Yes, I am well, Father." With those words my physical life on the planet Maldec began.

When I went to sleep some fifteen hours later it was in a new bedroom. The next day my mother and I discussed what I would need in the way of clothing. In the midafternoon of the second day after my awakening, I was visited by Brig-Stura, an emissary of the ruling council, who physically examined me and asked if I had any messages to impart to the council from our god (the el you call Lucifer and we called Baal). I had no such message.

My father had recently returned from the planet Sarus (Earth), where the construction of the Great Pyramids was nearly completed. I was informed that our entire family would be returning with him to the Earth to witness the setting of the astrastone spiel (capstone) on the largest of the three structures. I was present when that stone was put into place.

That day, with an escort of four krates and two servant Simms, I walked about the Giza Plateau taking in the sights and looking at the different types of off-world people who were milling about the place. Some had a psychic essence that was slightly tolerable, and others caused displeasing static in my wa (emotional harmony). I remember thinking then, *Why do such offensive people soil the physical universe?* I admired my krate escorts, who had been trained to tolerate otherworld races, some of which I thought then were the ultimate of physical and psychic ugliness.

Those who read this who harbor ill feelings about those not of their own race or religion might award me their sympathy and understanding [or appreciate] how I felt at the time. I can only say that my strong feelings toward other races were an extreme contrast to the joy and security I felt in the presence of my own people. Eventually my observations of otherworld peoples were influenced by curiosity. Those observations could be easily compared to those you might make when visiting a zoo. Yes, we of Maldec of those ancient times considered humans not of our world to be nothing more than animals.

As you would milk a cow to gain nutrition for physical power, we saw no difference in emotionally milking inferior human animals for their psychic essence, which provided us with an expanded range of psychic power. In truth, it was a thrill to be among a group of one's own kind that collectively felt superior and had a goal to increase its superiority to the fullest extent. The English word that would have described each and every Maldecian of pre-Frequency Barrier times is "bigot," which means someone who is strongly partial to one's own group, religion, race or politics and is totally intolerant of those who differ.

Until the time that the teachers from the Hamp radiar (Uranus) plane-toids came to Maldec to teach us about sacred mathematics, things were very different for Maldecians. We lived in peace among ourselves on our beautiful world, which was four times the size of Earth. The planet had sev-eral oceans and a system of rivers and large freshwater lakes. Both the waters and the forest-covered land teemed with animal life. We of Maldec are monogamous and then, as now, oxygen-breathers.

The very first male and female of our kind were the only ones who did not mature to the age of puberty in a state of suspended animation, although all Maldecians who came afterward did. Newborns were first wrapped in various types of coverings and carried about for several years on the backs of their parents, who later deposited them unat-tended in natural caverns until they awakened. As the civilization devel-oped, attendants were assigned to the "awakening caverns," and much later in the development of the culture, those who were still to become part of the three-dimensional life remained in the care of their parents or relatives.

Our adverse ways and attitudes toward other races did not materialize in the molar level [third dimension] of perception until there occurred a dis-agreement among the elohim in higher levels of the universal life field. I understand that this great disagreement polarized the elohim into two fac-tions: those who would follow the original master plan of the creator of all that is and those who would employ their divine right of free will to develop and interact with the molar (five-sense) level of perception in any way they chose. The El of Maldec was one of the latter. All Maldecians who were born from that time on came into the three-dimensional universe prepared to implement the molar-level plan of universal conquest designed by the el/god you refer to as Lucifer.

From a platform of total control of the physical universe could be launched activities that could bring about changes in the higher levels of the universal life field. Our construction of the Great Pyramids on the Earth was a small part of the plan to conquer and control the physical universe. We were aware that there were people who originated from els who shared Lucifer's agenda and with whom we would someday unite when we encountered them in the three-dimensional state of life. I can tell you that there are millions multiplied by many more millions of these cultures that have already united and are fanatically bent on conquering the physical universe and those who oppose them. This alliance is sometimes referred to as the Confederation or the forces of darkness.

Darmins and the Uranian Teachers

Maldecians born prior to the great disagreement of the elohim were called *darmins*, which means, roughly, "the unordained." It was rare that a person would have two darmin parents, like Serp-Ponder, the krate who helped Jaffer Ben-Rob and his family escape execution along with the Cryberants who carved the Sphinx of Giza. Eventually darmins were sterilized at the order of the ruling council of Maldec, who proclaimed that they were acting under divine orders of the planet's el. The darmins did not resist.

The great teachers from the Hamp radiar system (Uranus) came to Maldec several thousand Earth years before my birth. The world at the time was mostly populated by darmins. Darmins were motivated by the desire to gain personal wealth and loved material things, but found it exciting to acquire such things by using their knowledge and by physical work, if necessary. A darmin would never break his or her word. It was these honest traits that attracted the great teachers to our world.

During the period that the great teachers from Uranus resided on Maldec, more and more *quains* (ordained ones) awoke. They demanded many things from the teachers, things that the loving teachers were not ready to give prematurely. One day a quain named Ordo-Sambilth demanded that his teacher, Frocent of Uranus, tell (teach) him something about the sacred numbers. The teacher replied that it would be covered over the course of a month or so later. In a rage, Ordo-Sambilth strangled the Uranian. The Uranian reaction to this crime was to pack up and leave the planet Maldec, never to return. During their preparation for departure they were attacked by a number of quains who wanted to obtain any written material about the sacred numbers that had not been previously imparted.

The Uranians, acting in self-defense, killed two of the attacking quains. No more Uranians were killed or injured. The act of killing another human being was devastating to the ultimately benign Uranians, who collectively felt ashamed to the depth of their souls. During their stay on Maldec they had contacted other races such as the Gracians. After these other explorer groups returned home and learned of the events that had taken place on Maldec, they too became remorseful. The Uranians later refused to procreate as penance for their actions on Maldec. Today no more than eighteen Uranians live in physical bodies in the molar (three-dimensional) level of the universal life field on the planet Simcarris, which orbits the sun/star you call Thurbal in the constellation of Draco, or the Dragon. Simcarris is also the present home of Trome of Sumer (Saturn) and Churmay of Wayda (Venus), both of whom provided you with accounts of some of their previous lifetimes on the Earth.

Maldecian Conquest

After the departure of the great teachers from Maldec, the military order of the krates was formed and our world leaders began to form plans for the conquest of the local star system. This plan was put into operation on the very first day that the space-traveling Gracians arrived on Maldec and willingly offered to transport our scouts and emissaries to the other two oxygen-breathing worlds of the solar system, Sarus (Earth) and Wayda (Venus).

Our leaders' plan for conquest was long-ranging, and because the gentle folk of Wayda would have offered only minimal resistance, they were placed second on the list after Sarus, whose people were expected to become adversarial when the noose was eventually tightened. In other words, the Earth was to act as our proving ground, and the expected various reactions of the people of Earth were to provide us with data that would assist in the development of methods that could later be employed to bring other off-world races under our control.

We were sure that others of our kind were doing the same thing in other solar systems located throughout the universe, and we longed for the day we would unite with them. I must say we were very disappointed to find that the learned Gracians and the highly technical Nodians did not have the same goals we did. A secret study was conducted to determine why they didn't and to determine if they had any weaknesses we could exploit for our benefit.

Maldecian Upbringing

Before continuing with my account of my first lifetime in the three-dimensional (molar) level of the universal life field, let me tell you of Doy of Maldec (my name at that time). First of all, I have no reservations about describing myself or my people, the Maldecians, and their first-lifetime attitudes. Nor am I hesitant in any way to describe our past actions, because that which was performed by the forces of light or darkness cannot be undone, and that which is so can still be changed by the same forces for better or worse. (Of course, the meaning of the terms "better" or "worse" depends on which side of the universal wheel of life one's consciousness resides.)

After tremendous torment and anguish, many Maldecians (both darmins and quains), including myself, have opposed the malevolent psychic program of our el and have switched our consciousness to the opposing side of the wheel, and in doing so have joined with the forces of light.

Beware, for there are those Maldecians (who outnumber us converts) who still believe in racial superiority and practice the ancient ways. They can be found today among those of dark-force worlds that ravage certain parts of the universe and cast a lustful eye at the planet Earth.

It has been speculated that the building of the Great Pyramid and the destruction of Maldec was permitted by the creator of all that is in order to disconnect the El of Maldec from the Maldecian newborns and save them from any malevolent indoctrination.

We of Maldec no longer spend any time in a state of suspended animation after physical birth due to the fact that our home planet no longer exists. It created changes in the universal life field that prevents our el from maintaining and indoctrinating any Maldecian newborns.

After Maldec was destroyed, any newborn Maldecians (those who had never before experienced human life) came to be called *chaire-salbas* (those on an uncharted path). There are about 35,000 of these Maldecians living today on a number of different worlds located in other solar systems. The Federation is presently assembling the chaire-salbas into one body on a moon of Uranus so they can form a civilized society that can be the basis of a new Maldecian culture composed of all types of Maldecians who wish to pursue the ways of the forces of light. *[The world where the seeds of this new Maldecian culture will be finally planted will be described later in this chapter under "The Replacement for Maldec." —W.H.B.]*

Rom Memory

In that lifetime I spent only about nineteen Earth days on my home planet of Maldec after my awakening and never returned to it at any time prior to its destruction. Most of what I presently know about the ancient human culture, physical features and animal life of my home world was obtained from mental roms (records) created by the staff of Opatel Cre'ator at the time he was the ambassador to Maldec and Earth. The art of rom-making was very primitive in those times, and the recorded sights and sounds of Maldec were accompanied by the rightfully suspicious feelings of a particular rom's Nodian producer(s). The Nodians' opinions of the Maldecians of those times were quite derogatory. My first experience with these recorded Nodian feelings and opinions made me very angry. Today my views would be almost, but not quite, similar to those ancient rom-makers. But their views and mine would now be influenced by many events and other developments that have occurred since those rom records were created.

A person relating to a mental rom is subjected to the rom's content in such a way that the recipient of the mental information actually represents the person (is the person) who created the rom. Only after the termination of the rom reading can a person reflect on the rom's content with his own feelings and knowledge. I say this in order to say further that anyone reading a rom record of any of my previous lifetimes would hear, see, smell, taste, physically feel and emotionally react exactly as I did at any time in any lifetime. During a rom reading session of any of my lives the rom reader would be Doy of Maldec and not himself in any way.

A lifetime of 200 years takes about four minutes in Earth time to be mentally experienced, although it would seem to the rom reader that he had lived through that lifetime and had experienced 200 years. Most persons, after reading and experiencing a mental rom pertaining to the first lifetime of a Maldecian quain, would be emotionally devastated afterward. The meaning of ultimate evil and the means required to perpetuate its existence in the universe might be too much for a person of light to handle mentally and psychically. A person experiencing a rom record of a quain's first lifetime necessarily encounters motivations and events influenced by the psychic program of the Maldecian el, Baal (Lucifer). From your point of view this would be like shaking hands with the devil and agreeing with everything he said, fanatically rendering him your full attention and spiritual service with joy. Did you know that the forces of darkness want your soul and want you to perform for them and provide them all of your creative psychic energy (life force) for all eternity? *[The word "live" spelled backward is e-v-i-l. When a person has "lived" contrary to the master plan of the creator of all that is, he could be called a d-e-v-i-l. —W.H.B.]*

On the day following the setting of the capstone of the Great Pyramid, my sister and mother left the Earth for Maldec and I remained behind with my father, Nass-Kolb, a member of the planning council, whose assignment was to advise the Maldecian governing bodies and military garrisons situated on various parts of the Earth. His work then included making sure that all our people knew what to do after the pyramid accomplished its purpose, which was to transmit Earth's reserve vril energy to Maldec.

It was expected that the native people of the Earth would react to this event in a number of hostile ways. It was estimated that after a short period of time, the loss of the Earth's vril energy would cause the native Earth people to become physically tired and confused. The Earth people who performed certain jobs would not be able to work, so they would have to be replaced immediately by darmins and Simms. It was also expected that many Earth people would die from psychic shock because they might become disconnected from the consciousness of their parent el. My father and his colleagues were very concerned with the unknown factors that could influence the aftermath.

I stayed behind with my father in order to better acclimate myself to three-dimensional life. I had been awake for only a little more than three Earth weeks. My father thought it would be good for me to observe him going about his business and to interact with those who had an important part in our grand project. He wanted me to experience the thrill of being part of a great Maldecian historical event.

For several weeks my father and I traveled by Gracian aircar to many places on the Earth. At each place we were dined and entertained by the local governor or military chief. We were treated even more grandly at the palace of the Maldecian high governor of the Earth, Her-Rood. Our visit to his palace could be compared to attending a 300-acre circus. It was my very first experience with excitement and continuous laughter.

Marduk of Maldec

The last stop on our trip was the palace of Prince Sant (he was a prince because he awoke in his fourth year after birth). In a large villa on Prince Sant's estate resided the living god of Maldec, Marduk. Marduk awoke and took up three-dimensional life after sleeping only seven months. He was cared for in his infancy by Misshemoo, the daughter of the supreme ruler of Maldec, the priest king Mic-Corru. Misshemoo herself had two royal sons named Delver and Dovey. (As you might know, only Maldecian males who awoke prior to their time of puberty were considered to be royalty and were given a single name.) Female royalty was bestowed on women who mothered such sons. A Maldecian was considered an aristocrat if he had such a prince in his ancestral line. Both my mother and father had royal princes in their ancestry.

Marduk was to play one of the most important roles in the transference of the Earth's vril energy to Maldec by way of the Great Pyramid of Mir (Egypt). It was for this reason that he was on the Earth and awaiting the day he would perform his holy duty. Marduk was at the time about fifteen Earth years of age. Living with Marduk was Prince Andart, who was also fifteen years old and who deliberately performed as Marduk's mental adversary. You might say that Andart was the counterpart of what you call the devil's advocate. It was Andart's job to argue the case of the forces of light and keep Marduk mentally sharp concerning his "divine" mission. These two young men were actually carrying on the same three-dimensional debate that is still going on to some degree in the macro level of perception between the els of darkness and the els of light.

Prince Andart was an unsterilized darmin who awoke in his eighth year. The rule was that you do not sterilize a darmin prince. I thought him to be the most beautiful man I had ever seen. (Prince Sant ran a very close second.)

My father and I were given an audience with Marduk, and it was during that audience that I first saw Prince Andart. He sat on a chair reading a book throughout the entire time we were in his company. On several occasions he looked up from his reading and smiled at me. My father and I knelt on one knee before Marduk until he told us to rise and be seated. If we had not been Maldecians of aristocratic blood, we would have been down on our hands and knees with our foreheads touching the floor.

Marduk seemed to have only two moods. He smiled occasionally and asked us if we were being well cared for. My father answered him in the affirmative, but added a few flattering phrases. Marduk raised both hands as a signal for my father to stop talking. It was then that Marduk became stern; not a muscle moved in his face and his words were actually like daggers. The various tones (frequencies) that composed his words actually physically hurt the joints of our bodies. I saw Marduk's single krate bodyguard and my father shake as tears ran down their faces. The only other two people who were present at the time were Andart and me, and we were not that emotionally affected. In fact, Andart wasn't affected at all.

Marduk's response to my father's flattery was: "Nass-Kolb, don't waste my time and bore me with flattering statements I have heard thousands of times before. If you wish to please me, prepare well for the things we must do." Marduk then became calm and spoke softly: "Nass-Kolb, I have seen that your daughter, Doy, has a heart hard enough to be a krate general. Her presence pleases me. You will leave her here to attend me when you leave. She will accompany me when I go to the Land of Mir. You may both leave my presence."

My father left for the Land of Mir within an hour after we met with Marduk. I occupied myself by walking the pathways of the estate. They took me through gardens of flowers and other forms of beautiful landscaping. I was sitting watching a beaver swimming about when I heard bells begin to chime, announcing that dinner would be served in about 45 minutes. As I was walking back toward the palace I saw a large black spacecraft resting on a section of lawn. It was at least twice the size of the Gracian craft that had brought my family and me from Maldec. At several points on the craft's hull were silver triangles that had double left sides. (I later learned that this type of triangle was the official logo of the Nodian Trading House of Cre'ator.)

Doy and Prince Andart

Walking across the lawn from the direction of the craft was Prince Andart and a white-haired, dark-complected man wearing black clothes cut in military style. Pinned on his tunic was a small silver triangle with a double left side. Around his neck hung a jewel that brilliantly emitted every color in the visible spectrum. I knew that the jewel was a faceted piece of astrastone, which was the same type of material from which the capstone of the Great Pyramid of Mir was fashioned.

The two men walked to my side. Prince Andart introduced me to his companion, who was Opatel Cre'ator, ambassador to Maldec and Earth from the planet Nodia. I knew who the Nodian was because I had seen him from afar on the day the capstone of the Great Pyramid of Mir was put into place. As we walked toward the palace, Prince Andart took my hand. I felt a small, soft flow of his psychic essence enter my soul. It was the custom for a man of my race to give an amount of his life force to a woman in which he truly had a romantic interest. (It means considerably more than giving flowers or candy, I assure you.) If I had removed my hand from his, all would be said and done about the matter and we would remain only friends, unless I returned the energy at some future time, at which time he had the right to refuse me. I did not take my hand from his and we briefly looked at each other and smiled. The Nodian walking with us knew our customs well, and was quite aware of what had transpired between my love and me.

The psychic bond made us radiate. Anyone of our race could, just by looking at either one of us, recognize immediately that we were in love. No man or woman of our race would ever approach us separately with any romantic interest unless our love for each other somehow came to an end. Prince Sant was the first to congratulate me on my new relationship with Andart. He said, smiling, "So it's a darmin prince for little Doy—and I was seriously thinking of taking your hand during dinner. What are you going to do during those endless times when your husband is occupied arguing with Marduk?"

I thought for a moment. *Maybe I can find out what they are arguing about. Maybe I can help my love, Andart, successfully plead his case.* When I had the last thought, I had a violently strong anxiety attack and became very sick to my stomach. This occurred every time I became curious about Andart's side of the argument. When Andart heard of this, he held me tightly in his arms and said, "Think only of how our love feels as it flows between us, and you might understand that a universe filled with people who love each other would be a much better place in which to live." I said aloud, "Inferior races of people can't possibly produce, express and feel the highest form of love as we of Maldec do." Andart then replied, "Yes, Doy, all the human races in the universe have the ability to express love to the fullest. This ability was given to all people of the universe by the creator of all that is. Don't trouble yourself with these universal matters and thus bring the wrath of

Baal down upon you." I then said, "I will leave you to deal with these things, my love; I would certainly die if I ever get that violently ill again."

As Andart and I talked, I saw Prince Sant still sitting at the dinner table watching us. He sat for a while, flicking the tip of his tongue on the center of his upper lip, as all of our race do when in deep thought. Then he suddenly rose from the table and hastily left the dining room, his massive chair toppling over and crashing to the floor with a loud thud. From the look on his face I concluded that he had been thinking, as I had, about things that displeased the El of Maldec.

The Land of Mir

It was a beautiful summer day when Marduk, Sant, Andart and I came together to board two large Gracian aircars for a visit to the Land of Mir. Marduk said, smiling, "Andart and Doy will not accompany me on the craft I travel in. I can't stand them. I wish they hated each other so they would be fun to watch." Then, "Does anyone here really hate someone?" Several hands went up in the air—even Andart's. Marduk laughed and said, "Yes, yes, Andart, I know you hate me. Good, your hate feels so good." He then pointed to an Earth woman with an upraised hand and said, "You, come be my companion as we fly to Mir and glory." The woman was so thrilled that she fainted. She did not go with Marduk, but he never intended for her to go with him, anyway.

Just before we boarded our aircars, the black Nodian spacecraft of Opatel Cre'ator silently passed over our heads, hovering for about thirty seconds. Then it moved up and away at a tremendous speed, carrying its Nodian occupants back to their distant home world. Marduk stared at the craft and said, "There goes Prince Sant's Nodian friends. When and if we see them again, things will be different."

Our flight to the Land of Mir was uneventful. During the first full day of our stay in Mir, Andart and I roamed and picnicked along the banks of the river now called the Nile (known then as the Sa by people of the area). We left the activity that was under way near and about the three Great Pyramids. The Gracians were still in the process of moving their equipment and some remaining Reltian (Jupiterian) workers to their city of Miradol (Teotihuacan, Mexico). We were amused to watch the Reltians running about catching fireflies and popping them into their mouths. When they opened their mouths they emitted a luminescent glow. I tried putting a firefly in my mouth to amuse Andart, but immediately regretted it. It tasted terribly bitter.

On the second day just after dawn we were visited by a krate messenger who informed Andart that Marduk had requested his presence in the large white tent in which he was preparing himself for the big event. We returned to the place where the pyramids stood and Andart went to see Marduk.

Vril Energy Experiment

Some three hours later Andart returned to our tent smiling. He told me that Marduk was getting strong feelings of hesitation about proceeding with the plan to send Earth's reserve vril energy to Maldec some two days hence. Andart said that he did everything he could to encourage Marduk to continue as planned, because he (Andart) did not personally believe the plan would work, and that such a failure would bring Marduk and the quain rulers of Maldec down a peg or two.

Believe me, Andart did not in any way think that his encouragement would lead to the subsequent disaster. Andart left Marduk still pondering the fact that it would be quite a number of years before Maldec (constantly moving in solar orbit) would again be in the best position (relative to the Great Pyramid) to receive the reserve vril energy that belonged to Earth. When we watched the elders of Maldec arrive at the site of the Great Pyramids and saw their personal vril sticks being unloaded and taken into Marduk's tent, we knew that Marduk had decided to go ahead with the plan.

I asked Andart, "Do you think it will work, or that it will fail? I hope it works, don't you?" Andart then said, "Doy, I don't know if it will succeed or not, and I really don't care which proves to be the case. I am concerned only with the fact that we of our race might have provided a physical weapon that our el, Baal, can use to attack and injure another el. I say, let the gods fight if they must, but leave us humans out of it." As I started to consider what Andart said, a wave of nausea came over me.

Andart and I visited with my father the day before the great event. He was pleased to see us and very happy that we had become mates. My father was also nervous about what was about to transpire the next day. Our visit comforted him and kept his mind somewhat off the possibility that he might have overlooked something during the countless number of inspections of the pyramids that Marduk had ordered and that he and his colleagues had conducted. He said several times, "The Gracians say all is well with the structures, and I can think of nothing more to do."

Andart and I stood on the eastern bank of the Nile along with several Gracians, who planned to leave for Miradol later in the day. One young Gracian aircar pilot asked us what we Maldecians were doing with the pyramids across the river. He asked if it was some sort of spiritual ceremony. Andart replied, "You might say so, but of a type I am sure you will not

Michael Tyree

understand." He had just completed his sentence when a pillar of fire shot skyward from the apex of the Great Pyramid.

All was silent, and the pillar of fire looked beautiful to behold. I was overjoyed and kept saying over and over, "It works, it works!" My joy ended when the ground beneath our feet began to shake violently. We could see people running from the pyramids; some jumped into the river. The air was filled with the smell of burning sulphur. Then a great flash of blinding light occurred in the sky. Andart and I fell to our knees trembling. We both wanted to die and end the misery that existed in the deep recesses of our spirits. The Gracians tried to give us aid and comfort, but they were totally confused about what had happened.

After the Explosion

The Gracian confusion was short-lived as the telepaths among them learned from some source that Maldec had exploded. For a few minutes the Gracians were more concerned with the fact that one of their outlying structures (now called the pyramid at Meidum) was falling apart. They milled about, shouting numbers at each other and at the heavens. Eventually their attention came back to us Maldecians, who were rolling around on the ground and wailing.

A Gracian woman doctor came to us, touched a tuning fork to our foreheads, and we passed out. Our sleep was filled with horrible sights and sounds. Several hours later we awoke in a clearing in the central part of the continent you call Africa. The Gracians told us again what had happened to Maldec and informed us that they hastily left the area of the Giza Plateau because the krates were killing everyone they saw. They told us that they had landed at this place in order to catch their breath and decide what to do next. They had decided to rest for a while and then fly on to Miradol to join with others of their race.

I thought of my mother and sister, who had been on Maldec when it shattered to bits. I also wondered about my father and even wondered about what had become of Marduk. The only thing Andart said was, "Don't break down and cry, Doy. Once you start to cry, you will cry yourself to death." I have since learned that my father was one of those who took poison after he learned that Maldec no longer existed. Marduk was blown into microscopic pieces, as was the planet on which once lived the people who thought him an infallible god.

At dawn the next day we rejoined our Gracian benefactors and flew with them to Miradol. Our craft was telepathically alerted that the krates were killing everyone in the city. Andart nevertheless asked to be taken there, hoping that by his royal authority he might stop the slaughter. The chief of the Gracians, who was named Baxer-Tolm, replied, "Prince Andart, I know you mean well, but my answer to your request is no. Tell me something: Do you Maldecians ever stop coming up with crazy ideas?"

Baxer-Tolm agreed to covertly drop us off near the palace of the Maldecian high governor, Her-Rood. The Gracian men gave us no departing words, but one of their women kissed Andart on the cheek and warmly embraced me.

Chaos at Her-Rood's Estate

It took us about three hours to walk to the gates of Her-Rood's estate. Krate guards at the gate asked us to wait in their guardhouse. They offered us strong alcoholic drinks, which we accepted.

Several minutes later a small aircar landed beside the guardhouse. From it came a krate officer who, upon entering the building, saluted Andart and asked us to follow him to the aircar. He flew us to the central palace. When we left the krate, he was shaking and crying. I turned to comfort him when Andart touched me on the shoulder and said, "You can't help him, Doy. If one of his comrades doesn't kill him and put him out of his misery, he will soon spend all his psychic essence and die anyway."

There were thousands of people sitting and milling about Her-Rood's palace. Some of these people were crying themselves to death and others, ignoring the grieving, continued to laugh and frolic about. On occasion we saw krates take the life of a friend or comrade. Human bodies covered the lawns and hallways. We either stepped over or walked on many a dead person in order to reach the central meeting hall of the palace. In the hall we waited with others whose shoes were, as ours, covered with blood. A krate officer spotted us and came to our side. He whispered to us to follow him. We followed him through a door and into a hallway devoid of bodies. Eventually we reached a room in which sat several high-ranking krates and Her-Rood himself.

Her-Rood was drunk and speaking in an incoherent manner. He tried to convince everyone present that Maldec had not exploded. The highest-ranking krate general in the room was named Hantbo-Crob. He came to us and said, "Prince Andart, due to the absence of Prince Sant and the obvious condition of Governor Her-Rood, we of the military council ask that you take over as high governor of Earth." Andart thought for a moment and then began to laugh. He then said, "A Gracian recently asked me if we Maldecians ever stopped coming up with crazy ideas. I guess we don't, sir. I guess we don't. What happens when Her-Rood sobers up or Sant shows up? What would you have me do, kill them?" The krate general instantly replied, "I will have them killed at your command. We need one of royal blood to take charge now."

Andart then said, "I am the highest born of everyone here. I will act as temporary regent for Her-Rood until he can once again take control. If he is given any form of intoxicant or injured in any way, I will crucify anyone who had a part in such actions. You generals are not thinking straight. You're going to need all three of us of royal blood to create any form of normal order." The general rose and saluted and said, "Command us, Prince Andart."

Prince Andart's Command

Andart's first order was, "Stop the killing at Miradol immediately." General Hantbo-Crob replied, "The killing at Miradol has stopped, my lord. There is no one left to kill."

Andart then said, "Search for Prince Sant and bring him here. Remove all dead bodies from the palace and surrounding areas. Have your soldiers do their mercy killings at least five miles from the palace. Put Her-Rood to bed with a guard to protect him. Arrange quarters for my wife and me. Find me one or more of those Trakians who spy for the Nodians. Don't injure them; I want them to telepathically contact the Nodians for us."

It took more than three days to clear the palace and its grounds of the dead bodies. Andart and I were kept informed hourly as to Her-Rood's condition. During the night of our fourth day as the sole supreme rulers of the Earth, Prince Sant and his Nodian friend Opatel arrived in a Gracian aircar they had come to possess. It was during this visit that Opatel took under his protection Nisor of Moor and the Nodian spacecraft operator, Sivmer-Binen.

Sant informed us that several Maldecian elders had not committed suicide, and several were of higher royal rank than Andart and himself. He said we were to expect them within two days' time. Their orders to Sant were, "Tell that darmin, Andart, to immediately cease giving orders like a quain prince. Put Her-Rood back in charge no matter what his physical and mental condition is. We are declaring martial law. Rolander and his brother Sharber are to be considered the highest-ranking krate generals."

Her-Rood took no time returning to his state of intoxication. He mainly spent his time overseeing executions, such as the executions of the Gracians Itocot-Talan and his grandson, Tixer-Chock.

The elders of Maldec did not show up at Her-Rood's palace as we had been told they would, but Rolander and Sharber did. They took control of every section of government and began to reorganize them. Sant was assigned to handle the Nodians and any other off-world culture that might have an interest in the Earth or in our harsh recovery actions. Andart was assigned the task of keeping track of the millions of off-worlders (Martians, Sumerians, Waydians and Trakians) that the Nodians were dumping onto the planet. His job was really only counting noses and where those noses were living.

Maldecian Off-World Policy

As time went on (about two years) things were pretty well back to the way they were before Maldec exploded. One day Andart and I were invited to a banquet given in honor of the Nodians Opatel Cre'ator and the wife of his brother Rayatis, Aranella Cre'ator. She was regal in her manner and a very beautiful woman who listened closely to everything that was said that night by Rolander, Sharber and Her-Rood. During the banquet a krate came to offer her a pillow, only to be roughly pushed aside by her Martian bodyguard Sharmarie. The Martian was about to pistol-whip the krate to death for approaching her without her permission. Lady Cre'ator quickly motioned to the Martian, who sheepishly holstered his gun and then proceeded to beat the krate with the pillow and kick him in the rump until he ran from the room. If it were not for Rolander and Sharber's wish not to offend the visiting Nodians, Sharmarie would have been attacked by as many krates as it took to kill him. [*Sharmarie adds: "There were not enough of them within a hundred miles of the place that could have done that job!"]*

On several occasions Lady Aranella visited with me while her brother-in-law, Opatel, and Andart discussed the off-world immigration situation. The Maldecian ruling council of Earth wanted the off-world immigration to stop. The Nodians were steadfast in their opinion that we Maldecians caused the problem in the first place and were responsible for the care of the now-homeless people of the solar system. The Nodians then began to threaten us with punitive actions if we in any way deliberately harmed the immigrants. These threats did not sit well with the ruling council. After all, they had heard only the Nodian ambassador Opatel Cre'ator making these threats on the behalf of his never-seen half brother, Rayatis Cre'ator, as well as two other unseen Nodians named Trare Vonnor and Carlus Domphey. Who did these men think they were?

Prince Sant, who had visited Nodia, tried his best to convince the ruling council not to underestimate the Nodians or what they might do. The ruling council's official reply to Prince Sant was, "If these Nodians take serious action only after seeking an affirmative light of divine direction from the creator of all that is, then we will wait to see if they receive such divine direction to attack us. We do not believe that lights of divine direction exist. We believe the Nodians use this myth only to justify their actions to others. If things don't go well in what they do to others, they can always say, 'The creator of all that is told us to do it.' Because we believe the Nodians to be arrogant opportunists who seek only material wealth, we will continue to conduct our affairs on the Earth in any way that pleases us."

Lady Cre'ator's Visit with Doy

It was on a day that my husband Andart was traveling away from home that Lady Cre'ator came to visit me accompanied only by Sharmarie, her Martian protector. During her visit we talked about our respective home worlds and our own personal life stories. I had little to say about my home world of Maldec because I had left it so soon after my awakening. I did tell her of my mother and sister, who perished when Maldec was destroyed. But then again, I had little to say about them because I had physically lived in their presence for only a few weeks. She said nothing when I told her that I respected my father's courage to take his own life after his dreams were shattered along with the world of his birth.

She told me how she had been born of poor parents, but was selected by the Nodian sage Linc Core to come and study with other selected Nodian children at his special school. It was at Linc Core's school that she met her husband-to-be, Rayatis Cre'ator, also a child of humble beginnings. At Linc Core's school she was trained to be a musical entertainer. This was a profession she practiced only briefly. I remember telling Aranella that Earth people went to schools, but we Maldecians awoke knowing how to read and write our native language, and many of us also awoke with special knowledge that others of our kind did not awaken with. Later the unknowing ones learned from associating with those who had knowledge. I also told her that my sister Sibrette awoke with the full knowledge of acting and singing. I said that I believed they would have liked each other very much had they met.

Lady Cre'ator then asked me what I awoke to be in life. It was a question no one had ever asked me before, not even myself. I tried to think, but I could only say, "I have no idea." As she described her daughter Falashakena, Sharmarie grumbled under his breath. Aranella said to the Martian, "You love her and miss her as I do. Admit it." Sharmarie answered with a deep sincerity in his voice. "Yes, I love her and miss her now that she has grown into an intelligent young woman."

I asked why her daughter had not come with her to the Earth. She told me that her daughter and her older half brother Dray-Fost hardly ever left their father's side. They were both being groomed to someday take over their father's rapidly expanding trading empire. Hearing this, Sharmarie said, "May the els of light protect us all."

I then ventured to ask Lady Cre'ator two questions that were burning in me to be asked. "Lady Cre'ator, would your husband, Trare Vonnor and Carlus Domphey attack the Earth and make war with us Maldecians?" She answered that they would do so instantly without any hesitation whatsoever if they received an affirmative light of divine direction to do so. This answer brought me to my second question, which was, "Would you tell me truthfully if lights of divine direction exist and can be received by human beings?" She replied that lights of divine direction were a reality, but could be obtained only by special people who had the ability to perceive the divine will of the creator of all that is. She said that Linc Core, who once was her teacher, had acquired this exceptional ability many years past.

The Storm

Andart had not returned home. Starting at dawn of the eighth day of his absence, the sky began to darken, followed by lightning and thunder. The electricity went off and I had no lights. I summoned servants, but they did not respond to my constant requests. I eventually found some candles and sat on a divan staring out a window at the ferocious storm. Hours went by before I heard a loud banging on my apartment door. I thought at first that Andart had come home. When I opened the door, standing before me was the Martian Sharmarie. He asked if Lady Cre'ator was with me. He was very disappointed to learn that she was not.

After a short time the wet and worried Martian said, "Come with me, Lady Doy. Many parts of the palace are collapsing. Soon it won't be safe anywhere in this place." I did not want to leave and possibly miss Andart when he returned home, but when a large tree branch came flying through the window and into the room, I was convinced to leave. The wind and rain now blew into the room.

Sharmarie and I moved down the dark corridors of the palace calling for Lady Cre'ator and Opatel. Our calls were useless because they were drowned out by other voices in the dark that called out for friends and loved ones and for servants to come to their assistance. Soon we began to bump into and stumble over people who had fallen. We eventually reached an area in the palace that had windows, allowing the lightning flashes to temporarily illuminate our way.

Nearing the main entrance, Sharmarie requested that we stop and wait for a few more lightning strokes. He thought he had caught a glimpse of Lady Cre'ator in the crowd by the light of a previous lightning stroke. He was right. In the dark she had been unknowingly walking toward us. When she was illuminated once again, we were able to see that she was close enough to reach out and touch. Without saying a word, Sharmarie took each of us under his arms and carried us out of the building, where he set us down and stood over us to protect us from the wind and the rain.

Lady Cre'ator asked Sharmarie if he knew where Opatel was. He told her that he did not know where her brother-in-law was, and suggested that he might be on his spacecraft. We noticed that there was a large aircar parked in front of the palace. We ran to it and joined the crowd trying to board it. As Sharmarie proved, a shouting Martian waving a gun is not to be ignored. He soon took charge of who would be allowed either to stay in the aircar or get on board. After he forced a number of krates out of the vehicle and others away from it, he sent Lady Cre'ator and me to the front of the car with orders to save him a seat.

As soon as his personal selection of passengers was completed, he closed the door. After coming to the front of the car, he shouted at the Earthman pilot to take off. At Sharmarie's order the pilot flew to the place where Opatel Cre'ator's spacecraft had been parked. When we arrived at the spot we found that the craft was gone. We flew about for hours before the exhausted pilot could no longer maintain control of the craft, which was being battered and heavily damaged by flying debris of every sort. Upon landing, Lady Cre'ator and Sharmarie decided to leave the craft and seek some other type of shelter. I decided to stay aboard the aircar. I was too frightened to move.

After my friends left, the car began to move in circles in the mud beneath it. The electric lights in the car went out. Then everything and everyone in the car fell toward the back of the vehicle as that part tipped over the edge of a very high cliff. The aircar hit the face of the cliff several times before it hit the rocky ground at its base. At the aircar's final impact with the ground, my neck was broken and I died instantly.

Fear not the coming comet, nor its companion,
for they are the objects of divine restoration.
—Brime of Rorfa

A Description of Maldec by Sanza-Bix of Gracyea

I am Sanza-Bix. I was about eighty Earth years of age (but appeared like a present-day Earth man in his early twenties) when our spacecraft landed on the planet Maldec. More than 300 years of space flights (thousands of them) between the planets Gracyea and Maldec had preceded our flight. I had never visited Maldec before. During the journey from Gracyea, which took about twelve Earth days, my companions and I reviewed again and again the plans we had for constructing buildings of sacred design on the planet you call Mars. We were to meet with our Maldecian associates and make final arrangements for beginning the Martian phase of our project.

It might interest you to know that one of our purposes for constructing pyramids on the Earth, Mars and Venus was to use the finished structures to transport people (body and soul) and goods instantly from one planet to another, thus eliminating spacecraft and the time required to make interstellar trips.

The Maldecians told us the truth when they said that it had been the desire of our mutual teachers, the Uranians, to establish this stargate form of transportation between the peoples of various solar systems for the benefit of all. It is now known that the Uranians had successfully completed one such stargate link* with the third planet of the sun/star system Bantivail. This link was dismantled after they suddenly broke off relations with the Maldecians and retired to a state in which they will no longer reproduce their own kind or have anything to do with other races (except, on rare occasions, the Nodians). Although it was our intention to complete

---

*Much of the technology employed today to propel interstellar and intergalactic spacecraft was developed from studies of universal-life-field factors that would have harmoniously participated in the function of pyramid-generated stargate links.

the stargate project that the ancient teachers from Uranus had once proposed, the Maldecians had other plans, kept secret from us, for building pyramids on Earth, Mars and Venus.

A Brief Stay on Maldec, Living in Uranian-Built Structures

I was one of thirty-six Gracians who arrived on Maldec during my first lifetime. We remained aboard our craft until we were physically contacted by Karyo-Belum, who was then the Gracian ambassador to the people of Maldec. Within an hour Karyo-Belum arrived along with his Gracian assistant, Halp-Donax, and two Maldecians (one was a darmin, the other a quain). The quain, Ottannor-Micdin, was assigned to us as our caretaker and guide. It took the two small Gracian aircars about fifteen trips to move us and our personal belongings to our assigned residence. Each round trip took more than an hour.

The residence was a beautiful thousand-year-old structure that had been built by the Uranians. It stretched out over and under more than thirty acres of land. One could walk over mounds of mowed grass and suddenly come upon a part of the building, which seemed to be in the process of erupting or birthing from under the surface. Occasionally a skylight was encountered on the top of a mound. These skylights consisted of a transparent membrane that slowly expanded and contracted. During its expansion the membrane silently vented any molecules of gas that were nonessential to the living environment within the building.

When we entered the structure, we encountered a variety of what you would refer to as wild animals that were allowed to roam free throughout the building. These large felines, canines, pachyderms and many other species (all animals of Maldec) displayed no form of aggressive behavior toward people or each other—that is, as long as they were within the building. However, when outdoors they returned to their natural aggressive behaviors. Many of the animals of Maldec were similar to those of the Earth of today, only they were about twice as big. The only Maldecian creature I know of that never had a similar counterpart on Earth had short white-and-blue-spotted fur. It looked like a cross between a rabbit and a fork-tongued dinosaur. It hopped about and was about four feet tall. Our Maldecian caretaker and guide Ottannor-Micdin, like every other of his race, would not enter the building. He left us at the entrance after turning us over to the care of a Simm named Pallobey. I have always enjoyed the company of Simms. Their home planet, as you know, is located in the same sun/star system (Lalm) as my home planet of Gracyea.

About 200 Simms and 500 Gracians lived in that ancient Uranian architectural marvel. The corridors, halls and chambers of our residence were constructed of both natural and synthetically created materials. Some of the blocks of synthetic material absorbed the gases vented by the skylight membranes described earlier. Others produced light when touched. Some produced either cold or heated air. By touching a synthetic stone framed by natural emeralds, beautiful music could be heard, but only by the person who touched the stone. Simple thoughts could increase the volume or stop the music. (I wish I knew now what the composition of those synthetic stones were, and from whence came that soothing music.) We Gracians ate our meals with the Simms in any number of dining rooms. The food was obtained, prepared and served by the Simms.

Each of us Gracians had a private bedchamber and bath. The interiors of these chambers as well as every other room or corridor in the building could be enlarged or shrunk in size. In the center of most rooms was a block of synthetic stone that stood about waist high. Set in the block were a number of tuning forks. When one or more were sounded, walls of stone weighing as much as 100 tons silently moved up, down or sideways. Knowing the proper tones permitted a person to enlarge or shrink the size of a room. Many a time I lost my way when a corridor I had previously used no longer existed because someone had parked a wall in it, sealing it off. I eventually learned what the ancient Uranian symbols for "proceed in this direction" were.

It was summertime at this latitude and every morning (of a 34-hour day) we Gracians would assemble in a large green tent with a number of Maldecians who were our link to their leaders. During our meetings we discussed what would be required to begin our constructions on Mars. After approximately two and a half Earth months we concluded that we were ready to begin.

As a parting gift, we Gracians were taken by our Maldecian caretaker, Ottannor-Micdin, on an aerial guided tour of some of the ancient Uranian buildings that dotted the surface of the planet. More than 30 percent of these buildings were empty—that is, the Maldecians would not enter them. They said that this was their way of showing respect and reverence for those who built them. The remaining 70 percent of the buildings were used by the Maldecians. We later learned that the quains could not tolerate the benign vibrations originating from the universal life field that some of the buildings attracted. We also learned (too late) that the buildings the Maldecians utilized had been remodeled to a degree that was undetectable even to a highly trained eye. The Maldecians intended to alter all the ancient buildings on their planet.

When we left Maldec every Gracian except our ambassador, Karyo-Belum, and his assistant left the world for two separate destinations—Earth and Mars. This was my first and last visit to the planet Maldec. It took about eight Earth days to catch up to the planet Mars as it sped along in its solar orbit.

Arriving on Mars to Begin the Pyramid Project

Our trip from Maldec finally ended when we Gracians, 334 in number, landed on the Martian plain you call Cydonia. We were greeted by two of our kind, one of whom had a black eye. Both carried Martian shields. They said they had begun carrying the shields to ward off the stones that the Martian children occasionally threw at them. They pointed to a pile of shields nearby and advised us each to take one. The shields were a gift from the Martian zone-rex, Rancer-Carr.

At dusk the top of the walls of the building complex that you refer to as the Citadel (the headquarters of the zone-rex) were lit by torches that burned until dawn. We newly arrived Gracians were told by those who came before us to put any thoughts of entering the Citadel out of our minds. We were, of course, very disappointed to hear that we were not welcome to view and study the numerous ancient Uranian buildings that lay within its walls.

We Gracians spent our first night on Mars aboard our spacecraft. When we rose at dawn to face the rising sun to pray, I noticed a lone figure standing at a considerable distance near a kneeling camel. When we completed our prayers, I watched the man mount his camel and ride it toward the Citadel. As he approached it, the great gates opened and two Martian guards dropped to one knee while holding fast with both hands the hilt of large broadswords that were stuck in the ground before them. It was not difficult for any of us to conclude that the camel rider was Rancer-Carr, the zone-rex of the planet Mars.

Among those Gracians who came first to Mars was Tixer-Chock, who, along with several others, had already completed "toning" the natural materials of the area and had fashioned the tuning forks we builders would need as tools to cut, dress, move and set the building blocks into their particular buildings. When Tixer-Chock departed for Earth, he strongly advised us not to visit the Martian sacred mountain of Daren and to be on our best diplomatic behavior with the Martians. The procedure for solving any problem with the local Martians was to send Gike-Nex, our Martian-speaking comrade, to the gates of the Citadel to yell out our concerns. If within the hour a camel rider came out of the Citadel and rode in the direction of the city of Graniss, we could be sure that the zone-rex was doing something about our problem. If no rider left the Citadel, we took this to be a sign that the zone-rex was expecting us to deal with the situation any way we could.

The Arrival of the Reltian Laborers and
Carving the Face of Sormel

About one Earth month after I arrived on Mars, our Reltian labor force (from the planetoids of Jupiter) began to arrive in several stages. After the Reltians and all of our construction equipment were assembled on the plain of Cydonia, we began our work. In honor of our ancient Uranian teachers, we began to carve the face of one who was the chief of those teachers who first came to our home planet, Gracyea. His name was Sormel. It was our hope that this monument would please the teachers and bring them back to us from wherever they were. We wanted them to see that we, their students, were carrying forward their divine plan. The Martian zone-rex approved of this monument to the teachers. The Maldecians secretly did not approve, but could do nothing about it at the time. If the Maldecian plan for the pyramids had been successful, they probably would have destroyed the great face of Cydonia or disfigured it in some way. I am sure it would have been a diabolical thrill they would have been unable to resist.

It was while we were carving the great face of the teacher Sormel that I met Nisor of Moor, who had come to Mars from Wayda (Venus) as a representative of the Nodian Trading House of Domphey. I watched with my friend Soakee-Loom as Nisor left Mars inside an obviously malfunctioning spacecraft belonging to the Nodian Trading House of Cre'ator.

The Day of Destruction

Our work on Mars began about eighteen Earth months before our construction of the pyramids of Mir (Egypt) and the city of Miradol (Teotihuacan, Mexico) were begun on the Earth. We had very little to complete on Mars when Maldec was destroyed. It was nighttime at Cydonia when it happened. During the disastrous event many of our buildings that had been constructed on the order of sacred geometry sent forth earsplitting sounds. Clouds of dust rose over the area, making it very difficult to see more than a few feet. By morning everyone knew what had happened.

We communicated telepathically with our people on the Earth, only to learn that they were being slaughtered by the Maldecian krates. We had only four spacecraft available to us on Mars, and they were immediately sent to Earth with every aircar we had to help our people in any way possible. The majority of our local space fleet had been based on Maldec.

At noon that day the zone-rex sent for us Gracians to assemble within the Citadel. After entering the complex, we were met by the sight of a black spacecraft bearing the symbols of the Nodian trading houses of Cre'ator and Vonnor. The craft had landed sometime during the night without being seen by us. On a stone platform in the center of the complex stood the Martian zone-rex, Rancer-Carr, and five Nodians. A Nodian who spoke our language told us that spacecraft from Nodia would soon arrive on Mars to take those Gracians who wished to leave back to our home planet. They informed us that they were sorry that they could neither help any of our people on the Earth nor take any of us there.

In the days that followed, Nodian craft arrived as promised. I was one of those Gracians who was aboard the first "blackbird" (as we called Nodian spacecraft) to leave Mars. I have never lived a lifetime on the planet Earth, so I will be of no help describing past Frequency Barrier times on the planet.

Several other things might be of interest to those who have been following the various accounts of events that took place on Earth after the destruction of Maldec. The husband of Doy of Maldec, who was known as Prince Andart in his first life, has been identified during a recent embodiment on the Earth as Colonel Klaus von Stauffenberg. It is known that Colonel von Stauffenberg was responsible for placing and detonating a bomb in the presence of Adolf Hitler. This assassination attempt failed and Stauffenberg (Andart) was later captured and executed. It appears that Andart was still trying to stop the killing.

Comments on Comet Hale-Bopp

Before concluding, I will discuss a very important happening presently under way in your local star system [March 1997]. I do this at the request of Doy of Maldec. It has come to our attention that many persons on the Earth are aware that a comet (Hale-Bopp) and a body about four times the size of the Earth (called the "companion") are traveling toward the orbits of the three existing inner planets of your solar system. I, Sanza-Bix, understand that since the comet and its companion were first seen from the Earth and their course was determined, there has been much fearful concern and speculation generated about these two bodies. I wish to address the reports made from several sources on Earth that the companion body is a large spacecraft filled with living beings.

First of all, this is simply not so, because no spacecraft with any dimension of over 500 miles has ever been constructed by any culture of any world in any solar system that exists in any of the millions of galaxies ever visited by explorers originating from some point in the Federation. Any such craft built in a solar system visited by the Federation would have been detected millions of times over by different cultures as it traveled from its origin to your solar system. No such detections were ever reported.

A mothership over 500 miles long cannot come too close to a planet without its mass and propulsion forces causing weather and tidal problems on the planet. Crafts of this size generally enter a solar system and permit themselves to be naturally drawn toward the central sun, but before they come too close to any planet that they might disrupt, they are physically propelled by their operators back toward the outer boundaries of the system, where they once again are allowed to be naturally attracted back toward the center of the system by the gravitational pull of the system's sun. One such operational cycle consisting of a natural drift period and powered-up reversal period can be designed to last several years. Some smaller motherships can assume an orbit about a radiar system such as Saturn. Think about it—if a mothership with a diameter of 500 miles can drastically disrupt the natural functions of a planet, imagine what a ship with a 100,000-mile diameter would do to the weather and tides of a planet much smaller than it is. There are many reasons I could give (but writing space does not permit) that would instantly dispel even the slightest notion that the so-called companion is a spacecraft built and controlled by either intelligent humans, lizards or gigantic orange bunny rabbits.

The Replacement for Maldec: Hale-Bopp's Companion

So you ask, "If the companion is not a spacecraft trailing the Hale-Bopp comet, what is it, and why does it sometimes disappear and then reappear at other times? The companion is the three-dimensional manifestation of the planetary replacement for the once-destroyed planet known as Maldec. What is truly being observed is an act of divine restoration. The divine manifestation of this new world began in higher (invisible) levels of the universal life field. The cycles of appearance and disappearance of the companion relate to the creative process seemingly required for the cosmic birth of the new world. That is, the new planet periodically goes from the three-dimensional level of the omnipresent, all-permeating universal life field into its higher levels and then returns once again to the visible three-dimensional level of the universal life field.

As you are aware, a comet is composed of frozen gases. In some types of comets the gases are the same as those that comprise the atmospheres of several types of living planets. As a comet approaches a sun, these frozen gases begin to thaw. In the case of the Hale-Bopp comet, its gases will thaw to become the atmosphere of the new Maldec.

This is the sixth time since the destruction of the original Maldec that the Hale-Bopp comet and its companion have materialized in your solar system. On the previous two occasions it disappeared when it crossed the orbit of the original Maldec as it headed both toward and away from the sun. The most recent three-dimensional appearance of these bodies took place 13,005,623.8 Earth years ago.

We of the open state of perception hope that the new Maldec at this time in its manifestation will remain in the three-dimensional level of the universal life field and take up an orbit about the sun in the same orbit of the original planet Maldec. If this occurs now or anytime in the future, the planets and radiars of the solar system will reshuffle into their original orbital positions, after which the planets and planetoids of the solar system will once again return to life and provide homes for their native souls.

The presence of the comet and its companion at this time in history and the possibility of divine restoration of the total solar system look promising, because the companion has appeared more frequently this time than it has ever done in previous appearances, and also because this is the companion's first appearance since the birth of the Christ. Is it not prophesied? "There will be a sign in the heavens that will herald the second coming of the son of man."

I, Sanza-Bix of Gracyea, have given these words to be written. Doy of Maldec will come to you soon. May our separate paths once again join and create good and powerful things as do the paths of the most holy numbers.

I am Doy of Maldec and I now live on the planet Nodia, where I presently serve as one of nine ambassadors representing the living people of Maldec to the Federation. I have given an account of my first life experience on the Earth and am prepared to tell you of several lives I lived on the Earth thereafter. I am pleased that you [W.H.B.] are once again physically well enough, one of Cre'ator, so that we can continue with that which we have agreed to do together.

Tamta of the Australian Benfyvees and Earth's Geography of My Time

My father's name was Fronk and my mother's was Salta. In the order of birth I was their fourth and youngest child. My name was Tamta. Sanza-Bix has estimated for me that this lifetime I will tell about took place some 29 million years ago. *[Sharmarie: Knowing Sanza-Bix, he could be off a day or two one way or another.]* The human population of the Earth at that time is estimated to have been about 4.75 million. Sixty-five percent of this population lived on the landmass you call Australia. In those times the continent was one-third larger than it is today, as was the continent of South America, whose additional landmass extended westward. Parts of Antarctica, now beneath the sea, were connected to the southwestern part of South America. One could say that South America and Antarctica at the time were really one landmass. The Pacific Ocean was not as deep as it is today. A great deal of the Earth's water was frozen in mountains of ice at the planet's geographical poles. There was then a number of island chains throughout the Pacific. Most of these islands were less than 200 miles apart. Australia was then separated from the island of Borneo by about 80 miles. Traveling in stages by boat, one could travel quite easily from island to island, from Australia to North and South America. I know of several of these islands that exist today, though greatly reduced in size. You call them Easter Island, Cocos Island and the Galapagos. It is not my intention to give you a lesson in ancient geography, but only to establish clearly that today's Earth surface was very different during that lifetime of mine.

At that time, Australia and the island chains that ran in every direction from that continent represented about 70 percent of the landmass that has become known as the original continent of Mu. When Mu was at its maximum size, it had a population of about 65 million people. During a period of about 2800 years, the ancestors experienced a number of progressive decreases in detrimental Frequency Barrier effects. In other words, the people of the original Mu lived in what is now referred to as one of the rare golden ages. During this particular golden age the effects of the Frequency Barrier were so minor that spacecraft from the planet Nodia and elsewhere landed periodically on the Earth, and the Trading House of Cre'ator actually maintained a base on the planet. The Cre'ator base was really operated by people born on the Earth, because even though the Frequency Barrier was very weak, after a few months it bothered open-state persons to some degree.

Off-world people usually left the Earth before they experienced intense headaches and a decrease in their mental abilities, which were always accompanied by soul-frightening dreams. These unavoidable effects occurred even more rapidly to those born on the Earth who might have traveled to an open-state planet. Such Earth-born persons would become completely mad in less than four days. Their only hope for recovery was to return as soon as possible to the Earth.

Space Conflicts between the Forces of Light and Dark
During that particular golden age four great battles took place in the

solar system between the forces of light and the forces of darkness. In each case the Federation repelled the invaders and prevented them from taking physical possession of the Earth. A description of the aftereffects of these conflicts would be too lengthy for this writing. But I can say that from that time to the present, the Federation has made every effort to prevent such warfare from occurring again in the vicinity of planet Earth.

About 200 years after the last conflict in space, the Earth began to change geologically. The temperatures began to rise and the planet began to wobble on its axis. The ice at the poles started to melt and the levels of the oceans rose considerably. With these events came major mental and physical changes in the people living at those times. Eventually it was no longer possible for open-state people to visit or live on the planet.

Three thousand years later the extreme geological changes to Earth ceased and a new golden age began to develop. It was during this period that I, Doy of Maldec, was born and became known as Tamta of the Benfyvees.

The group of about 350,000 people, of which I was a member, called themselves Benfyvees, meaning "descendants of the gods." This group had been formed several hundred years prior to my birth at a place that today would be southeast of the city of Perth. The first of our kind grouped together because they had mental abilities very superior to the majority of people living on the Earth at the time. Our relationship to the other types of people of the Earth was not good. They mostly feared us and avoided coming into contact with us. Somehow sparse knowledge of ancient Mu and the battles of the gods survived over time, and they were the basis for many of their stories and legends. They considered that we were somehow related to the fearful events that had taken place in the mysterious past.

We had learned by telepathic communication with people of other worlds about the Frequency Barrier and its history. We also realized that at any time, our superior mental abilities could be lost, even those of our descendants.

We possessed the technology to generate electricity, and we illuminated at night the streets of our one and only city, Murphakit. Our seagoing vessels were powered by sails and electrical power generated by both wind and sun.

Our 22-Year Journey for a Suitable Home

Our society was totally communistic and my father Fronk was a member of the governing council, which consisted of about a hundred members. When I was sixteen my entire family, along with about 500 other Benfyvees, set out on a sailing trip that would take us around the world. The purpose of this trip was to learn more about the planet and its natural resources to help us determine if there was a place more suitable to live. There was no time limit placed on this journey.

During this trip we visited many islands and continents, and by the end of the trip I had married a man named Ramcace, by whom I had a son we named Jercaro. On many occasions we came ashore and trekked inland to find and explore the ruins of ancient cities built by various cultures that had come and gone since the destruction of Maldec. I walked the lanes of the city you call Tiahuanaco [Bolivia] and the streets of Teotihuacan (the Gracian Miradol). I also stood at the base of the Great Pyramid of Giza when its four highly polished limestone faces still glistened like mirrors. It was in the land now called Egypt that I died along with many of my fellow Benfyvee travelers. Our deaths followed a period of uncontrolled physical trembling and fever. I was about thirty-eight at the time, so we had been traveling for more than twenty-two years.

The first sixteen years of my life as a Benfyvee were spent becoming educated in our customs and ways. My education was in archaeology and anthropology. My husband had been trained in archaeology and physics. Nearly every Benfyvee was an archaeologist. We rightfully thought at the time that more could be learned and reinvented faster by studying the artifacts of previous Earth cultures. The world at the time was filled with things (instruments and vehicles) that no longer functioned. In most cases we had no idea what the purpose of many of these ancient devices had been. Our requests to our extraterrestrial contacts as to what the purposes of certain ancient devices were and how the instruments actually worked were usually responded to with the statement, "You will have to figure the thing out by yourselves. For us to assist you would violate the Federation's Prime Directive and the master plan of the creator of all that is."

Even without open-state help we were able to reproduce or at least understand some of those devices that had survived from the various times that were, to us, our very ancient past. Remember, the artifacts of which I speak, those that an Earth person even today would consider highly technical and far beyond comprehension, were scattered about the surface of the planet. Many of these instruments were manufactured by cultures that existed thousands and even millions of years apart.

I know you have the question, "Where did all these buildings and high-tech devices disappear to?" There are a number of reasons why this evidence, which proves without a doubt that many ancient cultures possessing exceptional technology existed at various times on the Earth: (1) Frequency Barrier effects helped cause their decay. (2) The effects of the elements over time caused natural erosion and decay. (3) Geological changes covered many of them by soil, lava or water. (4) The main reason for the disappearance of high-tech artifacts on the Earth is that the Federation has either destroyed them where they once lay, or physically removed them from the Earth during a period of over several million years.

Why would the Federation do that? Well, they viewed such things as potential troublemakers. Earth people who had the telepathic assistance of those of the dark side could gain the necessary references about a device that might give them a superior military advantage over other Earth inhabitants. Imagine what the world would be like today if the Nazis had developed the atomic bomb first. It was those of the open-state dark side who were helping the Nazis develop jet-powered warplanes and field-drive spacecraft when World War II came to an end.

Even after millions of years many ancient devices and artifacts have escaped the Federation's detection and still remain intact at some great depth beneath the planet's surface. *[Machined objects such as metal screws have been found in coal deposits estimated to be millions of years old. In the 1960s and 1970s a number of paperback books were published that listed many ancient artifacts that scientists were unable to explain. —W.H.B.]*

Only buildings designed and constructed on the order of sacred geometry have been spared the sonic cannons of the Federation. The Federation will not permit the Prime Directive to be violated and will do everything in its power to keep the noncomplying forces of darkness from violating it in any way. The ancient underground city of Trelba Sye and its contents have been left undisturbed by the Federation so that someday it can be used as physical evidence to support what we have told you.

In my first lifetime I and my husband Andart visited Trelba Sye and the underground city of Shalmalar, "the city of the sleeping sea." Our reasons for making these visits pertained to the duties he was then performing as the Maldecian chief of off-world immigration.

At the beginning of my twenty-two year journey and explorations of the Earth, we sailed eastward and stopped at numerous islands to search for ancient artifacts. The people of these islands were amazed by our four vessels, the largest of which was nearly 500 feet long; the other three were about 300 feet long. During these island visits we found the remains of many well-built roads that disappeared at the ocean's edge, then appeared once again on another island. This is to say that many sections of these ancient roads even then lay on the ocean floor at depths of several hundred feet. The islands themselves had originally been hills over which the road at one time ran between one point and another.

We did find some ancient artifacts on these islands, but getting the natives to part with them was not easy. They considered many of these things holy relics. I am sad to report that we plied them with strong alcoholic drinks unfamiliar to them in order to pack up and sail away with their treasures before they became sober.

From the start of our trip our fleet was occasionally circled by open-state spacecraft of several types. I can tell you now (though I didn't know then) that they were Gracian and Federation-provided Saturnian (Sumerian) space vehicles. I also know now that some of the spacecraft we saw, especially in Egypt, were those operated by persons whose consciousness resided on the dark side of the universal life field.

There is a universal saying: "Where there is honey, you will find the bees." Similarly, when a golden age appears to be developing on the Earth, there you will find the Federation and also those who practice the ways of the dark side. On several occasions we witnessed Sumerian crafts rise from the depths of the ocean, sending forth millions of drops of water that acted as prisms, sparkling with every color in the visible spectrum. It was quite beautiful to see. Visitations of open-state spacecraft of all types occurred at least every week of our 22-year trip.

Easter Island

We eventually came to the island now called Easter Island. This place was dotted then by the numerous statues found there today, but only the very tops of these carvings could be seen. I am aware that it is believed that the ancestors of the present natives are credited with the carving, moving and erection of these statues. The truth of it is, they are responsible for putting some of the existing stone hats on some of the statues before they dug them out of the burial spots in which they stood for quite some time before the island last became repopulated by seafaring people from the south Pacific.

These statues were already several million years old when we Benfyvees first discovered their tops protruding a foot or so above ground level. We had no idea at the time how big they were, and we didn't bother to dig one up to determine its true size. Because we found nothing else on Easter Island that interested us, we left after only a three-day stay.

The coast of South America extended in some places as much as 1200 miles to the west. The boundary of the present continent and its one-time western extensions is now represented by what is called the Marianas Trench, which is about 13,000 feet deep. *[Several years ago it was reported in the press that a scientific expedition that was taking underwater pictures at the bottom of the Marianas Trench snapped a picture of a building that had several Greek-like columns as part of its structure. After this initial report nothing more was said about the picture or the images it contained. —W.H.B.]*

In those times the Andes mountains were not nearly as high as they are today. They gradually rose to their present height as the western part of the continent began to break away and sink under the waves of a rising Pacific Ocean. What you presently know about tectonic plate movements and the various interactions the plates have with each other explains fairly well how the west coast of South America gradually sank and the Andes mountains rose.

South America was then, as it is now, of great scientific interest to the Federation. During the nearly six and a half years we Benfyvees spent exploring the western part of the continent, we saw as many as fifty open-state spacecraft flying in formation during both daytime and evening hours. These flights were mostly made by Sumerians who were engaged in removing some species of plants and animals from the Earth and reintroducing certain types of the same, which they had concluded would once again survive on the planet. On one occasion we saw two black disks resting on top of a hill. I felt very uneasy about their presence. Though I could not think of a reason why, I felt a bit frightened of the star people and hoped I would never meet one physically.

Tiahuanaco (Bolivia)

It was during the six years or so we roamed South America that I married and had my son Jercaro. When we first visited the city called Tiahuanaco (in present western Bolivia)—it was then called Prycobra by its approximately 400 inhabitants—there were then three women for every male inhabitant. A strange disease had been killing off the mature men at an alarming rate. Fortunately, this disease did not affect any of the men in our group. At Prycobra we came upon a vault filled with about fifty broken wooden rods covered with metal prongs that once held fine gemstones.

When I first saw these artifacts, my heart raced. I now know that it was to Prycobra that the Maldecian elders came after Maldec exploded and from which they issued their orders to Prince Sant that my husband Prince Andart should surrender his temporary post as Maldecian high governor to the Earth. It was also from this place that they issued their orders to the krate generals Sharber and Rolander to kill the Gracians and any off-worlders who had had anything to do with the construction of the Great Pyramid of Mir. The wooden rods we found had been the personal vril sticks of the Maldecian elders. Twenty-eight pairs of these vril sticks had been used to send the reserve vril energy of the Earth to Maldec. It is now known what that energy did to the planet Maldec.

Among the broken vril sticks were the petrified remains of the wooden hilt of a Martian broadsword. How this artifact came to be among the broken vril sticks I still don't know. I mention it because the hilt had become petrified, but the wood from which the vril sticks had been fashioned had not. When I picked up a piece of a vril stick, a bolt of electricity went through my body. It took the total strength of a Benfyvee man standing close to me to free the rod from my hand. The inhabitants of the city wanted the sticks and the metal that was attached to them, so we gave them the rods.

As you might remember from my account of my first lifetime on the Earth, Andart, myself and a number of krate generals had been informed that the Maldecian elders would come to Her-Rood's palace within a few days and take over the governing of the Earth, but they had never arrived, nor were they ever seen again.

Nazca, the Hub of Earth's Ancient Magnetic Grid

We left Prycobra and its problems and went to the place now called the Nazca plain (located in present-day Peru). At Nazca we observed small Sumerian spacecraft come within a few feet of the ground, hover for a minute or two and suddenly take off in various directions. Nazca was then and is now a key hub in the Earth's ancient magnetic grid. The Nazca plain was later etched with depictions of animals and lines that ran in various directions. Both the images of the animals and the directional lines played an important part in the navigation of the Sumerians, who drew them to certain points in the ancient magnetic grid of the planet, even though the presence of the ancient magnetic grid was undetectable by any open-state equipment that existed then.

Using animals to locate certain points in the old grid worked very well. The images and lines of Nazca were drawn to correspond to the DNA programming (biological memories) of certain kinds of animals, then used to locate certain points in the planet's magnetic grid in the way that dogs are used to sniff out the location of hidden contraband or how a homing pigeon returns to its nest. (When a small magnet is taped to the pigeon's head before it is released, the bird will fly in circles until it becomes too exhausted.) Salmon and eels display their own unique abilities to navigate by way of the Earth's magnetic grid lines. Eels come from the Norwegian fjords to spawn in the Sargasso Sea in the Caribbean, where their cellular memories instruct them to go, even though the river(s) in which their ancient ancestors once spawned no longer exist due to geological changes over many years.

Many of the buildings (or parts of restored buildings) and roads attributed to the Inca were built by much earlier cultures millions of years before the Inca culture existed.

We spent two more years exploring the eastern part of South America, which was of considerably more interest to us than the continent of North America. For a period of time the area now covered by the Amazon rain forest was nearly twice its present size. The plants and animals of the forest lived undisturbed by humans. The Sumerians (Saturnians) had reintroduced many pre-Frequency Barrier plants to the area. One of these plants reacted even to the weak Frequency Barrier effects of the time, mutating to grow to four inches and producing a fruit that resembled cranberries. Birds ate these berries without any ill effects, but once the juice of the plant was exposed to the air, it chemically changed. When this biochemical extract came in contact with other plants, it caused them to produce the same type of fruit alongside their usual flowers, but the juice of these second-generation berries did not have the same biochemical properties as the berries from the original plant.

The reason I recall this plant extract is that when it touched certain metals and types of stone, it caused them to liquefy. If a person acted quickly, he could square a stone by scraping away any irregular protrusions. After about fifteen minutes the hot stone cooled and remained in the form in which it had been fashioned. We Benfyvees were aware that this was how some previous cultures had shaped and fitted many of their building blocks. Some blocks shaped in this manner can be seen in the walls of several structures erroneously attributed to the Incas. This plant does appear from time to time in small patches within the Amazon rain forest, but it does not always produce berries that liquefy metal and stone.

During the time we Benfyvees were in the vicinity where these plants were growing, there were very few people living there. Those few had no ambition to build anything out of stone and had absolutely no idea that they could have used the berry juice to reshape it. *[Spanish conquistadors reported that on at least one occasion their boot buckles and spurs were turned to liquid after walking through a patch of foul-smelling plants. They also reported that gold (but not silver) was one of the metals unaffected by the berry juice. —W.H.B.]*

Teotihuacan and the Masemors

We traveled north overland as far as Teotihuacan (Miradol). During this phase of our journey we encountered many artifacts from previous civilizations, especially from the time when Mu was experiencing a golden age. The name "Mu" in the universal language of the human soul means "mother," and the term "Mu Ma" means "the greatest form of vril energy that can be expressed or directed from a pure female source" (goddess energy).

We also came upon many buildings that had been constructed by the Gracians in pre-Frequency Barrier times. Many of these buildings had been covered over by the Federation or by natural events such as volcanic eruptions and floods. At Teotihuacan we found a tribe of about 3500 people busily digging into the mounds that contained the ancient Gracian buildings constructed on the order of sacred geometry. This tribe called themselves the Masemors. They had developed an alphabet and number system and were obsessed with keeping very accurate records of their history. We stayed about a year and a half with them and learned their language. Much of the tribe's history was filled with accounts of encounters with the "sky gods." They told of children being fathered by the gods and later becoming their leaders. The validation of this was the fact that their leaders were taller than the average tribal person and had a lighter complexion.

The Masemors had reproduced musical instruments that had first been made by an earlier culture who once lived there. During the evenings the melodies from their flutes, whistles and stringed instruments caused a breeze that was clearly created by the sacred music and its interaction with the uncovered Gracian buildings there. We observed that this "sacred wind" caused the branches of the trees that had rooted on the still-to-be-excavated mounds to sway to the rhythm of the sacred music. While the music was playing, the animals of the surrounding forest were quiet and we humans were in a state of euphoria. The music of the Masemors was of a type now called Ra music, which is composed of musical tones (frequencies) revealed by the sacred geometry embodied in the Great Pyramid of Giza and other ancient Gracian buildings. [Sanza-Bix: Music is a thing of the fourth dimension (the micro level of perception, which is a higher level of the universal life field) because it requires time to be completely expressed from its beginning to its end.]

During our stay with the Masemors, no one living in the city became ill in any way. In fact, the Masemors didn't know what sickness was. The oldest of them was about 350 years old (their water had very little, if any, deuterium in it). Only about two children a year were born to the Masemors, but we of the Benfyvees experienced a remarkable increase in our birth rate while we were living in the ancient city! When we were ready to depart, the chief of the tribe brought to us four Masemor teenagers (two boys and two girls) and requested that we take them with us, which we did.

The Bimini Area and Its Sacred Temple

By traveling to the east, we came to the coast. In those days Florida and most of the Caribbean islands such as Cuba and Haiti were still part of the same landmass. The island of Bimini was also part of this landmass; that is, it was not an island at the time. There were two things of importance about the area of Bimini: (1) There were a number of natural artesian springs that originated deep in the Earth and that definitely contained no deuterium. (2) A town was there that had originally been built by pre-Frequency Barrier native Earth people. Though the stone palaces and buildings had not been built on the order of sacred geometry, they were very attractive. The town's population had overflowed into surrounding huts made of just about anything their builders could get their hands on. The ruins of this town were excavated much later by those of the golden-age kingdom of Atlantis. The so-called Bimini wall or Bimini road is all that remains of this ancient place today. It is reported that on occasion the natural deuterium-free artesian springs bubble from the seabed. This has given rise to the legends of the area about the so-called fountain of youth.

In this ancient Earth town was the "most holy temple of Terron, the Lord God El of the planet Earth." During our visit to this temple we found it to be in ruins and stripped of its roofs of gold and copper. It was on one of the rooftops of this temple that Kevinar-Kale of Earth and his friends had seen the great flash of light appear in the sky when my home world of Maldec exploded.

We camped for about two months on the eastern shore of the ancient landmass while we waited for our ships and their crews to locate us. They had sailed from the Pacific to the south Atlantic through a network of waterways that connected the two major bodies of saltwater. These waterways were then part of the combined landmasses of Antarctica and South America. Our ships had completed their navigation of these waterways years before and had sailed to what would become India to deposit others of our Benfyvee explorers. They did so with the understanding that they would pick us up at a predetermined time and place. After pickup our destination would be the ancient sites on the much larger continent of Africa. In fact, what is now called India and the island of Madagascar were then a part of Africa. We expected to join the others of our band in the land now called Egypt. Our fleet of ships was a week late due to the fact that we had to remain at anchorage to repair some storm damage.

Africa and the Telepathic Bormians

When we reached Africa we found it to be inhabited by a vast variety of people. Some were so mentally primitive that we Benfyvees looked to them only as some type of creature that might be good to eat. This is the first time in our travels that we armed ourselves for protection.

From the very first day of our arrival in Africa we saw open-state spacecraft flying about continuously, day and night. It was not at all uncommon to encounter as many as five of these vehicles resting on the ground. Whenever any black disks of the Federation appeared, the other types of spacecraft were conspicuously absent.

We came upon four blond males who were dressed in identical green robes. They were telepathic and spoke our Benfyvee language. Without introduction they addressed many of us by our personal names. They told us that they were open-state people from a planet called Borm and were able to tolerate the Frequency Barrier only to a certain extent. They said that they were on the Earth to make certain biological and geological studies on behalf of the Federation. They also said it would be several weeks from the time of our meeting before they would have to leave the Earth, because they estimated that by that time they would begin to feel ill. They asked for and received our permission to physically examine the four Masemor youths we had brought with us from Miradol (Teotihuacan). It was from the Bormians that we learned that both Masemor girls were with child.

The Bormians thought nothing of bringing down a primitive human with tranquilizer darts, examining him or her, then leaving their specimen to sleep it off and awake to find beside them a bag of sweet candies laced with vitamins and various types of medications.

We Benfyvees, upon the Bormians' request, donated samples of our DNA. A day later they told us that everyone in our group was a Maldecian darmin except me, who was a Maldecian quain. We had heard the story of the destruction of Maldec from our parents, who had received the information telepathically from people of the open state. But this was the first time we learned that our most ancient DNA ancestry began on the planet Maldec. No one but me reacted with adverse feelings to hearing this. Sensing my feelings, one of the Bormian quartet came to comfort me. He soothed me with words that were both physical and mental. When we parted I felt good once again. Before he turned to walk away, he said, "I wish you well, Doy of Maldec, now in the person of Tamta of the Benfyvees. I hope that the creator of all that is blesses you during this life and all of your lives yet to come."

When the time came for the Bormians to leave us, we were invited by them to attend their departure. We traveled about twenty miles from the place we first met them to a spot where we found a seven-foot-high circular stone platform with a 75-foot diameter. Within three hours a black disk bearing scorch marks on its hull landed upon the platform. The Bormians donned clothing with transparent faceplates. Before entering the craft one of them said, "We wish you well. Beware of those who operate the triangular spacecraft that bear the symbol of a man with a broken arm." As the blackbird slowly rose from the platform, I wondered what the worlds of the open state were really like. When the spacecraft instantly disappeared from my view, I felt a deep feeling of loneliness.

Coming "Home" to Egypt

We traveled north some two years later to the land now called Egypt, which was then referred to as Ethromal, the land of the pyramids. When we arrived at the pyramids we were met by the members of our group that had explored the country to the east, now called India. They had arrived only a few days before we did.

We of the Benfyvees loved the country of Ethromal and the ancient buildings dotting its landscape. The bed of the Nile was several hundred feet lower than today, so the forested plateau on which the pyramids stood was that much higher above the river. It was decided almost immediately that we had found the place to which all of the Benfyvees should emigrate.

We began to construct a town to the west of the pyramids and sent a message to our ships anchored to the far south. The message that contained a historical description of our long trip and our decision to permanently settle in the land of Ethromal was to be carried back to our homeland by the fleet. We knew that it could take as long as six or seven years before we saw more emigrants from our homeland.

Like so many who came before and after us, we were astounded by the pyramids. We spent a great deal of time trying to figure out how to gain access to their interiors without damaging them.

A tough but nonaggressive group of hunters ranged the forests and fished in the numerous lakes that then existed in the immediate area of the pyramids. We eventually began to trade with the brutes, who behaved like puppies in the presence of a Benfyvee woman. The local people numbered about 9000; the closest thing they had to a religion was the worship of the gods who flew about in the bellies of the metal birds. They were quite surprised to learn that we did not fall to our knees as they did every time an open-state spacecraft flew overhead.

The first wave of about 20,000 Benfyvee emigrants began to arrive when we expected. Within a year's time many of us became very ill and began to die. I did not sicken right away; I lived to see both my son and later my husband pass away. The symptoms of their sickness as well as mine were at first similar to those of malaria, then palsy, followed at the end by epileptic seizures.

Just before I began to experience the seizures that finally killed me, I remember staring at the Great Pyramid. I was torn between hatred for it and wanting to become a loving part of it and understand all it represented.

Every time I felt hate for it, a voice that seemed to come forth from its sacred form would softly whisper, "Rest you, Doy of Maldec. Know that I love you. I am the creator of all that is."

Rarla of Rome

I was born in the year A.D. 11 to Vadius Gromius and his wife Aprela in the city of Rome. They named me Rarla. My father was an armorer for the elite Praetorian Guard of Emperor Tiberius. He also served as the postmaster for the guard, arranging the delivery of personal letters of the guardsmen to their families and friends. Letters for any guardsman were first delivered to our house before being taken to the imperial palace three times a week by my father.

We were considered a wealthy family because we owned about eighteen slaves. All but six were men who worked for my father in his armor- and weapon-making shop. The other six were girls who worked within our house. I learned to read from my mother, who learned from her mother before her. I loved to watch food being cooked, but never attempted to do any cooking myself. It was a sign of aristocracy for a woman to recite recipes of things they had tasted and watched being prepared. I so much wanted to be an aristocratic lady and ride about Rome in a litter, looking at the things that went on in the various markets.

For my fifteenth birthday my father arranged for my dream to come true. He arranged for my mother, himself and me to be carried in a litter from one end of Rome to the other at a full run. It took every slave he owned or could borrow to perform such a Herculean task. Running slaves were sent in to replace those who were about to collapse by horse-mounted guards that both herded the litter bearers and cleared our path of pedestrians. I later learned that this cross-town litter trip was the subject of a large bet that my father had made with several of his friends. I also learned later that for weeks before the "great litter race," every freeman and slave in Rome who could was placing a bet on whether or not the litter would reach its intended destination on time.

My father won his bet, and to celebrate took me (my mother wouldn't go) on the following day to a private gladiatorial contest. I soon learned why Mother did not want to watch such an event. Large sums of money were again bet on the outcome of the matches. Three pairs of men fought each other to the death. Even the three victors were badly wounded. As their reward for winning, they were shot down by arrows from the audience. That night I drank wine until I passed out.

The Emperor Tiberius had become a recluse and resided on the island of Capri. In the year A.D. 28 I was seventeen years old when fresh troops of the Praetorian Guard were suddenly called to relieve their fellow guardsmen who protected the emperor on Capri. The sudden order left much mail and armor undelivered. This made it necessary for my father to go to Capri to deliver the mail and tons of personal items that the replacements had left behind.

Our entire household, slaves included, left Rome and went to Capri. My father noted that in the course of our trip we never met any of the relieved praetorians marching back to Rome. The closer we got to Capri, the more encounters we had with large bands of legionnaires (regular Roman soldiers). Our wagonloads of mail and armor were searched again and again before we were allowed to move on.

The answer to this mystery was solved when the captain of the ship that would take us to the island of Capri told my father that an attempt had been made on the emperor's life by a large military force led by a Roman nobleman. Most of the emperor's Praetorian Guard were killed defending him. The invading assassins were defeated when a mainland-based garrison of regular legionnaires came to the emperor's rescue. The attempt on his life was at first ordered to be kept secret, but the news eventually leaked out.

On Capri only a handful of the original praetorian garrison were still alive, and their bravery caused the emperor to raise them all to officer rank. Among these newly made officers was a young man named Geonius. A little over a year later (in A.D.30) he would become my husband.

My life on Capri began when the emperor put my father in charge of the scribes who would copy by hand hundreds of outgoing imperial proclamations and handle all incoming messages. My father got this assignment because the man who had done the job before him had been killed during the recent ill-fated invasion.

In the year A.D. 32 I had a one-year-old daughter I named after my mother. That was the year that twenty-year-old Gaius Julius Caesar Germanicus came to live with the Emperor Tiberius. This fellow was also referred to as Caligula. *[The name "Caligula" was a nickname given to him by the soldiers of his father, Germanicus Caesar. It meant "little baby shoes."* — *W.H.B.]* Even though Tiberius had ordered Caligula's mother, Agrippina I, and his two older brothers killed during a purge, Caligula found favor with the old emperor, who still felt a sense of gratitude for the military support that Caligula's father had given during several attempted coups. Because

Caligula physically resembled his father and carried his name, I believe this saved him from the same fate as his mother and brothers. When Tiberius died, Caligula proclaimed himself emperor and began killing anyone related to Tiberius who might someday make a claim to the imperial throne. It has been believed by some that Caligula became mentally unbalanced due to an illness he had had in A.D. 37, but I tell you, that fellow was *always* out of his mind! The crazy, cruel and horrible tortures that he ordered need not be recounted here.

Truthfully, my father in that lifetime was loving to his family, but was overjoyed seeing men kill each other in gladiatorial combat. In A.D. 40 Caligula had my father beheaded because he suspected that he was part of a conspiracy plotting to overthrow him. He erroneously accused my father of changing the content of military dispatches he sent to his commanders who were fighting in what is now Germany. Because the Germans had beaten the Roman soldiers, who were following Caligula's divine military instructions (issued from a good distance), the only possible reason for their defeat in Caligula's mind was that his orders had been altered by someone before they were dispatched. Thus my father was on the very top of the list of Caligula's scapegoats.

In A.D. 41 I was thirty years old. Caligula was twenty-nine when my husband Geonius, along with several other officers of the Praetorian Guard, hacked him to death with their swords. The Praetorian Guard then proclaimed Caligula's uncle, Claudius I, emperor of the Roman Empire. Claudius was not too bad a ruler, but his choice of a successor was almost Caligula reembodied. His name was Nero. Nero was the adopted son of Claudius and the natural son of Agrippina II (Caligula's sister), who was Claudius' second of two wives. It is true that when Agrippina was positive that Nero would succeed Claudius, she poisoned her husband to hasten Nero's crowning.

Nero became emperor when he was seventeen years old and I was forty-three. My twenty-three-year-old daughter was also married to a praetorian guardsman and had two infant sons. Nero, following the advice of his mother Agrippina and her cohort Burrus, the prefect (chief commander) of the Praetorian Guard, ordered all praetorian guardsmen who participated in the assassination of Caligula to be put to the sword along with their families. Agrippina and Burrus did not want any of these guardsmen getting ideas about doing the same thing to their puppet, Nero.

When it came my time to be executed, I looked into the face of the young praetorian who was poised ready to strike me with his sword. For several moments he hesitated. In those moments his dress and attire changed before my eyes. He became a beautiful blond youth with the golden cobras of the royal Maldecian krate upon his forefingers and who had tears were running down his cheeks. When I regained my senses my praetorian executioner was also spilling tears. When his sword struck me I felt no pain.

Sapeena of the Seneca

I will tell of the brief lifetime I had on the Earth as Sapeena of the Seneca. I speak of this life because it is the last one I experienced on your planet and the last time I lived under the influence of the unnatural Frequency Barrier.

I was about seven years old when my father, Black Turtle, went to war in the company of our redcoat allies, the British. That was during the winter of 1775 during the American Revolution. My father never returned from that war, and in 1777, at the age of nine or ten, I died in a hail of Yankee musket balls.

We were members of a division of the North American Indian tribe called the Seneca. The Seneca were one of the five nations that composed the Iroquois League—the Oneida, Cayuga, Onondaga, Mohawk and Seneca. These nations had in common similar cultures and the same language (Iroquoian). Our group of Seneca lived near the banks of the Genesee River, in what is now the state of New York.

I spent a great deal of time as an infant lying on my back, sometimes with other infants, peering through cornstalks or some other crop, searching for my mother, who was busy working nearby with other women of our tribe. My early years of that lifetime were filled with bewilderment. Even after learning to walk and talk, I existed in a state of total confusion. My detachment from reality was quite obvious to everyone around me. My odd behavior brought curious medicine men from far and wide to follow me about and watch my every move. They all concluded that I had been touched by the Great Spirit—they concluded that I was crazy.

Though I was well-fed and -cared for, I could not resist taking other people's food or belongings. If anything disappeared, the party to which the item belonged simply came to my house to retrieve it. I never hid anything I took. I would openly place any item that I "borrowed" on a pile beside our house. I was not punished for my acts because it was believed that if I were punished, the Great Spirit would become very angry with whoever dealt out the punishment. People who saw me coming would rush to me and give me something in the hope that I would go away before I burned their house down or did something else just as bad.

I was about five years old when two canoes filled with white men from the north landed on the banks of the Genesee. One of the white men who came to our village wore a black robe. He went by the name Father Pierre. His mission to our village was to attempt to do what others of his kind had tried to do many times before: convert us Senecas to the Christian religion.

When Father Pierre heard of mad Sapeena, he paid me a visit. He spoke Iroquois quite well as we sat with my mother next to my pile of loot. I asked him if he had brought me a gift. After a moment of thought he took a medal that bore the image of a saint on it out of a small pouch and handed it to me. I held it in my hand throughout his interview. I learned soon after that he reported to our chief that I had not been touched by the Great Spirit, but was instead possessed by the devil. He volunteered to drive the evil spirit from me, and the chief gave him permission to try. [Sharmarie: "The chief was probably an old Martian soul and thought, What the hell, why not give it a shot?"]

The time of my exorcism was quite an occasion in my village. Hundreds of my people gathered about my house and began to beat on drums. When Father Pierre arrived, he told them to stop their drumming. The priest brought with him a small metal statue of the Virgin Mary, a wooden crucifix, candles and what seemed to be an endless supply of holy water. After purifying our house with smoke and holy water, he began to pray in Latin. I soon found myself praying with him in the same tongue. When he realized that I was praying with him in fluent Latin, he went into a state of shock and began to pray for angelic protection in his native French. I thought I would give him some help, so I repeated everything he said in French. The poor man first thought that I had the ability to mimic, so he tested me by asking several questions in French, Latin, Celtic and German. He was more astonished when he learned that my knowledge of these languages was even more extensive than his. He gave up trying to drive the devil out of me and resigned himself to listen to me speak in French of what I knew about the life and death of Jesus Christ. After more than two hours he asked me if I had ever encountered Satan (the devil). I answered that I was sure I had, in many forms—once as Marduk and once as Caligula.

Father Pierre requested that I go with him to a place called Montreal, but the chief denied his request. When the chief asked him whether I was touched by the Great Spirit or possessed by the devil, Father Pierre answered him honestly, saying that he still did not know which was the case. My people took Father Pierre's rapid departure from our village as some sort of victory for them—a victory that I, Sapeena, was responsible for. The gifts I received now came with requests for all manner of spiritual guidance and assistance. The chiefs of the five nations each came to me seeking "battle powers" that they assumed I could give them.

Eventually one of the conditions our chiefs put upon the British commanders before they would provide them with military assistance was that the commanders either come and visit me or send me a valuable gift. I soon had a good-sized collection of clay pipes, teacups, spoons, blankets and the image of King George III painted on just about anything you could imagine.

The only British commander to visit with me in person was Colonel St. Leger, who came by our village to seek more of our warriors to fill his ranks. We spoke to each other in English. He noted that some of the English words I spoke were archaic and had not been part of the English language for several hundred years. Colonel St. Leger had the habit of looking in disgust at his dysfunctional pocket watch every five minutes or so. I had seen a watch before, but none that beautiful. I asked him to let me hold it. Its case was of solid gold. When I gave his timepiece back to him, it was working fine. He held it to his ear, smiled and said, "Thank you, Sapeena. I thought the only place I could have had this watch repaired was in London. How are you with unruly horses?"

Before Colonel St. Leger left our village, he gave me a broken music box that had a ship painted on its top. When he gave it to me, he said, "I don't give this to you because it is broken. I can't fix it or find anyone who can. Maybe your magic will bring it back into repair." The colonel mounted his horse and I opened the box, which immediately began to play the melody of some sort of sea chantey. He laughed hilariously and repeated several times, "There you are, Sapeena, there you are, you little witch."

Both my mother and I missed my father. We had not seen him for more than a year and a half. One morning we awoke to find his moccasins filled with feathers outside the entrance to our house. They had been placed there by one of his comrades to inform us that he was dead.

Because most of our menfolk were off fighting the Yankees, it was decided that our band would divide into several groups to travel to other Seneca villages farther to the north and west because there would be safety in numbers. My mother and I were with a group of about twenty that set out for Canada under the leadership of an old half-breed named Louis. On the fourth day of our journey we were spotted by a troop of about fifteen armed Yankees. They opened fire on us. We were in a clearing and there was no cover. Both my mother and I were shot and fell dead as we tried to run into the forest. This ended my life as Sapeena of the Seneca.

In the Earth year I estimate to have been 1827, I began to live again in the three-dimensional plane of the universal life field. I was born then to darmin Maldecian parents on the planet Nodia. Therefore I am presently about 170 Earth years of age.

It is my fondest wish that my accounts of some of the past lifetimes I experienced on the Earth will be of value to those who read them. I thank Sanza-Bix of Gracyea and you [W.H.B.], one of Cre'ator, for helping me record my memories.

I am Doy of Maldec.

P A R T　　　T W O

It Has Begun

The time has come when events both on and off the Earth are occurring at a rate that is quite overwhelming for me. The telepathic levels of the universal life field (ULF) are nearly filled to capacity with the mental activity of extraterrestrials communicating to extraterrestrials and extraterrestrials communicating to their contacts upon the Earth. Being in the mental presence of such activity can be quite psychically disturbing as well as physically tiring. From time to time I must remind my open-state friends to take it easy and take into account that I'm the one who's on the Earth. It is I who have to deal with the Frequency Barrier and the unnatural conditions and restrictions imposed by those in control of the planet who make it very difficult to carry out my part in informing people about the past purposes that the extraterrestrials have had and presently have for visiting Earth.

"It Has Begun" is an announcement that the third of four phases of preparation that the extraterrestrials must complete before becoming totally involved with a new planetary culture (such as that of Earth) has in fact begun. Nearing the end of this third phase, physical contact between the extraterrestrials and Earth people of their choice will openly occur. In the meantime sightings of their spacecraft will increase dramatically. The purpose of this increase of extraterrestrial overflights is to get the people of the planet, even the average person, to accept their presence as commonplace. There will definitely be a time when fear of a so-called invasion will prevail, but the extraterrestrials have their ways of dealing with and alleviating any fearful concerns. After all, with their advanced technology they could have invaded and taken control of this world long before this had they been so inclined.

One such extraterrestrial phase-three overflight took place on the night of March 13, 1997, at Phoenix, Arizona. An eyewitness to this event, interviewed on MSNBC on Sunday, June 22, 1997, reported that numerous types of UFOs were sighted in the skies both over the city and its outskirts. The most impressive of the sightings was that of an extraterrestrial spacecraft estimated to be a mile or more in length! This gigantic spacecraft, captured on videotape, displayed a line of bright white lights. I must say, the videotape that depicts this spacecraft is very impressive. One reason why thousands saw the immense spacecraft is because they were looking toward the sky more frequently than usual, hoping to glimpse Comet Hale-Bopp as it streaked across the heavens.

The witness described the vehicle as being triangular and black, and he recognized it was solid when it was illuminated by the light of the then-quarter moon. Many residents of Phoenix and towns in the vicinity saw this vehicle as it slowly and silently passed over their heads. The articulate witness added that this same spacecraft was sighted by people living in Sedona, 100 miles to the north.

The four phases of preparation rarely take the extraterrestrials more than three Earth years to complete, but in the case of the Earth, the beginning and ending of the third phase had to be synchronized with the progressive diminishment of the Frequency Barrier. The beginning of the third phase tells us that the extraterrestrials believe that the Frequency Barrier will soon be gone and thereafter no longer prevent people of the planet from using the mental frequencies required to be active in higher levels of the universal life field.

Several recent events that have occurred on the Earth have caused the extraterrestrials to be anxious to communicate their feelings and warnings in respect to these matters. These events include the suicide of the Heaven's Gate 39 during the passage of the Hale-Bopp comet and its companion body, the successful cloning of a sheep in Scotland and the suppression of the fact that the nine so-called S.E.T.I. messages are actually real messages transmitted to the Earth from an extraterrestrial source more than twelve light-years away.

Of these three major events, the one that disturbs the extraterrestrials the most is the successful cloning of an animal and the fact that scientists of the Earth are seriously considering cloning human beings. I have hesitated to accept the responsibility for passing on the extraterrestrial warnings to others because my knowledge about those subjects is either sparse or nonexistent. After a brief period of extraterrestrial persuasion I have agreed to try my best to document the reasons for their concern. The basic theme of their persuasion was simply, "Phase three has begun and time is rapidly running out."

As I begin this writing project, the proverbial statement about the blind leading the blind has come to mind several times, so as I continue it is my sincere hope that first I, then you, the reader, will be able to comprehend the information the extraterrestrials impart to us. My preparatory communications have informed me that the extraterrestrial concerns are somewhat out of the frame of reference of most people. That is, for us to understand their information, we must accept the existence of unseen things governed by higher forces that are not under their control or ours. As you read this, keep in mind that the extraterrestrials are calling on millions of years of collective knowledge from a countless number of extraterrestrial cultures. Even if this book were ten miles thick, I am sure there would not be enough pages to record all the reasons the extraterrestrials have for their concern.

In Part Two, a number of extraterrestrials help us gain an understanding of these matters. This group will be collectively referred to as the Committee. The eight-member Committee consists of the following: Serbatin of Gee, Tillabret of Emarin, Ombota of Mars, Krive of Dacsa, Vilasin of Trake, Prancacotta of Sumer, Latmigful of Corray and Rendowlan of Nodia. Some of these extraterrestrials have visited the Earth in very ancient times, and in some cases more recently, but none have spent any lifetime on Earth that was influenced by the Frequency Barrier.

They will mainly present both their personal opinions and the opinions of Federation officials about the affairs on Earth today and what will most likely happen in the near future. They will tell what they know about the Federation and dark-side agendas for the planet.

Thousands of people who have read *Knowledge from the Stars, Dragons and Chariots* and the foregoing accounts previously published in the *Sedona Journal* have contacted me, saying, "I already knew that these events in the Earth's ancient past were true. I don't know how I knew. Can you explain it?"

The answer is quite simple. These readers have been receiving the same telepathic messages that I have been receiving for more than thirty-five years, but on a more subconscious level. All that my writings really do is arrange the facts in a comprehensive order and bring them to a person's conscious attention. When this is done, a link between the conscious mind and subconscious memory becomes established. My friends, you will be surprised to learn that you know more than you think you do about extraterrestrials and their relationship to the history of the Earth and the local solar system.

Wesley H Bateman
June 24, 1997

T E N

Serbatin of Gee

Worlds are as grains of sand in the glass that
measures cosmic time, and the Earth will be the
last to settle in the glass before it is turned once
again by the creator of all that is. Then our spirits
will once again be quickened and sparkle with wonderful, divine purposes that we have never known
existed.
—Ther-Mochater of Parcra

I am Serbatin of Gee. My first birth occurred about 7400 Earth years
after the destruction of the planet Maldec on the planet that my people call Gee. Gee is the eighth of twelve life-sustaining planets in the
sun/star (solar) system we call Jatha. The solar system of Jatha is located
about 169,000 units you call light-years from your solar system in the
direction of the center of the galaxy. Utilizing the two most advanced systems of spacecraft propulsion (manipulated light and stargate piping), the
distance of 169,000 light-years can be traveled in as little as 87.5 Earth
hours or, by an alternate route, 32 Earth days. *[Sharmarie: Guess which
route I would take.]* The minimum time factor could someday be reduced
if and when any new stargate portals are found that terminate in either of
our respective solar systems or in a solar system nearby.

In my first lifetime space travel throughout the solar system of Jatha was
commonplace, but interstellar flight had not yet been achieved. The first
race to develop space flight in our solar system were the Morfs, who

resided on the fourth planet in our system (Morfa). The Morfs and we of Gee are both oxygen breathers, as are the peoples of all the planets of the system except those of the eleventh and twelfth planets, who are nitrogen breathers.

In that first lifetime I was trained in the field of animal and human biology. I was one of a large group of scientists from several worlds in our solar system who had just begun to conduct experiments in all types of cloning, when a large Federation mothership entered our solar system and rapidly dispatched emissaries to the peoples of our various worlds. Within about two Earth years, each and every world in our solar system had become a member of the Federation. When my group was apprised of what the Federation had learned from millions of other cultures on the subject of cloning, we were glad that we had not attempted to clone a human being, primarily because we learned that such an act would "not please the elohim."

The Consequences of Cloning Humans

We also learned that such an attempt to clone a human would not have been totally successful, because no human psychic essence would animate the clone unless the founder (source of the biological material from which the clone was created) died and thus freed his or her psychic essence to instantly reembody in the clone.

Each human body born naturally or cloned must establish a harmonious relationship with the universal life field. Such a relationship takes about twenty-eight Earth days after birth (or biological activation, in the case of the clone). In a natural birth this twenty-eight-day period is called the neonatal period. Many infants die during this time because one or more of their body organs did not establish a totally harmonious relationship with the universal life field. The organs of a human clone that contain no animating human psychic essence have never established a complete and harmonious relationship with the universal life field.

Simply, the clone eventually dies unless the founder dies first and psychically animates it. The longer a clone is biologically active, the weaker will become its founder's relationship with the universal life field. When the founder's body can no longer maintain a harmonious relationship with the ULF, he or she will die and, by universal law, be forced to animate the clone. When this animation occurs, the traumatic effects caused by the animation process can kill the clone (depending on its level of maturity) or cause various forms of biological defects such as mental retardation and physical deformities. Believe me, the founder of the clone would be better off dead!

The care and maintenance of a human clone up to the point of its full maturity is very difficult, even with a medical technology that has been developed millions of years beyond that presently employed on Earth. Sterile conditions must always prevail because a clone's body is susceptible to infection caused by agents that would be harmless to a human body that was sexually procreated.

The obvious question is: If this is so, why are we of the open state concerned about your attempts to clone a human being on Earth? To understand our reason for concern, one must first accept the fact that the Frequency Barrier is a unique condition that exists only on Earth. No similar condition is known to exist anywhere else in the universe.

The Universal Life Field (ULF) and the Frequency Barrier

Within the Frequency Barrier's sphere of influence many things can be physically done that could not be accomplished anywhere else in the universe. This is because the Frequency Barrier distorts the universal life field. The ULF distortion is greater at the center of the Earth's core and diminishes over distance. The planet Mars on occasion is subjected to subtle Frequency Barrier effects that originate from Earth. The degree of ULF distortion in the vicinity of Mars is relative to the distance between the two planets.

After many thousands of years of studying biological samples originating on Earth, it has become quite evident to us that the effects of the Frequency Barrier cause considerable biological mutations from time to time that would not be considered normal anywhere else in the universe. These cell mutations, though present in many types of life forms, might not become physically evident for thousands of years. There is also the fact that all life forms on Earth naturally reevolve generation after generation (in response to the diminishing of the Frequency Barrier) toward the biological conditions that prevailed prior to the beginning of the Frequency Barrier.

Therefore both natural and unnatural biological changes are taking place on Earth. Some of these changes occasionally connect and reinforce each other for better or worse, sometimes even canceling each other, which ends any further developments, good or bad, in that life form. The fluctuating power of the Frequency Barrier affects all forms of life and can be rightly referred to in your language as the greatest biological mutator that has ever existed. *[Note: Because the Frequency Barrier causes subtle biological changes in all forms of life, the Martian Sharmarie sometimes refers to it humorously as the Freaky Barrier. —W.H.B.]*

The universe perpetually operates as a system governed by certain laws.

From time to time humans produce conditions (creations) that are incompatible with the universe's operating system. The destruction of the planet Maldec and its aftermath can certainly be considered a human creation that was incompatible with the orderly function of the universe as a whole. What affects one thing in the universe will affect the total universe. Therefore we of the open state are looking forward to the eventual positive manifestation of the Christ reality in the molar level of the ULF. When that new reality is established in the third-dimensional level, it will become an influential spiritual part of all other things that exist in that ULF level of perception.

Because of the Frequency Barrier, Earth is not compatible with the universe's natural operating system. The universe relates to planet Earth only through universal laws unaffected by the Frequency Barrier (such as the law of gravity). Because the universal laws that strictly govern biology elsewhere in the universe are affected by the Frequency Barrier, these universal laws are not always enforced on Earth. It would be as if an hour ago it was against the law to steal or kill someone, but not at present, and not until the law is once again enforced by the universe. When the Frequency Barrier is gone, Earth will return to full compatibility with the universal operating system and will be subjected to all its laws, including those that govern the creation of all forms of life.

The Dark-Side Agenda

Those we refer to as the forces of darkness view these temporary suspensions of the universal laws of biology on Earth as windows of opportunity they can use to produce (create) one or more new forms of life that could be created nowhere else. Their reason for pursuing the creation of new life forms not approved by the elohim is because they know, as do we, that such an achievement would elevate them to a superior status that would give them creative powers equal to that of the els. If they ever accomplish this, the rest of us can expect molar lifetimes filled with miseries I don't really care to think about or describe.

Among all things in existence, physical life forms offer little resistance to limited modification or manipulation by humans. The endless variety of life forms in the universe provide those of the dark side with a biological playground, and the human life form interests them the most. They have several times in the past attempted to use the Frequency Barrier as a mutating agent to (1) produce new forms of DNA and (2) produce a totally new type of being by combining genetic materials obtained from humans and animals that can in turn sexually reproduce. The latter is their ultimate goal. One of their more recent attempts was conducted in an underground facility located near Dulce, New Mexico. Thankfully, this facility is no longer under the control of those of the dark side.

One of the Maldecians' purposes for building the Great Pyramid was to use the creative vril energy, which the pyramid draws and accumulates, to manipulate genetics. Their purposes were symbolized by the part-lion and part-human form of the Sphinx. We are now aware how that program eventually ended.

The beings referred to as Grays (corts), as you know, are clones, but they are unable to reproduce sexually. For this reason their creators do not qualify as gods. The Grays were genetically engineered by those of the dark side to tolerate the Frequency Barrier, and in several ways physically act as their agents on Earth.

The Grays' Experiments with the Sasquatch, Then Humans

One of the Grays' assigned tasks was to physically abduct some Earth people to obtain certain types of Frequency Barrier-influenced biological material. The Grays' obvious interest in pregnant Earth women and the reason they impregnated them in some cases is based on an earlier program they had conducted with the females of the life forms called the Sasquatch (Bigfoot). Pregnant Sasquatch females were placed in the Frequency Barrier by the dark side to determine what effects it had on fetal development. After the birth both the mother and child were taken off the Earth for further study.

Based on the results of their Sasquatch studies, the dark side switched to the study of certain types of pregnant Earth women to determine how the Frequency Barrier affected fetal development. To track the location of the women they had artificially inseminated with biologically altered sperm, they implanted their victims with coded transmitters. For similar reasons Earth males were also tagged with locator implants. These implants enabled the Grays to locate these abductees for subsequent sampling to determine how the unnatural biological material they had introduced had been changed by the Frequency Barrier.

(Warning: Do not attempt to remove or alter the function of a dark-side implant if that implant is more than two years old. Some implants are not locators, but biological monitors that also contain biological regulating programs. Removal or disruption of their function could lead to illness or premature death.)

[Note: For further information about dark side and Gray activities on Earth, see my book, Knowledge from the Stars, *particularly the chapter "Dulce: How Sweet Is It?" Also refer to "The Autopsy of a Cort" (Sedona Journal, November 1995) and "The Rom Masters" (Sedona Journal, July 1995). —W.H.B.]*

We who serve the master plan of the creator of all that is have for millions of years successfully opposed, both spiritually and physically, every evil thing those of the dark side have tried to manifest into the third-dimensional level of perception and thereafter impose on those who are not of their kind. Handling the forces of the dark side in the open state generally amounts to countering their military attempts to conquer world after world for the purpose of controlling or psychically vampiring the psychic energy of the people living on those worlds or of simply acquiring raw materials. But when it comes to the Earth and its Frequency Barrier, the dark side as well as ourselves face many unknowns. The dark side is willing to dare the unknowns in the hope of gaining something by chance. The dark side does not care if their activities cause pain and suffering to others. (I can tell you, it is rare to find a Maldecian such as Doy who sincerely regrets that race's part in creating the mentally restricting Frequency Barrier that exists on the Earth today.)

A Warning against Human Cloning;
Our Own Biological Sampling

For many reasons we of the light feel we must take certain actions on Earth to stop any dark-side activity that has even the slightest possibility for success. Therefore we advise that you oppose in any way possible the attempt to clone human bodies, because such an attempt just might be successful. Believe me, such a success will open up a biological Pandora's box. The universal ramifications of such an accomplishment are impossible for even those of the open state to comprehend. The bottom line is, we don't want that which the dark side deliberately wishes to do ignorantly accomplished by well-meaning Earth scientists.

The elohim do not disapprove of cloning animals when they themselves provide the psychic essence to animate them. The manipulation of genetics, as done in the practice of transgenetics, might be permitted by the el of one world and not by the el of another. Transgenetics is the science of combining the genes of one type of animal with those of another type. This might be done in an effort to produce more milk, meat or eggs. We of the open state do not know exactly what type of transgenetic products would be approved of by the Lord God El of the Earth.

We of the light also take biological samples from every type of life form that exists on Earth, mostly from plants and animals. We do not do this to gauge the diminishment of the Frequency Barrier because there are several much easier ways to do this.

We have several purposes for taking and analyzing human biological samples obtained on Earth. Earth humans have differing types of DNA, in most cases because their DNA is not native to Earth. This means that sometime in the past they had an ancestor that was not an Earth native. Among people with dominant Earth DNA, there are many who possess strong Martian, Waydian, Sumerian, Reltian, Trakian and Maldecian strains.

Any knowledge gained from these studies that tells us how a certain DNA type is faring biologically within the Frequency Barrier is very useful to us when we assign our research personnel for temporary missions there. If Martian DNA is standing up to current Frequency Barrier conditions better than any other type, then our research craft will be staffed by Martians. In case of mishap, a Martian crew would stand a better chance of surviving until they could be rescued.

The unpredictability of Frequency Barrier effects once caused us to take frequent samples, but at present nearly all off-world DNA reacts equally to the current effects of the Frequency Barrier. This is an indication that it is stabilizing and that it will soon disappear. We are using this data in initiating phase three of our preparations for contact.

Samples of plants and animals taken from Earth help us determine if any native species now extinct can be reintroduced into its natural habitat. I am certain we have a dodo bird or two that would find its home world a very nice place to live.

[Note: A species of elephant that stands eleven feet at the shoulder and has two very large humps on its head has been found recently in the wilds of Nepal. This creature is called by the natives "rajah gaz," meaning "king elephant." DNA samples from this animal have linked it with an extinct species. The rajah gaz is one of the animals that was reintroduced to its native Earth by the extraterrestrials because it can now live and thrive on the Earth in the current Frequency Barrier, which is far weaker than that which prevailed two million years ago, when it contributed to this creature's extinction. —W.H.B.]

Monitoring a Jess, a Biological Agent (HIV) of the Dark Side

I believe you have covered in previous writings the reason why we humanely slaughter cattle and remove from them certain organs that we later analyze. Even though you have covered this subject before, I will touch on it briefly once again. We do this to monitor the Frequency Barrier effects on a biological agent called a *jess*. The particular jess we are monitoring was created by those of the dark side when they operated their underground base near Dulce, New Mexico. This biological agent was intended to temporarily deactivate a person's immune system to prevent the body from rejecting foreign biological material such as animal organs. Another name for this jess is HIV, which is a virus that usually deactivates the body's immune system. When this occurs, the infected person is said to have AIDS.

[Note: For information about how the HIV/jess got into our living environment and why the organs of cattle are being studied by the extraterrestrials, see my book, Knowledge from the Stars. *When reading that material, take into consideration the recent occurrences of what is called Mad Cow and Mad Swine disease. —W.H.B.]*

If a human body is successfully cloned on Earth, the regulating biological laws of the universe will have to adjust to the new biological reality, just as the spiritual laws of the universe will have to adjust to the third-dimensional manifestation of the Christ reality. This means that anyone anywhere in the universe who has the technological ability could successfully clone human bodies and that those cloned bodies would have no difficulty in achieving ULF attunement.

Unrestricted human cloning will certainly lead to the production of many identical clones biologically founded by one person. The younger ones could be used by the founder to replace his or her blood from time to time or harvest organs whenever one of the founder's organs became diseased and began to lose ULF attunement. At the founder's death he or she could even resume third-dimensional life immediately by animating a clone with his or her psychic essence (soul or micro-level self). The problem of which clone to psychically animate would be easily solved by terminating all the clones except the most mature one. The terms "kill" and "murder" would never apply to the termination of a clone.

Changes in the biological laws of the universe might permit those of the dark side to achieve their goal to create new forms of life and thus become superhuman, gaining powers that they would use to rule over others.

[Sharmarie interjects: I like the old-fashioned way that people have used to make people. I firmly support the existence of the biological barriers that prevent different types of animals and humans from mating with each other. Can you imagine meeting someone for the first time and saying, "I'm part porcupine and part alligator, and this is my wife, who is part rattlesnake and part canary"?]

The biological laws of the universe are quite complex. No one really knows what role the successful human cloning on Earth would actually play in the alteration of universal law, but we of the open state are not willing to take any chances. Are you?

Successful cloning of a human being on the Earth will not be a snap, because there is quite a bit of difference in the biological makeup between one human body and another. These differences could be adjusted for with the biological knowledge that we of the open state possess, but biologists on Earth do not yet understand our task of keeping those of the dark side from passing on this key biological information to those on the Earth who have publicly stated that they will attempt to clone a human body.

We hope that before any human clone is successfully produced, the Frequency Barrier will no longer exist and the universe will again fully enforce its biological laws on the planet. When that happens, the cloning of a human body will not be possible. I am Serbatin of Gee.

E L E V E N

Tillabret of Emarin

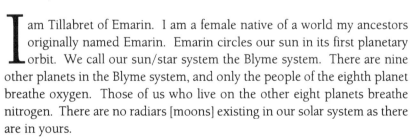

Worlds are as grains of sand in the glass that
measures cosmic time, and the Earth will be
the last to settle in the glass before it is turned
once again by the Creator of All That Is. Then our
spirits will once again be quickened and sparkle
with wonderful, divine purposes that we have never
known existed.
—Ther-Mochater of Parcra

I am Tillabret of Emarin. I am a female native of a world my ancestors originally named Emarin. Emarin circles our sun in its first planetary orbit. We call our sun/star system the Blyme system. There are nine other planets in the Blyme system, and only the people of the eighth planet breathe oxygen. Those of us who live on the other eight planets breathe nitrogen. There are no radiars [moons] existing in our solar system as there are in yours.

In my present lifetime I am about twenty-seven Earth years old and unmated. I am presently, as I have been during previous lifetimes, a member of the council that governs our world. My position on the governing council is that of overseer of off-world trading-house relations. For this reason I claim that I am qualified to communicate to you, one of Cre'ator [W.H.B.]. I know of your relationship with that Nodian trading house, as do the others of this committee of which I am now a member.

I do want you to know that prior to the establishment of this contact, I tried but failed to lay some ground rules concerning any possible unnecessary interruptions by the Martian Lord Sharmarie. If he says something funny, I can't promise not to, as you might say, crack up. The subject I have chosen to address is a very serious one and I sincerely hope to be able to give it my full concentration and rely on your full mental attention.

[Sharmarie: Very well, I promise not to interrupt again after I make one request, which is, can't we go back to the subjects of cloning versus sexual reproduction? I really want to hear what Tillabret has to say about both these subjects.] [Note: Tillabret made no comment. —W.H.B.]

The "Companion" of Hale-Bopp, the New Maldec and the Dark Side's Experiment

As you are aware, a comet named Hale-Bopp, followed by an object four times the size of Earth, recently became visible from the surface of your world. The object that trails the comet was named the Companion. It is also known that the mass suicide of the Heaven's Gate 39 was timed to the arrival of the comet and its crossing over the orbits of the three inner planets (Mars, Earth and Venus) on its natural path toward the Sun.

What has not yet been considered is the fact that the exact time of the first suicide coincided with the time that the Companion crossed the solar orbit in which the now-shattered planet Maldec was once located. It must also be noted that there was nearly a full eclipse of the Earth's moon (Luna) also under way at the time the suicides were taking place.

The suicides of the Heaven's Gate 39 was actually a well-planned dark-side experiment. Through the leader (Applewhite), those of the dark side convinced the group that the "companion" body that accompanied Hale-Bopp was actually a spacecraft that their spirits could use as a vehicle to reach higher dimensions. How they convinced the group that they would need a space vehicle (built of third-dimensional matter) to transport their disembodied consciousnesses to a higher dimension of the ULF I cannot even imagine. Neverthe-less it is evident that the dark side succeeded in convincing the group that a third-dimensional vehicle was required to transport their souls to paradise. Here is a case where half-truths were impressive enough to convince 39 people to take their own lives.

[Note: "When the truth is ugly, a lie can appear to be beautiful," a line spoken in the motion picture Demetrius and the Gladiators. —W.H.B.]

The dark side wanted the souls of the Heaven's Gate 39 to rendezvous with the Companion, not because it is a spacecraft, but because it is the manifesting replacement of the original planet Maldec. I will explain why the dark side wanted this to occur.

The fact that the so-called Companion (New Maldec) disappears from time to time and then later reappears has led to the theory held by some on Earth that it is a spacecraft that was for some unknown reason coming and going from the comet's tail. In fact, the reason that the planet is sometimes visible and sometimes invisible is due to a divine birthing process. This phenomenon is occurring because the molecular rotational speed of the matter that composes the new planet speeds up for one cycle, making the body invisible, then slows down again, making the body visible.

The planet seems to be invisible when the planet's molecules are spinning faster than the visual/mental scan rate (window of perception) of a person who is living on Earth. This is similar to looking at a fan blade rotating at high speed. When the speed of the fan exceeds a person's visual/mental scan rate, the fan blade seems to disappear. I might say here that the Companion is nearly always visible to those of the open state because our visual/mental scan rate is higher than that of an Earth person whose physical third-dimensional perception is presently impaired by the Frequency Barrier. Although our visual/mental scan rate is presently greater than yours, the so-called Companion sometimes vibrates beyond the limits of our senses and becomes invisible to us as well.

Eventually the molecules of the new planet Maldec will slow down and remain rotating at a pace more compatible with the third-dimensional level of the ULF. It is expected that when this act of divine restoration is completed, the new planet will assume the planetary orbit once occupied by the original planet Maldec. Thereafter the other planets and radiars of the solar system will slowly return to the original orbits they enjoyed prior to the destruction of the original Maldec. It is also expected that once the planets and radiars return to their natural positions, they will once again be able to sustain life.

At this point I think I can be more exact about why the dark side wanted the Heaven's Gate 39 to commit suicide at that precise time. In order to make this clear, we must consider what was occurring on and off the Earth at that time, and the relationship that these occurrences had with the ULF.

The Cosmic Event Caused by
the Companion's Crossing Maldec's Past Orbit

Off the Earth, Comet Hale-Bopp and its companion (New Maldec) crossed the orbital path of the original Maldec, which produced certain unique ULF responses. The presence of the new planet at a spot that the old planet once occupied caused what could be called a cosmic shudder in the ULF. This cosmic shudder, coupled with the fact that the destruction of the original planet Maldec was the sole reason why the Frequency Barrier manifested on the Earth in the first place, precipitated an expected cosmic event. This cosmic event was expected by both ourselves and those of the dark side, because it had occurred many times before in the past whenever the comet and its companion crossed the Maldecian orbit. During the most recent time when Hale-Bopp and its companion crossed the orbit of old Maldec, the Companion's core, as before, began to vibrate in sympathy at the same rate at which Earth's Frequency Barrier-producing core was vibrating. The cores of the two planets vibrated sympathetically for a number of hours thereafter. For that period of time one could say that the Frequency Barrier existed on two planets, the Earth and New Maldec. This sympathetic state that would exist between the two planets was a key ingredient in the dark side's experiment, as were the Heaven's Gate 39 and the partial eclipse of the Earth's moon. For a number of reasons, the Earth's moon affects the Frequency Barrier, and at the time it also affected the condition that temporarily existed on New Maldec.

At the time of their deaths the Heaven's Gate 39 were dressed in identical black clothing. The color black represents the highest degree of material completeness, whereas the color white represents the highest degree of spiritual perfection. The official colors of the Federation are black and silver. The black clothing and the twenty quarters (containing some silver) were indications that Marshall Applewhite and his followers were under the false impression that they were in contact with the Federation. I assure you that they definitely were not. Even the twenty coins were symbolic, as were the black and white Nike shoes that the group was wearing.

[Note: What I say now is solely for the purpose of documentation. I am aware that fewer than ten people on Earth will be able to understand the meaning of the statement, "Twenty is in the field." In the future there might be time and writing space to cover the meaning of this statement. —W.H.B.]

Each of the coins found on the bodies bore the word "Liberty," which represented the Heaven's Gate 39's way of saying that what they did had liberated them from the Frequency Barrier and other restrictions of the world that kept them from obtaining their full spiritual potential. The Latin phrase "E Pluribus Unum," which means in English "from many, one," was meant to tell us that they were of one mind in what they did. "In God We Trust" tells us that they were trusting in God to assist them and bless their actions. Beneath the image of the eagle is the image of an olive branch that symbolizes the peace they hoped to find after leaving the physical confines of Earth. The black and white Nike shoes worn by the Heaven's Gate 39 symbolically referred to Nike, the mythological Greek goddess of victory.

During the cosmic window opened by the sympathetic relationship that the Earth and New Maldec had with each other at the time of the suicides, the dark side was sure that the psychic essence of the Heaven's Gate 39 could leave the confines of Earth's Frequency Barrier and be drawn to New Maldec, where their psychic presence would become part of the planet's third-dimensional birthing process. Since the beginning of time only the elohim have provided the human essence of life to a newly created planet. If the dark side were able to accomplish that which is the sole right of the elohim to create, they definitely would become gods. All divine purposes for the restoration of the planet Maldec would have been altered or totally destroyed. Furthermore, the Frequency Barrier conditions that existed on both planets would become permanent for all eternity. Those of the dark side would not have cared if such a condition were permanently established in the universe. What they wanted to accomplish was that the higher powers of the universe recognize that they alone created this new reality.

I am very pleased to inform you that this dark-side experiment did not succeed. We of the open state are not totally sure why. Most of us feel that this failure was due to the fact that the coins found on the bodies of the Heaven's Gate 39 were a late addition to their plan and were an addition that the dark side would not have approved had they known. When the Heaven's Gate 39 decided to use the symbology of the coins to tell the world of the contempt they had for it, they also unknowingly eliminated themselves from the dark side's project by the very fact that coins bore the statement "In God We Trust."

The psychic essences of the Heaven's Gate 39 presently exist in the disembodied state with the micro level of the ULF as that level of perception presently relates to the planet Earth. I am Tillabret of Emarin.

The Heaven's Gate 39

In 1965 my wife and I, who were in our late twenties, founded and directed the M.I.N.D. Research Foundation in Hollywood, California. Some of our experiences from that time can be found in my book, under the heading "Hooray for Hollywood."

The M.I.N.D. center's capacity was 114. Our nightly audiences consisted of government agents, television script writers, UFO researchers from various other organizations and an endless supply of "flower children." Each night we presented a slide program and a number of 16-mm motion pictures, which were copies of the four television shows we did with attorney Melvin Belli, in which we predicted (with extraterrestrial help) a number of earthquakes and their associated UFO sightings. The fact that these predictions proved to be true made our organization very popular at the time.

Our nightly program began about 8 P.M. and lasted until the last person in the audience left (sometimes as late as 4 A.M.). I soon came to know the diehards by name. Many of the people who were obviously very interested in what we had to say were invited to special meetings that were arranged at more suitable times.

During these special meetings the inevitable question was asked, "I want to learn to mentally communicate with the extraterrestrials. Will you teach me how?" Eventually we conducted tests to determine if anyone in the requesting group could be trained as a telepath who could then communicate to the extraterrestrials. My personal thought about training others to become telepathic was, the more the merrier.

Today I am aware of the sacrifices and drastic changes in lifestyle that a person will experience who communicates telepathically with any type of extraterrestrial. Many cannot emotionally handle these experiences. Once a person is able to communicate telepathically with extraterrestrials, he is open to receiving communications from those who serve the master plan of the Creator as well as those of the dark side. Believe me, knowing how to tell the difference is not easy. Neither type will lie to you, because telling a lie costs them too much of the psychic energy that both sides value very highly. Though those of the dark side will not lie to you, they will try to cause you to lie to yourself by skillfully leading you on about a subject until you come to false conclusions.

Among those I tested and trained freely in the 1960s to communicate telepathically with the extraterrestrials was a man who came to the M.I.N.D. center with a lady friend who rarely spoke. One day this pair came to me and asked if they could have a copy of our slide program and its accompanying audiotape. They said they were going to make a cross-country trip and wanted to show the program to groups of people as they traveled. I gave the couple what they requested as well as a spare slide projector. I never saw them again.

The man's name was Marshall Applewhite; his lady friend's name I do not recall. I am fairly sure her name was not Bonnie Nettles, the woman who later joined Marshall Applewhite. I did read and learn by word of mouth of a pair of people using the names Bo and Peep traveling about the country promising people to take them to heaven on an extraterrestrial spacecraft. I never thought for a minute that Bo was the Marshall Applewhite I had trained to be an extraterrestrial telepath. I never knew (for thirty-two years) what became of Marshall Applewhite and never heard of the organization he founded, known as Heaven's Gate, until he and thirty-eight of his followers committed suicide and the event became international news.

I remember Marshall Applewhite as a somewhat timid but very enthusiastic soul. When I heard that he had developed into a person with considerable persuasive abilities, I immediately realized that his personality had been changed by years of telepathic extraterrestrial communication, as mine had been. The question was, what type of extraterrestrials did he communicate with?

At this point in my writing I want to tell the readers to beware of extraterrestrial messages that are received and passed on by anyone, *including me.* A skepticism that is sound, not based blindly on some fanatical belief that gets in the way of reason, is a good thing. I will rely on the "knowing that surpasses all understanding" that resides within us all to inform you if what I say is true or false. —W.H.B

T W E L V E

Rendowlan of Nodia

I have pulled taut many bows and loosed
arrows against my fellow men. In lives past,
from within forts, castles and starships have I
waged war. I have wielded swords and
experienced their piercing pain and
the darkness that followed.
I have prayed that I would not again be called forth by
trumpets and drums, but the banner with its triangle
has been raised and flutters again in the cosmic wind.
So a soldier I will be once again.
—Tin-Tamin of Grailbot

[I have mentally communicated with Rendowlan of Nodia on an almost daily basis for the past thirty-three years. The information pertaining to extraterrestrial spacecraft propulsion that is found in Dragons and Chariots *originated with him. Rendowlan is continuously assisting me in my understanding of extraterrestrial science and technical matters. Our friendship began many lifetimes ago in the distant past. —W.H.B.]*

I am Rendowlan. As you know, this account of my first life experiences is one of several that will be given to you from others who presently live off the Earth. All these persons lived their first lives more or less during the same 600-year period. The Committee has decided that during future contact we will relate our personal experiences during that 600-year period only. Those of us who had a direct personal experience of any major event that occurred within the open state or upon the Earth will initially describe that event. The rest of us will interject only if we can add something of significant worth.

During lives that followed our first lifetimes, we have each been somewhat aware of what was happening on the Frequency Barrier-affected Earth. We will attempt to chronicle the Frequency Barrier from its beginning to the present. In this way the times of the golden ages will be stated accurately. The open-state reaction to certain events that occurred during the history of the Frequency Barrier will also be described in those accounts.

Once again we [the Committee] converse; may the elohim be pleased with our purpose for doing so. I am Rendowlan, Lord of Devisement 617, of the Trading House of Cre'ator. *Castor flex sim vara gol vim larpa. Costrina blac sace mor mar rit trover.*

During my first human lifetime I lived nearly 600 Earth years. My death did not occur naturally, and the cause of that death will be described at some later point.

Beginning in my twelfth year* of life on the planet Nodia, I was an uneducated orphan boy among thousands who labored in the construction of thousands of miles of pipelines, artificial channels and aqueducts that carried water from higher elevations to many places on the world where it was vitally needed. It was a time when Nodia began to bloom and its villages were rapidly becoming large cities whose off-world inhabitants outnumbered the natives.

It was from these countless numbers of off-worlders that much of the Nodian technology originated. That is, our race had and still has the knack of taking things from several different types of cultures and coming up with something new and useful. We accomplished this by befriending, respecting and learning the ways (when possible) of all types of off-worlders. Because of this talent for diplomacy we were able to act as intermediaries for off-world cultures that would otherwise never have associated with each other or shared their various forms of knowledge due to cultural and language differences. Our ability to act as cultural chameleons allowed us to found the institution generally referred to as the Federation. May the elohim continue to bless its existence.

During that period when I was employed (paid in food and clothing only) as a pipeline worker, I was chosen to be part of a detail assigned the job of unloading various forms of building materials that had been manufactured on the planetoid Vitron, which orbited the giant Ampt radiar, which in turn orbited in the fourth planetary position the central sun/star Sost. (Nodia occupies the third planetary position.)

I remember how excited I was as I walked up the ramp and through the

---

*All references to hours, days and years are in Earth units.

massive cargo doors of the large spacecraft. I had seen these craft both in flight and on the ground, but I had never seen the interior of one before. I cursed the ignorance that prevented me from becoming one of those who flew in these marvels to distant worlds. But luck was with me when I was chosen to accompany an aircar we had loaded with pipe to its distant destination.

Several hours later in the twilight night* my companions and I unloaded the aircar's Vitronian cargo and then sat on the ground next to a portable kitchen that was locked and unstaffed. One of us realized that we had been left behind at a desolate location without food or water. We shouted as loud as we could at the aircar as it disappeared over the horizon. Every attempt we made to break into the kitchen failed. Soon after, we began to express our fears that we would eventually die of hunger or thirst.

I was one of three who climbed to the highest hill to look for some form of salvation. For as far as we could see, the barren terrain was lifeless. When we returned to the others sitting by the kitchen, we huddled together to keep warm. We all began to cry.

I awoke from sleep to hear the sound of a voice calling to us in a strange language. I could make out the silhouette of a large man who walked toward us carrying an electric lantern. Behind him at a distance was another large man, who was straddling an air scooter occasionally illuminated by a soft, flashing blue light.

As the stranger came closer and stood over us, he called once again to his companion in heavily accented Nodian. "Rhore, come here and see what we have found. It's a pack of stray Nodian poons!" (a poon is a monkeylike creature).

The propulsion system of the scooter hummed and its rider brought it to a sudden stop, so close to us that we fell over each other as we attempted to avoid being struck. Our clumsy attempt to get out of the way of the speeding scooter caused the two men to laugh.

The man on the scooter spoke to us clearly in Vic Nodian, which was then the language of the lowest class. Most off-worlders spoke Vic because it provided them with swear words that did not exist in the pure Nodian language of Sol-Tec. We of the stranded group had no trouble understanding what the man was saying.

---

*One day and night on Nodia is a little more complicated than on Earth. There are bright days when the planet is illuminated by both the central sun and the light of the Ampt radiar. Sometimes both hemispheres are illuminated to some degree. Twilight days and nights, which are only a little darker, are the most numerous. Periods of completely bright days and dark nights occur about every 32 Earth days and last about 4 days. Nodia rotates on its axis once in about 38 Earth hours and takes about 3.7 Earth years to orbit the central sun. Nodia has no moons.

Rescued by Sharmarie and Rhore

When the electric lantern was turned to a higher setting, the area became brightly lit, revealing to us that the two men were definitely off-worlders of a type I had never seen before. They were tall, with skin the color of bronze. They wore dark red-leather skirts and sandals. Each had long, black shining hair that was braided. The braids were arranged on top of their heads and held together by daggers made of copper. We took them to be very wealthy lords. One of my companions nudged me and pointed at a glittering metal medallion on the side of the scooter. The medallion bore the emblem of the Trading House of Cre'ator. This was an emblem we had seen many times before.

The strangers introduced themselves as Sharmarie and Rhore. I asked if they were of the House of Cre'ator. This question was answered with a laugh and the statement, "It might be said we have a very loose relationship with that organization. As you see, we ride about on a scooter and not in some luxurious aircar." The one called Sharmarie then said, "You poons look hungry and thirsty. Let's all of us have a feast. After all, that's why we dropped by."

As if by magic, a large pistol appeared in his hand. Without hesitation he fired it several times. Each shot sent a metal window shutter on the kitchen sailing through the air.

In a short time, the one called Rhore began to pass hot platters of food out one of the windows. It was delicious, not the usual fare provided for common laborers. It was apparent that Rhore acquired the prepared food from the private pantry of the project's engineers and high supervisors.

A smiling Sharmarie walked among us and sprinkled a mustard-colored powder on our food. He said this additive would help warm us up. It sure did. As time went by, everyone in the camp appeared to be moving in slow motion and our words became meaningless. Six hours later the central sun rose in the west and we found that our visitors were gone. We tried in vain to relate to each other our personal experiences and strange dreams of the night before.

Several hours after dawn two large cargo ships landed nearby and several types of mobile equipment began to roll out of their cargo doors. A group of project supervisors approached us. Upon seeing the condition of the kitchen, they became very angry and began to slap us around, while loudly demanding how we low-class idiots were able to gain entrance to it.

The sound of an air scooter moving at high speed brought our chastisement to an abrupt end. As Sharmarie and Rhore dismounted the scooter, our tormentors froze in their tracks. Among a string of Vic Nodian swear words Rhore managed to say, "What are you men doing to our pack of poons?" Each astonished supervisor managed a quick bow and excused themselves with the statement that they had very important work to perform.

I later learned that Sharmarie and his companion Rhore anticipated the early arrival of the supervisors and concealed themselves out of sight in order to humorously observe what their reaction would be to the condition of their laborers and field kitchen.

The area soon began to fill up with hundreds of laborers and strange-looking equipment. On Rhore's command a large air-conditioned building was assembled, in which we all sat comfortably and ate an endless supply of wonderful food.

Sharmarie then announced that it was now time for each of us to tell our life stories and get to know each other more personally. He said that the telling of a person's life story was a very important event on his home world, and those who listened to such a story actually showed the narrator the highest form of respect.

We sat in total fascination as Sharmarie and Rhore told us about their home world Mars and related their life stories. Two more rest periods occurred before I was called upon to speak.

I told my audience how my early life with my parents and siblings was pleasant up until the time they all died, along with thousands of other Nodians who ate food prepared from an imported off-world grain that had been preserved by a chemical toxic to Nodians. After it had been chemically treated, the producers of the grain ate it without experiencing any ill effects. I escaped that fatal breakfast because I was living with my maternal grandfather some thirteen days' walking distance from my home. My grandfather lived beside a lake among a group of old men who spent their time fishing and philosophizing.

The House of Cre'ator and My Family Connection

Two of my grandfather's friends were Howaren and Rayatis, who were, respectively, the maternal and paternal grandfathers of Rayatis Cre'ator, the founder of the Trading House of Cre'ator.

I realize that the names Cre'ator and Creator could be mistaken as meaning one and the same by those who will read this writing. The meaning of Cre'ator in the language of Nodia means fisher or fisherman (*crea*, fish; and *torr*, man). By the way, the meaning of the surnames of the other two great Nodian trading houses are Vonnor (to brighten) and Domphey, the name of a small, colorful Nodian bird.

My grandfather and I shared a room in the small house of Howaren, who was actually my grandfather's second cousin. I lived there for two more years after my family died. Then my grandfather also died. Howaren gave me a written message and told me to take it to the nearest village and give it to the headman. When I arrived in the village, the headman was not to be found. The man in charge of the place was there recruiting laborers to build a pipeline that would drain the lake where I had previously lived. I tried to visualize what the place would look like after the lake was drained and wondered how Howaren would react to such a thing.

Not being entirely stupid, I signed up as a laborer in order to obtain transportation back to the lake. I was already sitting in the cargo section of an aircar when I learned that the new labor recruits had been divided into several groups, and my group was destined to be taken to a building site some 12,000 miles away. I learned later that this was a common practice. It kept the laborers from quitting and going home whenever they wanted to.

When I completed my life story, Sharmarie asked me if I still had Howaren's message. I took it from by shoulder bag and handed it to him. I immediately regretted it, not thinking to tell him to be careful, as its folds were held together by a fishhook. Sharmarie removed the hook from his finger with a twist and a quick pull. He said nothing as he looked at the words, which were meaningless to him. He then gave the message to Rhore, who then commented, "I can't read this thing either, but I think it's a message to Rayatis Cre'ator from his grandfather." Rhore then left the building taking the message with him. He returned without it.

Just after the next dawn we were well into the life story of one of my companions when a voice requested permission to enter our quarters. Rhore yelled out his permission. A man wearing the uniform of a high-ranking military officer entered and addressed Sharmarie: "Honored one, please come with me and bring with you he who bears the name Rendowlan." Everyone followed the officer.

Several hundred yards away rested a silver and black craft. It was the most beautiful thing I had ever seen. We all got aboard a topless aircar that was used to move construction equipment about. The car silently carried us toward the waiting spacecraft and to a future that none of us had ever even imagined. The carpeted ramp of the craft was already lowered. At its base stood several soldiers.

Meeting Rayatis Cre'ator and Living Underground

The first person to walk down the ramp was a black-haired youth wearing the black military uniform of the House of Cre'ator. His uniform lacked any insignias of rank. Following him was a tall man wearing loose-fitting, tan-colored trousers and shirt. This man was holding the hand of a red-headed little girl. Sharmarie tapped me on the shoulder and said, "That's Rayatis Cre'ator. The young man is his son Drayfess and the little girl is his daughter Falashakena."

With a shove, Sharmarie started me moving in the direction of the descending Cre'ators. Sharmarie and Cre'ator grasped each other by the hand. Then Cre'ator looked at me and held out his hand while saying, "I have been told we are of the same blood. Come, let us leave this place." I turned to look at my sorrowful companions. Cre'ator beckoned to them with a wave of his arm, "Come, all of you, get aboard." Only a reprovisioned Rhore stayed behind to continue to ride his scooter to who-knew-where. After depositing my companions and me in a room filled with plush sofas and chairs, Rayatis Cre'ator and daughter disappeared.

When we landed about twenty minutes later, we were met by a red-faced, cotton-haired off-worlder named Rick-Charkels, who took us in tow and marched us to what first appeared to be a square metal building that had a door but no windows. By voice command the door slid open, revealing a moving escalator that carried us first downward and then moved rapidly horizontally for almost an hour. The conveyance had fold-out seats. We stepped off the escalator onto a platform leading to another door. This door also opened in response to Rick-Charkels' voice.

Nodians and off-worlders were engaged everywhere in some form of work or conversation. Before passing through one particular area, Rick-Charkels ordered us to be totally silent. Later we were told that the area consisted of plush cubicles in which the elite Lords of Devisement conducted telepathic communications with spacecraft and Cre'ator outposts located on what was then considered to be far-distant worlds.

We were quartered in one large barracks-type room, one level up from the inner sanctum of the Lords of Devisement. We did not see the surface of the planet for more than eight Earth months. We were ordered to bathe and were given plain white-colored trousers and what you would refer to as turtleneck sweaters. We began to feel very important. Everyone we came into contact with showed us respect and kindness. Then the dream of every ignorant Nodian boy came true. After being given a number of mental tests and medical examinations, we were informed that we would be going to school.

The Martian Sharmarie did visit us from time to time. He even attended some of our classes. He finally confessed that he attended because he had been ordered to do so by Rayatis Cre'ator, not to check on our progress but, as he put it, Cre'ator had said, "What good is there in having a Martian genius about when he doesn't know anything?" (Sharmarie, of course, emphasized the word "genius.")

Adriannaro, My Companion

I was paired with another one of the poon pack named Adriannaro. The purpose of the pairing was to provide each of us with a study mate and confidant. After months of mental rom input and live instruction, we became totally transformed from the low-class boys we were when we arrived to educated, socially polished young men who were eager to accomplish great things.

One day we were escorted to an elevator that took us up more than nine levels. When the elevator stopped, we found ourselves in the famous bakery of the lady Tanforan. It was a bright Nodian day and the place was filled with finely dressed Nodians and off-worlders who were sitting at tables talking and eating bread and pastry. The aroma of the baked goods caused us to actually drool.

We were greeted by a pretty young Nodian woman who knew our names and took us to the only unoccupied table in the place. We were served again and again whatever our heads desired. About the time we had reached full capacity, we were approached by a very old Nodian woman who carried a broom. She told us her name was Gertaeva and that we should follow her. She moved slowly, so Adriannaro took her arm in an attempt to help her walk. In response to his kind gesture, she whacked him hard across his back with the handle of her broom. When out of the public eye, Gertaeva did not get any younger, but she stood up straight and walked quite swiftly, stopping on occasion to use her broom to sweep some invisible object out of our path. She also stopped in front of doors and put her ear to them. Soldiers saluted her when they passed and walked faster to avoid a whack from her broom in return. We were later informed that Gertaeva was the chieftess of the Cre'ator intelligence service; in other words, she was the organization's top spy.

She eventually ushered us to the open door of a fine four-room apartment and told us to wait inside. She then locked us in. An audible recorded message described the various features of the apartment, even down to the name of the artists and designers who had contributed to its beauty. The message continued, informing us as to which one of the two bedrooms was assigned to us individually. The message ended with the order that both of us should dress in one of several uniforms that were to be found closeted in our respective bedrooms. After dressing we spent about ten minutes sternly looking into each other's eyes and continuously saluting. To this day we still accuse the other of being the first to blink and break out in laughter.

About an hour later the door was opened by two soldiers wearing plain black uniforms with thin dark blue braids on their sleeves. We knew them to be Vitronians. One of them said in precise Nodian, "Come with us, honored ones. It's dinnertime."

The dining hall was paneled with polished wood that had originated on numerous worlds on which existed a Cre'ator trading post. The harmonious combinations of the colors and texture of the woods were wondrous to behold. The panels served to convey the fact that when natural things from many worlds are displayed together, their combined individual beauty exerts the powerful feeling of divinity. There were about 200 people present in the dining hall and not one spoke above a whisper. It was truly as if we were dining in the presence of the creator of all that is.

At the head of the table sat Rayatis Cre'ator. It appeared that he was still wearing the same clothes we saw him in some eight Earth months earlier. On an elevated seat to his right sat his daughter, who from her perch could, if she wished, look directly into her father's eyes.

Cre'ator's Plan Revealed

My companion, Adriannaro, was seated to the girl's left and I was seated to Cre'ator's right. About two hours later I could not remember eating. Adriannaro told me that I had indeed eaten everything that had been placed before me. I never saw Cre'ator put anything into his mouth, but he must have because I recalled that empty platters were removed from in front of him and his drinking cup was constantly being filled. Being in the presence of this powerful person does account somewhat for my state of mind at the time. His conversation was filled with humor. He told me that he had a confession to make to Adriannaro and me. It was his idea to pair us because he and I were blood-related and Adriannaro was blood-related to his wife Aranella. His experiment had two parts. The first part was to see if we were able to get along without inflicting bodily harm on each other. When he described the second part of his experiment, his tone became more serious as he gestured in the direction of his daughter. He continued to say that she was of both bloodlines and had a direct kinship to both Adriannaro and myself.

Rayatis Cre'ator was a young man in his late twenties, but he spoke of dying someday. He pointed out that even his numerous assistants (Lords of Devisement) would someday reach old age and die, or possibly crack under the strain of their offices. It was therefore important to train their replacements as well as his own replacement as soon as possible. He told us that it was his wish that both his daughter Falashakena and son Drayfess jointly assume his position as the prime director of the trading house. He added that if it was the will of the elohim that someone yet unknown assume his position, so be it. He intended to leave his successor an organization that was up to the task of maintaining itself and expanding to unimaginable limits.

He asked both Adriannaro and me if we would accept his offer to be trained as Lords of Devisement. He added, "Maybe at some future time one of you will take my place. If you accept my offer, expect my daughter to join you in your training when she reaches puberty." Cre'ator did not wait for our answer. He simply rose and walked unattended from the dining hall, leaving his daughter in her seat. The child spoke for the first time, saying, "I'll tell Father that you both said yes." Shortly after, Sharmarie entered the hall and gathered her up into his arms. She first looked as if she were going to cry, then she ordered him to put her back into her chair so that she could listen to a live musical presentation that was about to begin. Sharmarie's response to her demand was that he would sing her a song, and if she still wanted him to leave her alone he would do so, after placing her on a distant mountaintop.

About six years later Falashakena joined us in our training; she was then about thirteen years old. During the following year she married, and two years later married once again. In both cases her young husbands attained the "infinite thought" (highest form of extrasensory perception) and became one with the consciousness of the creator of all that is. Because her first husband was her soulmate, her aura took on a soft gray hue. People who have such an aura are referred to as neuts. Neuts are very trustworthy, so a vast number of them serve the Federation in the capacity of temporary administrators whenever their unique services are required.

After Falashakena's second marriage she no longer trained with us. When we saw her physically she was occasionally accompanied by her mother, but always accompanied by an off-worlder named Akite. Several years later Akite also attained the infinite thought. He chose not to be absorbed into the Creator's divine consciousness and remained in human form to provide spiritual consultation to Falashakena—and does so to this very day.

Lords of Devisement

I was assigned my position as a Lord of Devisement before Adriannaro was given any official position in the trading house. One day we had a brief social meeting, after which he simply disappeared. Even with all of my newly acquired power I could not find out where he was. I was concerned for his life, because those were the days when assassination attempts on the life of Rayatis Cre'ator were commonplace. Sometimes a Lord of Devisement was an assassin's target. Several years passed before I learned that Adriannaro was the chief of an elite group of telepaths (Eperone net) that were each located at strategic locations within the Cre'ator trading structure. These telepaths were Cre'ator's personal and most secret means of communication. Eventually the Eperone net developed into a spy network, and remains so today. At this time the Eperone net's members and their locations are known by the Federation, which from time to time also makes use of its services. A similar Cre'ator organization, whose name translates to "gray razor," exists and functions likewise.

In order to describe my early life as a Lord of Devisement, I must refer from time to time to Rayatis Cre'ator, so I will make a few basic comments about him.

He was a middle-class Nodian who was (is) a master at organization. He recognized the latent talents of persons of any planetary culture whom many of his peers would have ignored. To the amazement of those close to him, he was able to speak fluently the language and recite the laws of any off-world culture. It took several years of association before he admitted to me that this ability was supported by a database of mental roms that acted as a form of memory. Without this personal mental source of information he would have been totally in the dark as to what many off-worlders were actually saying. He revealed this to all the Lords of Devisement because the technology had developed to the point that thousands of people could mentally tap the same data source simultaneously and thus be instantly more efficient in their off-world dealings and diplomatic relations. He admitted that his decision to reveal the source of his great knowledge was also prompted by the fact that the Federation demanded that he share this secret "technology" with them.

Once the total body of the Lords of Devisement were able to tap the Cre'ator rom banks, the trading house and its possessions began to expand at an unbelievable rate. Even though we all had the power and means that was once available only to Rayatis Cre'ator, he was still the most experienced of us all in making decisions. A mite's worth of knowledge is priceless.

During my earliest times as a Lord of Devisement my duties were very light, and there were long periods during which I had little or nothing really to do but study and think about finding a wife. I mentally rejected several beautiful candidates of high station and chose as a bride a young woman who was from the village of my birth. Her name was then, and is now, Prantisa. Upon hearing of my marriage, Rayatis Cre'ator sent me the following message. "Congratulations on your marriage. Prepare immediately for an off-world trip." The handwritten message was accompanied by a container filled with common clay cups (some were broken). I learned much later that Cre'ator had made them himself.

Several days later Prantisa and I walked up the boarding ramp of a large spacecraft. We were greeted at its entrance portal by Opatel Cre'ator (older half brother to Rayatis). Several hours passed before we lifted off from Nodia. During this time Opatel told me that our mission was a diplomatic one, and that our destination was a solar system some nine flight days distant. More specifically, our destination was a planet called Maldec in that solar system.

Mission to Maldec

During the course of the flight to Maldec we were introduced to the others who were part of our mission. The majority were Trakian telepaths trained on Nodia who were natives of planetoids that orbited the Trake radiar, located in the solar system we were heading for.

Halfway through the trip we were introduced to Sant, the Maldecian prince. Our first meeting was brief. After we left the meeting, Prantisa said, "Prince Sant seemed to be very pleasant, but thinking about him makes me feel deeply depressed. Why do you think this occurs?" I replied that the Maldecian prince had the same effect on me, and added that it might be best for us both to avoid him when we could diplomatically do so. Little did we know that we were about to encounter millions of his kind, each one naturally able to psychically make any off-worlder feel quite miserable.

At first our Maldecian hosts wanted to quarter us in a compound they had exclusively designed to house off-world visitors to their planet. Opatel Cre'ator rejected even the most magnificent palace they had to offer in the compound. I remember that he later told his staff that if he had accepted the Maldecian palatial quarters it would have been like "being in prison in paradise." Second, getting out of the compound in order to get to our spacecraft would have been no easy matter. Then again, this inconvenience was what the Maldecians had in mind.

Lord Opatel chose to house his staff and himself aboard the spacecraft, where, to the dislike of our planetary hosts, we could come and go as we pleased. We often suddenly lifted off, orbited Maldec for a few days and just as suddenly returned to our original landing spot, which was a high hill within sight of the off-world compound. Although no Maldecian said a word, we were amused by the fact that they were curious about what we were doing during the periods we were in orbit. Actually, it was during these orbits that our Trakian telepaths were downloading information to Nodia.

Although we were escorted by krates to various beautiful areas and sites for both recreation and business purposes, only Prince Sant made visits to our space-vehicle headquarters. Our landing site and the area within a two-mile radius were declared off limits to any off-worlders or unauthorized Maldecian.

Once a full Maldecian orchestra assembled and performed outside our craft. Among the musicians there were several poorly disguised krate espers, who could no more overcome our defenses and mentally scan our craft's interior than they could play a piccolo. After the real musicians left the area, the Maldecian espers remained oblivious to the fact that the others had departed. When they came to their senses they left, murmuring to each other.

Visit to Earth

During the first of two visits I made to the Sol system and Maldec in my first lifetime, I also visited the Earth a number of times. On my first visit to the Earth our craft made an aerial survey of the planet's entire surface area. We also spent nearly a full day parked near the site where the Great Pyramid was then under construction. We watched thousands of labor gangs composed of natives of the planetoids of the Relt radiar (moons of Jupiter) moving about the building site. We were pleasantly entertained by the musical tones emitted by the Gracian tuning forks used to both cut the stone blocks and elevate them into their designated locations within the magnificent structure.

Within an hour or two after we landed we were visited by a group of Gracians (a race never considered shy). By means of telepathy we conversed for several hours. It was then we first learned that the Gracians were involved with the Maldecians in a similar building project on the planet Mars. This information was later telepathically related to Nodia. We asked if we should physically investigate the building project on Mars. Cre'ator replied, "No, the Trading House of Vonnor will look into this matter."

A brief time later I found myself on Earth once again, sitting in a small boat that bobbed about on the waves of the river you now call the Nile. I impatiently waited within the boat while Opatel Cre'ator held a conversation on the riverbank with the Earthman, Jaffer Ben-Rob. Later Lord Opatel related to me how sad he was about refusing Jaffer's request for Nodian military intervention to remove the Maldecians from his world.

A later visit to Earth was made in response to an official Maldecian invitation to witness the placement of the beautiful astrastone capstone on top of the Great Pyramid. This was a very brief visit, and after leaving the area of the pyramid, we found the path leading back to our spacecraft strewn with the dead bodies of animals. This was clearly some sort of Maldecian message we were left to decipher emotionally. We ignored their gruesome insult.

From that time forward Lord Opatel and those of our mission constantly discussed the Great Pyramid. All were emotionally inspired to refer to the structure's simple but overwhelming beauty. The real purpose for our discussions was to try to determine exactly why the Maldecians had built the structure. Maybe if we had uncovered their purpose in those early days, Jaffer Ben-Rob's plea for Nodian help would have been instantly heeded.

Maldec's Explosion and the Subsequent Loss of Aranella and Sharmarie

I was on Nodia when the news came that forces transmitted by the Great Pyramid caused the planet Maldec to explode. This news meant very little to the average inhabitant of Nodia, native and off-worlder alike. Because the planets and radiars of the Sol system did not feel the first effects of the destruction of Maldec until many years later, little attention was given to those who expressed concern or were scientifically capable of predicting the eventual aftermath. When the doomsayers (who proved to be right) warned that the Sol system would eventually begin to adjust to the loss of Maldec's mass from its midst, they were scoffed at. I know for sure that the leaders of the major Nodian trading houses took these warnings seriously, making private studies and designing contingency plans based on all possible disastrous scenarios.

These studies and plans proved to be very valuable when the Sol system actually began to change drastically—to the point that most of its planets and planetoids could no longer support any form of life. When catastrophic events began to occur on the planets and planetoids of the system, I participated in executing the plans to move their endangered populations to the Earth for safety. As these transportations were coming to an end, I accompanied Lady Aranella Cre'ator, Lord Opatel and the Martian Sharmarie on a space journey from Nodia to the planet Earth. My job on Earth was to evaluate the effect that these various populations were having on each other and on the native population of the planet.

I found all types of peoples of the Earth to be mostly totally incompatible with each other, mainly due to their cultural and language differences. Truly, the planet Earth was in a state of cultural chaos. I concluded that correcting these problems should begin by encouraging each off-world group to form a leadership that we, the Nodians, could deal with directly and that would also act as mediators with the leaders of any other off-world culture. This arrangement would help in the distribution of special foods and other types of physical needs, which vastly differed from culture to culture. I must confess, I was glad I was on Earth to evaluate the situation, not do anything about it. I knew that an army of cultural experts would soon arrive on the planet and take things in hand. I prayed that this benign invasion would take place quickly before things got worse. Race wars are very hard to bring to an end. I personally related my findings and suggestions to Nodia telepathically.

I passed on visiting the palace of Her-Rood the Maldecian, ruler of the Earth. I instead decided to live aboard our spacecraft. The weather was excellent during the first three days after our arrival, and the crew and I spent most of our time walking about and eating in the open air. I had difficulty sleeping. I shrugged the problem off as being related to the differences that exist between an Earth day and night and the various forms of day and night that occur on my home world of Nodia (like cosmic jet lag).

After the third day of the visit, light rain occurred off and on around the clock. The rainshower activity kept up for several days more, then the sky turned dark gray. It began to rain harder, and thunder and lightning could be heard and seen in the far distance. We were aware that rainstorms of this magnitude were an unnatural occurrence for the latitude and time of year.

We were physically visited by Opatel Cre'ator, who told us that we should prepare to leave the Earth as soon as he returned with Lady Aranella Cre'ator and Sharmarie. During the following two days and nights the rain continued to fall relentlessly. Lightning and thunder occurred, one flash and clap after another. Several earthquakes shook our craft violently. We all were anxious to see the rest of our party arrive so that we could leave the dark and frightening world.

An exhausted and wet Opatel Cre'ator did eventually return to our spacecraft, along with an equally exhausted Trakian. Opatel related that the Trakian had learned that Lady Aranella Cre'ator, Sharmarie and a Maldecian woman named Doy had boarded an aircar. The decision was made to lift off and search for any aircar flying about in appropriate areas. After taking to the air, we searched for several hours but never spotted even one aircar in flight. Lightning struck our craft several times and made the craft difficult to control. We were forced to gain altitude to avoid further possibly fatal lightning strikes.

From our great height we did observe the aircar we were seeking hovering over the spot where our spacecraft once was parked. Each attempt we made to reduce our altitude was met with lightning strikes, which caused the outer hull to glow reddish orange and the interior to fill with pungent toxic fumes. We climbed above the Earth's atmosphere into space. Below was a sight I will never forget. Millions of lightning strokes were occurring at the same time. The display was awesome. We remained in orbit for about a day and made what internal repairs we could. All the while the Earth appeared to be ablaze beneath us. It took thirty-eight Earth days for our crippled spacecraft to reach a world where there existed a Cre'ator trading facility. We waited on that world only one day before a spacecraft came from Nodia to pick us up and take us home.

Both Lord Opatel and myself personally reported the loss of Lady Aranella and Sharmarie to Rayatis Cre'ator. He cried, but made no sound. We sat with him for a period of time until he interrupted the silence by saying, "Maybe she is still alive. I'm going to find out for myself." I tried to describe the conditions on the Earth that we saw. As I began, Opatel touched my arm and whispered, "It won't make any difference to him what you might say. Rayatis Cre'ator is no longer in the same universe with the rest of us. It is best that Falashakena and Drayfess assume control of things. Let us hope he recovers from his insanity."

Rayatis Cre'ator did recover, but he had long periodic bouts of mental depression. He was killed when a spacecraft he was aboard crashed into the surface of the planet Earth. He had visited the planet several times before, not to insanely search for a living Aranella but to sanely search for her spirit.

When it came to drastically dealing with the forces of darkness, there was no equal to Falashakena Cre'ator. She equally shared the top chair of the trading house with her half brother Drayfess, but when a situation arose that involved the forces of darkness, she merely had to say, "I'll handle this." Drayfess, who was of very strong character himself, never gave her an argument. They were a visibly striking pair, he with black hair and she with red, among the rest of us with hair as white as snow.

During that ancient lifetime I fathered two daughters, who were named Pensala and Grenta, and a son named Roecerlin.

Restructuring the Organization of the Federation and the Trading Houses

By necessity the duties of a Lord of Devisement had to become more defined. There were so many of us autonomously doing something that in many cases we were unknowingly working against each other.

On the other hand, because the Federation's Lord of Devisement structure had more discipline built into it since the institution's foundation, it was logical for the trading houses to redesign their administrations and operating procedures within a framework similar to that of the Federation. Compatible telepathic links between the Lords of Devisement of the Federation and counterparts within the trading houses had to be created. When all facts and factors (too numerous to list) were considered, this was not an easy task.

When the Lords of Devisement began to become specialized, some of us old-timers realized that we really had no special expertise in any field. Our training and experience was established by generally dealing with any situation that might have been instantly thrust upon us to handle. I think you might say that we were jacks of all trades but masters of none. Those of us who fell into this category found ourselves employed in organizing the telepathic bridges between our trading house and the Federation as well as to all the other existing trading houses.

Each trading house in reality functioned originally within an economy that they alone created and totally controlled. Each house had the considerable expense of supporting its own vast military organization. The existence of these powerful military organizations were of great concern to the Federation. Something had to be done that would permit these organizations to exist and perform for their individual trading houses, but also take unhesitating action on behalf of the Federation when required.

In addition, conversion of the trading house economies to the single economy of the Federation had to be started. This operation was and is still quite complex. Too many cultures that the trading houses dealt with had individual economies that worked well only with the original trading house economies.

Reorganization of the trading houses took centuries of time— during which those of the dark side also organized.

[At this point Rendowlan requested that I present my own personal understanding of what the forces of darkness actually are and why they exist. He asked that I relate what I understand about those who follow the ways of the dark side of life, knowing that my version was originally acquired from my open-state sources over a period of thirty-five years, and little if any more open-state information would improve my understanding of the subject to any greater degree. — W.H.B.]

The Dual Structure of Our Universe

Neither I nor anyone else who lives within the Frequency Barrier* of the planet Earth can fully understand every facet of universal reality. We live in a universe that has a dual structure, where everything consists of a plus and minus component such as black-white, left-right, positive-negative, male-female, action-reaction, light-darkness, matter-antimatter, proton-electron, sharp-dull, truth-lie and good-evil ad infinitum, even emotions.

The creator of all that is represents all things that exist, counterbalanced by absolutely nothing. This means that nothing is something. Because nothing (the void) exists, everything must exist in a dual form at some level.

Human beings are subcreators and have a natural Creator-given right to mentally access any level of perception in the universal life field (ULF), which is omnipresent and all-permeating. This means that our psychic essence is constantly one with (in tune with) all knowledge. (The human body is totally in harmony with the ULF after 28 Earth days, the neonatal period.) Therefore the universe and the ULF not only exist around us but within us. The primary purpose for third-dimensional life is to manifest knowledge acquired from higher levels of the ULF and employ it in the third dimension.

I understand that when all higher ULF realities are manifested into the third-dimensional level of perception by human beings, the master plan of the creator of all that is will be completed. In this way the positive-negative natures of reality will be balanced (neutral). When all existing realities are present in a physical form in the third-dimensional level of perception, so will be the total consciousness of the creator of all that is, because the Creator is all reality. I leave it to you, the reader, to imagine the meaning of this divine event.

The preparation for the Creator's manifestation into the third-dimensional level of perception has already begun and the extraterrestrials are fully aware of it. The foundation of this preparation was established on the planet Earth and is presently referred to as the Christ reality. There are several superlogical reasons why the foundation of this new reality was laid out within the Frequency Barrier of the planet Earth. I will mention only the single and most evident reason, which is security.

The Restrictions of the Frequency Barrier

For thousands of years harsh Frequency Barrier conditions made it impossible for any useful telepathic contact to take place between people of the Earth and any type of extraterrestrial. But over the past hundred years or so, the strength of the Frequency Barrier has gradually weakened, allowing for better and better telepathic contacts to be established and maintained. The greatest technological achievements that we on Earth enjoy today were realized and developed during this same period.

The existence of the Frequency Barrier has prevented both benign and evil extraterrestrials from physically visiting the Earth in large numbers. Only specially equipped spacecraft provide temporary protection for them during any visits they make to this planet. Those of the "other side of the wheel" (evil ETs) have tried to circumvent the physical restrictions imposed on them by the Frequency Barrier by using expendable surrogates such as the Grays [not the Zetas], who are genetically engineered to physically function for them within the Frequency Barrier. Other than causing considerable emotional disturbances for many Earth people, the activities of the Grays have served to falsely promote the worldwide belief that they are the only extraterrestrials we have to deal with here.

Both the physical and mental restrictions of the Frequency Barrier have in the past kept both types of extraterrestrials from influencing the lives of Earth people or in promoting any sort of off-world agenda. These conditions have so far protected the manifesting Christ reality from any "evil open-state" attempt to devalue it or foul its true relationship to all other forms of reality. Up to now extraterrestrials have done little one way or the other to affect the manifestation of the Christ reality. We of Earth are solely responsible for the state of development that the Christ reality has reached. Our record to date is very good in spite of the efforts by some to "churchify" the reality. I need not state why these special interests pursue these goals.

Every reality manifested into the third dimension brings its counterpart, so a Christ reality must be accompanied by an Antichrist reality. Such realities can affect humans only if they are provided with psychic energy by humans. By not supporting the Antichrist reality with psychic emotional energy, it will become impotent and without any great influence. Humans have within them the ability to be either ultimately good or ultimately evil. There are those living in the open state who practice the ways of evil to the fullest extent. Compared to them, Hitler or Stalin would hardly rate.

The End of the Frequency Barrier

Now that the Frequency Barrier is nearing its end, both organizations are becoming extremely interested in the Earth and its people. They are specifically interested in whether the Christ reality or the Antichrist reality will win the emotional attention of the planet's inhabitants before the Frequency Barrier is gone. If the Christ reality prevails as the stronger reality, it will manifest first into the third dimension and those of the dark side will back off and keep their distance from the Earth. I am pleased to report that my extraterrestrial contacts have informed us that the emotional attention given to the development of the Christ reality over the past 2000 years is greater than that given to

---

*Frequency Barrier: The accidental destruction of Maldec, through the Maldecians' activating the Great Pyramid, caused a ringing-like reaction in planet Earth, which shut down the human brain's ability to receive higher frequencies for a very long time.

its evil counterpart. Unless something drastically changes, the last days of the Frequency Barrier will not be filled with the hardships, misery and torment that were biblically described as the "time of tribulation."

Before closing, I would like to leave you with some meaningful humor. At the time I was attempting to understand that the dual nature of the creator of all that is is both everything and nothing, the Martian Sharmarie said, with due respect, "It's like the words of that old song: 'I've got plenty of nothing, and nothing's plenty for me.'" —W.H.B.

The House of Cre'ator after Aranella's Death

In the years following the time that Petrimmor will describe [in the next chapter], we of the trading house I served (and now serve) suffered and mourned the loss of Aranella Cre'ator and Sharmarie and later, under different circumstances, Rayatis Cre'ator. Opatel Cre'ator continued to serve as a roving ambassador for the House of Cre'ator, which was then directed by Rayatis Cre'ator's daughter Falashakena and her half brother Drayfess. Several times I had the opportunity to travel to the Earth with scientific expeditions conducted by the Federation. Each time, I would refuse the Federation's requests for me to take part in these expeditions. Even if I had been ordered to do so by my superiors, I would have used every bit of power I could muster to have any such order rescinded.

The time just before Maldec exploded to several hundred years thereafter represented a period of rapid change due to the fact that all areas of Nodian technology were developing at a tremendous pace. Understanding and applying these new technologies to useful purposes was hectic. Many people had to be trained to build, maintain and operate these things throughout the Federation and trading house systems. More and more people of millions of races undertook the schooling necessary to understand the correct procedures and personal safeguards required to be employed as telepaths for these organizations.

Because what you call hardware was becoming phased in with mental command forms of activation and control, new types of mental specialists had to be created. The use of a person's psychic energy to operate hardware mentally can be a risk to his health and even his life. Exposure to the effects of intergalactic travel also held the same risks. As more knowledge of these things became progressively evident, the risks and dangers subsided proportionately. In order to encourage qualified persons to embark on careers that required considerable amounts of their personal life force, they were enticed with great material rewards. In other words, in those days if you wanted to become rich, first become a telepath or some type of mental-energy-expending specialist.

How Economics Determined the Use of New Technologies

The economies of the Federation and the trading houses were taxed to their limits because of the costs of training and maintaining these specialists. It took more than 2000 years before the economies of the Federation and trading houses began to grow once again. How things held together until the resurgence occurred is still a mystery to me. The growing economy allowed for bigger and more advanced spacecraft to be built. For the first time new spacecraft propulsion systems that had been designed as much as a thousand years previously were able to be put into service.

As time went by, scientific data obtained from more than a millennium of observations of the Earth helped us realize that the Frequency Barrier existed there and that it was progressively diminishing in strength. It was thousands of years after my first lifetime that the Earth's spiritual importance was recognized and plans were begun to protect and be part of the world's spiritual destiny.

I was part of the initial realization that the future operation of the Federation and the trading houses would require continuous change until the growth of technology reached its peak or came to a stop, because there was no way for humans to sensibly use or control it. People who are continually forced to learn as fast as they can usually stop learning.

Even now new technology that was conceived from millions of bits of technology developed over hundreds of thousands of years is still emerging. Our original fears that open-state technological advancements might surpass the ability of humans to use and control it have proved unfounded. We now believe that the creator of all that is is pleased that we manifest technological things to assist us in fulfilling our purpose for existing with the universe.

During my first lifetime I lived nearly 600 Earth years, as did many of the then-living Lords of Devisement who served Rayatis Cre'ator. I became a diplomat, and there was noplace within the Federation I could not go, even if only on a whim. As time passed, the years I spent traveling about on Cre'ator or Federation motherships surpassed any number of years I spent living on any one planet. I took every opportunity to visit Cre'ator trading facilities whenever I found myself in their vicinity. I enjoyed these visits because they permitted me to give executive assistance to many who operated the facility and also learn from the people of the world on which they operated.

The Death of Opatel Cre'ator

It was near the end of that lifetime that I returned to Nodia for a brief stay. After paying my respects to Falashakena and Drayfess Cre'ator,

Falashakena told me that her uncle, Opatel Cre'ator, was also present on Nodia but in ill health. His illness was due to the effects of considerable intergalactic travel, for which there was then no remedy.

Opatel was not bedridden. I found him walking in the garden of the private home of Drayfess Cre'ator with Drayfess' daughter Illena. I had never met the woman before, but she greeted me by name. Opatel was pale and his eyelids and lips were bright red and dark purple. These were definite signs of what was then called galactic sickness. The condition was caused by numerous conversions of the human body from matter to antimatter and back again during intergalactic space flights.

We sat at a table under a tree and Illena left us. Opatel immediately began to scold me about the many intergalactic flights that he knew I had made over the years. He advised me to remain on Nodia and give up any future intergalactic travels I might have had in mind. He was terribly concerned that I too would acquire the same affliction. He rattled off names of many of our generation who had died from the sickness.

We then spent several hours talking about our times on Maldec and the Earth and about Rayatis and Aranella Cre'ator and Sharmarie. We also spoke about those last days and our friendship with Petrimmor and his group. Opatel, even after several hundred years, showed anger when he recalled how Dell had been so cruelly murdered by the Maldecian Kamer-Ostsen. He told me that he was sorry that Prince Sant did not manage to leave the Earth with us. He also expressed sorrow over the fact that he was unable to bring the Maldecians to their knees and give the Earth back to Jaffer Ben-Rob and his people.

Before we parted he smiled and said, "Do not take my state of being so hard. I know I will die soon, but I have heard from the wisest that I have met on many worlds that this life is not the last, and that it is the will of the elohim and the creator of all that is that we live again and again. I know within the deepest place of my being that we will meet again in a future lifetime. I hope that we are permitted to remember this life."

Several days later I was summoned to the House of Cre'ator. Falashakena met me personally and asked that I follow her, which I did. After a short aircar flight we walked to a secluded room lit by candles. Only Drayfess and Illena were there sitting by a casket that held the body of Opatel Cre'ator.

Falashakena whispered, "Please tell no one that Lord Opatel is dead. To many who would be our enemies the thought of his being alive will keep them subdued." I fully accepted this wisdom. This sad occasion was the last time I saw Falashakena and Drayfess Cre'ator during that lifetime.

An Unsuccessful Rescue Attempt

I left Nodia and resumed my travels to distant Cre'ator outposts. Many more years passed. Then the time came when I was informed by the commander of the mothership Sobdret, in which I was living, that we were destined for a solar system in which an interplanetary war had broken out. There presently existed a cease-fire. It was the plan of the Trading House of Cre'ator to take advantage of the ceasefire to visit the Cre'ator outpost and move any of its personnel off the planet to the safety of the mothership.

In order not to incite the warring parties to resume their hostilities, it was decided that only the armed spacecrafts and a few unmanned passenger drones would be sent to pick up the outpost personnel. Against the strong objection of the mothership's commander, I decided to go along with the rescue team aboard the armed command craft. Earlier, after I had awakened, I had noticed that my fingernails had turned purple. I, of course, realized that this was the first sign of galactic sickness. This knowledge motivated my decision to be of as much use as possible to the living before the illness took my life.

The command craft was placed in orbit about the planet on which the outpost was located and then the drones, which were operated remotely, landed. The drones were still being loaded when several spacecraft of one warring faction began to attack us. We could not leave our orbital position, because to do so would mean we would have to abandon the drones. Some of the drones were already lifting off. To break contact with the unmanned craft would have allowed them to fall back to the planet's surface, killing their passengers in the process.

We returned defensive fire at our attackers. This did not stop their attacks. Our strategy was to hold them off long enough to get all of the drones out of the planet's atmosphere and rapidly tow them to safety, or at least to a distance where we could be joined by other armed craft sent to our aid from the mothership.

The spacecraft I was in was struck on its underside by an enemy bolt of energy. The interior of the craft began to get very hot. The commander ordered those who controlled the drones to attempt to reland them on the planet's surface. He no sooner gave this order when were once again struck by enemy fire. This was followed by a brilliant flash of light and a tremendous heat that instantly consumed every molecule of air in the craft as well as our lungs. Within less than a second all aboard the spacecraft were also vaporized.

In this way did I perish in that first lifetime. Since then the elohim have placed me into many molar-level lifetimes. I am Rendowlan, Lord of Devisement 617 of the Trading House of Cre'ator.

T H I R T E E N

Petrimmor
of Cartress

Ready yourselves, you of the world called
Earth, for that time soon to come when the
skies will sparkle with the presence of a host of
starships. Fear not, nor worship those who cause
them to wing about. Know that their spirits are no
greater exalted than yours and
that they will come in peace.
—Ebbestee of Meklar

At a recent time my home was honored by a visit from the Nodian Lord Rendowlan. While he was present a great crowd assembled around my dwelling, so you now know we of the planet Cartress are a curious lot.

Rendowlan's recent flight from his home world of Nodia took a little more than three Earth days to complete. If this flight had taken place during my first lifetime, it would have taken about seventy-one Earth days and the Nodians would have been met with suspicion and possibly considerable hostility. Such was the case when the first spacecraft from another world landed on our planet and its occupants came into contact with our astonished and fearful reaction.

During his visit Rendowlan requested that I tell you about this encounter and the subsequent conditions that have affected my many lifetimes ever since. I am pleased to do so, and my spirit quickens at being elevated to such a degree of importance.

Our First Visit from the Nodians

At the time the triangular craft landed on Cartress, I was about thirty-seven Earth years of age, married, with four children, and employed as a policeman. We were just beginning to light our cities with electricity and communicate by telephones and radio. We had no means to travel by air, but had developed electric-powered automobiles and ships.

Our religion, which was centered on nature, was administered by those who possessed mythical powers they never explained or discussed with those outside their group. It was from this group we learned, hundreds of years earlier, that our local solar system, as well as other suns, had planets that also contained human life. The general attitude was that we would make no attempt to physically contact any other off-world civilization and would rid ourselves of the like if they physically contacted us. Little did we know that our development of radio would make our world interesting to a race of feather-wearing, cigar-smoking, space-traveling off-worlders known as Gracians.

The Gracians landed their large mothership in a remote area of our world and made their presence known by buzzing several of our largest cities with brightly painted aircars. These sightings, which continued for several days [*a Cartressian day is about twenty-eight Earth hours* –W.H.B.], filled the populations with fear.

Eventually the location of the Gracian mothership was reported. I was assigned the command of a brigade of armed policemen who later ringed the vessel and trained our weapons (similar to your bullet-projecting rifles) on it. I was ordered to fire one round at the spacecraft and see what the results might be. When the projectile struck the craft's hull, it ricocheted downward and raised a small cloud of dust.

From the spacecraft came a heavily accented voice that spoke in our native language, "Please do not do that again." I fired at the spacecraft again. I soon regretted my action. A tone of sound radiated from the spacecraft and caused my vision to blur. My entire brigade began to see double and became nauseous to the point of throwing up. The smell of the regurgitation of several thousand men was overwhelming, and we retreated to quite a distance.

The voice from the spacecraft once again boomed: "You will recover. Bring to us the shirel woman named Shyreldane."

There was no one on our planet who did not know that Shyreldane was the prime religious consultant to the highest leaders of our government. It took nearly five days for the grand lady to join us. As we awaited her arrival we were occasionally treated by beautiful tones emanating from the Gracian starship that made us feel good. We hoped they would continue, and they did.

During the fourth day of our wait, five Gracians came out of their craft and erected a blue canopy under which they placed a table and a number of chairs. While four of them went about this activity, the fifth probed the ground with a metal rod looking for my spent bullets. After finding both, he and the others reentered their vehicle.

The area was silent when Shyreldane and her two young male assistants began to walk toward the open port of the spacecraft. They stopped walking when a man came from the craft wearing clothing and a headdress that were made of bright-colored plumes. He was a striking figure. When he reached Shyreldane, they embraced as if they were long-lost friends. They held hands as they walked to the canopy, where they sat for several hours discussing what later proved to be a very serious subject.

At the completion of their talk a large sky-blue aircar appeared and landed nearby. One of Shyreldane's assistants came to me with the order that I should get onboard. At the thought of doing so, I nearly shook myself out of my shoes. I was met by the feather-bedecked Gracian, who first gave me a broad smile and dropped my two spent bullets into my hand saying, "Yours?" I sheepishly nodded in the affirmative. As the aircar gained altitude, I looked at the spacecraft and the thousands of people below. I was at first in a trance. When I realized that I was flying, I began to shake noticeably. The Gracian sitting one row in front of me touched my hand, saying, "Don't worry. I do it all the time."

As we flew in the direction of the setting sun we were entertained by soft music that seemed to originate from the ceiling of the craft. Suddenly my right hand experienced a sharp burning pain. With a painful cry I dropped the bullets I had been holding. They were glowing red when they struck the floor and rolled, leaving trails of smoke. The Gracian chief, Somast-Choke, pointed a small tuning fork at the metal balls and turned a knob on the fork's handle until the vibrations it was emitting exceeded the range of my hearing. The bullets appeared to cool and return to their natural appearance. Even so, I gave no thought to picking them up.

A Painful Gift from the Universal Life Field

Somast-Choke looked at my blistered palm and said, "Those things were bound to hurt somebody." He activated his tuning fork once again and touched it to my left temple and then my wrist. Immediately thereafter, I no longer felt any pain from my wounds. Within minutes the blisters and inflammation around them disappeared, leaving dark brown marks. At close inspection, these marks were in the form of strange symbols. For the remainder of that lifetime I was actually sought out by Gracians for the purpose of looking at the symbols, as well as to kiss and shake that hand.

I later learned that there were tones within the Gracian music I had been listening to that stimulated certain areas of my brain and momentarily linked my consciousness to the macro level of the universal life field. Vril energy from that level reacted naturally with the elemental composition of the bullets and caused them to heat up as they did. I was actually taught a lesson by the elohim that related to my violent act of shooting at the Gracian spacecraft. But along with that punishing lesson came a gift, a divine gift, that has served me and others of the light lifetime after lifetime. Later in my account I will describe how this gift gave me occasional macro consciousness and made me quite a celebrity.

My first trip in a Gracian aircar ended after it swooped down and flew between the walls of a deep canyon. When this happened I was able to make a good guess about our final destination. Within minutes my guess proved correct when the aircar landed at the city of the mystics, a place called Worg.

Worg was not exactly a forbidden city, but I knew from a very early age, as did every other Cartressian, that arriving there uninvited would only produce ire in the city's inhabitants. And these were people you definitely did not want to be mad at you.

City of the Mystics

The place was lit by powerful lights situated on the walls of the canyon. These lights illuminated the numerous entrances that led to the underground metropolis. Some of these portals were at least 300 feet wide and 150 feet high, framed by gigantic carvings of animals as well as blocks of stone containing the fossil remains of plants, animals and gigantic humans who had lived millions of years earlier. A man wearing a dark yellow tunic blessed the aircar and then, after waving his arms in a circle, pointed at an entrance. The aircar rose once again and flew into the ancient city. As it did so, the lights on the canyon walls flashed off and on, changing color with every flash. This was a sign of welcome.

I was the last to leave the aircar. Only Shyreldane waited for me. The Gracians and her attendants walked on ahead. I was amazed at the sight of the most beautiful buildings I had ever seen. Fountains and waterfalls cascaded down the sides of some buildings as well as the natural walls of the gigantic cavern in which they were contained. I immediately noticed that the falling water produced no sound. In fact, I could not hear any form of sound except those I produced myself, such as my footsteps. Shyreldane said, "This is a place of beauty. Shortly you will see and feel things of even greater beauty. Though you are not yet aware, you have become one of us, who have the privilege to live in and among this glory. Of course, those of your family are welcome to live here also."

She then went on to explain that she, as well as others of the city, had carried on a telepathic relationship with the Gracians for nearly forty years (Earth time). She also told me that the buildings that lay ahead (many still under construction) were designed on the order of sacred numbers, and that the knowledge of these numbers and their uses were imparted telepathically to her and several others of her kind by the Gracians.

The Gracian visit had two purposes: to inspect the completed sacred buildings and those still under construction, and to choose one or more Cartressians to travel with them to another world where they were constructing a number of pyramids based on the sacred numbers. It was their hope that the accompanying Cartressians would learn by observation certain construction techniques that they could in turn teach their people when they returned to their home world.

We stepped onto a narrow path that entered a grove of trees. I felt an overwhelming sense of security and privacy. All about us were soft flashes of light that were produced by fireflies. The path led to a spot where there was a bed and a table, on which were two ceramic containers, one blue and the other burnt orange. Before leaving me, Shyreldane told me that my dinner was in the blue container and my breakfast was in the orange container. She also informed me that about fifty yards farther on down the path was a bathing pool fed by a waterfall.

Orbaltreek and Dell, an Off-World Child

After eating my dinner, I ventured down the path to the pool. There I found a number of men and women who had also just arrived by means of another Gracian aircar. These people were a strange mixture of off-worlders who were attempting in every way possible to communicate with each other. I sat under a tree and observed them as they continued to arrive at the pool. Compared to my size (about seven Earth feet), some were shorter (to about three feet), and others were taller (to about eight feet). A Cartressian named Orbaltreek eventually came to the pool from the same direction I had. Spotting me, he came to my side and introduced himself. He was clean-cut and expensively dressed. When he attempted to tell me what his occupation or position in life was, he could not remember. This lack of memory bothered him only momentarily. He sat with me under the tree and exchanged comments about various off-world individuals who were now beginning to enter the bathing pool, nude in some cases, others in various forms and degrees of dress.

Our discussions were interrupted by a little off-worlder wearing what you might call a metallic green jumpsuit. At first I could not determine if our visitor was male or female. Later I correctly determined that our new acquaintance was male. His skin color was as white as milk. His eyes were dark green and his hair was eggshell white, which at times looked slightly pale green. Pointing to his chest, he stated his name, which was Dell. He stood before us, smiling and making gestures as would a mime, in an attempt to encourage us to speak to him.

I could detect no seams in his one-piece suit of clothing, which included his shoes, nor could I figure out how he got into the thing or how he relieved himself. He seemed to know what I was thinking. He lifted his arm and pulled downward on a metal tab. When he did, his clothing separated as if he had cut it with a sharp knife. When he reversed his action the fabric once again united as if it were one continuous piece. What Orbaltreek and I had seen for the very first time was the operation of a zipper. We took turns opening and closing it as our new friend stood like a mannequin with an upraised arm.

Within the course of this activity, Dell noticed the symbols that had been branded into the palm of my hand earlier that day by the red-hot bullets. He took my hand and placed it palm down on the top of his head and began to chant in soft tones. When he completed his chant, I actually jumped back away from him in fear when I noticed that his eyes no longer had pupils. Even so, he apparently could still see. When I became somewhat composed, I was further amazed by the succession of golden symbols that appeared and disappeared from his snow-white eyes. I soon realized that the symbols were exact duplicates of those that were then permanent features of my right hand.

Suddenly the phenomenon ceased and Dell's dark green pupils returned once again and sparkled in unison with the flashes of a firefly that had perched on his forehead.

Dell was the first to speak. When he did, it was in fluent Cartressian, a language that he had been unable to speak a word of twenty minutes earlier. He also knew my name as well as the names of every one of my living relatives, and could describe every experience I'd had since I began to think and talk.

He then told me that by the same procedure he would someday teach me the language of his home world of Ry. Orbaltreek asked Dell if he would do the same for him. Dell shook his head and verbally said, "Not until you regain all the memories that you have recently lost."

Dell then asked to become a permanent companion of Orbaltreek and me, adding, "I am the only one of my kind who will go with the Gracians, and with you as friends I will not be lonely." Orbaltreek and I spontaneously lifted up the tearful little fellow between us and assured him that from that moment on we would never part, until the time came for us to return to our native worlds.

Later Dell sat in the fetal position with his head between his legs and fell to sleep. We left him and returned to our respective rest areas.

I was about to eat my breakfast when both Dell and Orbaltreek arrived. Dell was wearing a brown tunic and knee-high boots of the same color. Over his shoulder hung a large dark blue duffle bag. Orbaltreek was as I saw him the day before, except for the wet remains of a melon that circled his mouth. He sat down at my table and continued to gnaw away at the meat of the fruit. When I opened my breakfast container, I was disappointed to find that it did not contain any melon.

Varbreen's Arrival with Information about Orbaltreek

During my breakfast Shyreldane's assistant, Emler, came to us and requested that we come to the place where the path entered the grove. When we arrived at the spot there were many off-worlders milling about. Then I heard a familiar voice calling my name. It was the voice of my wife, Varbreen. After telling me that our children had been left in the care of my parents, she informed me that the people of our world were filled with fear over the arrival of the Gracians and that all forms of industry had come to a standstill. After assuring her that things were really not as bad as they seemed, I then introduced Varbreen to my two new friends. After hearing the name Orbaltreek, a strange look came across her face. She pulled me to the side and whispered, "That man's a wanted criminal. I learned from a radio broadcast that all police units throughout the world are looking for him." I asked her, "For what offense?" After several moments she answered, "I can't remember, I just know it was for doing something terrible." Shyreldane's assistant, Emler, standing nearby, overheard Varbreen's whispered message and spoke to us. "While he is within the confines of this city he cannot be arrested for any crime."

Emler then motioned for us to follow the crowd. We later boarded several electrically powered topless buses. As we penetrated deeper into the city of Worg, the forms of the buildings began to radiate a captivating affect. We were so attracted by the sight of these structures that we paid no attention to the fact that the sides of the streets were lined with people who were straining to get a look at us as we went by.

After about forty minutes the caravan of buses came to a stop in front of the most magnificent structure I had ever seen. It seemed to have an intelligent life of its own, and it caused all who looked upon it to wish they could communicate with it. You just knew that it had wonderful things it wanted to tell you. I realized that whenever I looked at the building, the thought of anyone I knew brought about a feeling of love for that person. In some cases the feeling was greater and in other cases the feeling was not as great. I tested this effect by thinking of the most hideous criminal I had ever known during the course of my profession as a policeman. A slight feeling of love eradicated all thoughts of disgust and hatred I'd always had when thinking of that person.

I then realized that these feelings of love were not really mine, but the feelings that the building had for those I thought about. It was then that I became aware that I, Petrimmor of Cartress, had experienced the presence of the consciousness of the creator of all that is. By the demeanor of the others around me, I knew that only I had been so blessed.

Somast-Choke, the Gracian Chief

The Gracian chief, Somast-Choke, dressed in a simple purple-colored sarong and sandals, was sitting on a dressed block of stone talking with several Cartressian masons. As he talked, he was placing small yellow feathers in his long black hair. After completing his decorating, he stood up on the block and motioned to all to leave the buses and join him on a tour of what would later be named the "the place where angels rest."

I will not degrade the beauty of the place by attempting to describe it in any language. Even Sol-Tec, the language of the soul, would not serve well to make a worthy description.

As we followed Somast-Choke in silence, he occasionally stopped to tap his tuning fork on a block of stone that was destined to be placed at some location in the structure. He expressed joy when the fork's musical tone informed him that block had been cut and dressed precisely to divine specifications. At the end of our tour he announced, "All is well in this place, is it not, Petrimmor of Cartress?" I answered with a shout, "Yes, all is well in this place, Somast-Choke of Gracyea."

Later we returned to the grove and found that my single bed had been replaced by one that could sleep two and that there were two blue ceramic dinner containers on the table. I wondered what we might be having for breakfast.

We spent several hours at the bathing pool learning from Dell about his home world of Ry. When we asked him if he was married, he broke out in laughter and said, "I am too young to be married." When we asked him his age, we learned that he was just over eight Earth years old. When Orbaltreek asked him if he liked the female sex, he blushed and put his fingers in his ears.

My wife could not restrain herself any longer. She asked Orbaltreek if he knew that the police were looking for him in order to arrest him. Orbaltreek stared vacantly as he sincerely tried to remember. He eventually answered her question by saying, "I can't remember. I hope that it wasn't a crime that I will have to die for." With that, I declared the subject officially closed.

We were awakened from our sleep by Emler, who informed us that it was time to leave the city of Worg and begin our journey to worlds that circled a distant star. I wondered where Dell and Orbaltreek might be. As we approached the Gracian aircar, I was pleased and relieved to see that they had arrived there before us.

Before our aircar landed beside the Gracian mothership, I noticed that only a few Cartressians were still present in the area, which was now littered with abandoned vehicles and weapons. The Cartressians were moving about in small groups that stopped on occasion to absorb the soothing tones of sound that still emanated from the gigantic spacecraft.

The interior walls of the mothership were made entirely of polished woods. Many of the wooden panels were covered with exquisite carvings of strange, yet beautiful animals. I learned later that these animals did in fact exist on the Gracian home world.

We ate breakfast with Dell and about twenty other off-worlders. I asked Dell if he knew where Orbaltreek might be. Before he could answer, Varbreen offered, "The Gracians probably arrested him." Dell then said, "Orbaltreek ate earlier and he is in the place where they control the flight of this spacecraft. The Gracians are teaching him how to direct its course."

Varbreen and I freely roamed about the spacecraft and engaged Dell as our interpreter. He seemed to have no problem at all talking to or understanding any off-worlder we encountered. We learned that all of the off-worlders had been living onboard the Gracian spacecraft for more than an Earth year, and during that period had visited seven other worlds on which the Gracians were constructing sacred buildings. From each world one or more of its natives became part of the ship's off-world population.

It never really occurred to us that we were actually entering and leaving one solar system after another until we came to a part of the spaceship where a large section of its hull was transparent. Our first view of another world was marvelous. The surface of the gigantic sphere was green and blue and at places was obscured by fluffy white clouds.

The Gracian mother craft circled the planet only once before landing. The landing site was ringed by buildings whose structural forms could have been inspired only by the Gracians. I was certain that they had been here before.

The world was called Sute by its natives. Their appearance was similar to those races on the Earth known as Chinese and Japanese. When compared to us of Cartress, these people were more technically advanced, having such things as television, jet-powered aircraft and helicopters.

Our group found the Sutes to be likable people. They were very polite and informative. When they spoke it sounded as if they were reading from a prepared script. There was always a pause of a few seconds between their sentences.

As he had done on Cartress, Somast-Choke visited several building sites for the purpose of inspection. This tour took about twelve Earth days. At one impressive site we encountered hundreds of Gracians. This was the first time we had ever seen Gracian women. The Gracians were actually building an entire city. The surrounding area was a lush rain forest.

During our stay on Sute I spent a great deal of time backtracking in search of my wife. My search time was shortened whenever I could recall where I had last seen an operating television set. She was fascinated by the things. When we departed the planet, a number of additional Gracians and four male Sutes left with us. As a parting gift, a Sute woman gave Varbreen a small portable television set. She was able to view Sute television programs onboard the Gracian spacecraft for about three days until the signal suddenly stopped. The spacecraft had switched to its stellar propulsion system (based on manipulated light) and immediately entered another solar system. Varbreen was highly disappointed. She asked me if the place we were going to had television. Of course I had no idea.

Offloading on Mars and Arriving on Earth

Seven Earth days after initiating stellar drive, we entered the solar system in which our journey would end. Less than an hour later the Gracian spacecraft landed gently on a sparsely vegetated plain. In the distance could be seen an ocean of waist-high grass. The cloudless blue sky contained numerous flocks of birds that flew up from and disappeared back into the grass. The planet was the one you now call Mars.

We remained onboard until five large Gracian aircars landed beside us. Only Somast-Choke left the ship to greet the new arrivals. Then many Gracians left the spacecraft along with numerous pieces of construction equipment. Later we watched two aircars fly off in the direction of the setting sun, each carrying equipment suspended by cables. The equipment, which was many times larger than the aircars, swung in wide circles within the force field that propelled the vehicles.

When the remaining aircars were loaded with their various cargoes and lifted off, the Gracian mothership did likewise. Within minutes the planet Mars was left far behind.

We had been looking through a transparent section of the craft's hull when, to our surprise, our view of Mars and the stars became blocked by a large black object. Suddenly the object was illuminated by powerful beams of light that were projected from the underside of the Gracian mothership. This illumination allowed us to see clearly that we were being followed by a spacecraft that was at least twice the size of ours. We were traveling at our maximum speed when it overtook and passed over us. A Gracian standing beside me pointed to the disappearing vehicle and said, "Nodians." When I asked the Gracian if Nodians were native to this solar system, he replied that they were not. When Varbreen asked what the Nodians looked like, he told her that he could not say because he had never seen one in person. He added, "The Maldecians tell us that the Nodians are dangerous and should not be trusted." He anticipated our next question, and before we could ask it, said, "You will be among the Maldecians very soon."

The Gracian walked away, bowing as he passed two others of his race who were walking together in our direction. One was Somast-Choke and the other was introduced as Tixer-Chock. Tixer-Chock was one of those who came aboard the spacecraft during the time it was on Mars. He looked very tired. During a later conversation he said that he was very glad to have left Mars because the people's dispositions could change instantly from being humorous and gentle to hot-headed and brutish. He added that he personally seemed to bring the worst out in them.

Our landing on Earth was ignored by hundreds of Gracians and Reltians, who were too occupied with leveling the landscape where they intended to construct a living site and several sacred structures. The place would later develop into a city that the Gracians called Miradol and that is presently referred to as Teotihuacan, Mexico.

I recall that it was a cloudy day, and a warm mist shrouded the surrounding forests. Only the Reltians seemed to tolerate the humidity. All but the Gracians remained onboard the spacecraft, and after two days of rainfall I saw the sun for the first time from the surface of the planet. It was slightly larger than the sun that gave light to my home world of Cartress.

The ground was soft, and on occasion we had to walk around pools of water. The Gracians were interested in those pools because they identified depressions in the ground that would have to be filled before they started to build.

Varbreen and I were assigned to live in one of about 200 fabric-covered, dome-shaped buildings that had been erected. The domes had been placed in concentric circles, and our home was located within the second-largest ring.

One afternoon the Gracian mothership rose into the air and flew out of sight. Both Varbreen and I felt a bit sad. We later realized that our feelings were based on the fact that the spacecraft was our only link with our home world and our children. We also had a feeling of helplessness.

Later that afternoon, as Varbreen and I sat outside the door to our dwelling, I spotted Dell and Orbaltreek walking in our direction. For several hours into the night we talked about our recent experiences, speculating about what the future might have in store.

Itocot-Talan, the Master Builder

In the days that followed, our group wandered about the place, stopping and observing whatever activity we found to be of interest. Dell informed us that the building of the city was under the direction of a Gracian master builder named Itocot-Talan. We then made it a quest to look for this master as we went about our explorations. As time passed we noticed that lines of Gracians seemed to come and go from a spot just behind a small natural mound some distance from the building activity. We decided to walk to that spot to satisfy our curiosity.

The Gracians we met en route greeted us warmly when we passed them. When we reached the top of the mound we were startled by two men who seemed to appear out of thin air. They wore silver breastplates trimmed with gold and helmets of the same metals decorated with plumes of white feathers. I was familiar with the expressions on their faces. I had seen similar expressions on the faces of my police colleagues when they were cautiously considering a dangerous situation. I reacted naturally by moving myself between these strangers and my wife. After a few minutes of frozen silence the facial expressions of the strangers changed. One even gave us a slight smile as he motioned us to continue on.

Our path now led downward in the direction of several oblong fabric-covered buildings and some canopies that covered groups of tables and chairs, where Gracians sat engaged in conversation. Under one canopy was a Gracian aircar that was capable of carrying about fifteen passengers. Believing that there was nothing more to see at this place, we turned to leave. As we did a voice from below called out my name. I turned to see Somast-Choke motioning to us to meet with him at the bottom of the hill. He waited with his hands on his hips.

As we approached Somast-Choke, he spread his arms, saying, "All is well in this place. Is it not Petrimmor of Cartress?" Before giving my answer I glanced briefly at the strange men standing on the top of the mound with the colors of the setting sun reflecting from their armor. Somast-Choke patted my shoulder and with a serious tone said, "Those are Maldecian soldiers, who are called krates. They are being exceptionally vigilant because one of their chiefs is here visiting with our chief, Itocot-Talan."

Somast-Choke invited us to join him in his boxlike home for an evening meal. During the period we spent with him he enthusiastically told us about his people's plan to build the city of Miradol as well as several large pyramids at a place on the planet some surface distance from where we were at the time.

In response to sounds of voices and movement outside his home, Somast-Choke rose from his chair and asked us to follow him outside. The area was now lit with soft lights. We watched as two men walked toward the aircar between two ranks of Maldecian krates, who stood at full attention. In a low voice Somast-Choke said the taller man wearing a loose, dark-green robe was his chief, Itocot-Talan, and the other, who wore white trousers and jacket, was the Maldecian general known as Sharber.

After the Maldecians departed, our group walked to Itocot-Talan, who, after seeing Somast-Choke, spoke to him with a slightly angry tone, "The Maldecians want us to put our total labor force, as well as our greatest efforts and time, into building the pyramids and less time into building Miradol. I have insisted that we keep to our original timetable."

Somast-Choke explained later that in order to comply with the Maldecian demands, many additional Gracian experts would have to be summoned from other projects then under way on other worlds, thus leaving those equally important projects incomplete. Many of these experts were scheduled to arrive on the Earth at various times in the future, when their duties elsewhere were either completed or could be temporarily suspended. The Gracian added that additional construction equipment and human laborers would also be needed to speed up the pyramid construction.

I asked Somast-Choke, "For what purpose was I brought to the Earth?" He answered by saying, "In a few days we will go to the place where we are building the pyramids. There you will meet Liferex-Algro, a holy man of my people, who, after looking at the symbols in the palm of your hand, will tell you what your future purpose is to be.

Leaving for the Mir Pyramid Construction Site

Only Varbreen, Dell and I sat in the passenger section of the Gracian aircar when it left Miradol for the place where the Great Pyramids were beginning to be built. At the controls of the aircar was the recently Gracian-trained Orbaltreek, who fumbled several times when attempting to automatically set the craft's course. Varbreen's confidence in him was totally shattered. She asked me, "How do we know he can operate this air-

car, and how do we know he will get us to where we are supposed to go?"
I did not answer her. I had the same questions.

Our aircar trip took several days. Twice we witnessed the sun rise in the
east. Varbreen was sure that we were flying in circles. I thought that she
might be right until I noticed a screen that had become illuminated with a
bright yellow X. A much-relieved Orbaltreek informed us that the automatic activation of this screen was exactly what he had been waiting for. He
told us that the yellow X symbol would eventually shrink to a dot that
would continue to pulse. The pulsing dot would mean that we had reached
our destination and that the car would then have to be flown and landed
manually. We all stared endlessly at the slowly shrinking yellow X. It was
about noon on the third day when the expected pulsing dot finally
appeared on the screen.

Below us for as far as the eye could see was a tropical forest. Its treetops
presented a beautiful patchwork of every shade of green one could ever
imagine. The forest was separated into two parts by a wide river. It was
impressive to see sunlight reflecting off its dark blue waters.

Orbaltreek informed us that he would now follow the course of the
river to the north. Eventually the craft slowed, came to a stop and hovered.
To our right we could see a village and to our left, on the west bank of the
river, rows of fabric-covered buildings. We landed about 100 yards south
of that place.

We stood beside the aircar until we were approached by two Gracians
who had little to say to us except, "Where have you been?" They then
entered the aircar and flew off to the west, leaving us glaring at a sheepish
Orbaltreek.

We entered the city of tents and inquired of the first Gracian we met
directions to the holy man, Liferex-Algro. The Gracian we asked for directions first stood stiffly, then turned his body to the cardinal points of the
compass. After turning a full circle, he pointed toward the river and
informed us that we would find Liferex-Algro in that direction.

After reaching the river's edge, we of course could go no farther without
a boat. One of several cigar-smoking Gracians sitting near us on a rock,
after hearing us mention the name Liferex-Algro, said, "We are the great
one's assistants. Wait with us if you wish. He will come from the other side
of the river before the sun sets and will lead us in prayer."

After hearing my name, the Gracians asked to look at the palm of my
hand. Afterward they took turns shaking my hand and then looking at
their palms.

A woman then asked, "Who is your interpreter?" As she asked her question, she held her palm in front of my eyes. On it numerous symbols began

to appear. Dell, who was standing beside me, took the woman's hand, placed it on his head and began to talk to her in her native language. He brought his reading to a sudden stop and shook his head with vigor in the universal gesture for no. Even so, the woman was beaming. She then began to unload herself of her jewelry and other prize processions and lay them at my feet.

By the time Liferex-Algro's boat was spotted on the river, every Gracian present had shook my magical hand and obtained a reading from touching the top of Dell's head. At my feet were many things of great value, including a mountain of Gracian cigars. After Varbreen held and inspected each item, she reluctantly accepted my order that Orbaltreek was to be put in charge of the treasure.

Liferex-Algro, the Gracian Stolfa

Liferex-Algro was a man of great age. He wore a long gown made of tiny black feathers. He immediately embraced me and called me by name. As we walked toward the campsite, he said, "We of Gracyea would be honored if you would live among us, not only to amaze us with what you know of our individual life histories and what our futures might hold, but it is our wish that you might get a Maldecian to willingly seek to know these things as well. I suspect that Maldecians' historical life and future reading would be quite a revelation. If you accept this request, be very cautious. Be patient and do not give a Maldecian any indication that you have any interest in giving him or her a life reading."

Liferex added, "Your interpreter, Dell, wisely refused to speak of that time when any Gracians who were read would surely die. We accept that the time of our deaths should be known only by the elohim and those such as yourself, whom they have chosen to serve them."

I asked the stolfa (Gracian priest) if I might take a little time to consider his request, and he accepted my condition. Liferex-Algro took us to a vacant dwelling in the midst of the Gracian part of the camp. It had several compartments. He told us that the living arrangements would be only temporary. He then left us to conduct a prayer service for his people. The service ended as the setting sun disappeared below the treetops in the west.

During the evening Dell told me he had learned that each and every Gracian we read was destined to die on the Earth in three to four years' time. After hearing this, I felt very sad. I felt overwhelmed in wanting to help the Gracians any way I could.

That very night I told Liferex-Algro that I would patiently wait for a Maldecian to ask me for a reading. Hearing this, the Gracian stolfa said he would provide me with whatever I might need to accomplish my mission.

Just after dawn I stepped out of our dwelling to find Orbaltreek occupied with inspecting and dusting off a small aircar that could hold an operator and eight passengers. He was exuberant when he said, "This car is ours to use as we will. The Gracian who delivered it said that we should go to the nearby village of Pankamerry and seek out the Earthman Cark Ben-Zobey." After Orbaltreek satisfied Varbreen that all the treasure we accumulated the previous day was still intact and onboard the aircar, we flew southwest about fifteen miles. After landing we went about searching for the village headman, Cark Ben-Zobey.

Cark Ben-Zobey and a Year in Pankamerry

He was a kind and gentle person. Wherever he went he was followed by his wife, who hid her face behind a veil. Following her was an unveiled young woman and several young men. These three were their children.

Cark Ben-Zobey and his family escorted us to a spacious house that had been built of wood. As they started to leave, I absent-mindlessly extended my hand as a gesture of farewell. The Earthman stepped back saying, "No, thank you. I need not be told what I already know about myself, and maybe my future will hold things I do not as yet wish to know." After touching two fingers to his lips as a salute, he and his band departed. Even when they were some distance away we could hear them chattering to each other.

At the time I thought, *If these Earth people fear my gift, what chance would there be that one of their shrewd Maldecian masters would become curious enough to request that I demonstrate my powers?*

Our stay at Pankamerry was at first very uneventful. We had no visitors except for Cark Ben-Zobey's oldest son, Arcdent Ben-Cark, who from time to time came to inquire about our needs.

To break the monotony, one morning we took an aircar trip, first to the Gracian encampment and then south along the river. The encampment had grown to more than ten times its size since we had last seen it. The area was also filling up with construction equipment. We later learned that the added dwellings were not actually occupied at the time and had been built to house others who were yet to arrive.

We traveled just above the treetops for several hundred miles south along the river. During this flight we learned that the land the natives called Mir was the home to an abundant variety of animal life. We were most impressed by the animals you call elephants. When compared to elephants that live on the Earth today, I would estimate that those of that ancient time were at least twice as large. At one point we startled several Earth people camped on the riverbank as we flew over. After they recovered, they shouted and gave us a friendly wave. Varbreen thought that they were inviting us to land and visit them. We circled them once more and I dropped a container of Gracian cigars and several large containers of Gracian popcorn. They continued to wave to us as we turn northward in the direction of our home in Pankamerry.

A few days later the village began to fill with large numbers of Earth people, who set up shop in the village marketplace. These merchants were forbidden to visit the site where the pyramids were going to be built.

A small group of Gracians and a larger group of Reltians also came to the village to construct prefabricated warehouses and level an area where larger Gracian aircars and spacecraft could land. The Reltians[1] were interesting little black-skinned people. The Gracians advised us to keep our eyes on our possessions whenever the Reltians were nearby. They had no idea what ownership was all about. We never had a bad experience with a Reltian, mainly because they usually ran away whenever they saw us approaching them.

For more than a year we lived in Pankamerry. We occupied ourselves by shaking hands and giving life readings to any Gracian who came to our door and asked for one. Business usually began immediately after I turned downed Orbaltreek's daily request to use the aircar to fly about Mir on "practice flights." The first time he asked to use the car I permitted him to do so. He returned about two days later, along with three Earth women wearing Gracian jewelry that once had been part of our treasury. Beside that, the presence of the unveiled river women brought an angry outcry from the villagers. To make things worse, he did not return for two more days after taking his lady friends back to their tribe.

As the days passed in Pankamerry I became concerned about the fact that no Maldecians ever came to the place. I decided that we would take a trip to Miradol so that I might be able to find a Maldecian who was curious about his or her future. After filling our aircar with about five percent of our treasure (it could hold no more), we left the rest of it with Cark Ben-Zobey and set out for the city of Miradol.

Before heading west we took a look at the building progress of the three great pyramids. By word of mouth we had heard that they were growing in size and would eventually be extremely large. This flight over the area allowed us to observe thousands of Reltian workers moving about the area and blocks of stone being moved by rail cars. The river was filled with barges full of dressed blocks of stone, which were being towed by aircar to receiving stations located on the west bank of the river. The water of the river was not the deep blue color we had originally observed! Now it was murky brown from the mud dislodged by the block barges when they were forcibly run aground on the riverbank.

Hand-Reading at Miradol

A day later we arrived at Miradol (a day and a half faster than it took us to get from Miradol to Mir). We actually landed near Itocot-Talan's headquarters and found the place overflowing with Maldecians.

Several new features had been added to the local area—scale models of the city of Miradol, the Mir pyramids and Gracian constructions on Mars. As we walked toward the campsite we saw Gracians and Maldecians walking among the models, stopping at times to point at a feature and converse.

Itocot-Talan and his grandson, Tixer-Chock, received us. I did not have to tell either of them why we had come to Miradol. They assisted me by spreading the word that a man with the power to tell a person's past and future had come to visit. Before too long, lines of Gracians appeared before my house daily. Gracians, Gracians and more Gracians, but no Maldecians.

I did find pleasure in walking about the growing city of Miradol. It was actually a relief from my work because no Gracian would stop his holy construction work and ask me for a life reading. Orbaltreek had become bored with Miradol and wanted to return to Mir and his friends who lived along the river. One night he seriously suggested that he might kidnap a Maldecian and force his victim to shake my hand. Truthfully, I did consider his plan, but I failed to come up with a way to deal with the dire ramifications that could develop from such an act. I did file Orbaltreek's plan away in my mind as my very last resort. The idea lost its appeal when I realized that I never saw a Maldecian alone. They always seemed to travel in pairs or larger groups.

Dell no longer needed to tell me that all the Gracians we had read during a particular day were soon to die. He merely gave me a nod before he left the reading room to take his nap.

It was late spring when Tixer-Chock informed us that a considerable number of high-ranking Maldecians would assemble in Mir within three weeks to witness the setting of the capstone of the great pyramid. He thought these new arrivals might be in a more festive mood because they were making arrangements to house and entertain Maldecian children. Maybe Dell and I could pass ourselves off as harmless entertainers. After burying the treasures we acquired in Miradol, we departed two days later for Mir. On our arrival we met immediately with Liferex-Algro to tell him about our plan.

The Great Pyramid

We met again that night and sat for a time bathed by torchlight several hundred feet from the Great Pyramid. Its beauty and spiritual power caused me to become spellbound. Liferex-Algro pulled me to my feet and

asked me to walk with him to the base of the structure. As we walked, neither of us said a word.

With my toes touching the bottom of a white casing stone at the base of the apothem line[2] of the south face of the pyramid, I leaned forward and placed the palms of my hands and my body on the stone's slanted side, because everyone's bodies were then, and are today, phi-proportioned. Phi (1.618033989) is a most sacred number of the elohim. With my body pitched in the manner I just described, it was exactly angled at 51 degrees, 51 minutes and 14 seconds, which was then the angle of the pyramid's faces. In this position I felt weightless and euphoric. My ecstasy was interrupted by the voice of Liferex-Algro, who asked, "Is all well with this place, Petrimmor of Cartress?"

I was about to answer yes when a dark feeling passed through my very soul. When I regained my senses I was lying in the fetal position and feeling very cold. Liferex-Algro covered me with his feathered cape and held my head in his lap and stroked my brow. He softly asked, "What have you learned?" I asked that Dell be summoned to interpret, but Liferex responded to my request by saying, "You will not need his help, nor would you want to subject him to the same experience." After a few minutes of silence I gave my reading of the Great Pyramid of Mir. I started by saying, "All is not right at this place, Liferex-Algro of Gracyea. Someone has committed a great blasphemy, for at places within the holy structure the mortar that binds its stones contains human blood. And for this violation of the master plan of the creator of all that is, the Creator in the future will need to be born as a human and die by the shedding of blood.[3]

Thereafter we cried, and our tears burned our cheeks as if they were composed of acid. Liferex-Algro rose and shouted, "The Cryberants, the Cryberants added the blood to the mortar for those Maldecian scum!" As he left running, he called back to me, "I can't let them set the capstone. I've got to stop them from doing so."

For days the Gracians searched for their high priest, but he was never found, alive or dead. Now only I knew the terrible secret of the mortar of blood. I was at a loss as who to tell. I was certain that the Maldecians had murdered Liferex-Algro, and I did not want to experience the same fate. It was my hope that Tixer-Chock or Itocot-Talan would come to Mir before the time the capstone would be set so I could impart my secret to one of them. I felt that telling any Gracians who were working on the pyramids in Mir about what I knew could cause them harm. This thinking was supported by the fact that the banks of the river on both sides for as far as the eye could see were becoming covered by white Maldecian tents, mostly occupied by their soldiers.

We eventually left the site of the pyramids and returned to our house in Pankamerry, where we at once resumed our friendship with Cark Ben-Zobey and his family. Cark Ben-Zobey introduced us to an Earthman named Jaffer Ben-Rob and his wife, Alfora. Alfora was of the river people, but out of courtesy for the local villagers wore a veil fastened by a pin in the shape of triangle with two left sides. She also carried an infant in a cloth slung over her back.

As we developed a trust for each other, Jaffer confided to me that he was actually hiding out in Pankamerry and had once been in charge of seeing to the needs of the Cryberants who carved the Great Sphinx, but had been forbidden to associate with those who mixed the special mortar for the pyramid. He told us how he had been hired as a companion for a young Maldecian and spent some time living in an off-worlder compound on the planet Maldec. Finally he told us about meeting with the Nodian Opatel Cre'ator one night on the banks of the river. He pointed to the triangular pin that held his wife's veil and described it as the symbol of a large house of merchants to which Opatel Cre'ator belonged. He estimated that the day Liferex-Algro disappeared was the same day the Cryberants were marched north to a place where they were put to death. Even after becoming close friends I did not tell him what I knew about the mortar of blood.

As the time for setting the capstone grew close, we left the aircar behind and walked the fifteen miles to the site of the pyramids. We actually arrived less than an hour before the event occurred. As we came to the clearing, we were met by the sight of a gigantic shiny black spacecraft that bore a triangle on its hull. The triangle had a double left side like Alfora's pin. We watched as a number of tall white-haired men came out of the vehicle. They were met by a single Gracian stolfa, who led them off toward the pyramids and the crowds of people that surrounded them.

Though I did not know it at the time, two of about twelve Nodians who followed the stolfa were Opatel Cre'ator and Rendowlan.

I had a terrible sinking feeling as the Maldecian aircar lowered the pyramid's capstone into place. I could not get the thought from my mind that the mortar that would bind the capstone to the body of pyramid would have as part of its composition the flesh, bones and blood of the Gracian Liferex-Algro.[4]

Orders to Leave

Before that fateful day when the Maldecians attempted to send the creative vril energy of the Earth by way of the Great Pyramid to their home world, a troop of Maldecian krates came to the village of Pankamerry. Their mission was to inform all off-worlders to leave the area by any means possible. They also announced that four days hence, any off-worlder not directly part of their pyramid project who was found within a 60-mile radius of Pankamerry would be dealt with most harshly.

We were packing our treasure into the aircar for another flight to Miradol when several krates paid us a personal visit. It was immediately obvious that they wanted us to give them our aircar. While they made their demand to me, Orbaltreek, who was already sitting at the controls of the craft, suddenly lifted off and flew south. Varbreen's realistic reaction to Orbaltreek's departure helped convince the Maldecians that our rotten air-car pilot had betrayed and abandoned us. The krates even smiled about our situation. They found it amusing because treachery was something they understood and admired.

We spent several hours sitting in front of our house talking with Cark Ben-Zobey and his family. I told him that he could keep the treasure we had previously entrusted to him as well as that still located in the house. It had become too inconvenient to carry the stuff around. Then Varbreen did something unexpected. She went into the house and returned wearing a veil. Our guests applauded her. Marthree, the wife of Cark Ben-Zobey, removed Varbreen's veil as well as her own and said, "We are family now."

Our conversation was interrupted by a voice from the shadows. As I expected, it was Orbaltreek, who had returned when he was sure the Maldecians had gone. Dell was the first to say good-bye to the Earth people. He said, "It is best we leave. I don't feel well about this place."

When we reached the aircar we found that we had another passenger. Her name was Cimiss. Orbaltreek introduced us. Within a few hours Varbreen and Cimiss were talking as if they had been long-lost sisters.

When we arrived at Miradol we found the place to be considerably quiet. There was absolutely no construction work going on. The Gracians, Reltians and Maldecians had separated into their respective living areas.

Miradol, and Revealing the Maldecians' Secret

I told Itocot-Talan and Tixer-Chock about the blood mortar used in the construction of the Great Pyramid of Mir and that I believed that Liferex had been murdered by the Maldecians. They then told me that any further attempt to get a Maldecian life reading would not serve any real purpose. What the Maldecians were and what they were all about was becoming very clear to them. They urged me to take my wife and friends and leave Miradol. They told me to watch for Gracian or Nodian spacecrafts and make contact with their crews. Itocot-Talan assured me that a crew of either race would do their best to return us to our home worlds.

Itocot-Talan and Tixer-Chock asked to shake my hand and obtain a life reading. After Dell interpreted their readings, he rose abruptly to leave the room. As he passed me he nodded twice, and there were tears streaming down his cheeks. From the expression on their faces I knew that the Gracians were aware that they would soon die. We left Miradol during the night and flew south, looking for a place where we might find some friendly Earth people like those we had recently left in Pankamerry in the Land of Mir.

Finding a New Home to the South

About midmorning we spotted a town of considerable size and flew over it. The stone buildings were two and three stories tall. We circled one of exceptional size surrounded by a courtyard filled with people. On the edge of the town rested a triangular-shaped Gracian spacecraft. Overjoyed, I asked Orbaltreek to land near the craft. He turned in his seat saying, "Look closer, I don't think we should land near that spacecraft." Taking a second and much closer look, I could then see hundreds of Maldecian krates walking about the vehicle. Because we were in a Gracian aircar they paid us little attention, probably thinking we were also Maldecians. Farther on and still within sight of the spacecraft, we saw a small village. We observed only a small number of people moving about and decided to land there.

Two men arrived at our landing site and stood with their heads bowed as we stepped out of the aircar. They had a look of disappointment on their faces when they learned that they were not greeting a carload of Maldecians.

We secured the aircar, took some trade goods from our treasure stores and sought out a place where we might find someone from whom we could obtain some information about the place as well as what was happening at the Gracian spacecraft.

We found an inn and entered it. At first no one seemed to be there, but then an elderly veiled woman came to us from another room. She was nearly blind and came to the sound of our voices. She told us that she was sorry that she would not be able to serve us any food or drink. She asked us why we were not in the town to see the Maldecian royalty who had arrived the night before. She informed us that we should not miss the opportunity because she understood that they were going to leave for the Land of Mir at sunset.

We took several rooms in the inn. We were fortunate because they were the last rooms available. That night the occupants of those rooms began to return for dinner and a night's rest. We found the innkeeper and paid him for our rooms and evening meal with a small Gracian red jewel that hung from a thin gold chain. He was overwhelmed by our extravagance and mistakenly thought that we were paying in advance for at least a couple of months.

Signs of Disaster

Two nights later, as we were sitting under a large tree in front of the inn, a section of the northern sky became very bright. Within seconds there were deafening, piercing screams and cries of forest animals. A dog ran past us whimpering and disappeared under the building. The occupants of the inn came running into the yard, yelling and praying aloud. Many of them in different states of dress, thinking the noise was due to some local problem, began to walk the road in the direction of the nearby town.

Just after dawn the forest was again still. Each of us looked miserable after coming to the end of a sleepless night. Eventually people started to return to the inn, each with his own version of what had happened the night before. Finally the truth was learned: The planet Maldec had exploded into pieces and all who were living on its surface at the time had been killed. For many days the inn was a place of gloom. Those who sought solace in drinking intoxicating liquor slowly became festive. Within a week or so they were toasting the Watchers (Maldecians) and wishing their spirits well.

The first week after Maldec exploded, bands of Earth merchants began to arrive at the inn. Among their wares were beautiful feathered capes, in some cases silver armor and helmets once worn by Maldecian krates. I confess that I was pleased to see this empty armor, since it meant that the Gracians killed at least a few of the devils.

When I asked one of the merchants where he got these items he said, "In the city to the north called Miradol. These things are there for the taking from the thousands of corpses that now lay rotting in the place. If I had an aircar to carry the treasures of the place away I would become very wealthy."

After hearing the merchant's story, I called Orbaltreek to my side and told him to find a place to totally conceal our aircar.

One morning a merchant with a large aircar landed to acquire water for his crew and Reltian slaves. The Reltians looked starved, so Varbreen and Cimiss took them food. I attempted to buy the Reltians from the merchant with some of our Gracian treasure. He laughed and said, "I already have mountains of what you offer." I firmly grabbed his hand and shook it.

I then told him that Dell and I could tell his future. He wholeheartedly agreed that we do so. I then told him that if we could read his past correctly, his payment would be four of his Reltian slaves. We haggled and he finally agreed to give us two slaves as payment. I watched him place his hand on Dell's head and listened to the verbal reading. When the reading was concluded, the merchant pointed to the Reltians and said, "Take any two you want." I chose a young woman and a middle-aged man.

Dell looked at me smiling, crossed his eyes and nodded again and again. Several people observed us give a life reading to the merchant and spread the news of our powers far and wide.

Stranded on Earth

We spent about twenty-one Earth years at that spot, giving life readings and growing very wealthy, all the while living with the hope that the Gracians would return to take us home. During that period Orbaltreek and Cimiss had a son and daughter and Varbreen and I had son we named Marle. Dell was now a young man, but did not find the local women to be of any great interest. He said many times that he longed to return to his home world to find a bride. As for the Reltians, they also produced a son they called Oken. He and Marle grew up as close friends.

When we all agreed it was safe, we dug out our buried aircar. Orbaltreek undertook the job of teaching Marle and Oken to fly it. Seldom did we venture into the local town, though we had many clients who lived there and had often invited us to their homes. On one occasion we accepted such an invitation. Marle flew Varbreen, Dell and me to town in the aircar. After we left the car at the edge of town, we had to walk a distance to our destination. Our attention was captured by some loud voices.

We found the source of the voices just in time to see a giant of a man whack a Maldecian krate on his chest armor with a large broadsword. The krate went flying, bouncing several times off the cobblestone street. Two other krates were on their toes like ballet dancers moving about the giant, while two other giants were beating on their chests and waving their swords over their heads in slow circles. I had never heard a Maldecian moan in pain and obviously neither had his companions. Still on their toes, they backed up to their fallen comrade and looked down at him in bewilderment. One of the krates took off like a gazelle as the other stood watch over his fellow trooper. The giants continued to swing their swords and yell at the krates in a very strange-sounding language. This scene continued until four krates, led by one of their officers, arrived.

With this group of Maldecians was a tall white-haired man wearing a tight-fitting black uniform. The four krates lifted their wounded friend between them. The man in the black uniform shouted a few words at the giants, causing them to lower their weapons. After he had a few words with the krate officer, he turned to look in our direction. He then started to come our way as the krates left in the opposite direction.

Rendowlan

In the language of the Earth he introduced himself as Rendowlan of Nodia. He caught me glancing at the now-sedate giants. He cocked his head in their direction and said, "My wayward Martian bodyguards. It takes me all the diplomatic power I have to get them out of trouble. I think one of them has just broken some Maldecian ribs."

I told Rendowlan of our appointment and he asked if he could walk with us to our destination. I, of course, told him that he was welcome to do so. We must have been an odd sight for the people we passed. I learned later that some we passed thought we were prisoners of the three giants who walked behind us with broadswords resting on their shoulders.

I asked Rendowlan if he had, in fact, said that the giants were from the planet Mars. He confirmed that he had indeed said so. I then related that my group, by way of a Gracian spacecraft, had landed on Mars to unload some construction equipment before coming to the Earth. I added that I never saw any human Martians while I was there, only Martian birds. Rendowlan replied, "You might not have seen any Martians, but I would wager heavily that they saw you.[5]

After reaching the home to which we had been invited, we loudly announced ourselves, as was the custom. Then came a reply from within, "We are frightened of the giants. Please send them away." I assured our host that they would leave shortly.

Before leaving, Rendowlan asked if he might visit with me and my group at the inn the next day. I agreed. My mind was filled with the thought that this meeting might lead to our obtaining passage to our home world of Cartress.

The very first thing I asked Rendowlan was whether could he arrange for us to be taken to our home world. He thought a minute or so and finally said, "I don't know where Cartress is. We will have to locate a living Gracian navigator to point us out the way. We don't even know where Gracyea is. The best I can offer is passage to Nodia. We might be able to figure out how to get you home from there."

Rendowlan then told us how the radiars were malfunctioning and the planets and planetoids of the local solar system were becoming uninhabitable. He also informed us that the Nodians were moving the human populations from these worlds to the Earth. He pointed out that his three Martian bodyguards were some of the first emigrants. He requested that we help him establish a reception station for these off-world refugees at the inn. He read my thoughts and added, "The Maldecians won't give us or you any trouble."

Petrimmor's Station and the Arrival of Rancer-Carr

In the years following, the area about the inn developed to the point that it overtook the nearby town. The area was named Petrimmor's Station by the Nodians. The station was only one of several hundred stations that received thousands people who were natives of the Trake radiar (Neptune) planetoids and the planets Mars and Wayda (Venus). Refugees from those places were also received at stations where those of the planetoids of the Relt (Jupiter) and Sumer [Saturn] radiars were received.

Those first to arrive in great numbers were the Martians. No matter how long ago this time occurred, I remember it as if it were yesterday.

The first month with the Martians was living hell, until that wonderful day when a black Nodian spacecraft landed at the station and off stepped he who wore the crown of the Red Dragon, Rancer-Carr, who by divine right was the zone-rex of all Sol Four (fourth planet of the sun Sol, or Mars). I thank the elohim to this very day.

The presence of the people of the scarlet light unintentionally interrupted even our dreams as they passed the worlds where we maintained our lives. We knew in our hearts that they truly meant to be good, and by thought wished them safe passage to their new home.
—Creppit of Argial (companion planet to the world known as Mollara)

Martians of old were not a race to accept instruction or even listen to simple reason. If there was anything that their migration to the Earth6 accomplished, it united them into one people. They put aside the ways of war they had used against each other on their home world. Consequently this left a vacancy in their psyches that drove them to find a new enemy toward whom they could direct their pent-up aggressions. Hundreds of years of harsh rule by their bar-rexes (warlords) caused them to resent authority. Therefore, because I was somewhat of an authority figure, I was at the top of their list of potential enemies. My insurance against bodily harm was the fact that they thought me to be a fool, for only a fool would try to assert authority without a military force to back him up.

The Martian Immigrants

Things might have been easier to contend with if the Martians had arrived in smaller numbers, but that was not the case. Thou-sands of them arrived per week. This was also the case at receiving stations located elsewhere on the planet. The individual Nodian transporters, after being assigned their missions, acted independently. They made as many round trips as was possible, as fast as they could. They wanted to complete the operation quickly and depart the solar system, just as my group and I wanted so much to do.

Because the Martians did not allow us to individually register them on arrival—as they had agreed to let us do before they left Mars—we had no idea who was who. All we had to work with was the Nodian head count and some Martian lists that neither we nor a common Martian could read. Dell spent many days searching the mobs of Martians in vain for someone who could read the Martian passenger lists. Beside these lists was a number in Nodian mental roms that identified each Martian (visually), along with his or her name and historical background. The problem was that we had no telepathic Nodian, Trakian or any instrument that would permit someone to read the mental rom records. We asked each Nodian spacecraft commander who deposited his cargo of Martians at our receiving stations if he could spare someone who could help us out. In every case we were turned down. I soon realized that these commanders had no intention of subjecting any of their crew members to the obviously chaotic conditions that prevailed at our location on the planet Earth.

The Nodians eventually came to realize that we could not handle any more Martian emigrants and began to deposit the stragglers (those who originally resisted being transported) at other locations throughout the world, but not before they unloaded on us thousands of Martian sheep as well as hundreds of camels. Within days of their arrival, the greatest number of these animals died. They could not tolerate the changeover from breathing their native air to breathing the air of Earth as easily as their human relations. Later, off-world animal life was brought to the Earth in preparatory stages. These efforts only slightly increased their survival rate.

Many older Martians developed all kinds of respiratory ailments. We did not have an adequate number of medical personnel of any race who could deal with these problems, and as a result, many ailing Martian humans also died within weeks after their arrival. It was then the practice of the average Martian to cremate their dead, but preserve and entomb those of higher station. The mass cremations rapidly depleted the area of natural combustible material and they reluctantly resorted to mass burial.

Low food supplies led to the Martians' ranging far and wide, raiding farms and places where the Earth natives stored food. Our only means to notify Nodia of these happenings was by way of telling a Nodian spacecraft crew and hope that they could inform the Nodian authorities by means of telepathy about the situation.

I did not isolate myself from the Martians, much as I wanted to. Instead I went among them in hope of finding one of their kind whom they respected and who would help me to establish some kind of beneficial organization that could do something about their particular problems.

Then three things happened that started to turn things around. The first thing was that, except for a few survivors, many of those in the Martian raiding parties were not returning to their encampments. The survivors related that they had encountered and battled very large units of Maldecian krates, who outnumbered them and had superior weapons. The Maldecians were intent on keeping the Martians pinned down until they starved to death.

The Arrival of Gracian Olbey-Cobex

One afternoon Dell arrived at our headquarters with a young man dressed in Martian attire. I knew immediately that this fellow was not a Martian, but a Gracian. His name was Olbey-Cobex. He related that he had been taken prisoner on Mars by the Martians just before the last Gracian spacecraft left the planet. He was a spacecraft pilot and, most important, was a pretty good telepath.

Olbey-Cobex was an answer to my prayers. He first mentally contacted Gracyea and learned that the Gracians and the Nodians had met and united. A decision had been reached between the two races that was based on the fact that because the Gracians were hated by the Maldecians and resented by the Martians, it would be best to leave any physical dealings with these people to the Nodians. One thing I learned from this news was that the Nodians now knew where Gracyea was located in the vast universe, so maybe they also knew where my home world of Cartress was located.

I began to inquire of each Nodian spacecraft crew who landed at the station if they were scheduled to return to Nodia in the near future. In each case they informed me that they themselves were waiting to be relieved by other crews. They told me that a large Nodian mothership loaded with food, medicine and other survival items specifically formulated for every type of off-world emigrant would arrive in the solar system and take up an orbit around the Sumer radiar (Saturn). I decided to await this mothership's arrival and then make every possible effort to hold Rendowlan to his promise to take my group to Nodia and then home to Cartress. The problem here was that I had not seen or heard from Rendowlan for years.

Late one afternoon the sky turned a dull gray and funnel clouds began to form. Not even a native of Earth had ever seen such a phenomenon before. Several of these whirlwinds swept through the Martian encampments and ripped the roof off the inn in which my group lived and tried to carry out our duties. The tornadoes killed many and left the area devastated. The Martians believed that the tornadoes were recently developed Maldecian weapons. At the time I thought they might be right.

After the tornadoes there was no real way to hold the Martians together. They eventually broke up into bands, which then spread out in every direction. Their logic was that they would be less vulnerable to this "new Maldecian weapon" if they were not concentrated in one area. After they dispersed, their original numbers dwindled to about one percent of what they had been. We had no way of telling where the Martian groups had gone or how they were dealing with their survival on the Earth.

One day two Nodian spacecraft landed at the station. The first one brought the Martian supreme ruler Rancer-Carr, and after several hours the second craft brought the representatives of the Nodian Trading House of Domphey, Nisor of Moor and his wife Ivatcala. They had come to prepare us for the coming of emigrants from yet another dying world of the solar system, the planet Wayda (Venus).

The Martian zone-rex seemed to me unlike any Martian. He spoke fluently the language of the Gracian Olbey-Cobex and the languages of the Nodians, Maldecians and the people of Earth. The crew of the spacecraft he came in was reduced to the minimum required for operating the vehicle. This was done to make room for several Martians the zone-rex had selected to join him in his aerial search for those Martian bands that had recently departed from our station. This act temporarily provided me with about twenty-five Nodian-trained Trakian telepaths. They were selfishly motivated to telepathically inform the Nodians that they wanted to leave the Earth as soon as possible. The Trakian numbers decreased with each departure of a Nodian spacecraft. Even now I remember vividly the reaction of the Martians at the station when they first laid eyes on their zone-rex. They stood in absolute and most respectful silence. The silence made me realize just how much noise I had become accustomed to.

After the zone-rex commanded his people to accept my authority, he then informed them that he would return as soon as possible to take them to yet another world in a far distant solar system where they might better survive.

A New Home for the Martians: Mollara

The visit of the zone-rex was brief. As his craft disappeared over the southern horizon, I remember wondering how things would have gone with his people had he arrived a year or so earlier. I later learned that during this time he had been on Nodia making plans to move his people from the Earth to a world called Mollara. The Nodians suggested Mollara as a new home for the Martians and agreed to help them get there. The first problem was finding and assembling a sufficient number of spacecraft that could be assigned to the task. Many of these vehicles were advanced in age and had to be modified to accommodate the special needs of their would-be passengers. Additionally, these vehicles were designed to carry cargo, not passengers, and for many, the long trip from Earth to Mollara would be the last trip though space they would ever make. Among these expendable second-class vehicles would have to be a number of first-class ships that would return the Nodian crews to Nodia. Ships that carried technicians and tools to repair any breakdowns during the trip also had to be committed to the project. After being modified, the second-class vehicles would really be of no further use to the Nodians. Some transporting crafts could be used to generate electrical power for the Martians on their new home world. The others would have to be junked or in some way used on Mollara as temporary shelters or warehouses.

There was an initial problem with getting the various Nodian trading houses to agree to modify hundreds of spacecraft and then trash them. In this case the force of spirituality rapidly defeated the force of materialism. I also learned that the Martian zone-rex had already been to Mollara to get an idea about how his people might fare. He left a number of Martians on Mollara to prepare for the arrival of others who had survived their deadly stopover on the planet Earth.

Nisor of Moor put a stop to the Trakian telepath desertions. With great diplomatic persuasion he actually got six Trakians to volunteer to stay with us on the Earth and act as our communication link with Nodia. Nisor and his wife Ivatcala, a woman who had been blessed by the elohim, were part of a group that were sponsored by the Nodian Trading House of Domphey, who were conducting the transportation of the people of Wayda (Venus) to the Earth.

The Waydian Arrivals

Comparing a Martian to a Waydian would be somewhat like comparing an eagle to a butterfly. The soft and gentle Waydians evoked a totally different set of emotions, those that one naturally employs when dealing with inquisitive and frightened children. The Waydian presence at the station served as a tranquilizing sedative for the remaining Martians. Martian and Waydian children were instant friends. The Martian youngsters enjoyed playing camel and racing about, sometimes blindfolded, with a Waydian boy or girl on their backs. At first the Waydian kids resisted being part of this game, but later learned to steer their "Martian camels" by pulling on their long black hair.

It was a status symbol for a Martian boy or girl to actually have their very own Waydian to ride around. Many a fight occurred between the Martian boys over whose female Waydian rider was actually the prettiest or smartest.

My life had become less hectic and I was able to take stock of things of a more personal nature. Both my wife and I wanted to find a way to contact someone who could tell us about our children (now grown) that we had left behind on Cartress in the care of my parents. The Trakian telepaths did make many an unsuccessful effort to help us.

The young Gracian Olbey-Cobex contributed to contacting telepaths on his home world of Gracyea. He eventually confided in me that he did not enjoy telepathically communicating with his people because their spirits were filled with deep sorrow over being tricked by the Maldecians, allowing them to become an instrument that had brought about such destruction and misery. He learned from his mental conversation with his people that they had given the Nodians certain technical knowledge that pertained to life-support systems they had previously developed to move large numbers of different types of off-world construction workers from planet to planet. He told us that the Nodians were using this knowledge to modify the spacecraft that would eventually be used to transport the remaining Martians from Earth to Mollara.

The Meditations of Olbey-Cobex

One morning as the sun rose, Varbreen and my son Marle woke me and directed me to look out my bedroom window. There in the yard under a tree sat Olbey-Cobex, who was reciting a string of numbers that were meaningless to me. I first thought that the Gracian was saying his morning prayers. It was Dell who told me that Olbey-Cobex was conducting a ritual that would eventually take his life. He was reciting the value of the constant you know as pi, the most sacred number of the creator of all that is. The value of pi (3.141592+) is, as you know, a string of numbers that is believed to never end anyplace in the universal life field that is comprehensible to the human mind. Pi is also known as an irrational number (cannot be written as a fraction). Olbey-Cobex was attempting to reach the divine consciousness of the creator of all that is by following the path that he believed these numbers provided to the birthplace of infinity.[7]

Dell pointed out that Olbey-Cobex was essentially committing suicide, because he would neither eat nor sleep until he had completed reciting this sacred number. *[To say that it would take a person forever to recite the numerical value of pi could easily be a gross understatement. —W.H.B.]*

It took about twelve Earth days for Olbey-Cobex to pass from us. He dropped his head after uttering the words zero, zero, zero. I sent Dell to find my son Marle and have him bring a Gracian feathered cape in which we would bury our departed friend. As I placed the cape over the body of Olbey-Cobex, it ignited into flames and instantly evaporated into a small cloud of blue smoke. Everyone present was amazed to see the body also become transparent and then totally disappear. It was Orbaltreek who ended the event by saying, "For you, Olbey-Cobex of Gracyea, I will tell all I meet from this time forward that all that you have ever said about the sacred numbers is true."

The Martian Exodus and Maldecian Slavers

After Olbey-Cobex went to count the stars, Oken and his Reltian father and mother, Tou and Nebe, requested that they be allowed to go along with the Martians. Hearing their request, my son Marle also added his name to the list of those who wanted to go to Mollara, not necessarily to stay and live on that distant world, but to be among the Nodians who would take them there. He hoped to learn what he could about space navigation and possibly in some way reach our home planet of Cartress, joining the brothers and sisters he had never met. Varbreen and I gladly agreed to these requests.

The day finally came when a considerable number of Nodian spacecraft landed at the station. After many lifetimes I can truthfully say that I had never seen a more motley fleet of space vehicles. More than a third of them had to receive considerable repairs before they could make their final journey to Mollara.

Even after the last spacecraft of the great Martian exodus left our station, we still had a small population of Martians living among the Waydians. Some of these Martians were those who for one reason or another did not want to go to Mollara. Others were those who arrived at the station too late. We were one of the first stations to send off our Martians, and we were aware that other stations elsewhere on the Earth would be doing likewise in weeks to come. We did have some minor success in getting some of the latecomers to these other locations before they missed the "boat" again. Before they left the solar system, all the exodus spacecraft joined in Earth orbit, then joined with other craft that had recently left Mars with their cargo holds filled with every type of Martian plant and animal.

With the Martians gone, the station became the target of Maldecian slavers who saw our gentle Waydians as unresistant victims. This activity required us to concentrate our charges into one single group. The slave raids stopped when a small army of Sumerians, Trakians and some Martians, led by Nodians, ringed the Waydian population. This militia attempted to teach the Waydians to defend themselves, but they would rather have become slaves or die before they would hurt anyone. The sad part of this was that there was noplace known at the time anywhere in the universe where the Waydians were more suited to live than the Earth, and in order that they do so in peace, something had to be done about the Maldecians. The militia was well-organized, and I pointed out to its commanders that they should assume full command of the station.

They accepted my suggestion, which left our group free to take a much-needed vacation. Our old Gracian aircar was once again uncovered from its underground hiding place by Orbaltreek and Dell.

Flying South to Other Stations of Off-Worlders

I had not seen the station from the air in many years. Where once there had been beautiful forests as far as the eye could see, now there was barren land, tilled with ruts produced by flows of unabsorbed rainwater. It appeared that the Earth below us had been clawed and wounded by some gigantic beast. Amidst the eroded landscape could be seen some patches of tilled soil, which was evidence that the Waydians were trying their best to grow what food they could.

Our destination was the yet-unmolested wilderness that we knew existed to the south. We had also learned that there were other off-world receiving stations located in that direction. We thought we would visit these stations to learn how our colleagues there dealt with certain problems that we surely had in common. Within an hour after leaving our station, we all confessed to a sense of guilt for leaving our Waydian children in the care of the militia "baby tenders" so that we could fly off on a vacation. I occasionally had the feeling that I had forgotten to turn the water off in a plugged bathtub. Our feelings later proved to be correct, because we never returned to the place named Petrimmor's Station.

Most of the stations we came to in the course of our flight had been abandoned. Evidence showed that most of these places had been vacated in haste. Other places were occupied by small numbers of Waydians and Martians who had not seen a station administrator in over a year. We were told that these small groups were supplied from time to time by Nodian spacecraft that contained Earth air. After the Nodians left supplies, they picked up the sick and dying and flew them many thousands of miles to the east and gave them into the care of the Sumerians, Trakians, Reltians and cooperating Earth people.

The Maldecians rarely bothered this large off-world alliance that was well-organized and was increasingly well-supplied and -armed by the Nodians. Everyone in the alliance knew that the Maldecians were duplicating advanced forms of weapons and would eventually launch a major attack against the off-world alliance before it became too strong or decided to attack and subjugate them. The Maldecians were certainly correct to expect that the off-world alliance would someday come after them with all their military might. This day was put off time and time again because the off-worlders were physically affected by the environment, tormented by the Earth's four seasons of weather and the lack of home-world food. The latter problem caused ill health. The Maldecians, untroubled by these environmental problems, decided to wait until the Earth conditions, unhealthy for the biological makeup of the off-worlders, took their toll. The Nodians knew that the Maldecians hoped that some off-worlders might survive their biological ordeals and provide breeding stock for future slaves.

In the meantime the Nodians were hard at work building spacecraft and making plans to use those vehicles to move every living off-worlder off the planet Earth. It was also in the Nodian plan that when each and every off-worlder had been moved safely from the Earth, they would themselves attack the Maldecians.

Despite all the Nodian efforts and good intentions, the Earth suddenly began to undergo great cataclysms that resulted in the eventual physical manifestation of the Frequency Barrier.

When the woman known as Doy of Maldec asked Aranella Cre'ator if her husband and others of her world would order an attack on her fellow Maldecians living on the Earth at the time, Lady Aranella told Doy she could expect such an action if the Nodian military received a "light of divine direction" to do so. Aranella Cre'ator at the time knew full well that in anticipation of receiving a positive light of divine direction, the Nodians were preparing to attack the Maldecians without mercy. Opatel Cre'ator had already been selected to lead the attack on the Earth-based Maldecians. The war craft from which he hoped to direct his warfare he named "The Jaffer Ben-Rob" after the Earthman who, years before on the banks of the river you now call the Nile, had sadly refused to assist in ridding the Earth of the Maldecians.

The positive light of divine direction that the Nodians awaited was never received. As you have often heard said in the words of the language you now speak, "God works in mysterious ways." Only in the most recent times have we of the open state of perception come to realize the meaning of those mysterious ways and how they relate to the future of both the planet Earth and the entire universe.

Surveying the Stations, Avoiding Maldecians

During our excursion south of Petrimmor's Station, we found some bands of off-worlders living near what were once receiving stations. They did so in the hope that some form of assistance would come to them from the sky. We also saw bands of off-worlders roaming about and living as they could off the land. We made no effort to contact these roaming bands because we knew that we could do them no good. We also considered that such personal contact with these desperate people could prove to be dangerous. The only areas we found to be functioning in a civilized manner were areas under the control of the Maldecians. That is, everyone living in those areas, mostly native Earth people, appeared to be well-fed and - clothed.

Running short on food, we eventually landed in a small Maldecian-controlled village. We bartered some of our long-ago-acquired Gracian jewels for food and then went about preparing and eating it beside our aircar. The Gracian aircar attracted the attention of four Maldecian krates, who came to us with smiles on their faces. They first asked if they could see our Gracian treasure, pretending that they wanted to trade with us. We knew that it was our aircar they really wanted.

Orbaltreek slowly entered the aircar and fully retracted its transparent canopy. By this action he identified himself as the vehicle's pilot. The smiling krates walked backward to the car and then got into it. It was then that I noticed Orbaltreek putting on his seat harness. This was something I had never seen him do before. The aircar rose at its maximum rate of climb and at about 600 feet flipped over. I will never forget the screams of those four krates as they tumbled, with arms and legs flailing, to their death. [*Sharmarie interjects, "It's obvious that those Maldecian krates never heard the slogan, Buckle up for safety."*]

Orbaltreek landed at the spot from which he had taken off. We quickly reloaded our Gracian treasure and recently purchased food. Later we landed again and rested near a small stream of water. The next morning we continued on our journey.

After traveling in wider and wider circles for two days, we again came close to a large Maldecian settlement. In the outskirts of this town were several estates. Resting on a lawn of one these estates we saw a large black spacecraft. This craft bore on its hull the symbol of the Nodian Trading House of Cre'ator. We landed our aircar behind a line of trees and I alone cautiously walked a short distance to the spacecraft. The side portal of the craft was open.

I first whispered, then shouted, "Is anyone inside?" An elderly Nodian came to the portal and put his forefinger to his lips, symbolically saying, "Be quiet." He then said: "If you are that Cartressian who has been flying around in a Gracian aircar, you had better take off and find someplace to lay low. The Maldecians have put out the hue and cry to apprehend you and your friends. They say that you are wanted for the sneak attack and murder of one Maldecian krate, two Earth women and a small child."

I replied, "What? They didn't accuse me of raping some pregnant woman while she was in labor?" He gave a stifled laugh and said, "If no one turns you in soon, I'm sure that too will be added to their list of charges." He motioned to me to enter the spacecraft. When I did, he closed the port to the outside world.

The circular Nodian craft at its widest point had a diameter of about 110 feet. It had three upper decks that had progressively smaller diameters. Soft lights came on in front of us as we walked and went off behind us, leaving the rear areas we passed in total darkness. We ascended a small flight of steps and arrived at a well-lit landing. Beyond the landing was a crescent-shaped room. There sitting on plush furniture sat several Nodians.

One of these Nodians was Rairol. He recognized me immediately as the Cartressian fugitive. He talked in haste, explaining that the spacecraft would soon be filled with Maldecians who were going with him to a conference that would pertain to Maldecian and Nodian affairs. He told me that he could not take the chance of my people or me being sensed by some Maldecian esper. He then took a copy of a map and circled a spot on it. He told me to meet him and Rendowlan at that spot at dawn twelve days in the future. He also advised that we keep our aircar well-hidden until we needed to get to the spot he had marked. He then added, "Be there, Petrimmor, and we will take you and your people home to Cartress."

Encountering Sharmarie and Rendowlan in Evercass

Our continued journey brought us to a town within 60 miles or so from the place Rairol had marked on the map. It was our plan to seclude the aircar and mingle with the people of the town. We decked ourselves out in Gracian jewelry in order to pass as some kind of wealthy merchants. Orbaltreek landed the aircar at the edge of the town and left us there. He then flew off to find a place to hide our vehicle. Cimiss and Varbreen walked together and Dell and I followed behind at a distance, keeping them in sight.

The name of the town was Evercass. The majority of the population consisted of Earth people. The next largest segment were Maldecians. From time to time we passed an off-worlder, who appeared well-dressed and well-fed. We also saw groups of strange off-worlders—that is, they were from worlds that were not part of the local solar system. My multiple questions, how had they gotten to the Earth and who brought them and why, were answered when we spotted a couple of Nodians dressed in black uniforms who were walking with a taller man wearing the same cut of clothes but in dark red wine color.

My pulse raced a bit when I recognized one of the Nodians as Rendowlan. Dell and I caught up with Cimiss and Varbreen and passed them in order to catch up with our old Nodian acquaintance. We were within about thirty feet of him when the taller man spun around to face us with a pistol pointed directly at my head. Women screamed and Earth people dropped to the ground. Varbreen came to me and stood by my side, staring into the eyes of our would-be executioner.

A smile came across Rendowlan's face and he called to me, saying, "You can either join us for some refreshment or just stand there and allow Sharmarie to shoot you." The menacing weapon disappeared in a flash.

A short time later our expanded group sat under a canopy in an open-air restaurant and talked softly as we watched the changing street scenes. Before our eyes passed wagonloads of farm products and merchandise as well as groups of Reltian and Waydian slaves on their way to market. Small troops of Maldecian krates also passed our way. When we realized that these small troops were joining into a larger body farther down the street, the pistol that could have sent me to help Olbey-Cobex count the stars now rested openly on the tabletop.

Other than the Martian zone-rex, I had never seen or conversed with a more sophisticated Martian than Sharmarie. He didn't apologize for scaring us as he had, but explained his threatening actions as the result of years of responding to possible assassination attempts on his employer's wife, Aranella Cre'ator. He explained that he had come to the Earth with her and her brother-in-law, Opatel Cre'ator, who were presently guests at the palace of Her-Rood, the Maldecian governor-general of the Earth. Sharmarie told us that the events at Her-Rood's palace were not to his liking, so he decided to travel about searching for someone who could tell him where he might find some of his people or tell him how they coped with being packed up and taken away to Mollara.

I told him about my association with his people at Petrimmor's Station and the food and Maldecian problems they experienced. When I told him how his people reacted to the arrival of the zone-rex, a look of pride formed on his face. He then said that he planned to go to the planet Mollara and spend some time with his people soon after he returned Lady Cre'ator to Nodia. He also said he would seek out my son Marle, who had gone with the Martians to Mollara, tell him of our meeting and see to his welfare.

The afternoon turned to dusk and there was still no sign of Orbaltreek.

Hearing about our concern for our companion, Rendowlan spoke into the ear of the other Nodian, whose name was Shayoler. Shayoler rose and walked toward the company of krates still milling about where they had assembled early that afternoon.

Rendowlan told us that the Nodians were trying to encourage the Maldecians to let them help the world's populations of off-worlders more directly with both expert assistance and technology. He also confided that the Nodians were gravely concerned with the fact that the Maldecians were now mass-producing weapons of types they had never used before.

The State of Weaponry

I can explain this weapon problem by using the Martians, Maldecians, Gracians and Nodians as examples. The Martian bar-rexes had always had small standing armies. From time to time these warlords would clash with each other, using what we would now call primitive weapons such as swords, spears, bows and arrows. They thus developed the practice of war to no greater degree than they found absolutely necessary.

The Maldecians, on the other hand, never fought among themselves. The only reason they formed krate military units was to intimidate their subjects of the Earth. Facing the possibility of warring with organized off-world groups that might be armed with superior Nodian weapons caused them to start copying and producing any weapons they could get their hands on.

Gracians, being a space-traveling race, entered into many solar systems where they found populations of a single world fighting each other with all manner of weapons. The Gracians also encountered solar systems where interplanetary war was under way between the populations of two or more planets. If a world was important to them, they would chance making contact with the people of that world no matter how hostile the people might be. They did this in the case of my home world of Cartress. Our development of firearms occurred during a fifty-year period of warfare that resulted in the establishment of a one-world government and economy.

The Gracians developed defensive weapons based on the use of sound waves. I myself experienced the effects of Gracian sound weapons that day on Cartress when I fired two bullets at their spacecraft. The Maldecian krates who went about slaughtering the Gracians at Miradol also got a taste of these defensive sound weapons. I know now how regretful the Maldecians were when they realized they had killed every Gracian who knew how to use those weapons.

The Nodians also traveled between the stars and encountered war wagers on single planets as well as between worlds in the same system.

Unlike the Gracians, the Nodians attempted to make peace between the warring factions. If negotiations did not succeed, the Nodians were famous for lending their might to one side or the other to bring the fighting to an end.

Orbaltreek's Capture by the Maldecians

Shayoler returned to us with the news that Orbaltreek and our aircar had been captured by the Maldecians, and both had been taken to the palace of the Maldecian governor. Rendowlan asked for silence as he began a telepathic conversation. We soon learned from Rendowlan that he had mentally contacted Opatel Cre'ator, who was at that very moment at the governor's palace. Opatel told Rendowlan that he would do everything possible to keep Orbaltreek from being killed or tortured. He also said that he would make a strong effort to gain his freedom.

Cimiss, upon hearing of her husband's capture, broke down. No words could calm her. Sharmarie reached into a small pouch that hung from his belt and extracted what looked to me like a small piece of dried tree bark. He squeezed Cimiss' cheeks until she open her mouth. He placed the bark on her tongue and immediately she went into a deep sleep.

Rendowlan again sent forth a telepathic message, and several minutes later a Nodian aircar landed in the street directly in front of us. Two armed Nodians got out of the car and stood facing what was probably the town's full garrison of krates. The krates did nothing but stare back at them as Sharmarie lifted Cimiss and cradled her in one of his arms. Holding her in this manner allowed the hand of his other arm to be free to point his pistol in any direction. No words had to be said.

We automatically rose from our seats and hurried to the open hatch of the waiting aircar. After the Nodian soldiers got in, the craft's pilot caused the vehicle to rise and head directly at high speed toward the krates at head level. Just before hitting them, he pulled up suddenly. Sharmarie shouted to the pilot. "Do it again!" This order was countermanded by Rendowlan, who then instructed the pilot to set his course for the palace of the Maldecian governor.

I remember Sharmarie then saying to Rendowlan in low tones, "Once a poon, always a poon" [a monkeylike creature]. The flight to the palace took place during the darkness of night and seemed to be quite brief. We circled the palace and its well-lighted surroundings several times before traveling about thirty miles farther west. The aircar stopped and hovered, then suddenly became illuminated by lights projected from a very large Nodian spacecraft resting in a clearing beneath us.

We rested the remainder of the night aboard the space-traveling headquarters of the Nodian ambassador to the Earth, Opatel Cre'ator. With thoughts of Orbaltreek on our minds, no one actually slept. At dawn we were visited by Rendowlan, accompanied by two Nodian women who brought with them black Nodian uniforms with Cre'ator insignia for Dell and me and some fine gowns for Varbreen and Cimiss. Rendowlan swung a third uniform over his shoulder and said, "If we are lucky, Orbaltreek will be wearing this before the sun sets." We left Cimiss still sleeping soundly and, along with Rendowlan, boarded an aircar fully loaded with Nodian men and women for a short flight to the governor's palace.

A Visit to the Grand Palace

The Grand Palace and its surrounding palaces and gardens covered more than a square mile. What had once been beautiful rolling lawns and gardens that circled these magnificent buildings were now covered by pre-fabricated buildings of Gracian design and thousands of white tents that housed tens of thousands of krates. Here and there could be seen some Gracian aircars parked in groups as well as some aircars that appeared to be newly built by the Maldecians. In fact, they were copies of Gracian vehicles that had been built for the Maldecians by mechanics who were Earth natives. Varbreen was sure she had spotted our old aircar among the hundreds we'd passed over. I never doubted her.

We landed in a large square courtyard located within the center of the Grand Palace. The Nodians who came with us broke up into groups. Each group had its own Maldecian welcoming party. Our particular group had a welcoming party that included a line of twelve krates and an equal number of Cre'ator dartargas (Federation soldiers). These troops represented, respectively, the personal guard of the Maldecian Prince Sant and the Nodian ambassador Opatel Cre'ator.

Opatel embraced Rendowlan and squeezed Sharmarie's upper arm. Sharmarie then left us to locate Lady Aranella Cre'ator. Lord Opatel addressed each of the remaining members of our group by name and immediately informed us that Orbaltreek was safe and unharmed and that Prince Sant had assured him that he would obtain Orbaltreek's release as soon as he could get an audience with the governor. Opatel suggested that we stay with him until then and not wander off on our own. From that moment on Varbreen walked so close to him that she could have been mistaken for his shadow. The place frightened her because it was filled with trash, broken furniture and discarded clothing.

As we entered the corridors, we encountered people stumbling about or lying about in a state of alcohol or narcotic intoxication. Many of those on the floor were actually dead. No one seemed to care. At times our party would stop and wait while krates removed a body or two from the path of their prince. We finally reached a large room that was magnificently decorated with wall hangings and statuary. The Maldecians left us. It was several hours before Prince Sant returned to tell us that the governor wanted to meet with all of us.

The room to which we were ushered was very large. It seemed even larger because it contained very little furniture and was occupied by a very small number of people. The Maldecian governor did not greet us, but surveyed us with bleary eyes. I had never seen a Maldecian in such a mentally disoriented or weakened physical state. Rendowlan whispered to me, "Be careful. He still has the last word."

Standing beside the governor was an elderly Maldecian who was obviously very excited. He moved from side to side on the balls of his feet and continuously flicked his tongue against his upper lip. His name, which I will never forget, was Kamer-Ostsen. It was he who first spoke to us, saying, "It has come to the governor's attention that there are those among you can read the past and future of a person, and he wishes to be entertained by a demonstration of these wondrous talents." I thought to myself, *Orbaltreek never could keep his mouth shut!*

Lord Opatel responded by saying, "I am sure that my friends would be willing to demonstrate their unique abilities for the governor, but first let us resolve the matter of the man called Orbaltreek." This response clearly irritated the governor and Kamer-Ostsen. After receiving several hand signals from the governor, a krate left the room on a run. Within minutes he returned with a smiling, relieved Orbaltreek. Kamer-Ostsen told us that Orbaltreek was now free.

Dell and I spent several hours giving readings to Earth people who were called to the hall for that purpose. No Maldecian would allow himself to be read, simply because to obtain such a reading he would have to shake the hand of a lowly off-worlder. Every time a specific event in the life of an Earth person was described by Dell, the person reacted with excitement and reported aloud, "That was so. That is exactly what happened." These announcements brought a smile to the face of the governor. Her-Rood's supply of Earth people for us to read seemed endless. It was I who pleaded to give Dell time out so that he could rest.

Kamer-Ostsen pointed out that Dell's readings made no mention of what the future would hold for those who were read. I told him that we did not feel that reading the dull futures of the Earth people would have any entertainment value for the illustrious governor. He then walked to Dell and said, "I will read this little man's future." He reached out for Dell's hand and grasped it, saying, "This man will soon die." In an instant a device fashioned in the form of a cobra sprang from his sleeve and raked Dell's hand with its metal fangs. Dell immediately died without a sound and fell to the floor. Kamer-Ostsen then turned and look straight into my eyes and said, "If you want to accurately predict the future, create the future yourself."

We were at first frozen in a state of shock. It was Varbreen who then went to place Dell's head on her lap and closed his vacant eyes. Lord Opatel walked to within inches of Kamer-Ostsen and yelled, "Why?" The Maldecian backed away and said, "The governor will not tolerate anyone who has a power that he cannot control." Her-Rood was now bored and totally disinterested. He dismissed us with a wave of his hand.

When we left the room Orbaltreek was carrying Dell's body. The Nodians were furious. Just as we were about to enter the courtyard of the palace, we were met by the Maldecian Prince Sant. He was very much aware of what had happened. He opened the conversation with Opatel by saying, "I might be the only one of my race who still has the power to reason. I will not ask you what you are going to do. I know that nothing I can say will prevent your people from attacking my people. What I do ask of you is that when you leave the Earth, take me with you. I might be of value as a consultant. In that capacity I might help you bring the forthcoming conflict to a quick end." Opatel embraced the Maldecian prince and told him, "Get ready to leave within the next six days."

Orbaltreek's Story

We returned to Opatel's spacecraft headquarters, where Orbaltreek united with his wife, Cimiss. It was the first time in many years that I heard them openly talk about missing their now-grown children, who had gone many years before to the lands in the east to live among the Sumerians.

That night Orbaltreek and I sat and reminisced about the past. As we did, he puffed on a very stale Gracian cigar. During our conversation it came to my mind to ask him if he ever remembered why he had been or might still be sought on our home world of Cartress for some great crime he'd committed before we met. He thought for a minute, then answered my question with a yes.

Orbaltreek then went on to say, "In a state of drunkenness, my twin brother and I released all the animals from the zoo, including those that were wild and dangerous. Many people were killed and even eaten, including my brother. When I sobered up, I attempted to hang myself, after I could not find a beast that would do the job of killing me. I was about to commit suicide when a shirel [a Cartressian religious figure] came to me and commanded me to stop. I told him that I could not bear living with what had happened as a result of my stupid actions. The shirel then told me he would touch me, and I would forget what had happened, and anyone else I came in physical contact with who knew of the event would also be unable to recall what I had done. The shirel told me he was blanking out these memories because the elohim appreciated the fact that my brother and I freed the animals from their unnatural confinement and wished that I also would remain free to pursue a useful life. The next thing I remember after he touched my forehead was spotting you sitting by the bathing pool in the holy city of Worg."

I thanked him for revealing his past to me and then attempted to lighten things up for him by telling him that I was placing him under arrest. He smiled only slightly at my ill-timed humor. I then asked him if he would mind if I told Varbreen his story. This time he seemed somewhat amused and said, "Go ahead and tell her, but I'm sure that Cimiss or Dell already did years ago." I responded by saying, "Why didn't you tell me?" To this he answered, "This is the first time you ever asked."

Our Fatal Attempt to Leave Earth

As the day for our departure from the Earth neared, we preferred to remain within the secure confines of the Nodian spacecraft. We occupied our time by talking about returning to Cartress. We described as much as we could remember about our home world to Cimiss, who, being a native of the Earth, had never been to that distant world. During the course of our descriptions it came to me that she had probably heard all that Varbreen and I were telling her from her husband, Orbaltreek, many times before. I also realized that that did not matter to her, because our stories kept her mind off what had happened to Dell, whose body now rested in the cargo hold of the spacecraft.

On occasion we sat before a transparent section of the spacecraft's hull and watched as Nodian technicians inspected such things as the craft's landing gear and a vast number of devices attached to the ship's outer hull. These devices popped up for service, but when they were restored to their "hosts," their covers closed without revealing a seam. Both Orbaltreek and I wondered aloud, "How do they do that?"

One afternoon, while a technician was watching, Cimiss called our attention to the fact that the sky was darkening. Soon thereafter torrential rains began to fall with such a force that we could no longer peer through the water that cascaded down our window. Orbaltreek activated a device that projected a blast of compressed air designed to clear the window from the outside. The device worked for only a few minutes before it stopped functioning.

Several hours later Rendowlan came to us with a request. He informed us that every Nodian aircar but one was engaged in a search to locate Lady Aranella Cre'ator and the Martian Sharmarie to bring them back to the spacecraft. He asked Orbaltreek to fly the remaining aircar and join the search. Orbaltreek, of course, agreed to do so.

Cimiss did not want to be separated again from her husband and insisted to be taken along on the search. Varbreen and I suggested that we should accompany them because they might need the additional eyes we could provide.

It took Orbaltreek nearly an hour to figure out how to fly the Nodian aircar. Its controls differed from those of the Gracian aircar he had grown so familiar with over the years. We sat silently as we waited for him to feel confident about flying the car. Any attempt to talk was overcome by the sound of the rain striking the craft's canopy. The noise was nearly deafening. Varbreen said, "It's not going to be possible to find anyone under these conditions. Let's return to the spacecraft." I told her that we had to try.

I now know that that spacecraft was the last to leave the Earth during those terrible times. If I had heeded her request, our spirits, by the power of universal law, would not have had to live as humans time and again within the confines of the Frequency Barrier of the planet Earth.

We were about twenty minutes into our flight when the aircar was struck by lightning. I tried to take the controls from an unconscious Orbaltreek as the car began to spiral rapidly toward the ground. As I tried to move him, I felt Varbreen tug on my shirt and say, "What's the use? Come here and hold me." I dropped back into my seat and held both her and Cimiss to my chest. It was the very last thing I remember of that first lifetime.

I will return when you wish me to relate another lifetime I thereafter experienced on the Earth. Until then I will await your mental presence once again. I am Petrimmor of Cartress.

*The British wore red, the French were in blue
and we Prussians were donned in black.*

My Prussian Lifetime

Those before me chose to begin their accounts of their past lifetimes from the first lifetime to the most recent lifetime they experienced on that world. I would like to reverse the account of my many lifetimes on the Earth by relating the very last one that I can recall. During that last lifetime on the Earth I was known as Ralph Karl Lont. I was born in the year 1789 in Berlin (then the capital of the kingdom of Prussia) during the reign of Frederick the Great (Frederick William II). During his reign my father, Karl Rinehart Lont, rose to the rank of a minor officer in the Prussian army. His duties pertained to purchasing, training and the veterinary care of the army's horses.

Because of my father's position in the military, I was permitted to go to school at the age of eight to learn what was then called a military trade. At this school I learned to read, write and use simple arithmetic. DurIng that four years of schooling I lived at home with my parents and younger sister, Marie. My father was very happy when I was accepted by the school because he knew that I would eventually be assigned a military job, such as in the supply corps, that would keep me mostly behind the lines during battle.

At the age of twelve I was taken into the army as one who repaired harnesses, saddles and bridles. Later, by age sixteen I too became a minor officer, and my duties were expanded to include purchasing or manufacturing new tack as well as overseeing a group of blacksmiths. Keeping the army's horses fit and equipped was very important, and my efficiency brought me to the attention of the Prussian general staff. One day a general asked the question, "Who is this Ralph Lont that we are entrusting so much money to?" I was called before the general staff to make a full accounting. After they saw how I and my small staff had frugally spent our funding without any evidence of corruption, they brought my office into the general staff headquarters. Within a year my father became a part of my personal staff.

When I was twenty-three years old I married a Polish girl named Salla and began to put on considerable weight. My next promotion was to the staff of General Gebhard Leberect von Blucher in 1814, a year after he came out of retirement. The general of the Hussars was truly fond of me because, like himself, I had little formal education and rose in rank by using my basic intelligence and working very hard.

After having some drinks, the general could be urged to imitate his good friend General von Scharnhorst, who, when excited, would stutter. Von Blucher would at the end of his performance always apologize to his absent friend and propose a toast to him.

In 1814 I was one of Blucher's military aides when he marched on Paris. For this military effort he was raised to the royal rank of prince. Then came June 16, 1815, which was the day in Belgium when we Prussians met in battle the French army commanded by Marshal Michel Ney. During this battle, which is called the Battle of Quartes Bras, General Blucher was wounded. In reality, the French had us beaten, but because of the heavy rain they did not try to finish us off or rout us. Believing that he had successfully prevented us from joining the troops of the English Duke of Wellington near Waterloo, Marshal Ney ordered several units under Emmanuel Grouchy to keep us pinned down and overtake us if we attempted to reach Wellington. Blucher ordered us not to retreat, but to march at full speed in the direction of Waterloo. By the time the French realized that we were pulling out of our positions, more than half our army was several hours ahead of them. The French attempted to cut us off, but the ground they had to cross was covered with mud. As we marched toward Waterloo, Grouchy was always an hour or so behind us.

We reached Waterloo in the late afternoon of June 18, 1815, and once again faced Marshal Ney. This time it was he who gave ground. We eventually overwhelmed Napoleon's right flank.

I was on horseback at General Blucher's side and was very tired. From our high vantage point we watched as Wellington launched the final offensive that drove the French from the battleground. General Blucher called my attention to what he thought was a French soldier who was wandering around somewhat aimlessly. This deranged fellow was stopping from time to time to bayonet dead horses and dead soldiers. Several of the bodies he was stabbing were what I thought at the time were his own fallen comrades. Blucher said to me, "Ride down there, Ralph, and tell that man to stop. Tell him that the battle is over."

I rode up to the man, who gave me a salute. It was then I noticed that this man was not wearing a uniform of any of the armies that fought that day at Waterloo. His uniform was mustard green and trimmed with pale blue. As he raised his rifle, I thought to myself, *The English are in red, the French in blue and we Prussians are wearing black. Who is this man?* Then I felt his bullet strike me in the throat, and everything went black. I later realized I had been shot by a member of our own Dutch contingent.

When I once again resumed three-dimensional life, it was as newborn baby on my native world of Cartress. I am Petrimmor of Cartress.

A u t h o r ' s   N o t e s

1. Reltians were then natives of the planetoids or the Relt radiar. The Relt radiar is now called the planet Jupiter. For more information about the Reltians, see Ruke of Parn: *Through Alien Eyes*, part 5, August 1996.

2. The apothem line is in the center of each of the four faces of the pyramid. It is the shortest path that a drop of water would take if released at the peak of the structure and allowed to run down a face of the base.

3. In ancient Mesoamerica human sacrifices conducted on the tops of pyramids was commonplace. It is said that some people actually volunteered to have their living hearts cut out as an offering to the gods. This practice had a misinterpreted historical relationship to the fact that human blood was used in some of the mortar of the Great Pyramid of Mir (Egypt).

4. The formula for the mortar used in the Great Pyramid has never been detemined. It has been reported that the blocks of stones it binds will shatter before the mortar will give way.

5. This article is being written April 5, 1998. On April 6 the Mars Orbital Survey is scheduled to transmit to Earth close-up, high-resolution pictures of the gigantic face and five-sided pyramid located at Cydonia on Mars, revealing the ancient past told in *Through Alien Eyes*.

6. Martians emigrated because their planet was becoming uninhabitable due to the explosion of Maldec.

7. Infinity defined: (1) The quality or condition of being infinite. (2) Unbounded space, time or quantity. (3) An indefinitely large number or amount. (4) Mathematics. The limit that a function f is said to approach at $x = a$ when for x close to a, $f(x)$ is larger than any preassigned number.

F O U R T E E N

Ombota of Mars

Every existing law of nature can be described
by the sacred language of numbers, and every
law of nature is expressed in the activities
of a single atom.
—Ralbux Ducsur of Gracyea

I was born into three-dimensional life on the planet you call Mars about 69 Earth years after the planet Maldec was shattered. I grew to the age of nine Earth years on my native planet before I was carried with others of my family and race to the Earth by the Nodians. Later I was one of those of my kind who left the Earth and went to dwell on the planet Mollara. I will tell you of those times. Be patient with me, for I am a woman of simple stock. If you need to know why the grass is green and the sky is blue, I am not the one to ask.

Freeing the Nomadic Tribes before the Evacuation of Mars

When I was first born, my parents were no longer subject to the rule of any bar-rex (local warlord) and were free to live pretty much as they pleased. Our tribe still traveled the banks of the waterways for hundreds of miles in one direction before crossing the water to travel the same distance in the opposite direction. This was necessary to keep the grass from becoming overgrazed by our flocks of sheep.

Within the course of our travels we still had to pass through the stronghold of a bar-rex in order to cross the waterway. Though we were not subject to being taxed or considered subservient, we still voluntarily gave part of our herd to him. This was done somewhat out of a habit formed over several thousand years of forced practice and for several practical reasons. One reason was simply that we had too many sheep and had no way to keep them from reproducing except to slaughter and waste them. The only option for those who lived in the strongholds would have been to leave the stronghold and raise their own flocks or take our sheep forcibly from us. All in all, it was decided by our tribe's leaders that the best way to handle the potential problem of hungry strongholders was to give them some sheep twice a year and keep them off the grasslands. Those who remember the times before were pleased with the arrangement, because instead of the bar-rex and his cohorts dictating and demanding how we should live, they were now totally subject to our generosity.

After the destruction of Maldec and the departure of the Gracians from our planet, the zone-rex of our world, Rancer-Carr, took full control of our government. He did not punish those bar-rexes who had plotted with the Maldecians to eliminate him from being the divine figurehead he once represented. He instructed the bar-rexes to maintain their strongholds, but not to force their will on any of the nomadic tribes that were once under their jurisdiction. The zone-rex realized that he needed the intelligence and organizational ability of these men to help formulate his plans for a total evacuation of the population to the Earth.

The zone-rex made numerous personal visits to the various nomadic tribes in search of people who could be of value in organizing such a move as well as to educate the people about what the Earth was like and what hardships they might have to endure. In some cases persuasion would be required, since many were afraid to travel in space or did not totally appreciate the dangers that would be faced by those remaining behind on a planet about to experience tremendous geological changes.

Changes in the planet's weather were becoming evident. Rainfall decreased considerably and the levels of the waterways dropped in turn. Wind velocities increased and the air became filled with dust. This affected breathing to a point where it was necessary to wear scarves over our mouths and noses. Many animals suffocated.

The older ones of my tribe pointed out that the great stars (the sun and radiars) were getting smaller. This was due to the fact that with each orbit of the sun, our planet Mars was moving away from it and the radiars were also assuming new solar orbits, adjusting to the absence of Maldec's planetary mass in the sun's gravitational pressure field.

Being as young as I was, it was difficult for me to understand why from time to time the men of our tribe would stand in clusters and point to a bright star in the sky and talk in an excited manner, or why my mother and other women were crying as they packed our belongings into sheepskin bags and bundles, only to have them set aside by the men, who informed the women that there would be no room for these packages aboard the spacecraft that would take us to Earth. Many times I heard my mother say, "How will we live without our cooking utensils and tent?" My father assured her that these things would be replaced once we reached the Earth. She complained further, "The replacement pots will probably be much smaller than those that we already have." When we finally left Mars, my mother's largest cooking pot was situated on my father's head and his much-prized leather helmet was to be found on our pile of discards.

But much more happened before we departed for the Earth. I vividly remember the day that the zone-rex visited us. He came riding on a camel with a large troop of soldiers who were also so mounted. With him were several white-haired men and women, whom he introduced as people who were native to a distant world called Nodia. He informed us that the Nodians were going to take us to the Earth in their spacecraft and that those then present would remain with our tribe until the time came for us to leave.

The Nodians spoke Martian and used projected pictures of Earth and the interior of their spacecraft to prepare us for what lay ahead. They also gave us medical examinations and answered every conceivable question, such as, "Would the god of Mars and the spirits of our ancestors be able to accompany us to Earth and feel welcome there?"

The Nodians were exciting to me because of their ability to project pictures and talk about different worlds. Every evening I was part of the crowd that assembled to see the Nodians project their pictures and tell us of the Earth. Though the presentations were the same every night, I still found them fascinating. I especially enjoyed seeing animals of the Earth that I never realized existed.

The Beginning of the Meteorite Bombardment; Stabilizing the Orbit of Mars with Two Artificial Moons

One evening just after sunset, brightly lit objects with red-and-green tails streaked across the sky. We of Mars had never seen anything like it before. You would call these objects meteorites. The Nodians told us that they were actually pieces of the planet Maldec. In time, larger and larger pieces of the shattered world began to strike the surface of Mars. These strikes caused even more dust to rise into the atmosphere, to the point where the sun appeared to be only a bright spot in the midst of a brown haze. The warm summer nights that we once enjoyed began to get very cold.

At night the stars were very faint, but two large ones appeared to be the brightest of all. The Nodians told us that what we thought were stars were actually two large spacecraft that were in orbit about our world. These craft were providing mass that exerted drag on the planet's magnetic poles. This was done to slow down the unnatural wobbling motion the planet was beginning to exhibit. If left unchecked, the planet would have continued to wobble faster and faster until it reached the point where it would have flown apart. The second reason for exerting drag on the magnetic poles was to stabilize the planet's orbit, which was becoming more distant from the sun with every solar cycle. In other words, the Martian year was getting longer and longer.

Several years after we evacuated the planet, the Nodians replaced their orbiting spacecraft with two artificial moons that were designed to handle the planet's wobble and solar orbital problems. From Greek mythology you know these artificial moons as Phobos (fear) and Deimos (terror), which are the names of the two ferocious dogs of Mars, the ancient Roman god of war (Aries to the Greeks), that are chained at the gate of hell.[1] *[Other authorities state that Phobos was a human attendant of the god Mars. — W.H.B.]* Phobos is actually a partially hollowed-out piece of Maldec and Deimos is a solid piece. Astronomers of the Earth have suggested that these moons are captured asteroids.

Eventually the weather conditions made it impossible for the Nodians to project their pictures to crowds in the open air. We were asked to tell anyone who had seen their presentation to educate those who had not. I took this as a request directed personally at me. I spent my time searching for people who were unaware of the marvelous things I had learned from the Nodians. The fact was, I found very few who would take the time to listen to me tell them about the Earth and its people as well as the various

---

1. Phobos is the larger of the two satellites of Mars. The orbit of Phobos is of low eccentricity (0.015) and inclination (1.04 degrees) and lies at a mean distance of only 9378 km (5824 mi) from the center of Mars, or less than two Mars' radii above the planetary surface. The satellite's period of revolution is less than one-third of Mars' rotation period, and the moon appears to rise in the west and set in the east as seen from Mars. This moon's orbit is in the opposite direction from that of any other moon in the solar system.

Phobos is a body of very irregular shape, roughly 27 x 21.5 x 19 km (18 x 13 x 12 mi), and it always keeps its long axis pointed toward Mars. Phobos' mean density of 1.9 06 g/cu cm and its low reflectivity are suggestive of the most primitive meteorites or C-type asteroids. The surface of the satellite is covered with craters and exhibits elongated depressions, peculiar parallel linear striations and chains of craters, all tending to parallel the orbital plane.

kinds of Earth animals we would soon encounter. Most thought that my stories were only fantasies that stemmed from the mind of a little girl.

Most of the Nodian cargo ships that would take us to Earth were too big to land on Mars or assume a Martian orbit. Their mass in orbit would have affected the wobble-control program. This required our population to be ferried in small numbers quite a distance into space where the larger crafts were waiting. Once one of these large spaceships had reached its capacity, it would depart for a three-and-a-half-day trip to the Earth. Orbiting the Earth was not a problem, but it was still necessary to ferry us and our belongings to the Earth's surface in smaller ships.

There was nothing orderly about our departure from Mars. Some became fearful, hesitating at the last minute to board the ferry craft. Others tried to take personal possessions that they had earlier been informed they could not take. Whenever a dispute arose, the commanders of the shuttle would shut their doors and wait until some kind of order was restored. These problems led to families becoming separated, because a father or son would be ordered by the zone-rex to stay behind on Mars to participate in the enforcement of martial law. Many people were injured because they had never experienced being in a highly concentrated crowd before. The emotional state of affairs caused many tempers to get out of hand, and some deaths occurred due to violence.

Creating the Martian Coate-Grol Unit within the Federation

Not all the military peacekeepers later left Mars for the Earth. Several thousand of them accepted an offer from the Nodians to become Federation soldiers and, as a unit called the Coate-Grol, were later taken to a solar system near one of the stars that makes up the Belt of Orion. The plan was that this group of soldiers would learn what they could from the Nodians and eventually join other Martians on the planet Mollara.

Loudspeakers blared out and repeated a list of names of those who were to assemble near a ferry craft that was to lift off the following day. In most cases it took nearly a day to get through the crowd. As time went on, the crowd would stand back and provide a fairly clear path for a departing family if they shouted, "It's our time!" When it was our time, we had little difficulty reaching the shuttlecraft. I remember how my father walked boldly past men who joked about his wearing my mother's best cooking pot on his head. This inspired many women to demand that their husbands and children place pots on their heads.

Shuttling to and Living on a Mothership

My father lifted me onto his back, where I could see over the crowd and advise him what direction we should walk. From my vantage point I could see through the brown haze to the orange glow of cooking fires and blazing funeral pyres. It was cold, and we all enjoyed the warmth we found inside the shuttlecraft. The craft we boarded held only about thirty people. After making numerous trips, the Nodians had learned that in order to eliminate panic during a flight, all ports that allowed an outside view had to be covered. Every one of our group was at first silent, then one of the men began to knock in rhythm on the cooking pot on his head. He was soon joined by a chorus of "pot-knockers." This activity caused many of us to laugh.

About an hour later and after feeling a few sharp bumps, the door of the shuttlecraft opened once again, revealing an area filled with people. Here and there were cooking fires. The first thing I realized about this place, when I compared it to the place we had just left, was that the air was clean and fresh.

The large cargo area in which we were deposited was circular and had a diameter of about 200 feet and a dome-shaped ceiling about 70 feet high. The perimeter of this room was ringed by a number of terraced metal platforms crowded with people. Under these bleacher-type platforms were toilet facilities and first-aid stations.

The central area of the room was also circular and had a diameter of about 65 feet. This area also contained people mostly coming and going from a station that dispensed food and water as well as information about how to obtain required medical assistance. Because of the excitement, many pregnant women went into labor. I heard it said that the ship had another cargo hold filled to capacity with livestock, even animals and birds native to Mars that were not domesticated.

We spent several days waiting for more shuttlecraft to arrive. After the craft was considered totally loaded, we had to wait several more days while the Martian-type air was gradually replaced by Earth-type air (much richer in oxygen than it is today). This was a time of misery for many, especially the elderly. It took days before any of us felt like moving and eating. We learned that more than 85 percent of our livestock had died due to the air changeover. The upside was that the animals that survived were in good health and were expected to do well and reproduce on the Earth.

From the moment we arrived, the soft female voice of a Nodian named Freattha, speaking in Martian, was heard throughout the area, reminding us to be courteous to each other, to speak softly and hold down the noise. This same disembodied voice made other public announcements and paged individuals for any number of reasons. When the voice did begin to say something, you could hear nothing but the cries of the newborn. These cries were great morale boosters because they represented new Martian life and proof to us all that our race could and would survive.

Off to Earth

I had just been put to bed by my mother when the voice of Freattha announced, "We are now leaving for the Earth. We will arrive in three and a half days. May the elohim bless our journey." I wondered who the elohim were.

During the trip to Earth I saw very little of my father, who spent his time meeting with other men of our world to plan and discuss how we were going to live on the Earth. Their main concern pertained to how the livestock would be protected and later, as they multiplied, equally distributed among the people. Our ages-old tribal way of distribution had to be tested on the Earth. They had to take into consideration what we and our animals were going to eat and drink until there was enough livestock to consume without reducing the numbers of breeding stock. There were more types of grass and plants on the Earth than on Mars, and the Nodians were unable to tell us if any specific types of Earth vegetation would be harmful to us or our stock. The thought of raising sheep in one location, rather than moving them continually along the waterways of Mars, was perplexing to my father. He could not visualize a place where there were millions of square miles of forests and grasslands.

The Nodians also told us during their orientation lectures that we would join people from Wayda (Venus) and the planetoids of the Sumer (Saturn), Relt (Jupiter) and Trake (Neptune) radiars. This concerned us in several ways: Would they steal our livestock? Would their stock compete or prey on ours for food? Would their gods get along with ours, and would the spirits of their ancestors get along with the spirits of our ancestors? Each day my father told us about at least one more thing that he and the other men were worried about.

The three-and-a-half-day journey to Earth passed very slowly. During this time we all experienced the physical condition of extreme perspiration. It was unnatural for us to sweat so profusely. This condition was brought on by the biological changes in our bodies, which were the result of breathing Earth air. The odor became overwhelming, and the Nodians retaliated by dispensing rivers of pleasant-smelling liquids and disposable towels. My mother continuously swabbed me down.

It was Freattha's soft, assuring voice that informed us that we had assumed an orbit about the Earth. She told us that we would be given some pills to help those who might experience some discomfort in adjusting to the new planet's atmospheric pressure and stronger gravity.

It took one more day before the center of the large cargo bay began to lower slowly and guardrails rise to prevent anyone from falling forty feet to the deck below. On that lower deck could be seen hundreds of smaller spacecraft of various sizes and shapes. None were larger than the open area between the decks.

We were informed by Freattha to stand away from the guardrails. We soon learned why. Spacecraft from the lower deck rose one at a time to the level of our deck and extended a ramp so that those whose names were called could board it. Once loaded, the craft moved downward and horizontally to a tube that led into space. None of these shuttlecraft could carry more than 100 passengers. It took another two Earth days before my parents and I left the mothership and landed on the Earth. The length of each shuttle trip varied because it was determined by where the mothership was in orbit relative to the designated landing site.

Landing and Adjusting to Earth Life at Petrimmor's Station

When we stepped upon the Earth for the first time, we were amazed. The horizon was at a greater distance than on Mars. It was cool, and the smell of the place was very pleasant. I immediately began to look about for the strange animals I had seen in the Nodian pictures. All I saw was an elderly Martian couple waving and calling to us and several other Nodian shuttlecraft landing on the grass-covered plain. I remember my father, with a sweep of his arms, saying, "I hope the sheep can eat this. If they can, all will be well."

The Martians who greeted us directed us to walk westward until we came to the encampment at what they called Petrimmor's Station. My father asked the Martian man if Petrimmor was some kind of bar-rex. The old man chuckled a bit when he said, "No, but he is working at it."

We walked for more than an hour, but also rested from time to time to catch our breath and allow my father to take the atmospheric pressure pills the Nodians had given us. Neither my mother nor I had any such problem, but the increase in gravity caused our muscles to ache after walking some distance. This discomfort eventually waned as we became accustomed to the stronger gravity.

We first became aware of the encampment because of the sounds coming from it. Funeral pyres were already lit and receiving the bodies of those who had died from lack of tolerance for the atmospheric pressure and increase in gravity. The encampment was a sight to behold. It stretched for as far as one could see. Strange machinery dotted the landscape as well as stacks of lumber and other forms of building material. My people kept their distance from these things, fearing that the metal monsters would eat them or put an evil curse on them.

It took quite some time before the word got around that the machines would make bricks. At Petrimmor's direction, a number of Earth people tried to teach us how to operate the machines. We thought this ridiculous because we had never lived in a house. Tents that we could fold and carry with us had always been our form of shelter. The Earth people pleaded with us to take them seriously about what a winter on the Earth amounted to. Everyone was too physically and emotionally exhausted to pay them much attention. Besides that, the thoughts of winter only caused worry about how the animals would survive. After all, how could one build houses for thousands of sheep?

Petrimmor's request, then demand, to dig latrines was complied with out of personal necessity. Crews of Earthmen worked continuously digging water wells. This activity was my favorite form of entertainment because they used elephants to move things about. Once, at the command of its handler, an elephant lifted me by its trunk over its head (some seventeen feet from the ground). I was thrilled, but eventually was chased away because I constantly pestered him to repeat the experience.

In the evenings we would meet in groups and inquire of recent arrivals from Mars about the present conditions there. The accounts became worse and worse. We began to realize that we were fortunate to be on the Earth and that we should begin to fully adjust to the fact that we had to make the best of it. When this realization sank in, we began to build. I became part of a gang of children who pulled small wagonloads of bricks from where they were made to the places where they were used. Our pay was in hard candy, dried fruit, felt hats and jump ropes. Jumping rope was an exercise designed to help the children strengthen their muscles to deal with the stronger gravity of the planet.

Experimentally, a flock of Earth sheep was mixed with a small flock of Martian sheep. The results of this experiment were at first disastrous for the Earth animals. Martian sheep were nearly twice their size, and the Earth rams were no physical match for the Martian rams. Eventually the Earth ewes began to give birth to crossbreed lambs. Many of these larger lambs had to be born surgically at the cost of the mother's life. When the crossbreeds grew to maturity and began to breed among themselves, their offspring were what could be called biologically stable. The four-horned rams of this crossbreed were mean critters and had no problem dealing with the rams of pure Martian or Earth stock. The numbers of this crossbreed grew slowly, but my father and the other herdsmen were pleased with this new development.

Swimming, a New Experience

On Mars it had been forbidden for more than a thousand years to cross a waterway at anyplace other than a bar-rex stronghold. The fact that such a law did not exist on the Earth allowed us Martians to enjoy an experience we had never had before, which was swimming. It was my interest in the work elephants that brought this sport to my attention.

It was midmorning when a group of my friends and I followed several elephants and their handlers to a narrow river several miles from the borders of our encampment. We sat on the riverbank and watched the giant animals roll about and spray water on themselves with their trunks or lie on their sides as their handlers scrubbed them down with brushes. Nearby several Earth children were also splashing about and propelling themselves through the water by paddling with their arms and kicking their feet. We decided to move closer to these Earth kids and figure out how they kept themselves from sinking.

As soon as their veiled mothers saw us coming, they called their children to them. The women then began to wave us away—that is, all but one, who was not veiled. This lady was taller (about the size of my mother) and wore green trousers, whereas the other women wore skirts. This lady separated from the others and walked toward us, bringing with her a small boy and girl. As she came close she said hello and spoke to us in heavily accented Martian. She told us that her name was Ala and that she too was an off-worlder who had recently come to the Earth from one of the planetoids of the Trake radiar. She was the prettiest lady I had ever seen.

We sat around her and on occasion she called to the Earth women to join us. After some persuasion the other women and their children began to come to her call. The Earth women inspected us with a look of disgust. One patted the head of one of our boys, which caused a considerable amount of dust to rise. After a bit of chatter the boy was pulled toward the water. He stood naked and stiff as a board as two Earth women began to wash him with soap and water. A laughing Ala encouraged the rest of us to enter the water. We bathed and splashed about until the late afternoon. Some of us even tried our luck at swimming.

Walking back to camp, I felt wonderful. My companions, now clean and shiny, looked beautiful. Their once-matted hair was now blowing like black silk in the soft summer breeze. My mother and father were amazed at my appearance and fascinated with the account I gave them of my afternoon at the river. Several days later they too spent a day beside the river's flowing waters. This soon became a weekly ritual. The Earth people were friendly, but the women were standoffish because my mother did not wear a veil. My father told us not to be concerned about the custom because he had heard that the Earth women wore veils because they were too ugly for their husbands to look at.

The house-building in the encampment was moving slowly because the physical labor was difficult for many of our adults. Youngsters like myself were faring very well on Earth foods such as fish and dried fruit. Although crossbreeding our sheep with Earth sheep was successful, the attempt to do likewise with our larger one-humped camels with the two-humped Earth camels did not work at all. The number of our camels decreased. My father said that it was just as well, because our camels were too weak to ride or use for work.

Food Problems

As time went on, the amounts of rice, beans, dried fruit and fish began to get smaller. This was because the Earth people, under orders from the Maldecians, would not sell these things to Petrimmor for distribution to us. Petrimmor was at a loss as to what to do about this growing crisis. By the time the Nodians began to supply us with food suitable for our race, it was too late coming, and when it did, it was not enough to last very long. This condition forced us to slaughter our sheep's young and thus reduce our breeding stock. There was a point where we had to stop this practice.

The Earth people began to avoid us. They ceased making bricks for us and left our encampment, taking with them their tools and elephants. I really missed those elephants. Our first encounter with the Maldecians occurred when our people attempted to capture fish from the nearby rivers. First the Maldecians, from a safe distance, shot arrows and bullets at our fishermen and killed a number of them. When our men began to fish under the protection of bow-carrying Martian soldiers, the Maldecians were not to be seen, but their covert activities were evidenced by the fact that the riverbanks were littered with the bodies of fish they had poisoned. Those who ignorantly ate these dead fish became very sick and later died.

Our menfolk were infuriated and prepared to go to war to obtain food and punish the Maldecians for their horrible crimes. Petrimmor tried to dissuade our warriors from taking action and asked that we wait for emergency food supplies that the Nodians promised to deliver soon. He also told us that our zone-rex, Rancer-Carr, would soon arrive to take us to the planet Mollara.

My father, mother and myself were among of a group of my race who sat about Petrimmor's headquarters at the old inn and listened to his plea for restraint. My father was one of the few who asked the others to be patient. It was at that meeting that I once again saw the Trakian lady, Ala. I also learned that her husband, Zomuter, served the station as a telepathic communicator to the Nodians. I was amazed that it was possible for one person to talk to another person with their minds over vast distances. I vowed to myself that one day I would learn to communicate in the same way. (The fact that we are speaking to each other telepathically now shows that I have kept this vow.)

Our War against the Maldecians

Petrimmor's plea for patience fell on a majority of deaf ears. That night I lay awake listening to the sound of thousands of Martian broadswords being sharpened and solo voices here and there throughout the encampment singing ancient Martian ballads of war.

When I awoke at dawn the hut was vacant. I found my mother sitting by herself outside, as was the custom of our women whose husbands or sons had gone to battle. She would remain alone, fasting in silence until her husband either returned alive or until his comrades brought her his body or his empty sandals. She remained in her vigilant position for about five days and nights.

It was my exhausted father who lifted her into his arms and carried her into our hut. Later I saw my father do something I'd never seen him do before. He cooked a lamb stew to which he added his share of the spoils of war, which was a handful of rice. As he poured the rice slowly from his hand, he said to me, "As you eat this rice, remember those who gave their lives for it." He waited with me in silence until the stew was ready. He ladled some into two small bowls, handing me one of them and carrying the second to my mother.

He had left behind the bag in which he had carried the rice. The soft leather bag was maroon, its seams piped with velvet of the same color. The bag was closed by two buckles of solid gold. I lifted the bag and found that it still contained things that seemed heavy to me. I put the bag back where my father had left it. Later by firelight he dumped its contents onto the ground before us.

The first item to catch my eye was a highly polished silver dagger that had a handle of gold in the form of two intertwined serpents (later in life I learned that the intertwined serpents were the emblem of the Maldecian krates). Attached by silver chains to the dagger's scabbard were a number of small silver boxes. My father opened one of the boxes and stared at its contents for a moment before he quickly snapped it shut. He forbade me from ever looking into any of the boxes without his permission. It was some ten years or so later on the planet Mollara that I looked inside those boxes to find the tiny body parts of a human infant. It was obvious that the krate who was once the dagger's owner had used his newly acquired weapon for the first time in some diabolical bloodletting ritual.

My father went to war many times during the months that followed and each time returned to us unharmed. With the coming of winter our men were worn out and had no physical strength to wage war with the Maldecians. This was exactly what the Maldecians hoped would happen. In spring we experienced the devastating effects of several tornadoes, and thereafter a dark sense of foreboding dominated us all. Many of our people formed separate groups and set out in the directions of the four winds to find food.

I recall that during the summer, the first several hundred Waydians (Venusians) were delivered to Petrimmor's Station. The Waydian presence uplifted our spirits. They stood up bravely to our common hardships. They were pleasant little people. Their largest adults reached the height of my outstretched arm. The Waydian children mingled easily with their Martian counterparts and quickly learned our language, whereas we stupidly did very little to learn theirs. They were able to hold their breath for as long as twenty minutes and could swim underwater like fish.

In midwinter a large number of black Nodian spacecraft filled with food and medicine landed at Petrimmor's Station. After they unloaded their cargoes, all but one left the Earth. This craft remained until early spring to act as a deterrent to any possible Maldecian attacks. Nodian aircars patrolled the countryside daily, looking for signs of Maldecian troops. They never found any. We often wondered what they would have done if they had.

It was near the end of the Earth month you call May when our zone-rex, Rancer-Carr, arrived at Petrimmor's Station. I remembered him from the time that he came to us on Mars and told us we had to go to Earth to survive. This time he told us that we must leave Earth and once again travel through space to a very distant world. He told us that the world we would go to was very much like Mars and that he had been there recently. He assured us that we would like living on the world he called Mollara.

When the spacecraft of the zone-rex left Petrimmor's Station, my entire family was onboard. Among us were also several Nodian espers who mentally scanned the Earth beneath us for a sign of those of our race who had left Petrimmor's Station before the zone-rex arrived. Several very large Martian encampments were found in what you now call South America. The zone-rex decided that the Martians who lived in these camps would not go to Mollara with the first departure but would wait at least another year on the Earth, thus giving the Nodians more time to assemble another fleet of spacecraft. This second fleet never materialized.

Some of the roaming groups were found and given enough provisions to return to the station. After our search was complete, we retraced our flight path and picked up the sick or injured from the slow-moving groups and flew them back to our encampment.

The Second Evacuation

Within the next two months, Nodian spacecraft of every size and model began to land at Petrimmor's Station. Some of these vehicles would act as shuttles to carry us to larger spaceships waiting in orbits circling the Sumer (Saturn) radiar. Those smaller ships that were equipped with interstellar propulsion systems would join the larger ones and form a fleet before departing for Mollara. While this operation was under way shiploads of Martian animals that had never been on the Earth joined the fleet. All Martian animals of any type were left behind for the Sumerians living on Earth to either remove later or humanely destroy at their discretion.

When the Nodian spacecraft left the solar system they were filled to capacity with nearly one million surviving Martians out of about 29 million living on Mars before the destruction of Maldec. Another 1.4 million were left behind on the Earth because there were not enough Nodian spaceships to transport them to Mollara. Not openly mentioned was the fact that the sudden environmental impact of more than a million Martians joining the native population of Mollara would have been very detrimental to the planet. I found out much later in that lifetime that the Nodians could also have transported probably a fifth of those left behind, but decided to give those of us who actually went to Mollara a better chance.

The Nodians were, in their minds, being practical. At that time they were planning to invade the Earth and subdue the Maldecians. They saw 1.4 million Martians as ground-based allies. They secretly began to organize and arm those Martians (as they did with the Trakians and Sumerians then living on the Earth) into military groups led by Nodians such as Abdonel the Coate-Grol (meaning "the sun cat" in the Martian language). These groups were also assigned Trakian telepaths who kept them periodically in communication with Nodia.

Adventures on the Way to Mollara

It took about nine Earth months to travel from Earth to Mollara, and once again we went through the process of converting from breathing one type of atmosphere to another. The air of Mollara was exactly the same as that of our home planet Mars. We humans experienced no ill effects, but less than 50 percent of our animals that had lived on Earth survived the reconversion. Fortunately, thousands of sheep and other native Martian animals brought directly from our dying world did not need to risk the biological problems experienced by those animals subjected to air changes

(Mars to Earth or Earth to Mollara). When these animals were set free from the spacecraft that brought them to Mollara, they made themselves at home by gorging themselves on the new planet's miles of lush blue-green grass. The months spent getting from Earth to Mollara were filled with adventure. Many times the fleet came to a complete standstill because one or more of the spacecraft broke down. These breakdowns usually occurred during an attempt to accelerate to the light speed necessary to propel a craft instantly from one solar system to another. A damaged craft and its crew were often left behind after a fully functioning craft was sent back for its cargo of Martians or their animals. The spaceships that carried the animals were older and more prone to breakdowns. By the time we reached Mollara we were living with our animals and constantly stepping around them and their droppings. I, of course, was on the patrol that picked up buckets of animal waste and delivered it to a Nodian named Recrothis, who seemed overjoyed with my presents. He placed the stuff in a machine that broke it down into its basic molecules. The machine's output was packaged in different-colored wrappers and stacked like bricks. By the time we reached our destination only a narrow path between ceiling-high stacks of bricks led to and from Recrothis and his fascinating machine.

On several occasions our fleet was visited by spaceships belonging to civilizations living on planets of solar systems we had to pass through. Most of these encounters were friendly. The size of our fleet in some cases discouraged any of these people from giving us trouble. In two separate incidents we were intercepted by large fleets of spacecraft native to the solar system we had entered. In both cases the locals had more spacecraft than we did. We were left to continue on our way after the Nodians sent emissaries to the key planets of that solar system. The Nodians were silver-tongued devils. I often wondered what toll they paid or promises they made that convinced those menacing visitors not to do us harm. (The rumor is that they showed them a picture of Sharmarie.)

During our passage we were entertained by landscapes of Mollara and pictures of the world's natives. The Mollarans had features and skin color exactly like ours. The most remarkable difference between us was our height. Whereas our men ranged to above eight Earth feet, their men were considered tall if they were three and a half Earth feet in height. *[Jonathan Swift, who wrote* Gulliver's Travels, *mentioned that Mars had two moons. He wrote about these two moons many years before they were actually discovered from the Earth. Is it possible that Swift was recalling events of a previous lifetime? The Martians' and the Mollarans' differing heights does bring to mind the story of Gulliver and the Lilliputians. —W.H.B.]*

Mollara was actually 1.8 times larger than Mars and had a native population of about nine million people. They loved us, as we did them, and still do in the present.

Settling on Mollara

On arrival our people were divided into groups that were settled in five towns. Each town was separated by equal distances. When we arrived, those towns were about 80 percent completed by Martians who had preceded us by about two Earth years. A Mollaran day is about 18 minutes longer than a present Earth day, and its year is about three Earth days longer than an Earth year. Like Earth, Mollara has four seasons.

I estimate that I was a little more than 13.5 Earth years old when I arrived on Mollara. My father, mother and I first lived in the town of Acmiss (a Mollaran name meaning "on an incline"). The slightest slant of a hillside was considered steep by the tiny Mollarans. Over the years that followed, the Nodians provided us with many forms of technology. Their mental rom method of teaching was embraced and greatly appreciated. They provided us initially with all the information they could about our home planet Mars and its history. The Nodians never attempted to force their ways upon us. They provided anything we wanted to know about them or other off-world civilizations, but only upon requests made to them through our governing councils.

Farming large areas of land and fishing in the planet's saltwater seas became the first new occupations for us Martians. Later our industries grew to match those of any sophisticated off-world culture. We built aircars and eventually spacecraft of Nodian design. We were able to share our advanced technologies with the Mollarans and the eight other human cultures of our adopted solar system. (Mollarans call their sun Task. The Nodians call it Cordovan.)

Near the age of fifteen Earth years I became the first and only wife (as was my mother to my father) to a man of my race known as Toltarreg. He was about nine years older and was an official in the high court of the zone-rex. His job was to interact with the five governing councils on behalf of the zone-rex, especially in matters that pertained to agriculture. One of the conditions the Mollarans insisted on prior to our coming was that our population would always remain at half the size or less than theirs. When I married, our people had refrained from having children in order to comply with the agreement. Our race was then (and still is) polygamous, and birth control was no easy matter. It got to the point that news of two more Mollaran births became very important to us. Even so, those of us who wanted to have children had to ask permission of the local council. Eventually the kind-hearted Mollarans changed their conditions, first to allow our population to be equal to three-fourths of their numbers, then eventually to 100 percent. Today the Martian population on Mollara is about 258 million and the Mollarans number some 417 million.

I have been informed that the Earth presently hosts 62 percent of all living Martians, 92 percent of all living Maldecians, 100 percent of all living Reltians (Jupiterians), 37 percent of all living Trakians (Neptunians), 84 percent of all living Sumerians (Saturnians) and 77 percent of all living Waydians (Venusians). The Earth also hosts persons who psychically stem from thousands of off-world races, but their individual numbers are very low compared to Earth's overall population.

When I was sixteen years of age I gave birth to a son that I named Tremmet. This made my son a cot, the name given to Martians born on Mollara. It was just before his birth that we learned of the catastrophes that had befallen the Earth and all who lived there. We had no idea at the time what the Frequency Barrier was that developed on the Earth. It was also about that time that another 150,000 Martians arrived on Mollara. These latecomers had left the Earth with us, but had become stranded along the way due to spacecraft breakdowns. These people were found by the Gracians and transported to Mollara along with their descendants. The descendants were multiple breeds, composed of Martians, Nodians, Vitronians, Trakians and various mixtures of races who had hosted them on their worlds until the Gracians found them.

The Five-Star Mini Galaxy near the Milky Way

The sun of Mollara was one of five stars that could be accepted as members of the Milky Way galaxy, but because these stars are located some distance from the edge of the galaxy and move opposite to the galactic spiral motion, they are not recognized by some authorities as part of the larger galactic formation. These same authorities say that the five-star system is a mini galaxy in its own right. The rotational speed of the system relative to the Milky Way's opposite rotational speed is such that the two celestial systems constantly maintain the same distance and location relative to each other.

Four of these stars each have nine planets and the fifth star, named Bantivail, has twelve. The solar system of Bantivail was a mysterious place. Its only human inhabitants were a variety of different races who lived on its twelfth planet and maintained a small military outpost for the Federation. The surfaces of the other eleven planets were waterless deserts devoid of all forms of life. On all these barren worlds were found the ruins of long-abandoned cities. On the third planet of the system, obviously at one time the most populated, was a cluster of gigantic man-made pyramids. When the Gracians began to visit the five-star system regularly, they identified the builders of these pyramids as their ancient teachers, people who once lived on the planetoids of the Hamp radiar (Uranus). The question of what happened to the missing Bantivailians was not to be answered until many thousand years later.

The Astrastone Lode on Bantivail 3, Protected by the Federation

The third planet of Bantivail also became of major importance to the Federation when a new type of crystallized carbon was found there. This crystal, called astrastone, has no known rival in the mineral kingdom when it comes to hardness. A piece of it can be reduced in size or faceted only by a concentrated focus of pure psychic energy. A jewel created in this manner is brilliant and very beautiful.

It was quickly realized that the astrastone capstone that the Maldecians provided the Gracians to place on top of the Great Pyramid on Earth had been somehow acquired from Bantivail 3. The Gracians, during their association with the Maldecians, had not known about the existence of the five-star system and played no part in shaping the capstone. These facts, added to the fact that the Maldecians originally had not developed any form of space-traveling vehicle, and the question of who provided the tremendous amount of psychic energy to cut the stone so precisely in the required shape for the pyramid capstone also adds to the mystery.

The discovery of the rare astrastone attracted prospectors and every other type of adventurer who had the means to travel through space and make it to Bantivail 3. The Federation outpost on Bantivail 12 was constantly sending spacecraft to intercept the waves of freebooters who attempted to penetrate the system. Many of these rogues fought each other to the death for the sake of obtaining this precious stone. Others lost their lives when they ignored warnings not to enter the system and engaged the Federation in battle, only to have their spaceships blasted into oblivion. Any who reached Bantivail 3 and later left the system were allowed to go peacefully on their way, no matter how much astrastone they carried with them. It was believed that anyone who could get to Bantivail 3, land there and live long enough to leave the place, had to be favored by the elohim.

These times have been memorialized by the poem whose first stanza in English is as follows:

"The Bantivails are red and gold, but they have no souls, so I've been told. And yet a man would go along just to dress his love in an astrastone. If this stone he did find and did not leave his soul behind, then to her he can sing this rhyme, and his love will last until the end of time."

As I presently recall this ancient rhyme, I am fingering a faceted piece of astrastone about half the size of a grain of rice, which now hangs from a chain of natural Martian copper around my neck. This wonderful possession was presented to me by my husband and son.

The Tar Spikes

Many of the freebooters, crippled by fights among themselves or the Federation, were forced to land on Mollara or on another of the thirty-five inhabited worlds of the five-star system. The largest group of off-worlders who sought sanctuary on Mollara after attempting to visit Bantivail 3 are now called the Tar Spikes (roughly translated to English from the Nodian meaning of black fingernails). Both the males and females of their race have shaven heads and are covered with tattoos. They could be compared pretty much in appearance and manners to members of biker gangs on the Earth, only these bikers have IQ levels that would challenge that of a Federation Lord of Devisement. The Tar Spikes were highly intelligent, but we still thank the elohim that in those early times they didn't know they were.

We were amazed to learn that the Tar Spikes were visitors from a distant galaxy named the Big Circle, a place later visited by Federation explorers. This galaxy is about eight times larger than our own Milky Way galaxy. The Federation learned a great deal from these intergalactic travelers. The Tar Spikes' greatest contribution to the Federation was their version of an intergalactic propulsion system. This system was about five percent of the size of the intergalactic propulsion system then used by the Federation and trading houses. This Tar Spike system allowed smaller spacecraft to travel between galaxies.

The Tar Spikes were and still are scavengers and junk dealers. There is no piece of equipment they can't identify or repair. They have the ability to locate any derelict spacecraft and strip it as vultures would a carcass. Though these characters were hard to get along with, they were good to know. We of the five-star system as well as the many worlds of the Federation became their willing customers.

The Riff Barrier between Matter and Antimatter and Its Tunnels

It was from the Tar Spikes and a group with which they had a fond relationship, called the Driznafalians, that we learned about the cultures living within the Big Circle and about the barrier of energy called the Riff that separated the positive-matter universe from its counterpart, the negative-matter universe.

The Driznafalians were known to stretch the truth a bit, but if a Tar Spike said that something was so, you could accept his or her word without a doubt. The Tar Spikes volunteered to travel to our home world of Mars and survey its condition. With their crafts they could have made a round trip from Mollara to Mars in about twelve days. The Nodians talked them out of traveling to our home world.

The next offer the Tar Spikes made us was to take a group of our people with them on a trip to the Riff. This offer was accepted. When our people returned to Mollara, they related what they saw and also brought us mental roms they had made. I experienced the contents of these roms, as did many of my friends. The sights of the Riff were the subject of our conversation for many years thereafter.

The Riff looked like a veil composed of woven ribbons of flowing gold. Within the fabric of the veil of energy were pulses of lightning of every color that exists in the visible spectrum. The Riff extended in every direction as far as the eye could see. It gave me the impression that our universe is within the golden shell of a cosmic egg. From time to time the Riff was indented. These indentations were like tunnels that allowed a spacecraft to penetrate into the Riff's energy field for millions of miles. These tunnels were filled with the junk and lost treasures of our universe.

What fascinated me and many others of my acquaintance were the numerous ancient spaceships that had gravitated into these tunnels, where they resided for millions of years. I wish there were the time and space to tell you about all the strange and wonderful contents of the Riff tunnels. I will describe the contents of a mental rom I recall that pertained to the boarding of a gigantic mothership of some unknown culture estimated at the time to have been more than 400,000 years old.

The Ancient and Mysterious Giant Mothership

This vessel had been entered many times before by armies of Tar Spikes who were progressively and methodically stripping the ancient queen of anything of worth. Even so, there was much of interest and beauty left to see on her decks and in her lush apartments. Before I describe the contents of that exciting mental rom, I must tell you that when this ancient vessel came up in conversation, everyone presented their own versions of how this great human achievement was produced and how it met its fate. In truth, even today no one knows who built that great mothership or, for that matter, the thousands of others (obviously the products of different ancient races) that are similar and have been found in the tunnels of the Riff during the eons that followed.

One thing we know for sure is that hundreds of thousands of years before the Nodians began to travel between galaxies there existed races that had made the same technological achievement. The question remains, what happened to these people? If they still exist, where are they? I believe that these ancient races were once intimate with those people of the planetoids of the Hamp radiar (Uranus). I don't actually know this to be true, but some part of me that existed long before my first lifetime believes that this is so. I feel that it is a time forgotten or divinely erased from our eternal consciousness, a time that will be remembered a cosmic moment before we individually become one with the creator of all that is.

(I have been advised by Sharmarie, who monitors our conversation by thought, not to get carried away by including too many details in my description of that ancient mothership. As you might say, "Oh, shucks.")

When experiencing the contents of the mental rom that pertains to the ancient mothership I mentioned earlier, one begins the experience in total darkness. The sound of a Tar Spike voice requesting light is heard. Several bright globes of light are activated and rolled down a corridor. The senses are immediately overwhelmed by what is illuminated. The walls of the broad passageway are covered with murals that depict animals that no one even today can identify. On the horizon of the painted landscapes could be seen buildings, some of which were in the shape of pyramids.

Nowhere within the ship could be found any human remains or the painted or recorded images of any human. Only the surviving furniture—chairs, tables and beds—served to indicate that those who used them were humans of average open-state size. No evidence was found that could tell us what these ancients ate or if in fact they consumed any three-dimensional types of food at all. No form of organic matter or human fingerprints (other than those of the Tar Spikes) were to be found.

A number of building and landscaping tools were found, but there was nothing that could have been classified as a weapon. The youngest derelict ships (much smaller in size) in the Riff that were thought to have been built by the same ancient culture were also absent of any form of weaponry. This wonderful spacecraft had several decks, upon which once rested its "litter" of thousands of smaller spacecraft. None of these vehicles were to be found. It was like finding an abandoned ocean liner with all its lifeboats gone.

Other ships of younger ancient cultures found in the Riff did contain smaller armed spacecraft on their litter decks. The propulsion systems of these craft proved inferior to the systems used by the most advanced cultures of the time.

The propulsion system of the great mothership was totally dead. The containment tubes that once radiated one of the key forces of gravity (weak nuclear force) into subtle magnetic fields that could be regulated were clogged with clumps of metal slag consisting mostly of the element thallium and to a lesser degree the elements lead and mercury. (At the present time the Federation employs spacecraft propulsion systems that use plasmas created from the element thallium.[2])

The prevailing theory is that this ancient vehicle was not originally built in the positive-matter universe in which we presently live, but in the negative-matter universe. The people who built the craft attempted for some unknown reason to leave their universe and pass through the Riff to enter our universe. During the course of this attempt they abandoned their mothership to escape some unexpected danger. Even though they themselves did not make it through the Riff's energy barrier, their mothership did after its structure and contents somehow converted from antimatter to matter. The presence of younger craft of the same culture found in the numerous Riff tunnels tells us that they attempted to come through the Riff many times, but failed. [Sharmarie adds, "There is something to the statement, If at first you don't succeed, try, try and try again."]

The Danzar Gate

Within the past twenty-five Earth years, using a propulsion system that employs the energy of the Riff barrier itself, the Federation has sent expeditions through a thin part of the Riff that is now called the Danzar Gate. These expeditions returned unharmed. Their findings have not been made general knowledge. Lack of permission by way of lights of divine direction have prevented the Federation from visiting the antimatter universe ever since.

It is said that only one craft exists that can pass through the Riff. Where this craft is based in the universe is considered the greatest of Federation secrets. A first-class spacecraft can travel from the Sumer radiar (Saturn) to the Danzar Gate in about 80 hours. The solar system closest to the Danzar Gate is protected and administered jointly by the Federation and the Nodian Trading House of Isotrex.

I lived nearly 110 Earth years during that first lifetime. My father died about twenty years before me and my mother about one year. My husband Toltarreg lived some six years longer than I. During that lifetime my son Tremmet provided me with four grandchildren, who in turn elevated me to the title of great-great-grandmother. My mother's death occurred after she lost her mental focus on reality. One day she sat in the front of our house

2. Matter can exist in four different states: solid, liquid, gas and plasma. Plasma is produced when an element is heated to about 100,000°F or more. The largest percentage of matter that exists in the entire universe is in the plasma state.

and refused to eat, but promised me that she would eat just as soon as I returned home from warring with the Maldecians.

My first lifetime, which took me from Mars to Earth and then on to Mollara, comes to mind more than any other happier lifetimes I have experienced since. That first lifetime ended when my heart stopped during my sleep. The last thing I remember was dreaming that I was once again a child playing with other children on the bank of a Martian waterway. In my dream I heard my mother's voice call my name. As I parted the tall grass with my hands, I saw her standing before me smiling. She lifted me in her arms and said, "We must hurry on, Ombota. Your father has come home to us."

May you in the future meet only with those from friendly stars. I am Ombota of Mars.

A   p   p   e   n   d   i   x   A

The Great SETI Con Game

Oh, what an evil Web site we weave when first we practice to deceive!

What if you received nine radio messages from an intelligent extraterrestrial source and could not figure out what the messages said? Answer: Post the messages on the Internet as a game, thus tapping the intellect of thousands of people for any possible translation or clue that might permit you and you alone to understand what the messages said. (As you will see from reading the messages on SETI's Web page at the end of this article, they do not reveal the frequencies of the tones in the message, merely symbolizing them with alphabetic characters and keyboard symbols.)

This is exactly what the organization known as SETI [Search for Extraterrestrial Intelligence] has done. One thing that the person or persons who devised the scheme did not take into consideration was this: Anyone who had the ability to actually translate the messages would also have the ability to see through their deception. Maybe the organization might want to change its name to the Search for Egotistical Terrestrial Idiots. They wouldn't have to look any further than their own organization.

I can tell you truthfully that the nine messages are from an extraterrestrial intelligence and are intended for *all* the people on the Earth and not for a self-important few who have access to the radio telescope that received them. SETI has definitely underestimated the extraterrestrials, who have been preparing for twenty-two years to send the messages in the form of radio waves (a method that is to them crude). That is, the extraterrestrials have made sure that the means to translate the messages already exists on the Earth.

This preparation was in the form of over twenty-two years of telepathic communication to several people on Earth to whom they gave information that would later provide the means to translate these messages. That information is the Ra system of mathematics, the same system used in the design of the Great Pyramid of Giza as well as other ancient buildings on both the Earth and Mars—and more recently in the designs of the crop glyphs, or crop circles, that have mysteriously been impressed in English grain fields.

The question of why the extraterrestrials would resort to sending nine coded messages to Earth by way of radio is easily answered. The time has

Ra Table of Nines

(1)	0.027	(10)	0.270	(19)	0.513	(28)	0.756
(2)	0.054	(11)	0.297	(20)	0.540	(29)	0.783
(3)	0.081	(12)	0.324	(21)	0.567	(30)	0.810
(4)	0.108	(13)	0.351	(22)	0.594	(31)	0.837
(5)	0.135	(14)	0.378	(23)	0.621	(32)	0.864
(6)	0.162	(15)	0.405	(24)	0.648	(33)	0.891
(7)	0.189	(16)	0.432	(25)	0.675	(34)	0.918
(8)	0.216	(17)	0.459	(26)	0.702	(35)	0.945
(9)	0.243	(18)	0.486	(27)	0.729	(36)	0.972
				(37)	0.999		

come to validate their Earth contacts and the Ra system of mathematics. They want the people of the Earth to open their ears and minds to what these human contacts have to say about many subjects that the extraterrestrials have schooled them in.

An extraterrestrial message that validates my twenty-two years of Ra mathematical research also validates the fact that I have truly been in personal contact with those extraterrestrials who sent the messages. Furthermore, the fact that I (and now others) can translate those messages should strongly indicate to the reader that the extraterrestrial accounts of Earth's ancient history in Part One and the book *Knowledge from the Stars* are true and not figments of a fertile imagination.

I have rarely spoken out about the secret government and Majestic 12 in the hope that if I left them alone they would leave me alone and I could get my work done. I had no wish to discover a venomous snake in my bathtub (as I had once) or sit beside my deathly ill daughter in an intensive-care unit for six months as she fought to hang onto life—because she had been poisoned by an undetectable substance. I assure you, these people play a deadly game.

The lie that the nine messages SETI received are not authentic messages from intelligent extraterrestrials is another attempt to keep the public in the dark about what is really going on. As for me, enough is enough!

If you should hear stories that I am a drug dealer, child molester or that I died after being struck by lightning, don't you believe it. These are usually the methods Majestic 12 employs to discredit or silence those who might provide even the slightest evidence that supports the truth that extraterrestrials do exist and have been visiting the Earth since prehistoric times. Two of Majestic 12's purposes for keeping this secret are, first, to protect the global economy and, second, to protect the powerful religious institutions. After all, money and religion are the bases of their power and control.

Before I unravel the SETI con game, I do want to thank them for delivering my extraterrestrial e-mail. And, incidentally, by the time they read this article (and I'm sure they will) this information will have been e-mailed to thousands of people located in just about every country on Earth. (I wonder what in hell they are going to do about *that!*)

The SETI Messages

SETI set the stage for their "imaginary" extraterrestrial messages by stating that no messages have *really* been received from Tau Ceti (a real star located about 12 light-years from Earth) but that decoding these messages "will show us how far we have to go before we will be able to understand any *real* messages we receive." I will do my very best to prove to anyone who cares that the messages are authentic.

The first two extraterrestrial messages received by SETI will be shown later. I have added hyphens to separate the first nine sequences to help show that the G symbols are obviously brackets that separate the units of information. Notice that the messages all begin and end with the symbol G. (This is so obvious that SETI also recognized it.) It will become evident later that the G represents the seventh number in the Ra Table of Nines, or 0.189. The number 7 in the case of the messages has a relationship to the seven periods of the Periodic Table of Elements (electron shells K to Q).

I am going to deal only with the first two extraterrestrial messages, because that is all I need to prove my point. I will hereafter use SETI's own description of all nine messages to make several important statements.

SETI: "The message is being broadcast on a wavelength of 21 cm, the so-called magic frequency."

The wavelength mentioned above has the related frequency of 1,420,405,752.7 cycles per standard second of time, *which is the well-known hydrogen resonance frequency.* This frequency has long been considered the most likely frequency any extraterrestrial culture would use to communicate to any other culture living elsewhere in the universe.

The extraterrestrials knew that SETI's radiotelescopes would be tuned to this frequency. To add weight to their messages, the extraterrestrials added unmistakable data about the hydrogen atom that could not be missed by any knowledgeable person who translated the messages.

In the Ra system the frequency of the so-called "magic wavelength" is simply the square root of 2 times 1 billion cycles per *natural second of time*[1]. Expressed in five of the seven Ra formats, this frequency reads, in natural seconds of time: 1.40625 (omega major units), $1.41371\overline{666}^2$ (red units),

---

1. The unit of time nature uses, based on the speed of light. The natural second is slightly longer than the human-devised one (300,000 vs. 299,792.8 km/sec ± 1.1 meter). The Ra system is based on

1.414213562 (green units), 1.4147106633 (blue units) and 1.4$\overline{222}$ (omega minor units).

The Ra system of mathematics has several unique features, such as *repitans*, which are fractions of the number 27 (1 ÷ 27 = 0. $\overline{037}$, 2 ÷ 27 = 0. $\overline{074}$, and 3 ÷ 27 = 0. $\overline{111}$ and so on), as well as plus and minus sequences such as: 1 ÷ 0.81 = 1.$\overline{234567m901}$ (a plus sequence) and 1 ÷ 0.81 x 8 = 9. $\overline{8765432m09}$ (a minus sequence).[3] Notice that the numbers 8 and 1, respectively, are missing (*m*) from these two Ra sequences.

An important number relating to the hydrogen atom is known as the *fine structure constant*. The Ra value for this constant is 0.001371742112 when identified by the following procedures: 1 ÷ 27 = 0. $\overline{037}$, which, when squared, is 0.001371742112, or 1 ÷ 729 (27 x 27) = 0.001371742112.

All 27 Ra repitans and all Ra plus and minus sequences are multiples of the value for the fine structure constant for hydrogen as per the following examples: 0. $\overline{037}$ ÷ 0.001371742112 = 27; 1.23457*m*901 ÷ 0.001371742112 = 900; or 9.8765432*m*08 ÷ 0.001371742112 = 7200.

When the Ra value for the fine structure constant is multiplied by 8, we arrive at the value of 0.01097393690, which is the Ra value for the Rydberg constant. (The Rydberg constant is used in simple equations to determine the wavelength of the spectral lines emitted by hydrogen, from the infrared to the ultraviolet.)

Knowledge of the Ra Table of Nines and five of the seven Ra formats is also required for translating the extraterrestrial messages. The Ra Table of Nines consists of 37 numbers starting with 27 and ending with 999—that is, 27, 54, 81, 108, 135, 162 and 189, continuing to 999 (I am omitting the decimal points for simplicity). Notice that when these numbers are added horizontally, they always total 9. (The number 9 is the key number in the Ra system of mathematics, and the extraterrestrials make this point by transmitting exactly nine messages.)

Now that you have a basic understanding of the 27 Ra repitans, the 37 numbers in the Ra Table of Nines and the Ra values for the fine-structure and Rydberg constants for hydrogen, it is time to look at the first two extraterrestrial messages. (Remember that I have added hyphens between the first ten units of the first message just to show how the G's function to

---

expressions, and its seven formats are derived from the seven periods in the periodic table of elements, which recognizes the seven electron orbits. When electrons jump from one orbit to another, the atom itself is changed. Each orbit has a specific natural function (for example, one is related to human brain activity). The two formats not dealt with here are called *irrational red* and *irrational blue*.

2. A line above a three-number or longer sequence indicates that the sequence is repeated to infinity, a "repitan."

3. Those wishing to check the calculations from a computer keyboard will use the slash (/) instead of the usual division (÷) symbol.

divide them.)

The original message consisted of 571 characters, a long pause of 17.71 seconds, then a repeat of the sequence. The characters are here arranged by pitch. There were 19 unique tones in the original message, here labeled A through S. A is the lowest tone and S is the highest. Each tone lasts about 0.492 seconds. The entire sequence, including pause, took 298.61 seconds, or about 4 minutes and 59 seconds.[4]

Original Message—30 January 95

```
GBG-GBBG-GBBBG-GBBBBG-GBBBBBG-GBBBBBBG-GBHBBHBG-
GBBHBBBHBG-GBHBBBHBBG-GBHBHGGHBHBGGBB
HBBBBHBBGGBBIBIBGGBIBIBBGGBBJKBKJBGGBJKBKJBBGGBBBBJKBB
BKJBGGBBBBIBBBIBGGBLBLBGGBBLBBBBBBLBBBGGBLBBLBBGGBBBBB
BMBBMBBBGGBBMBBBMBBBBBBGGBBBBBMBBMBBGGBBMBBMBBBBGGB
BBBBBNOBBONBBBGGOBBOLOBBBBOLOBBOGGBPBPBGGBBPBBPBBGGBB
BPBBBPBBBGGPQAQPGGBPQBQPBGGBBPQCQPBBGBBBPQDQPBBBGGBB
BBPQEQPBBBBBGGBBBBBPQFQPBBBBBGGBBBBBBPQBABQPBBBBBBGGBB
BBBBBPQBBBQPBBBBBBBGGBBBBBBBBBPQBCBQPBBBBBBBBGGBBBBBB
BBBPQBDBQPBBBBBBBBBGGBBBBBBBBBBBBBPQCACQPBBBBBBBBBBBB
GQBQHQDQHQCQGGRQBQHQQHQBQRGGSQBQHQDQHQBQSGGRQQIQBQIQB
QRGGSQCQIQCQIQBQSG
```

Now let's begin with the first message, which consisted of 19 separate tones that were assigned capital letters (A to S) as a means of identification. These 19 tones actually represent the first 18 numbers in the Ra Table of Nines and zero (27 to 486 plus 0): A = 27, B = 54, C = 81, D = 108, E = 135, F = 162 , G = 189 and H = 216 and so on. This is confirmed by SETI's description of the second extraterrestrial message.

In the second message, there are 18 new characters, for a total of 37 characters used so far. The new characters are represented by the letters T through Z and a through k. T is higher in pitch than S and so on. This message is 874 characters long. Again, each tone takes 0.492 seconds, and the pause is 17.71 seconds between repetitions. The message length is 447.67 seconds, or 7 minutes and 28 seconds.

Second Message—2 February 95

```
GQCQTQBQTQDQGGQDQTKQBQKTQCQGGQDQTQBQTQEQGGQEQTKQBQKTQ
DQGGQEQUQBQUQDQGGQDQUKQBQKUQEQGGQDQUQBQUQCQGGQCQUKQBQ
KUQDQGGVQBQHXHQBQVGGWXPQCQPXWGGVXHQDQHQBQVGGWXPQCQP
XWGGVQBQHQBQHXVGGWXPQAQPXWGGXPYPZPaPbPcPbPaPZPYPXGGQ
BABQNOQBABQONQBQGGOQBABQOPdBdPOQBABQOGGQCQLdCdLOQBABQ
```

4. The bolded paragraphs are from the SETI Web site, www:ibiblio.org/lunar/alien.html.

OGGOQDQOPdCdPOQDQOGGOQBAAABQOPdBABdPOQBAAABQOGGQBQHQ
BdBABdBQHOQBAAABQOGGOQBABQOHdBBBdHOQBAAABQOGGQCQeQCQ
eQBQGGQBQeOQCQOeQCQGGQBABQeQCQeQDQGGQDQeOQCQOeQBABQGG
QCQfOQCQOfQBQGGQBQfQCQfQCQGGQBABQfOQCQOfQDQGGQDQfQCQfQB
ABQGGRiRiRGGRiSiSGGSiSiRGGSiSiSGGRjRjRGGRjRjSGGSjRjRGGSjSjS
GGKRKPSPKRKGGKSKPRPKSKGGQAQhgBDADBgjgEDADEghQAQGGdDdhg
BAAABgjgFAAAFghdDdGGdBCABBFBBACBdhgDADgjgFDADFghdBCABBF
BBACBdGGQBQhgAgjgBAAAAABghQBQGGRgAgPgBAAAAABgPgAgRGG
SgDADgPgFDADFgPgDADgSGGKQBQKhgDAAADghKQBQKGGKdBCABBFB
BACBKhgCDADCgjgDDADDghKdBCABBFBBACBdKGGKdDdKhgCAAACggE
AAAEghKdDdKGGQBQkgBDADBgkQBQGGKQBQKkgEDADEgkKQBQKGGQAQ
kgAgjgDAAADgkQAQG

   In the first message the zero value is symbolized by S, or 513 (27 x 19). When 18 additional symbols are introduced in the second message, the symbols then total 37, the exact count of numbers in the Ra Table of Nines. The S is then replaced by the 37th and last number in the Table of Nines (0.999), which will represent zero in the second message. When the 82nd symbol is introduced, it will represent zero and will continue to do so in every extraterrestrial message yet to come. Knowing what numerical values to assign the first 37 tones is the first key to translating messages.

   Now let's turn our attention to what SETI says are fictitious extraterrestrial time units. It is implied that the game maker invented these units as part of the game. Really? The Ra value for the duration of each tone is 0.492075 natural seconds, and the Ra value for the duration of the pause between a repeat of any of the extraterrestrial messages is 17.7147 natural seconds. When the *pause* of 17.7147 natural seconds is divided by the *duration* of 0.492075 natural seconds, the result is exactly 36 (4 x 9).

   These time units prove that the nine SETI messages did indeed originate from an intelligent extraterrestrial source. Take my word for it, the odds are astronomical that anyone could come up with such a fictitious time unit that would be in perfect mathematical harmony with the Ra system of mathematics.

   I really don't have to go beyond this first calculation to prove that the SETI messages are not fictitious, but let's go on.

   Starting with the first section of the original message (GBG, or 54) we have 54 ÷ 0.492075 (duration of the tones) = 109.739369 (changing only the decimal placement, which is also the value of the Rydberg constant.) In addition, if this result (quotient) is divided by 0.001371742112 (fine-structure constant for hydrogen, *fsc*) the result is 80 thousand. (If you think this is a coincidence, I advise you to apply to SETI for membership.)

   What a way to start things off! The extraterrestrials are transmitting on the hydrogen resonance frequency, so why not say something right up front about a number that can be used in simple equations to determine the wavelengths of all of hydrogen's spectral lines?

The second sequence of the first message reads: GBBG, or 108 (known later as tone D); 108 ÷ 0.492075 (Ra duration of tones) = 219.478,738 ÷ 0.001371742112 [fsc] = 160 thousand units.

The third to sixth sequences in the first message are, respectively GBBBG (162, identified later as tone F, or 6), GBBBBG (216, identified later as tone H, or 8), GBBBBBG (270, identified later as tone I, or 10), GBBBBBBG (324, identified later as tone J, or 12).

Notice that when the values of the above sequences are divided respectively by SETI's time unit (0.492075 Ra natural seconds) and the results of those divisions are divided again by the value of the fine structure constant for hydrogen, the final results are simply 240, 320, 400 and 440! This fictitious alien time unit, which I will call *fat* [0.492075], times the *fsc* (0.001371742112) [or *fat* x *fsc*] = 0.000675 (25 x 27). I will use the product of *fat* x *fsc* (675) without the decimal and zeros to avoid having to repeat the same string of numbers.

One might well ask, how do we handle these symbols/numbers? That is, how do we know when to add, subtract, multiply or divide them? First of all, it's neither time-consuming nor difficult to add, subtract or divide the numbers of any sequence between the G brackets. Those familiar with the Ra system of mathematics might, by using one or more types of mathematical procedures, isolate recognizable Ra values. After all, why include three more tones to represent addition, subtraction or division, perhaps confusing the total tone-value picture? For instance, because there are only B's in sections one to six leaves one no option but to add the values of the B's.

As the messages are translated, a pattern might emerge that reveals exactly what type of mathematical procedure is to be employed to extract every bit of data from a particular sequence.

The extraterrestrials knew it would require someone with a strong knowledge of the Ra system to translate their messages. They also knew that anyone who could translate their messages would be spiritually committed to sharing it with anyone and everyone on Earth.

In section seven (GBHBBHBG) of the first message, the tone H (216) is introduced. I have here applied only simple addition to the sequence. Thus we have 54 + 216 + 54 + 54 + 216 + 54 = 648. Dividing 648 by 0.000675 (*fat* x *fsc*), we simply get 960 thousand units. One might also look at the seventh sequence in this way: 216 ÷ 54 = 4 (result one) and 216 x 108 (54 + 54) = 23,328 (result two). Result two divided by result one = 5832 (result three) x 54 = 314,928 (result four). If we divide result four by SETI's *fat* (Ra 0.492075), the result is exactly 640 thousand time units.

(Result three [5832] is a very important number because there are 583,200 square green ra feet in the base areas of both the Great Pyramid of Giza and the Pyramid of the Sun at Teotihuacan, Mexico. The height of the Great Pyramid is also 5832 green ra inches.)

By including Ra pyramid data (familiar to many Ra Society members) in their messages, the extraterrestrials knew that when the messages were translated, it would be obvious that they knew about the Great Pyramid on the Earth and that the structure was built using the Ra system of mathematics. How could an extraterrestrial culture know such things unless they have visited Earth, traversing vast distances in space (don't forget, both coming and going)? According to Earth scientific views, it would take anyone light-years to travel the distance between the stars. Don't you think these views ought to be rethought?

The extraterrestrials also know that unless the Great Pyramid is destroyed, the Ra data embodied in it will always be available for true scholars on Earth to compare with the data they send in their messages. It is evident that by choosing the mathematics embodied in the Great Pyramid as a key to any or all of their messages, the extraterrestrials pass us information about their technology, their abilities and the true history of planet Earth. In other words, the questions raised by these translated messages can be answered only by acknowledging certain astonishing facts—facts that Majestic 12 does not want you to know at this time. Yes, I am certain that Majestic 12 will eventually remove the cloak of secrecy from the existence of extraterrestrials. Why? Soon they will have no other choice, and they know it. Lucky for us, the extraterrestrials are working with their own timetable and not Majestic 12's.

In the eighth sequence we have GBBHBBBHBG. I offer the following as only one of several possible translation procedures: B + B (54 + 54) = 108. H (216) ÷ 108 = 2 (result one). Then B + B + B (54 + 54 + 54) = 162; H (216) ÷ 162 = 1.333 (result two). Multiplying result one by result two, we arrive at 2.$\overline{666}$ (result three). Dividing result three (carried to nine decimal places) by the value of the last tone (B) in that sequence (54), we get 0.049382716. The last but probably not the final result expresses at least two very important Ra numbers: 0.049382716 x 21.6 (the value of H is 216) = 1.0$\overline{666}$, which is the omega minor value for H-bar[5]. The number 0.049382716 x 64 = 3.160493824, which is the omega minor value for pi.

---

5. H-bar is used in quantum physics equations to determine such things as an electron's orbital velocity as well as other dynamic electron activities.

If 0.049382716 is multiplied by 28.8 (32 x 9 = 288), we arrive at 1.4$\overline{222}$, or the omega minor version of the square root of 2. (The square root of 2 x 1 billion cycles is the Ra value for the hydrogen resonance frequency on which the nine extraterrestrial messages were transmitted.)

On the other hand, if we divide result three by 6.75 (*fat* x *fsc*), we obtain the value 0.395061728 (1 ÷ 8 omega minor pi). When 0.395061728 is multiplied by 2, the result is the Ra plus sequence 0.7$\overline{m901234567}$

The Ra values for H-bar are 1.0546875 (omega major), 1.0602874 (red), 1.060660172 (green), 1.061032974 (blue) and 1.0666 (omega minor). The red value for H-bar (1.0602875) was used as a unit of Ra measure (red rams) to lay out the dimensions of the pyramids of the pre-Columbian city of Teotihuacan and the three major pyramids at Giza. This unit of measure has been named the *hunab* after the Aztec god of measure, Hunab Ku, according to Hugh Harleston Jr. in Peter Tompkins' *The Secret of the Mexican Pyramids*.

The average alpha brain wave produced by a meditating human being is 10.602875 cycles per natural second of time. This frequency is the same for the most frequently occurring natural ELF wave generated by lightning. Because of this frequency's unique relationship to the average human alpha brain-wave frequency, when we multiply it by 10 to 106.02875 cycles per natural second of time, the tone is an octave above A in the Ra musical scale.

The first six numbers of the green value (1.060660172) might be recognized by some as the value of Dr. Buckminster Fuller's *synergetic constant* (S1). The H in H-bar represents the value of Planck's constant, which is known as the *universal unit of action*. The Ra values for Planck's constant are 6.591796875 (omega major), 6.626796875 (red), 6.229126071 (green), 6.631456091 (blue), and 6.$\overline{666}$(omega minor).

An ancient Egyptian papyrus known as the Rhine papyrus contains mathematical information that gives the value of pi as 3.16. The Ra values for pi are 3.125 (omega major), 3.141$\overline{592}$(red), 3.142696806 (green), 3.1430801409 (blue), 3.160493830 (omega minor). (The omega minor format is the format in which crop glyphs are designed. The famous Barbury crop glyph of several years ago had three small circles whose combined areas were 316 square feet, the same as the area of the fourth and largest circle of the four that composed the glyph.)

The ninth sequence is GBHBBBHBBG, which redundantly expresses the same final result as the previous sequence. This was arrived at in the following way: H ÷ B (216 ÷ 54) = 4 (first result), and 216 ÷ 162 (6 x 27)

= 1.$\overline{333}$ (second result); 4 (first result) x 1.$\overline{333}$ (second result) = 5.$\overline{333}$ (third result). When the third result (using nine decimal places) is divided by the sum of the values of the remaining two B symbols in the sequence (54 + 54 = 108), the final result for the ninth sequence is the same as that of the eighth: 0.049382716. This redundancy tells us to take notice of this number, because it will play an important part in the deciphering of the remainder of the first message.

To continue with my exposure of the great con game, I must familiarize the reader with the Ra values for the speed of light in the natural second of time: 300,000 (omega major), 301,592.$\overline{888}$ (red), 301,698.893430 (green), 301,804.935230 (blue) and 303,407.$\overline{407}$ (omega minor). It is scientifically accepted that a wavelength divided into the speed of light will identify its frequency and vice versa. The Ra system does not disagree with this physical fact, but offers other data about wavelengths and frequencies that are too lengthy to present in this article.

We need only divide the wavelength of the most intense line of hydrogen, which is the ultraviolet line known as Lyman M2 (with a wavelength of 1215 omega major angstroms) into the omega major value for the speed of light (300,000. omega major kilo rams per natural second of time). Doing so, we obtain Lyman M2's associated frequency, which is 246.913580247. Then if we divide SETI's time unit of 0.492075 (Ra natural seconds) into the wavelength of the same hydrogen line, we get 2469.13580247, ten times the Lyman M2's frequency. (Hey, SETI, where did you guys really get your fictitious alien time unit?)

The remaining seven extraterrestrial messages are found in the complete printing of SETI's Web page at the end of this article.

The next question I have is, why would SETI want or need to come up with names for fictional time units? For a "game," ticks and tocks are good enough for me.

The total number of characters used by the extraterrestrials to form their nine messages is stated by SETI to be 82. In reality, there are only 81 active numbers (characters, or tones). The 82nd character or tone eventually becomes the final representation of zero. The number 81 (9 x 9) is 1 ÷ 2 of 162 (phi) and is also the number that, when used as a divisor, produces Ra repitans and sequences.

When we multiply the number of messages (nine) by the number of active symbols used in the messages (81), we arrive at 729 (27 x 27)—which is the reciprocal of the fine-structure constant for hydrogen.

It's just a matter of time before the nine extraterrestrial messages are totally translated. If I accomplish the translation of any or part of a message you will find that translation on my Web page, *www.realmofra.com*, now under construction. I hope that the remaining parts of the nine extraterrestrial messages relate to the measurements and geometry of the Great Pyramid. If so, our translation of the messages will not be too difficult.

I am truly sorry to be the one to inform you that there are people who believe themselves to be of an intellectual elite, who also believe that they have some divine right to trick, use you and keep you in ignorance of one of the most important events to have happened in known human history, which is that extraterrestrials exist and have made a sincere effort to contact everyone living on the planet Earth.

The extraterrestrials who sent the nine messages to Earth are now fully aware of how their messages were dealt with. If ever the person or persons who devised the great SETI con game sees a black disk in the skies over their head, I strongly advise them to run like hell.

SETI obviously chose Tau Ceti as the source of their imaginary extraterrestrial culture because of the similarity of the names "Seti" and "Ceti." Such an association of names helps support their presentation of the messages as being merely a game. Ironically, the transmission of these *real* nine extraterrestrial messages came from a star system located beyond, but quite near, Tau Ceti. That star is Lalm, and the planet from which the messages were sent is called by its human inhabitants Gracyea. I have no idea what the star Lalm is called by Earth astronomers.

The ancient Egyptian pharaoh Seti I of the 19th Dynasty (1294-1279 B.C.) was another person who demanded that his subjects think only as he told them to think and no other way. He was a major force in the attempt to totally eradicate the religious philosophy of the so-called heretic pharaoh, Akhenaten, who proposed that there was only one god, whom he called Aten (symbolized by the sun disk), not an army of gods. Whether or not Akhenaten's god Aten was real or false really doesn't matter. What worried several succeeding pharaohs was that he offered the people a different way to worship and think. It seems that there are those of the present day who, like Seti I, are worried about what the average person might think or discover before *they* do.

I would sure like to know who paid for that radio telescope that SETI used to receive the nine extraterrestrial messages, wouldn't you?

Patience, my friends, it will soon all come to a sudden end. Wes Bateman, GAAG.

The Contact Project—Why?*

Why are we doing this? What is this all about? Well, obviously, no messages have really been received from Tau Ceti. However, I urge you to leave reality behind for a little while, and help us try to understand the message. This should be a lot of fun for all involved, and I hope it will show us just how far we have to go before we will be able to understand any real messages we receive.

There have been projects like this before. However, they have always been (in my opinion) fairly simple tests, being very anthropomorphic in nature. What I hope I have achieved [sic] here is something different. Through a lot of time and effort a message has been developed that is fairly simple in content, but very unusual in the way it is put together. It should be very difficult to understand the way in which the message is written . . . even if you understand its contents. In fact, there are ways it could be made even more . . . alien . . . but then I don't think anyone would get it. As it is, I predict it will take a few weeks anyway.

Then there's the other thing that differentiates this project from earlier ones: you. Anyone can participate, and I hope anyone does. You can try anything you like to decode the message . . . write computer programs, show the message to your friends, use books on cryptography . . . anything. Just remember to share what you are doing and what you are thinking with all of us. Use the Discussion Page! This should be an interactive group project involving people from around the planet. With the talent out there, it should be possible to solve this first message.

Yes, I did say *first* message. There will soon follow others. Over time, we will hopefully learn a good deal about the denizens of the Tau Ceti system. Of course, that all depends upon you . . .

The original message consisted of 571 "characters," a long pause of 17.71 seconds, then a repeat of the sequence. The characters are here arranged by pitch. There were 19 unique tones in the original message, here labeled A through S. A is the lowest tone and S is the highest. Each tone lasts about 0.492 seconds. The entire sequence, including pause, took 298.61 seconds, or about 4 minutes and 59 seconds.

In the second message there are 18 new characters, for a total of 37 characters used so far. The new characters are represented by the letters T through Z and a through k. T is higher in pitch than S and so on. This message is 874 characters long. Again, each tone takes 0.492 seconds, and the pause is 17.71 seconds between repetitions. The message length is 447.67 seconds, or 7 minutes and 28 seconds.

*What follows is from the Web page "The Contact Project," www.ibiblio.org/lunar/alien.html.

The third message is the longest so far with 1514 tones for a message length of 12 minutes, 42.5 seconds (762.5 seconds). Again, each tone is the standard length, as is the pause. We should come up with names for these time units. There are 25 new characters, for a total of 62 used so far.

The fourth message is shorter again, with 515 tones for a message length of 4 minutes and 31 seconds (271.06 seconds). Again, each tone is the standard length, as is the pause. There are six new characters, for a total of 68 used so far. In order of pitch (lowest to highest), the new characters are: %!#@$*

The fifth message is shorter, with 413 tones. There are three new characters, in pitch order (low to high): :^~

The sixth message is slightly shorter, with 407 tones, for a message length of approximately 3 minutes, 38 seconds (including pause). There are five new characters (from low pitch to high pitch): ;?[]{

The seventh message is even shorter, with 351 tones, for a message length (including pause) of about 3 minutes, 10 seconds. There are three new tones, in order: -+} (for a total of 79 characters used so far).

The eighth message is long again, with three new characters: \./ (in order). A total of 82 characters have been used so far.

The ninth message is the shortest yet and uses no new characters. The message is being broadcast on a wavelength of 21 cm, the so-called "magic frequency."

Third Message—7 February 95

GIPQDdBADDAFAFADDABdDQPlGGlPgDAAADgPlGGILgBDADBgLOQCQOG
GQBdDdBQLgEDADEgLIGGOQAQOPmPOQAQOGGGXhgDADghXGGQBEBQeXe
pGGpPQBFdBEBDBEBdFBQPpGGGGXhgBAAABghXGGQFQeXepGGpPQBEBQ
PpGGGGpPQAQPpGGoBAAAAAAAAAAAAAAAAAAAoGGGGpPQBQPpGGoA
BBBBBBAAAAAAAAAAAAAoGGGGpPQCQPpGGoAAAAAAABBBBBBBBBB
BBoGGGGGpPQCQPpGiGqPgAgPqGiGrPgDAAADgPrGGGoAAAAAAABBBB
BBBAAAAAoGGGnAABBBAAABAAABABAAAAABBAAAAABBAAAAAB
ABAAABAAABBBAAnPoAAAAAAAAAAAAAAAAAAAABBBBBBBBBBBB
BBBBBBoGGQAQsQBQsQAQGGQCQsQBBBQsQCQGGQBQtQAQtQBQGGQBBB
QtQCQtQBBBQGGQBQPQBQPQBQGGQBQKPKQCQKPKQBQGG6PKPKP6GGQ
AQuQBQuQAQGGQAQuQAQuQAQGGuPsjPPuGGQBBBQvQCQvQBBBQGGQB
BBQvQBBBQvQBBBQGGGvPtjPPvGGQCQ5A5QBQ5A5QCQGGGQCQ5B5QCQ5
B5QCQGGGQCQ5C5QEQ5C5QCQGGGQCQ5D5QBCBQ5D5QCQGGoBBBAAABA
AAAAABAAAAABAAAAAAABBBAAAAAAAABBAAAAAAAAABBBAAA
AAAAAABAAAAAAAAAAAAAAAAAAAAAAAAAAAAAAABAAAAAAA
AAAAAAAAAABAAAAAAAAAAAAAAAAAAAAAAAAAAAAAAAAAA
AAABBBAAAAAAAAAAAAAAAAAAABAAAAAAAAAAAAAAAAAAAA
AABBBAAAAAAAAAAAAAAAAAAAAABAAAAAAAAAAAAAAAAAAA
AAAAAAAAAAAAAAAAAAAAAAAAAAAAAAAABBBAAAAAAAAAA
AAAAAAAAAAAAAAAAABAAAAAAAAAAAAAAAAAAAAAAAAAAA
ABBBBBAAAAAAAAAAAAAAAAAAAAAAAAAAAAABBBAAAAAAAAA
AAAAAAAAAAAAAAAAAAABBBBBAAAAAAAAAAAAAAAAAAAAAA
AAAAAAAAAAABBBAAAAAAAAAAAAAAAAAAAAAAAAAAAAAAAA
AABBoGGxzxPoBBBBBBBBBBBBBBBBBBBoPxzxGGwywPoBoPwywGGz
yzPoBBBAAABoPzyzGGzyzPoBBBBBBBoPzyzGG1y1PoBoP1y1GG1y1Po
BBBAAABoP1y1GG1y1PoBBBBBBBoP1y1GGW2PB1y1BP2WGGW797PC
1y1CP797WGGW898PD1y1DP898WGGW323PE1y1EP323WGGW434PF
1y1FP434WGGW4y4PBAB1y1BABP4y4WGG0PoBABBABBABABABAB
ABABAABABBABAABAABBAABBAABABABABABAAABAAABBBAAABAA
ABBABAABABBAAAABAAABAABAAAAAAAAAAAAABABAAAAAAAAA
AAAAAAAAAAAAAAAoP0G

Fourth Message—17 February 95

G%P!%!QBDBQ!%!P%GG%P!%!QECEQ!%!P%GG%P!%!QBBCBBQ!%!P%G
G%P!%!QBEDEBQ!%!P%GGV!Q!VGGW!Q!PQBQP!Q!WGGQB#B#BQPQBABQ
PQB#B#BQGGQB#C#BQPQBAAABQPQB#C#BQGGQB#D#BQPQBAAAAA
BQPQB#D#BQGGQB#E#BQPQBAAAAAAABQPQB#E#BQGGQB#F#BQPQB
AAAAAAAAABQPQB#F#BQGGQC#C#CQPQCAAACQPQC#C#CQGGGQQLQ
X#Y#XQLQBAB5Y5BABQGGV@oBo@VGGW@oBo@PQBQP@oBo@WGGV@
oBBAABAAo@VGGW@oBBAABAAo@PQDQP@oBBAABAAo@WGGV@oBA
ABAABAAAAABAAAAAo@VGGW@oBBAABAABAAAAABAAAAAo@PQ

FQP@oBBAABAABAAAAABAAAAAo@WGGV@0@VGGW@0@P!@!QBEBQ
!@!P@0@WGG!@!e!$!e!%!GG*P!$!QBFDECEEAABDBDBAAEECEDFBQ!$!P
*G

Fifth Message—24 February 95

GGXPQBQ:QCQ:QDQ:QCQ:QBQPXGGRQBQ^X^QBQRGGSQFQ^X^QFQSGGRQ
BQ:QDQ:QBQ^X^QBQ:QDQ:QBQRGGSQBQ:QCQ:QDQ:QEQ:QDQ:QCQ:QBQ^X
^QBQ:QCQ:QDQ:QEQ:QDQ:QCQ:QBQSGGRX^QBQ:QCQ:QDQ:QEQ:QDQ:QCQ
:QBQ^XRGGRQBQ:QCQ:QBQ^X^QBQ:QCQ:QBQRGGRQCQ:QDQ:QCQ^X^QCQ:
QDQ:QCQRGGRQBQ:QCQ:QDQ:QCQ:QBQ^X^QBQ:QCQ:QDQ:QCQ:QBQRGGS
QAQ^X^QAQSGGG0^w^0GG1y1^KwK^1y1GGxzx^KwK^xzxGGw^m^wGGK
wK^m^KwKGGwyw1y1^wywGGzyz^1y1^zyzGGR1t~t1RGGS1v~v1SGG
*P11$11P*GGQAQP~Q~PQAQG

Sixth Message—1 March 95

G1PK~KP1GG~PK1KP~GG;m;P!;!QBBDBBQ!;!P;m;GG;KmK;P!;!QAQ!;!P;
KmK;GG;xzx;P!;!QBEDD#D#DDEBQ!;!P;xzx;GG;2;P!;!QDCCAAACCDQ!;!
P;2;GGxPK4KPxGG4PKxKP4GGx^xzx^xGG4^m^4GG7P1$1P7GG8P~$~
P8GG7PK8KP7GG8PK7KP8GGG?B?PoBABBAAABAAAAAAAAAAAAAoP?
B?GGV[?B?[VGGW[?B?[P![!BCDABdEEECEAECEEEdBADCB![!P[?B?[WGG
]PoBABBAAAAAAAAAAAAAAAAoP]GG{PoAAAAAAABAAAAAAAAAA
AoP{GG[][P![!BCDAAdEEECEAECEEEdAADCB![!P[][GG[{[P![!B![!P[{[GG{
H?B?H]GGGm^3^mG

Seventh Message—9 March 95

G!@!QDDEBAFEAFEFAEFABEDDQ!@!^2^!@!QDDBAFEAFEFAEFABEDDQ!@!
GG-HPQBQ:QCQ:QDQ:QCQ:QBQP-H-GG-IPQDQ:QCQ:QBQ:QCQ:QDQP-I-
GG-P-PGXPQBQPXGP-PGG!@!L!@@@!L!@!GG!@!5C5!@@@!5C5!@!GG!@
!5D5!@@@@@!5D5!@!GG!@!e!+!e!%%%!GG!+!QBAdBAEABdABQ!+!^2^!
+!QBAdBAEABdABQ!+!GG!}!P![!QECdBCBDFE#BAAAB#EFDBCBdCEQ![!P!
}!GG!}!QDdEFADE#FBF#EDAFEdDQ!}!^2^!}!QDdFADE#FBF#EDAFEdDQ!}!G

Eighth Message—14 March 95

G9^0^9GG!X!QYQ!X!P!X!Y!X!P!X!QYQ!X!GG2PoBAAAAABBBBBBBBBBBBo
P2GG;oBAAAAAAAAAAAAAAAAAAAAo;P!;!DBBCECBBD!;!P;oBAAAAAA
AAAAAAAAAAAAo;GG;oAAAAAAABBBBBBBBBBBBBo;P!;!DDCBEBCDD!
;!P;oAAAAAAABBBBBBBBBBBBBo;GGw^2^wGGw^797^wGG0^2^0GG0K^
K797K^K0GGQBQ{QBQ^?B?^QBQ{QBQGQCQ{QCQ^?C?^QCQ{QCQGGQDQ{Q
DQ^?D?^QDQ{QDQG;.?ECE?.;P!;!DEFFCEFFFED;!P;.?ECE?.;GG;/?ECE?/;
P!;!DEFFFEFFFED!;!P;/?ECE?/;GG;/?ECE?/;P!;!BACCEBBBECCAB!;!P;/
?ECE?/;GG;\?ECE?\;P!;!BACCEBDBECCAB!;!P;\?ECE?\;GG/^z^/GG\^
z^\GG\6/6\GGzPK.KPzGGR\^zyz^\RGGR/^zyz^/RGGS.^zyz^.SGG^wyw
^\RGGR/^wyw^/RGGR.^wyw^.RGG2-2-0-22GG-m-PGQAQHXHXGP-m-
GG-m-^3^-m-G

Ninth Message—1 April 95

G9PoABBBBBBBABABABABABABBBBBBBBBBBBBBBBBBBBBBo
P9GGQCQ9QCQ^0^QCQ9QCQGGGA%AGG3-m-2im-m
3GGA^2^AGG3$3GG3H?B??BCB??B?i3H$GG3-*-2i?B??BCB??B?-
*3GGxGG

A p p e n d i x B

Have You Dummies Heard the Latest?

The United States Air Force at the time of this writing [June 1997] intends to announce that in 1947 the people of Roswell, New Mexico, who claimed to have seen the bodies of aliens that were recovered from a spacecraft that crashed in the area, did not see alien bodies, but had actually seen a number of dummies that had been thrown out of an airplane in order to determine how a real person would end up after being ejected from a jet and parachuting to the ground. The problem with this story is, the Roswell UFO crash occurred in 1947, but the Air Force parachuting-dummy experiments did not take place until six years later in 1953. It appears to me that the Air Force is conducting another type of dummy experiment by releasing this story—they want to determine if we are dumb enough to swallow it. The Air Force has had fifty years to tell the public about their dummy project. Why did they wait until now?

I also wonder why the Air Force needed caskets that could be hermetically sealed to transport their dummies under armed guard to medical labs so that they could be autopsied.

I would wager that whoever came up with the "dummy" cover story for the Air Force also has a job as a consultant for the Search for Extraterrestrial Intelligence (SETI), another group of people who think that the average person is really stupid.

Dealing with the SETI Messages

Since the publication of the article, "The Great SETI Con Game" [see Appendix A], our translation project pertaining to the nine extraterrestrial messages received by SETI via radio telescope in 1995 is well on the way to completion.

This is what I can tell readers about the messages and their contents so far. The messages are certainly not in code. The symbolic tones the messages consist of certainly represent the thirty-seven numbers in the Ra Table of Nines as well as numbers of greater value that are multiples of the number nine. Because knowledge of the Ra system of mathematics is a requirement for translating the messages and only a relatively small number of people living on the Earth have this knowledge, it is obvious who the extraterrestrials expected to translate their messages.

So far several new numbers have been identified that have not been recognized during our past twenty-two years of studying the Ra system. The addition of these numbers of importance to our Ra knowledge has opened up many new things to consider. The extraterrestrials want us to give strong consideration to the number 26,244. We are fairly sure we know the reason why.

The Triangular Stone over the Entrance and the Diagonal Cross Section of the Great Pyramid

Illustrations that depict the triangular stone (prism-shaped) are found in Vol. 2, book A, pages 113 and 118 of *The Rods of Amon Ra*. Also on page 113, the area of the triangular stone is stated to be 2.6244 square green

rams. There are 26244 omega major angstroms in the wavelength of the Brackett M6 spectral line of hydrogen. A wave and a small circle (located in a trough of the wave) are deeply inscribed on the face of the stone. It is presently believed that the shape of the wave represents the frequency signature of the wavelength of Brackett M6 that is produced when that particular wavelength of light passes through a prism that has the dimensions and angles (scaled down) of the triangular stone. The carved wave could otherwise represent a wave associated with the movement of an atomic particle at a particular velocity. (Such a particle is possibly represented by the circle.)

The area of the diagonal cross section of the Great Pyramid is 26244 square green ra feet. Therefore the diagonal cross section represents the same dimensional factors of the triangular stone located over the pyramid's entrance, only on a much larger scale.

When white light (which contains all wavelengths) is directed through a prism, the light breaks up into the wavelengths that compose it. Each individual wavelength will bend (deviate) at a particular angle from the angle that the light enters. The degree that a particular wavelength bends is called the wavelength's *angle of deviation*. Wavelengths considered to be red deviate the least, and wavelengths considered to be violet deviate the most. We need to know what the angle of deviation is for Brackett M6 after it passes through a prism that has the scaled-down dimensions of the triangular stone or diagonal cross section. We are pursuing this information.

This data, combined with the Ra frequency of sound data that we already understand, will assist us to understand how the massive stones were raised and positioned in the pyramid by the Gracians. At this time [June 1997] we have not received any type of response from the SETI organization concerning our accusations. This was expected, because their present option of response would be to stand fast with their story that they made up the messages and that only a crackpot would say differently. It should be obvious to SETI that any adverse response they might make (other than an admission that they should have been honest about the reality of the extraterrestrial messages that came into their possession) will be countered by undeniable data that would only make things look worse for them.

The Ra data and its obvious relationship to the nine messages found, "The Great SETI Con Game" in the appendix will also help the SETI group translate the nine extraterrestrial messages and any others they might have lying around gathering dust. After all, that is what they really wanted to do in the first place.

New York Times

NEW YORK, WEDNESDAY, JUNE 25, 1997

Air Force Details a New Theory in U.F.O. Case

By WILLIAM J. BROAD

No bodies. No bulbous heads. No secret autopsies. No spaceship. No crash. No extraterrestrials or alien artifacts of any sort. And most emphatically of all, no Government cover-up.

The Air Force yesterday made public its latest report on the famous 1947 incident in the New Mexico desert near the town of Roswell that is at the heart of claims by flying-saucer fans that extraterrestrials have visited Earth and that has become a celebrated part of American popular culture.

The report, in voluminous detail, says the supposed mountain of evidence about aliens is a mirage.

Just as old sightings of squids and whales spawned tales of sea monsters, so too, the Air Force says, the shadowy doings of brave fliers, high-altitude balloons, lifelike crash dummies and saucerlike craft in the southeastern New Mexico desert at the dawn of the space age were glimpsed and embellished over the decades into false evidence of aliens.

For instance, one serviceman who crashed in a test balloon 10 miles northwest of Roswell suffered an injury that caused his head to swell and resemble the bulbous cranium of the classic science-fiction alien, the report says. This secretive 1959 mishap, it adds, apparently led decades later to tales of a crashed extraterrestrial that walked under its own power into a military hospital.

So, too, dummies were routinely dropped from balloons to test parachutes and were sometimes lost in the desert and disfigured in suggestive ways, their hands often missing a finger. A distinguishing characteristic of the aliens supposedly sighted near Roswell, the report notes, is four fingers.

Some critics fault the Government for addressing the topic of alien visitations, dismissing it as ludicrous.

But other experts say the United States' obsession with unidentified flying objects has never been greater and praise efforts to combat what they view as a dangerous mania. They note the recent suicides of 39 members of the Heaven's Gate cult, who believed an alien spaceship passing near Earth would take them to an ethereal paradise.

Not surprisingly, true believers in Roswell are unshaken, seeing the new report as evidence of the most egregious Government cover-up of all time.

"This is the biggest story of the millennium, a visit to the Earth by extraterrestrial spacecraft and the cover-up of the best evidence, the bodies and the wreckage, for 50 years," said Stanton T. Friedman, who has written about the Roswell incident and who is to be a featured speaker at the upcoming gala.

In an interview, Mr. Friedman accused the Air Force of false reasoning, selective use of data and lying.

"The evidence is overwhelming that planet Earth is being visited by extraterrestrial spacecraft," said Mr. Friedman, who lives in New Brunswick,

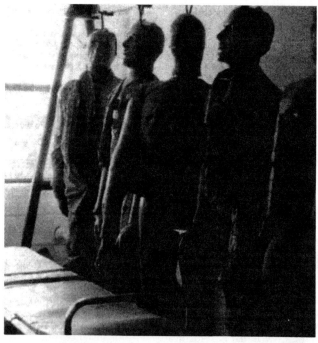

Identified Flying Objects

U.S. Air Force Photo

U.F.O. buffs say officials covered up a 1947 visit by aliens. But the Air Force said yesterday that the mysterious happenings in the New Mexico Desert involved crash dummies and spy balloons.

Canada, and whose 1992 book, "Crash at Corona," is in its sixth printing. (Corona is a village near the purported crash site.)

Critics of the new report bridle at its main thesis that civilians are confusing military activities that took place over

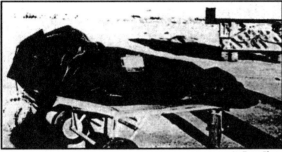

An insulation bag for balloon test dummies may have been mistaken for a body bag, according to the Air force.

Air Force Photo

more than a decade and falsely recalling them as a single incident. Such memory failures, critics say, are highly unlikely.

But the Air Force says the witnesses are often recalling events more than four decades old and could have easily mixed up the dates.

Joseph W. Kittinger Jr., a retired Air Force colonel who was much decorated for his pioneering jumps from balloons high over the New Mexican desert, praised the report as exhaustive and overdue.

"I'm insulted at how this fraud has been perpetrated and delighted that the Air Force has taken it on," Colonel Kittinger said in an interview.

The much debated incident took place on a desolate stretch of desert that was surrounded by several secret military bases. Increasingly, the site or sites (the faithful disagree on its exact location) are today ringed by tourist attractions that play on the extraterrestrial theme.

More than 100,000 sky watchers and conspiracy theorists are expected to visit Roswell for a celebration of the incident's 50th anniversary during the first week of July. Festivities are to include a soapbox derby of homemade alien vehicles.

The hullabaloo got started in July 1947 when a ranch foreman, W. W. Brazel, found strange, shiny material littering the ground. Mr. Brazel gave it to the sheriff, who turned it in to the military authorities at the nearby air base.

On July 8, the Roswell Army Air Field issued a news release about the crash of a flying disk, prompting a newspaper, The Roswell Daily Record, to run an article under the headline: "R.A.A.F. Captures Flying Saucer."

Military officials retreated the next day, calling the curious debris merely a downed weather balloon. With that, the matter was largely forgotten until the late 1970's with the birth of what eventually became a small industry of experts, books, articles and television shows recounting alien visitations and conspiracy theories.

Under growing pressure from true believers and curious Congressmen, the

Air Force Photos

The mock space probe at White Sands missile base may have been seen as an alien spaceship.

Alien or Test Dummy?
Eyewitness descriptions of aliens

EYES
"His eyes was open.
atring blanky."

EARS
"No visible ears, just a rise there and then a hole."

SKIN
"Their skin coloration a bluish-tinted milky white."
Vern Maltans

FINGERS
"They didn't have a little finger."
Gerald Anderson

"They had four fingers."
Vern Maltan

The dummies were often damaged from the drops.

CLOTHING
"They looked like thy had some sort of bandages on 'em ... over his arm" "around his mid-section and partially over his shoulder."
Gerald Anderson

In some test, the arms and legs of the dummies were secured with tape and nylon webbing.

Parachute-Testing Program Fueled the Rumors
The parachute-testing program probably contributed to alien theories because the dummies were not always recovered immediately: some were never found. This increased the chance that non-military personnel might have come across one and misidentified it.

Air Force in February 1994 began to investigate just what took place many decades ago.

A 23-page report made public in September 1994 said the silvery wreckage in the desert had been part of a top-secret system of atomic espionage. That admission made the 1947 story about a weather balloon a white lie. Carried into the atmosphere by balloon, the spy sensors listened for weak reverberations from Soviet nuclear blasts half a world away.

But the 1994 report said nothing about extraterrestrial beings, who in various accounts of the Roswell crash number between two and eight, dead and sometimes alive. The silence arose because the Air Force found nothing in the balloon saga to account for the reports of aliens, so it ignored the topic at the time and only later came up with a detailed and intriguing explanation.

The new Roswell report, titled "Case Closed," was written by Capt. James McAndrew, an intelligence officer assigned to the Secretary of the Air Force's Declassification and Review Team. Its 231 pages are designed to go beyond the 1994 report by revealing more about Federal work in the desert and examining what apparently inspired sightings of not only alien artifacts but of the extraterrestrials themselves.

In places it is grim. For instance, it describes the crash of a KC-97G military plane near Roswell that killed 11 fliers, leaving their bodies badly burned and reeking of fuel. The stench was so foul that identification work at the Roswell air base was moved from the small hospital to the commissary, which had a large refrigerator.

The Air Force report suggests that this crash, recalled decades later by- a civilian who visited the air base and talked to workers there, prompted his account of small, black, mangled, dead aliens who smelled so bad that their autopsies were moved from the base hospital to a place better suited to the dissections.

This civilian, W. Glenn Dennis, has been called the "star witness" of the Roswell incident. Mr. Dennis is president of the International UFO. Museum and Research Center, which was founded in 1991 in Roswell.

The new Air Force report focuses on military work and accidents from 1947 to 1976 and says many of the claims about extraterrestrials are based on faulty memories and, in fact, are pieced together from military work that took place over many years.

The finding of shiny wreckage in 1947, it says, "was the first of many unrelated events now collectively known as the 'Roswell Incident.'"

The desert work focused on the development of spy gear and high-altitude escape systems. Starting in 1950, for instance, balloons rising as high as 19 miles dropped dozens of lifelike dummies to perfect parachutes for pioneering pilots, including those in the X-15 rocket plane and the U-2 spy plane. The dummies landed all over the New Mexico desert, and several were lost.

The report quotes one witness as saying of the Roswell aliens, "I thought they were plastic dolls."

Starting in 1957, test pilots began to join the dummies in bailing out at high altitudes, culminating in Colonel Kittinger's 1960 leap from a balloon nearly 20 miles up, which remains the highest parachute jump ever.

At times this human research was also quite suggestive of aliens.

A balloon flight in 1959 ended in an accident that caused Capt. Dan D. Fulgham's helmet to shatter and his head to swell. His eyes became mere slits in a puffy face. He was taken to the Roswell base with a high-security escort and was eventually transferred to Wright-Patterson Air Force Base in Ohio for treatment.

The new Air Force report says this accident probably accounts for reports of an alien that walked into a Roswell air base hospital under its own power, and of the shipment of aliens to the Wright-Patterson base, where, according to Roswell lore, they underwent close scrutiny.

The report also tells of other activity

in New Mexico that conceivably was mistaken for extraterrestrial craft. A V-shaped balloon flown in 1965 bears a striking resemblance to the sketch of an alien spacecraft drawn by an anonymous witness.

And the report notes that desert balloons between 1966 and 1972 lifted and dropped mock interplanetary probes. The program was designed to aid space agency research, but to the untrained eye the probes looked like flying saucers.

"The incomplete and inaccurate intermingling" of actual events, the report concludes, over the decades has resulted in a "sensational story" about aliens crashing in the desert at Roswell. But the tale "cannot withstand close scrutiny when compared to official records."

It seems unlikely that the Air Force report will end the debate between the Federal Govern-ment and flying-saucer fans. If anything, as the 50th anniversary of the Roswell incident draws near, the subject is likely to become as hot as the smoking wreckage of an alien space-ship.

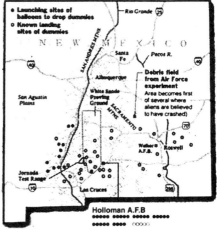

"The arguments of the critics collapse of their own weight," said Mr. Friedman, the Roswell author, who added that he had not yet read the new Air Force report. "I hope it doesn't have as many lies as the previous one."

Continued from

New York Times
WEDNESDAY, JUNE 25, 1997

What Aliens? A 2-Part Explanation

Believers call it the Roswell Incident: an alien crash-landing in the New Mexico desert in the summer of 1947, followed by a diabolical Air Force cover-up. The Air Force released a 231-page report yesterday intended to debunk claims of alien sightings. Theses pictures and diagram lay out the basis of its case.

JUNE 1947: THE INCIDENT A secret Air Force experiment leaves debris 75 miles northwest of Roswell which is mistaken for debris from an alien spacecraft.

People From Another Time

After matching key people in Mr. Denuis's account to personnel who served in Roswell, the Air Force found only one who was there at the time of the incident.

The "missing" nurse 1st Lieut. Eileen M. Fenton.	"Capt. "Slats" Wilson" Composite of two individuals: Capt. Lucille C. Slattery and Maj. Isabelle M. Wilson	The "pediatrician" Capt. Frank B. Nordstrom.

"Big redheaded colonel" Col. Lee F. Ferrell	When person was at base Mr. Dennis's description Person matching description

43 launchings of dummies

'Aliens' At the Hospital

The "star witness" for believers in an alien landin, the Air Force says was W. Glenn Dennis, a 22-year-old mortician in 1947, who claimed that the Air Force recovered alien bodies and performed autopsy on them. The report sys his accounts clearly refers to events that happened years after 1947, and to people who were there years later.

Source: "The Roswell Report: Case Closed," U.S. Air Force

Victims of Two Accidents Were Mistaken for Aliens ▶

❶ KC-97G Plane Crash, June 26, 1956

GRISLY AUTOPSY

Mr. Dennis said a nurse at the base hospital told him she witnessed an autopsy on three "very mangled," "black little bodies." The Air Force says this was the part of the autopsy of the victims of the crash of a KC-97G plane.

A KC-97G plane

SUSPICIOUS CARGO

▼**WRECKAGE** The Air Force says that items Mr. Dennis believed to be wreckage from an alien spacecraft in the back of military ambulance were actually equipment used in a parachute-testing program.

"HIEROGLYPHICS" Mr Dennis described markings that looked like hieroglyphics. The Air Force says that they were most likely poorly stenciled labes.

❷ Manned Balloon Accident, May 21,1959

LARGE-HEADED ALIEN

The Air Force believes that the image of bulbous-headed aliens with slits for eyes, below, probably originated from sightings of Capt Dan D. Fulgham, who was injured in a balloon-ing accident. He is shown at far right after blood was drained from his scalp.

Archie Tse and Juan Velasco/ The New York Times

D i c t i o n a r y

63-92 Sharmarie's telepathic and teleporting Nodian friend, whom he met on the ship that took him to Nodia; he also visited Ivatcala to give her brief instructions about her future readiness to understand the elohim

A

Abdonel first assistant to Tasper-Kane and a Nodian ambassador who in disguise called himself Coate-Grol in order to lead Martian warriors to resist Maldecians on Earth

Abdu Roash site north of Giza where Rededef tried to build a pyramid, the only king of the Fourth Dynasty who did so

Acmiss town on Mollara for Martians

Adolfro Blaclotter a Nodian Lord of Devisement and designer of the present economic system of the trading houses

Adriannaro Nodian classmate and companion to Rendowlan when they were young

Adthro son of Kevinar-Kale

Agrathrone father of Sharmarie in an Earth life, one of twelve Earth emperors

Agrippina II mother of Nero, Caligula's sister and second wife of Roman emperor Claudius who, with the prefect Burrus, put to death the murderers of Caligula and their families, which included Geonius and his wife Rarla/Doy and their daughter and grandchildren

Akhenaten ("beneficial to Aten"), the name taken by Amenhotep IV when he established the worship of one god and a new capital

Akhetaten ("horizon of Aten"), the new capital established by Akhenaten; its ruins are now called Tel el-Amarna

Akite Falashakena's second husband, who attained the infinite thought but chose to remain in human form to be her spiritual consultant

Aknostros Silmikos' farmer stepfather

Ala off-world woman from Trake radiar/Neptune, living on Earth

Alfora Jaffer's orphaned wife from the Nile near Giza

Alperians speechless inhabitants of the Sost solar system

Altranmis a Greek scholar visited by Pythagoras

Alysybe Churmay's stepmother in her first life

Ambis Dora/Churmay's father in a lifetime in France

Amel a strong man of Parn who deliberately flunked the Gracians' test

Amenhotep II seventh king in the 18th Dynasty, whose tomb was robbed by Churmay and others in an Egyptian lifetime

Amenhotep II ninth king in the 18th Dynasty, father of Tutankhamen, as claimed by his mother, Queen Tiye

Amenhotep IV tenth king of the 18th Dynasty, son of Queen Tiye; he took a new name, Akhenaten, when he established the worship of one god and moved the capital

Ameth-Thuth a vizier who ruled in Khufu's name, as the latter was usually drunk

Amon a god of Egypt during Churmay's Egyptian lifetime

Ampt radiar in the Sost solar system; Vitron is a huge planetoid, the only one in the radiar; Nodia is a planet in the Sost system

Andart a Maldecian darmin prince who was assigned as debating partner of Marduk; at fifteen chose Doy as a mate

Ansomore a Waydian city, seat of the world government

Aprela mother of Rarla/Doy and also the name of Rarla's daughter

Aranella wife of Lord Rayatis Cre'ator, mother of Falashakena and Drayfess

Arbel introduced gold and later, taxes to town of Bratel and embroiled Mosh/Jaffer in a get-rich scheme

Arcdent Ben-Cark oldest son of Cark Ben-Zobey

Ari-Lionent father of Sharmarie in his first lifetime

Arita wife of Carlus Domphey

Armonamuri one of the Babylonians who helped decipher an inscription inside the Great Pyramid during one of Tixer-Chock's Earth lives

Artaclean father of Sharmarie as Rembeylian in Sparta

Asentel a Sumerian/Saturnian aircar pilot for Jaffer

astrastone a crystallized carbon found by the Federation only on Bantivail 3, third planet of a sun in a five-star mini galaxy near the Milky Way; used to make the capstone of the Great Pyramid; workable only by a concentration of pure psychic energy

astrastone spiel capstone of the Great Pyramid

Aten personified by the sun disk, the only god Amenhotep IV, or Akhenaten, declared would be worshiped in Egypt

Ath a planet in the Mel star system, home world of Fan and Frate

Atlan Atlantis

Atlanians inhabitants of the two Atlans, or Atlantis

Atrelos Tamos/Thaler's father in a life in Alexandria, who became the First Deputy Minister of Trade to Ptolemy XII

Aye a high priest of Amon, uncle of Tutankhamen, whom he succeeded on the throne as the thirteenth king of the 18th Dynasty, and who in turn was succeeded by his general, Horemheb, also known as Rameses I

B

Baal Maldecian name for Lucifer

Babbor aircar navigator in Thaler's Tibetan lifetime

Babs elected representatives on each of the inhabited planetoids of the Sumer radiar/Saturn, who together made up the Council of Seven Lights

Balis   Thaler's wife on his home world

Bangur   capital city of Sumeria in Trome's life there

Banlon and Nylo   two Neptune planetoids that now orbit past Pluto

Bantivail   a star system, one of five that make up a mini galaxy near the Milky Way; another of the five is Carrdovan; the system has twelve planets, eleven of which are now uninhabited deserts with ruins of ancient civilizations; a small military outpost is maintained by the Federation to protect the astrastone

Bantivail 3   the third planet in the system, the only source of astrastone; contains giant pyramids made by the Uranians and a stargate linked to other stargates, including one on Earth, so that individuals could star-travel without spaceships, a macro-level transference

Barco   from Morza in the Lalm star system, a black-skinned population; he and his race were put in charge of the Reltian workers who helped construct the Great Pyramids

Barla   daughter of Jaffer and Alfora

bar-rex   a Martian warlord

Baxer-Tolm   chief of the Gracians at Giza

Becrickta   Churmay's mother on Wayda

Bellarbus   Trome's uncle in an Earth life, who could read the crystal ball that came from off-world

Bello   Trome, in a Sumerian lifetime

Bel Nec   the only radiar of the star Lalm, in its sixth solar orbit

Belps   spiritual people of the Ee system's second planet who visited Moor

Bemiss   Tamos/Thaler's mother in a lifetime in Alexandria

Benfyvees   the advanced tribe of Tamta/Doy in her Australian life

Benner   Sharmarie's twin son, brother of Quandray, in current lifetime

Benranefifti   a daughter of Khufu who was cheated out of a queenship by Myva

Bent Pyramid   at Dashur, where King Snofru, Queen Hetepheres and son King Khufu are buried

Beverjoanon   Earth merchant who hired people to strip valuables from the murder victims of the krates after Maldec exploded

Bey-Cannor   Earth physician, uncle of Tarm, who married Churmay in her first life

Bhafdat   an Indian who was with the twelve Babylonian visitors to Saqqara; a mathematician who helped Melth-Nakhefra solve a number problem

Big Circle   a huge distant galaxy, home of the Tar Spikes

Black Turtle   Seneca father of Sapeena/Doy

Blyme   a star with ten planets, the first of which, Emarin, is the home of Tillabret

Boinkalix-Ralsever   assistant to Tarvmole, the Gracian chief building engineer

Booke-Tasser   Sharmarie's father in current lifetime

Borm   a planet whose people were called Bormians

Bormen Dora/Churmay's husband during a lifetime in France

Bormians people who worked for the Federation to track the biology and geology of Earth

Bove Charon, now orbiting Pluto; originally orbited Neptune and had the largest population within the Trake radiar

Brace Thaler's name during a Tibetan Earth life when he was a furniture maker and in the air force

Bralph the Waydian gift rooster that Morris named after a male relative

Branya wife of Gra Moy/Nisor

Bratel a town in Poland where Mosh/Jaffer settled

Braymark Maldecian leader in Egypt during the early Atlantean lifetime of Mac-Densel/Trome; killed by a spaceship for disobeying orders

Bredef-Karnut older son of Melth-Nakhefra/Tixer-Chock and Tertmis

Brevracarliss wife of Tixer-Chock, daughter of a rich Gracian tobacco farmer

bright eyes term for those who could communicate telepathically in Thaler's Tibetan life

Brig-Stura an emissary of the Maldecian ruling council

Brike Ben-Demus an Earthman whom Nisor met after his spaceship crashed

Brockmel from Trake radiar/Neptune, consultant to Gracian Itocot-Talan, telepath for House of Cre'ator, killed by Maldecians

Brugrey a slave assigned to Naya/Churmay and her father during her Egyptian lifetime

Bulon Trome's father in his first life

Burr a mountain-dwelling Martian tribe during Sharmarie's first lifetime

C

Callrus husband of Taydeena/Churmay after she moved to Luxor

Cap-Tonelarber stepfather of Sharmarie in his first lifetime

Cark Ben-Zobey headman of Pankamerry, a village east of Giza

Carlus Domphey Nodian founder of the Trading House of Domphey and its First Lord of Devisement

Carma Torge's wife

Carrdovan "Carr's star," also called Task, third brightest star in what we call the Pleiades constellation, though it is beyond our galaxy; its second planet, Mollara, became the Martians' home; part of a five-star mini galaxy

Cartress the planet of origin of Petrimmor and Orbaltreek

Cartressian natives of Cartress, seven feet tall

Catransa Rancer-Carr's daughter

chaire-salbas ("those on an uncharted path"), Maldecians born after the destruction of Maldec

Christ reality, the a reality desired to be manifest in the molar state of reality by all who are in the open state

Churmay   a woman from Wayda/Venus evacuated to Earth after the planetary disturbances began; was taught to sing by the Maldecians and saved from a drug-induced death by Sant, Tarm and Opatel in a game of Shadows with her owner Jorhisa; presently lives on Simcarris

Cimiss   Orbaltreek's Earthborn mate

Citadel   present name for the plain on Mars that is the site of the pyramid and the Face; ancient headquarters of the zone-rex, Rancer-Carr

Cleopatra   childhood playmate of Thaler during his lifetime in Alexandria

Clovis   the first king of the Franks; uncle of Dora/Churmay's mother in a lifetime in France

Coate-Grol   ("sun cat"), Abdonel the Nodian, who founded the Martian warrior league to combat the Maldecian Earth overlords; the name became associated with the league itself; Martian soldiers who as a group became Federation soldiers, taken to a system near Orion's Belt for training

Commiva   a Federation mothership

Corboslate   giant servant of Opatel Cre'ator

Cordovan   Nodian name for the sun Task

cot   a Martian born on Mollara

Council of Babs   Omurayan elected council in the Sumer/Saturn radiar

Council of the Seven Lights   composed of elected representatives from the seven planetoids of Sumer/Saturn

crare   a rare metal found on the Trake planetoids

Crax-Milanto   Tixer-Chock's father in his first lifetime

Crennamer   Earth trader of goods with the Maldecians

Criltrenos   a Greek in Italy, friend to Cronopius/Nisor

Croma   Ruke of Parn's wife during his first lifetime

Cronopius   name of Nisor in Italian lifetime when Vesuvius erupted

Cro-Swain   an orna Maldecian, father of teenage son Sou-Dalf and daughter Debettine, neighbors to Jaffer; later the military dictator of his area

Crubbo   old priest-scribe assigned to Melth-Nakhefra as translator and spy by the high priest of Ra

Cryberants   those who built the Sphinx for the Maldecians and were murdered when it was completed; from Lyra

Cyper-Dale   a Nodian who took Nisor to Mars

Cyrol   a Greek tutor of Cleopatra during Thaler's life in Alexandria

Cyrus-Orbey   king of Sumeria during Bello/Trome's Earth life there; taken off-planet for a period as was the custom for Sumerian kings

D

Daamutyty   wife and queen of Khafre, mother of Menkaure, died at his birth

Dackeys   villagers in a Turkish town in Trome's Earth life

Dankmis   a Waydian city

Danzar Gate, the a thin part of the Riff barrier

Daren sacred mountain on Mars, which is now called Olympus Mons

darmins ("the unordained"), Maldecians who were born before the polarization of the els into two factions

Darrie a woman in Trome's Earth life who was given a crystal sphere by the "gods"

dartargas Federation soldiers

Dashur site of the Bent Pyramid and the Red Pyramid

Debettine orna Maldecian, wife of Cro-Swain, mother of Sou-Dalf and Valneri

Dell from Ry, an eight-year-old when he met Petrimmor; short with dark-green eyes and white/pale-green hair; Petrimmor's psychic interpreter

Delme mother of Mosh/Jaffer

Delver son of Misshemoo and grandson of Maldecian ruler Mic-Corru

Denbrevra daughter of Tixer-Chock and Brevracarliss

deviser counselor on Nodia

Deybal Ben-Volar former police chief of Tigrillet during Jaffer's life on Earth; an organizer of the freedom fighters

dids blue strips used as scrip, issued to pyramid construction workers to exchange for goods

Dimathra a Christian aunt of Criltrenos

Distra home planet of Nisor's present wife

Djenifre-Ptah also called Rededef, the third king in the Fourth Dynasty

Djoser Third Dynasty king of Egypt in one of Churmay's Egyptian lives

Dogons present descendants of a black race from the radiar now called Sirius B, which orbits the star Sirius A

Dora Churmay's name in a lifetime in France, during which she became a Christian

Dovey son of Misshemoo, grandson of Maldecian Mic-Corru

Dovinta wife of Kevinar-Kale

Doy Maldecian woman who visited Earth 19 days after awakening as a 15-year-old on Maldec; became engaged to Prince Andart; perished on Earth during the Great Catastrophes; now lives on Nodia

Drancusus Sharmarie's tutor, a road contractor, in his Roman lifetime as Granius

drat a Martian beer

Drayfess son of Rayatis Cre'ator and wife Aranella, older brother to Falashakena; black-haired, unlike the usual Nodian white hair; he, with Falashakena, inherited the administration of the Trading House of Cre'ator

Dray-Fost half brother of Aranella Cre'ator

Driznafalians friends of the Tar Spikes, intergalactic travelers

Drucall planet in a distant system where Churmay's family was relocated

Druma sun of the planet Simm

Dthermas   an old, wise Egyptian scholar-priest who greeted Pythagoras and his party

Durdler   a skate who assisted the underground resistance on Earth headed by Coate-Grol

E

el   one of the elohim

El, Lord God El   a great spirit and consciousness governing a specific planet

elohim   an order of beings who govern planets; for example, the El of Mars

Emarin   the home planet of Tillabret

Emler   Shyreldane's assistant

Eperone net   an elite group of telepaths in the Cre'ator trading structure

Ermtay   an elderly Moorian woman who was one of the first two people to meet off-worlders

Estrelmis   wife of Pythagoras

Ethbo   son of Mosh/Jaffer

Ethromal   the name for Egypt in the time of Tamta/Doy

Evercass   town with mostly Earth inhabitants south of Miradol

F

Falashakena   red-haired daughter of Rayatis Cre'ator and Aranella, guarded by Sharmarie in his first lifetime; with brother Drayfess inherited the administration of the Trading House of Cre'ator

Fan   a telepath from Ath who worked for the House of Domphey and who taught telepathy to Nisor and Ivatcala and others

Farneen   Ymet/Churmay's father in an Egyptian lifetime

Fe-Atlan   North Atlantis island continent

Federation   the Federation of Worlds, formed when the Nodian trading houses became too adversarial

ferts   name meaning "monsters" given to the children born with superior mental powers in the time of Gra Moy/Nisor

Filbrius   master of Cronopius/Nisor

Fogtra   an elderly Moorian woman who was one of the first two people to meet off-worlders

Forn   father of Ruke in his first lifetime

Framer   Thaler's father in his first life

Franet   a planetoid of the Jupiter/Relt radiar, now called Ganymede

Frate   telepathic daughter of Fan and Eighth Lord of Devisement for the House of Domphey

Freattha   female Nodian announcer on Mars-to-Earth trip

Frequency Barrier   a debilitating frequency state on Earth caused by the Maldecian attempt hundreds of millions of years ago to steal Earth's life essence, destroying Maldec and later causing other planets in this system to change orbits and become lifeless, leaving only Earth habitable; Earth's core would later vibrate alternately more—which caused devolution in human DNA and an amnesia about former lives—and less, which allowed golden ages to develop. Earth was thus mentally and physically detrimental to anyone who might visit. Those not subject to the Frequency Barrier are in "the open state."

Frocent one of the wise, ancient Uranian teachers who was murdered by the Maldecians

Fronk father of Tamta/Doy

G

Gee the eighth planet of twelve inhabited planets in the Jatha star system, 169,000 light-years toward our galactic center from Earth, home world of Serbatin

Geonius an officer of the Roman Praetorian Guard who married Rarla/Doy and later, with fellow officers, murdered the emperor Caligula

Gertaeva a Nodian woman, chieftess of the Cre'ator intelligence service

Gike-Nex a Gracian on Mars who could speak Martian

Gracians six-foot tall, beautiful, black-haired, fair-skinned telepathic natives of Gracyea in the Lalm star system, master engineers who were hired by the Maldecians to build the Great Pyramids at Giza, Teotihuacan and Mars; they wore sandals and feathered clothing and smoked cigars

Gracyea fourth planet of the star Druma, home to the Gracian engineers of sacred buildings

Graforet wife of Trome in his first life

Gra Moy ("Bear's Eye"), Nisor's name in an Earth life in Tennessee area almost six million years ago

Graniss area on Mars now called Cydonia, ancient capital of chief warlord Rancer-Carr and Mars' only neutral territory

Granius Sharmarie's name in a Roman lifetime

Great Catastrophes, the the 1750 years of Earth calamities that began some 80 years after the destruction of Maldec

Great Rens, the the three Great Pyramids at Giza

Green Jacket a young Martian on Earth who helped spy on Maldecians, companion of Prince Brone

Grenta one of Rendowlan's two daughters on Nodia

Gretrama one of the wives of the Waydian herdsman who greeted the first spacecraft to visit Venus

H

Halp-Donax Gracian assistant to Karyo-Belum

Hamarebuti leader of twelve Babylonian scholars who visited Saqqara to understand the sacred geometry there during a Tixer-Chock lifetime

Hamp radiar Uranus and its planetoids, the origin of the teachers who first brought sacred knowledge to Gracyea, Maldec and other planets and galaxies

Hantbo-Crob   a high-ranking krate general at Her-Rood's palace

Harcar   Naya/Churmay's father in an Egyptian life

Harn Sloves   ("Dry Shoes"), leader of the Prenpossas, Gra Moy/Nisor's tribe

He Who Casts No Shadow   a spy with psychic abilities who helped the Earth freedom fighters

Heb-Sed   a celebration held during certain years of an Egyptian king or queen's reign

Her-Rood   Maldecian governor-general of Earth, whose headquarters were in the area of southern Venezuela

Hetepheres   queen to Snofru, mother of Khufu and great aunt to Melth-Nakhefra

hi   a Martian stronghold or territory governed by a bar-rex

Hocrolon   an elected representative from Churmay's Waydian village

Horemheb   a general of the Egyptian army under the reigns of the Amenhoteps, later seizing the throne and taking the name Rameses I; last king of the 18th Dynasty

Howaren   maternal grandfather of Rayatis Cre'ator

I

Iberlotin   a Waydian village

Ibolue   Thaler's mother in his first lifetime

Illena   Drayfess Cre'ator's daughter

Imhotep   adviser to King Djoser in the Third Dynasty during one of Churmay's Egyptian lives; spent time off-planet with the Nodians and, with their advice, released Marduk's soul from its imprisonment in the Great Pyramid

infinite thought, the   when achieved, one reunites with the consciousness of the creator of all that is; the highest form of psychic perception

Isotrex   a Nodian trading house

Itocot-Talan   the chief of the Gracian builders on Earth and a great scholar, also Tixer-Chock's grandfather

Ivatcala   Nisor's wife and coworker in House of Domphey travels

J

Jaffer Ben-Rob   of Earth, born in the village of Tigrillet, off present Portugal coastline, chosen as companion to teenage Maldecian Sou-Dalf; married Alfora before living on Maldec; returned and joined the freedom fighters

Jaguar's Tongue   the Mayan priest-king whom Smoke Bird/Tixer-Chock and his father served as stonemasons

Jasaul   Sharmarie's brother in an Earth life

Jatha   a sun in this galaxy, one of whose planets is Gee, home of Serbatin

Jercaro   son of Tamta/Doy and Ramcace

Jorhisa   sister of Her-Rood, ruler of Earth-based Maldecians

Juliopo   Churmay's half brother on Wayda

Jupiter   the Relt radiar, called Robe by the people of the planetoid Parn

K────────────────────────

Kalt-Rapanine   oldest son of King Rabbersinus and leader of a group of scholars, teachers and inventors during Trome's Earth life

Kaltros   father of Silmikos/Tixer-Chock

Kamer-Ostsen   the Maldecian elder who killed Dell

Kanius   Jaffer's richest farmer uncle

Karyo-Belum   the Gracian ambassador to Maldec

Keerey   husband of Naya/Churmay in an Egyptian lifetime

Kelneto   Ymet/Churmay's abusive stepfather in an Egyptian lifetime

Kevinar-Kale   of Earth, who gives an eyewitness account of the day of Maldec's destruction in chapter 8

Key Shi   husband of Ting Sue/Churmay in a Chinese lifetime

Khafre   or Chephren, the fourth king of the Fourth Dynasty, succeeded by his son Menkaure; Khufu's younger half brother by father Snofru's second wife; conducted wars to regain control of territories; trusted Crazy Melth-Nakhefra, his childhood classmate (Tixer-Chock's Egyptian life), to find entrance to the pyramids

Khamerernebty II   queen and wife of Menkaure, mother of King Shepseskaf, last of the Fourth Dynasty

Khufu   second king in the Fourth Dynasty, succeeded by son Rededef; father of Tertmis, also by his third wife, Myva

Klaus von Stauffenberg   the Nazi colonel who tried to kill Hitler, a recent lifetime of Prince Andart

Knoore   city south of Turkey, to which Trome's people emigrated

Koffraf   Supreme Minister of Trade under Ptolemy XII; Thaler's father was next in authority

krates   Maldecian soldiers

L────────────────────────

Lady Cre'ator   Aranella, wife of Rayatis, mother of son Drayfess and daughter Falashakena, who was guarded as a child by Sharmarie

Lake Samm   on Venus/Wayda

Lalm   the central star of Simm, its second planet, and Gracyea, its fourth of five, and Bel Nec, the radiar in the sixth orbit, which has eight planetoids, one of which is Morza, home of Barco

Lamuma   ("the Great Mother"), the Domphey mothership that visited Wayda

Land of Mir   Egypt's name during the time of building the Great Pyramids

Land of Ser   Egypt's name during the time of early Atlantis, or the Atlans

Leeva   a Martian woman of high station who was among the group, including Tasper-Kane, Abdonel, Trome and Jaffer, that tried to unite the off-world refugees brought to Earth

Liferex-Algro   holy man of the Gracians located at the Egypt pyramid site

Linc Core   a Nodian sage who was a telepath and teleporter

Loctensa   Churmay's sister on Wayda

Lord God El   supreme deity or dimensional ruler of a planet

Lords of Devisement   originally Nodian, later included planetary businessmen from galaxies increasingly distant

Luna   Waydian and Trakian name for Earth's moon

M

Mac-Densel   Trome's name in an Atlantean lifetime, when he joined the army and explored Egypt; a mind reader

Macrantor   younger brother of Sharmarie in Atlantean life as Socrantor the Younger

macro level   the level where the els interact

macro monks   term denoting a devolved yet superior species, originally from Reltians left on Earth

Macshallow-Brunto   Ninth Lord of Devisement of the Federation, who provided an addendum to Chapter 7

Maldec   the fifth planet originally orbiting our sun; destroyed millions of years ago when the Maldecians attempted to steal Earth's psychic energy; an oxygen world

Maldecians   an eight-foot-tall, blue-eyed white-skinned blond race from Maldec whose intention was to eventually rule the universe, beginning with its neighbor, Earth

Malura   the small moon of Maldec

Marcela   wife of Tamos/Thaler in his life in Alexandria; half Greek and half Roman

Marduk   the living god of Maldec, a Maldecian youth considered a god by his people; inside the Great Pyramid at the time of the destruction of Maldec, his soul was imprisoned for eons until Imhotep was told how to free it

Marle   mother of Jaffer Ben-Rob of Earth, second wife of Rob Ben-Rob

Marle   Varbreen and Petrimmor's son

Marqua   a teenage girl in Trome's Earth life who could read the crystal ball; later became queen and high priestess

Martcra   ("Cherry Flag"), a planet-traveling businesswoman who brought Rhore the Martian to Nodia

Marthree   Cark Ben-Zobey's wife

Martians   eight feet tall, with a bronze complexion and black hair; warlike; either lived in strongholds governed by bar-rexes or lived a nomadic existence along the waterways with their sheep and camels

Masemors   a tribe that lived at Teotihuacan during Tamta/Doy's lifetime

mastaba   Egyptian tomb

Masyna   Trome's mother in a Turkish lifetime

Meko Larm   ("Turtle's Shadow"), father of Gra Moy/Nisor

Melcenta   slave mother of Cronopius/Nisor in an Italian life

Melth-Nakhefra   Tixer-Chock's name in Egyptian lifetime, related to the throne through his mother Solmara, and whose father was teacher of math and architecture to King Snofru and son King Khufu; he became friend King Khafre's sleuth to enter the Great Pyramid, though he was so unbalanced, people added "Crazy" to his name

Menkaure   fifth king in the Fourth Dynasty in Egypt, also called Mycerinus, succeeded by his son; son of Khafre and Daamutyty, he was motherless from birth and was reared with the two sons of Tertmis and Melth-Nakhefra

Menneva   mother of Rembeylian/Sharmarie in Sparta

mental roms   devices that can download in virtual reality planetary or personal histories on any subject matter in minutes

Mercury   originally orbited Jupiter, then called Sovia

Merelre   a fellow artist who was Ymet/Churmay's mate in an Egyptian lifetime

Mermatha   mother of Silmikos/Tixer-Chock

Mern   a Neptune planetoid, Trake's home world, now called Triton

Merp   woman who raised Mosh/Jaffer

Merthran   mother of Urais/Sharmarie in an Earth life

Mestvuker   a Gracian physician in the pyramid area of Egypt; vaccinated Alfora

Mic-Corru   supreme ruler of Maldec

micro level   the mental or fourth-dimensional level

Mill   Alfora's adoptive father

Mills-Bant   a krate officer and suitor of Valneri

Milly-Anet   Mac-Densel/Trome's wife in his Atlantean lifetime

Miradol   now called Teotihuacan in Mexico, where the Gracian engineers constructed a city

Misshemoo   daughter of Mic-Corru, the supreme ruler of Maldec, and caretaker of Marduk in his infancy

Moantalax   one of the Gracians who were the first to visit Parn

Mogent   an old Martian used as a translator

Mokaben   a distant Earth governor in an Earth life of Urais/Sharmarie

molar level   the level at which people on Earth operate because of the Frequency Barrier

Mollara   second planet of star Carrdovan/Task in the five-star mini galaxy near the Milky Way, where Martian refugees found a home; birthplace of Jaffer in his present life; Bantivail is another of the five stars in this mini galaxy

monitor zero   office second in authority to the Martian zone-rex, held by Sharmarie in his present lifetime

Mont-Bester   Mac-Densel/Trome's son in his Atlantean lifetime

Moor   ninth planet of star Ee, home world of Nisor, whose natives are over seven feet tall

Morfa   the fourth planet in the Jatha solar system

Morfs   the residents of Morfa

Morris   a Nodian leader of the House of Domphey second-phasers, who visited Mern and spoke to Thaler and also visited Wayda and Oote

Morza   second planetoid of the Bel Nec radiar of the star Lalm, home of Barco

Mosh   Jaffer's name in a primitive Earth life around Poland; became a metalworker

Moytensa   Sharmarie's name in a lifetime as an Anasazi at Canyon de Chelly

Murphakit   the only city of the Australian Benfyvees

Myva   scheming mother of Rededef and Tertmis and wife of Khufu

N

Nadja   Taydeena/Churmay's mother in her lifetime in Jerusalem, Alexandria and Luxor

Nansa   Ymet/Churmay's mother in an Egyptian lifetime

Nass-Kolb   Doy's Maldecian father

Naya   Churmay's name in an Egyptian life, when she was regarded as the beloved of Sobek

Nedart   the telepath from Sumer/Saturn who communicated for Ruke

Nefertiti   queen and wife of Amenhotep IV, daughter of his maternal aunt; she bore three sons and six daughters, two of whom married Tutankhamen and Rameses I; later became part of the household of Aye

Neftener-Lype   a Nodian official based on Mars who perished when the defective Nodian craft crashed on Earth, with only Nisor and Sivmer-Binen surviving

Nella-Vo   female commander of the Nodian mothership Shalope, from Orkintu in the Tagmer solar system

Neptune   the Trake radiar

neuts   Nodians who have a soft gray aura and are trustworthy; Falashakena was one

New Corn   mother of Six Uncles/Nisor

New Maldec   the "companion" of Hale-Bopp, presently being prepared to resume its original orbit

Nisor   from Moor, which was saved by off-worlders from extinction caused by pollution; affiliated with the House of Domphey, under whose orders he visited Wayda/Venus to train and later evacuate them; helped build Martian pyramid; presently the 862nd Lord of Devisement of the House of Magail

Nivers   a red-headed race with six-fingered hands who worked for the Maldecians during Gra Moy/Nisor's lifetime

Nodia   third planet of the sun Sost in the Milky Way galaxy; where the trading houses, and later the Federation, began

Nodians   the people of the planet Nodia, who had brown complexions and snow-white hair; three Nodians founded the first trading houses, whose ships traveled the universe

Nort   Torge's father, headman of Bratel in Poland, where Mosh/Jaffer settled

nubs   hairless rodents on Parn

O

Ock   head metalworker in Mosh/Jaffer's group

Ogalabon   one of Sharmarie's three soulmates in current lifetime

Oken   son of Reltian slaves Tou and Nebe; boyhood friend of Marle

Oker   father-in-law of Ruke of Parn in his first life

Olbey-Cobex   Gracian pilot and telepath taken prisoner on Mars when things got bad

Olma   Torge's widowed sister who had a son, Retvo

Ombota   a female Martian first evacuated to Earth, then Mollara

Omuray   Titan, a planetoid of Saturn, or the Sumer radiar, where Trome first lived

Oote   Wayda's moon, inhabited by the Whars

Opatel Cre'ator   Nodian ambassador to Maldec and Earth, older half brother of Rayatis; Nodian contact to assist the freedom fighters; a witness to Great Pyramid capstone setting

open state   one's mental state when one is unaffected by the Frequency Barrier on Earth

Orbaltreek   a Cartressian, companion to Petrimmor, pilot of aircar on Earth

Orbeleen   a female Simm servant on Maldec

Ordo-Sambilth   the Maldecian quain who strangled his Uranian teacher, Frocent

Ordover   a Waydian village

Orja   mate of Rick-Charkels

Orkintu   a planet in the Tagmer system, home world of Commander Nella-Vo

Orma   Doy's Maldecian mother

orna   an Earthborn Maldecian educated on Maldec

Orydebbsa   Tixer-Chock's mother in his first lifetime

Ostrocran   a Nodian who asked for Trakian volunteers to spy on the Maldecian Earth overlords

Osypala   Silmikos/Tixer-Chock's sister

Ottannor-Micdin   a Maldecian quain on Maldec who was a guide and caretaker for Gracians

P

Pactra   a Federation mothership on which Ruke of Parn currently lives and works

Pallobey   a Simm servant on Maldec assigned to Gracian Sanza-Bix and his group

Pankamerry   Earth village east of Giza, a trading center and landing port

Parn   a planetoid of Jupiter/Relt radiar now called Callisto, where Ruke first lived

Pen-Dronell   a Nodian commander of the Federation forces on Earth at the time of the evacuation of the Martian refugees; the Second Lord of Devisement of House of Cre'ator

Pensala   one of two daughters of Rendowlan

Petrimmor   policeman on his home world Cartress, taken to Gracyea; he was given the gift of knowing the past and future of anyone he touched

Philolaus   took charge of Pythagoras' school during the latter's journey to Egypt

Picer   Thaler's friend on his home world

Ponalix   an elderly Gracian stationed in Pankamerry

poon   ("monkey"), Sharmarie's nickname for the Nodian lads who were stranded on a building project on Nodia

Prantisa   wife of Nodian Rendowlan

Prenpossas   ("walking trees"), the tribe of Gra Moy/Nisor, who were seven feet tall, black-skinned, with oriental eyes

Prime Directive   universal law forbidding interference in the natural development of a planetary culture

Prince Brone   a Martian dwarf, son of a bar-rex, companion of Green Jacket, brought to Earth with other emigres

Prince Sant   a Maldecian nobleman who was their contact with the Nodians

Princess Rytoon   daughter of Queen Soroona

Proteus   a piece of Maldec now orbiting Neptune

Prycobra   ancient name for Tiahuanaco

Ptolemy Auletes   illegitimate son of Ptolemy IX who overthrew Ptolemy XI by bribing the Romans to assist during Tamos/Thaler's life in Alexandria

Pythagoras   mentor of Sepore, who went to Crotone and Egypt, accompanied by Silmikos/Tixer-Chock

Q

quains   ("ordained ones"), Maldecians who were educated by their el in superiority and arrogance

Quandray   one of Sharmarie's three soulmates in current lifetime

Queen Soroona   of Egypt, or Ser, in the time of early Atlantis during Mac-Densel/Trome's Earth life

Queen Tiye   wife and widow of Amenhotep II, claimed infant Tutankhamen was her and Amenhotep III's child

Quintus Fabius Maximus Verrucosus   Roman general during Sharmarie's lifetime as Granius

Qutata   Bello/Trome's mother in a lifetime in Sumeria

R

Ra   Egyptian sun god, also called Amon Ra

Rabbersinus   king of the city of Knoore, south of Turkey, in Trome's Earth life

rad atmosphere   the air formula in a spacecraft that serves a variety of nitrogen-atmosphere breathers and, after an initial special atmosphere, oxygen breathers

Radiant Ones, the   the term Earth people gave to the Maldecians

radiar   system of inhabited satellites around a planet; for example, Saturn, the

Sumer radiar

Rail "god" of storms in Sumeria during Trome's life there

Rainbow nickname of artist Ymet, Churmay's name in an Egyptian lifetime

Raind Thaler's employer on his home world; she was a skate and an architect-builder

Rairol Nodian who expected to rescue Petrimmor on Earth

Rallee daughter of Ruke of Parn in his first lifetime

Ralno fellow shipwreck survivor and companion of Cronopius/Nisor

Ralph Karl Lont Petrimmor's name in a Prussian lifetime, a military aide of General Blocker who, with the British, defeated Napoleon at Waterloo in 1815, his last Earth life

Ramcace South American husband of Tamta/Doy

Rameses I General Horemheb, after he became king of Egypt

Rancer-Carr the "Red Dragon," supreme leader or zone-rex of the Martians

Rarla Doy's Roman name

Rayatis Cre'ator founder of the Trading House of Cre'ator, whose wife is Aranella, stepson is Drayfess and daughter is Falashakena; also, his paternal grandfather of the same name

Recrothis Nodian who treated animal waste on the journey from Earth to Mollara

Rededef third king in the Fourth Dynasty, succeeded shortly by his uncle, Khafre; son of Khufu and Myva, who was the third of Khufu's four wives; brother of Tertmis, who was wife of Tixer-Chock/Melth-Nakhefra

Regalians inhabitants within the Sost solar system

Regalus a Federation mothership that presently orbits Saturn

Relt radiar Jupiter and its planetoids, one of which was hurled after Maldec's destruction into an orbit close to the sun and is now called Mercury

Reltians inhabitants of the Relt radiar, all about four feet tall and black-skinned, brought to Earth by the Gracians as the only ones small enough and serene enough to help build the Great Pyramids; they claim as descendants the Aborigines

Rembeylian Sharmarie's name in Spartan lifetime

Remissa a maid of Dimathra who sexually initiated Cronopius/Nisor

Rendowlan Nodian witness to Great Pyramid capstone setting, called a poon by Sharmarie when he was a youth; trained to become a Lord of Devisement by the Trading House of Cre'ator

Retkitta one of Sharmarie's three soulmates in current lifetime

Retvo son of Olma, who grew up in the care of Arbel, became head man of Bratel

Rhore a Martian warrior and often companion to Sharmarie

Richard the Lion-Hearted Richard I of England, whose Third Crusade failed to recapture Jerusalem, but made a treaty with Saladin allowing Christians access to their holy places

Rick-Charkels   a red-headed off-worlder on Nodia

Riff, the   barrier of energy separating the matter and anti-matter universes

Rig-Nastbin   a Nodian-Vitronian who visited Moor and saved the planet's inhabitants

Rish   son of Mosh/Jaffer

Rita-Meesa   Mac-Densel/Trome's mother in his Atlantean lifetime

Ro-Atlan   South Atlantis

Rob Ben-Rob   Jaffer's father in his first lifetime, a provincial magistrate and deputy police chief of Tigrillet

Robarius   Sharmarie's father in Roman lifetime as Granius

Robe   the name given the Relt system/Jupiter by Ruke's people on Parn

Rocree   Moytensa/Sharmarie's brother in Anasazi lifetime

Rocreenal   Moytensa/Sharmarie's brother in Anasazi lifetime

Roecerlin   son of Rendowlan

roibe   a Maldecian born on Earth who had never visited Maldec

Rolander-Crobe   a ruthless Maldecian krate general, twin brother of Sharber

rom recorders and players   learning devices through which one can directly experience another person's recorded thoughts or learn any knowledge in minutes

Rort   Ymet/Churmay's artist master in an Egyptian lifetime

Rosey   mother of Urais/Sharmarie in Atlantean lifetime

Rosolan   Churmay's father in her first life

Rubdus   a Simm servant of the Maldecian family of Cro-Swain on Earth

Ruke   from Parn, a planetoid of the Relt/Jupiter radiar; joined other Reltians who were brought to Earth by the Gracians to build the Great Pyramids

Ry   Dell's home world

S

Sa   name given to the Nile by those living near it during the pyramid construction

Saara   Rancer-Carr's only wife, a great beauty

Sabber   a priest of Amon in Naya/Churmay's Egyptian life, who, with Imhotep, departed to live with the "gods"

Sacriba   Churmay's sister on Wayda

Sake-Kover   Maldecian krate commander of the barracks at the villa of Maldecian Cro-Swain and his family

Saladin   called "the Magnificent"; the Islamic leader who expelled from Jerusalem the army of the Second Crusade in the twelfth century

Salta   mother of Tamta/Doy

Sant   a Maldecian prince and friend of and interpreter for Opatel Cre'ator; he had an extensive estate on Earth, where Marduk had a villa

Sanza-Bix   a Gracian who shares his memories of Maldec in Chapter 9

Sapeena   a Seneca life of Doy, who lived a short life during the American

Revolution; regarded as crazy, she could speak and understand all languages and "repair" broken watches and such things

Saqqara ("place of holy work"), where Imhotep lived during Churmay's Egyptian life

Sarus ancient name for Earth

Sata wife of Mosh/Jaffer

Saturn the Sumer radiar

Savacanopy Earth high temple priest

Scenra mother of Sharmarie in first lifetime

Scora widow with whom Cronopius/Nisor stayed in Greece

Semnaftut-Kanutra father of Melth-Nakhefra/Tixer-Chock and King Snofru's and King Khufu's teacher of math and architecture; married to Queen Hetepheres' niece Solmara

Sencreta Trome's mother in his first life

Sepore slave of Aknostros, an Egyptian accountant, former student of Pythagoras; accompanied Silmikos/Tixer-Chock to Italy to join Pythagoras, then Egypt

Ser Egypt, as called by the Atlanteans during Trome's life

Serakus Bello/Trome's father in a Sumerian lifetime

Serbatin of Gee, a planet in the Milky Way galaxy, a biologist with an interest in cloning

Seron a planet on which Nisor is presently stationed, near the farthest Federation boundaries

Serp-Ponder a krate officer who saved Jaffer; born to darmin parents

Shabdar father of Taydeena/Churmay in her lifetime in Jerusalem, Alexandria and Luxor

Shadows a Maldecian telepathic game enjoyed by Jorhisa

Shallo Bain ancient city in Tibet where Brace/Thaler was once born

Shalmalar ("the city of the sleeping sea"), an ancient underground Earth city

Shalope ("lullaby"), a Nodian mothership that visited Thaler's home world

Sharber a ruthless Maldecian krate general, twin of Rolander

Sharmack Rancer-Carr's son

Sharmarie a Martian warrior who offers comments throughout the book; an anomalous Martian, he was bodyguard to Nodian Falashakena, daughter of Rayatis Cre'ator, when she was a child and also guarded her mother Aranella Cre'ator; employed by the Trading House of Cre'ator

Shavmenus Bello/Trome's uncle in a Sumerian lifetime

Shayoler a Nodian who accompanied Rendowlan

Sheila Sharmarie's slave mother in Roman lifetime as Granius

Shem a Martian nomadic tribe during Sharmarie's first lifetime

Shepseskaf son of King Menkaure and Queen Khamerernebty II, succeeded his father; last king of the Fourth Dynasty

Shih Huang-ti warrior and emperor during Ting Sue/Churmay's Chinese lifetime; he built parts of the famous Wall of China

shirel a Cartressian religious leader and consultant

Shray mother of Parn in his first lifetime

Shrenala Brace/Thaler's wife in a Tibetan lifetime

Shrives Nisor's clan, which controlled the ground and water transportation on Moor

Shyreldane a Cartressian woman, the prime religious consultant/shirel to the government leaders

Sibrette Doy's Maldecian sister

Silmikos a Greek lifetime of Tixer-Chock, when he studied and traveled with Pythagoras

Simcarris eighth planet of Thurbal, a star in the constellation Draco, where Churmay and Trome and his family now live and also the eighteen remaining Uranians who are still in physical bodies

Simm a planet orbiting Duma, whose gentle people became personal servants to the Maldecians; Gracyea is also located in that system

Simms from the planet Simm; a tall, thin, gentle race who became servants of the Maldecians

Sitshay a goat-headed god of Sumeria; a priestess of Sitshay adopted and reared Bello/ Trome's sister, who married the king of Sumeria and ruled it alone for 112 years

Sivmer-Binen the spacecraft operator who took Nisor from Mars to Earth and crashed, the two being the sole survivors

Six Uncles Toltec name of Nisor in Mexican lifetime

skates the governing council of all Trake/Neptune planetoids, tattooed master illusionists/educators who could draw power from the macro level of perception of the ULF where the elohim interact

Smenkhkare eleventh king in the 18th Dynasty who reigned briefly prior to his younger brother, Tutankhamen

Smoke Bird the name of Tixer-Chock in a Mayan lifetime

Snofru first king of the Fourth Dynasty; succeeded by son Khufu by Hetepheres; also father of Khafre, fourth in the line of kings, by a different wife; the first king that Melth-Nakhefra/Tixer-Chock's father taught

Soakee-Loom a Gracian involved in building the pyramid on Mars; took Nisor sightseeing

Sobdret a Cre'ator mothership

Sobek Egyptian crocodile god; Naya/Churmay was known as "beloved of Sobek"

Socrantor the Elder Sharmarie's father in Atlantean lifetime

Socrantor the Younger Sharmarie's name in an Atlantean Earth life

Soldulah an officer in Saladin's army who obtained Taydeena/Churmay for his

504 ❖ Through Alien Eyes

harem; later assigned duty in Alexandria

Solmara   mother of Melth-Nakhefra/Tixer-Chock in his Egyptian lifetime; cousin to the king

Sol-Tec   language of the soul, a Nodian language in contrast to Vic Nodian, a language of the lower classes

Somarix-Tol   the Gracian in charge of fine-tuning the Great Pyramid

Somast-Choke   chief of the Gracians on Cartress

Somencar   son of Kevinar-Kale

Somife-Rallee   Maldecian krate commander at Giza

Soogee   Trome's wife in a Turkish life

Sormel   chief of the Uranian teachers who first came to Gracyea; it was his likeness that was chosen for the face on Mars

So-Socrey   medicine man, Sharmarie's teacher in his first lifetime

Sost   star of the planet Nodia in the Ampt radiar, in the Milky Way galaxy

Sou-Dalf   son of orna Maldecians Cro-Swain and Debettine and brother of Valneri; to whom Jaffer was a paid companion; supervisor of the murder of the Cryberants who built the Sphinx

Sovia   originally orbited Jupiter but was hurled from its orbit and is now called Mercury

spiel   capstone (of the Great Pyramid)

Stenee   daughter of Trome in his first life

Stoc   Thaler's name in a life in northern Europe 9 million years ago, born into the only tribe whose leaders had psychic powers

stolfa   a Gracian priest

Stone Snakes   father of Six Uncles/Nisor

Subto   a slave assigned to Naya/Churmay and her father in an Egyptian lifetime

Sumer Basic   current name for the spoken language of the Omuray planetoid of Sumer/Saturn

Sumer radiar   Saturn and its twelve planetoids, seven inhabited, in ancient times

surac   Egyptian term for a king

Sute   a planet the Gracians visited when Petrimmor was aboard; its inhabitants looked oriental and were technically advanced

Sybra   Naya/Churmay's mother in an Egyptian life

T

Tagmer   the star around which the planet Orkintu orbits

Taina-Soy   Abdonel's mother

Tamos   Thaler, in a life in Alexandria, when he was in the shipping trade to Greece

Tamta   Doy's name in her Australian lifetime, a member of the advanced Benfyvee tribe

tane   a military overseer under a Martian bar-rex

Tanforan   a Nodian woman who had a famous bakery

Tar Spikes   ("black fingernails"), off-world scavengers, visitors to Mollara from the Big Circle galaxy; whose intergalactic propulsion system furthered the Federa-tion's explorations

Tarm   an Earth noble who won Churmay from Jorhisa by winning a game of Shadows

Tarnbero   an old male Simm servant on Maldec

Tarvmole   Gracian chief construction engineer for the Great Pyramids

Tasido   Trome's father in Turkish lifetime

Task   sun of Mollara, which the Nodians call Cordovan

Tasper-Kane   leader of the Nodian planners who moved the Sumerians to Earth

Taydeena   Churmay's name in her lifetime in Jerusalem, Alexandria and Luxor

Teen   Waydian name for Earth

Tee-Robra   aunt of Sharmarie in his first lifetime

Tel el-Amarna   the ruins of Akhetaten, the new capital established by Akhenaten

Tenny   the woman who was murdered by Arbel in his enforced tax collections

Terron   pre-Frequency Barrier name of the "Lord God El" of planet Earth, whose temple was at Bimini, and on whose rooftop Kevinar-Kale observed the lighted sky when Maldec exploded

Tertmis   sister of Rededef, daughter of Khufu and Myva; wife of Melth-Nakhefra/Tixer-Chock

Thaler   from the planetoid Meru/Triton of the Trake radiar/Neptune; he and his wife Balis were trained to be telepaths on the planet Vitron so he could join the Earth freedom fighters and keep the Federation informed

Thurbal   star of the planet Simcarris, where Trome of Sumer and Churmay of Wayda now live

Ticaree   Nisor's mother in his first lifetime

Tigrillet   birth village of Jaffer in his first life, west of Portugal

Tillabret   a female native of Emarin, a planet in the Blyme star system

Ting-Sue   Churmay's name in a Chinese lifetime, when she helped build the Great Wall

Tixer-Chock   a Gracian sent to help with pyramid-building on Earth, grandson of Itocot-Talan

Tobet   Ymet/Churmay's brother in an Egyptian life

toibe   a Maldecian born on Earth and who had never visited Maldec

Toltarreg   Ombota's husband, an official in the high court of Rancer-Carr on Mollara

Toray   a name for Egypt during a Sharmarie life on Earth

Torge   a tribal leader in Mosh/Jaffer's lifetime around Poland

Toriata   wife of Sharmarie in an Atlantean life as Socrantor the Younger

Trading House of Cre'ator   founded by Nodian Rayatis Cre'ator

Trading House of Domphey   founded by Nodian Carlus Domphey

Trading House of Magail   a division of the Trading House of Domphey

Trading House of Vonner   founded by Nodian Trare Vonner

trading houses   commercial interstellar traders originating on Nodia

Trake radiar   Neptune and its eleven planetoids, also called the Crobet radiar by the Federation; it had three large planetoids before Maldec's destruction, two of which are now Pluto and its moon, Charon; two of its smaller planetoids, Banlon and Nylo, now orbit beyond Pluto; Trakians are those who inhabited this radiar

Tramesant   Nisor's father in his first lifetime

Trare Vonner   Nodian founder of the Trading House of Vonner and brother-in-law of Rayatis Cre'ator

Tra-Vain, Hol-Canter, Serc-Rhis and Misshemoo   three male princes and a female princess who, with Mic-Corru, the supreme ruler, were the governing board of Maldec

Trelba Sye   an underground Earth city located in what is now Idaho

Tremmet   son of Martians Ombota and Toltarreg living on Mollara

Treno Domphey   brother of Carlus Domphey

Tricklelemla   Gracian mate of Cyper-Dale

Triton   present name for Mern, one of the original planetoids of the Trake radiar

Trocker   Sharmarie's other son, twin of Quandray, in current lifetime

Trohawker   a Martian warlord

Trome   lived on planetoid Omuray of Sumer/Saturn during his first life; became well-known for his invention of a photosensitive fertilizer; came with other refugees to Earth and joined Tasper-Kane's attempt to assist émigrés; now lives on Simcarris, where he has assisted the Federation to monitor the Frequency Barrier's effect on Earth's plant and animal life

Trowfor   a half-Maldecian and half-Earthling man who taught Churmay singing lessons

Tunertha   Subto's wife in Egypt

tur   term for gold in Mosh/Jaffer's lifetime

Tura   a site on the Nile where the fine white limestone was quarried that encased the Great Pyramid

Tutankhamen   son of Queen Tiye and Amenhotep III, who succeeded his brother Smenkhkare to the throne of Egypt

U

ULF   universal life field

Urais   Sharmarie's name in an Atlantean Earth life

Uranians   wise ancient teachers from the planetoids of Uranus who traveled to planets to share their wisdom and knowledge; after the Maldecian treachery they disappeared; only eighteen are still living in physical bodies, on Simcarris

Uranus   the Hamp radiar

Utherium   village near Rome during Sharmarie's Roman lifetime as Granius

V

Vadius Gromius   father of Rarla/Doy; an armorer and postmaster of the elite Roman Praetorian Guard of Tiberius

Valbra   Philolaus' daughter and wife of Silmikos/Tixer-Chock

Valneri   daughter of orna Maldecians Cro-Swain and Debettine and sister of Sou-Dalf

Varbreen   Petrimmor's wife

Varman-Den   father of Mac-Densel/Trome in Atlantean life

Vass   the planet on which Nisor and Ivatcala received their education

Vitron   a large single planetoid of the Ampt radiar in Sost solar system, which is also home of the Nodians

Vitronians   inhabitants of Vitron

Vormass   a Maldecian telepath who questioned Churmay on Wayda

vril rods   charged with vril energy, the highest form of energy in the universe, used by the Gracian stolfas in levitating stone blocks with sound and also by the Maldecians when they tried to send Earth's psychic energy to Maldec

W

wa   a Reltian word signifying a person's most satisfactory state of being; a Maldecian word for emotional harmony

Watchers, the   one of the names given to the Maldecians by Earth dwellers

Wayda   Venus, an oxygen world

Whars   inhabitants of Oote, the Waydian moon

Worg   underground city of the mystics on Cartress

Wren-Shanna   younger sister of Sharmarie in his present lifetime

Y

Yalput   Naya/Churmay's brother in an Egyptian life

Ymet   Churmay's name during an Egyptian lifetime as an artist

Z

Zains   primitive peoples during Trome's Earth life in Turkey

Zomuter   Ala's husband, a telepath communicator to the Nodians

zone-rex   the top warlord or supreme authority on Mars during Sharmarie's first lifetime, who was Rancer-Carr

WES BATEMAN, FEDERATION TELEPATH

Wes Bateman is a telepath with direct, open contact to ETs from the open state, who are not subject to Earth mankind's Frequency Barrier-caused closed brain and limited consciousness. Bateman has 30 years of ongoing information on the open state; the Federation; the Frequency Barrier and how it affects humanity; ETs and evolution; a wide spectrum of technical and scientific information, including mathematics and the universal symbolic language; and the three trading houses of this system—all part of the true history of this part of the galaxy and beyond.

DRAGONS AND CHARIOTS

DRAGONS AND CHARIOTS

An Explanation of Extraterrestrial Spacecraft and Their Propulsion Systems

By Wesley H. Bateman

This book contains descriptions of a number of extraterrestrial spacecraft and their various types of propulsion systems. This data was obtained over a period of 28 years by way of telepathic communication with extraterrestrials who have been visiting our planet in spacecraft we have come to call "flying saucers" or, as they are generally referred to, unidentified flying objects (UFOs).

SOFTCOVER 65P.
$**9**95 ISBN 0-929385-26-8

Chapter Titles:

- Introduction to Saucer Propulsion
- Gravity
- The Interplanetaries
- The Dragon

- The Dragon Seeds
- Manipulated Light
- The Interstellar Motherships
- The Intergalactic Motherships

KNOWLEDGE FROM THE STARS

The author of *Dragons and Chariots* and the four Ra books shares his thirty-year adventure as a Federation telepath and the wisdom brought to Earth through his telepathic connections.

- Flight 19
- Secret of flying saucers
- Vril energy
- Universal life field
- Dulce
- ETs
- Frequency Barrier
- Several ET inventions
- Trading houses
- How the Federation works
- Christ reality
- and much more

SOFTCOVER 171P.

$11 95 ISBN 0-929385-39-X

Chapter Titles:

DRAGONS AND CHARIOTS

This book contains descriptions of a number of extra-terrestrial spacecraft and their various types of propulsion systems. This data was obtained over a period of 28 years by way of telepathic communication with extraterrestrials who have been visiting our planet in spacecraft we have come to call "flying saucers" or, as they are generally referred to, unidentified flying objects (UFOs). **SOFTCOVER 65P.**

$9⁹⁵ ISBN 0-929385-26-8

DRAGONS AND CHARIOTS
An Explanation of Extraterrestrial Spacecraft and Their Propulsion Systems
By Wesley H. Bateman

Chapter Titles:

- Introduction to Saucer Propulsion
- Gravity
- The Interplanetaries
- The Dragon
- The Dragon Seeds
- Manipulated Light
- The Interstellar Motherships
- The Intergalactic Motherships

KNOWLEDGE FROM THE STARS

The author of *Dragons and Chariots* and the four Ra books shares his thirty-year adventure as a Federation telepath and the wisdom brought to Earth through his telepathic connections.

- Flight 19 • Secret of flying saucers • Vril energy
- Universal life field • Dulce • ETs • Frequency Barrier
- Several ET inventions • Trading houses
- How the Federation works • Christ reality
- and much more **SOFTCOVER 171P.**

$11⁹⁵ ISBN 0-929385-39-X

Chapter Titles:

- Sasquatch
- The Finding of Flight 19
- Flight 19 Update
- The Secret of the Flying Saucers
- The Frequency Barrier
- Vril Energy: The Psychic Charge Force
- The Universal Life Field: Levels of Perception
- The Forces of Light and Darkness
- Dulce: How Sweet Is It?
- Extraterrestrials: Now You See Them, Now You Don't
- I Am Darafina
- Yesteryear, a Million Times Yesteryear
- Mental Investigations of New Dimensions
- Hooray for Hollywood
- The Mind Center
- The Patrax Projects: Part 1
- The Patrax Projects: Part 2
- The Patrax Projects: Part 3
- The Patrax Projects: Part 4
- Introduction to the Federation
- The Trading Houses: This for That
- The Trading Houses, Part 2
- The Christ Reality
- Not on Your Life or Mine

THE EXPLORER RACE SERIES

ZOOSH THROUGH ROBERT SHAPIRO

Superchannel Robert Shapiro can communicate with any personality anywhere and anywhen. e has been a professional channel for over twenty-five years and channels with an exceptional- clear and profound connection.

The Origin...
The Purpose...The Future...of Humanity

If you want to understand every nuance of your behavior, of the world around you; if you want to be stimulated, clarified; if you want to experi- ence revelations; if you want to be excited; if you want to be stimulated; if you want to be cheered up, you have come to the right place. We do not promise that you will have the greatest experience you have ever had. But if you are at all open mentally or philosophically, you will be thrilled, or at the very least intrigued.

—Zoosh through Robert Shapiro

If you have ever asked questions about who you really are, why you are here as part of humanity on this miraculous planet and what it all means, the books in the Explorer Race series can begin to supply the answers—the answers to these questions and to all your other questions.

Now the amazing story of the greatest adventure of all time can be told— the epic of the Explorer Race. And told it is, by beings ranging from par- ticles to the Mother of All Beings.

The scope, the immensity, the mind-boggling infinitude of these chroni- cles by beings who live in expanded realities beyond our imagination will hold you enthralled. Nothing even close to the magnitude of the depth and power of this all-encompassing, expanded picture of reality has ever been published.

Light Technology Publishing is pleased to present this magnificent Explorer Race Series of books by Zoosh and a cast of hundreds through superchannel Robert Shapiro.

the
EXPLORER
RACE

Zoosh, End-Time Historian
through Robert Shapiro

Book 1...
The Explorer Race

The Explorer Race is the story of you, of the E
of humanity, past, present and future. Feel th
and the power of discovering your purpose, o
covering why you are here. A radiant new ad
ture awaits the graduates of this creator s
called Earth, and those illuminated graduate
you, the Explorer Race!

SOFTCOVER 574P.

$2500   ISBN 0-929385

Chapter Titles:

THE HISTORY OF THE EXPLORER RACE
- The Genetic Experiment on Earth
- Influences of the Zodiac
- The Heritage from Early Civilizations
- Explorer Race Time Line, Part 1
- Explorer Race Time Line, Part 2
- The Experiment That Failed

GATHERING THE PARTS
- The ET in You: Physical Body
- The ET in You: Emotion and Thought
- The ET in You: Spirit

THE JOY, THE GLORY AND THE CHALLENGE OF SEX
- Emotion Lost: Sexual Addiction in Zeta History
- Sex, Love and Relationships
- Sexual Violence on Earth
- The Third Sex: The Neutral Binding Energy
- The Goddess Energy: The Soul of Creation

ET PERSPECTIVES
- Origin of the Species: A Sirian Perception
- An Andromedan Perspective on the Earth
  Experiment
- The Perspective of Orion Past on Their Role
- Conversation with a Zeta

BEHIND THE SCENES
- The Order: Its Origin and Resolution
- The White Brotherhood, the Illuminati, the
  Dawn and the Shadow Government
- Fulfilling the Creator's Destiny
- The Sirian Inheritors of Third-Dimensional

TODAY AND TOMORROW
- The Explorer Race Is Ready
- Coming of Age in the Fourth Dimension
- The True Purpose of Negative Energy
- The Challenge of Risking Intimacy
- Etheric Gene-Splicing and the Neutral Part
- Material Mastery and the New Safety
- The Sterilization of Planet Earth

THE LOST PLANETS
- The Tenth Planet: The Gift of Temptation
- The Eleventh Planet: The Undoer, Key to
  Transformation
- The Twelfth Planet: Return of the Heart Ene

THE HEART OF HUMANKIND
- Moving Beyond the Mind
- Retrieving Heart Energy
- The Creator's Mission and the Function of
  Human Race

ok 2...
s and the EXPLORER RACE

s book, Robert channels Joopah, a Zeta Reticulan now in the
dimension, who continues the story of the great experi-
—the Explorer Race—from the perspective of his race. The
would have been humanity's future selves had not human-
created the past and changed the future. SOFTCOVER 237P.

$14⁹⁵ ISBN 0-929385-79-9

Joopah, Zoosh and others
through Robert Shapiro

pter Titles:

Great Experiment: Earth Humanity
alk to Contactees
ming One with Your Future Self
teraction with Humanity
s and Abductions
True Nature of the Grays
vering Questions in Las Vegas
Encounters in Sedona

• Joopah, in Transit,
  Gives an Overview
  and Helpful Tools
• We Must Embrace the Zetas
• Roswell, ETs and the Shadow Government
• ETs: Friend or Foe?
• ET Presence within Earth and Human Genetics
• Creating a Benevolent Future
• Bringing the Babies Home

ok 3...ORIGINS and the
NEXT 50 YEARS

Volume focuses on humanity's origins and the near future.
ers the oribins of this creation, why negative attributes
needed and how various races came to be. it also delves
he physical bodies—the masculine, the femine and the
of the child. SOFTCOVER 339P.

$14⁹⁵ ISBN 0-929385-95-0

Zoosh, End-Time Historian
through Robert Shapiro

pter Titles:

gins of Earth Races
Creator and Its Creation
White Race and the Andromedan Linear Mind
Asian Race, the Keepers of Zeta Vertical
ught
African Race and Its Sirius/Orion Heritage
Fairy Race and the Native Peoples of the North
Australian Aborigines, Advisors of the Sirius
tem
Return of the Lost Tribe of Israel
Body of the Child, a Pleiadian Heritage
ting Sexual Balance for Growth
Origin of Souls
xt 50 Years
New Corporate Model
Practice of Feeling

• Benevolent Magic
• Future Politics
• A Visit to the Creator of All
  Creators
• Approaching the One
Appendix
• The Body of man
• The Body of Woman
Origins of the Creator
• Beginning This Creation
• Creating with Core Resonances
• Jesus, the Master Teacher
• Recent Events in Explorer Race History
• The Origin of Creator
• On Zoosh, Creator and the Explorer Race
• Fundamentals of Applied 3D Creationism

SHAMANIC SECRETS for MATERIAL MASTERY
Learn to communicate with the planet

This book explores the heart and soul connection between h
and Mother Earth. Through that intimacy, miracles of heali
expanded awareness can flourish.

To heal the planet and be healed as well, we can lovingly
our energy selves out to the mountains and rivers and int
bond with the Earth. Gestures and vision can activate our
to return us to a healthy, caring relationship with the land
on.

The character and essence of some of Earth's most power
tures is explored and understood, with exercises given t
nect us with those places. As we project our love and l
energy there, we help the Earth to heal from man's destr
of the planet and its atmosphere. Dozens of photographs, maps and drawing
the process in 25 chapters, which cover the Earth's more critical locations. SOFTCOVER

$19⁹⁵ ISBN 1-891824

Chapter Titles:

- Approaching Material Mastery through Your Physicality
- Three Rivers: The Rhine, the Amazon and the Rio Grande
- Three Lakes: Pyramid Lake, Lake Titicaca and Lake Baikal
- Mountains: Earth's Antennas, Related to the Human Bone Structure
- Three Mountains: The Cydonia Pyramid, Mount Rushmore and Mount Aspen
- Mountains in Turkey, Japan and California
- Eurasia and Man's Skeletal Structure
- Greenland, the Land of Mystery
- Africa and North America
- South and Central America and Australia

- Shamanic Interaction with Natural Life
- Africa and the Caspian and Black Seas
- Mauna Loa, Mount McKinley and Shiproc
- The Gobi Desert
- Old Faithful, Cayman Islands, Blue Mount and Grandfather Mountain
- Meteor Crater, Angel Falls and Other Uni Locations on the Planet

PART II, THE FOUNDATION of Oneness

- The Explorer Race as a Part of Mother Ea Body
- Spiritual Beings in a Physical World
- Earth Now Releasing Human Resistance t Physical Life
- Healing Prisoners, Teaching Students
- The Shaman's Key: Feeling and the Five S
- How to Walk, How To Eat
- Breathing: Something Natural We Overlo
- How to Ask and Let Go, and How to Sleep
- Singing Our Songs
- Some Final Thoughts

..MANIC SECRETS for ..SICAL MASTERY

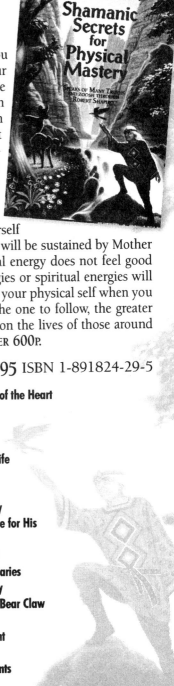

COMING SOON

The purpose of this book is to allow you to understand the sacred nature of your own physical body and some of the magnificent gifts it offers you. When you work with your physical body in these new ways, you will discover not only its sacredness, but how it is compatible with Mother Earth, the animals, even ..arby planets, and plants, all of which you now recog- ..s being sacred in nature. It is important to feel the .. of oneself physically before one can have any lasting ..cal impact on the world. The less you think of yourself ..cally, the less likely your physical impact on the world will be sustained by Mother .. and other being physical energy as well. If a physical energy does not feel good .. itself, it will usually be resolved; other physical energies or spiritual energies will ..ve it because it is unnatural. The better you feel about your physical self when you .. work in the previous book as well as this one and the one to follow, the greater ..ore lasting will be the benevolent effect on your life, on the lives of those around ..nd ultimately on your planet and universe. SOFTCOVER 600P.

$**19**95 ISBN 1-891824-29-5

CREATORS AND FRIENDS
THE MECHANICS OF CREATION

Creators and Zoosh
through Robert Shapiro

Book 4...CREATORS and FRIEN
The Mechanics of Creation

As we explore the greater reality beyond our planet, our dim
our creation, we meet prototypes, designers and creator
explain their roles in this creation and their experiences befc
beyond this creation. Join us in the adventure of discov
mind-stretching! SOFTCOVER 435P.

$**19**95 ISBN 0-89182

Chapter Titles:

- Andastinn, Prototype of Insect Beings
- Kazant, a Timekeeper
- Founders of Sirius, Creators of Humanoid Forms
- A Teacher of Buddha and Time Master's Assistant
- Designers of Human Physiology
- Avatar of Sea Creatures; and Quatsika, Messenger for the Dimension Makers
- The Empath Creator of Seventeen Planets
- Shapemaker of Portals
- Creator of the Inverse Universe, Our Creator's Creator
- Creator of the Void, Preamble to Individuality
- The Tornado-Shaped Creator of Creators
- The Center of Creation
- The Heart Council
- Creators of Gold Light and White Light
- Creator Talks About Itself and the Explorer Race
- Creator Talks About His/Her Friends

- Creator Speaks of the Stuff of Creation
- Creator Discusses Successes and the Outw of Negativity
- Synchronizer of Physical Reality and Dime
- Master of Maybe
- Master of Frequencies and Octaves
- Spirit of Youthful Exuberance
- Master of Imagination
- Zoosh, the End-Time Historian
- Master of Feeling
- Master of Plasmic Energy
- Master of Discomfort Speaks of Himself a Explorer Race
- Master of Discomfort Discusses Light Transference

Appendix: The Lucifer Gene

Book 5...
PARTICLE PERSONALITIES

All around you are the most magical and mystical beings. They are too small for you to see as single individuals, but in groups you know them as the physical matter of your daily life. These particles remember where they have been and what they have done in their long lives. We hear from some of them in this extraordinary book in the series. SOFTCOVER 237P.

$14⁹⁵ ISBN 0-929385-97-7

Chapter Titles:

- A Particle of Gold
- The Model Maker: The Clerk
- The Clerk; a Mountain Lion Particle; a Particle of Liquid Light; and an Ice Particle
- A Particle of Rose Quartz from a Floating Crystal City
- rticle of Uranium, Earth's Mind
- rticle of the Great Pyramid's Capstone
- rticle of the Dimensional Boundary
- ween Orbs

- A Particle of Healing Energy
- A Particle of Courage Circulating through Ea
- A Particle of the Sun
- A Particle of Ninth-Dimensional Fire
- A Particle of Union
- A Particle of the Gold Lightbeing beyond
- A Particle of the Tenfold Wizard
- A Particle of This Creator

ok 6...EXPLORER RACE
and BEYOND

r continuing exploration, we talk to Creator of Pure ngs and Thoughts and the other 93% of the Explorer We finally reach the root seeds of the Race (us!) and we are from a different source than our Creator and a different goal; and we end up talking to All That Is! COVER 360P.

$14⁹⁵ ISBN 1-891824-06-6

pter Titles:

- tor of Pure Feelings and Thoughts, One Circle
- Creation
- Liquid Domain
- Double-Diamond Portal
- ut the Other 93% of the Explorer Race
- hronizer of Physical Reality and Dimensions
- Master of Maybe
- ster of Frequencies and Octaves
- it of Youthful Enthusiasm (Junior) and Master
- Imagination
- sh

- The Master of Feeling
- The Master of Plasmic Er
- The Master of Discomfo
- The Story-Gathering Ro of Light/Knowledge
- The Root Who Fragm
- The First Root Retur
- Root Three, Compar
- The Temple of Know
- The Voice Historia
- Creator of All Th

the n
nize
value
physi
physi
Earth
about
dissol
do th
and r
you a

Cha
- Cell
Ev
- Cell
- Iden
- The ND
- Lear
iends
h
hapiro

- Lear
M
- Seeim the Library
- Rel
- Thea Living Temple
- The
- Foosecond Root
Giver of Inspiration
ided the First Root

Book 9...EXPLORER RACE and JESUS

The immortal personality who lived the life we know as Jesus, along with his students and friends, describes with clarity and love his life and teaching on Earth 2000 years ago. These beings lovingly offer their experiences of the events that happened then and of Jesus' time-traveling adventures, because the being known as Jesus had full consciousness. So heartwarming and interesting you won't want to put it down.

$14⁹⁵ ISBN 1-891824-14-7

Chapter Titles:

- Jesus' Core Being, His People and the Interest in Earth of Four of Them
- Jesus' Life on Earth
- Jesus' Home World, Their Love Creations and the Four Who Visited Earth
- The "Facts" of Jesus' Life Here, His Future Return
- The Teachings and Travels
- A Student's Time with Jesus and His Tales of Jesus' Time Travels
- The Shamanic Use of the Senses

- The Child Student Who Became a Traveling Singer-Healer
- Other Journeys and the Many Disguises
- Jesus' Autonomous Parts, His Bloodline and His Plans
- Learning to Invite Matter to Transform Itself
- Inviting Water, Singing Colors
- Learning to Teach Usable Skills
- Learning about Different Cultures and Pec
- The Role of Mary Magdalene, a Romany
- Traveling and Teaching People How to Find Things

Book 10...EXPLORER RACE: EARTH HISTOR and LOST CIVILIZATIONS EXPLAINED

Zoosh reveals that our planet Earth did not originate in this solar system, but th water planet we live on was brought here from Sirius 65 million years ag Anomalous archaeological finds and the various ET cultures who founded what w now call lost civilizations are explained with such storytelling skill by Speaks Many Truths that you feel you were there!

$14⁹⁵ ISBN 1-891824-20

Chapter Titles:

- Lost Civilizations of Planet Earth in Sirius
- Ancient Artifacts Explained
- Ancient Visitors and Immortal Personalities
- Before and after Earth Was Moved to This Solar System from Sirius
- The Long Journey of Jehovah's Ship, from Orion to Sirius to Earth
- Jehovah Creates Human Beings
- Beings from the Future Academy
- Sumer
- Nazca Lines
- Easter Island
- Laetoli Footprints

- Egypt and Cats
- Three More Civilizations
- Medicine Wheels
- Stonehenge
- Carnac in Brittany
- Egypt
- China
- Tibet and Japan
- Siberia
- Natural Foods/Sacrament of Foods
- SSG's Time-Traveling Interference in Israe Imperils Middle East: How to Resolve It

THE ANCIENT SECRET OF THE FLOWER OF LIFE

DRUNVALO MELCHIZEDEK

Drunvalo Melchizedek's life experience reads like an encyclopedia of breakthroughs in human endeavor. He studied physics and art at the University of California at Berkeley, but he feels that his most important education came after college. In the last 25 years, he has studied with over 70 teachers from all belief systems and religious understandings.

For some time now, he has been bringing his vision to the world through the Flower of Life program and the Mer-Ka-Ba meditation. This teaching encompasses every area of human understanding, explores the development of mankind from ancient civilizations to the present time and offers clarity regarding the world's state of consciousness and what is needed for a smooth and easy transition into the 21st century.

VOLUME I

Once, all life in the universe knew the Flower of Life as the creation pattern, the geometrical design leading us into and out of physical existence. Then from a very high state of consciousness, we fell into darkness, the secret hidden for thousands of years, ncoded in the cells of all life.

w we are rising from the darkness and a new is streaming through the windows of percep-
This book is one of those windows. Drunvalo
izedek presents in text and graphics the
r of Life Workshop, illuminating the mys-
of how we came to be.

red geometry is the form beneath our being
oints to a divine order in our reality. We can follow that order from the invisible to the infinite stars, finding ourselves at each step. The information here is one but between the lines and drawings lie the feminine gems of intuitive under-
ing. You may see them sparkle around some of these provocative ideas:
COVER 228P.

$25.00 ISBN 1-891824-17-1

pter Titles:

<table>
<tr><td>embering Our Ancient Past</td><td>• The Geometries of the Human Body</td></tr>
<tr><td>Secret of The Flower Unfolds</td><td>• The Significance of Shape and Structure</td></tr>
<tr><td>Darker Side of Our Present and Past</td><td>• When Evolution Crashed, and the Christ Grid Arose</td></tr>
<tr><td>Aborted Evolution of Consciousness and the eation of the Christ Grid</td><td>• The Measuring Stick of the Universe: The Human Body and Its Geometries</td></tr>
<tr><td>t's Role in the Evolution Consciousness</td><td>• Reconciling the Fibonacci-Binary Polarity</td></tr>
</table>

by Drunvalo Melchizedek

VOLUME II

The sacred Flower of Life pattern, the primary geometric generator of all physical form, is explored in even more depth in this volume, the second half of the famed Flower of Life workshop. The proportions of the human body, the nuances of human consciousness, the sizes and distances of the stars, planets and moons, even the creations of humankind, are all shown to reflect their origins in this beautiful and divine image. Through an intricate and detailed geometrical mapping, Drunvalo Melchizedek shows how the seemingly simple design of the Flower of Life contains the genesis of our entire third-dimensional existence.

From the pyramids and mysteries of Egypt to the new race of Indigo children, Drunvalo presents the sacred geometries of the Reality and the subtle energies that shape our world. We are led through a divinely inspired labyrinth of science and stories, logic and coincidence, on a path of remembering where we come from and the wonder and magic of who we are.

... first time in print, Drunvalo shares the instructions for the Mer-... step techniques for the re-creation of the energy field of the ev... huma... ... to ascension and the next dimensional world. If done love, this ... breathing prana opens up for us a world of tantalizing sibility in this ... protective powers to the healing of oneself, of other even of the planet. ... ver a memory or a fleeting reflection of yours the following topics:

- The unfolding of the third i... ...stem
- Whispers from our ancient heri...
- Unveiling the Mer-Ka-Ba mediation
- Using your Mer-Ka-Ba

- Connecting to the levels of self
- Two cosmic experiments
- What we may expect in the forthcoming dimensional shift

SOFTCOVER 228P.

...**500** ISBN 1-891824-

Chapter Titles:

- **Spirit and Sacred Geometry**
- **The Left Eye of Horus Mystery School**
- **Ancient Influences on Our Modern World**
- **The Mer-Ka-Ba, the Human Lightbody**
- **The Mer-Ka-Ba Geometries and Meditation**
- **The Mer-Ka-Ba and the Siddhis**

- **L... ...ealing**
- **The L...vels of the Self**
- **Duality Transcended**
- **The Dimensional Shift**
- **The New Children**

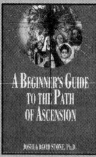